P9-CIT-127

S S⁰ Em
/

THE IMPACT OF
WAR ON AMERICAN LIFE

The march on the Pentagon, October 21, 1967.   (United Press International)

THE IMPACT OF WAR ON AMERICAN LIFE

The Twentieth-Century Experience

Edited by
KEITH L. NELSON
University of California, Irvine

HOLT, RINEHART AND WINSTON, INC.
New York Chicago San Francisco Atlanta Dallas Montreal Toronto London Sydney

JUL 20 1972
UNIVERSITY OF THE PACIFIC

LIBRARY
JUL 20 1972
UNIVERSITY OF THE PACIFIC
252530

Copyright © 1971 by Holt, Rinehart and Winston, Inc.
All Rights Reserved
Library of Congress Catalog Card Number: 72–146925
ISBN: 0–03–083056–7
Printed in the United States of America
1 2 3 4   006   9 8 7 6 5 4 3 2 1

For
JANE
and
KATHERINE ELIZABETH

CONTENTS

BIBLIOGRAPHY: IMPORTANT WORKS ON
THE IMPACT OF WAR   371

PERSPECTIVES
ON THE EFFECTS OF WAR

War is father of all and king of all, and some he shows as gods, others as men;
some he makes slaves, others free.

    HERACLITUS

In peace and prosperity both states and individuals are actuated by higher
motives, because they do not fall under the dominion of imperious necessities; but
war which takes away the comfortable provision of daily life is a hard master,
and tends to assimilate men's characters to their conditions.

    THUCYDIDES

When war is undertaken in obedience to God, who would rebuke, or humble,
or crush the pride of man, it must be allowed to be a righteous war; for even the
wars which arise from human passion cannot harm the eternal well-being of
God, nor even hurt His saints; for in the trial of their patience, and the
chastening of their spirit, and in bearing fatherly correction, they are rather
benefited than injured.

    AUGUSTINE

From war comes tardy gain and speedy loss;
What's bad war swiftly turns to what is worse;
A host of evils follow war, but not
A single benefaction; war's a curse.

    AIMERIC DE PEGUILHAN

War has the higher significance that by its agency, as I have remarked
elsewhere, "the ethical health of peoples is preserved . . . ; indeed, just as the blowing
of the winds preserves the sea from the foulness which would be the result of
a prolonged calm, so also corruption in nations would be the product of
prolonged, let alone 'perpetual,' peace."

    G. W. F. HEGEL

Introduction

There can be little doubt that the last few years have witnessed a remarkable and widespread growth of interest in war as an agent of historical change. Under the impact of the Cold War and particularly of the Vietnamese conflict, men of many different fields—journalists, historians, psychologists, sociologists—have turned in increasing numbers to the study of war's consequences. Whereas before the 1960s little serious attention was given to this subject, today one encounters relevant courses, symposia, articles, and monographs on all sides.

To be sure, libraries throughout the world have long been filled with books dealing with war. Yet strangely, very little of this earlier writing is concerned with what the process of the struggle actually *does* to the participants. Much of it is battle history. More of it is devoted to assessing blame for having failed to prevent the conflict in the first place. Most of it treats war as if war were little more than a game of rational decision-making, with a payoff, plus or minus, at the end.

Americans would seem to have been among the worst offenders in this regard. Our practicalism, presentism, and lack of tragic experience have long conditioned us to write and read our history as if we had become what we are because we had earlier decided to be this way. As a nation, one of our fondest myths (the frontier thesis notwithstanding) is that our political, economic, and social system is mostly the product of conscious choice on the part of our leaders and our voters. That the United States is also the unintended result of misapprehended wars, historical drift, and processes only partly noted has largely been beyond our ken.

Now we as well as other peoples are finally beginning to face this possibility. Indeed, not only our new concern with war but also the general growth of comparative studies would seem to be an obvious indication of this fact. By the very act of comparing different histories we imply that there are kinds of past behavior, previously considered acts of will (that is, free), which will now be seen as conditioned by their contexts (that is, not fully free).

Even so, there is no good reason why such behavior cannot be better and better understood. If our models are still embryonic, our data impressionistic, and our tradition unsympathetic to the study, much the same could have been said about the state of science itself three hundred years ago. Hopefully, in groping our way through an increasing number of comparisons, we shall begin to find, as scientists did, that predictable patterns of relationships can be discerned. Hopefully too, with intelligent manipulation on our part, these patterns can more frequently become our building blocks instead of obstacles.

This anthology has been designed to further the study both of American wars and of war in America. Thus, the volume is arranged so that at least three of its four sections—that is, those on World Wars I and II and on the Cold War —can be read *seriatim* and as a supplement to books which may not devote sufficient attention to these subjects. Yet, at the same time, the subdivision of the three sections into corresponding area fields (political, economic, social, and cultural) is intended to make structural comparisons possible, if not almost inevitable. Moreover, the questions which introduce each area field have been arranged to provoke thought not only about the relationships *within* a war, but also about similarities *between* (or among) the conflicts. Of course, for thorough comparative work, a sample from only three, recent, American wars is rather culture-bound and slim, but it is also true that there are advantages for the student in taking somewhat deeper soundings and in holding the cultural factor constant.

Let it only be added that in no case have the materials for this volume (except those on the Warfare State) been selected because they represent a given point of view, but always instead as a result of their being among the most comprehensive and thoughtful essays available on the topic. In some instances there has been a chance to introduce alternative interpretations of events, but in general the study of war is so new and undeveloped that most historio-graphical debate must be carried on by inference. The brevity of the articles is also less a tribute to the editor's skill at cutting than a witness to the fact that the scrutiny of such wars as these is still so young an art.

It remains, then, to offer the student a few suggestions as to the kinds of characteristics wars may share, the types of effects and impacts they may generate, and the sorts of limiting variables which may be relevant. In other words, it remains to give some indication of the hypotheses he may wish to test in his comparisons.

To start with, however, it should be noted that the very use of the word "war" for two separate and distinct events indicates that we *already* perceive something similiar in each. In effect, it is as if we had agreed among ourselves that whenever we employ this designation, certain things will have transpired (for example, hostility and violence among organized human groups). This commonsense consensus is the beginning of a theory as to what war is and does.

The real question is, how far can we get beyond a recognition of obvious similarities among conflicts toward a systematic understanding of the features which they share? Or, to borrow an analogy, to what extent can we emulate the psychiatrist who, when confronted with neurosis, is able to offer more than that his patients are "unhappy"? To what extent can we develop a diagnosis and prognosis for the process we call war?

This is not an easy question to answer. In the best of all possible worlds, perhaps, we might have long since possessed a model which, given specified factors, could be used to show what kinds of things would then occur (or, for historians, would *have* occurred). As it is, in the world of the 1970s, we are only just beginning to discover and invent the models which the scholars of the future will be testing.[1]

If, in spite or because of this, the student of war wishes to start out with a model, his strategy in the matter cannot be timid. He must be willing to borrow and to steal from his comprehension of whatever processes he knows in order to help himself envisage the relationships he encounters. Anything is fair for mining—the thoughts of contemporaries, the reconstructions of historians, the ideas of engineers and scientists, the metaphors of everyday conversation—as long as, in the end, his definition itself is rigorous and his testing is severe. Is war like a game? A disease? An explosion? A revolution? Or, must a model of war be built from the bottom up, out of small and middle-range hypotheses?

Of course, it is not essential that a model be developed before interesting comparisons can be made as to functions and effects. In the past even the most perceptive observers of war have usually confined themselves to limited and unrelated descriptive statements. Alexis de Tocqueville, for example, contended in the nineteenth century that "war . . . must invariably and immeasurably increase the powers of civil government; it must almost compulsorily concentrate the direction of all men and the management of all things in the hands of the administration," but Tocqueville's explanation as to why was only fragmentary.[2] More recently, Arthur Marwick, in an illuminating study of World War I, has suggested that for Britain there were seven major consequences of the conflict: loss of life, loss of capital, disruption of trade and finance, reorganization and reorientation of society, awareness of deficiencies, postponement of reform, and excitement for the populace. Again, these statements appear to have been derived without much theory.[3] And lately, Gordon Wright, in what is now our standard treatment of the Second World War, has speculated brilliantly but impressionistically about such effects of that struggle as, for instance, its having "reinforced trends toward a mood of lawlessness, toward a confusion and corruption of values, toward a decline in man's belief in a rational universe."[4]

The student too may decide to work without explicit models. The soundest tactic after all may simply be, first to describe as carefully as possible what the impact of a war upon an area of activity actually *was*, and then, taking the resulting generalization, apply it to an analogous area of activity in either the same or another war, in order to ascertain the degree of parallelism or similarity at hand. A third and final stage, of course, is the attempt to determine just what the factors were which made the two effects so different or alike. Thus, if World War I contributed to centralization of the governmental apparatus and to the strengthening of the executive, did the conflict

[1] As many readers will be aware, most of the work which has been done in comparing sizable historical phenomena has dealt with the problem of revolution. For the great "classic" in this field, cf. Crane Brinton, *The Anatomy of Revolution* (Englewood Cliffs, N.J., 1938), and for an indication of more recent scholarship on the subject, cf. Chalmers Johnson, *Revolutionary Change* (Berkeley, 1965).

[2] Alexis de Tocqueville, *Democracy in America* (New York, 1945), II, 284.

[3] Arthur Marwick, *After the Deluge* (London, 1968), pp. 289–90. In a subsequent work, *Britain in the Century of Total War* (London, 1968), Marwick attempts to reduce his categories of generalization to what he calls four "*modes* through which war affects society": (1) by material loss or gain; (2) by challenging and testing the efficiency of a country's institutions; (3) by increasing participation in activities and decisions; and (4) by offering an intense emotional experience.

[4] Gordon Wright, *The Ordeal of Total War, 1939–1945* (New York, 1968), p. 236.

work the same kind of changes on the *economic* organization of the country? If so, why, and if not, why not? And did World War II have an impact similar to that of World War I on *political* organization? If so, why, and if not, why not? Such a procedure as this may not take the student very far toward the building up of theory (though, as we shall see, it might be relevant), but it should prove to be of value in increasing his understanding of what occurred.

Having asserted this, however, we would nevertheless like to call attention to at least one existing model (or partial model) which, although strangely neglected in this context, appears peculiarly relevant to the study of war's impact. We refer specifically to "modernization" theory, or that body of ideas which has grown up in the attempt to explain what has happened to those nations which over the last four hundred years have become more "modern." Here, in our view, is a process and a formulation which can be used to throw perspective on the phenomenon we call war.

What then is modernization? As one might expect, there are a number of scholarly interpreters, each with his particular slant. To Marion Levy, "A society will be considered more or less modernized to the extent that its members use inanimate sources of power and/or tools to multiply the effects of their efforts."[5] Samuel P. Huntington, on the other hand, defines modernization as a process involving such socioeconomic changes as urbanization and industrialization, and such political alterations as "rationalization of authority, the differentiation of structures, and the expansion of political participation."[6] S. N. Eisenstadt sees

it as a movement toward "a high level of structural differentiation, and of so-called 'social mobilization,' and a relatively large-scale, unified and centralized institutional framework."[7] What all these interpretations have in common, it would seem, is the idea that, in modernizing, a society is consciously and/or unconsciously becoming more powerful, or efficient, at manipulating its environment.[8]

This, in turn, is the reason why the schema seems to fit so well with war. For what *is* war, from one point of view, but a quick attempt to maximize a nation's power vis-à-vis an enemy on the outside (i.e., to overpower him)? Therefore, though the specific forms of mobilization in the two processes may be different, it is plausible to expect that their general impacts might be similar. War could be called an accelerated (and in some ways more conscious) instance of the modernization process, except that in war, of course, variables such as defeat, destruction, and the like may intervene. Nevertheless, modernization may be a helpful measuring device for the student attempting to assess the changes wrought by war.

This is by no means to say that modernization should necessarily be considered an unqualified good. Since it is clear that increasing the power of the group is a process only loosely correlated with that of increasing the capabilities of individuals, it follows that, to the extent

[5] Marion J. Levy, Jr., *Modernization and the Structure of Societies: A Setting for International Affairs* (Princeton, 1966), I, 11.

[6] Samuel P. Huntington, *Political Order in Changing Societies* (New Haven, 1968), pp. 5, 32–35, 93.

[7] S. N. Eisenstadt, "Transformation of Social, Political and Cultural Orders in Modernization," *American Anthropologist* (April 1959), as cited in Eisenstadt, ed., *Comparative Perspectives on Social Change* (Boston, 1968), p. 257. For a handy listing of some of the more specific changes to be expected from the modernization process, see Wilbert E. Moore, *Social Change* (Englewood Cliffs, N.J., 1963), pp. 90–105.

[8] No one contends, however, that modernization affects all aspects of a given society at the same rate, and indeed some theorists (e.g., Huntington) suggest that uneven rates of modernization are a prime cause of worldwide instability.

that modernization is defined *only* in terms of group power (as opposed to the rights and abilities of the citizen), it is open to our criticism. To a certain extent the two objectives are bound to overlap—i.e., more powerful nations will mean more capable individuals, and vice versa—but such congruency cannot be complete. It is possible to conceive, for example, of a world like that of George Orwell's *1984* in which a society is considerably effective in organizing certain kinds of power, and yet in which individual citizens have been deprived of all but the barest minimum of rights. Moreover, the very power and unhappiness of the United States at the present time are another proof of this same point: that modernization and utopianization (as one might describe the process by which the general capabilities of individuals are enhanced) may be related but are not synonymous. Thus war, if it is like modernization, can help to create a *stronger* nation, perhaps, without necessarily helping to bring about a *better* one. And war can result in a great expansion of national power while leading to only a slight increase, if any, in the prerogatives and versatility of the citizen.

To be sure, whatever the model or definition of war one uses, there will always be *historical* factors to consider in dealing with a specific conflict. Some of these have to do with the character and situation of a nation as it enters upon the war, and are therefore largely antecedent to the struggle (though not unrelated to its causes nor unaffected by its course). Others have to do with the war itself, and are therefore more dependent on its development as well as on the antecedent factors.

Among the antecedent factors are the following:

1. the phase and configuration of a nation's development at the time the war occurs
   e.g., extent of urbanization, stratification, industrialization, centralized control
2. the objective of the war
   e.g., independence, expansion, self-preservation
3. the type of enemy encountered
   e.g., strong, weak, confident, desperate
4. the kind and number of allies
   e.g., helpful, independent, dependent
5. the kind of national leadership
   e.g., conservative, reformist, revolutionary
   e.g., ordinary, charismatic
6. the extent of internal unity and commitment regarding strategy and tactics

Among the dependent factors are these:

7. the extent of resources employed and the intensity of employment
   e.g., limited, unlimited
   e.g., cold, hot
8. the length of the war
   e.g., days, weeks, months, years (note the length relative to anticipation)
9. the amount of destruction incurred
   e.g., deaths, debts, damage
10. the amount of postwar obligation or control
    e.g., victory, stalemate, defeat

If at first such a list might seem forbidding, still the model-building student should not despair. Indeed, if one is willing to assume a limited and definable variation within these categories, it is at least theoretically possible to construct a matrix indicating the total number of ways in which the factors may combine. The first six categories, for example, given three variations each, will fit together in 729 different profiles, while the latter four, given the same number of internal variations, will combine in 81 alternative ways!

Moreover, on the basis of one's examination of particular conflicts (and utilizing the descriptive statements derived from modernization theory, from other models, or from specific observations), one ultimately might be able to hypothesize some of the outcomes to be expected as a result of various combinations. Thus, the equation would be as follows:

If there is x (given y), then z will result

Or, if there is a particular combination of factors directly conditioning or limiting the process of war, 7, 8, 9, 10, given a particular combination of prewar factors, 1, 2, 3, 4, 5, 6, there will be a particular combination of results.

Or, to use more specific examples,

1. if there is an intensive war of some length, resulting in military victory with little internal destruction for a relatively modern nation, substantially united, under reformist leadership with reformist objectives, possessing vigorous allies and fighting powerful, relatively modernized enemies (e.g., the United States, 1941–1945), there will be certain kinds of effects (e.g., greater internal consensus, slowing of reform impulse, increased psychological lift) within that nation,

   whereas,

2. if there is a limited war of some length, resulting in military stalemate with little internal destruction for a relatively modern nation, seriously disunited, under reformist (later, conservative) leadership with reformist (later, conservative) objectives, possessing few allies and fighting elusive, semi-modern enemies (e.g., the United States, 1965–1971), there will be other kinds of effects (e.g., growing political polarization, weakening of traditional standards, loss of confidence).

Or, in abbreviated form (attempting to hold as many factors as possible constant and citing only the apparently critical elements), with reference to certain specific results,

1. it may be that war will drive relatively modernized societies (e.g., Germany, 1914–1918) much further toward modernization than it will premodern societies (e.g., Turkey, 1914–1918);
2. it may be that war against a relatively modernized society (e.g., China against the United States, 1950–1952) will have a more modernizing effect on a nation than war against a premodern enemy (e.g., China against India, 1965);
3. it may be that war which results in considerable physical destruction (e.g., Germany, 1939–1945) will clear more of a path for economic change than war that does not (e.g., Germany, 1914–1918);
4. it may be that a successful war (e.g., Germany, 1871) does a great deal more to strengthen the national status quo than an unsuccessful war (e.g., France, 1871).

In the final analysis, then, by adding categories for historical factors to our original ideal-type (i.e., to our conception of war as revolution, or modernization, or whatever), we may have developed a more useful model than we had previously possessed. *Without* such categories, clearly, an ideal-type is hard to employ (or test), since it must always be involved with neutral, or average (or ideal) historical material (e.g., nations, leaders). *With* these categories, on the other hand, we can compensate more effectively (though never to the point of completely satisfying a conscientious historian) for the fact that no belligerent and no war is ever really "typical."

Of all the possible effects which war could produce, perhaps the most serious would be *more* war. For this reason, and because the Cold War today is so often described as being self-perpetuating, it has been thought desirable that we include in the anthology a separate section on the "warfare state." Here the question is specifically raised as to whether or not a war can create interests and/or needs which serve in turn to maintain the conflict.

As the readings will reveal, many of the current accusations about such "interests" are nothing new. Rulers, soldiers, and businessmen, for example, have long been viewed as peculiarly dependent or susceptible to war, and whole traditions of suspicion have grown up regarding their activities. Usually each has been distrusted separately (the politicians and the soldiers by the liberal; the capitalist by the radical), but in the years immediately preceding both world wars there was an increasing tendency to see three groups (political, military, and industrial) as cooperating against the peace.

Though this fourth section is focused primarily upon the contemporary debate, enough selections have been taken from earlier periods to enable the student to view the issues somewhat comparatively. The author regrets that he could not include more material with which to judge both the validity of the traditional fears and the accuracy of the prewar suspicions. The justification can only be, first, that there are fewer writings of quality for the earlier years than for the present, and second, that the current situation is sufficiently complex to require a maximum of attention. Neither the emphasis nor the selection is intended to influence the student's judgment regarding (1) the extent to which socio-structural changes were and are occurring, and (2) the extent to which any changes were and are either the result or cause of war.

In the preparation of a volume such as this, one inevitably acquires many debts. My special thanks are due to my research assistants, David Heifetz, Richard Robertson, and Paul Pearson, for their help in finding and analyzing relevant materials, and to my typist, Catherine Smith, for her considerable labors in preparing the manuscript for the press. I would also like to acknowledge the generous and constructive suggestions of my faculty colleagues at UCI, Richard Stryker and Michael Butler, and of my editor at Holt, Rinehart & Winston, Clifford Snyder. My wife, Jane Wallace Nelson, has been of very great assistance, not only as part-time typist and letter-writer, but also as a "second editor." Let me only add that I am grateful to the authors and publishers who granted me permission to reproduce their work.

K. L. N.
University of California, Irvine
June 21, 1971

Part One

THE IMPACT OF WORLD WAR I

The First World War, it has now become clear, was an extraordinary turning point in history. Indeed, in a sense, this conflict stood to the nineteenth century as the French Revolution had stood to the eighteenth, representing, like that cataclysm, both the climax and the destruction of a tradition of optimism which had gradually taken root within Western culture. In addition, however, and to a much greater extent than the Revolution, World War I marked the beginning of an era in which violence became endemic. For this, the war itself and the fear and hatred it engendered must bear a major portion of the blame.

In its size and cost the First World War was quite literally unprecedented. In the four years of fighting, from August 1914 to November 1918, over 65 million men were called to arms, and of these over 8 million lost their lives —more than twice as many as had died in all the major wars from 1790 to 1913. By the time of the Armistice, twenty-eight nations (Britain, France, Italy, Russia, the United States, and their allies versus Germany, Austria-Hungary, Bulgaria, and Turkey) comprising over 90 percent of the world's 1.8 billion people were involved in the struggle. It has been estimated that the direct financial cost of the war was almost $200 billion in the currency of the time, and roughly four times that much in 1970 dollars.

The repercussions of this terrible bloodbath were enormous. To begin with, of course, it completely refashioned the political and institutional map of Europe, shaping that continent as never before along nationalist and republican lines. Simultaneously, however, it severely distorted the internal politics of the participating nations, and in several instances brought revolutionary and reactionary regimes to power. It undermined the colonial empires of the victors and destroyed those of the vanquished. It taught new techniques of organization and control to the belligerents even while transferring the center of financial wealth from the Old World to the New. It reduced or reversed population trends in many countries and subjected traditional familial and social relationships to unexpected stress. And, as we have noted, it brought about a major dislocation of spirit and of attitude.

The United States, unlike Europe, was struck only a glancing blow by the war. Due to our late entry into the conflict (April 1917), this country was actively engaged as a belligerent for only one year and seven months. Our losses, beginning in November 1917, came to 116,000 dead out of 4.7 million mobilized and approximately 2 million sent to Europe (from a population of 100 million). (This compares with 618,000 dead out of 4.2 million mobilized on both sides in the American Civil War.) The money cost for the United States was $33 billion, a figure which indicates that our financial and our industrial power was far more significant to the outcome than was our manpower.

Yet the war had an important impact on the United States. Even before 1917 our sales to the Allies and our own rearmament had led to an expansion of the economy as well as to a slowing of reform. After 1917, and our belligerency, the effect of the war was to become much more pronounced. The needs of mobilization, for example, justified a systematization and coordination of the economy which previously would have been inconceivable and which later, when abandoned, left much in disarray. This in turn resulted in a rapid if temporary growth of governmental power that was to become a noteworthy precedent for the future. Socially, the exigencies of war created extraordinary pressure for conformity by minorities, at the same time giving them unusual opportunities to improve their status. Intellectually and emotionally, the nation gave itself over to an orgy of idealism, which quickly turned to shock and disillusionment with the disappointment of the peace.

The Swift Growth of Motor Transportation

This double-column advertisement from a big eastern daily tells a graphic story of a new industry.

A year ago regular inter-city motor truck transportation was virtually unknown.

Today it is an established thing in every section of the country.

Motor truck transportation has become an important factor in the industrial and commercial fabric of the nation. By shouldering a big share of war work it is taking a tremendous burden from the railroads.

'Nobby Cord'
for Trucks
United States Tires and Truck Service are keeping pace with swift-growing motor truck transportation as they have with passenger service.

'Nobby Cord' Truck Tires are the finest development of pneumatic tires for fast, long-distance trucking. Their enormous strength and extreme durability are combined with unusual resiliency.

Where solid truck tires are desired, United States quality is equally dependable.

The complete service organization of United States Tires is one of the factors that have made large-scale inter-city motor truck transportation possible.

United States Sales and Service Depots are everywhere.

For passenger cars—'Royal Cord', 'Nobby', 'Chain', 'Usco' and 'Plain'. Also Tires for Motorcycles, Bicycles and Airplanes.

United States Tubes and Tire Accessories Have All the Sterling Worth and Wear that Make United States Tires Supreme.

United States Tires are <u>Good</u> Tires

The war greatly stimulated the American automobile industry, especially following the Federal Roads Act of May 1916 which appropriated $75 million in matching grants for "strategic" highways.   (New York Public Library)

Douglas Fairbanks warms up a crowd of prospective bond buyers during a Wall Street rally in 1917. Four Liberty Loans and a Victory Loan raised over $21 billion for the Treasury and encouraged widespread public acquaintance with security issues.   (National Archives)

Chapter One

ECONOMIC EFFECTS OF THE WAR

Taken together, the five authors of this section show how profoundly the First World War affected such aspects of the economy as the attitudes of business and labor, the organizing abilities of government, the productive capacities of industry, the distribution of national income, and the structure of international finance. In the first selection, Rexford G. Tugwell makes a convincing argument that, as a result of the conflict, American industry "experimented with a kind of voluntary socialism —and liked it." In related fashion, Joseph Dorfman demonstrates that economic mobilization gave impetus to the government's use of professional economists, the systematic collection of economic statistics, and central economic planning generally. George Soule discusses several other specific changes which occurred, including the expansion of automobile production, the decline of the construction industry, the inflation of credit and prices, and the extinction of foreign debt. John D. Hicks contends that, though labor profited from the war, many of its gains were lost in the period immediately following the armistice, with the result that its demands became increasingly radical. In seeming agreement, John M. Clark suggests that the quick advantages which some groups realized from the struggle were more than offset by the ultimate costs of overproduction, disruption of trade, depletion of resources, and finally, depression.

QUESTIONS:
1. Compare the economic changes wrought in America by our actions as a neutral (1914–1917) with those which resulted from full participation in the war (1917–1918).
2. Rexford G. Tugwell has described what he calls a kind of "voluntary socialism" brought on by the war. In what ways was the system really "voluntary" and in what ways was it not?
3. On the basis of your reading here and elsewhere, which of the effects of the war would you say represented a speeding up of previously existing trends, and which a slowing down or reversal?
4. To what extent was the war's impact on the economy immediate, and to what extent was it deferred?
5. How would you differentiate between what the war did for business and what it did for labor?

1

Rexford G. Tugwell
WAR-TIME SOCIALISM

"America's War-Time Socialism," Nation, Vol. 124 (April 6, 1927), pp. 364–366.

Rexford G. Tugwell (1891–   ), an economist, political scientist, and longtime professor at Columbia University, gained his greatest fame as a member of President Franklin D. Roosevelt's "Brains Trust" in the 1930s. Now a senior fellow of the Center for the Study of Democratic Institutions, Santa Barbara, California, he is the author of many books, including *The Economic Basis of Public Interest* (1922), *Industry's Coming of Age* (1927), *Battle for Democracy* (1935), *The Place*

of *Planning in Society* (1954), *The Democratic Roosevelt* (1957), *The Enlargement of the Presidency* (1960), and *FDR: Architect of an Era* (1967).

A year before we went to war, industry began to get ready. The Naval Consulting Board and the army's Kernan Board were making industrial surveys early in 1916; and in the summer the Council of National Defense was set up. In the first months of 1917 the Munitions Standards Board and later the General Munitions Board came into existence. Out of the problems met by these early industrial bodies arose the demand for coordination which resulted in a unique economic experiment—the War Industries Board. President Wilson may have conceived the function of this body in military terms, as issuing orders and penalizing their non-fulfillment. If he did, Mr. Bernard Baruch, the chairman, had a different idea. To him the enterprise of war was a vast cooperation. The industrial system was to run as one well-oiled machine, but it was to run on a volunteer basis with plenty of play for individuality.

To understand why he succeeded, it is necessary to appreciate the situation into which he stepped. American industry, by 1917, had had the three swiftest years of its history. Greatest activity, greatest price changes, greatest profits, greatest building programs, greatest internal changes set these three years apart. Cautious attitudes toward over-equipment, customary wage-levels, trade secrecy, and hallowed management practices had all been modified. There was an ever-expanding demand; no one needed to worry about markets. Profits were high and certain. All that had to be done was to make the wheels go round and the product come out, faster and faster and faster. If there was any difficulty about technique, technicians, workmen, and plans were provided. On the whole, the war was an industrial engineer's Utopia.

Each of the great industries formed a committee with headquarters in Washington. Here they were brought into contact with the source of orders—for soon all the Allies' buying was concentrated and apportioned. Needs were classified. Each unit of industry was given the work which it could do best. Industries which furnished raw or semi-finished goods to finishing industries were gradually brought in. Industries which made goods for civilian consumption had also to become part of the system, since, in so many ways, they were linked to the ones which were doing outright war work. Before the Armistice, the system was nearly perfected and a mission had gone abroad to tie up our national system with that of the Allies. We were on the verge of having an international industrial machine when peace broke.

The Railway, Food, and Fuel administrations had been functioning throughout almost this same period. In many ways their work closely paralleled that of the War Industries Board, with jointures here and there. For the railways needed cars, locomotives, and rails; food is a factory product; and fuel is raw factory power. The organizations came closer and closer administratively until a productive coordination was effected.

It would be a mistake to assume that this revolution took place without costly errors, some recalcitrance, even some dishonesty; but a ten-year perspective makes it more impressive, to me at least, than it seemed when we were in the midst of it. Then all seemed disorder and meaningless change; now, across the gulf of post-war chaos, there appears to have been a remarkable industrial achievement. For the thing worked. Goods were produced. An army of two million was carried across the sea, well fed and well clothed, the civil population was

so prosperous that it disgusted the soldiers, and to the Allies were sent some billions of dollars' worth of materials.

This achievement required a revolution in our customary arrangements. The essence of our economic theory had been distilled into the Sherman Act, with later additions in the Clayton and Federal Trade Commission acts. We conceived voluntary activity and free competition as guardian angels which hovered over business everywhere, adjusting functions to one another, protecting individuals and groups in their mutual dealings, and stimulating all concerned to the requisite enterprise. This ideal sought to dominate a rebellious reality; and, having its source in the authoritative texts of the economists and in the minds of statesmen, its existence had been secured even down through "the new freedom" of the pre-war Wilson. Most of the work of the Department of Justice and of the Federal Trade Commission had, until 1917, consisted in breaking up the "trusts." It was about the most consistent single governmental policy we had. But this whole ideology had to be modified if industry was to accomplish more in war than it had in peace.

So it was that the old system melted away in the fierce new heat of nationalistic vision. The Government now, so far as industry was concerned, was staffed by big-business men who had few hampering ideas but a singular flair for administration. There were none who thought the competitive system sufficient for war. The industries, drawn together in the various committees of the War Industries Board, discovered that they had most of their affairs in common. There ensued an era of combination such as put the pale efforts of the nineties to shame. And where outright combination did not develop, trade associations, under various names, perfected working organizations and began to exchange information of all kinds, including the most jealously guarded of trade secrets. So far as operations were concerned they were as close-coupled as the units of a single organization. There came to be a free reservoir of technical knowledge which even yet has not been drained. And where the various units of industry held back from this new intimacy the new Government officials—not the Department of Justice, which was hunting first spies and later Reds—found ways, sometimes gentle, sometimes a little rough, of forcing the very combinations which had always been thought to be unholy.

It soon became apparent that industry under its coordinated guidance and with its new cooperative efficiency possessed not only an enhanced power to produce but a dangerous advantage in the markets. The strength developed for the sake of production could be used —and was—for the purpose of exploiting the buyers of its products. Part of this difficulty was met by the consolidation of all government buying in the coordinated subsections of the War Industries Board. This was not enough. The Government bought enormously; but private buying was always much greater. In order to keep down the price of steel, it was necessary to do more than fix a price for what the Government required. Much steel was going into machines, automobiles, building construction, and other industries which, although only indirectly connected with the war, were none the less essential. Nor could wages be kept down on government contracts, many of which were of the "cost plus" variety, if food prices kept rising. These new problems were met quite calmly. The same group which had set out so unheroically to create a productive machine determined to keep it from clogging its own progress with prohibitory prices.

If they ever meant to abolish profits, they were unsuccessful. But there is nothing to show that they meant to do this. They intended rather to set a price high enough to include the producers who made the "marginal goods" —in the economists' phrase—those produced under conditions of greatest expense, which it was nevertheless necessary to have. That there would still be profits—large ones—for those concerns whose costs of production were low was obvious. But if the old competition for prices in the market could be transformed into a competition for lowered costs, that would be a valuable service. So the big profits were in a sense a sign of efficiency rather than of gouging consumers. This system developed gradually. Part of it had to wait for the organization of statistical staffs and the collection of hitherto non-existent data. Part of it came directly under the board; part was assimilated more nearly to the Food and Fuel administrations. It got under way in 1918; and only the Armistice prevented a great experiment in control of production, control of price, and control of consumption. As it was, the whole process was left at a somewhat inconclusive stage when demobilization began.

Control of production and price proved easier than control of consumption. Ordinarily, rising prices could be trusted to act as a check as goods grew scarcer. With prices held down, some other method had to be devised. The priorities system regulated the flow of goods. But it was different when it came to persuading workmen not to buy pianos or silk shirts with their much-advertised high wages—which some, at least, were getting. We never reached the stage of allotment by a rationing system, such as the other nations used; or of forbidding the manufacture of silk shirts. We depended upon publicity campaigns—for low-milled bread, for resoling old shoes, and for gasolineless Sundays.

Old clothes became, for a time, almost fashionable; and one went motoring with a guilty conscience. It was costly, but effective. Perhaps it would not have survived years of struggle; certainly it depended considerably upon emotional response to the heavy odor of melodrama in the Wilsonian phrase. And it was always more effective among those with a typical middle-class stake in events than among the workers, who were surprised and pleased by their new access to hitherto unattainable goods.

The one thing in this elaborate system of control which was never seen clearly was the financial policy it called for. It seems to me that we should have paid for the war out of taxation as we went along and that we should never have made governmental loans to our Allies. This would have been possible. The process of producing goods engenders the income to buy them. It was only a question of getting the income into the Treasury. We could have got it there as well by taxation as by liberty loans; the same funds were available for either use. But we were afraid to tap the obvious sources of surplus—corporation profits. We preferred to dally with taxes on ice-cream cones and movie tickets.

We did issue loans and we permitted them —through the rediscounting machinery of the new and untried Federal Reserve System—to add to an already alarming inflation. Workers —and manufacturers too—suffered from the price-vagaries to which this inflation contributed throughout the war and post-war periods. It was the great element of uncertainty in the whole system of control. And if we had never made loans to our Allies but had frankly presented them with war-materials we should not have been under the still present illusion that we were carrying on purely commercial transactions with them for which we should eventually be paid. The need for financial administration failed to call forth the organizing genius which built up the other controls which were on the whole so successfully devised.

This system of coordinations and voluntary controls, it must be remembered, was imposed upon an industry which had, for several years, been producing war goods at the height of its haphazard capacity. There was a jumble of orders and prices, the Eastern industrial region was more crowded with war orders than other regions, the Allies competed with each other to place contracts, manufacturers bought where they could in the quantities they could get regardless of others' requirements; all this it was the function of an industrial general staff to straighten out. Gradually, plants for making gas-holders were converted into airplane factories; carpet manufacturers began to make blankets and duck; automobile-makers produced airplane parts; lumber mills cut and shaped ship-timbers and airplane spruce; refrigerator factories made field-hospital tables; furniture-plants made ammunition-boxes; shirt-factories made mosquito-nets and signal flags.

The normal progress of a decade was compressed into every year. Much of the accumulated technical knowledge which had been piling up from the time of Frederick W. Taylor's first inventions suddenly became accessible through the opportunity to rebuild plant, replan processes, and introduce a completed serialization. These impulses to change ran like a regenerative flame through the old industrial structure. Progress was accelerated by a number of factors: (1) The certainty of demand and of profits; (2) the ease of obtaining funds; (3) the pooling of trade secrets; (4) the simplification and standardization of materials and processes; and (5) the coordinations of war-time control.

"The profits of all corporations in the United

States," David Friday says in his "Profits, Wages and Prices," "had never exceeded $4,000,000,000 until 1913. Under the stimulus of war demand, with its high prices and increased production, profits reached the astounding figure of $10,700,000,000 in 1917." Not all kinds of industry participated, of course, in this prosperity. It was concentrated mostly in the mining and manufacturing industries; but for these "the earnings in 1917 were almost exactly 330 per cent of those of 1913, the highest pre-war year."

With profits on this scale rolling in, and with price levels always rising and thus promising higher ones, it is no wonder that some voluntary reorganization of industry took place through the efforts to expand for greater volume of production. When there was superposed on this mighty drift a concerted effort toward internal technical efficiency and a subordination of formerly independent units to a coordinated plan, a new industrial revolution could be said to be well under way.

Industries which did not readily respond to an invitation to combine were actually called together in Washington and read curtain lectures by officials of the Government for not doing what they would have been punished for a few months earlier. Each industry pooled its techniques, standardized its tools, machines, styles, qualities, and processes on the best, took its orders, and proceeded to make goods as they were never made before—or since.

It must have been sheer momentum which carried us into the middle of 1920. For as soon after the Armistice as they could get away, the dollar-a-year men drifted out of Washington. The control staffs were broken up, price and consumption restraints were removed, and the railways were handed back to their owners. There was, of course, need for abnormal amounts of peace goods to repair war-time loss

or neglect, and there were shortages because of the time involved in shifting productive processes again. But before long the inevitable headache began. Prices had risen in crescendo after the controls were abandoned; the European market was cut off because buyers there lacked the wherewithal to pay, except with goods, and these we banned by tariffs. Suddenly we discovered that our tremendous productive power was flooding the markets with goods which could not be sold with any profit. And so we proceeded into several years of depression.

Under war-pressure industry had experimented with a kind of voluntary socialism—and liked it. It liked the substitution of solidarity for suspicion, of unity for compelled disunion, of cooperation for competition, of a common purpose for haphazard growth. But when the war was over, old ideas which had been in suspension again stirred in politicians' minds, the Department of Justice turned from hunting Reds to hunting trusts, tariffs were raised. The Supreme Court drew a long breath and eyed the war powers arrogated by the Administration with the chilly disfavor which recently found expression in the Tyson case,[1] decisively turning back legislative efforts to regulate prices, excusing its former complaisance in such cases as the New York rent laws by using the phrase "controlling emergency."

As a result of this post-war lassitude and the recrudescence of old ideas, we have returned—as far as the Government can effect it—to the days of 1910. But industry, in spite of obvious handicaps, has not slipped all the way. It finds itself with an overcapacity caused by faulty coordination and restricted demand, and with other maladjustments. And it has frankly gone back to its policy of price-competition, which is so wasteful and so damaging to consumers'

[1] In *Tyson and Brothers v. Banton* (1927) the Supreme Court invalidated a New York law regulating resale theater ticket prices.—Ed.

interests. But its internal operating technique, as contrasted with the technique of its organization, improves steadily. Research, standardization, machinization, serialization, personnel administration—all have continued to go forward since the war.

2

Joseph Dorfman
NATIONAL MOBILIZATION

From The Economic Mind in American Civilization, *Vol. III, 1865–1918, pp. 473–485 by Joseph Dorfman. Copyright 1949, by Joseph Dorfman. Reprinted by permission of The Viking Press, Inc.*

Joseph Dorfman (1904–   ), born in Russia and educated in the United States, has been a professor of economics at Columbia University since 1931. An authority on the history of economic thought, he has published a study of *Thorstein Veblen and His America* (1934) as well as a magisterial survey of *The Economic Mind in American Civilization* (5 vols., 1946–1959).

The First World War brought this country face to face with its first major international responsibility, and there was inevitably a great deal of confusion in every area of thought and action. For economics, in the broadest sense, it was only slowly seen that national mobilization must go beyond the mustering of men to effective use of the nation's whole industrial resources. Furthermore, in carrying out this mobilization, it was in time evident that "common sense" was not enough; recourse was therefore had to the services of men whose professional interest had led them to study the economy of the country.

The utilization of economists by the govern-

ment in the 1917–18 period was often grudging and inefficient; their advice, when accepted, was not always put into effect. The government and the public, nevertheless, made some important discoveries: they felt the effect of a concerted national effort, which was in part the result of planning, and in this they found an added usefulness for the services which could be rendered by professional economists. . . .

The government had definitely embarked on a defense program as early as 1916, but little of a concrete nature was accomplished. The Naval Consulting Board appointed a committee to make a comprehensive survey of the industrial plants of the country, but it did not "appear to have been as useful in practice as might have been expected." Congress provided in the same year for a Council of National Defense, consisting of six members of the cabinet, to co-ordinate "industries and resources for the national security and welfare" and to create relations which would make possible "in time of need the immediate concentration and utilization" of the country's resources. The act at the same time provided for an advisory commission appointed by the President on the recommendation of the Council. For some time little more than conferences occurred. But with the approach of war large numbers of subordinate committees were established, composed primarily of business executives who served without pay.

Though this variety of organizations covered the entire economy, a systematic plan was lacking. Even after the declaration of war in April 1917 there was no effective co-ordination among the numerous supply divisions of the Army and Navy. In the Army alone ten separate procurement agencies were bidding against each other for supplies. And purchases by the Allies increased the confusion. Bernard Baruch, chairman of the reconstituted War Industries Board, recalled later that the various Army contracting agencies "fought each other as bad as they fought the Germans, and then they fought me just as hard, and fought the Navy just as hard." In fact, it took more than a year to achieve some sort of effective co-ordination.

The problem of essential industries became very perplexing. Every business considered itself essential, and so many priorities were issued that by 1918 there was a danger of breakdown. In general, the business community wanted changes in the economy to be gradual. The New York *Annalist* stated that while the notion of "business as usual" should not be allowed to interfere with winning the war, still labor should not be taken from one industry until another was ready for it.

For some time after the United States entered the war the railroads were left to their own devices. They attempted to meet the need for unified action by a voluntary organization, called the Railroad War Board, composed of five railroad executives. This proved ineffective, and in December 1917 President Wilson commandeered the roads. In July 1918 the government took over the telephone and telegraph lines; later the cables, and just a few days before the Armistice, the express business was placed under government operation.

Even after the War Industries Board was given sweeping powers in March 1918, its activities were still governed by "expediency in individual instances" rather than "by an established policy for which the whole administration took responsibility." In an attempt to bring about unity, more and more boards were created. The quality of many of these boards gave rise to the *bon mot*, "A board is long and narrow and wooden."

In recalling this period, Baruch stated that "the greatest deterrent to effective action" during the war was the lack of facts. For prosecuting the war, as Professor Allyn Young said, the government required statistical information

for the "measurement of our national resources . . . ; the determination of our actual and potential output of the immense variety of things that are important directly and indirectly in the conduct of the war; the gauging . . . of our own needs and those of our allies and of the other countries that have to be recognized as in some measure dependent upon us," but when the country entered the war our "federal statistics were woefully incomplete and inadequate." Remedying the defects was no easy task. There was a real need for a central statistical commission to supervise and co-ordinate the work of the numerous independent statistical bureaus and to supplement their activities. Only in June 1918 was a Central Bureau of Planning and Statistics established, with Edwin F. Gay of Harvard as chairman. It set up a clearing house of statistical activities, appointed contact men to keep in touch with the statistical work of the war boards and certain of the permanent departments, and to supervise questionnaires in an effort to eliminate excessive duplication. In the end [Wesley] Mitchell could say: "When the Armistice was signed we were in a fair way to develop for the first time a systematic organization of federal statistics."

The needs of the government for prosecuting the war and the complaints by consumers of rapidly rising prices resulted in ever-widening government control of prices. But the system of control, as in other fields, was developed in a piecemeal fashion as "expediency dictated." After all, government price-fixing ran counter to the habits of the business community and some of the most firmly entrenched doctrines in political economy. . . .

The price-control program did, to some extent, prevent runaway prices. An index number of 573 commodities brought under price control at various dates from midsummer 1917 to the Armistice dropped from 209 in July 1917 to 189 in June 1918. Thereafter, with moderate advances permitted, the index rose again, but it did not rise to the pre-price-fixing point.

As Professor Mitchell has well said, the price-fixing authorities might have accomplished more had they "realized their power earlier, brought more commodities under control, and insisted upon more drastic reductions." But he thought that their success demonstrated that within quite wide limits the price level was susceptible to direct control by the government when supported by public opinion.

As for war financing, there was a danger at the start that the government would to an overwhelming degree have recourse to loans rather than taxes; and taxes of a character primarily in the nature of excises and custom duties rather than income and excess profits taxes. On the eve of America's entrance into the war Senator [F. M.] Simmons of the Senate Finance Committee was reported to have said that it had been the country's custom to pay its war bills by bond issues and he saw no reason for a shift in that policy. But this attitude soon changed. This modification of policy was in great part due to the vigorous campaign instigated by O. M. W. Sprague, professor of banking at Harvard. Sprague was, in general, a conservative, and was not even an expert in public finance. Yet he aroused the public and the profession to protest against the original congressional policy. He began his campaign as early as 1916, with a speech before the American Economic Association. The objection to financing the war primarily on loans, he said, was that loans had the defects of paper money. Individual borrowings for the purchase of bonds and bank investments in bonds would occasion expansion of the volumes of credit, thereby tending toward inflation. While a taxing policy would reduce demand for unneces-

sary consumption, and hold down the money costs of war, easy monetary conditions, needed to float loans, would enable many to borrow without reducing consumption; and the resultant uneven advances in prices would give rise to undesirable variations in income, to "undeserved and temporary gains" for extravagance in consumption.

Sprague pointed out with some asperity that a loan policy gave higher consideration to property than to life. Since modern warfare required the conscription of men, he said, it should logically and equitably require conscription of all income above that absolutely necessary. Under the loan policy the stay-at-home could convert his surplus into an interest-paying loan, to which the soldier, if fortunate enough to return, would have to contribute. Furthermore, the stay-at-home very often received a higher income and a better position, while the returning soldier would find it difficult to secure his old position or its equivalent. . . .

Though the tax program as enacted did not come near the "fifty-fifty" idea [loans and taxes] which was the real heart of the Sprague demand, it was generally acknowledged afterward that the vigorous expression of the proposal at an opportune time had brought salutary results. It is noteworthy that [E. R. A.] Seligman, one of the most vigorous opponents of Sprague's viewpoint, wrote that, with all its faults, the Revenue Act of October 1917 (with its heavy income and excess profits taxes) was based on "democratic principles hitherto unrealized in fiscal history. To impose the great burden of taxation on wealth and luxurious consumption rather than on the expenditure of the mass of the people was to take an appreciable forward step in the direction of realizing the principle of ability to pay."

Each successive revenue measure raised the tax rates, with especial emphasis on personal income taxes and excess profits taxes. Thus in 1916 the normal income tax rate was 2 per cent, with a surtax on incomes exceeding $20,000 ranging from 1 per cent to 13 per cent on incomes in excess of $2,000,000. By 1918 the normal rate was 6 per cent on net incomes up to $4000 and 12 per cent on higher incomes, with a surtax ranging from 1 per cent on incomes exceeding $5000 to 65 per cent on incomes over $1,000,000. The business and financial community did not let this "dangerous tendency" toward "excessive taxation" go unchallenged. The Chicago banker George M. Reynolds complained at the time of radicals urging excessively high taxes to relieve the middle class and little business. He said: "Do they not know that if the wealthy and big business are oppressed and harassed through excess taxes and price reductions that are beyond reason, and depression is brought upon us, the poor and middle classes and little business will be the chief sufferers? Having less power of resistance, they will be the first to feel the pinch of hard times. It will be like a panic or fire. The strong are able to care for themselves, but the weak go down in the crash." And Mortimer Schiff of Kuhn, Loeb and Company declared that the government must not hamper enterprise by "unwise or too onerous taxation." Capital as well as labor must be permitted, according to him, to earn a fair return. The government must also offer a fair return of interest on its bonds, reasonably close to other prime and readily salable investments. The Federal Reserve System should provide additional currency to support both government and industrial needs. As he outlined the situation, current savings were inadequate; the various classes must borrow from their banks to invest in government bonds; the banks, in turn, must rediscount their customers' notes with the Federal Reserve banks. The money thus received the government would return to the people through the channels of trade and

would again become available for investment in government bonds. This pyramiding process was sound, he thought, for it would be self-liquidating as the people would repay their debts from savings and from the proceeds of their production. But in spite of the heavy increases in taxation and of numerous pronouncements from President Wilson on down that there should be no profits from the war, substantial profits were reaped, for, as [Frederick W.] Taussig pointed out, the legislation was not created with the expected speed nor on the expected scale.

Control of labor was even more gropingly applied. The need for unified administration of the labor supply and for centralized treatment of labor questions was belatedly recognized. The government had to face the problem of the I.W.W. pacifism, and attempted to solve it by mass arrests of the leaders. Upon this Alvin S. Johnson, in discussing why America lagged in the war effort, commented that labor in the Northwest was pretty well infiltrated with I.W.W. ideals, and it was necessary to employ I.W.W. men and their sympathizers to obtain the essential wood supply for airplanes and ships. "And it is worth noting that those I.W.W. laborers have done important pieces of our war work in record time. The actual producers have found it not impossible to do business with men of I.W.W. leanings and to get them to agree to sink their private predilections for sabotage for the country's good." Yet the Department of Justice fell upon their leaders with indictments of conspiracy. "Believe what you will against these I.W.W. leaders; many of them were to be counted on to hold labor in line; and the rank and file of workers in sympathy with the organization now feel suspicious of the government and all its works."

In general, however, the government was not hostile to labor unions, and they flourished. There was a proliferation of boards—for mediation, policy, and labor standards—but only toward the end of the war was the machinery becoming comprehensive and fully effective. Despite the slow method of trial and error the government's experience was of great value for subsequent action.

3

George Soule
INDUSTRIAL GAINS AND LOSSES

From Prosperity Decade: From War to Depression–1917–1929, *pp. 59–63, by George Soule. Copyright 1947 by George Soule. Reprinted by permission of Holt, Rinehart and Winston, Inc.*

George Soule (1887–1970), journalist, author, and educator, was editor of the *New Republic* magazine from 1924 to 1947 and professor of economics at Bennington College from 1949 to 1957, when he retired. His particular interests were social and economic history and the problems of labor and industry. Among his many books were *The Coming American Revolution* (1934), *Sidney Hillman, Labor Statesman* (1939), *Prosperity Decade* (1947) (volume 8 of the ten volume *Economic History of the United States*), *Time for Living* (1955), and *Planning U. S. A.* (1967).

The war . . . exerted effects on the economy that became manifest in subsequent years. . . . Here some of the more important may be briefly noted. The movement for standardization of products and processes, the interchangeability of parts, and reduction in the number of sizes and styles made rapid headway, and the attention of many was called to the savings that could thus be effected. Scientific management received governmental encouragement, and more attention began to be devoted to the arts of managing industrial personnel. The industry committees formed with the encouragement of the War Industries Board and the Food Administration constituted the basis of the subsequent growth of trade associations.

The war marked a great increase in the physical plant of American manufacturing. Expenditures for new buildings and equipment rose from $600 million in 1915 to $2.5 billion in 1918. Some of these additions represented special-purpose facilities useful for war only, and some were devoted to industries like shipbuilding and aircraft production, which suffered a drastic shrinkage in the postwar period. Nevertheless, a fairly large proportion of the new investment provided plants and machinery capable of being turned back to peace production without difficult problems of reconversion. The war therefore occasioned a large and permanent increase in manufacturing capacity.

Naturally, some industries boomed while others were adversely affected. It is not easy in all cases to separate from the normal trend the effects of the war on a specific industry. During the period there was a rapid growth of the relatively new automobile industry. Production of passenger cars rose from 460,000 in 1913 to 1,750,000 in 1917. In 1918, production was reduced by government order, but not eliminated. The adoption of this new method of transportation created a stimulus in many other directions. There was a proliferation of oil wells and refineries, pipe lines, filling stations, and garages. State and local governments built many miles of roads, mostly on borrowed money. All of this naturally helped to accentuate the war boom.

It is possible to learn something about the relative growth of industries by changes in their physical output between 1914 and 1919. Neither of these years is ideal as a bench mark, because both were characterized by slumps of physical production. Nevertheless, they are chosen because they were years when the quinquennial census of manufactures was taken.

The industry which showed the greatest growth of all in this period was motor vehicles, which more than quadrupled in output. Next in order came rubber goods, with an increase of 186 per cent, due largely to the demand for automobile tires. The only other industry that more than doubled was condensed and evaporated milk, with a growth of 134 per cent. Other heavy gainers were petroleum refining, linoleum, iron and steel, slaughtering and meat packing, explosives, soap, hats, motorcycles, canning and preserving, manufactured ice, paints and varnishes, woolen goods, silk manufactures, and pianos. Industries that declined during the period were largely associated with construction. They included brick, cement, clay products, lumber, cast-iron pipe, turpentine, and rosin. A few industries showed the effect of permanent declines in demand, like cotton lace goods. A few others, like fertilizers, cordage and twine, and jute and linen goods, reflected shortages of materials resulting from the war.

The shrinkage of housing construction, while the population continued its growth, laid the basis for the future housing shortage and building boom. Those who enjoyed larger real incomes on account of the war constituted an active market for luxury goods and created higher standards of living that later affected wider circles of consumers. While the President and the Secretary of the Treasury during the war were asking people to curtail their expenditures for patriotic reasons, business interests conducted a nation-wide anti-thrift campaign with billboards and full-page advertisements urging liberal buying of consumers' goods.

Allied buying before 1917 virtually extinguished the net debt of Americans to foreigners, and the amounts loaned to their associates in the war consisted almost entirely of an expansion of the Allied debt. Approximately $643 million of Allied borrowing was used to repay the short-term notes obtained by the

Allies through American banks before the entry of the United States into the war and interest before the end of the war period amounted to over $700 million more. The rest was paid for commodities and services in the following order of importance—cereals and food, munitions, cotton, other supplies, transportation and shipping, and miscellaneous. The former debtor position of the United States was thus dramatically changed to a creditor one, and American producers became accustomed to a large export surplus financed on credit.

Few gave any thought at the time to the question how these loans were to be repaid or what would happen to exports when the stream of foreign lending stopped. It was not until later that people began to be aware of the difficult problem of transferring payments for the Allied debt. The controversy that subsequently arose concerning this matter and the long train of misfortunes set in motion by postwar readjustment were not foreseen.

The credit inflation that accompanied the governmental policies in financing the war, and the rapidly rising prices that resulted, naturally had a direct bearing on the economic history of the next few years.

Finally, the eyes of many who had participated in the war planning, or who had observed it with understanding, were opened to the possibilities of managing the economy for chosen ends. Whereas in previous years the behavior of the economic order had seemed like a series of unpredictable and uncontrollable natural phenomena, it now was analyzed with the aid of masses of new statistics and more detailed examination of cause and effect. It began to be possible to speak in terms of relative magnitudes and large aggregates, and to apply deliberate social controls by policies of priority and other devices. Toward the end of the war, a relatively few people began to ask why, if production and distribution could be governed even by a hastily improvised organization for war purposes, even better results might not be achieved over a longer period for purposes regarded as desirable in peace.

This attitude, however, did not at the time gain the adherence of those who held power, and failed to attract a wide popular following. The literature of reconstruction in the United States was far less voluminous and had a much smaller circulation than it did in England and other countries. No influential advocate of economic planning appeared. Mr. [Herbert] Hoover and Mr. [Bernard] Baruch had emphasized that everything being done was for the emergency only. They saw no peril in a rapid abandonment of controls. Planning even for demobilization and reconversion had made little headway within government circles when the end of the war arrived. Most of the war agencies themselves were staffed by volunteers who were eager to get back as soon as possible to their customary pursuits. The overcrowded and distracted atmosphere of Washington seemed to be an evil from which everyone would be glad to flee at the earliest possible moment. Nevertheless, the experience of war planning exerted a permanent influence on the thinking of the economists and engineers who participated in it.

4

John D. Hicks
LABOR AND THE POSTWAR REACTION

From John D. Hicks, Rehearsal for Disaster; The Boom and Collapse of 1919–1920 (*Gainesville: University of Florida, 1961*), *pp.* 34–41.

John D. Hicks (1890–   ) taught at the Universities of Nebraska and Wisconsin before coming to the University of California at Berkeley, where he was Morison Professor of American History from 1942–1957, and has since been emeritus professor. A specialist in recent politics and the agrarian movements of the American West, he is the author of *The Populist Revolt* (1931) and *Republican Ascendancy 1921–33* (1960), as well as co-author (with Theodore Saloutos) of *Agricultural Discontent in the Middle West, 1900–1939* (1951).

Labor, on the whole, profited greatly from the war. Wages rose even more rapidly than prices, so that in terms of purchasing power, or "real wages," the worker as the war ended was getting a better return for his labor than he had received before the war. The menace of unemployment seemed likewise to have disappeared. Membership in trade unions had almost doubled. Union treasuries were full, and labor leaders, counting on the liberal provisions of the Clayton Act of 1914, felt a reasonable security in their right to bargain collectively, and to strike if need be without fear of hampering injunctions.

Labor confidence got its first rude shock with the brief recession that followed the signing of the armistice; the status of war workers and of peace workers, it soon appeared, could be vastly different. During the war period every effort had been made to tap new sources of labor supply. With so many men in service, and with European immigration at a standstill, employment agents had induced Negroes and poor whites to leave the South in great numbers for jobs in the northern cities. Mexicans, Puerto Ricans, and Filipinos were likewise in great demand. More and more women had gone to work outside the home, replacing men not only in white-collar jobs but also in such unskilled activities as freight handling. The United States Employment Service of the Department of Labor, formerly interested mainly in securing jobs for immigrants, had organized local boards in nearly every community, and had funneled off the available labor supply to the points of greatest need. Altogether, civilian employment figures by the time of Armistice Day had reached about forty million persons, of whom nearly one-fourth were engaged in some kind of war work.

With wages at unheard of figures, most workers assumed, quite mistakenly as events proved, that their newly found prosperity would last on indefinitely. Then, immediately after Armistice Day, the cancellation of war contracts touched off a cycle of wholesale dismissals. In the midst of a hard winter, thousands of men who had no resources except the daily wages they earned found themselves without jobs. They were soon joined by thousands of ex-servicemen in search of employment, and by a smaller, but still considerable, number of former federal employees, particularly those discharged by the rapidly evaporating war boards. Some of the women who lost their jobs could return to their domestic duties, and some of the rural workers who had come to the cities could return to the farm. But great numbers of war workers found themselves stranded in a strange environment, and with little prospect of re-employment. By February, 1919, an estimated 3 million workers were out of jobs.

The government did little to help this unfortunate situation. At this juncture the United States Employment Service could have been of inestimable assistance, but Congress, in its eagerness to turn its back on war developments as rapidly as possible, chose January, 1919, as the time to curtail the appropriations for this agency by some 80 per cent, and thus to hamper its activities when they were never more greatly needed. [President] Wilson, however, did call a conference in Washington of governors and mayors to discuss the problem of unemployment, but the sentiment of the gathering was probably well expressed by Governor Calvin Coolidge of Massachusetts, whose verdict on the returned veterans was that "more than 90 per cent" of them were able to "take care of

themselves." The President also urged Congress to institute a public-works program, including reclamation projects, but the economy-minded Republican majority refused to follow his advice. When in the summer of 1919 business began to take on a new lease of life, unemployment declined, but it by no means disappeared.

There were other disturbing considerations. Among them was the thoroughgoing inflation of the price structure that had followed the war. The rise in prices as an inevitable accompaniment of the war was one thing, but their continuing rise after the return of peace was quite another. Prices had begun to climb in 1914 with the outbreak of the war in Europe, and by 1917 when the United States entered the war they were about 70 per cent above the averages of 1913, the last full year of peace. The trouble was that after Armistice Day, with government controls relaxed and deficit financing still in operation, the upward trend persisted. During 1918 the average of prices had risen to approximately 100 per cent over prewar figures, while during 1919 they rose by another 24 per cent. It might be possible to prove statistically that wages had risen correspondingly, but, whatever the averages might show, prices for many workers had far outrun wage increases, and the problem of making ends meet had become extremely precarious. As *Life* commented wryly, "When we receive one of those bulletins showing that foods haven't increased in price, we realize that you can prove anything with figures."

Moreover, the attitude of employers was far from reassuring. Their rejoicing over the demise of the War Labor Board, which for the duration had defended the rights of labor, was open and unashamed. They seemed to regard the reappearance of "a convenient margin of unemployment" as a blessing rather than a curse. Mr. [Samuel] Gompers, said one of their spokesmen, might as well forget the Clayton Act, for labor was a commodity after all. Peace meant a glutted labor market, and with the law of supply and demand back on the throne, labor would have to accept lower wages whether it wanted to or not. Also, the time had come to halt the process of unionization, which had profited altogether too much from government favoritism during the war. Employers should at last feel free to run their businesses without the handicap of outside interference.

Was labor to lose all the gains it had made during the war? Not if it could help it. Fighting a war on the slogan "to make the world safe for democracy" had had some unanticipated results. Why should employers not understand that "their day of absolutism in industry is gone, the same as absolutism in government is gone?" "What shall it profit a man if he gain democracy for the whole world, and lose his own at home?" Why should the sound doctrine "that every individual had the right to regular and continuous employment at a wage sufficient for the maintenance of proper living conditions" be so coldly received in business circles? Sensing the changed atmosphere, Mr. Gompers reluctantly broke off his pleasant cooperation with the capitalists, and resumed his time-honored role as labor leader. But the armies of labor he sought to command were no longer so content with his methods. New conditions, some of the younger and more radical leaders insisted, called for fundamental changes in the pattern of labor organization. The rapid technical advances of the war years had made possible in many industries the use of much unskilled or semi-skilled labor, not classifiable by trades or crafts. Why should these workers not be organized into all-embracing industry-wide unions? To Gompers and his conservative associates, firm disciples of the trade-union principle, this proposal was far too revolutionary to be tenable. But the fact remained that the American Federation of

Labor accounted for only 4 to 5 million workers, perhaps not more than one-eighth of the total American labor force. Did not democracy require that the other seven-eighths also have a voice?

There was considerable disagreement, also, as to the political role that labor should play. Why should American workers forever adhere to the Gompers policy of "voluntarism," with no defenses except economic pressure and the pitting of the older parties against each other in quest of minor favors? What help could labor expect from either the Democrats or the Republicans, "rival lackeys to the great monopolies"? Why should American workers not follow the example of British labor, to say nothing of the Soviets, and form a party of its own? "If labor doesn't organize politically," one disillusioned worker observed, "it ought to be enslaved—and probably will be." But against such radical views Gompers and the old guard held the line with firm consistency. At the meeting of the American Federation of Labor in Atlantic City, June, 1919, Gompers was re-elected with only one dissenting vote, and his policies were upheld, but the existence of a strong undercurrent of discontent was too obvious to be overlooked. Predictions were rife that revolutionary changes in policy only awaited Gompers' death or resignation.

Indeed, railroad labor, in its enthusiastic support of the so-called "Plumb plan" for the reorganization of the railroads, seemed unwilling to wait even that long. This plan was drawn by Glenn R. Plumb, an attorney for the railroad brotherhoods, and was officially presented to the government and the public in 1919 as railroad labor's solution for the railroad problem. The plan revealed, first of all, that the brotherhoods were "in no mood to brook the return" of the railroads to private control; instead, they proposed that the government should float 4 per cent bonds from the proceeds of which to purchase all the railroads of the nation at prices ultimately to be determined by the courts. Operation of the railroads as one united system was to be vested in a corporation owned by the government, but controlled by a fifteen-member board of directors, one-third to be appointed by the President to represent the public, one-third to be elected by the operating officials, and one-third by the classified employees. Surplus earnings after expenses were to be divided equally between the government and the employees, with automatic reductions in rates whenever the employees' share of the surplus should exceed 5 per cent of the gross operating expenses. Railroad rates would continue to be supervised by the Interstate Commerce Commission, and the customary rights and privileges of labor were to be duly safeguarded.

Naturally, this radical proposal met with a barrage of opposition. The New York *World* denounced it as "a new form of class industry in which the public provides the capital and the workers take the profits." Such a program might well precede, as some of its proponents no doubt intended, "a drive for the democratization or nationalization of all basic industries such as mines, steel mills, packing industries and other enterprises of a national character." It was socialism, or worse, and should be defeated at all costs. Defeated it was, with Gompers and other labor conservatives joining the opposition, and by the Transportation Act of 1920 the railroads were returned to their private owners. But the fear of the radical program inherent in the Plumb plan disturbed conservatives for a long, long time, and was to bear fruit in the ruthless suppression of the Railroad Shopmen's strike of 1922.

As a matter of fact, the year 1919 was the worst year for industrial strife that the United States had ever known. It would be difficult even to list all the strikes that occurred in the nation during that year. According to one computation, the total reached 2,665, and the number of employees involved, 4,160,348. Strikes or lockouts directly affecting the state of New York alone numbered 608 during the first quarter of the year. The first of three strikes by New York's 16,000 harbor workers began on January 9, and ultimately idled 50,000 longshoremen as well. Later in the month 35,000 dress and waist makers went out. In May the ladies' cloak and suit makers struck; in July, the cigar makers; in August, the Brooklyn surface, elevated, and subway workers; in September, the pressmen; and so on throughout the year. The demands of the strikers varied, but they included such items as higher pay, a shorter workday or week, regular wages instead of piecework pay, and recognition of the union. In the settlement of the New York strikes and of those staged elsewhere in the country there was a general tendency to yield a little to labor, especially in view of the still mounting cost of living.

5

John M. Clark
THE COST OF THE WAR

From John M. Clark, The Cost of the War to the American People (New Haven, Conn.: Yale University Press, 1963), pp. 278–283. Reprinted by permission of the Carnegie Endowment for International Peace.

John M. Clark (1884–1963), after teaching briefly at Colorado College, Amherst College, and the University of Chicago, was appointed professor of economics at Columbia University in 1926. He served in that capacity for more than twenty-five years, becoming (John Bates) Clark Professor of Political Economy shortly before his retirement. His published works include *Alternate to Serfdom* (1948), *Guideposts of Change* (1949), and *Economic Institutions and Human Welfare* (1957).

The problem of the effect of the War . . . may be set forth in two questions: have we been richer or poorer since the War than we should have been if the world had remained at peace; and have we been richer or poorer than we should have been if the War had come as it did, but we had remained neutral? The first question can be answered, after a fashion and with all necessary reservations, by an appeal to "normal" trends, prolonged into the post-war period; the second question involves so many uncertainties that it is virtually unanswerable.

As to the first question, it is possible, though far from certain, that the peak of our post-war prosperity was not only the highest in our history but higher than anything we should have experienced if there had been no war. But it is also morally certain that the depressions of 1921 and 1930 cut deeper than any that would have occurred if the War had not disrupted the economic life of the world. And with every week that the present depression continues, the moral certainty increases that the effect of the War in deepening our depressions outweighs its conjectural effect in heightening our post-war boom; and that we have on the average been poorer since 1919 than we should have been if peace had continued. It is even possible that we have been poorer since 1922.

The question of the effect of our participation in the War, assuming the existence of war in Europe in any case, is hopelessly conjectural because it depends on what would have happened had we remained neutral. Would the Central Powers have won the War, and if so, what effect would that have had on our

international position? Such questions are probably idle. What seems fairly certain is that our exceedingly profitable neutral trade would have been seriously hampered or crippled, and we should have emerged without the enormous volume of debts owing to us which are hampering the resumption of normal economic relations at present. This might have been a blessing in disguise. And Europe would still, after the War, have been in urgent need of our funds and our goods, which we should have been in a position to supply. Hence there is no adequate reason for supposing that our prosperity would have been any less than it has actually been. Whatever the outcome of the War if we had not entered it, Europe could hardly have been worse disorganized than the Peace of Versailles left it, nor international economic relations more disrupted.

Perhaps the main reason for thinking that the peak of our post-war prosperity was higher than we should have enjoyed if there had been no war consists in the fact that Europe had such need of our goods that she bought them on credit and so enabled us to continue marketing a large export surplus in spite of the fact that we were now a creditor nation and would naturally be receiving an excess of goods rather than sending it out. Thus the process was cumulative, Europe falling increasingly into our debt. We have seen . . . that such a credit demand affords, while it lasts, probably the greatest possible stimulus to production; but it is in its essence a temporary condition. The present state of Europe indicates that the process is coming within sight of the natural limits set by the credit capacity of the European nations. From now on, we must probably get on without a large part of this extra and temporary stimulus; and therefore we may have to resume, after the present depression, from a lower level than the post-war trend hitherto would indicate. This is especially true if the international debt situation remains unchanged, since it constitutes a serious obstacle to the resumption of normal international trade relations.

This whole international debt situation has entered upon a new chapter with the "Hoover plan" for a one-year moratorium, on which negotiations are being carried out. . . . This proposal constitutes the first practical recognition on the part of the United States of the fact that German reparations and interallied debts are, after all, bound together; and also that the terms of the settlements cannot, under all conditions, be literally carried out. Whether the temporary concessions made now will be sufficient, from the bare standpoint of preserving Europe from fiscal and political shipwreck or whether some more permanent adjustment will be necessary—this remains to be seen. The recent fall in prices has automatically increased the real burden of the debts by an enormous amount. And the whole situation increases the uncertainty as to whether it will prove practicable for us to collect the full amount of the payments due us under the terms of the Young Plan. There can be no question but that full collection would be an evil for the civilization of which our country forms a part.

And even granting fiscal repayment as practicable, it is far from certain that we can collect these sums in a form which will mean a net addition to the wealth our nation would otherwise be producing and consuming. There is a large probability that at least part of our collections may, directly or indirectly, displace domestic production rather than add to it. If Europe sends us goods, some of them will compete with our own industries which are now working at part capacity for lack of markets. And if Europe cannot send us goods, she can buy less from us, thus tending to reduce the output of our export industries which are

in a similar condition. Our balance of trade is now being maintained by a reduction of Europe's purchases from us: a situation from which we do not gain. Thus the collections harm Europe without clearly and certainly benefiting us. In short, on these doubtful matters of our post-war prosperity as affected both by domestic and international conditions, the balance sheet of the War probably shows a loss, though this may not be susceptible of proof.

There remains our domestic war debt, and the very real and tangible billions of losses from death and disability, whose fiscal counterpart is found in the budget of the Veterans' Administration. This last is the chief clear and demonstrable burden to the national economy remaining from the War. The paying off of 23 billions of war borrowings, with possibly 13 to 14 billions of interest, disbursed to our citizens after being collected from our citizens as taxes—this involves burdens on our national economy, no doubt. But it is not a net loss of 23 billions nor of 36 or 37 billions. Whatever net burdens there may be, they are . . . not capable of demonstration or measurement. Aside from the aftermath of death and disability, the measurable national effects were for the most part borne while the struggle was going on. In that respect we were the most fortunate of the major participants.

We were fortunate, first of all, in the period of our neutrality. Instead of plunging at once into the conflict, we had some two years— discounting the preliminary depression—in which we sold munitions at high profits and received a general stimulus to our own production through the diffused and cumulative effects, with the result that we were able to consume more and at the same time to save enormously more; building up without felt abstinence the greater part of the productive plant for munition-making which was of actual service in fighting the War. In general, productive equipment which we had to install after our own entry into the War produced little effective output before the armistice; and if we had had to rely solely on such equipment, we should not have been able to congratulate ourselves so heartily on our performance.

The year 1916 was notable not only for general prosperity, but especially for the number of very large incomes and the size of the few largest. "Profiteering" was not yet effectively limited by war taxation. The rich had plenty of funds, either to pay as taxes, to subscribe to government bonds, or to devote as capital to essential war production.

From our entry into the War to the end of the fiscal year 1921 this country spent, through Federal, State, and local governments and private agencies, very nearly 40 billion dollars on war demands of one sort or another, of which possibly 35½ billions was on account of the World War, and the rest mainly pensions to veterans of former wars and the normal peace-time outlays of military and naval establishments. Of the 35½ billions some 32 billions represented outlays of goods and services by the national economy as a whole, and not mere fiscal transfers such as payment of interest on the public debt to our own citizens. These war-time dollars may be thought of as roughly equivalent in buying power to post-war dollars of 1922–28. About half of this effort was concentrated in the calendar year 1918, constituting more than one-fourth of our national income in that year.

We have estimated that some 13 billions of this war cost came out of increased productive effort during the years 1917–19, . . . and 19 billions came out of decreased consumption. . . . The years 1920–21 witnessed a shrinkage in the national output of wealth which would go far toward wiping out the increase in the years 1917–19. Indeed, over the whole period

from 1917 to 1922, and allowing for a normal upward trend, it is more than doubtful if the War caused any increase in our national volume of production above what it would otherwise have been, by way of compensation for its costs. On that basis the cost all came out of decreased consumption, but the retrenchment was spread over a longer time than the war effort.

The increased output in 1917–19 was made possible largely because, in spite of fewer workers attached to private employments, there were more persons actually at work in them. This came about simply through lessened unemployment. Furthermore, those in essential industries put in a great deal of overtime. In human terms as well as in money terms, this was more than usually costly output.

The workers who produced it naturally did not receive their full share of the increase—naturally, that is, in view of the need of diverting one-fourth of the whole to the Government. The purchasing power of salaries shrank by billions, inflicting on this class the most pinching economic burdens borne by any major group. The *total amount* of salaries increased, even in buying power, simply because there was such an increase in numbers working for the Government. As for wages, wage *rates* probably failed to keep full pace with rising costs of living, but annual earnings per worker showed some gains, because workers were more fully employed. In this form of added work done, wageworkers made a contribution which the figures of national income fail to show.

Farmers gained over 5 billions in the years 1917–19, and might be said to have been paying for it ever since. Business incomes, including corporate savings, mounted enormously, though only a moderate increase found its way to individuals as interest and dividends. The true worth of these corporate savings it seems impossible to measure, owing to uncertainties as to the real meaning of net incomes reported in a time of great inflation, and the difficulty of choosing an appropriate index number to deflate them. In any case, the shrinkage of consumption came for the most part out of salaried workers and security holders. The latter paid, not through shrunken incomes, but in loans and taxes. And, of course, they retained their equities in an increased corporate surplus, and some billions of government bonds, on which they probably received as interest something more than they had to pay as taxes to meet this same interest on the bonds held by themselves and their neighbors.

Besides the economic outlays, made at the time the War was fought, in the shape of increased efforts and decreased consumption, there were also valuable coal and ores taken out of the ground and destroyed. Such costs as these bear on the future, and their amount is hardly measurable. But our estimated 32 billions was disposed of at the time. What was left over included a mass of fiscal obligations requiring us to collect money as taxes and disburse it as interest or other forms of payment, all to the same general body of citizens from whom the taxes came, though not in the same proportions. The more material post-war burdens for the nation as a whole consisted of the task of demobilizing industry from war and remobilizing it for peace; and the burden of the dead and injured.

Ketten in the New York Evening World

WORK or FIGHT

APPLIES TO BOTH!

"While Congress did not pass the proposed 'work or fight' amendment to the Draft Bill, it is clear that the President . . . is determined to enforce its principle in dealing with strikers or employers."—*The Outlook, Sept. 25.*

In April 1918 Woodrow Wilson created the National War Labor Board, giving it unprecedented powers to arbitrate in all disputes involving war-related industries. Later, when the occasion demanded, he backed up the rulings of the Board by seizing plants, threatening management, and threatening to blacklist strikers.   (*Outlook Magazine*; New York Public Library)

Eugene V. Debs being formally notified in the Atlanta Penitentiary on May 31, 1920 of his fifth nomination by the Socialist Party for the Presidency of the United States. At the time, he was serving the second year of a ten-year sentence for having violated the Sedition Act of 1918 by giving speeches in opposition to the War.   (Underwood & Underwood)

Chapter Two

POLITICAL
EFFECTS OF
THE WAR

In this section we encounter a variety of perspectives regarding the scope and merit of the changes wrought in the institutions of government and in political relationships. Mark Sullivan, for one, is very much impressed with the exorbitant cost of the war both in liberties forfeited and in dangerous precedents for the future. Carl B. Swisher, on the other hand, though equally impressed with what occurred, is considerably less fearful than Sullivan in describing the growth of presidential power, as is Seward Livermore, who argues that party politics were largely unaffected by the conflict. Still, it is not irrelevant to Sullivan's fears that, as Alfred H. Kelly and Winfred A. Harbison point out, the Supreme Court was confined at the time to an almost insignificant role in interpreting the prerogatives of the government. As for politics, Richard Hofstadter sees the war, and the way Wilson fought it, as an important factor in bringing about the disintegration of the Progressive movement, while George Mowry, who basically agrees with Hofstadter, puts particular emphasis upon the debilitating effects of the reconversion process. William Leuchtenburg, in the end, finds consolation in the contention that the experience of war later proved to be a valuable inspiration for many New Deal reforms.

QUESTIONS:

1. In what areas was the President most eager to increase his powers during World War I, and in what areas was the Congress most loath to surrender powers?
2. Is it possible to reconcile the notion that the government's balance of power among its three branches was altered during the course of the war with the suggestion that partisan politics went on virtually unaltered? How?
3. Can you explain why a war might undermine the momentum of political movements which are dedicated to domestic reform? In answering, you might bear in mind that the First World War was apparently responsible for bringing socialists to power in Germany and communists in Russia.
4. Why would the experiences of war prove to be useful in contending with an economic depression?
5. Did the First World War leave the country more "modernized" politically?

6

Mark Sullivan
SUBMISSION TO AUTOCRACY

Reprinted by permission of Charles Scribner's Sons from Volume 5, Our Times, pages 489–491. Copyright 1933 Charles Scribner's Sons; renewal copyright © 1961 Mark Sullivan, Jr.

Mark Sullivan (1874–1952), a graduate of the Harvard class of 1900, became one of the most successful political columnists and social commentators of the years between the two world wars. He is particularly remembered for his *Our Times: The United States, 1900–1925,* published in six volumes (1926–1935), and for his autobiography, *The Education of an American* (1938).

Of the effects of the war on America, by far the most fundamental was our submission to autocracy in government. Every male between 18 and 45 had been deprived of freedom of his body—for refusing or evading the surrender, 163,738 were apprehended and disciplined, many by jail sentences. Every person had been deprived of freedom of his tongue, no one could utter dissent from the purpose or the method of war—for violating the sedition act, 1597 persons were arrested. Every business man was shorn of dominion over his factory or store, every housewife surrendered control of her table, every farmer was forbidden to sell his wheat except at the price the government fixed. Our institutions, the railroads, the telephones and telegraphs, the coal mines, were taken under government control—the list was complete when, after the war and preceding the Peace Conference, Wilson took control of the trans-Atlantic cables. The prohibition of individual liberty in the interest of the state could hardly be more complete. "In the six months after our entry into the war the United States had been transformed from a highly individualistic system . . . into what was almost a great socialistic state in which the control of the whole industry, life and purpose of the nation was directed from Washington. It was an amazing transformation, for nothing like it had ever been attempted before on any such scale, and the process was wholly antipathetic to our ordinary ways of doing things."[1] It was the greatest submission by the individual to the state that had occurred in any country at any time. It was an abrupt reversal of the evolution that had been under way for cen-

---

[1] James Truslow Adams in "The Epic of America."

turies. Since Magna Charta, substantially all political change had been in the direction of cumulative taking of power from the state for the benefit of the individual. Now in six months, in America the state took back, the individual gave up, what had taken centuries of contest to win.

It was not merely that we had passed through the experience of enforced submission or voluntary surrender or both. The results remained with us. Government had learned that we could be led to do it, had learned the technique of bringing the individual to give up his liberty, the cunning of propaganda, the artfulness of slogans, and the other methods for inciting mass solidarity and mass action, for causing majorities to insist on conformance by minorities.

The purpose for which we did this, as described by the one who urged us to it and led us into it was "the destruction of every arbitrary power anywhere," "to make the world safe for democracy," a purpose to save the peoples of all nations, including and especially Germany, from autocratic government;[2] a purpose to have the individualist ideal of society (France) triumph in a struggle against the ideal of regimentation (Germany).

That purpose, reviewed fifteen years later in the light of what had meantime happened in the world, seemed very ironic indeed— Germany and Italy under dictators, Russia under a dictatorship called proletarian but more extreme in its deprivation of individual liberty than any personal dictator or absolute monarch attempted, American industry and social organization in the beginning of what was aimed toward regimentation.

[2] "Liberation of [all] peoples, the German people included, from autocratic governments."—Wilson, address to Congress, April 2, 1917.

7

Carl B. Swisher
COMPETITION FOR POWER

From Carl B. Swisher, "Control of War Preparations in the United States," American Political Science Review, Vol. 34 (December 1940), pp. 1085–1098.

Carl B. Swisher (1897–1968) held the Thomas B. Straw Chair in Political Science at The Johns Hopkins University from 1938 until his retirement in 1967. A specialist in the Supreme Court and the Constitution, he was the author of *American Constitutional Development* (1944) and *The Growth of Constitutional Power in the United States* (1946). He also served as special assistant to the Attorney General of the United States from 1935 to 1937.

. . . A prominent characteristic of governmental behavior [during the war] was competition for power between the President and Congress, with victory usually in the hands of the President. Closely allied characteristics were the steady growth in the centralization of power as experience in the handling of war preparations was developed, and a progressive decline in the unwillingness of Congress to permit drastic interference with rights of liberty and property. . . .

One of the emergency agencies first established and most frequently involved in political controversy was the Committee on Public Information, which was set up for the control of publicity. It owed its origin, not to an act of Congress, but to an executive order of April 14, 1917 (eight days after the declaration of war), issued pursuant to a request of the Secretaries of State, War, and Navy. The Committee was to consist of the three secretaries mentioned, or of persons delegated by them, together with a civilian chairman.

Under the direction of George Creel, a magazine writer and former newspaper man who was appointed chairman, the Committee on Public Information operated as a loosely-knit and ever-changing but always powerful organization, in spreading information and propaganda and molding the beliefs of the American people. It published an organ called the *Official Bulletin* by which public documents and digests of information were circulated among the departments, bureaus, and offices of the government, displayed in post-offices, and sent to such subscribers as would pay the subscription price. The Committee had no direct power of censorship, but it exercised a restrictive influence in many ways. The Administration relied heavily on its judgment as to the information which should be given out. The chairman was given representation on the Censorship Board established under the Trading with the Enemy Act. Furthermore, he was in such close contact with the Postmaster-General and other government officials in positions of authority that it was unwise for any publication to flout his policies.

Congress took no responsibility for the Committee on Public Information. At the time of the establishment of the agency it was said that Administration officials considered recommending to Congress a simple bill to give the Committee statutory authority to carry out its rulings. Congress discussed the subject of control of information at length in connection with the omnibus measure which came to be known as the Espionage Act, but, whether because of its own concern about the preservation of freedom of speech and of the press or because of pressure from the newspapers of the country, it did nothing to sanction the establishment of the Committee. Drastic censorship proposals were made and rejected, and Congress included no provision in the Espionage Act concerning an agency to control public information. Bills subsequently introduced for that purpose died in committee.

The Committee on Public Information continued to function, in spite of the absence of legislative sanction, amid criticism from Congress and from the press. During most of the period of its existence its expenses were paid, not out of an appropriation made directly for its use, but out of a fund allotted to the President for use at his discretion for general defense purposes. Its prestige would doubtless have been enhanced had Congress given it formal recognition, but it was not seriously handicapped by the lack of it. In the summer of 1918, Congress did recognize its legitimacy to the extent of making an appropriation for its expenses.

Of the other committees, commissions, and administrations set up for war purposes, many had a common parenthood in the Advisory Commission of the Council of National Defense. Provision for the establishment of the Council of National Defense had been made in the Army Appropriation Act of 1916. The Council consisted of the Secretaries of War, Navy, Interior, Agriculture, Commerce, and Labor. The Advisory Commission was to consist of not more than seven members nominated by the Council and appointed by the President. Each of these members was to have special qualifications, such as knowledge of some industry or public utility or the development of some natural resource. The Council was authorized to make investigations of industry and transportation as related to national defense and to make recommendations to the President and the heads of the executive departments.

The fact should be emphasized that as far as the cabinet officers serving on the Council of National Defense were concerned, the legislation gave them no important new powers.

It merely provided an organization in which they might meet and coordinate the performance of their normal functions if war should be declared. Furthermore, the powers of the Advisory Commission did not go beyond the giving of advice. It was intended that the Commission should bring to the political officers of the government the information and the best judgment of men in the several branches of business and industry, but authority was left with the executive. The fact that Senate action was not required in connection with appointments is doubtless explained largely by the fact that no real powers were conferred upon the persons selected. It was a useful arm of the executive for the execution of authority already held. In May, 1940, President Roosevelt, acting pursuant to the same statute, revived the Advisory Commission to deal in the same advisory manner with the conditions of another crisis.

In spite of its lack of formal authority, the Advisory Commission became an extremely important agency in organizing the country for war. It created large numbers of committees to assemble facts in terms of which production and transportation of war materials were to be planned. These committees educated personnel for the task of coordination. Some of them received broad powers through presidential order or provided the basis for the establishment of other agencies by executive order or by statute.

The organization of what came to be known as the Food Administration, one of the agencies that evolved out of the Advisory Commission, provoked a sharp conflict between the President and Congress. It was discovered during the summer of 1917 that the food supply of the country had already been curtailed by shipments abroad and by reduced production due to unfavorable weather conditions. The President decided that authority over the distribution of food ought to be allotted to a Food Administrator serving under direction of the President and responsible only to him. He had in mind for the task Herbert Hoover, who had already won fame through his management of Belgian relief.

In requesting the enactment of legislation, the President asked for power to fix prices both to encourage production and to secure consumers against extortion. He concurred in Hoover's belief that these objectives could be achieved through voluntary cooperation, but he nevertheless asked for full powers of enforcement, saying: "It is absolutely necessary that unquestionable powers shall be placed in my hands." He assured Congress that the regulation was to continue "only while the war lasts." It was to be a demonstration of democracy at its best. "The last thing that any American could contemplate with equanimity would be the introduction of anything resembling Prussian autocracy into the food control in this country."

In spite of pressure for hasty enactment, the measure was debated over a period of several weeks. A minority opposed it bitterly. Senator James A. Reed of Missouri declared: "The power demanded is greater than has ever been exercised by any king or potentate of earth; it is broader than that which is exercised by the Kaiser of the Germans; it is a power such as no Caesar ever employed over a conquered province in the bloodiest days of Rome's bloody despotism." The bill was handicapped in the Senate by the opposition of Senator Thomas P. Gore, chairman of the Committee on Agriculture, who denounced the provision for one-man control. "I maintain it is unconstitutional legislation," he said. "It would turn over the business of our country to one individual." The Constitution ought to be cherished in times like these, he argued, lest in other times of crisis it be needed to protect us against a dictator, "and to protect us against subserviency of a Congress that might be willing to lick the dust at the feet of such a dictator."

The Senate at first refused to sanction the plan for an administrator chosen by the President alone and passed the bill with a provision for a Food Control Board of three commissioners, to be appointed by the President by and with the advice and consent of the Senate. The bill as approved by the Senate left to the President the selection of the chairman of the board from the three commissioners, so that Mr. Hoover could still be placed at the head of the board if the Senate would accept him as one of the three commissioners. His authority would be subject to check by the other two commissioners, however, and the possibility of swift and vigorous action would be greatly reduced.

The Senate made its position on this part of the bill overwhelmingly clear. A proposal to return to the President's plan for a single administrator received the support of only ten votes as against sixty-three votes in the negative. Another attempt was made, but the vote registered was sixty to twenty-three against the President's plan. The President had won in the House of Representatives, however, and he was determined to win the battle in the conference committee. "If I can help it," he wrote to a friend, " 'there ain't going to be no Food Control *Board*.' I think that it will come out in conference. It makes the bill practically unworkable." Under pressure from him, a majority of the conferees accepted his decision. They had "received their orders," said Senator Gore, who refused to fall into line.

Administration leaders sought to force the immediate acceptance of the report of the conference committee. "The lash, forever and eternally the lash, is laid across the legislative

back," shouted Senator Reed in protest. "More and more we cringe. More and more we whine and crawl between the legs of those who master us." The report was accepted. The President appointed Hoover to the position of Food Administrator, in which he exercised sweeping authority throughout the period of the war.

In the form in which it originally passed the Senate, the Food Control Bill contained another provision which was highly objectionable to the President. It provided for a Joint Committee on Expenditures in the Conduct of the War, and represented the uneasiness of the Senate at the expansion of unchecked presidential powers. A precedent was found for a congressional check upon war expenditures in the fact that during the Civil War Congress had established a Committee on the Conduct of the War.

The subject of congressional participation in the management of the war had been brought to the attention of the Senate on April 9, 1917, three days after the declaration of war. At that time Senator John W. Weeks, a Republican from Massachusetts, offered a joint resolution providing for a joint committee to be known as the Joint Committee on the Conduct of the War. The Committee was to "make a special study of the problems arising out of the war," and to "confer and advise with the President of the United States and the heads of the various executive departments." Senator Weeks explained that this was the general course followed during the Civil War. The Committee would furnish a direct connecting link between the executive and legislative branches of the government. This was no reflection on the president or the heads of departments. It was part of the duty of Congress to have some knowledge of methods by which the five or six billions of war appropriations would be expended and to determine whether expenditure was being made in accordance with the purpose of Congress. The resolution submitted by Senator Weeks was referred to the Committee on Rules, where the Democratic majority rewrote it to limit it more specifically to consideration of expenditures and changed the title to Joint Committee on Expenditures in the Conduct of the War. The report of the Committee was adverse, however, and no further action was taken on the resolution.

In the meantime, Senator Weeks offered the original draft of his resolution as an amendment to the food control bill. When the amendment came up for consideration, Senator [Robert L.] Owen, a Democrat, asked the substitution of the draft as reported out of the Committee on Rules, and Senator Weeks accepted the substitute. With no debate whatsoever, a vote was taken and the amendment was adopted, 53 to 31. The amendment was a part of the bill when it went to conference committee. . . .

The President hurled the weight of his opposition against the proposal. The plan for the Joint Committee, he wrote to Representative [Asbury] Lever, would render his task of conducting the war almost impossible. "The constant supervision of executive action which it contemplates would amount to nothing less than an assumption on the part of the legislative body of the executive work of the Administration." He referred to the Civil War experience as an ominous precedent wherein President Lincoln had suffered distressing harassment. The proposed cooperation of Congress with the President was not practicable. "The responsibility rests upon the Administration. There are abundant existing means of investigation and of the effective enforcement of that responsibility." He asked a friend in the Senate to aid in preventing his management of the war from "being put under an

espionage committee." The President was again victorious. The proposal for the Joint Committee of Congress was abandoned.

The President averted a possible struggle with Congress over methods of managing railroads by taking over control of the railroads of the country and establishing a railroad administration while Congress was in recess for the Christmas holidays at the end of 1917. Government operation of transportation lines had been recommended by the Federal Trade Commission in a report made on June 19, 1917. The government was slow to act, no doubt partly because of a current movement for permanent government ownership and operation. The railroad field was one of many in which it was feared that the war might be used as a pretext for bringing about changes that would become permanent in spite of the opposition of conservative interests.

The railroads themselves had sought to bring about the necessary coordination of their facilities without resort to government control. Pursuant to the request of the Council of National Defense, leading railroad executives had met in Washington a few days after war was declared and established their own coordinating agency in the form of a committee called the Railroads' War Board. A member of the advisory commission of the Council of National Defense and a member of the Interstate Commerce Commission were ex officio members of the Board. Throughout the remainder of 1917, the Board sought to bring about the maximum of cooperation among roads which had hitherto been encouraged to compete and had been denied the privilege of any high degree of cooperation. For a number of reasons, the Board was unable to bring about the desired coordination, and traffic congestion became one of the most serious problems connected with speedy preparation for war. Railroad finances, furthermore, were in a serious state, and the raising of funds for the railroads' use threatened to interfere with the floating of loans for government purposes. . . .

The President postponed action until December 26, 1917, when he issued a proclamation taking possession and assuming control of the railroads of the country as of December 28, 1917. Administration was vested in the Secretary of the Treasury, William Gibbs McAdoo, not in his secretarial capacity, but in a new position as Director-General of Railroads. Existing statutes and orders of the Interstate Commerce Commission affecting railroads were to continue in operation, said the President's proclamation, but "any orders, general or special, hereafter made by said Director, shall have paramount authority and be obeyed as such."

The statute under which the action was taken [the Army Appropriation Act of 1916] made no provision for the management of traffic on the roads or for compensation to the owners. It had been enacted, not with the expectation that all railroads would be taken over, but to insure the ability of the government to transport troops and equipment to the Mexican border if the occasion required. Some additional legislation for the guidance of the government was obviously necessary. President Wilson appeared before Congress on January 4, 1918, to request the enactment of such legislation, and Administration bills to achieve the desired end were introduced simultaneously in both houses. There was sufficient disagreement concerning the measure to prevent the completion of enactment until March 21, 1918, but no substantial change was made in the organization for management of the railroads which had been set up by the President.

In point of numbers, the government had all the organization it could conceivably need

for the management of the war; yet plans went awry, programs of production and distribution broke down, frantic agencies got in each other's way, and competing government purchasing agencies fought for the possession of the same materials. Materials were said to have been carried to Europe, and then carried back again because of need for ballast in otherwise empty ships. Men trained for battle were sent abroad and had to be provided with clothing and guns by the Allies whom they went to assist. Hearings before the Senate Committee on Military Affairs disclosed gross inefficiency at critical points. In spite of the fact that criticism of the government was denounced as giving aid and comfort to the enemy, such criticism was voiced in Congress and publicized by the press.

The great need, it was said, was not for more agencies but for over-all supervision, coordination of activity from the top. The President, it was argued time and again, was already burdened with more responsibility than any man could possibly carry. He should be provided with right-hand assistance in managing the mass of organizations subject to his control. The Committee on Military Affairs did not return to the plan for a joint congressional committee to aid the President, but proposed the creation of a Ministry of Munitions and of a war cabinet of three men. . . .

Although the President had staunch defenders in Congress, it began to appear that criticism of delay and apparent inefficiency in getting ready for active participation in the war might result in the enactment of legislation to which the President was opposed. Under his direction, therefore, a bill was prepared authorizing him to coordinate or consolidate executive agencies for the period of the war and to create new agencies by executive order to which functions might be transferred. The Democratic floor leader thought it gave the President too much power and refused to introduce it. Senator Lee S. Overman introduced the bill, which thereafter bore his name. It was referred to the Committee on the Judiciary, of which he was chairman.

The introduction of this Administration bill had the desired effect of postponing further consideration of the measures to which the Administration was opposed. It stirred great excitement in the Senate and in the press. Senator [Gilbert] Hitchcock declared that it "would mean nothing but an abdication by Congress of its law-making power." Senator Reed Smoot thought there would be nothing left but to make the President a king. Other senators sputtered about the proposed congressional abdication of power. The *New York Times* said of the bill: "It outstrips in its delegation of power the authority contemplated in the War Cabinet Bill and the measure for a Director of Munitions together."

The more violent protests against the bill took their tone from a provision which authorized the President to create new agencies by executive order and "to vest therein the performance of such functions as he may deem appropriate." This drastic provision was eliminated by the Judiciary Committee. Other changes of lesser importance were made in the bill, and information was circulated that the principal desire of the President was to have unrestricted power for effective coordination of the War Department. The measure came to a vote in the Judiciary Committee on the last day of February. In spite of the fact that the President, in conferences with individual senators, had urged enactment of the measure, the Committee vote was a tie. Three weeks passed before the tie was broken and the measure reported favorably. Debate was prolonged, and it was not until May 20, 1918, that the Overman Act received the President's signature.

Under the powers of reorganization conferred by the Overman Act, the President brought about a number of changes in the government establishment. The principal change, which had to do with the War Industries Board, was decided upon and actually initiated some weeks before the Act was passed. The powers of the Board, or of its chairman, were expanded and its position was strengthened as a coordinating agency. The Board had originally been in the form of a committee under the Council of National Defense, by which it had been organized. It was therefore in no position to give orders to the Secretary of War or to other members of the Council. On March 4, 1918, while the Senate Judiciary Committee was deadlocked over the bill, the President wrote a letter to Bernard M. Baruch asking him to accept the chairmanship of the War Industries Board. The letter gave to the chairman full power and responsibility in most matters with the important exception of price-fixing, leaving the remaining members chiefly as advisers to the chairman. The President outlined the functions of the Board and the duties of the chairman as if it were now independent of the Council of National Defense. To all intents and purposes, it became independent immediately as a result of the President's letter. It achieved formal independence after the Overman Act was passed, when the President issued an executive order establishing the Board as "a separate administrative agency to act for me and under my direction."

In tearing the War Industries Board away from its creator—the Council of National Defense—and establishing it as an independent administrative agency, the President may have violated the spirit of the Overman Act, in view of the fact that the authorization to create new agencies and transfer powers and functions to them had been stricken from the bill. However that may be, the Board, through Chairman Baruch, became an extremely powerful agency during the last months of the war. Grosvenor B. Clarkson, the historian of the Board, has said that through it the United States "had in the end a system of concentration of commerce, industry, and all the powers of government that was without compare among all the other nations, friend or enemy, involved in the World War."

8

Seward Livermore
PARTISANSHIP IN CONGRESS

Copyright © 1966 by Wesleyan University. Reprinted from Politics is Adjourned, *by Seward Livermore, pp. 1–4, by permission of Wesleyan University Press.*

Seward Livermore (1901–   ) served in the Department of State and in the Central Intelligence Agency between 1944 and 1965, after having taught American history for a number of years. He has since returned to teaching, and is currently a professor at Towson State College (Baltimore). His chief areas of research are American diplomatic, political, and intellectual history, particularly of the early twentieth century.

On the evening of October 24, 1918, President Woodrow Wilson retired to his study in the White House and tapped out on his typewriter a brief message to the people of the United States. It contained a sharp indictment of his political opponents for their obstructive behavior during the war and concluded with an appeal, almost a peremptory demand, for the election a few days thence of a Democratic Congress. The gravamen of his charge was that the Republican leaders in Congress, although pro-war, were anti-administration and thus incapable of giving him the support he needed to see him through the critical period ahead. "At almost every turn, since we entered the war," he said, "they have sought to take the choice of policy and the conduct of the war out of my hands and to put it under the

control of instrumentalities of their own choosing. This is no time either for divided counsel or for divided leadership."

The publication of this document the next day in the nation's press produced an appalling uproar from one end of the country to the other. It astonished a good many Democrats, enraged all the Republicans, and brought into focus a bitter political controversy that had been going on for many months despite a great amount of pretense to the contrary. In the noisy outburst of abuse and recrimination that followed the appearance of the message, the "instrumentalities" mentioned by Wilson were largely lost to sight or obscured by other issues raised by the warring parties, and the matter has escaped attention ever since. Consequently, out of this omission or neglect has sprung one of the sturdiest and most enduring myths in American history—the myth that Wilson by his appeal had revived partisan politics which had automatically and miraculously come to an end when the country entered the war on April 6, 1917.

Wilson's appeal is considered all the more opprobrious because it presumably violated the partisan truce established as a result of his famous "politics is adjourned" statement of May 27, 1918. Besides presupposing a state of affairs without parallel in American experience, this interpretation does not explain why such a truce was necessary in the first place if all partisan activity had already ceased. Nevertheless, it has remained the most popular and widely accepted explanation of the disaster which overtook the Democrats at the polls on November 5. Many otherwise reputable accounts of that critical period make it appear that the President had enjoyed the most harmonious bipartisan cooperation in the stupendous task of forwarding the war program of the government. Republicans and Democrats are pictured working shoulder to shoulder in patriotic support of the Great Crusade without a thought of political advantage or disadvantage arising to mar this remarkable display of transcendent national unity, except perhaps for some welcome constructive criticism from certain quarters. Wilson's appeal, therefore, far from rallying the people to his cause, justly infuriated the hitherto loyal Republican opposition, alienated the electorate, and brought about one of the most significant political upsets in American history.

That other factors might be responsible for this denouement has occurred to a few commentators on the period, but their observations have done little to dispose of the legend of Wilson's allegedly irrational behavior. For the most part, the entire World War period has been sadly neglected on the political side. In the case of the 1918 elections, too much reliance has been placed on the official propaganda put out by both parties in the hectic closing days of the campaign. In the frenzied insults that were exchanged, neither side paid much attention to the truth; and in the post-mortems that followed the election, nothing was done to set the record straight. The victorious Republicans naturally felt called upon for no explanation of their unexpected and stunning success other than the obvious one of the appeal. The unhappy Democrats, on the other hand, beyond claiming to be the innocent victims of foul play, were disinclined to indulge in any painful public analysis of their mistakes, since it would not alter the outcome. Consequently, the pre-election image carefully fostered by Republican propaganda of selfless and wholehearted cooperation in the war effort has remained undisturbed, and statistics are frequently drawn from this source to demonstrate that as many, if not sometimes more, Republicans as Democrats voted for military appropriations and other war measures. Statistics alone, however, do not convey

any idea of the bitter and prolonged struggles that preceded the adoption of many of these measures, indeed all of the major ones, and gave a strong partisan coloration to the proceedings despite all the solemn disavowals to the contrary.

Hence, too much stock cannot be put in the protestations of Republican leaders like Senator Henry Cabot Lodge, whose latest biographer [John A. Garraty] accepts at face value the senator's assertion that during the war he cast no party vote and made no partisan speech until his partisan passions were unleashed by Wilson's provocative action. The little space that is devoted to the World War phase of Lodge's career is concerned primarily with trying to demonstrate that patriotism precluded any political shenanigans on the part of Wilson's deadliest senatorial foe. While true up to a point, it overlooks the wily Lodge's penchant for working behind the scenes whence he could direct, with no danger to himself, the partisan activities of his more truculent colleagues such as Senator Lawrence Y. Sherman of Illinois, a windy obstructionist of great virtuosity. When Sherman's habit of undermining public confidence in the administration at every opportunity while certifying at the same time to his own patriotic loyalty brought upon him the well-merited censure of the New York *Times*, Lodge warmly defended his obstreperous colleague as "eminently sound in his views" and not afraid to say "many true things that more timid men won't say."

If politics were actually adjourned, and the Republicans including Lodge and Sherman had indeed yielded the last full measure of devotion to the common cause, then Wilson truly deserved the tragic consequences of his action. If, on the other hand, the situation was different and the President had good reason to believe that his cause stood in mortal danger from intense but crudely camouflaged political activity, the course he adopted emerges as a logical corollary. At least it was taken in response to specific conditions, and while perhaps not the wisest course in the circumstances, it was not the result of megalomania or incipient mental decay, as some of his detractors have alleged.

Neither the newspaper files for the war period nor the pages of the *Congressional Record* nor the private correspondence of the principal statesmen involved reveal a suspension of political activity or indicate any serious effort in that direction. One earnest New Yorker in a pamphlet entitled "Trifling with the War" took his fellow countrymen severely to task for their frailty in this respect. "The Patriot," he complained, "has not yet driven the Political Partisan out of the American's heart." Many citizens deplored this scandalous state of affairs but generally absolved their own side from any responsibility in the matter. The war, therefore, far from constituting a moratorium on politics as is so widely believed, merely presented the two parties with a different set of issues and imposed a minimal amount of restraint and caution on their behavior. There was some feeling that any undue display of partisan animus would distract public attention from the major business of defeating the foe, a thing that had happened within living memory in the congressional elections of 1862 and 1864. Instead of forcing politics into the background, however, this sentiment became the occasion for an elaborate camouflage that enabled politicians to ply their trade with little fear of public censure. Behind a smokescreen of patriotic oratory, professing loyalty and devotion to the common cause, the flag, and the boys in the trenches, candidates for office carried on much as usual in the halls of Congress and on the hustings. In the ensuing struggle for power, few punches were pulled or political tricks left unturned.

Shortly after the start of the war, one newspaper was moved to remark of the debates in Congress on vital war measures that "they have been disgraced by personal or political or sectional or factional contentions which are utterly discreditable at the same time they waste precious time."

9

Alfred H. Kelly and Winfred A. Harbison
PATRIOTISM ON THE BENCH

Reprinted from The American Constitution, Its Origins and Development *by Alfred H. Kelly and Winfred A. Harbison, pp. 662–675. By permission of W. W. Norton & Company, Inc. Copyright 1948 and 1955 by W. W. Norton & Company, Inc. Copyright © 1963 by W. W. Norton & Company, Inc.*

Alfred H. Kelly (1907–   ) has been a professor of history at Wayne State University since 1935, and specializes in foreign policy and constitutional studies. In addition to co-authoring *The American Constitution* (1948) with W. A. Harbison, he has edited a book of essays entitled *Foundations of Freedom* (1958) and published an analysis of *Quarrels That Have Shaped the Constitution* (1962).

Winfred A. Harbison (1904–   ), also an historian, has taught at Wayne State since 1929 and has served as Vice President of Academic Administration at that institution since 1953. He is a student of the Republican Party in the Civil War period, as well as of the Constitution.

The important decisions bearing upon the extent of the federal war power were made by Congress and the President without guidance of the Supreme Court. Most of the critical war measures never came before the Court; and with one exception, the few that did reached the Court well after the Armistice, when the constitutional issues involved were no longer of immediate significance. As in Civil War days, it would have been difficult or impossible for the Court to challenge successfully the constitutionality of a federal war activity while the war was in progress. One may assume that had the Court passed unfavorably upon vital war legislation while the war was still going on, ways and means would have been discovered to ignore or to circumvent the decision.

In the *Selective Draft Law Cases*, decided in January 1918, the Court unanimously upheld the constitutionality of the Selective Service Act of 1917. Chief Justice [Edward] White found the constitutional authorization to impose compulsory military service in the clause empowering Congress to declare war and "to raise and support armies." He held that the power was derived, also, from the very character of "just government," whose "duty to the citizen includes the reciprocal obligation of the citizen to render military service in case of need and the right to compel it." He then pointed to the long historical record of compulsory military service in English and colonial law and in the American Civil War, to bolster his assertion that the power to draft men into military service was a necessary incidence both of the federal war power and of federal sovereignty. The Court's decision was obvious and inevitable, since it was evident that an adverse ruling upon the constitutionality of the draft would have interposed the Court's will directly athwart the national war effort.

Later decisions also sustained a broad interpretation of federal war powers. In the *War Prohibition Cases*, decided in December 1919, the Court upheld the validity of the War Prohibition Act, although the law had been passed after the signing of the Armistice. Justice [Louis] Brandeis in his opinion simply assumed the validity of the act under the federal war power and held further that the signing of the

Armistice did not make the statute inoperative or void, since the war power was not limited merely to insuring victories in the field but extended to the power to guard against renewal of the conflict. A few months later, in *Rupert v. Caffey* (1920), the Court again upheld the law. Brandeis' opinion rejected the plea that the act was an invasion of the states' police powers with the observation that "when the United States exerts any of the powers conferred upon it by the Constitution, no valid objection can be based upon the fact that such exercise may be attended by the same incidents which attend the exercise by a state of its police power." . . .

The war brought into the open once more the old conflict between the Bill of Rights and military necessity. For all the conflict over the Alien and Sedition Acts and over Lincoln's policies, the wartime status of the first nine amendments was, in 1917, still vague and confused. Two things, however, could be said with certainty. First, the state of war did not suspend operation of the Bill of Rights; in fact, the Third and Fifth Amendments specifically mentioned wartime conditions. Further, the efficacy of the Bill of Rights in wartime had been confirmed in *Ex parte Milligan* (1866). With this precedent in mind, the Wilson administration in 1917 immediately renounced any intention of suspending the Bill of Rights for the duration of the war. Second, it was equally clear from Civil War practice that the guarantees in the Bill of Rights were not necessarily the same under wartime conditions as in peacetime. Between these two extreme positions there was a vague and confused area of conflict between civil rights and the federal war power.

To an even greater extent than in Civil War days, it was the First Amendment, with its guarantees of free speech, free press, free assembly, and petition that caused most difficulty. Certain restrictions on freedom of speech and of the press were recognized by military and governmental officials as imperatively essential, both because of military necessity and because of the requirements of public morale. Furthermore, controls were demanded by an overwhelming proportion of the people, who were in no mood to listen to those opposing war with Germany.

While Congress adopted no general censorship law during the war, it did enact two statutes which, among other matters, imposed certain limitations upon press and speech. The Espionage Act adopted on June 15, 1917, included certain provisions for military and postal censorship. The amendment to the Espionage Act, which became law on May 16, 1918, and was often referred to as the Sedition Act of 1918, was more comprehensive and general in character.

The Espionage Act carried two principal censorship provisions. One section made it a felony to attempt to cause insubordination in the armed forces of the United States, to attempt to obstruct the enlistment and recruiting services of the United States, or to convey false statements with intent to interfere with military operations. The other established a postal censorship, under which treasonable or seditious material could be banned from the mails at the discretion of the postmaster general. A great many publications, including the *Saturday Evening Post* and the *New York Times*, as well as many radical and dissident periodicals and newspapers, were banned temporarily from the mails under this provision. . . .

The Supreme Court first passed upon the military censorship provisions of the Espionage Act in *Schenck v. United States* (1919), in which the Court borrowed the "rule of proxi-mate causation" to create the "clear and present danger doctrine." The case involved an appeal from a conviction in the lower federal courts on a charge of circulating antidraft leaflets among members of the United States armed forces. Appellant's counsel contended that the Espionage Act violated the First Amendment and was unconstitutional.

In reply Justice [Oliver W.] Holmes wrote an opinion, unanimously concurred in by the Court, upholding the constitutionality of the Espionage Act. The right of free speech, he said, had never been an absolute one at any time, in peace or in war. "Free speech would not protect a man in falsely shouting fire in a theatre, and causing a panic." When a nation was at war, he added, "many things that might be said in time of peace are such a hindrance to its [war] effort that their utterance will not be endured so long as men fight," and "no court could regard them as protected by any constitutional right."

But Holmes made it quite clear that the Espionage Act did not supersede the First Amendment. He carefully distinguished between permissible and illicit speech in wartime, and in so doing brought to bear the doctrine of proximate causation of illegal deeds. "The question in every case," he said, "is whether the words used are used in such circumstances and are of such a nature as to create a clear and present danger that they will bring about the substantive evils that Congress has a right to prevent. It is a question of proximity and degree."

Thus the Court for the first time gave expression to the clear and present danger doctrine. Nearly forgotten during the remainder of the World War I period, the doctrine was to experience a powerful revival after 1937, and to become the principal judicial guide rule in First Amendment cases.

About two thousand cases involving the Espionage Act arose in the lower federal courts during the war. Unfortunately, in nearly all of them the rule of proximate causation and the clear and present danger doctrine were ignored. Vague statements criticizing the war, the administration, or the American form of government were usually accepted as having a "bad tendency" or constituting "intent" to bring about insubordination in the armed forces. Under the act, for example, pacifists were convicted for expressing a general opposition · to all war; and a movie producer was convicted for showing a film on the American Revolution to a civilian audience. The Socialist leader, Eugene V. Debs, was convicted for merely exhorting an audience to "resist militarism, wherever found." If Holmes' later opinion in the Schenck case was correct, convictions of this character were based upon an incorrect interpretation of the law and were an unconstitutional infringement of the First Amendment.

In *Pierce v. United States* (1920), the Court adopted the "bad tendency" doctrine, ignoring "clear and present danger." The case, the last of a series rising out of the Espionage Act, involved a Socialist pamphlet attacking conscription and the war. It could not be shown that there was intent to interfere with the draft, nor was it shown that circulation of the pamphlet had any proximate effect on the war. Yet the Court, speaking through Justice Mahlon Pitney, held that the pamphlet might well "have a tendency to cause insubordination, disloyalty, and refusal of duty in the military and naval forces of the United States." Brandeis, with Holmes concurring, dissented vigorously. Quoting the Schenck opinion, Brandeis argued that it was necessary to prove "clear and present danger," and that mere "bad tendency" was not enough. . . .

The Court had its first opportunity to pass on the Sedition Act of 1918 in *Abrams v. United States* (1919). Here the Court reviewed a conviction of appellants charged with violating the act by the publication of pamphlets attacking the government's expeditionary force to Russia. The pamphlets denounced the "capitalistic" government of the United States, called on the allied armies to "cease murdering Russians," and asked a general strike to achieve this purpose.

The majority opinion, written by Justice John H. Clarke, upheld the conviction and the statute. The purpose of the pamphlet, Clarke said, was to "excite, at the supreme crisis of the war, disaffection, sedition, riots, and . . . revolution." No such right could be protected by the First Amendment.

Justice Holmes, joined by Brandeis, dissented vigorously in the most eloquent and moving defense of free speech since Milton's *Areopagitica*. He thought that it had not been shown that the pamphlet had any immediate effect upon the government's war effort, or that it had been the appellant's purpose to have such effect. "Now nobody can suppose," he said, "that the surreptitious publishing of a silly leaflet by an unknown man, without more, would present any immediate danger that its opinions would hinder the success of the government arms or have any appreciable tendency to do so." If the sedition law were to be construed, he added, so as to prohibit all vigorous criticism of the government and its officials, there was clearly nothing to distinguish this law from the Sedition Act of 1798, long considered unconstitutional. He concluded with a powerful defense of the philosophy of free speech in a republican society:

Persecution for the expression of opinions seems to me perfectly logical. If you have no doubt of your premises or your power and want a certain result with all your heart you naturally express your wishes in law and sweep away all opposition. To allow opposition by speech seems to indicate that you think the speech impotent, as when a man says that he has squared the circle, or that you do not care wholeheartedly for the result, or that you doubt either your power or your premises. But when men have realized that time has upset many fighting faiths, they may come to believe even more than they believe the very foundations of their own conduct that the ultimate good desired is better reached by free trade in ideas,— that the best test of truth is the power of the thought to get itself accepted in the competition of the market; and that truth is the only ground upon which their wishes safely can be carried out. That, at any rate, is the theory of our Constitution. It is an experiment, as all life is an experiment. Every year, if not every day, we have to wager our salvation upon some prophecy based upon imperfect knowledge. While that experiment is part of our system I think that we should be eternally vigilant against attempts to check the expression of opinions that we loathe and believe to be fraught with death, unless they so imminently threaten immediate interference with the lawful and pressing purposes of the law that an immediate check is required to save the country.

The significance of the Pierce and Abrams decisions is evident. Thereafter, a general sedition act might be regarded as not unconstitutional under the First Amendment. In wartime the national government can probably punish as seditious any act which it regards as interfering in any manner with the war effort. The First Amendment, in short, does not altogether protect "open discussion of the merits and methods of a war." Whether this is a socially and politically desirable situation is hardly a legal or constitutional question. It involves rather the issue of the extent to which control of public opinion is necessary to the safety of the state in modern war.

10

Richard Hofstadter
THE WITHERING OF PROGRESSIVISM

Excerpts from The Age of Reform, *by Richard Hofstadter, pp. 273–280. Copyright © 1955 by Richard Hofstadter. Reprinted by permission of Alfred A. Knopf, Inc. Published in Great Britain by Jonathan Cape Ltd.*

Richard Hofstadter (1916–1970), perhaps the most outstanding of that group of American historians which came of age after the Second World War, received his doctorate at Columbia University in 1942 and taught at that school from 1946 until his death. In the course of his career he was the recipient of many awards and recognitions, including the Beveridge Prize (1942) and the Pulitzer Prize (1964). Among his writings were *The American Political Tradition* (1948), *Social Darwinism in American Thought* (1955), *The Age of Reform* (1955), *Anti-Intellectualism in American Life* (1963), and *The Progressive Historians* (1968).

Participation in the war put an end to the Progressive movement. And yet the wartime frenzy of idealism and self-sacrifice marked the apotheosis as well as the liquidation of the Progressive spirit. It would be misleading to imply that American entrance into the war was in any special sense the work of the Progressives, for the final movement toward war was a nationwide movement, shared by the majority of Americans in both major parties. What is significant, however, is that the war was justified before the American public—perhaps had to be justified—in the Progressive rhetoric and on Progressive terms; and that the men who went to work for George Creel (himself a crusading journalist) in the Committee on Public Information, whose job it was to stimulate public enthusiasm for the war, were in so many instances the same men who had learned their trade drumming up enthusiasm for the Progressive reforms and providing articles for the muckraking magazines. By 1912 the Progressive spirit had become so pervasive that any policy—whether it was entrance into the war as rationalized by [President Woodrow] Wilson or abstention from the war as rationalized by [Senator Robert] La Follette—could be strengthened if a way could be found to put it in Progressive language. In the end, when the inevitable reaction came, the Progressive language itself seemed to have been discredited.

In the course of the long struggle over neutrality Wilson is the key figure, not merely because of the central power of leadership he exercised but because he was, on this issue, a representative American and a good Progressive citizen who expressed in every inconsistency, every vacillation, every reluctance, the predominant feelings of the country. He embodied, too, the triumph of the Progressive need to phrase the problems of national policy in moral terms. At first, while sharing the common reluctance to become involved in the struggle, he eschewed the "realistic" formula that the whole struggle was none of America's business and that the essence of the American problem was to stay out at all costs. Even his plea for neutrality was pitched in high moral terms: the nation must stay out in order to be of service, to provide a center of sanity uncorrupted by the strains and hatreds of belligerence. It must—the phrase was so characteristic —maintain "absolute self-mastery" and keep aloof in order that it might in the end bring a "disinterested influence" to the settlement.

Then, as the country drew closer to involvement under the pressure of events, Wilson again chose the language of idealism to formulate the American problem—the problem not only whether the United States should intervene, but what might be the valid reasons for intervening. One view—a view widely shared within the Wilson administration and among thoughtful men in the country at large—rested chiefly upon the national interest and cool calculations of the future advantage of the United States. According to this view, a victory for imperial Germany would represent a threat to the long-term interests of the United States in some sense that a victory for the Allies would not. It was expected that a victorious Germany would be more aggressive, more formidable, more anti-American, and that after the defeat of the Allies and the surrender of the British fleet it would either turn upon the United States at some future time or at least present so forceful and continuous a threat as to compel this country to remain a perpetual armed camp in order to protect its security. Therefore, it was argued, it was the business of the United States, as a matter of self-interest, to see to it that the Allies were not defeated— acting if possible as a nonbelligerent, but if necessary as a belligerent. Another view was that intervention in the war could not properly be expressed in such calculating and self-regarding terms, but must rest upon moral and ideological considerations—the defense of international law and freedom of the seas, the rights of small nations, the fight against autocracy and militarism, the struggle to make the world safe for democracy. To be sure, the argument from self-preservation and national interest and the argument from morals and ideals were not mutually contradictory, and both tended to have a place in the course of public discussion. But Wilson's course, the characteristically Progressive course, was to minimize and subordinate the self-regarding considerations, and to place American intervention upon the loftiest possible plane. He committed himself to this line of action quite early in the game when he rested so much of his diplomacy on the issue of the conduct of German submarine warfare and the freedom of the seas.

This was quixotically formulated because it linked the problem of American intervention or non-intervention to an issue of international law—though one entirely congenial to the Progressive concern over lawlessness. To Wilson's critics it seemed hypocritical because in purely formal terms British violations of maritime law were about as serious as German violations. American concern over them could never be pressed so vigorously because such a course of action would trip over the more urgent desire to do nothing to impair the chances of Allied victory.

Our experience after the second World War suggests that in the long run there was nothing Wilson could have done to prevent a reaction against both the war itself and the Progressive movement that preceded the war. But this too seems almost certain: that by pinning America's role in the war so exclusively to high moral considerations and to altruism and self-sacrifice, by linking the foreign crusade as intimately as possible to the Progressive values and the Progressive language, he was unintentionally insuring that the reaction against Progressivism and moral idealism would be as intense as it could be. For he was telling the American people, in effect, not that they were defending themselves, but that as citizens of the world they were undertaking the same broad responsibilities for world order and world democracy that they had been expected, under the Yankee ethos of responsibility, to assume for their own institutions. The crusade for reform and for democratic institutions, difficult as it was at home, was now to be projected to the world scene.

Wilson turned his back on the realistic considerations that might be offered as reasons for intervention, and continually stressed the more grandiose idealistic reasons. He did more than ignore the self-regarding considerations: on occasion he repudiated them. "There is not a single selfish element, so far as I can see, in the cause we are fighting for," he told the people shortly after American entry. "We are fighting for what we believe and wish to be the rights of mankind and for the future peace and security of the world." Again: "We have gone in with no special grievance of our own, because we have always said that we were the friends and servants of mankind. We look for no profit. We look for no advantage." "America," he said, all too truthfully, during the debate over the treaty, ". . . is the only idealistic Nation in the world." . . .

It was remarkable that Wilson should have succeeded even for a moment in uniting behind him as large a part of the country as he did in an enterprise founded upon the notion of American responsibility for the world. But it is in no way surprising that he should have been resoundingly repudiated in the election of 1920—more resoundingly than any administration before or since. Not long after they began to pay the price of war, the people began to feel that they had been gulled by its promoters both among the Allies and in the United States. In this respect the historical revisionists of the postwar period were merely tardy in catching up with them. The war purged the pent-up guilts, shattered the ethos of responsibility that had permeated the rhetoric of more than a decade. It convinced the people that they had paid the price for such comforts of modern life as they could claim, that they had finally answered to the full the Progressive demand for sacrific and self-control and altruism. In repudiating Wilson, the treaty, the League, and the war itself, they repudiated the Progressive rhetoric and the Progressive mood—for it was Wilson himself and his propagandists who had done so much to tie all these together. Wilson had foreseen that the waging of war would require turning the management of affairs over to the interests the Progressives had been fighting—but this was hardly the change that he had imagined it to be, for only on limited issues and in superficial respects had the management of affairs ever been very far out of those hands. The reaction went farther than this: it destroyed the popular impulse that had sustained Progressive politics for well over a decade before 1914. The pressure for civic participation was followed by widespread apathy, the sense of responsibility by neglect, the call for sacrifice by hedonism. And with all this there came, for a time, a sense of self-disgust. By 1920, publishers were warning authors not to send them manuscripts about the war—people would not hear of it. When at last they were willing to think about it at all, they thought of it as a mistake, and they were ready to read books about the folly of war.

11

George Mowry
THE POLITICS OF NOSTALGIA

From The Urban Nation *by George Mowry, pp. 35–39. Copyright © 1965 by George E. Mowry. Reprinted by permission of Hill and Wang, Inc. Published in Great Britain by Curtis Brown Ltd.*

George E. Mowry (1909–   ), a leading authority on the Progressive era, taught at UCLA for seventeen years before moving east to become Kenan Professor of History at the University of North Carolina, Chapel Hill, in 1967. He is the author of, among other volumes, *Theodore Roosevelt and the Progressive Movement* (1946) and *The Era of Theodore Roosevelt* (1958).

The almost universal social malaise following World War I was well calculated to inspire a "retreat to the past." Abroad the world in 1920 was anything but the peaceful and secure one that Wilson had promised for his war to end war and his peace with justice and without victory. In Europe, Ireland was in rebellion against British rule, Poland was waging a full-scale war against the Soviets, and Rumania had just ceased her military occupation of Hungary. With the franc falling disastrously, French cabinets were made and unmade with alarming regularity. Both the Communists and Mussolini's newly organized Fascists threatened the Italian government, and in Munich a Nationalist *coup d'état* had just missed being successful. Elsewhere, as Communist votes mounted, rightist dictatorships rapidly replaced the democratic governments sponsored by the peace settlements.

In the United States the economic transition from war to peace had been anything but smooth and had borne exceedingly bitter fruit. With little or no reconversion plan the government abruptly terminated war orders, almost before the ink on the armistice had dried, and rescinded much of the regulation in effect during hostilities. These actions created first unemployment and then ballooning prices as the pent-up demand for consumers' goods established a wild sellers' market. As wages fell behind skyrocketing prices, a wave of strikes further unsettled normal economic processes, the coal strike during the severe winter of 1919 in particular causing severe shortages and actual distress. Seeking to counter the rapid inflation, the Federal Reserve Board in late 1919 and 1920 tightened credit, an action which brought on a deflationary cycle. Well before the Presidential election the country was in the first stages of the so-called primary postwar depression. During the summer of 1920 farm prices as well as the inflated values on agricultural land skidded dangerously, and by late fall unemployment in the cities was rapidly rising.

For eighteen months before the election of 1920 the industrial scene had been violently disturbed by a bitter, protracted struggle for power between organized labor and capital. Attempting to protect and extend the gains made during the war, labor sought to organize the mammoth steel industry, as well as scores of lesser industrial opponents. But labor's challenge was met by a grim management determined to stop further organization and intent on returning the country, if possible, to the open-shop philosophy of the nineteenth century. Exciting the labor-capital issue almost to the flash point was the baleful threat of the Russian Revolution and the rise of world radicalism. Despite the many attacks inspired from the West against the new Soviet state, its chance for survival appeared to be more than even in the summer of 1920. No one knew at that time whether the Communist tide might not overwhelm many existing governments of Eastern and Southern Europe. With the publication of British Labour's 1919 program calling for nationalization of the nation's major industries, even that traditional home of conservatism appeared to be in danger of falling before the radical thrust. To frightened American conservatives it seemed as if the United States was next on the radical timetable. In 1919 the Plumb Plan for modified government ownership of railroads was advanced by the Railroad Brotherhoods and supported by President Wilson's son-in-law, Secretary of the Treasury William G. McAdoo. Almost simultaneously the striking miners voted overwhelmingly for the nationalization of the mines. In 1919 an American Communist party was formally organized. Although not a party member at that date, William Z. Foster, a future Communist leader, was then heading the striking steel workers in their battle against the industry's low rates and its standard twelve-hour day.

Meanwhile a wave of bombing atrocities swept the country, aimed at a score of political and financial leaders. But the most frightening episode of all the year's ominous harvest was the Boston police strike of September. If the police walked out, the question was repeatedly asked, what was to become of private property and of the social order? It was against such a background that Attorney General A. Mitchell Palmer organized his "ship or shoot" campaign against all alien radicals, and that over twenty state legislatures passed criminal syndicalist laws providing for heavy fines and prison sentences for advocating or inciting assaults against public officials, destruction of real or personal property, and the overthrow of government. A committee of the New York legislature solemnly proposed that "every strike is a small revolution and a dress rehearsal for a big one." In such an atmosphere it is small wonder that the leaders of the industrial and financial community were able to convince themselves and much of the public that the labor movement was crowded with agitators advocating the overthrow of the Constitution and asserting that the open shop was a basic ingredient of "the American way."

A good many other developments excited the imagination of the conservative and the timid during the election year of 1920. After five years of little immigration from abroad over 400,000 immigrants entered the United States, and wild predictions appeared in the press that unless radical restrictions were made from 2 to 5 million refugees from war-torn Europe would descend on the country in the following twelve months. The same stories invariably recalled that Wilson had vetoed a literacy test for immigrants, and that many of the radicals violently disturbing the domestic scene had European backgrounds. Closer to home, a series of ugly race riots broke out on the fringes of the war-born Negro communities in a number of Northern and Western cities. And although in 1920 most of the massive revolt against prewar moral standards was yet to come, the publication of Sherwood Anderson's *Winesburg, Ohio* and F. Scott Fitzgerald's *This Side of Paradise* had ushered in the new jazz age. While the Volstead Act enforcing the Prohibition amendment was but six months old, by midsummer of 1920 it was already being flouted openly. Meanwhile the automobile and the Hollywood movie, both enthusiastically received by the public, were rapidly contributing to the erosion of manners and morals, especially among the young.

Leaving a Republican National Committee meeting in 1919, Boies Penrose, the cynical and outsized Republican Senator from Pennsylvania, predicted that the leading issue in the 1920 elections would be "Americanism." When asked what that meant, Penrose was alleged to have replied, "How in the hell do I know? But it will get a lot of votes." Uncommonly frank at times, Penrose was probably honest in voicing his perplexity over an exact definition of Americanism. But the Senator was unerringly accurate in predicting the public's emotional response to the term and its value in vote getting. Both national parties, in fact, sensed the nostalgic mood of the country, and in their platforms and their choice of candidates they honored Penrose's judgment. Neither party dealt in any realistic way with present or future problems; they contented themselves with arguments about past issues. Only on the League of Nations question was there an attempt to grapple with the future. But by November, when the candidates and their followers were through discussing or avoiding this vital question, no one, whether friend or foe of the League, knew precisely how to vote to obtain the desired result.

12

William Leuchtenburg
INSPIRATION TO REFORM

The passage from "The New Deal and the Analogue of War," by William E. Leuchtenburg, was originally published in Change and Continuity in Twentieth-Century America, *edited by John Braeman, Robert H. Bremner, and Everett Walters, pp. 84–90. Copyright © 1964 by the Ohio State University Press. All rights reserved.*

William E. Leuchtenburg (1922–   ) has taught American history at Columbia University since 1952, and has served as consultant to such diverse institutions as the National Broadcasting Corporation, the Social Security Administration, the Ford Foundation, and the John F. Kennedy Memorial Library. His publications include *Perils of Prosperity, 1914–32* (1958) and *Franklin D. Roosevelt and the New Deal, 1932–40* (1963).

In tracing the genealogy of the New Deal, historians have paid little attention to the mobilization of World War I. Instead, they have centered their interest on two movements: populism and progressivism. Both were important antecedents—a reasonably straight line may be drawn from the Populist sub-treasury plan to the Commodity Credit Corporation, from the Pujo Committee to the Securities and Exchange Commission. Yet in concentrating on populism and progressivism, writers have given too little attention to the influence of the wartime mobilization, which may have been as great as the example of the Progressive era and certainly was more important than populism.

Much of the experience of the Progressive era proved irrelevant to the task facing Roosevelt in 1933. Very little in the Populist and Progressive periods offered a precedent for massive federal intervention in the economy. Many of the reforms of the prewar generation were modest ventures in regulation or attempts to liberate business enterprise rather than ambitious national programs of economic action. Moreover, in these years, reformers thought the state and the city more important arenas than the national capital.

World War I marked a bold new departure. It occasioned the abandonment of laissez faire precepts and raised the federal government to director, even dictator, of the economy. The War Industries Board mobilized production; the War Trade Board licensed imports and exports; the Capital Issues Committee regulated investment; the War Finance Corporation lent funds to munitions industries; the Railroad Administration unified the nation's railways; the Fuel Administration fixed the price of coal and imposed "coal holidays" on eastern industry; and the Food Administration controlled the production and consumption of food. The Lever Food and Fuel Control Act of 1917 gave the President sweeping powers: to take over factories and operate them, to fix a maximum price for wheat, and to license businesses in necessaries. By a generous interpretation of its powers, the War Industries Board supervised pricing, compelled corporations to accept government priorities, and forced companies to obey federal edicts on how to dispose of their products. "This is a crisis," a War Industries Board representative scolded steel-industry leaders, "and commercialism, gentlemen, must be absolutely sidetracked." Actions of this character, as well as the proliferation of public corporations ranging from the United States Housing Corporation to the Spruce Production Corporation, proved important precedents for New Deal enterprises fifteen years later.

The field of labor relations may serve as a single example of the difference in importance of the Populist and Progressive experience and that of World War I. Prior to the war, no serious attempt had ever been made to empower the federal government to uphold the right of collective bargaining. Federal action was limited to peripheral areas. When class lines were drawn in labor disputes, progressives frequently aligned themselves against the unions. But in World War I, the War Labor Board proclaimed its support of union rights and, to the discomfiture of businessmen, enforced these rights. Many of the labor policies pursued in the war months would have been inconceivable a short while before. When the Smith & Wesson Arms Company of Springfield, Massachusetts, insisted on its prerogative to require workers to sign yellow-dog contracts, the War Department commandeered the plant, even though the Supreme Court had upheld the legality of such contracts. The government even dared to seize Western Union when the president of the firm denied his employees the right to join the Commercial Telegraphers Union. The panoply of procedures developed by the War Labor Board and the War Labor Policies Board provided the basis in later years for a series of enactments culminating in the Wagner National Labor Relations Act of 1935.

The war gave a home to the new class of university-trained intellectuals which had emerged in the generation before the war. While some of them had found a career in public service in state governments before 1917, few had worked in the national government, chiefly because there was so little in Washington for them to do. After the United States intervened, Washington swarmed with professors, until, one writer noted, "the Cosmos

Club was little better than a faculty meeting of all the universities." In all countries, he observed, professors "fought, and they managed affairs, thus refuting the ancient libellous assumption that they constituted an absent-minded third sex. . . ."

Public administrators of this type represented a new force in American politics. They were advisers and technicians but, more than that, men of influence and even of power. At a time when class conflicts were sharpening, they did not reflect particular classes so much as the thrust for power of *novi homines* who had a significant role to play on the national stage. Some like Gifford Pinchot had made their appearance in Washington between the war, and still more like Charles McCarthy had been active in such reform capitals as Madison and Albany, but it was the war which offered them an unparalleled opportunity. Randolph Bourne noted perceptively the "peculiar congeniality between the war and these men. It is as if the war and they had been waiting for each other." Phenomena almost wholly of the twentieth century, they came by the 1930s to have a crucial part in shaping legislation and in manning the new agencies which their legislation developed. The passage of the Wagner Act in 1935, for example, resulted less from such traditional elements as presidential initiative or the play of "social forces" than from the conjunction of university-trained administrators like Lloyd Garrison within the New Deal bureaucracy with their counterparts on senatorial staffs like Leon Keyserling in Senator Wagner's office.

This new class of administrators, and the social theorists who had been advocating a rationally planned economy, found the war an exciting adventure. The *New Republic* liberals rejoiced that the war produced a novel kind of democratic state which was creating a radical new order based on the democratization of industry. ". . . During the war we revolutionized our society," the *New Republic* boasted. These liberals distinguished themselves sharply from the New Freedom reformers who aimed only to achieve minor changes in the nineteenth-century tradition. Nationalists and collectivists, they looked toward a centralized state which would use its powers to reshape the economy in the interests of labor and other disadvantaged groups.

Many progressives believed that Wilson's war measures signified both a fulfillment of Progressive hopes and a happy augury for the future. Enormously impressed by "the social possibilities of war," John Dewey observed that in every warring country, production for profit had been subordinated to production for use. "The old conception of the absoluteness of private property has received the world over a blow from which it will never wholly recover." Thorstein Veblen, who worked for the Food Administration in 1918, thought the war created new possibilities for far-reaching social change. Economists viewed the War Industries Board as "a notable demonstration of the power of war to force concert of effort and collective planning," and anticipated that lessons from the war could be applied in times of peace. When Wesley C. Mitchell closed his lectures at Columbia University in May, 1918, he remarked that peace would bring new problems, but "it seems impossible that the countries concerned will attempt to solve them without utilizing the same sort of centralized directing now employed to kill their enemies abroad for the new purpose of reconstructing their own life at home." "What we have learned in war we shall hardly forget in peace," commented Walter Weyl. "The new economic solidarity, once gained, can never again be surrendered."

The mobilization of 1917–1918 saw the first widespread use of intelligence examinations in the United States with the Army test being given to over 1,727,000 recruits.   (National Archives)

Chapter Three

SOCIAL EFFECTS
OF THE WAR

The readings in this section explore the ways in which the First World War altered both the character of, and the relations among various groups within American society. To start with, John F. Carter, Jr., discusses the "generation gap" of the early 1920s, suggesting that the experience of the preceding years had exercised a strong influence in changing the values and behavior of young people generally. Next, Preston W. Slosson calls attention to the advance of the feminist movement and to the accelerated entrance of women into industry as a direct result of wartime demands. Ethnic minorities were less fortunate, say Horace Peterson and Gilbert Fite, because the intolerance born of war rapidly burgeoned from an attack on German-Americans to an assault on all alien elements, including "that permanent alien element in America, the Negro." Yet John M. Clark argues, with much plausibility, that the wartime migration of large numbers of Negroes from the rural South to industrial areas of the North and West brought favorable as well as unfavorable effects in its train. This was hardly the case with public education, according to Willard Waller, for the war not only disrupted the schools at all levels but also emasculated the teaching profession.

QUESTIONS:

1. Why would World War I have affected the young so differently from the way in which it affected their elders? Or did it?

2. Would you say that the young people of 1919–1920 learned the same sorts of things from the First World War that the present generation of youth is "learning" from Vietnam? If so, what are those things?

3. Why do you think so much hatred developed against certain minorities during World War I? And why was the direction of this hatred apparently transferred so easily from group to group?

4. Considering our current experience with "women's liberation" as well as what happened after World War I, do you suppose that there are aspects of war other than increased opportunity for employment which tend to stimulate women's desires for equality?

5. Might it be argued that Mr. Waller, in describing the "disruption" of the schools, takes too narrow a view of the "educational experience"? Do you think so? Why?

13

John F. Carter, Jr.
THESE WILD YOUNG PEOPLE

From John F. Carter, Jr. "These Wild Young People: By One of them," Atlantic Monthly, Vol. 126 (September 1920), pp. 301–304.

John F. Carter, Jr. (1897–1967) led a varied career as social critic, author, newspaperman, and government official. After a brief postwar stint in the American embassies in Rome and Constantinople, he held positions with *The New York Times* (1923–28), *Liberty Magazine* (1932–34), the Department of State (1928–32) and Agriculture (1934–36), and the National Broadcasting Company (1938–39). He wrote a newspaper column ("We the People") from 1936 until his death, and was the author of such books as *Man is War* (1926), *What We Are About to Receive* (1932), and *The Future is Ours* (1939).

For some months past the pages of our more conservative magazines have been crowded with pessimistic descriptions of the younger generation, as seen by their elders and, no doubt, their betters. Hardly a week goes by that I do not read some indignant treatise depicting our extravagance, the corruption of our manners, the futility of our existence, poured out in stiff, scared, shocked sentences before a sympathetic and horrified audience of fathers, mothers, and maiden aunts—but particularly maiden aunts.

In the May [1920] issue of the *Atlantic Monthly* appeared an article entitled "Polite Society," by a certain Mr. Grundy, the husband of a very old friend of my family. In kindly manner he

> Mentioned our virtues, it is true,
> But dwelt upon our vices, too.

"Chivalry and Modesty are dead. Modesty died first," quoth he, but expressed the pious hope that all might yet be well if the oldsters would but be content to "wait and see." His article is one of the best-tempered and most gentlemanly of this long series of Jeremiads against "these wild young people." It is significant that it should be anonymous. In reading it, I could not help but be drawn to Mr. Grundy personally, but was forced to the conclusion that he, like everyone else who is writing about my generation, has very little idea of what he is talking about. I would not offend him for the world, and if I apostrophize him somewhat brutally in the following paragraphs, it is only because I am talking of him generically; also because his self-styled "cousin" is present. . . .

I would like to say a few things about my generation.

In the first place, I would like to observe that the older generation had certainly pretty well ruined this world before passing it on to us. They give us this Thing, knocked to pieces, leaky, red-hot, threatening to blow up; and then they are surprised that we don't accept it with the same attitude of pretty, decorous enthusiasm with which they received it, 'way back in the eighteen-nineties, nicely painted, smoothly running, practically fool-proof. "So simple that a child can run it!" But the child couldn't steer it. He hit every possible telegraph-pole, some of them twice, and ended with a head-on collision for which *we* shall have to pay the fines and damages. Now, with loving pride, they turn over their wreck to us; and, since we are not properly overwhelmed with loving gratitude, shake their heads and sigh, "Dear! dear! We were so much better-mannered than these wild young people. But then we had the advantages of a good, strict, old-fashioned bringing-up!" How intensely *human* these oldsters are, after all, and how fallible! How they always blame us for not following precisely in their eminently correct footsteps!

Then again there is the matter of outlook. When these sentimental old world-wreckers were young, the world was such a different place—at least, so I gather from H. G. Wells's picture of the nineties, in *Joan and Peter.* Life for them was bright and pleasant. Like all normal youngsters, they had their little tin-pot ideals, their sweet little visions, their naive enthusiasms, their nice little set of beliefs. Christianity had emerged from the blow dealt by Darwin, emerged rather in the shape of social dogma. Man was a noble and perfectible creature. Women were angels (whom they smugly sweated in their industries and prostituted in their slums). Right was downing might. The

nobility and the divine mission of the race were factors that led our fathers to work wholeheartedly for a millennium, which they caught a glimpse of just around the turn of the century. Why, there were Hague Tribunals! International peace was at last assured, and according to current reports, never officially denied, the American delegates held out for the use of poison gas in warfare, just as the men of that generation were later to ruin Wilson's great ideal of a league of nations, on the ground that such a scheme was an invasion of American rights. But still, everything, masked by ingrained hypocrisy and prudishness, seemed simple, beautiful, inevitable.

Now my generation is disillusioned, and, I think, to a certain extent, brutalized, by the cataclysm which *their* complacent folly engendered. The acceleration of life for us has been so great that into the last few years have been crowded the experiences and the ideas of a normal lifetime. We have in our unregenerate youth learned the practicality and the cynicism that is safe only in unregenerate old age. We have been forced to become realists overnight, instead of idealists, as was our birthright. We have seen man at his lowest, woman at her lightest, in the terrible moral chaos of Europe. We have been forced to question, and in many cases to discard, the religion of our fathers. We have seen hideous peculation, greed, anger, hatred, malice, and all uncharitableness, unmasked and rampant and unashamed. We have been forced to live in an atmosphere of "to-morrow we die," and so, naturally, we drank and were merry. We have seen the rottenness and shortcomings of all governments, even the best and most stable. We have seen entire social systems overthrown, and our own called in question. In short, we have seen the inherent beastliness of the human race revealed in an infernal apocalypse.

It is the older generation who forced us to

see all this, which has left us with social and political institutions staggering blind in the fierce white light that, for us, should beat only about the enthroned ideal. And now, through the soft-headed folly of these painfully shocked Grundys, we have that devastating wisdom which is safe only for the burned-out embers of grizzled, cautious old men. We may be fire, but it was they who made us play with gunpowder. And now they are surprised that a great many of us, because they have taken away our apple-cheeked ideals, are seriously considering whether or no *their* game be worth *our* candle.

But, in justice to my generation, I think that I must admit that most of us have realized that, whether or no it be worth while, we must all play the game, as long as we are in it. And I think that much of the hectic quality of our life is due to that fact and to that alone. We are faced with staggering problems and are forced to solve them, while the previous incumbents are permitted a graceful and untroubled death. All my friends are working and working hard. Most of the girls I know are working. In one way or another, often unconsciously, the great burden put upon us is being borne, and borne gallantly, by that immodest, unchivalrous set of ne'er-do-wells, so delightfully portrayed by Mr. Grundy and the amazing young [F. Scott] Fitzgerald. A keen interest in political and social problems, and a determination to face the facts of life, ugly or beautiful, characterizes us, as it certainly did not characterize our fathers. We won't shut our eyes to the truths we have learned. We have faced so many unpleasant things already,—and faced them pretty well,—that it is natural that we should keep it up.

Now I think that this is the aspect of our generation that annoys the uncritical and deceives the unsuspecting oldsters who are now met in judgment upon us: our devastating and brutal frankness. And this is the quality in which we really differ from our predecessors. We are frank with each other, frank, or pretty nearly so, with our elders, frank in the way we feel toward life and this badly damaged world. It may be a disquieting and misleading habit, but is it a bad one? We find some few things in the world that we like, and a whole lot that we don't, and we are not afraid to say so or to give our reasons. In earlier generations this was not the case. The young men yearned to be glittering generalities, the young women to act like shy, sweet, innocent fawns—toward one another. And now, when grown up, they have come to believe that they actually were figures of pristine excellence, knightly chivalry, adorable modesty, and impeccable propriety. But I really doubt if they were so. Statistics relating to, let us say, the immorality of college students in the eighteen-eighties would not compare favorably with those of the present. However, now, as they look back on it, they see their youth through a mist of muslin, flannels, tennis, bicycles, Tennyson, Browning, and the Blue Danube waltz. The other things, the ugly things that we know about and talk about, must also have been there. But our elders didn't care or didn't dare to consider them, and now they are forgotten. We talk about them unabashed, and not necessarily with Presbyterian disapproval, and so they jump to the conclusion that we are thoroughly bad, and keep pestering us to make us good.

The trouble with them is that they can't seem to realize that we are busy, that what pleasure we snatch must be incidental and feverishly hurried. We have to make the most of our time. We actually haven't got so much time for the noble procrastinations of modesty or for the elaborate rigmarole of chivalry, and little patience for the lovely formulas of an ineffective faith. Let them die for a while! They did not seem to serve the world too well in its black hour. If they are inherently good they will come back, vital and untarnished. But just now we have a lot of work, "old time is still a-flying," and we must gather rose-buds while we may.

Oh! I know that we are a pretty bad lot, but has not that been true of every preceding generation? At least we have the courage to act accordingly. Our music is distinctly barbaric, our girls are distinctly *not* a mixture of arbutus and barbed-wire. We drink when we can and what we can, we gamble, we are extravagant—but we work, and that's about all that we can be expected to do; for, after all, we have just discovered that we are all still very near to the Stone Age. The Grundys shake their heads. They'll *make* us be good. Prohibition is put through to stop our drinking, and hasn't stopped it. [William Jennings] Bryan has plans to curtail our philanderings, and he won't do any good. A Draconian code is being hastily formulated at Washington and elsewhere, to prevent us from, by any chance, making any alteration in this present divinely constituted arrangement of things. The oldsters stand dramatically with fingers and toes and noses pressed against the bursting dykes. Let them! They won't do any good. They can shackle us down, and still expect us to repair their blunders, if they wish. But we shall not trouble ourselves very much about them any more. Why should we? What have they done? They have made us work as they never had to work in all their padded lives—but we'll have our cakes and ale for a' that.

For now we know our way about. We're not babes in the wood, hunting for great, big, red strawberries, and confidently expecting the Robin Red-Breasts to cover us up with pretty leaves if we don't find them. We're men and women, long before our time, in the flower of our full-blooded youth. We have brought back into civil life some of the recklessness and

ability that we were taught by war. We are also quite fatalistic in our outlook on the tepid perils of tame living. All may yet crash to the ground for aught that we can do about it. Terrible mistakes will be made, but *we* shall at least make them intelligently and insist, if we are to receive the strictures of the future, on doing pretty much as we choose now.

14

Preston W. Slosson
EQUALITY FOR WOMEN

Reprinted with permission of The Macmillan Company from The Great Crusade and After, 1914–1918 *by Preston W. Slosson, pp. 130–135. Copyright 1930 by The Macmillan Company, renewed 1958 by Preston W. Slosson.*

Preston W. Slosson (1892–   ) taught history at the University of Michigan from 1921 to 1962, and has been professor emeritus since that time. In 1918 and 1919 he served as assistant librarian on the American Commission to Negotiate Peace at Versailles. He has been a radio broadcaster since 1941, and was a Democratic candidate for the House of Representatives in 1948. Among his publications are *Twentieth Century Europe* (1927), *The Problem of Austro-German Union* (1929), and *After the War: What?* (1943).

Count Hermann Keyserling, one of the many distinguished European philosophers, authors and men of affairs who visited the United States after the World War, found as the most noteworthy of transatlantic marvels the complete and assured ascendancy of the American woman. In America, he wrote,

all *men* are supposed to be equal. But women as a class are candidly accepted as superior beings. Thus America is today an aristocratic country of a peculiar type. It is a two-caste country, the higher caste being formed by the women as such. And this caste rules exactly in the way higher castes have always ruled. . . . Her inspiration and influence stand behind all American educators, as it stands behind all American prohibitionists. Her influence accounts for the infinity of laws and rules. She directs the whole cultural tradition. She also dictates in the field of moral conduct. Who wants to study the real meaning and purport of a caste system, should today not visit India, but America.[1]

Of course, there was exaggeration here. The good count came from the country of Schopenhauer and brought with him not only the traditions of central Europe but, as a lifelong student of Oriental cultures, many of the views of eastern Asia as well. At almost any period of American history the position of women would have seemed strange to him. But his words are not too wide of the mark to call attention to the rapid advance of the feminist movement in the United States during and after the war. The most obvious change was the adoption of woman suffrage as the universal law of the nation. But the complete acceptance of the American woman in political life was only one phase of a general movement towards sex equality, older than the war and broader than America. The same generation that saw woman suffrage granted in the United States saw it granted also in most of the nations of northern Europe along with many other legal rights and privileges. Not in the field of politics, but in economic status and social prestige, did the American woman occupy her unique position. American feminism meant freedom from custom and tradition more than from positive legal restriction. Many European nations, for example, had enacted divorce laws as liberal as those of most American states, but in none of them (with the possible exception

[1] Hermann Keyserling, "Caste in America," *Forum*, LXXX (1928), 106.

of Soviet Russia) were divorces so frequently obtained by discontented wives. European schools and colleges had been generally opened to women, but only in the United States did women look upon a college education as a natural right. Nowhere else in the world could a respectable unmarried girl spend her time and money with so little adult supervision. Nowhere else did the middle-class housewife have so wide a margin of leisure for amusement, self-development, or public work as her fancy might dictate.

Though the entrance of women into industry began long before the war, it was undoubtedly accelerated by it. The census of 1920, coming conveniently just when the temporary labor displacements of war time had been mainly eliminated, showed eight and a half million women and girls over ten years of age engaged in gainful occupations, an advance of more than half a million since 1910. This was not in itself a notable increase, indeed it did not quite keep pace with the growth in the general population; but the decreases were in occupations long open to women, such as farm work and domestic service, while in practically all "masculine" occupations the number of female workers greatly increased both in number and in proportion. There was a marked decline in the number of women employed as farm hands, laundresses, tailors, music teachers, midwives, charwomen, general servants and cooks, and a corresponding gain in the number of women chauffeurs, cigar makers, bankers, police and probation officers, social workers, lawyers, college professors, elevator "boys," clerks, typists, bookkeepers and barbers. Almost one woman in four "gainfully employed" was married and presumably running a home as well as an outside job.

For various sorts of routine clerical work employers definitely preferred women; men tended therefore to drift into other occupations rather than face the competition of the cheap and competent woman worker. There were, for example, eleven women stenographers and typists to every man so engaged. The capture of the elementary schools by the schoolma'am had made the old-fashioned schoolmaster an almost extinct type. No doubt the men had a real grievance in the fact that wages were kept down by the hiring of women to do the same work at cheaper rates, but their grievance was rather against the employers who would not pay "men's wages" than against the women who frequently needed their jobs as badly as the men they displaced. Fortunately the rapid expansion of American industry made it usually possible for any adaptable man to find some occupation not yet unduly cheapened by feminine competition. Probably the worst effect of woman's invasion of industry was not the economic but the psychological; more men, perhaps, left such occupations as teaching and stenography from the feeling that their task was "no work for a man" than because of lowered incomes. One occupation after another had thus taken on a purely feminine color. A traveler from Europe shortly before the United States entered the war commented on how unnatural it seemed to him to see men running elevators and doing other work that European women had taken over when their men went to the trenches. In many trades this temporary effect of the war was merely an acceleration of the general tendency in industry. . . .

The institution of the home was affected in a hundred ways by the growing custom of American women to pursue a trade before matrimony and sometimes along with it. In some respects the influence was wholly constructive. No longer was marriage the inevitable way of getting a living. This set a higher standard for husbands than in the days when "old

maid" (a term fast disappearing from use) might mean penury as well as loneliness. On the other hand, a conflict frequently arose between the man's desire to support his wife according to the old American tradition and the woman's desire to have "a career." The business girl gave up much in abandoning a job where all her earnings were her own to manage a household whose necessary expenses might leave little margin for the small luxuries to which she was accustomed. If she kept at her former work after marriage the double burden of home work and office work might easily prove too much for her health, or one of her tasks must be scamped. Nearly every popular magazine printed articles and stories innumerable around the problem, "marriage, a career, or both?" An interesting evidence of the interpenetration of man's world and woman's was the theme of Dorothy Canfield's novel, *The Home Maker* [1924], which depicted a woman who had failed as a mother but made a success in commerce, while her husband, kept at home by an accident, found in educating his children the success which he had missed as a man of business.

15

Horace Peterson and Gilbert Fite
MINORITIES UNDER ATTACK

From Horace Peterson and Gilbert Fite, Opponents of the War *(Madison: University of Wisconsin Press, 1957), pp. 81-90. Paperback edition published by the University of Washington Press.*

Horace Peterson (1902–1952) was a professor of history at the University of Oklahoma from 1936 until his death. His major fields of concern were the post-Civil War United States and Europe after 1870. In 1939 he published *Propaganda for War*, a study of the management of news in the period 1914–1917.

Gilbert C. Fite (1918–   ) has taught history at the University of Oklahoma since 1945. A specialist on American agriculture, he is author of *George N. Peek and the Fight for Farm Parity* (1954), *Farm to Factory; A History of the Consumers' Cooperative Association* (1965), and *The Farmer's Frontier, 1865–1900* (1956), as well as co-author (with Jim E. Reese) of *An Economic History of the United States* (1959).

Hatred of the enemy is a thing striven for in wartime. It is also often accompanied by a hatred of all foreign people, of all who are alien in any way. The differences—the loyalties to strange nations, to strange gods—are ignored when men are at peace; but with war comes a passionate denial of the right of anyone to have any other loyalty, any other god.

The United States is a land of many races, many nationalities, many religions. It is only natural that a world war would bring about friction among these elements. The first and most obvious clash came in the realm of nationality. Theodore Roosevelt spoke for nationalists everywhere when he dealt with this issue on a number of occasions in 1917: "The Hun within our gates masquerades in many disguises; he is our dangerous enemy; and he should be hunted down without mercy." "Every man," he wrote in 1918, "ought to love his country. . . . [But] he is only entitled to one country. If he claims loyalty to two countries, he is necessarily a traitor to at least one country." "Weak-kneed apologists for infamy say that it is 'natural' for American citizens of German origin to favor Germany," Roosevelt wrote at another time; "this is nonsense, and criminal nonsense to boot." Then he added, "We can have no 'fifty-fifty' allegiance in this country."

Roosevelt notwithstanding, a man's love of his homeland is something deep and abiding that cannot be entirely changed by emigration or by naturalization papers. However much a man might wish to lose interest in the land of his birth, it is not easy to do so. An American might become a naturalized Briton, German, or Frenchman, but he would still—in spite of everything—retain something within himself that would be forever American and forever alien to his adopted country. He may not "favor" America, but he could not lose all his affection for her.

The same was true of people of foreign birth and background in the United States in 1917. Those who came from the Allied nations, and particularly from England, could be passionately devoted to the land of their birth and still pass as patriotic Americans. Those from Germany and Austria could not do this. To them, as Jane Addams has said, "a war between the United States and the fatherland meant exquisite torture."

In 1917 there were hundreds of thousands of Germans and Austro-Hungarians, or people of German and Austrian ancestry, living in the United States. There were also large numbers of foreign groups, such as Poles, Finns, and Russians, who felt indifferent toward the war or unsympathetic with the Allies. Many of these people were not yet citizens of the United States. Recognizing that residents of foreign background would have major problems of adjustment under circumstances of war, there were those in the United States who recommended tolerance and kind treatment for enemy aliens. A certain sympathy continued for a few months after war began, but by the end of the summer of 1917 the public's attitude had changed noticeably. Perhaps it would be better to say that the attitude of a section of the public had changed. The bitter opposition to conscription irritated nationalists, and they looked with especial suspicion upon any critic of this practice who was of enemy birth. Then there was the wild drive against radicals. Here again, when a man was a radical and also an alien no sympathy could be expected for him. Many newspaper stories dealing with aliens began to carry an overtone of dislike merely because of their foreignness. The Governor of Arizona in one of his early justifications for the Bisbee deportation accused the I.W.W.'s of being foreigners. . . .

Of the millions of aliens in the United States only about 6,300 were arrested. Of the 2,300 aliens who were interned by the military authorities, some were later freed or paroled. The method of handling many of these cases, however, was often shameful. Suspects were arrested and held without trial. In some instances the courts offered only scant protection, if any at all. Vigorous application of both legal and extra-legal methods against aliens, however, went a long way to suppress alien elements who opposed the war. According to the Attorney General, alien enemies were sometimes held "for a limited period to produce a disciplinary effect." This policy seemed successful, because he reported that detention and internment "has acted throughout the country as a powerful deterrent against alien-enemy activity."

The action taken against aliens underlined significantly what had come to be looked upon as normal, accepted human intolerance. During a war, mob hysteria spreads even to those who in more settled times, pride themselves on their sufferance and liberality. The demand for conformity and uniformity becomes pandemic. The results are so effective that the schoolboy mistranslation of Terence—"nothing foreign is human to me"—emerges with deadly irony as an accurate verbal map of the public state of mind.

Under the exigency of this universal demand that everything be alike and on one level, the public cannot see that widely differing elements in society strengthen it economically, intellectually, and culturally. And so, when the United States entered the war in 1917, prejudice burgeoned; its tentacles reached every-where. Extremists attacked not only the Germans, but all alien elements. And this assault naturally included that permanent alien element in America, the Negro. To be sure, race prejudice was no new phenomenon in American life, but the emotionalism and intolerance generated by the war served to intensify mob violence against Negroes.

As a result of the war boom, a shortage of labor in northern industries developed. Many employers turned to the South and actively recruited workers. Negroes went north in great numbers, beginning a migration which was to change the population make-up of several northern cities. At the same time, the point of view of many northerners was also changed. Factory and mining towns were flooded with colored workers only recently occupants of cotton patches.

As these men and women came into the North some of them thought they would be escaping from the race antagonism that had plagued them in the South. After all, was it not the North that had carried on the war to free the Negro from slavery? Would not the North give the Negro equality? And then there was another thing. The country was flooded with talk of this war being a libertarian war, a war for democracy, a war which would result in the suppression of autocratic people. Would it not result in less autocracy among the American whites?

Of this there were some doubts. The greatest preacher of this cause of liberty and democracy was President Woodrow Wilson, and the Negroes knew Wilson as a southerner. In April, 1917, a Negro minister wrote that "while the colored people were loyal citizens, few of them were enthusiastic in their support of the President and his Administration." To this Wilson replied, "Your letter was the first notice I had that many of the members of the colored race were not enthusiastic in their support of the Government in this crisis." But

Wilson had misunderstood. It was not the Government but the southern individual who was at the head of the Government who failed to arouse their enthusiasm.

Before long the Negro became aware that there was not much difference between the northern white man and the southern white man. In May, 1917, the newspapers carried the story of a Negro who was burned to death by a white mob in Tennessee. The man was accused of killing a girl. A week later, the *New York Times* of May 27 reported a small race riot in New York City. One Negro was killed and seven others were wounded. But the first major outbreak after this population movement began occurred in East St. Louis, Illinois.

During 1917 some 10,000 to 12,000 Negroes migrated to East St. Louis, many of them lured there by exaggerated advertisements of businessmen promising high wages. Others were imported as strikebreakers. Bitter racial feeling was aroused as scores of minor conflicts developed between Negroes and whites. A corrupt local political machine added further instability to the situation which began to explode in late May of 1917.

The height of this disgraceful race riot was reached on July 2. The previous evening one or two carloads of white men drove through the Negro section of the city shooting promiscuously into many homes. Although no one was hurt or killed, angry Negroes now armed themselves and set out to avenge the unprovoked attacks on their homes. Shortly, they encountered several police officers in a car. Thinking it was the car from which shots had been fired into their homes, the Negroes fired upon it, killing one policeman and mortally wounding another.

The next day, July 2, one of the worst race riots in American history erupted in East St. Louis. Negroes were killed indiscriminately as police and soldiers stood idly by or, in some instances, even participated in the fray. The instances of inhuman brutality to innocent people are too numerous to relate here. Besides, they have been fully recorded by a congressional committee. One or two instances are enough to indicate the actions of the emotion-maddened mobs. One Negro who was trying to escape from thirty or forty whites was "knocked down, kicked in the face, beaten into insensibility; and then a man stood over him and shot him five times as he lay helpless in the street." And the savage brutality was not confined to Negroes who were residents of East St. Louis. A Negro man with his wife and son were passing through that city when a mob grabbed them at Collinsville and Illinois avenues, beat the man to death, shot the 14-year-old boy, and scalped the woman. The mob, said the House Committee which investigated the affair, "spared neither age nor sex in their blind lust for blood." The attacks on individuals were aggravated by the burning of over 300 Negro homes. The exact number of people killed is not known, but at least eight whites and 38 Negroes lost their lives and hundreds were wounded and maimed. One estimate gave 110 as having been killed. Some convictions were finally obtained and various punishments were meted out. Eleven Negroes and eight white men were sent to the State Penitentiary. But no jail sentences or other punishment of guilty parties could undo the damage of those awful days. It was increasingly difficult for the Negro to accept the war as a war for freedom and democracy. "Race-riots in East St. Louis," said the *Literary Digest*, "afford a lurid background to our efforts to carry justice and idealism to Europe."

Other areas experienced riots during July, although they were minor compared to that in East St. Louis. On the third there was trouble in the San Juan Hill section of New York City when policemen had trouble with a colored guardsman. On July 25 riots occurred in Chester, Pennsylvania, where four Negroes were shot and sixty arrested. The next day three Negroes were killed and many were wounded. The rioting continued through July 28 when two more Negroes were killed.

These and other race riots aroused general public condemnation. Some newspapers attempted to blame the East St. Louis riot on organized labor while politicians occasionally hinted that German agents must have been behind the racial difficulties. But most editorial writers deplored the mob action. Theodore Roosevelt denounced the rioters and gained some praise. President Wilson received many protests and demands for remedial action. One writer said the riot was "worse than anything the Germans did in Belgium." After reading one complaint Wilson wrote that the particular individual "cannot feel more distressed than I do at the terrible things which have recently been happening." He said that he wanted to make a statement "if it can be made naturally and with the likelihood that it will be effective." Nevertheless, Negroes believed that the President did not take vigorous enough action to guard against future race disturbances.

Negroes held a protest parade in New York City and in many other ways attempted to arouse public opposition to such attacks. From Los Angeles a Negro group sent a telegram to President Wilson stating:

In view of the fact that our country is asking of us to give up our very lives for civilization against barbarism and to establish world democracy . . . we feel, as human beings, we could ask for nothing less . . . for back of all loyalty there must be love of country, but if the country will not protect us in the time of need, we feel that it is not humanly possible to nourish our hearts to loyalty by memory of cold neglect from [the] general government.[1]

[1] Forum of Los Angeles to Wilson, July 8, 1917, Wilson Papers.

Wilson asked his secretary to acknowledge the telegram, saying that the matter was "having my gravest and most anxious consideration."

When a group of Negro leaders in Maryland sought an interview with the President to discuss the East St. Louis riot, Wilson said he was too busy to grant the request. This prompted Professor Kelly Miller of Howard University to write the President, "The Negro feels that he is not regarded as a constituent part of American democracy. This is our fundamental grievance." Miller added that there was no use trying to spread democracy abroad while Negro citizens in East St. Louis, Memphis, Waco, and other places were being mobbed and killed. Finally, he accused Wilson of maintaining a "lukewarm aloofness from the tangled issues of this problem." On August 15 Wilson did issue a statement condemning acts of violence against Negroes.

Nonetheless, violence against Negroes continued. The next most serious riot occurred in Houston. With colored troops stationed near Houston, more or less continuous trouble had developed over the enforcement of the Jim Crow laws. There were instances in which the Houston police had mistreated Negro soldiers. The riot was set off on August 23 when police officers raided a dice game in the colored section. Some of the Negro soldiers fled and sought refuge in the house of a woman. When officers tried to arrest the woman, a Negro soldier attempted to interfere. He was handled roughly and arrested. Later in the day this same police officer had trouble with a Negro member of the military police who was shot at and arrested. News of this reached the army camp, and colored soldiers, seeking revenge on the Houston police, "left the camp armed, approached the town, and committed various murders, assaults, and acts of terrorization." Fifteen persons were killed. The military authorities moved quickly to restore order. Forty-one Negroes were given life sentences at

Leavenworth Penitentiary, and thirteen were hanged in an arroyo about two miles east of Camp Travis. Secretary [of War Newton] Baker later wrote Wilson that because of the "speed with which the death sentences . . . were executed, some feeling was aroused in the country." Baker recommended that in the future death sentences should be reviewed in Washington.

After the execution of the thirteen soldiers a Negro newspaper, the San Antonio *Inquirer*, carried an article signed by C. L. Threadgill-Dennis which said: "We would rather see you shot by the highest tribunal of the United States Army because you dared protect a Negro woman from the insult of a southern brute in the form of a policeman, than to have you forced to go to Europe to fight for a liberty you cannot enjoy. . . ." Although the editor, G. W. Bouldin, claimed he was out of the city at the time and knew nothing of the article, he was indicted for attempting "to cause insubordination, disloyalty, mutiny, and refusal of duty." Bouldin was sentenced to two years in Leavenworth Penitentiary.

16

John M. Clark
THE MIGRATION OF NEGROES

From John M. Clark, The Cost of the War to the American People (*New Haven, Conn.: Yale University Press, 1931*), *pp. 257–261. Reprinted by permission of the Carnegie Endowment for International Peace.*

John M. Clark (1884–1963), after teaching briefly at Colorado College, Amherst College, and the University of Chicago, was appointed professor of economics at Columbia University in 1926. He served in that capacity for more than twenty-five years, becoming (John Bates) Clark Professor of Political Economy shortly before his retirement. His published works include *Alternate to Serfdom* (1948), *Guideposts of Change* (1949), and *Economic Institutions and Human Welfare* (1957).

One of the definite effects of the War was a wave of negro migration to northern industrial cities, which has resulted in an approximate doubling of the pre-war negro population of the northern states. Between 1915 and 1925 the northern negro population increased by probably something like a total of 700,000 in excess of the pre-war rate of increase. Between 1915 and 1928 it is estimated that some 1,200,-000 negroes moved north, though not all of them remained. In 1910 the northern negro population was 1,036,000, and for the previous decade it had been increasing at the rate of about 16,000 per year. In 1916 the first wave of war migration started, and by 1920 the northern negro population had grown to 1,551,-000, indicating a movement of well over 400,000 in five years. Local school censuses and test counts point to the conclusion that this rate of increase was maintained, or nearly maintained, in the next five years. And since the rural negro population of the northern states has been actually declining, it can be said that the whole movement, or more, went to the cities.

In the meantime, while the total negro population of the south still showed a slight increase between census years, the increase was so small as to make it probable that there was an actual decrease from 1916 on. And the rural population showed a decrease, even from 1910 to 1920, indicating a larger decrease from 1916 on. Southern negroes also are moving cityward.

The causes of this movement are largely economic, though partly of other sorts. Cotton growing was facing difficulties. The ravages of the boll weevil were increasing during the war years, reaching their height in 1920–21 and causing heavy reductions in yield per acre. Social conditions in the south also created restlessness, and the development of negro publications tended to intensify this and make it more articulate. But the opportunity for the great exodus was created by the demand for labor in northern industries brought about by the War, coupled with the virtual disappearance of immigration from abroad. Changes in the northward movement of negroes have been definitely correlated with changes in foreign immigration, increasing when it fell off, and *vice versa*. They have thus constituted a small and partial offset to the changes in the larger movement of foreign labor to our industrial centers.

The northward movement came in two waves, with the depression of 1921 intervening. For the first wave, the demands of war production may claim a large share of the responsibility; for the second the War can still be held responsible, *via* the sharp curtailment of immigration which followed it, and which it may be said to have precipitated. Both the restriction of immigration and the northward movement of negroes might have come later in any case, but the War certainly hastened and intensified both changes.

One economic effect has been to raise the material standard of living of the negroes, both those who went north and those who remained behind. This is partly offset by the increase in material needs resulting from the change to the more rigorous climate of the north, and from rural to city living conditions. It is estimated that the cost of the New York city government, as indicated in the 1931 budget, lays a burden of $434 on an average family of five —more than the entire annual income of many rural families. Indeed, the increase in material wants and expenses due to city living conditions is one general offset to the increased *per capita* income which our population as a whole has been enjoying. After all due allowance has been made for this, however, a material raising of standards of living remains.

The effect of the exodus on the condition of the southern negro seems to have been wholly for the better. There were attempts to keep negroes at home, and to prevent propaganda and recruiting for the northward movement; but these seem to have exercised slight retaining effect. The actual decline of the rural negro population created a serious labor shortage; and the effort to combat this took its more permanent and significant form in efforts to improve conditions. Wages rose, naturally, but there was also a general formation of interracial committees for the promotion of closer and more harmonious relations and the removal of grievances.

Hundreds of these committees have been formed, under the leadership of the Commission on Interracial Cooperation. As a result, today "intelligent white and colored men know more about each other than at any time since the Civil War." The committees are working for legislation, schools, civic improvements, more efficient police protection (an element in the prevention of mob violence), hospitals, and "the elimination of petty injustices and discriminations that are the worst feature of the race situation in the south."[1]

Another effect of the changing conditions has been to hasten the decline of the plantation system in southern agriculture, with its perpetuation of semidependent conditions for the negro cultivators. The ultimate effect may well be to stimulate the development of the more diversified agriculture of which the south stands in so much need. In general, the position and treatment of the negro in the south appear to have materially improved.

In the north, aside from increased wages, the results of the movement were not so uniformly favorable. The increased industrial competition and general friction between the races

[1] Will W. Alexander, *The Negro in the New South, Annals,* CXXXX, 152.

led to trouble, including bloody race riots in East St. Louis, Chicago, and elsewhere. The living quarters the negroes were able to find were naturally in the least desirable sections of the towns—sometimes in vicious districts. Congestion at first was often quite serious. As the black belts formed and extended their boundaries, there was widespread unsettling of real estate values. Residential segregation of the races was undoubtedly sharpened, since one or two negro families in a white district now constituted a more serious menace than formerly, and stimulated efforts to secure their removal for the protection of the character of the district. Near the borders of an existing "black belt" this was a much more serious matter, and methods of protection were less refined. As the advance guard of the negroes secured a definite foothold, values fell heavily, followed often by some measure of recovery as the district was abandoned to the colored residents.

The northward movement has definitely brought the negro into industrial employments. One unfortunate element was the fact that the first entry of negroes was often made in the capacity of strikebreakers, with the natural result in the form of intensified hostility and resistance. "[Negro] steel workers in Pittsburgh increased from less than 100 in five plants in 1910 to 16,900 in 23 plants in 1923—21 per cent of all steel workers in the district. Ten per cent of all iron molders in Chicago are Negroes. In Detroit, there were 11,000 Negro workers in the Ford plant, before its remodeling for the new Ford car, and about the same proportion in the present organization."[2]

One result of the movement has been a reduction in employment of negro women and children. Many women formerly working on the soil are now not listed as gainfully employed. Families moving into northern states were forced to keep their children in school, though improved conditions in the south are also responsible for the marked decrease of negro child labor.

Though the negroes earn low wages, they seem to be in general no less self-sustaining than the foreign-born whites, as judged by the percentage in almshouses. This percentage is, however, heavily concentrated in the northern states, indicating that the 2 million and more of negroes who are attempting to gain an economic foothold in these states do constitute a dependency problem out of all proportion to their numbers. On the other hand, "the Metropolitan Life Insurance Company alone has 2,500,000 Negro policy holders, over one-fifth of the entire negro population, representing eventual assets close to a billion dollars."[3]

Another phase of the movement is the stimulus given to the struggle of the negro for recognition in the ranks of organized labor. Negroes have gained a foothold in labor unions, but are rather typically kept in segregated locals, and these frequently have no direct representation in governing bodies, being represented through white locals. The northern migration has undoubtedly made this issue more active.

To sum up, the War has forced on the north something like twice as large a share of the national problem of color as it had borne previously, creating large massed and segregated negro populations in the northern urban centers. This has created friction and some serious trouble; but on the whole it does not seem clear that it has been a misfortune for the nation as a whole. For the negro it has meant on the whole a step in the long journey toward

[2] Charles S. Johnson, "The Changing Economic Status of the Negro," *Annals of the American Academy of Political and Social Science*, CXXXX, 133, November, 1928.

[3] Johnson, 135.

freedom and an independent social and economic position—not without its setbacks and hardships. For the whites, it has meant all the difficulties of adjustment attendant on this same process.

17

Willard Waller
EDUCATIONAL DISLOCATION

"War and Social Institutions," in Willard Waller, ed., War in the Twentieth Century (New York: Dryden Press, 1940), pp. 498–502.

Willard W. Waller (1899–1945) taught sociology at the University of Nebraska and Pennsylvania State College in the early 1930s, and at Barnard College from 1937 until his death in 1945. A student of marriage and the family in times of stress, he was author of *The Family* (1938), *War and the Family* (1940), and *The Veteran Comes Back* (1944), as well as editor of *War in the Twentieth Century* (1940).

When we think of war we usually think of its more dramatic aspects, of battlefields strewn with the slain, or perhaps of widows and orphans, or of refugees, or of widespread starvation. There are other aspects of war which ordinarily go unconsidered in spite of their very great importance. For instance, war interrupts the educational process, turns the schools to new and unaccustomed uses, gives a certain age group a substandard education, and cripples the school system for many years.

It is easy to describe the effect of war upon school in those regions where the actual fighting takes place. War destroys the schools there, and puts an end to formal education. Even where there is no actual fighting, it may not be possible to carry on schoolroom instruction. If this situation is prolonged for a sufficient length of time, there arises a generation of children like the "wild" children of Russia in the post-war period. Largely freed of family ties and out of reach of schools, these children lived on the edges of society and led a life little better than that of beasts.

Visitors to Russia in the post-war years were struck by the numbers of such "wild" children, who thronged the markets and railroad stations, seizing every opportunity to beg or steal. They were largely the heritage of years of civil war. Their parents had been killed in battle or executed, or in some way the children had become finally separated from them. They were not true "feral" children, that is, children without any culture at all, but they were certainly out of touch with most of the control institutions of society. Naturally, many of them were juvenile delinquents of the most hardened and vicious type. Possessing great skill as stowaways, they migrated all over Russia. In 1925 their number was estimated at 300,000, but such an estimate is only a guess. The government waged a strenuous campaign to settle them in children's institutions, and they disappeared within a few years. Until they were thus domiciled, schooling was, of course, altogether impossible.

Even where the tide of war does not roll, war destroys or damages education. Routine is, and perhaps should be, sacred in the schools. War interrupts the routine of every citizen and of every institution. When war begins, the schools adapt to the situation and divert their activities to the task of winning the war. Classroom instruction revolves around the theme of war to a considerable extent, with incidental losses and gains. School children are organized into groups for various kinds of war work. If there is a shortage of metal or other goods, school children collect odds and ends to be salvaged. If there is a campaign for the Red Cross, the children not only join as junior members, but canvass the community for members. War-garden movements flourish in the schools and are mediated by the schools to the communities. There are hundreds of special activities, focussed every month on different objects; there are campaigns for writing letters to the men in the service, Liberty Loan letters, and so on endlessly. School children help to sell bonds, distribute propaganda, and in general help to organize their community for war. In all this, the school serves as an agency which organizes the local community to serve the ends of the more inclusive community, the nation.

When the school is thus metamorphosed, teachers, and especially administrative heads of schools, become community leaders. They head up committees; they make speeches; they try to enlist the support of their community for the national program. In many respects this contact with the community is no doubt vitalizing to persons who have spent much of their lives in a quiet eddy while all the main currents of life flowed by. Unfortunately any favorable effect which might be so produced is more than neutralized by other disorganizing influences at work upon the schools.

If the schools assume the function of organizing the local community for the national program, that is, for the war, it naturally comes about that the teacher who opposes the war or supports it lukewarmly must pay a heavy penalty. Academic freedom is almost nonexistent in war time. [Howard K.] Beale has described the suppressions which took place in the United States during the first World War as follows:

The World War itself raised important problems at the same time that it imposed rigid repression of freedom. Opponents of the War were effectively silenced. Not only government agents but all that stripe of men who enjoy shouting and bullying set up a hue and cry

against "disloyalty" in the schools. Not only teachers who openly opposed the War or had formerly been known as "pacifists," but all who were suspected of not giving vigorous support to it, were subjected to local pressures, investigated, and made to give positive proof of their "loyalty" to the war system. The charge of pro-Germanism was hurled at them . . . Pacifism was made synonymous with treason. The schools were used to breed hate and to circulate what recent studies of war propaganda have proved to be official lies invented to create a war spirit. Teachers who resisted the general unreason and popular hysteria were vigorously punished. Views about the War that historians and teachers generally hold today would have led to instant dismissal. Teachers, instead of standing for reason and critical thinking in time of general hysteria, were swept along by popular passion into actually helping to create the war psychology.

Educators joined in the violations of freedom . . . Instead of standing squarely behind free expression for teachers, the committee of the American Association of University Professors recently established to protect "academic freedom" gave its support to suppression of freedom in matters relating to the War. It acquiesced in the drastic wartime laws denying free speech . . . Teachers themselves demanded the dismissal of their fellows who opposed the War.[1]

During the World War of 1914 and the post-war period, the teaching profession in the United States was literally and figuratively emasculated. The army made heavy demands upon the profession for officer material; teachers made good officers. The multitudinous varieties of war work attracted yet others. Perhaps the most important cause of the threatened annihilation of the profession was inflation. Salaries were already low; prices went up

[1] Howard K. Beale, *Are American Teachers Free, An Analysis of Restraints upon the Freedom of Teaching in American Schools*, Scribner, 1936, pp. 22–25.

and salaries did not. Many teachers left the profession, very likely many of the best. Enrollment in normal schools fell off heavily. By 1919 the situation had become a national scandal. It was estimated that 143,000 teachers left the profession in that year. There was a nation-wide shortage of teachers. A survey by the United States Commissioner of Education showed that there were 18,279 schools closed because of lack of teachers and 41,900 taught by teachers said to be "below standard but taken on temporarily in the emergency." A different estimate placed the teacher shortage at 39,000 and the number of teachers employed but with defective qualifications at 65,000.

Increases in the pay of teachers and other measures remedied this situation in large part in the course of a few years. It should be emphasized, however, that this wartime dislocation damaged the profession in other ways that are not so easy to remedy. Many of the teachers who left the profession during the war years were among its most valuable members; such people cannot be replaced by merely increasing the output of normal schools. On the other hand, many persons entered the profession with substandard qualifications during the war years, and remained to handicap it for many years thereafter. The emasculation of the teaching profession is thus one of the costs of war. If the teaching profession suffered as it did in the United States, we can easily imagine what happened in the nations more directly affected.

The situation is naturally much worse in the colleges, where the students are of military age. The first World War worked havoc with collegiate instruction in Europe, and sadly disrupted it in the United States. Immediately after the declaration of war, American colleges were in a fever of patriotism. Students left in the midst of their courses to enlist; their teachers were not far behind them. Enrollments fell off heavily; in a few colleges more than fifty percent. Largely because of the loss of tuition fees and dormitory rents, the colleges had a very hard time financially. Social and athletic programs and other student activities were, of course, eliminated, curtailed, or greatly simplified.

After the initial period of disorganization had passed, it came to be realized that the colleges had to be supported as a part of the national effort to win the war, and every effort was made to repair the damage. It was recognized that students under draft age could serve their country best by continuing their education. Late in the war, collegiate and military instruction were combined in the Students' Army Training Corps. This experiment ran but a few months, and probably was not altogether successful. Women's colleges suffered far less than others in the upheaval of war. Enrollment did not suffer. Even here some effort was apparently needed to convince the students that they should complete their courses before plunging into war work. One pronounced effect of the war upon the women's colleges was the decline in the number of graduates who went into teaching, a change incidental to the opening up of new careers for women.

Some relatively permanent damage was probably done to American colleges by the war. There were numerous losses of promising faculty members and replacements on an inferior level; the new members were then protected by tenure rules. Some of the language departments sustained great damage. Here again the slow processes of peace have consumed years in repairing the ravages of war. In other professions the training period was sometimes shortened because of military needs. Many college careers were interrupted. Many students received collegiate credit for military service. The cumulative effect of such things was no doubt considerable.

Ernest Hemingway in a Milan hospital in September 1918, recovering from wounds received while serving as an ambulance driver on the Italian front. His experiences later became the inspiration for his novel A *Farewell to Arms*. (From *Ernest Hemingway: A Life Story* by Carlos Baker. Reprinted by permission of Charles Scribner's Sons. Copyright © 1969 Mary Hemingway)

Chapter Four

THE EFFECTS OF THE WAR ON THOUGHT AND CULTURE

The following selections demonstrate clearly just how awesome a break with the mood of the past the First World War represented. Randolph Bourne, in an impassioned piece written during the war, gives some indication of the shift that was occurring when he accuses intellectuals of rationalizing America's participation by means of a spurious and outworn idealism. Four decades later Henry F. May reveals even more of what was involved in describing how the war destroyed the moral certainty, the optimism, and the faith in progress which so long had dominated American thought. That this was a particularly vivid and meaningful experience for the young writers who had gone to war is attested by Malcolm Cowley, who speaks of the "loss of roots" which he and other participants felt, and by Alfred Kazin, who emphasizes the "new vigor and direction" which the postwar authors shared. Meanwhile, among the public at large, according to Norman Furniss, another effect of the war was to encourage American religious conservatives to take up the offensive in their century-long struggle with the forces of religious liberalism.

QUESTIONS:

1. Why, would you estimate, was such a large majority of American intellectuals willing to support the First World War? (See Richard Hofstadter's essay in the section on Government and Politics, as well as those by Bourne and May in this section.)

2. Henry May asserts that the culture of 1912 fell to pieces because "attack, combined with the challenge of events, brought to light its old inadequacies." What role did the war play in this?

3. If, as Alfred Kazin suggests, there was something light and gay about the literary debunking which went on after the war, might one be led to question how much "innocence" really had been lost?

4. In terms of reactions to events, how much do you think that the literary generation of the early 1920s had in common with the ordinary youth of that day, as described, for example, by John Carter in the preceding section?

5. Were the religious liberals rendered particularly vulnerable by the war? Or was it just that their opponents were now more courageous?

18

Randolph Bourne
THE INTELLECTUAL CRUSADE

"The War and the Intellectuals," The Seven Arts, Vol. 2 (June 1917), pp. 133–146.

Randolph Bourne (1886–1918) was a young writer and social critic who championed the "rebellion" of his age and fought back savagely when the First World War led American intellectuals to abandon progressive and pacifist ideals. Among his works are *Youth and Life* (1913), *Education and Living* (1917), and his posthumously published autobiography, *The History of a Literary Radical* (1920). A victim of bronchial pneumonia in the midst of the war, he rapidly became a martyr to his literary generation.

To those of us who still retain an irreconcilable animus against war, it has been a bitter experience to see the unanimity with which the American intellectuals have thrown their support to the use of war-technique in the crisis in which America found herself. Socialists, college professors, publicists, new-republicans, practitioners of literature, have vied with each other in confirming with their intellectual faith the collapse of neutrality and the riveting of the war-mind on a hundred million more of the world's people. And the intellectuals are not content with confirming our belligerent gesture. They are now complacently asserting that it was they who effectively willed it, against the hesitation and dim perceptions of the American democratic masses. A war made deliberately by the intellectuals! A calm moral verdict, arrived at after a penetrating study of inexorable facts! Sluggish masses, too remote from the world-conflict to be stirred, too lacking in intellect to perceive their danger! An alert intellectual class, saving the people in spite of themselves, biding their time with Fabian strategy until the nation could be moved into war without serious resistance! An intellectual class, gently guiding a nation through sheer force of ideas into what the other nations entered only through predatory craft or popular hysteria or militarist madness! A war free from any taint of self-seeking, a war that will secure the triumph of democracy and internationalize the world! This is the picture which the more self-conscious intellectuals have formed of themselves, and which they are slowly impressing upon a population which is being led no man knows whither by an indubitably intellectualized President. And they are right, in that the war certainly did not spring from either the ideals or the prejudices, from the national ambitions or hysterias, of the American people, however acquiescent the masses prove to be, and however clearly the intellectuals prove their putative intuition.

Those intellectuals who have felt themselves totally out of sympathy with this drag toward war will seek some explanation for this joyful leadership. They will want to understand this willingness of the American intellect to open the sluices and flood us with the sewage of the war spirit. We cannot forget the virtuous horror and stupefaction which filled our college professors when they read the famous manifesto of their ninety-three German colleagues in defence of their war. To the American academic mind of 1914 defence of war was inconceivable. From [Prussian general and author Friedrich von] Bernhardi it recoiled as from a blasphemy, little dreaming that two years later would find it creating its own cleanly reasons for imposing military service on the country and for talking of the rough rude currents of health and regeneration that war would send through the American body public. They would have thought anyone mad who talked of shipping American men by the hundreds of thousands—conscripts—to die on the fields of France. Such a spiritual change seems catastrophic when we shoot our minds back to those days when neutrality was a proud thing. But the intellectual progress has been so gradual that the country retains little sense of the irony. The war sentiment, begun so gradually but so perseveringly by the preparedness advocates who came from the ranks of big business, caught hold of one after another of the intellectual groups. With the aid of [Theodore] Roosevelt, the murmurs became a monotonous chant, and finally a chorus so mighty that to be out of it was at first to be disreputable and finally almost obscene. And slowly a strident rant was worked up against Germany which compared very creditably with the German fulminations against the greedy power of England. The nerve of the war-feeling centred, of course, in the richer and older classes of the Atlantic seaboard, and was keenest where there were French or English business and particularly social connections. The sentiment then spread over the country as a class-phenomenon, touching everywhere those upper-class elements in each section who identified themselves with this Eastern ruling group. It must never be forgotten that in every community it was the least liberal and least democratic elements among whom the preparedness and later the war sentiment was found. The farmers were apathetic, the small business men and workingmen are still apathetic towards the war. The election was a vote of confidence of these latter classes in a President who would keep the faith of neutrality. The intellectuals, in other words, have identified themselves with the least democratic forces in American life. They have assumed the leadership for war of those very classes whom the American democracy has been immemorially fighting. Only in a world where irony was dead could an intellectual class enter war at the head of such illiberal cohorts in the avowed cause of world-liberalism and world-democracy. No one is left to point out the undemocratic nature of this war-liberalism. In a time of faith, skepticism is the most intolerable of all insults.

Our intellectual class might have been occupied, during the last two years of war, in studying and clarifying the ideals and aspirations of the American democracy, in discovering a true Americanism which would not have been merely nebulous but might have federated the different ethnic groups and traditions. They might have spent the time in endeavoring to clear the public mind of the cant of war, to get rid of old mystical notions that clog our thinking. We might have used the time for a great wave of education, for setting our house in spiritual order. We could at least have set the problem before ourselves. If our intellectuals were going to lead the administration, they might conceivably have tried to find some way of securing peace by making neutrality effective. They might have turned their intellectual energy not to the problem of jockeying the nation into war, but to the problem of using our vast neutral power to attain democratic ends for the rest of the world and ourselves without the use of the malevolent technique of war. They might have failed. The point is that they scarcely tried. The time was spent not in clarification and education, but in a mulling over of nebulous ideals of democracy and liberalism and civilization which had never meant anything fruitful to those ruling classes who now so glibly used them, and in giving free rein to the elementary instinct of self-defence. The whole era has been spiritually wasted. The outstanding feature has been not its Americanism but its intense colonialism. The offence of our intellectuals was not so much that they were colonial—for what could we expect of a nation composed of so many national elements?—but that it was so one-sidedly and partisanly colonial. The official, reputable expression of the intellectual class has been that of the English colonial. Certain portions of it have been even more loyalist than the King, more British even than Australia. Other colonial attitudes have been vulgar. The colonialism of the other American stocks was denied a hearing from the start. America might have been made a meeting-ground for the different national attitudes. An intellectual class, cultural colonists of the different European nations, might have threshed out the issues here as they could not be threshed out in Europe. Instead of this, the English colonials in ·university and press took command at the start, and we became an intellectual Hungary where thought was subject to an effective process of Magyarization. The reputable opinion of the American intellectuals became more and more either what could be read pleasantly in London, or what was written in an earnest effort to put Englishmen straight on their war-aims and war-technique. This Magyarization of thought produced as a counter-reaction a peculiarly offensive and inept German apologetic, and the two partisans divided the field between them. The great masses, the other ethnic groups, were inarticulate. American public opinion was almost as little prepared for war in 1917 as it was in 1914.

The sterile results of such an intellectual policy are inevitable. During the war the American intellectual class has produced almost nothing in the way of original and illuminating interpretation. [Thorstein] Veblen's "Imperial Germany"; [Simon N.] Patten's "Culture and War," and addresses; [John] Dewey's "German Philosophy and Politics"; a chapter or two in [Walter] Weyl's "American Foreign Policies"; —is there much else of creative value in the intellectual repercussion of the war? It is true that the shock of war put the American intellectual to an unusual strain. He had to sit idle and think as spectator not as actor. There was no government to which he could docilely and loyally tender his mind as did the Oxford professors to justify England in her own eyes. The American's training was such as to make the fact of war almost incredible. Both in his reading of history and in his lack of economic perspective he was badly prepared for it. He had to explain to himself something which was too colossal for the modern mind, which outran any language or terms which we had to interpret it in. He had to expand his sympathies to the breaking-point, while pulling the past and present into some sort of interpretative order. The intellectuals in the fighting countries had only to rationalize and justify what their country was already doing. Their task was easy. A neutral, however, had really to search out the truth. Perhaps perspective was too much to ask of any mind. Certainly the older colonials among our college professors let their prejudices at once dictate their thought. They have been comfortable ever since. The war has taught them nothing and will teach them nothing. And they have had the satisfaction, under the rigor of events, of seeing prejudice submerge the intellects of their younger colleagues. And they have lived to see almost their entire class, pacifists and democrats too, join them as apologists for the "gigantic irrelevance" of war.

19

Henry F. May
THE END OF INNOCENCE

From The End of American Innocence, *by Henry F. May, pp. 393–398. Copyright © 1959 by Henry F. May. Reprinted by permission of Alfred A. Knopf, Inc. Published in Great Britain by Jonathan Cape Ltd.*

Henry F. May (1915–   ) is an historian of culture and religion who taught at Scripps College from 1947 to 1952 and who has been at the University of California, Berkeley, since that time. In 1963 he was appointed to the Margaret F. Byrne chair of American history. His books include *Protestant Churches and Industrial America* (1949) and *The End of American Innocence* (1959).

. . . At some time long after the Armistice whistles had stopped blowing, it became apparent that a profound change had taken place in American civilization, a change that affected all the contenders in the prewar cultural strife. This was the end of American innocence. Innocence, the absence of guilt and doubt and the complexity that goes with them, had been the common characteristic of the older culture and its custodians, of most of the progressives, most of the relativists and social scientists, and of the young leaders of the prewar Rebellion. This innocence had often been rather precariously maintained. Many had glimpsed a world whose central meaning was neither clear nor cheerful, but very few had come to live in such a world as a matter of course. Exceptions to innocence had existed in all camps—they had included unhappy elder thinkers like Henry Adams, rueful naturalists like [Theodore] Dreiser, and vigorous skeptics like [H. L.] Mencken. None of these had yet deeply affected the country's image of itself; all, including Henry Adams, who died in 1918, were to become influential in the twenties.

This change, on the way for a long time and precipitated by the war, is worth looking at very briefly as it affected several segments of the increasingly divided nation. The most obvious aspect of change was the complete disintegration of the old order, the set of ideas which had dominated the American mind so effectively from the mid-nineteenth century until 1912. The heresies of the nineties had undermined this set of beliefs; the Rebellion had successfully defied it; the twenties hardly had to fight it. After the war it was hard to find a convincing or intellectually respectable spokesman for the prewar faith. The old moral idealism had become a caricature of Woodrow Wilson; the old culture was an inaccurate memory of [William Dean] Howells.

Progress, right after the war, seemed to be equally shattered, and various types of reaction, long present beneath the surface, thrust militantly into the open. Racial violence reached an all-time high; the Fundamentalists made their most extreme and pathetic efforts to crush the liberalism which had seemed to them oppressive. A little later, in the mid-twenties, something else which had been latent before the war reached a position of great power: the ultra-practical, anti-intellectual, pseudo-idealistic gospel of Prosperity First.

Yet many have denied that progressivism perished completely. Certainly it would be foolish to say that Americans lost their capacity for social innovation: in different ways both the twenties and the thirties saw more changes than the century's first decade. What was gone was the prewar *kind* of progressivism with its supreme confidence. This had been closely linked to moralism and culture; it could not survive without them.

Later political history was to make this change and some of its meaning clear. In the twenties, a number of promising attempts to form a progressive coalition failed. Most of the components, including liberal leaders and several kinds of articulate discontent, were present. What was lacking was the old idealistic cement, the thing that had made representatives of opposing interests sing hymns for [Theodore] Roosevelt or wipe their eyes over a Wilson peroration. Even the New Deal, much more thorough in its innovations than prewar progressivism had ever been, suffered from a serious—in the long run, perhaps a disastrous—lack of ideology.

The general belief in progress as the direction of history suffered quite as much as political progressivism. In the twenties and after, progress in this sense was repudiated by many of the most admired American novelists and poets. Before the war, most of the literary rebels had believed in progress as strongly as their opponents, though they had defined it differently. After the war, typical attitudes of writers ranged from [T. S.] Eliot's religious conservatism to [Robinson] Jeffers's naturalistic despair. The precise moment of change can be seen in one famous case, the wartime metamorphosis of Randolph Bourne. Bourne did not move all the way, before his death in 1918, to pessimism.

He did, however, lose completely his confidence in the state. Formerly an exuberant, mystical, somewhat naive insurgent, he became in his last essays a sharp, courageous profound inquirer, a defender of freedom in what he had learned was a hostile world.

Bourne's change symbolized the decline of literary optimism; it also demonstrated the failure of pragmatism to produce a new consensus. Before the war Bourne, like many other intellectuals, had combined an allegiance to John Dewey with a number of incompatible elements. When Dewey announced his support of the war and began his attacks on pacifism, Bourne renounced pragmatism in a series of stinging essays. Its values, he charged, had depended on the easy consensus of a peaceful period. Under fire, its insistent practicality and emphasis on the possible deteriorated too easily into shallow opportunism.

Somewhat angrily, Dewey continued to attack impractical idealists and pacifists and during the war moved still further toward support of the Wilsonian program. Disillusioned in 1919, he turned against Wilson and the League, explaining his wartime position in terms that sounded almost apologetic.

Dewey and his followers went on after the war to some of their most important work, and to a new height of prestige in some circles. Yet for some kinds of people who had once admired Dewey, Bourne's wartime questions remained moot. Rejecting far more than pragmatism alone, Bourne had helped to drive a wedge between the values of art and those of practical betterment.

Is there something in these realistic attitudes that works actually against poetic vision, against concern for the quality of life as above machinery of life?[1]

[1] Bourne: "Twilight of Idols," *Seven Arts*, October, 1917, pp. 695–6.

Despite several generations of serious and some-times promising effort, this question has not been answered. Pragmatism became one of a number of contending views and not what its founders still hoped it might be: the basis of a new, progressive "common faith."

The Rebellion, in its innocent prewar form, was over. Having helped to destroy the nine-teenth-century credo, it perished with its old opponent. In a more general sense, the Ameri-can intellectual revolution was only beginning. This has moved in so many directions that its later history cannot even be suggested here. One thing that happened after the war was the re-emergence with new prestige of the two main nineteenth-century heresies, extreme nat-uralism and extreme aestheticism.

In the new, more complex, and less cheer-ful climate of postwar dissent, nearly all the chief leaders of the prewar movement found themselves feeling strange and uprooted. The Chicago poets, the first generation of Green-wich Villagers, the *Masses* radicals, the original New Republicans all felt disoriented after the war in the presence of their juniors. Some dis-appeared, some like [Floyd] Dell wrote well only about their prewar experiences, some like [Van Wyck] Brooks and [Walter] Lippmann moved slowly into very different careers. Two things seemed to bother them in the world of Fitzgerald, Hemingway, and Faulkner: real frivolity and real pessimism. The only prewar writers who were really comfortable later were those who had belonged from the start to the non-exuberant minority, those who had cen-tered their method not on spontaneity but on craft. Chief among these were [Ezra] Pound and his young protege of the prewar years, T. S. Eliot.

Finally, since Americans of all generations retain some tendency to moralize, it is im-possible to refrain altogether from passing some judgments. The prewar Rebellion is not hard to assess. It was fragile, contradictory, and usually shallow. Yet it was immediately very valuable, and in the long run its consequences were complex and momentous. It protested effectively against both rigid materialism and meaningless moralities. In its time, it won vic-tories that could not have been won by a more consistent and penetrating kind of insurrection. Even at its shallowest, it taught the truth that all romanticism teaches and that Americans had been forgetting, the truth that the world cannot be reduced to simple formulas. It pro-duced some excellent work in its own day, and it introduced a period of artistic and intellec-tual achievement that lasted and flowered for two decades.

The old culture is harder to come to terms with, since it lasted longer and ran deeper. In the nineteen-fifties nostalgia comes easily. It is not hard to see the uses of unquestioned moral consensus in a world too shaken to be even rebellious. The kindness and cheerfulness of prewar America at its best are more than at-tractive. Most of us feel that we cannot get along if some vestiges of these qualities do not survive.

Yet the civilization of 1912 condemned it-self. It failed to carry out its own evolutionary precept of adaptation to conditions. It shut its eyes to some glaring flaws in the general suc-cess of American society. It allowed itself to become closely linked with a hopeless program that contradicted its own best insights: the dominance of a narrow class and a minority "race." It became blind even to its own heri-tage, the best of the American past.

These mistakes were not accidents, neither were they parts of some mysterious, inevitable cycle of maturity and decline. They were the results of a permanent flaw in American nine-teenth-century thought: its inveterate opti-mism. Peace, economic expansion, and a large measure of general content were facts of the

American scene most of the time. These had become confused with inevitable upward evolution and even with the coming of God's kingdom on earth. The American culture of 1912 fell into pieces not because it was attacked but because attack, combined with the challenge of events, brought to light its old inadequacies.

Since this happened, American civilization has been less happy, less unanimous, and more precarious. Off and on, it has also been more interesting. Its least successful periods have been those like the immediate present, times of false complacency that caricature the old confidence. Its best periods have been those when it has most nearly come to terms with an unfriendly world.

The end of American innocence was part of a great tragedy, but it was not, in itself, an unmitigated disaster. Those who look at it with dismay, or those who deny that it happened, do so because they expect true stories to have a completely happy ending. This is a kind of innocence American history must get over.

20

Malcolm Cowley
THE LOSS OF ROOTS

From Exile's Return: A Literary Odyssey of the 1920's *by Malcolm Cowley, pp. 36–47. Copyright 1934, copyright © renewed 1962 by Malcolm Cowley. Reprinted by permission of The Viking Press, Inc. Published in the United Kingdom by The Bodley Head and reprinted by permission of Laurence Pollinger Limited.*

Malcolm Cowley (1898–   ) was among those American intellectuals who were expatriates in the 1920s but who returned to become prominent members of the literary scene. From 1929 to 1944 he served as associate editor of the *New Republic*, and since the Second World War he has been a visiting professor of English at various universities.

Among his writings are *Blue Juniata* (1929), *Exile's Return* (1934), *The Dry Season* (1941), *The Literary Situation* (1954), and *Think Back on Us* (1967).

During the winter of 1916–17 our professors stopped talking about the international republic of letters and began preaching patriotism. We ourselves prepared to change our uniforms of culture for military uniforms; but neither of these changes was so radical as it seemed. The patriotism urged upon us was not, like that of French peasants, a matter of saving one's own fields from an invader. It was an abstract patriotism that concerned world democracy and the right to self-determination of small nations, but apparently had nothing to do with our daily lives at home, nothing to do with better schools, lower taxes, higher pay for factory hands (and professors) or restocking Elk Run with trout. And the uniforms we assumed were not, in many cases, those of our own country.

When the war came the young writers then in college were attracted by the idea of enlisting in one of the ambulance corps attached to a foreign army—the American Ambulance Service or the Norton-Harjes, both serving under the French and receiving French army pay, or the Red Cross ambulance sections on the Italian front. Those were the organizations that promised to carry us abroad with the least delay. We were eager to get into action, as a character in one of [John] Dos Passos's novels expressed it, "before the whole thing goes belly up."

In Paris we found that the demand for ambulance drivers had temporarily slackened. We were urged, and many of us consented, to join the French military transport, in which our work would be not vastly different: while driving munition trucks we would retain our status of gentleman volunteers. We drank to our new service in the *bistro* round the corner. Two weeks later, on our way to a training camp behind the lines, we passed in a green wheatfield the grave of an aviator *mort pour la patrie*, his wooden cross wreathed with the first lilies of the valley. A few miles north of us the guns were booming. Here was death among the flowers, danger in spring, the sweet wine of sentiment neither spiced with paradox nor yet insipid, the death being real, the danger near at hand.

We found on reaching the front that we were serving in what was perhaps the most literary branch of any army. My own section of thirty-six men will serve as an example. I have never attended a reunion of T.M.U. 526, if one was ever held, but at various times I have encountered several of my former comrades. One is an advertising man specializing in book publishers' copy. One is an architect, one a successful lecturer who has written a first novel, one an editor, one an unsuccessful dramatist. The war itself put an end to other careers. A Rhodes scholar with a distinguished record was killed in action. The member of the section who was generally believed to have the greatest promise was a boy of seventeen, a poet who had himself transferred into the Foreign Legion and died in an airplane accident. Yet T.M.U. 526 was in no way exceptional. My friends in other sections where there was a higher percentage of young writers often pitied me for having to serve with such a bunch of philistines.

It would be interesting to list the authors who were ambulance or camion drivers in 1917. Dos Passos, Hemingway, Julian Green, William Seabrook, E. E. Cummings, Slater Brown, Harry Crosby, John Howard Lawson, Sidney Howard, Louis Bromfield, Robert Hillyer, Dashiell Hammett . . . one might almost say that the ambulance corps and the French military transport were college-extension courses for a generation of writers. But what did these courses teach?

They carried us to a foreign country, the first that most of us had seen; they taught us to make love, stammer love, in a foreign language. They fed and lodged us at the expense of a government in which we had no share. They made us more irresponsible than before: livelihood was not a problem; we had a minimum of choices to make; we could let the future take care of itself, feeling certain that it would bear us into new adventures. They taught us courage, extravagance, fatalism, these being the virtues of men at war; they taught us to regard as vices the civilian virtues of thrift, caution and sobriety; they made us fear boredom more than death. All these lessons might have been learned in any branch of the army, but ambulance service had a lesson of its own: it instilled into us what might be called a *spectatorial* attitude. . . .

On a July evening, at dusk, I remember halting in the courtyard of a half-ruined chateau, through which zigzagged the trenches held by the Germans before their retreat two miles northward to stronger positions. Shells were harmlessly rumbling overhead: the German and the French heavy batteries, three miles behind their respective lines, were shelling each other like the Brushton gang throwing rocks at the Car Barn gang; here, in the empty courtyard between them, it was as if we were underneath a freight yard where heavy trains were being shunted back and forth. We looked indifferently at the lake, now empty of swans, and the formal statues chipped by machine-gun fire, and talked in quiet voices—about [Stéphane] Mallarmé, the Russian ballet, the respective virtues of two college magazines. On the steps of the chateau, in the last dim sunlight, a red-faced boy from Harvard was studying Russian out of a French textbook. Four other gentlemen volunteers were rolling dice on an outspread blanket. A French artillery brigade on a hillside nearby—rapid-firing seventy-fives—was laying down a barrage; the guns flashed like fireflies among the trees. We talked about the Lafayette Escadrille with admiration, and about our own service bitterly.

Yet our service was, in its own fashion, almost ideal. It provided us with fairly good food, a congenial occupation, furloughs to Paris and uniforms that admitted us to the best hotels. It permitted us to enjoy the once-in-a-lifetime spectacle of the Western Front. Being attached to the French army, it freed us from the severe and stupid forms of discipline then imposed on American shavetails and buck privates. It confronted us with hardships, but not more of them than it was exhilarating for young men to endure, and with danger, but not too much of it: seldom were there more than two or three serious casualties in a section during the year—and that was really the burden of our complaint. We didn't want to be slackers, *embusqués*. The war created in young men a thirst for abstract danger, not suffered for a cause but courted for itself; if later they believed in the cause, it was partly in recognition of the danger it conferred on them. Danger was a relief from boredom, a stimulus to the emotions, a color mixed with all others to make them brighter. There were moments in France when the senses were immeasurably sharpened by the thought of dying next day, or possibly next week. The trees were green, not like ordinary trees, but like trees in the still moment before a hurricane; the sky was a special and ineffable blue; the grass smelled of life itself; the image of death at twenty, the image of love, mingled together into a keen, precarious delight. And this perhaps was the greatest of the lessons that the war taught to young writers. It revivified the subjects that had seemed forbidden because they were soiled by many hands

and robbed of meaning: danger made it possible to write once more about love, adventure, death. Most of my friends were preparing to follow danger into other branches of the army —of any army—that were richer in fatalities.

They scattered a few months later: when the ambulance and camion services were taken over by the American Expeditionary Force, not many of them re-enlisted. Instead they entered the Lafayette Escadrille, the French or Canadian field artillery, the tanks, the British balloon service, the Foreign Legion, the Royal Air Force; a very few volunteered for the American infantry, doing a simple thing for paradoxical reasons. I had friends in distant sectors: one of them flew for the Belgians, another in Serbia, and several moved on to the Italian front, where John Dos Passos drove an ambulance. Ernest Hemingway was also an ambulance driver on that front, until the July night when an Austrian mortar bomb exploded in the observation post beyond the front lines where he was visiting at the time, like a spectator invited to gossip with the actors behind the scenes. E. E. Cummings was given no choice of service. Having mildly revolted against the discipline of the Norton-Harjes Ambulance Corps, and having become the friend of a boy from Columbia University who wrote letters to Emma Goldman, he was shipped off to a French military prison, where he had the adventures later described in *The Enormous Room.* . . . But even in prison threatened with scurvy, or lying wounded in hospitals, or flying combat planes above the trenches, these young Americans retained their curious attitude of non-participation, of being friendly visitors who, though they might be killed at any moment, still had no share in what was taking place.

Somewhere behind them was another country, a real country of barns, cornfields, hemlock woods and brooks tumbling across birch logs into pools where the big trout lay. Somewhere, at an incredible distance, was the country of their childhood, where they had once been part of the landscape and the life, part of a spectacle at which nobody looked on.

This spectatorial attitude, this monumental indifference toward the cause for which young Americans were risking their lives, is reflected in more than one of the books written by former ambulance drivers. Five of the principal characters in Dos Passos's *1919*—the Grenadine Guards, as he calls them—Dick Savage (a Harvard aesthete), Fred Summers, Ed Schuyler, Steve Warner (another Harvard man, but not of the same college set), and Ripley (a Columbia freshman) first enlist in the Norton-Harjes Ambulance Corps, and then, when the American army takes it over, go south to the Italian front. In February of the last wartime year, Steve Warner reads that the Empress Taitu of Abyssinia is dead, and the Grenadine Guards hold a wake for her:

> They drank all the rum they had and keened until the rest of the section thought they'd gone crazy. They sat in the dark round the open moonlit window wrapped in blankets and drinking warm zabaglione. Some Austrian planes that had been droning overhead suddenly cut off their motors and dumped a load of bombs right in front of them. The antiaircraft guns had been barking for some time and shrapnel sparkling in the moonhazy sky overhead but they'd been too drunk to notice. One bomb fell geflump into the Brenta and the others filled the space in front of the window with red leaping glare and shook the villa with three roaring snorts. Plaster fell from the ceiling. They could hear the tiles scuttering down off the roof overhead.
> "Jesus, that was almost good night," said Summers. Steve started singing, *Come away from that window my light and my life*, but the rest of them drowned it out with an out of tune

Deutschland, Deutschland über Alles. They suddenly all felt crazy drunk. . . .

"Fellers," Fred Summers kept saying, "this ain't a war, it's a goddam madhouse . . . it's a goddam Cook's tour." It remained, for many of us, a goddam crazy Cook's tour of Western Europe, but for those who served longer it became something else as well.

Ernest Hemingway's hero, in *A Farewell to Arms*, is an American acting as lieutenant of an Italian ambulance section. He likes the Italians, at least until Caporetto; he is contemptuous of the Austrians, fears and admires the Germans; of political conviction he has hardly a trace. When a friend tells him, "What has been done this summer cannot have been done in vain," he makes no answer:

> I was always embarrassed by the words sacred, glorious, and sacrifice, and the expression in vain. We had heard them, sometimes standing in the rain almost out of earshot, so that only the shouted words came through, and had read them, on proclamations that were slapped up by billposters over other proclamations, now for a long time, and I had seen nothing sacred, and the things that were glorious had no glory and the sacrifices were like the stockyards at Chicago if nothing was done with the meat except to bury it. . . . Abstract words such as glory, honor, courage, or hallow were obscene beside the concrete names of villages, the numbers of roads, the names of rivers, the numbers of regiments and the dates. Gino was a patriot, so he said things that separated us sometimes, but he was also a fine boy and I understood his being a patriot. He was born one. He left with Peduzzi in the car. . . .

Two days later the Germans broke through at Caporetto.

The passage dealing with the Italian retreat from river to river, from the mountains beyond the Isonzo along rain-washed narrow roads to the plains of the Tagliamento, is one of the few great war stories in American literature: only [Stephen Crane's] *The Red Badge of Courage* and a few short pieces by Ambrose Bierce can be compared with it. Hemingway describes not an army but a whole people in motion: guns nuzzling the heads of patient farm horses, munition trucks with their radiator caps an inch from the tailboard of wagons loaded with chairs, tables, sewing machines, farm implements; then behind them ambulances, mountain artillery, cattle and army trucks, all pointed south; and groups of scared peasants and interminable files of gray infantrymen moving in the rain past the miles of stalled vehicles. Lieutenant Frederick Henry is part of the retreat, commanding three motor ambulances and half a dozen men, losing his vehicles in muddy lanes, losing his men, too, by death and desertion, shooting an Italian sergeant who tries to run away—but in spirit he remains a non-participant. He had been studying architecture in Rome, had become a gentleman volunteer in order to see the war, had served two years, been wounded and decorated: now he is sick of the whole thing, eager only to get away.

As he moves southward, the southbound Germans go past him, marching on parallel roads, their helmets visible above the walls. Frightened Italians open fire on him. The rain falls endlessly, and the whole experience, Europe, Italy, the war, becomes a nightmare, with himself as helpless as a man among nightmare shapes. It is only in snatches of dream that he finds anything real—love being real, and the memories of his boyhood. "The hay smelled good and lying in a barn in the hay took away all the years in between. We had lain in hay and talked and shot sparrows with an air rifle when they perched in the triangle cut high up in the wall of the barn. The barn was gone now and one year they had cut the hemlock woods and there were only stumps, dried treetops, branches and fireweed where the woods

had been. You could not go back"; the country of his boyhood was gone and he was attached to no other.

And that, I believe, was the final effect on us of the war; that was the honest emotion behind a pretentious phrase like "the lost generation." School and college had uprooted us in spirit; now we were physically uprooted, hundreds of us, millions, plucked from our own soil as if by a clamshell bucket and dumped, scattered among strange people. All our roots were dead now, even the Anglo-Saxon tradition of our literary ancestors, even the habits of slow thrift that characterized our social class. We were fed, lodged, clothed by strangers, commanded by strangers, infected with the poison of irresponsibility—the poison of travel, too, for we had learned that problems could be left behind us merely by moving elsewhere—and the poison of danger, excitement, that made our old life seem intolerable. Then, as suddenly as it began for us, the war ended.

When we first heard of the Armistice we felt a sense of relief too deep to express, and we all got drunk. We had come through, we were still alive, and nobody at all would be killed tomorrow. The composite fatherland for which we had fought and in which some of us still believed—France, Italy, the Allies, our English homeland, democracy, the self-determination of small nations—had triumphed. We danced in the streets, embraced old women and pretty girls, swore blood brotherhood with soldiers in little bars, drank with our elbows locked in theirs, reeled through the streets with bottles of champagne, fell asleep somewhere. On the next day, after we got over our hangovers, we didn't know what to do, so we got drunk. But slowly, as the days went by, the intoxication passed, and the tears of joy: it appeared that our composite fatherland was dissolving into quarreling statesmen and oil and steel magnates. Our own nation had passed the Prohibition Amendment as if to publish a bill of separation between itself and ourselves; it wasn't our country any longer. Nevertheless we returned to it: there was nowhere else to go. We returned to New York, appropriately —to the homeland of the uprooted, where everyone you met came from another town and tried to forget it; where nobody seemed to have parents, or a past more distant than last night's swell party, or a future beyond the swell party this evening and the disillusioned book he would write tomorrow.

21

Alfred Kazin
THE SENSE OF RELEASE

From "The Postwar Scene" in On Native Grounds, *pp. 191–193, copyright, 1942, by Alfred Kazin. Reprinted by permission of Harcourt Brace Jovanovich, Inc.*

Alfred Kazin (1915–   ), one of America's leading literary critics, has been Distinguished Professor of English at the State University of New York at Stony Brook since 1963. Prior to that year he had taught at Harvard University, the New School, the University of Minnesota, Smith College, and Amherst College. He has published numerous studies, including *On Native Grounds* (1942), *A Walker in the City* (1951), and *Starting Out in the Thirties* (1965).

Here, for Europeans too weary to care too much and for Americans too excited to be conscious of all its implications, was the final irony of the war, if any was needed: The period which was marked abroad first by a feverish experimentalism and then by a growing incommunicable sense of the common European tragedy was the same period which saw the public triumph of modern American literature at home. In his bitter war diary for 1917, Randolph Bourne had written darkly, thinking

himself a prophet of disaster: "The war . . . or American promise! One must choose. . . . For the effect of the war will be to impoverish American promise." Now the war was over, and if "the promise of American life," as Bourne and his generation had been prepared to understand it, had died in the war, a different kind of promise had come in its place. Something in American life had gone out with the war, as Bourne and all he represented had gone down in it: a contagious idealism, the dream of a new community in America, all the tokens of that brave and expectant fraternalism which had at one period marked the emergence of the modern spirit in America. But the literature of criticism and revolt that Bourne and [H. L.] Mencken had helped to build together before the war, the movement which had proclaimed as its first principle *Place aux jeunes!* —Make way for the Younger Generation!— that movement had not only not died in the war; it had been given a strange new vigor and direction by the restlessness that came after it. In Europe many brilliant young writers had been killed and many older writers morally shattered; in America the heady, booming, half-comic world the war introduced gave modern writers a prominence, a heedlessness, a boisterous pride in their liberation from convention, that was to enter into the very substance of their work. If it was America that "had won the war for Europe," as the popular legend had it, it was the new American literature, seizing the vitality that was left in the world, that made the victory its own.

It was above all this sense of release that came to American writers after the war, the exhilaration of the sudden freedoms they had won with the dissolution of the old order and the proverbial American colonialism, that now gave so distinctive a tone to the new literature. It was as if the writers themselves, like so many representative classes in American society, were for the first time feeling their oats, creeping out of the old parochial shelters and the old parochial ambitions; and with their release there came a carefree irresponsibility, a gaiety, a youthful perkiness, that gave comic undertones to their growling dissatisfactions with American society. Never in all history, as Edmund Wilson said, did a literary generation so revile its country; and never, as Mencken proved so unforgettably, was the abuse so innocent or so enjoyable. Fundamentally, of course, they were in their different ways all enemies of the conventional middle-class order, enemies of convention and Puritanism, members of the "civilized minority," rebels against all that conspired to keep down the values of art and thought. But they were at the same time children of the new boom world, the gay exploiters of a new privilege, provincials intoxicated with their release from provincialism; and it was this that gave such rollicking emphasis to their contempt for provincialism.

With the same American concentration, the same sense of having to revenge oneself on time, that Gertrude Stein brought to the disembodied abstract world of her "perfect sentences," these writers now tried to make up suddenly for all American writers had missed before, for all that the American world, seemingly, had denied free spirits before. Everything now came free in the heady world of the twenties: all the bitterness of small-town life; all that hunger for richness of experience that had been repressed so long; all that taste for ineffable wickedness and dissolution that had never had a chance; all the yearning to prove that American writers could be as ornate or saucy or satiric as they pleased. If they had a taste for splendor of style, like [Branch] Cabell and [Joseph] Hergesheimer and Thomas Beer, they made of their style a kind of baroque verbal magnificence that was somehow more magnificent than the alleged European magnificence. If they had discovered the mysticism

of sex, like Sherwood Anderson, all life now became circumscribed around it. If they were contemptuous of the official myths about great men that had been taught to them in school, they now discovered, in the luxurious skepticism of debunking, that there were no great men ever. If they had revolted against their native village life in the Middle West, all village life in the Middle West now seemed a cesspool of bigotry and corruption and even the very incarnation of joylessness. "Wait and see," Edgar Lee Masters had chortled in 1918, "Spoon River shall be Americee." And so it proved. If the younger generation had emerged from the war, as F. Scott Fitzgerald said, "to find all Gods dead, all wars fought, all faiths in man shaken," all America was now Spoon River, all the deceptions were out, and only the free creative sense of a few remained. But how much fun it was to say so!

22

Norman Furniss
THE FUNDAMENTALIST REACTION

From Norman Furniss, The Fundamentalist Controversy *(New Haven, Conn.: Yale University Press), pp. 23–26. Copyright © 1954 by Yale University Press.*

Norman Furniss (1922–1964), a professor of history at Colorado State University from 1950 until his death, was particularly interested in the development of intellectual and religious movements. He was the author of *Fundamentalist Controversy, 1918–1931* (1954) and *Mormon Conflict, 1850–1859* (1960).

The World War's great impact upon the nation strengthened in several ways the determination of [religious] conservatives to combat the new forms of knowledge. In the first place, the catastrophe caused many to reject the optimism once inspired by the theory of evolution, the concept of man's inevitable, continuous advance to a state of universal felicity, and instead focused their hope upon one of the five major points of the fundamental creed, the Second Coming. Again the propaganda of hatred, so useful in arousing passions against America's wartime enemies, produced during the subsequent years of peace an unanticipated harvest of bitterness and insecurity that lingered in the spirits of many orthodox people, preparing them for an ideological crusade upon unacceptable beliefs at home. And finally the Fundamentalists made use of the Allies' condemnation of the materialistic philosophy of Germany to brand modernism as an alien, perverting faith, since it was the product of an aspect of that philosophy.

The theory of evolution had provided men with a cheerful outlook as they entered the twentieth century, for it fostered the conviction that nothing could prevent the human race from creating, slowly or rapidly, a good society free of evils. The terrible sight of a world at war, arising so unexpectedly before the eyes of Americans, destroyed such expectations and led many, especially those who had never been satisfied with the assumptions of evolution, to subject the religious liberals' affirmations to hostile analysis. They decided that modernism, with its synthesis of Christianity and evolution, had displayed its complete fallaciousness, since it had been unable to prevent the holocaust despite its high-sounding aspirations for man's progress. Whereas numerous liberal churchmen took the lesson to be opposition to war in any form, the Fundamentalists demanded that the whole discredited theology be scrapped in favor of a return to the traditional beliefs of Christianity, valid for all time. In the words of a character in one of his books, George McCready Price summed up the con-

servatives' attitude: " 'But Colonel,' broke in the Pastor fervently, 'it is not merely that the evolutionists and the Socialists have a different account of the origin of the human race than is found in the Bible, but their substitution is entirely inadequate to meet the world's needs.' "

In reaction to the Modernists' optimism the Fundamentalists, convinced that the war presaged the end of the world, placed their hope upon the Second Coming of Christ. This tenet explained the evil days to their satisfaction, for it envisaged, so far as most Adventists were concerned, a period of devastation before the Return. But since the doctrine of Christ's reappearance on earth was one of the beliefs which the Fundamentalists felt to be jeopardized by the higher critics' tinkering with the Bible, the emphasis on millennialism demanded of them a spirited defense of the old faith and bitter opposition to the new. It was significant that many fervent champions of religious orthodoxy after 1918 were premillennialists.

Another phenomenon of World War days, the unreasoning hatred of ideas and men said by the nation's leaders to be inimical, became one more force behind the rise of the fundamentalist movement. Having learned well that intolerance was justified when the nation was combatting foreign enemies, the Fundamentalists in the subsequent years of peace found themselves no longer able to meet domestic crises, especially a serious challenge to their faith, with Galilean charity. Whereas in 1912 and 1913 the religious conservatives attempted to overcome heretical tendencies primarily by reasoned argument, after 1918 the Fundamentalists sought forcibly to expel the modernist traffickers from the various denominations and to impose rigid creeds upon all who remained. It is true that some conflict between orthodoxy and liberalism would have arisen in the 1920's even if the war had not intervened, but that great upheaval helped precipitate and intensify it. Violence in action and language had now become characteristic of the Fundamentalists.

Wartime propaganda produced an atmosphere of anxiety conducive to a clash between science and theology. In the words of one sociologist: "Wild stories of the underhanded scheming of the enemy with Mexico, Brazil, and Japan were deliberately circulated to keep up the morale of the nation. And when the struggle was over, there was left a residue of the alarmist attitude which has not yet spent its force." Such men as [William Jennings] Bryan and [William B.] Riley made the unknown enemies of postwar America among the evolutionists and Modernists real to their followers with indictments closely resembling Allied propaganda. They warned that theological foes were attempting to "tear the virgin faith [of the children] to shreds by raising all kinds of dark and insinuating questions," were about to "capture" such organizations as the Chautauqua and the YMCA, and had "filched" the educational institutions laboriously constructed by conservatives in the previous century.

In the 1920's the figure of the deceitful Modernist was as familiar to the conservatives as the gaunt, sharp-nosed Puritan to the antiprohibition forces. The *King's Business*, a publication of the Bible Institute of Los Angeles, observed of the "creeping critics": "These men do not knock at the door, make themselves known and reveal their purpose, but have *secretly slipped* in *sideways*; and once safely inside, they have secretly, shrewdly and satanically laid their plans to foist upon the saints their doctrine of denial of God's holy word." A parable jumped to Riley's mind in this connection: "The tares of Evolution have been surreptitiously sown. It was night, and under cover of darkness the enemy came, not in the early evening when people were moving about, lest he be detected, but later, when men slept and no courage was required to put over the dastardly deed." As during the war patriotic Americans felt the enemy secretly sapping the ramparts of the nation, so in the 1920's Fundamentalists continued to see those other agents of Satan, evolution and modernism, clandestinely trying to subvert all that was good.

In yet another way the World War played a part in the outbreak of militant fundamentalism after 1918. During the conflagration Americans had learned through atrocity stories and vague rumors of espionage to hate Germany as a barbaric nation. But to the Fundamentalists higher criticism was a product of the German materialistic philosophy. That nation, they further believed, had followed evolution's theory of the survival of the fittest to its logical conclusion in a ruthless attempt to conquer Europe. They concluded, accordingly, that modernism, combining higher criticism and evolution into an unholy caricature of religion, was only an expression on this continent of a philosophy which had produced the most destructive war of all time, and they carried over into their postwar attacks upon modernism both the hatred and the propagandistic labels used during the years of actual armed conflict. When condemning the theory of evolution they made repeated references to the notion that [Friedrich] Nietzsche and his disciples had merely put the hypothesis into practice. Modernism, they further asserted, had transformed Germany into a godless nation capable of any evil deed and would, if permitted, ruin the United States as well.

Part Two

THE IMPACT OF WORLD WAR II

The Second World War, though more extensive and more "total" than the First, was in some ways at least less devastating. In reality a series of parallel wars on widely separate fronts, the larger conflagration is usually considered to have begun in September 1939 with Hitler's attack on Poland, and to have ended in August 1945 with Japan's surrender to the Allies. If World War II seems, on the whole, to have been a less shattering experience than World War I for almost all concerned, this is probably due to the fact that it was waged by the victors with less guilt on their own part, less frustration militarily, less unrealism generally, and above all, after having lived through the moral "letdown" of the previous war. Still, there is no gainsaying the unbelievable cost involved, and there is no denying the impact of the struggle.

The human and material losses ran to several times those of the First World War. Approximately 35 million people died on this occasion, more than 80 percent of them in Europe. The Soviet Union alone lost some 20 million persons, and more than 5 million Jews were murdered by the Nazis. Military deaths, all told, came to over 16 million men out of the 80 million mobilized (from a world population which had reached 2.3 billion). Material damage to property, much of it the result of bombing raids, cost in excess of $2,000 billion.

To list even the more obvious consequences of the war is not easy. Politically, they include the enlargement of Soviet and Communist influence, the restructuring of both Germany and Japan, the triumph of socialism in Britain, the liquidation of European colonial possessions, the establishment of Israel, and the collapse of Nationalist China. Economically, there is no overlooking the almost total physical and financial exhaustion with which Europe ended the war, as well as the commanding position which America now assumed as a result of its productive accomplishments and its exemption from destruction. On the social side, perhaps the most impressive change was the westward migration of 16 million eastern Europeans, but also significant were the leveling of the social pyramid and the destruction of the old elites which occurred in many places. In intellectual terms, the impact of the war was to a great extent ambivalent, inspiring at one and the same time renewed commitment to traditional values, a greater respect for science (witness the "achievement" of the atomic bomb), and a resurgent enthusiasm for international cooperation.

Though the United States played a more central role in World War II than in the previous conflict, it once again escaped the worst part of the maelstrom. This time the country fought for three years and nine months (three years and six months in Europe), after having been attacked by the Japanese at Pearl Harbor on December 7, 1941. In that interval the United States raised an armed force of 15.2 million men and women (from a population of 135 million) and suffered 1,066,000 casualties and 393,000 dead, almost none of them civilian. Direct expenditures reached about $300 billion, or approximately nine times as much as in 1917–1918.

But this does not begin to tell the story. Lifted by war from the Depression, American industry established almost every kind of record as the Gross National Product (GNP) soared in four years from $91 billion to $166 billion per annum. Simultaneously, with "Dr. New Deal" giving way to "Dr. Win the War" (as President Roosevelt put it), conservatives returned to Washington in droves to man the expansion of the government. On the social front, as family stability declined, internal migration became extensive (particularly among Negroes), and the school system found itself both reappraised and (ultimately) expanded. If the country was calmer and more businesslike than twenty years before, most citizens had become more persuaded than ever that what the world most needed was a strong dose of American idealism.

David Lilienthal, director of the Tennessee Valley Authority, speaking at the completion ceremonies for Douglas Dam, March 1943. Construction of such dams was speeded up because of the great need for industrial power in World War II.　　(Tennessee Valley Authority)

Women workers in Detroit beveling armor plate with acetylene torches. Between 1940 and 1945 the number of employed women in the United States increased from 14 to 20 million. (Margaret Bourke-White; *Life Magazine* © Time Inc.)

Chapter Five

ECONOMIC EFFECTS OF THE WAR

The following articles, which are organized around the same general topics as those of the economic section on World War I, point up both the greater scope of the exertions required by the second conflict and the more permanent character of the changes wrought. In fact, in a piece written in 1942, Stuart Chase argues that the war had finally proved, as the New Deal never had, that governmental expenditures could put an end to a depression. (Chase would have found support for his beliefs in the Employment Act of 1946, with which, after the war, the government for the first time declared itself responsible for the maintenance of full employment.) Somewhat more cautiously, George A. Lincoln, William Y. Smith, and Jay B. Durst contend that an important effect of the country's unprecedented industrial achievement was to "cement" in place the reforms of the 1930s. On the other hand, A. D. H. Kaplan points out that the war increased concentration of ownership so much that after 1945 the Truman administration felt compelled to make a special effort to counteract the trend. Even so, Frederick Lewis Allen asserts that World War II gave an economic lift to farmers and workers and people with low incomes, while Thomas

R. Brooks suggests that the war greatly strengthened labor, and that the postwar readjustment
among labor, business, and government was
much less bitter than the one following the
First World War.

QUESTIONS:

1. To what extent was the economic development
of the war years affected by the fact that the nation was emerging from depression?

2. How might the war have been financed other
than the way in which it was? What would have
been the effects of these alternatives, both during
the war and after?

3. What types of governmental controls and organization were employed in the Second World
War which were not utilized in the First? With
what result?

4. What did World War II do to and for labor,
as compared with World War I? How do you
explain the differences?

5. Do you agree that the Second World War left
more permanent traces upon the American economy than the First? Why?

23

Stuart Chase
A NEW ECONOMY

*Stuart Chase, The Road We Are Traveling, Twentieth
Century Fund, New York, 1942, pp. 49–51.*

Stuart Chase (1888–   ) is an economist and
political scientist who has served in various capacities in business and with such governmental
agencies as the Federal Trade Commission and
the Tennessee Valley Authority. Since the 1930s
he has published a continuing stream of books,
including *Men and Machines* (1929), *The Economy of Abundance* (1934), *The Tyranny of
Words* (1931), *The Proper Study of Mankind*
(1948), and *The Most Probable World* (1968).

[Hitler's] panzer divisions released not only another world war, but a new economic tempo.

Observe the astonishing effects on the United
States. Back in the dear, dim days of the Presidential campaign of 1940, citizens by the millions said "you can't spend your way out of a
depression." They believed it. They voted on
that belief. They were supported by the highest
banking, business and economic authorities. In
due course, Congress appropriated 60 billion
dollars, more or less, for defense spending, and
Mr. [William S.] Knudsen [codirector of the
Office of Production Management] began
awarding contracts as fast as God and the army
bureaucrats would let him. The money flowed
around the economic machine in ever greater
volume. Retail sales began to jump, factories
began howling for men, unemployment figures
tumbled downhill, relief rolls declined, profits
picked up, shortages developed in machine
tools and certain types of skilled labor, prices
began to climb for many products—the back-
bone of the depression was broken. The President, Congress and Mr. Knudsen had combined
"to spend our way out of it." Oh, but the
terrible government debt? Another 7 billion
dollars goes for the Lend-Lease bill! Oh, but
the budget, the budget? Another 9 billions
goes for the army!

There is no business depression in Britain,
Canada, Australia, Germany, Italy, Japan, in
any nation where armament expenditures are
large. Consumers are rationed for many commodities, but money is racing around the economic circuit. Governments are now claiming
and spending anywhere from 20 to 70 per cent
of national income. In all belligerent countries
the figure soon climbs to well above 50 per
cent. In England there are only 200 persons
left who receive as much as $20,000 a year,
after taxes. In the great bull market, thousands
of Americans used to clean up $20,000 in a
five-hour trading day.

Congress before the attack on Pearl Harbor
had already appropriated more than twice as
much money for guns as the New Deal spent

for butter, and other things, in eight years to 1940. It had appropriated more than twice as much as was spent for guns in the last war, when we shipped two million men to France. Where's the money coming from? Nobody gives a damn. That is just the point. In the old economy, such reckless outlays would have spelled bankruptcy and ruin. Money came first and men came second. In the new economy, no nation will permit bankruptcy and ruin so long as men, materials and energy are available. Men first, money second.

You do not understand how this can be so? I will try to explain. Germany does not permit ruin and bankruptcy and has little use for gold. It is Germany we are up against now. Adam Smith may heave in his grave, but no nation in this dangerous world of 1942 is meekly going bankrupt because some textbooks say it ought to. It will go physically bankrupt when it runs out of food, coal, iron, oil, aluminum, and not before. Well, who is going to pay for it? It is being paid for right now with the mental and physical work of those who are producing and moving the goods. "Stuff and nonsense," you cry, your eye on the book. Put your book away, my friend. The books which will explain the new world we are entering have not been written.

24

George A. Lincoln, William Y. Smith, and Jay B. Durst

THE INDUSTRIAL ACHIEVEMENT

From American Economic History, *edited by Seymour Harris, pp. 224–230. Copyright © 1961 by McGraw-Hill, Inc. Used by permission of McGraw-Hill Book Company.*

George A. Lincoln (1907–   ), a career army officer from 1929 until 1969, taught social science at the United States Military Academy during the last twenty-two years of that period. He was military adviser to the Paris Peace Conference in 1946, and is currently the director of the Office of Emergency Preparedness in the Executive Office of President Nixon. He is co-author of *The Economics of National Security* (1954) and (with Norman Padelford) *The Dynamics of International Politics* (1962).

William Y. Smith (1925–   ) is an Air Force colonel who holds a doctorate in political science from Harvard University and has served on the faculty at West Point; with the staff of the Department of the Air Force; in the Office of the Chairman, Joint Chiefs of Staff; and among the advisers to the National Security Council. He is now Military Assistant to the Secretary of the Air Force.

Jay B. Durst (1928–   ), a colonel in the United States Army, received an M.P.A. from Harvard in 1955 and has taught political science at the Military Academy during two tours of duty there. He has also served with the Special Forces in Vietnam and on the Joint Staff at the Pentagon. His present assignment is with the Office of the Chief of Staff of the Army.

The magnitude of the World War II achievement soon dwarfed the accomplishments of World War I. In that war, 2 million men crossed the Atlantic, half of them transported in British bottoms, to fight their campaigns with French and British equipment. In World War II, we sent more than three times this number to every corner of the world, supplied and equipped them, and in addition provided large quantities of supplies and equipment to Allied personnel. Just a year after Pearl Harbor, we were producing more war material than all our enemies combined. This was a war of mass, of machines, and of attrition, to be won or lost by the record of achievement in timely and massive mobilization and production. The Germans and the Japanese won the initial campaigns. But they failed to achieve victory before America's total mobilization came to ensure their defeat.

True, massive manpower still counted. But

it was even more a war of machine against machine and of opposing technologies. Rommel, one of Germany's greatest field generals, summarized: ". . . the bravest men can do nothing without guns, the guns nothing without plenty of ammunition . . . the battle is fought and decided by the quartermasters before the shooting begins." As a corollary, this was the first war in modern history in which science and technology brought material changes in weapons and techniques during the war itself, changes dependent on production schedules to give them timely effectiveness in the battle zones. Skill in estimating supply requirements far in advance and allocating scarce supplies to the places of decision had become an important part of the art of generalship.

The World War II effort began from an economic base of underemployment. Time was available to consider foreign experience and to devise a control and management system before shortages required major allocation of materials and controls to limit inflation. There were over 8 million (17 per cent of the labor force) unemployed in 1939, and it was well into 1942 before unemployment fell to a level requiring the use of a significant number of submarginal workers.

In the initial instance then, and for much of the war, the task of managing the mobilization was a task of bringing the prodigious but unmarshaled industrial power of the United States to bear on the war effort. There were two broad categories of requirements: the military program and the civilian economy. The program in support of the war effort had three major components: (1) lend lease, (2) support of our own military forces, and (3) shipping which was a requirement derived from the requirements to move military resources and lend lease. Lend lease was monitored by an agency in the executive offices of the President, but the task of procuring for the program from private industry and government plants was undertaken primarily by the military departments and by the Maritime Commission which built the ships. Nearly $50 billion worth of lend lease was provided, approximately three-fifths going to the British Commonwealth, one-fifth to the Soviet Union, and the remainder to other Allies. About $9 billion worth of reverse lend lease was received from Allies. Shipping, more than combat units or any other military resource, was generally the bottleneck and principal determinant of strategy.

A large number of temporary war emergency agencies were created. Many of them were overlapping, and there was a confusing progression of combinations, divisions, and births of new agencies as the war went forward.

The claims and counterclaims upon resources were monitored by the War Production Board, which replaced the earlier established Office of Production Management. In addition to monitoring the basic division between civilian and military production and programming production, it established priorities and allocations for scarce materials. Its actions often caused friction with military agencies whose demands, estimated on the side of over-insurance, exceeded WPB's conservative estimates of the capabilities of the expanding United States economy. Another important category of boards with United States-United Kingdom or United States-United Kingdom-Canadian membership coordinated Allied supply matters. The Munitions Assignment Board, for instance, allocated our munitions production between our own forces and lend lease in accordance with strategic priorities set by the United States-United Kingdom combined Chiefs of Staff. As the war progressed and the problems of its prosecution became more complex, the President could not alone coordinate all the agencies managing mobilization. Hence in May, 1943, he created the Office of War Mobilization charged with central leadership of the mobilization. James F. Byrnes, its director, was often referred to as the "assistant President."

Having considered the management of mobilization, this discussion now turns to a summary consideration of the factors managed— men, money, materials, munitions, and morale. The last, pertaining as it does to human beings, is a function of management of all other mobilization components.

The Armed Forces mobilized approximately 14 million men and women during World War II with a peak strength of approximately 12 million. The occupational deferments from the Selective Service System of conscription contributed, particularly in agriculture, to maintaining a military-civilian balance in manpower skills. There was no shortage of manpower. The United States had, in 1941, over 6 million unemployed. Six million additional workers joined the labor force, from the young, the normally retired, and others not normally employed. Although an Executive order of February, 1943, extended the work week from 40 to 48 hours, the average work week in 1944 in manufacturing was only 45.2 hours. Female employment increased until fully one-third of the wartime civilian labor force was composed of women.

The major manpower problems were those of training, geographic relocation, job transfer, and the very high labor turnover. In 1944, labor turnover in manufacturing industries totaled 82 per cent, of which 61 per cent was voluntary and traceable to transportation problems, lack of housing, inability of inexperienced workers to sustain the requirements of the job, and search for higher wages.

What happened to productivity and to wages? These are items concerning which any conclusions need to be very qualified to avoid serious controversy. As to the farm industry,

the Department of Agriculture estimates that the use of machinery on farms increased materially during the war. Output per man-hour increased by 25 per cent in the period 1939–1945. Man-hours worked on the farms were lower than in World War I, but total output was 50 per cent greater. Worker productivity in the manufacturing and service industries is harder to judge. Any appraisal must recognize the large group of untrained workers motivated primarily by patriotism rather than by experience and competence. Notwithstanding, the Council of Economic Advisors estimated that a considerable increase in output per man-hour occurred between 1939 and 1944. Weekly earnings increased approximately 50 per cent during the war whereas the general price level increased only about 30 per cent. Much of this gain in earnings was due to the longer work week, but the precedent of higher earnings contributed materially to the powerful postwar pressures for further rounds of wage increases.

The program of price control and rationing of civilian items under the Office of Price Administration was inseparable from the problems of wages and wage control. Wage controls and price controls lacked strong enforcement powers and, like rationing, leaned heavily on the willingness of individuals and groups to exercise voluntary restraint.

The price rise of 30 per cent from 1938 to 1945 compares favorably with the 60 per cent rise from 1914 to 1919. But an equivalent inflationary surge came in the immediate postwar period, perhaps due in part to the overly precipitate relaxation of controls, particularly price controls. The large wartime savings and the postwar expansion of private industry provided a demand pull resulting in a rise from 130 to 170 in the Consumer Price Index in the 2½ years after June 30, 1946, when price control ended. (All indices for this subsection are on the base period 1935–1939 = 100.)

World War II was financed by taxation and by a program of borrowing which included major efforts to suck off purchasing power, thereby dampening the inflationary push. About 44 per cent of Federal income came from taxes. Of the remainder, about two-fifths was loaned by banks and the remainder by nonbank investors. Expenditures for the war effort were approximately $315 billion, and the public debt climbed from less than $50 billion to approximately $260 billion. Except for the scarce irreplaceable resources consumed, these were, of course, real economic costs to the United States only to the extent that the productive resources would have been used for increasing the national wealth and personal consumption of the United States had there been no war. Further, it must be recognized that a considerable component of the expenditure provided facilities and other productive capabilities of continuing economic use after the close of the war.

While total Federal taxes of all types did not rise above 25 per cent of national income, Federal expenditures exceeded 50 per cent of national income in 1943 and 1944 and exceeded 40 per cent in 1942 and 1945. Considering the high wages, high profits, and the constant or rising standard of living, there is a question as to whether taxes were high enough. It is significant that the wartime structure of income, corporation and other Federal taxes set tax precedents which continued indefinitely into the postwar period.

Returning briefly to the item of war cost, it might be added that certain indirect results of this war will persist for another century. If the Civil War is a valid example, the expenditures for debt interest and veterans' payments will be more than three times as great as the direct expenditures of the war itself. In such case, the ultimate money expenditures incident to World War II will exceed a trillion dollars.

Evidence after eleven years indicated that perhaps this translation of Civil War experience is valid. By 1956 the total expenditures for veterans' benefits and debt interest were $110 billion, or 35 per cent of the net war expenditures for the years 1941 to 1945.

Men and money are essentials. But there must also be a marshaling of facilities, machines, and materials in order that a mobilization may progress. The United States was devoting only 11 per cent of its national produce to war expenditures as late as 1941. Happily, by that date, conversions and expansions were well under way for the much greater effort of a total mobilization. Military appropriations of 1940 and 1941 totaled nearly $70 billion although expenditures were only $16 billion. Two years passed before the economy reached a plateau of maximum effort of approximately 42 per cent of the national product devoted to war. This was a national product expanding rapidly from an index of 100 in 1939 to 126 in 1941 and 172 in 1944.

Over $60 billion was spent for construction. Of this, some $10 billion was for military camps and airfields, and the remainder for government productive facilities. Under this program the prewar estimated value of the nation's manufacturing facilities was expanded by more than half, while all nonwar supporting construction was severely restricted.

With production expanding rapidly, the initial system of priorities for materials ceased to be effective. When there is an absolute scarcity, government priority is merely a hunting license to a harassed producer who instead needs an assured supply. Control was finally successfully effected by the ingenious Controlled Materials Plan under which three materials only—steel, copper, and aluminum—were allocated to producers through the government agencies guiding the war effort.

To alleviate our great dependence upon foreign resources for critical raw materials we implemented a massive program for stockpiling. After the war, this stockpile was continued and added to, particularly during the Korean conflict, and its planned value approached $10 billion in the late fifties. By that time there was some question as to its strategic justification. . . . The construction of 8 million dead weight tons of merchant shipping in 1942 and 19 million tons in 1943, together with success in the battle against submarines, made possible the timely deployment of war material to the battle zones. Railroad transportation, which had faltered badly during World War I, profited from its two decades of mobilization preparation. Under the general guidance of the Office of Defense Transportation, the railroads, in 1943, moved 2½ times the freight and 4½ times the passenger traffic of 1939. Even raw-material extractive industries, basically inelastic in supply, expanded production by approximately one-half.

A brief quantitative summary of the explosion of wartime production, its magnitude and effectiveness, is revealed by the Index of Industrial Production (1935–1939 = 100) which rose to 239 and, in durable manufactured goods which are the sinews of modern war, to 360. Hindenberg's statement after World War I, that "America's brilliant but pitiless industry had entered the service of patriotism and had not failed it," was an exaggeration of the impact of our seventeen-months' World War I effort. The statement, if applied to World War II, however, is a sound summary of the strategy for that victory.

Could more have been done if necessary? Some economists agree that an industrialized country can, if it so wills, devote over 50 per cent of its product to a survival effort. Britain devoted between 50 and 55 per cent from 1941 to V-E Day, and Germany devoted as much as 50 per cent in the latter part of World War II.

The United States devoted no more than 42 per cent of its product to the war. Nevertheless, given the mushrooming capabilities of United States industry, it was enough to ensure victory.

The structure of government controls faded rapidly away after victory. Inflation, rather than the postwar depression so gloomily forecast by some economists, followed. Undoubtedly, elimination of price controls in mid-1946 contributed to rising prices. Further, the civilian economy, spurred by savings, by the pent-up demand of years of depression and war, by the expended inventory of plant and machine tools, gave consumers renewed confidence. Impressed by the successes of wartime production, they quickly forgot the Depression of the thirties and adjusted to a peacetime prosperity. The total manufacturing index in 1948 was 198 (1935–1939 = 100). The labor force gained in skills from the wartime experience and gained further from the program of the GI Bill of Rights, which provided billions to give millions of veterans further education. College attendance boomed.

Our World War II mobilization organization was successful if success is measured by production and by military accomplishments. The organization and its programs of operation had important postwar effects. Means and methods for managing a free competitive enterprise system in time of crisis while still retaining that system had been demonstrated. No revolutionary social and economic changes came from the mobilization. Rather, the war experience cemented in place the changes of the thirties. As Walter Millis remarks, "Both liberals and conservatives alike were to be disappointed." The service of businessmen in the governmental agencies and the great response of industry to war needs revived the reputation of business and of businessmen, badly deflated during the Depression. The teamwork between government and industry bridged the fissure that had developed during the New Deal. But, venturing a summary judgment, whereas the mobilization could have shifted the control of the reins of economic power predominantly to management, or even more likely to labor, neither shift occurred. Elected and appointed officials of our government dominated the mobilization which set patterns for continued governmental guidance of the economy. If any group gained, it was neither Big Capital nor Big Labor, but Big Government.

25

A. D. H. Kaplan
INCREASING CONCENTRATION OF BUSINESS

A. D. H. Kaplan, Big Enterprise in a Competitive System, *revised edition, pp. 32–35, © by The Brookings Institution, published November 1964.*

A. D. H. Kaplan (1893–   ) is an economist who since 1945 has been a senior staff member of The Brookings Institution. During World War II he served on the Committee of Economic Development in the Office of Price Administration and on the special committee for postwar economic policy and planning of the House of Representatives. He is the author of *The Liquidation of War Production* (1944), *Small Business, Its Place and Problems* (1948), and *Big Enterprise in a Competitive System* (1954).

Although World War I had set a precedent in mobilizing big business support for the military, this was hardly comparable to the use made of big business in World War II. The major contribution of big business to national security was undisputed. But wartime requirements also contributed to a marked increase in the scale of big business. Of the $18 billion

of war plants constructed between 1940 and the end of 1943, nearly three-fourths were in units exceeding $10 million, and nearly one-third in units above $50 million. In addition, some $15 billion of war plants had been built and operated for the government by large private companies. Approximately $7.5 billion of government plant contracts were placed with thirty-one corporations, averaging over $200 million per corporation. The great bulk of prime contracts went to the larger companies. The Federal Trade Commission reported that, during the period 1940–46, the process of war mobilization and demobilization saw the merging of not less than 1,658 companies: nearly one-third of these were absorbed by corporations having assets of $50 million or more. These developments in turn implied that the disparity between big business and the rest of the economic structure had been accentuated by the wartime experience. With the end of the war, containment of the economic power vested in the large corporations was again given a place of major importance in public policy.

In his State of the Union message of January 1947, President Truman emphasized the impact of the war on the concentration of industrial power:

In 1941 the Temporary National Economic Committee completed a comprehensive investigation into the workings of the national economy. The committee's study showed that, despite half a century of antitrust law enforcement, one of the gravest threats to our welfare lay in the increasing concentration of power in the hands of a small number of giant organizations.

During the war, this long-standing tendency toward economic concentration was accelerated. As a consequence, we now find that to a greater extent than ever before, whole industries are dominated by one or a few large organizations which can restrict production in the interests of higher profits and thus reduce employment and purchasing power.

The new postwar problem of business concentration thus visualized, the government proceeded to attack it on two fronts. Under the Surplus Property Act of 1944, Congress hoped to redistribute competitive strength by the sale of wartime plants to newer or smaller companies, rather than to firms already dominant in their respective industries. Simultaneously, the Federal Trade Commission and the Department of Justice moved to enlist the aid of the courts in reducing the market power of industrial giants.

An effort to broaden the area of competition under the Surplus Property Act was made in several important industries. The aluminum plants built for the government by the Aluminum Company of America were leased or sold to two other companies, Kaiser and Reynolds, on terms designed to promote their development as substantial competitors. The huge Willow Run plant constructed by the Ford Company for airplane manufacture was leased to Kaiser-Fraser for manufacture of automobiles. The Geneva steel mill in Utah built by U.S. Steel was acquired by that company only when other practicable bids for the $200 million plant failed to materialize.

Overall, however, the nature of disposable facilities was frequently such that they were most salable to those firms which had operated them during the war, and only in a few instances was industrial structure materially affected by the disposal program.

In the postwar period, the courts continued to be faced with the necessity of defining the limits of legitimate corporate growth. Initially, the period was one of tighter judicial interpretation of antitrust. More recent decisions appear to have eased the rigidity of the early postwar years. In general, the period has been one of increased maturity and sophistication in the application of antitrust. . . .

26

Frederick Lewis Allen
THE DIVISION OF PROSPERITY

From pp. 167–170 in The Big Change *by Frederick Lewis Allen. Copyright 1952 by Frederick Lewis Allen. Reprinted by permission of Harper and Row, Publishers.*

Frederick Lewis Allen (1890–1954) established a considerable reputation before and after the Second World War as a journalist and a chonicler. A member of the staff of *Harper's Magazine* for many years, he served as editor of that journal from 1943 to 1953. During the last months of his life he became a vice-president of Harper and Brothers, Publishers, and director of the Ford Foundation. His works include *Only Yesterday* (1931), *The Lords of Creation* (1935), *Since Yesterday* (1940), and *The Big Change* (1952).

What happened to the national standard of living when the federal government poured into the national economy war orders by the billions, and then by the tens of billions, and then by the scores of billions? Roaring prosperity. During the nineteen-thirties the New Dealers had been conscientiously trying to "prime the pump" by government expenditures of a few billions a year; what they had done with a teaspoon was now being done with a ladle.

By 1943 the last appreciable unemployment —except of people transferring from job to job,

or waiting for a promised opening to materialize
—had been soaked up. By 1944 the signs of
prosperity were everywhere. It was hard to get
a hotel room in any city. Restaurants in which
it had always been easy to find a table for lunch
were now crammed by a few minutes after
twelve. Sales of fur coats and jewelry—many of
them for cash across the counter—were jump-
ing. Luxury goods for which there had been a
dwindling market were suddenly in demand:
the proprietor of a music store reported that
he was selling every grand piano, new or reno-
vated, that he could lay his hands on. And
visitors to New England mill towns which had
been depression-ridden since long before the
nineteen-thirties were noting newly painted
houses, fences in fresh repair.

This gush of prosperity was a strange phenomenon to witness in a nation supposedly
stripped down for the supreme effort of war—
a nation in which airplane spotters sat under
the stars of a cold winter's night to listen for
an improbable enemy; in which air-raid wardens
put on their armbands for practice blackouts,
and waited endlessly for the dreadful moment
when the word would go out, "Signal 50 received, post your wardens"; in which first-aiders
took lessons in triangular bandages and talked
sagely about pressure points; in which women
went stockingless because they were running
out of nylons, and cigarettes, butter, sugar, and
coffee were in short supply, and beefsteak became the rarest of treats, and draft boards
puzzled over the latest changes in the regulations from Washington, and the ubiquity of
soldiers and sailors in uniform was a constant
reminder of everybody's obligation to make
sacrifices for the common safety. The government was doing what it could to reduce spending and thus slow down inflation—through price
ceilings, rationing of scarce and essential goods,
wage freezing, excess-profits taxes, and record-

high personal income taxes—and with some
success. Yet the prosperity was there, paradoxically overflowing. And after the long drought
of the nineteen-thirties there was something
undeniably welcome about it.

Who was getting the money?
Generally speaking, the stockholders of the
biggest corporations were not getting very
much of it. These corporations were in many
cases getting huge war orders, and thus consolidating their important positions in the national economy; but excess-profits taxes, along
with managerial caution over the uncertainties
of the future, and with the recollection of the
embarrassing scandals of 1918 war profits, combined to keep their dividend payments at
modest rates. The stock market languished.
Big capital, as such, was having no heyday.

Some smaller companies which had barely
been able to keep alive during the Depression
and now were receiving big war orders were
making extraordinary money—subject both to
taxes and to renegotiation of their contracts.
There were also numerous small concerns, in
the textile business for example, that got no
war orders but profited hugely—again before
taxes. But other businesses were in definite
trouble. Tourist camps and roadside taverns
and automobile dealers, for example, suffered
because of gas rationing, and there were many
manufacturers and dealers who were hard hit
by shortages of materials, could not shift into
war production, and went deep into the red.
But what was more interesting than the sort of
concerns which were getting the money was the
sort of individual people who were getting it.

The rich were getting some of it, but those
of them who were honest were keeping very
little because of high income taxes. Most of
the extravagant spending which was manifest
in so many places was the result either of tax

dodging or of the lavish use of company expense accounts. "It's all on the government" was the theme song of many a sumptuous party. Although the war was making a few legitimate millionaires—mainly among oil men who by reason of "depletion allowances" did not feel the full weight of federal taxes—in general the rich *and* honest did not gain much.

People outside the war industries whose salaries or wages were frozen by the War Labor Board were not gaining at all, though some of them were helped by "reclassification of jobs" or by "merit increases," with or without quotation marks. People who were dependent on dividends and interest likewise were seldom among the gainers; indeed in many cases inflation brought a real deterioration in their circumstances.

The principal beneficiaries, generally speaking, were farmers; engineers, technicians, and specialists of various sorts whose knowledge and ability were especially valuable to the war effort in one way or another; and skilled workers in war industries—or unskilled workers capable of learning a skilled trade and stepping into the skilled group.

The farmers were in clover; and it was about time. For they had long been faced with adversity after adversity. During the nineteen-twenties few of them had had seats on the prosperity band wagon; a boom in the price of farm land after World War I had overextended many of them, the failure of numerous rural banks had been disastrous to these and to others, and the prices they had got had seemed perpetually inadequate. During the Depression these prices had dropped to ruinous depths; and just as recovery was setting in, a series of droughts and dust storms had desolated whole areas of the Great Plains, sending miserable "Okies" on the desperate trek to California, where at least there was a faint hope of some-

thing better. But now prices were good, the demand for farm products was overwhelming, the weather was favorable, their methods were vastly improved, and by 1943 their total purchasing power was almost double what it had been at the end of the nineteen-thirties.

The engineers, technicians, and workers in the war plants benefited by an interesting circumstance. Since at the beginning of the war emergency there had still been millions of unemployed men and women, there had been no need for an official allocation of manpower; the war industries could absorb large numbers of workers from other occupations without crippling the economy. And they lured them largely by offering high pay. A young chemist would find himself sought out by a chemical concern at a salary he hadn't expected to earn for many a year. Mrs. Smith's waitress would leave for a job in an electrical plant that would bring her $50 a week with evenings free. A soda jerker would double his income by walking down the street to the factory that was going to make parts for tanks. And a salesgirl at a department-store stocking counter would fetch up in an airplane plant at two or three times her store pay.

Later, it is true, workers in essential industries were "frozen" in their jobs and the rulings of the War Labor Board tended to keep their pay within bounds; but the essential fact remained that these war workers became, as a group, the chief beneficiaries of the new prosperity. Look at the figures for workers in manufacturing industries. Between 1939 and 1945 their average weekly earnings went up by 86 per cent. Meanwhile their cost of living went up by an estimated 29 per cent—but even so they were far better off than in 1939. They had experienced a sharp and welcome gain in "real wages."

By and large, what the war boom did, then

—with numerous exceptions—was to give a lift to people with low incomes.

27

Thomas R. Brooks
THE WORKER IN THE WAR AND AFTER

Reprinted from Toil and Trouble by Thomas R. Brooks, pp. 207–211, 223–224. Copyright © 1964 by Thomas R. Brooks and used by permission of the publisher, Delacorte Press.

Thomas R. Brooks (1925–   ), a free-lance writer who devotes most of his attention to labor, the schools, and the police, was formerly assistant editor of the Transport Workers Union *Express* (1953–56) and assistant labor editor of *Business Week* (1957–60). During the last decade he has contributed frequently to such journals as *Commonweal*, *Commentary*, the *Reporter*, and the *New York Times Magazine*. *Toil and Trouble*, from which this selection is taken, is his first book.

The trade unions came out of the war greatly strengthened. Union membership swelled from about 10.5 million when the Japanese bombed Pearl Harbor to about 14.75 million when the war ended in August, 1945. The new industrial unions of the CIO were firmly established in auto, rubber, steel, and other mass-production industries. The craft unions of the AFL were even more firmly entrenched and were organizing on an industrial basis as well. Union officials, as members of wartime advisory boards, gained a prestige they had not had before the war.

This strength was also reflected in the gains secured, as the unions vigorously prosecuted their cases for wage gains before the War Labor Board. The Board in many cases corrected wage inequities, set equal pay for equal work for women workers, allowed a pattern of fringe benefits to emerge, and made increases to prevent substandard living. These gains are reflected in the increase of real earnings. Average real weekly earnings in manufacturing, $24 in terms of the 1935–39 price levels in 1939, rose to $28.12 in 1941 and reached a wartime peak of $36.72 in 1944. Real hourly earnings rose from 64 cents in 1939 to 69 cents in 1941 and reached a wartime peak of 81 cents in 1944. The Wage and Hour Administrator reported in 1942 that 7.5 million workers received 40 cents an hour or less. The WLB automatically approved increases, first up to 40 cents and later to 50 cents an hour, so by the end of the war no workers got less than 50 cents an hour. These gains should be set against rises in corporate profit after taxes, from $6.4 billion in 1940 to $10.8 billion four years later.

The war also brought about a change in the pattern of Negro employment. When war broke out, Negroes were largely employed in agricultural, unskilled, or service jobs. A large proportion was unemployed. Although a shortage of workers soon developed, Negroes were frequently excluded from new job opportunities in the expanding war industries. Craft unions that controlled job opportunities also discriminated against Negro craftsmen. A. Philip Randolph, the venerated leader of the Brotherhood of [Sleeping] Car Porters, organized his March on Washington movement as a protest against the exclusion of Negro workers from defense industries. The threatened march brought a quick response from Washington. On June 25, 1941, President Roosevelt issued an executive order establishing a Committee on Fair Employment Practices to investigate complaints of discrimination. This also ordered that all training programs for defense production be administered without discrimination and that all defense contracts require a no-discrimination clause. In May, 1943, the FEPC was given increased authority and a greater budget. However, it never possessed the power needed to give full justice to the Negro worker.

In three years, the FEPC handled 8,000 complaints of discrimination in war industry and government employment and held 30 public hearings. Unfortunately, federal FEPC ended with the war. However, its wartime successes sparked a few states to do likewise, and in 1945 New York, New Jersey, and Indiana adopted state FEPC legislation. Some permanent progress had been scored but not enough.

World War II ended, for many, on an uncertain note. Beneath the surface cordialities of the Yalta and Potsdam conferences lurked the icy realities of an approaching Cold War. Over Hiroshima and Nagasaki mushroomed a new fear to cloud men's minds. Closer to home, fear of unemployment and reduced earnings troubled American workers as they welcomed the dawn of peace.

Even before the war had ended, cutbacks in war production resulted in joblessness for some workers and in increasing apprehension among others. "They've closed up Willow Run," declared the CIO *Economic Outlook* in the spring of 1945. "They gave the workers Army-Navy E's and told them to go home because the Government and Mr. Ford didn't want the plant anymore. Nobody wants Willow Run, the $95-million factory that produced almost 9,000 Liberator bombers. Nobody wants the 51,950 pieces of machinery. . . . And nobody wants the more than 20,000 human beings who go with the plant." The worried auto worker unionists were not the only ones concerned over the problems of reconversion. John W. Snyder, director of the Office of War Mobilization and Reconversion, predicted in August, 1945, that there would be five million

unemployed within three months and eight million by the following spring. Others put the figure even higher.

To such dour prospects were added labor's fears of an anti-union drive on the pattern of the open-shop drives of the 1920s. A flood of anti-union legislative measures filled Congressional hoppers. None was passed, but similar measures were enacted in a good number of state legislatures, especially in states where industrialization was limited and unionism weak. After the death of Franklin D. Roosevelt, the new President Harry S Truman, pleaded for a continuance of the no-strike pledge, at least until his labor-management conference could fashion machinery for the peaceful transition from the war to the new economy ahead. But the President's hopes for a successful labor-management conference were soon shattered. Labor quickly chucked the no-strike pledge. In the last four and a half months of 1945, mandays lost due to strikes shot up to 28,400,000, more than double the wartime peak of 1943, when the coal strikes wracked the nation. This was but a prelude to the great strike wave of 1946.

That year set the nation on the collective-bargaining road to a new corporate welfarism. Over four and a half million workers marched on the picket lines in 1946, a half million more than the previous peak, in fateful 1919. One hundred and thirteen million man-days of labor were lost, three times as many as in 1945 and the largest in our history. Nationwide strikes halted production in coal, auto, electric, and steel industries; maritime and railroad transportation ground to a halt. Yet, for all the ferment and wrathful exchanges at the collective-bargaining table, strikers on the picket line frequently assumed a holiday air. There was a great letting off of steam. But unlike 1919, there was no stoking of revolutionary fires. *Fortune*, in November, summed the year up: "The strikes and strike threats of 1945–46 generated violent emotions, but it was an impressive fact that for the first time a great wave of strikes stirred up almost no physical violence. The strikers of 1945–46 were not desperate men. On the public platform their leaders sounded off with booming phrases directed at the enemy Capital; but privately they, like the strikers, were calm, cool, even friendly warriors."

The difference in temper between 1919 and 1946 was no less striking than the changes wrought in the economy. The impact of unemployment, which rose over a million in 1945 and jumped to 2.3 million in 1946, was cushioned by unemployment insurance, which had not existed in the post-World War I decade. Ex-GI's were aided by the "52–20 Club," a full year of unemployment insurance at $20 a week. Others went off to college careers financed by the GI Bill instead of entering a weakened labor market. Wartime savings, too, helped to tide over many people. As for the unions, their organizational strength—both in membership and treasury—was far greater than that commanded by the unions after World War I. . . .

Immediately following the end of World War II, drives to organize in the South and among white collar workers by both the AFL and the CIO failed, victims of jurisdictional rivalries between the two federations and among unions. The great dreams of postwar expansion also came to grief because legislative changes in states where unions had little or no strength all but made it impossible to organize the unorganized. External pressures, such as those represented in the passage of the Taft-Hartley Act in 1947 and a host of state so-called right-to-work laws, coalesced with internal pressures, such as the conflicts over communists and corruption as well as inter-union raiding, to inhibit, if not prevent, any urge to expansion on the part of organized labor.

Much of the distaste caused by labor's wartime strikes still lingered when the great strike wave of 1946 rolled across the country. Much was made of this in the press, and considerable steam was generated for "reform" of the labor law. Feeling against unions at times ran so high that President Truman at one point during the 1946 rail strike, after the government had seized the railroads, secured the passage of a bill in Congress to draft labor during an emergency dispute, by a vote of 306 to 13. Fortunately, cooler heads prevailed, and after the immediate emergency had passed—the rail strike settled—the bill was allowed to die quietly. But the episode did illustrate something about the prevailing temper. Both the AFL and the CIO underestimated the widespread public feeling that the Wagner Act, passed in 1937, was not entirely suitable for the postwar era. Undemocratic procedures within unions, racketeering, denial of equal rights to Negroes, and other abuses, it seemed to many, cried out for some legislative action. But labor stood pat, opposing any reform of the labor law as pure and simple anti-unionism. By doing so, the unions forfeited the game to the more aggressive champions of "reform," who secured the passage of the Taft-Hartley Law over the veto of President Truman in June, 1947. The new law, perhaps, was more punitive than what the moderate majority would have preferred. At any rate, Senator Robert Taft, Senatorial sponsor of the new law, later became the willing backer of amendments, never adopted, designed to ease the law's impact on legitimate unionization.

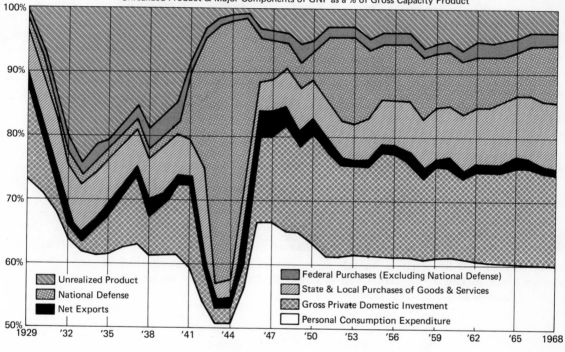

Unrealized Product & Major Components of GNP as a % of Gross Capacity Product

Legend:
- Unrealized Product
- National Defense
- Net Exports
- Federal Purchases (Excluding National Defense)
- State & Local Purchases of Goods & Services
- Gross Private Domestic Investment
- Personal Consumption Expenditure

Axis labels: 100%, 90%, 80%, 70%, 60%, 50%
Years: 1929, '32, '35, '38, '41, '44, '47, '50, '53, '56, '59, '62, '65, 1968

(Copyright © by TRANS-action, Inc., New Brunswick, New Jersey)

President Franklin D. Roosevelt in his role as war leader and commander-in-chief of
the armed forces, making an inspection tour of Camp Shelby, Mississippi in September
1942.   (Franklin D. Roosevelt Library)

Chapter Six

POLITICAL
EFFECTS OF
THE WAR

There is a significant amount of parallelism between the following interpretations and those which dealt with the political impact of the First World War. Once again, Carl B. Swisher describes the rapid concentration of power in the presidency, though this time Congress seems to have resisted the trend somewhat more forcefully and more successfully than it had in 1917–1918. Nevertheless, Thomas L. Stokes contends, like Seward Livermore before him, that war did not end partisan politics within Congress, and argues, in addition, that the conflict aided the conservative resurgence. At the same time, A. Russell Buchanan depicts the wartime "diminution" of the Supreme Court in terms that are strikingly analogous to those used previously regarding the earlier judiciary. Somewhat in contrast to these points of view, Eric Goldman maintains that the ebbing liberal movement lost as much of its strength from President Roosevelt's death as it did from "normal" postwar reaction. However, Arthur Ekirch, in an article which reminds one of those by Richard Hofstadter (World War I, Political) and Randolph Bourne (World War I, Thought and Culture), asserts that the liberals compromised themselves and their movement by their uncritical support of war, and were therefore themselves largely to blame for what befell them.

QUESTIONS:

1. To what extent and in what areas were the increased power and prestige which the presidency achieved during the war carried beyond 1945?
2. Why was there apparently more congressional opposition to the growth of presidential power in World War II than there had been in World War I? What was the net effect of this?
3. Why would you imagine that the reduction of the influence of the Supreme Court might be less marked and less prolonged in the Second World War than it had been in the previous conflict?
4. What could Roosevelt and Truman have done to minimize the conservative reaction both during the war and after?
5. What are the most significant similarities between the impact of World War I and the impact of World War II on the American political process?

28

Carl B. Swisher
ENHANCEMENT OF THE EXECUTIVE

American Constitutional Development, Copyright 1943 by Carl Brent Swisher, pp. 994–1002. Reprinted by permission of the publisher, Houghton Mifflin Company.

Carl B. Swisher (1897–1968) held the Thomas B. Straw Chair in Political Science at The Johns Hopkins University from 1938 until his retirement in 1967. A specialist in the Supreme Court and the Constitution, he was the author of *American Constitutional Development* (1944) and *The Growth of Constitutional Power in the United States* (1946). He also served as special assistant to the Attorney General of the United States from 1935 to 1937.

Although the masses of the people hoped and probably believed that the United States would

never again find it necessary to participate in a major war, the War Department and the military leaders of the country had no such illusions. Remembering the chaos of preparation for the equipment of an army after the declaration of war in 1917, and sensing that even to a greater degree the wars of the future would be wars of machines and of whole peoples rather than merely of trained army personnel, they began immediately to plan for rapid mobilization whenever the occasion required. They worked out plans for the conversion of peacetime industrial production to the production of war materials, and arranged for the allotment of so-called "educational orders" for war materials to enable plants to develop valuable preliminary experience. Evidently with the operation of the War Industries Board of the first World War in mind, they worked out plans for emergency governmental machinery to be co-ordinated under centralized leadership. They planned conscription of manpower for military service and effective control of labor in essential industries. Maximum wages were to be fixed and maximum prices were to be regulated, although without fundamental interference with the operation of the profit system. Through power to establish priorities and to commandeer equipment wherever necessary, the government was to maintain effective control over industry. Bills were drafted to be presented to Congress for speedy enactment if an emergency developed. The plan was subjected to much unfavorable publicity during the middle nineteen-thirties when it was sharply criticized by the Senate committee investigating the munitions industry. The sentiment of the committee and, evidently, of most of the American people was that the energies of the nation ought to be utilized in solving the problems of peace rather than in preparing for improbable war.

By the summer of 1939, although public sentiment was still divided, war clouds loomed so darkly that, in August of that year, President Roosevelt appointed a War Resources Board with a membership predominantly from eastern industrial and banking circles to act as a civilian advisory committee to the Army and Navy Munitions Board in developing industrial mobilization plans. The board worked behind closed doors for a period of months, during which war broke out in Europe, submitted a confidential report, and then disbanded. For reasons never publicly announced, the President made no further use of that board, but instead, on May 26, 1940, he returned to the device utilized at the beginning of the first World War, and, acting under the National Defense Act of 1916, he created a new advisory commission to the Council of National Defense. The Council of National Defense, consisting of six members of the cabinet, did not again become active as a separate organization, but the Advisory Commission, consisting of seven persons representative of various fields of activity, played an important part in the initial co-ordination of the resources of the country for national defense.

Because the commission was advisory only and possessed little or no authority in its own right, the opposition party in the presidential campaign of 1940 denounced the President's failure to establish machinery such as a War Industries Board or a Munitions Administration in which the administration of the rearmament program would be lodged. The President resisted such demands, however, until the allotment of power for administration could be segregated in a considerable degree from the power to make policy. Gradually, as lines of policy were clearly established, he strengthened the hands of his administrative agents. He co-ordinated newly established agencies for national defense with the program of reorganization carried out under the Reorganization Act of 1939. Pursuant to that act he brought together in what was called the

Executive Office of the President a number of agencies including the Bureau of the Budget, the Division of Statistical Standards, the Office of Government Reports, and the National Resources Planning Board. Along with these agencies he made provision for an Office for Emergency Management. The title was unique among permanent government agencies, but its use was understandable in view of the extent to which contemporary government had been government in terms of emergencies and was likely to continue so. Within the Office for Emergency Management, the President created a long line of new agencies for the performance of functions connected with national defense and war, including functions that were new and older ones that had previously been exercised by the Advisory Commission.

In the meantime, although the United States was not yet a formal belligerent, Congress began the enactment of measures reminiscent of or going beyond those of the period of the first World War. It authorized the expenditure of billions of dollars directly for the army and navy, for the equipment of plants for production of war materials, and for aid to nations which later became the allies of the United States. In line with slowly changing public sentiment, it eliminated neutrality legislation forbidding extension of credit to belligerents and other legislation prohibiting loans to nations which had defaulted on their obligation to us. It enacted a so-called Lend-Lease Act whereby the President was given almost unlimited power to transfer to Great Britain and other countries whose defense he considered essential to the United States almost any kind of equipment needed for conduct of the war, on a leasing basis or for any compensation the President might see fit to accept. Congress also enacted the first peacetime conscription act in the history of the United States. It provided for registration of all aliens in the country and strengthened legislation dealing with sedition and espionage. It required registration of propagandists of foreign governments, and enacted other measures for the mobilization of man-power and resources for national defense.

Although both the legislative and executive branches undertook sweeping measures for national defense, operations moved sluggishly until after the disastrous experience at Pearl Harbor on December 7, 1941. That attack brought the speedy enactment of a declaration of war against Japan which was followed by other declarations of war against the other Axis Powers. With a minimum of delay, Congress thereafter enacted a host of measures desired by the President. The flow of appropriations for war purposes developed into a torrent. "If appropriations could win this war," declared Senator [Arthur] Vandenberg, "victory is 'in the bag.'" Congress reinstated the provisions of the Overman Act of the first World War period, which authorized the President to reorganize the federal government virtually as he saw fit, and of the Trading-with-the-Enemy Act, which gave sweeping control over foreign trade and communications. Other measures strengthened the hand of the government in its control over raw materials, finished goods, transportation, communications, prices, wages, and so on.

In the executive branch of the government, the reorganization of agencies and their interrelationships continued at a rapid rate. Within the Office for Emergency Management an Office for Production Management, headed by two men, had been given authority to supervise the flow of materials which had been allotted to the several fields of military and civilian consumption. Because of need for greater speed and more freedom of action in that agency, the OPM was reorganized under one man as the War Production Board. Its position was

similar to that of the War Industries Board of the first World War, but the pressure on it from competing agencies was greater, its powers were greater, and it exercised them on a grander scale. An Office of Price Administration, which was closely co-ordinated with the War Production Board, developed great power over the distribution and the prices of civilian supplies. A director of economic stabilization was given authority in areas of conflict over governmentally controlled prices and priorities. A Lend-Lease Administration sent munitions, food, and other materials to our allies and to countries whose defense the President deemed essential to the defense of our own country, at the rate of some ten billion dollars a year.

The over-all purpose was to speed production and delivery of war materials, secure the proper allotment of raw materials for war and other purposes, and provide for uniform distribution of the limited stock of supplies for civilians. The government had to function under tremendous pressure from the several services for the immediate production and delivery of supplies, while providing for at least a minimum of civilian needs and making replacements in the machinery of production and transportation. It had to deal also with the competitive claims of Great Britain, Russia, China, and other allies, whose survival might depend upon a speedy delivery to them of supplies which were sought also by our own military and naval forces. It had to struggle with the seemingly insoluble problems of the proper allotment of man-power between the military and naval forces and the fields of industrial and agricultural production.

Management of the war effort called for a greater degree of executive rule-making and executive supervision of the life of the country than ever before. During 1942 the *Federal Register*, the official journal for publishing proclamations, orders, rules, and instructions of various kinds which have effect beyond the range of the issuing agency, turned out more than eleven thousand pages of what might be called law. The bulk was out of all comparison with that of the legislative output of Congress during the same period. The rulings issued by the Office of Price Administration alone made up a huge code of law, a code of which the contents were in such rapid transition as to require constant attention on the part of landlords, tenants, wholesalers, retailers, and consumers. Most rulings had, or were said to have, an ultimate basis in general statutes. Yet their specific provisions and the operations of the administrative machine were determined so completely by agencies in the executive branch of the government that members of Congress were hardly better informed about them than was the general public.

The continued concentration of power in the executive branch of the government is important not merely for the war crisis. It brings quasi-permanent entrenchment of administrative machinery and it grooves more deeply the already speedily developing trend in terms of which an administrative machine determines the nature of governmental operations and molds the life of the country. Furthermore, the decisions made within the administrative bureaucracy for the direction of the war effort will have tremendous influence on the post-war period. There is no possibility that a treaty of peace or federal statutes subsequently enacted can eliminate the post-war influence of such administrative decisions as the following: that war plants would be constructed in certain areas and not in others; that certain firms would receive huge war contracts of certain kinds, while other firms would receive contracts of other kinds, or none at all; and that housing adjustments would be made through the construction of new projects of chosen design, or through the improvement of transportation, or

by other means. Whether the work is done well or poorly, what may possibly seem like economic havoc in the post-war period will be the product of administrative decisions during the war period which will have been made under the strain of the crisis, without reference to nationally planned public policy.

The enhancement of executive power is not limited to the home field. As commander in chief of the army and navy in a total war, the President found it not merely possible but necessary to exercise far-reaching powers over foreign affairs. Commitments in plans worked out with our allies for the conduct of the war involved agreements on many matters not strictly military. Executive agreements, made often without publicity and even without the knowledge of Congress, governed matters which under other circumstances might preferably have been taken care of by treaty, in which event the concurrence of the Senate would have been necessary. As was indicated in the hearings and debates early in 1943 on extension of the Lend-Lease Act, the great popularity of that measure was qualified by suspicion that the almost unlimited power to aid allies and friends by distributing to them the resources of the United States was being or might be used to mold international policies which ought to be subject to legislative check. At hearings on the bill, an assistant Secretary of State remarked, "Many aspects of the arrangements made for mutual aid, through lend-lease and lend-lease in reverse, call for extended negotiations with foreign governments vitally affecting our political and economic relations with them." The lend-lease administrator said that "the State Department at the present time is in the process of negotiation with foreign governments on that whole question of the use of air fields after the war." From many other sources comes evidence of the extension of executive agreements as devices for the control of important aspects of American foreign relations. The trend of events may lead ultimately to a mode of procedure whereby most of the details of international arrangements will be determined by executive agreement, leaving the treaty-making power for exercise only in connection with major international compacts.

In his relations with Congress, the President maintained a position of clear dominance throughout the first year of our formal participation in the war. Few legislators voiced the belief, which had been held by some of their predecessors in the Civil-War period, that Congress should control policy and oversee administration of the war. The experience of enacting the President's "must" legislation in the New-Deal period had paved the way for general acceptance of presidential leadership in the war crisis. When, in the autumn of 1942, Congress, under leadership of the farm bloc, showed hostility to enactment of legislation to fix maximum prices of farm products at the parity level, the President declared sternly that, if Congress failed to enact the desired legislation within a specified time, he would take action without the support of new legislation:

> In the event that the Congress should fail to act, and act adequately, I shall accept the responsibility, and I will act. . . . The President has the powers, under the Constitution and under congressional acts, to take measures necessary to avert a disaster which would interfere with the winning of the war.

He explained his position by saying that the responsibilities of the President in wartime to protect the nation were very grave. The use of executive power was far more essential in this war than in any previous war. He could not tell what powers might have to be exercised in order to win. The American people could be sure, he said, that he would use his powers with

a full sense of his responsibility to the Constitution and to his country. When the war was won, the powers under which he acted automatically reverted to the people to whom they belonged. Congress enacted the desired legislation in spite of charges of presidential dictatorship.

The Democratic loss of a number of seats in both houses of Congress in the election of November, 1942, although resulting from many causes, marked the beginning of increased congressional resistance to presidential domination. Congress scolded the President for seeking broad grants of power for specified purposes and using the powers thereafter for purposes of which no hint had been given when the legislation was requested. As its term expired, the Seventy-Seventh Congress refused to enact a requested measure authorizing the President to do away with tariff barriers wherever he might deem such action desirable in promoting the conduct of the war. It was apparent that Congress would not refuse to give specific powers that were clearly needed; but its attitude was that the need must be shown and the grant must be specific rather than general.

In December, 1942, the same Congress forced a change in the leadership of the Office of Price Administration by the simple device of withholding appropriations. Early in 1943, using the suspicion of personal and political misconduct as an excuse, the Senate indirectly forced the withdrawal of the name of the President's nominee as minister to Australia. Congress cut off appropriations for the President's official national planning agency and a number of officials in high positions were threatened with similar treatment. Congress brought forward for serious consideration bills in many fields in spite of the fact that the President was known to be opposed to them. None of the proposed measures threatened basic interference with the management of the war, and no substantial group in Congress sought to take the basic control of the war out of the hands of the President; yet the series of petty conflicts between Congress and the administration showed that intra-governmental co-operation was at a low ebb at the time when it was most needed. Commentators who criticized what they regarded as executive usurpation of power watched uneasily the growth of negative criticism and petty sniping on the part of Congress and began to talk of the disastrous usurpation of power by Congress which had followed both the Civil War and the first World War, and in each instance had prevented the satisfactory solution of post-war problems.

It was clear to most critics of the administration both in and out of Congress that the war must be waged for the most part under presidential leadership. The necessities of secrecy and of speedy and flexible action could not be met by an unwieldy body such as Congress. Its basic function seemed likely to be that of continuing to enact legislation desired by the President while scrutinizing and debating both policy and details of administration in such a way as to incite speedier and more effective administration. In spite of presidential criticism of unfavorable analyses of the war effort by congressional committees, Congress continued to bring out information about the errors which clogged the wheels of administration and, incidentally, about laudable administrative achievements. It is questionable whether such problems as have arisen in relations between Congress and the Executive are as much problems of constitutional machinery as of the weaknesses of human beings when operating under heavy political pressure and the handicaps of wartime uncertainties, weariness, and strain. Clearer thinking, more self-restraint, and

more good-will, together with a self-denying attitude which seldom finds its way into high leadership, are greatly needed in both branches of the government.

29

Thomas L. Stokes
A DIVIDED CONGRESS

From Thomas L. Stokes, "The Congress" in Jack Goodman, ed., While You Were Gone, pp. 136–141. Copyright © 1946 by Simon & Schuster, Inc. Reprinted by permission of Simon & Schuster, Inc.

Thomas L. Stokes (1898–1958) was a Pulitzer Prize-winning Washington correspondent who began his career writing for three newspapers in his native Georgia and went on to become a syndicated columnist for the Scripps-Howard Newspaper Alliance, and later for United Features. At the end of World War II he published the following article in an anthology designed to familiarize returning servicemen with what had occurred at home "while they were gone."

In the first place, it can be pointed out that Congress, as a body, continually kept its composite mind separated into two fairly distinct compartments.

As to the war, it did everything asked for its promotion in the way of voting money and setting up and supplying the various special agencies [which provided] you as soldiers, sailors, and marines with what you required to fight and live as comfortably as is possible in modern combat. In connection with the war Congress performed a valuable service, too, in spying out weaknesses and inadequacies in the war program through numerous investigating committees, including the one once directed by then Senator Harry Truman. It ferreted out waste in time and methods and money and energy, exposed shortages and inadequate materials and equipment, and tracked down some of the profiteers and gougers on war contracts. We had our quota of the last. Senator Truman's theory was that Congress should investigate while the war was going on instead of waiting until afterward, as in the last war. This turned out to be wise. For the Truman Committee contributed much by helping to channel the war program and to check graft and corruption, as did special House Military and Naval Investigating committees.

On the other hand, and at the same time, Congress kept a close watch on the domestic economy and its direction, both of itself and as it was affected by the regimentation of war. This involved policies that had to do with our own everyday lives, then and hereafter.

Here was the irrepressible conflict. Broadly, on basic issues, it divided Congress into conservative and progressive camps. This conflict is not new, as has been said, and, as has also been said, it was intensified by the New Deal—by the fervent loyalties on the one side and the bitter antagonisms on the other aroused in the prewar years by the New Deal, its program, and its chief figure.

The conservatives continually raised the alarm that the New Deal was moving the country toward a centralized, planned economy. They sought to ease controls of various sorts—price-fixing, rationing, and the like—carrying on continued resistance to these established restrictions and vigorously opposing the imposing of others. As the war neared its end, they waged a constant campaign to shake off war controls and others prescribed earlier. . . . They feared that the war might be used to fasten a planned economy on the United States so tightly that it could never be shaken loose.

New Dealers are frankly for more planning in government. Only in this way, they argued

and still argue, can the complex machine civilization of today be directed properly to function so that everybody will have a job. They sought more government assistance [generally,] including unemployment benefits and social security (to cushion any shocks in reconversion from war to peace and to meet possible demands from future depressions) . . . public housing, expansion of public ownership and control of public utilities, [and] federal health and medical programs. . . .

The New Dealers and milder progressives had their heyday in the early years of the New Deal, writing into fundamental law that great body of reforms which has, for the most part, withstood assault. But their foes in Congress began to increase numerically and to put proportionately more vigor into their attack well before the war. In 1938, only two years after the tumultuous 1936 election in which President Roosevelt swept to victory with all but two states, Maine and Vermont, a reaction exhibited itself in the congressional elections. Republicans picked up 80 seats in the House and, for the first time since the New Deal came into power, began to approach the [dimensions] again of a major party, with 169 seats in the House compared with 262 for the Democrats. In the Senate Republicans had [had] but 17 members, an innocuous corporal's guard. They picked up six seats in the 1938 election to present a slightly more respectable front there. In President Roosevelt's decisive defeat of Wendell Willkie in 1940 Republicans backslid a bit in the House, with a loss of seven seats. They picked up five more in the Senate.

But, in 1942, even though the country was in the midst of war, Republicans took another spurt. They ran their House membership up to 209. This was nine short of the majority of 218, but it was better than it looked, [since] the Democrats, who had 222, discovered before long that their majority was really only on paper. . . . In the same wartime, mid-term election Republicans gained ten seats in the Senate, to bring their total there to 38. A majority in the Senate is 49.

The election was interpreted to indicate some dissatisfaction with conduct of the war. Republicans had stressed *that* as an issue, and we [Americans] *were* on the defensive all around the world. But there was reflected also, undoubtedly, the discontent with [a] regimentation to which we had not become accustomed. The election served as an outlet for lots of minor grievances in those days before we had found out how minor they really were and in what a big war we engaged. . . . There were, [moreover,] other circumstances which certainly had a part [in the result] and which must be taken into account, [if] for [no other] reason, because they had an interesting aftermath in bringing a new force—labor—actively into American politics.

For one thing, Democrats always had proved weaker in off-year congressional elections when President Roosevelt's name was not on the ballots, at the head of the ticket, to attract his followers to the polls. There was not the same keen interest. But beyond that there were other factors unfavorable to the Democrats in this particular 1942 election which, in so many ways, turned out to be such an important one for what followed in Congress.

Many persons who normally voted Democratic did not vote that year, beyond the customary falling-off due to Mr. Roosevelt's absence from the ticket. That was because of the migration of hundreds of thousands of workers from their homes into war industry in other states. They had to qualify anew under the laws of those states to which they had moved. This took a certain period of residence. Many did not qualify for this reason and some just didn't bother. There were, too, physical handicaps in voting in that many worked in plants

far away from their homes and far away from the polling places and so did not vote.

The Democrats and their labor allies woke up too late, to find themselves in an unfortunate, if not precarious, position in Congress, now the center of important battles affecting their interests, as they well knew. The C.I.O., which was loyally behind the President, decided to do something about failure to get the vote organized and out to the polls in the 1942 congressional election. They didn't want to see that happen again. The C.I.O. thereupon created its Political Action Committee (PAC), which developed by the 1944 elections into a really efficient, practical, political organization which deserved most of the credit it got for the re-election of President Roosevelt to a fourth term and the return of more comfortable majorities in the Congress which began to sit in January, 1945. [The] C.I.O. taught its members the elementary lessons in practical politics—in organization of voters, door-to-door canvasses, as well as the value of money in politics and elections. They learned how to levy on their membership at so much a head and saw how quickly many such small contributions can roll up into a nice fat wad for political organizing expenses.

But this was after some damage had been done them in Congress.

For conservatives were in the saddle, and effectively so, during most of the war years, and this had a particular relation to domestic issues in which New Dealers, their progressive satellites, and labor were interested. Even before the 1942 congressional elections the conservative influence was more potent than might appear from a bare list of party divisions. The reaction that occurred in Congress after the 1938 elections had other than strictly Republican sources. Southern conservative Democrats, who had long been irked over invasion of the South by such New Deal reforms as

TVA, wage and hour legislation, financial assistance to tenant farmers, and collective bargaining, finally began to break away and join common cause with Republicans in a coalition, first loose and occasional, but eventually fairly well organized. The Southerners, because of their peculiar legislative skill from long experience and because of their key positions through operation of the seniority rule, provided most of the leadership in this coalition. They supplied what came to be called in war agencies of the government "the know-how." They deserted the President, despite his popularity among the rank and file of their people back home, as demonstrated so conclusively in every election since he had entered the White House, and despite all that the New Deal had done for the plain people of the South. But now that they were reinforced in Congress, they did more boldly the bidding of their real masters—the industrial and planter oligarchy of the South. They were comparatively safe against the wrath of the masses in the South, first, because the people could not always find out how they were being betrayed and, second, [because] they were protected by the restricted suffrage through poll taxes and "white primary" laws. They had a select voting constituency loaded in their favor by the so-called "respectable element."

This coalition could outvote the Administration on strictly New Deal domestic issues even before Republican gains in the 1942 elections, and after that it was able to check any really progressive legislation. At the same time it made some gains of its own in tax and postwar legislation which become clearer as the country looks ahead to the problems of transition from a war to a peacetime economy. The coalition took care of its friends.

While New Dealers and their progressive associates could make no headway on fundamental social and economic measures during the war, they were able for the most part to hold the basic structure of reform erected in the early New Deal years. This was chiefly because those reforms had become so well entrenched with the people that the conservatives dared not attack them too openly and boldly for fear of political retaliation, though they have not given up the fight and you may look for its revival if, and when, the opportunity is offered. They have capitalized the natural reaction from reform that always follows such a dazzling era of change as that of the early New Deal. Likewise, they have exploited war weariness. They will overlook no chance here. You can be sure of that. . . .

30

A. Russell Buchanan
AN ACQUIESCENT COURT

From pp. 324–328 in The United States and World War II, *Vol. II, by A. Russell Buchanan. Copyright © 1964 by A. Russell Buchanan. Reprinted by permission of Harper & Row, Publishers.*

A. Russell Buchanan (1906–   ), a specialist in the study of war and of twentieth-century American history, has been a professor at the University of California, Santa Barbara, since 1938. In addition to writing *The United States and World War II* (2 vols., 1964), he has edited *The Navy's Air War: A Mission Completed* (1964).

The war years . . . witnessed a diminution in the strength of the judicial branch of the government, primarily through court decisions acquiescing in executive leadership. Early in the war, in the case of *United States v. Pink* [1942], recognizing certain Russian decrees as binding on property located in New York, the Supreme Court's decision raised an executive agreement to the status of a treaty and increased the President's power to by-pass the Senate in making international agreements.

On June 27, 1942, a German submarine

landed four saboteurs on the shores of Long Island, and four nights later another submarine deposited four more on the Florida coast. The Coast Guard and Federal Bureau of Investigation were alert and soon had the eight men in custody. President Roosevelt immediately appointed a military commission of seven Army generals to try the men and, in addition, issued a proclamation closing the courts of the United States to enemy aliens who entered this country to commit sabotage. An attempt was made to obtain civil trials by resurrecting *Ex parte [Milligan]*, a post-Civil War case which questioned the validity of military trial of persons far removed from the field of battle. The Supreme Court considered the matter sufficiently important to cancel its summer recess and reconvene. Its decision upheld the jurisdiction of the military commission, and within a few days six of the men were executed, a seventh received life imprisonment, and the eighth, who had not appealed, began a thirty-year term. The practical result of the case was that the Supreme Court had signified its approval of military tribunals during the war.

Inevitably, restrictions upon American citizens of Japanese parentage came to the attention of the Supreme Court. The first case involved Gordon Kiyoshi Hirabayashi, an American citizen who had violated the curfew set by General De Witt on the West Coast. The court upheld De Witt's action in setting a curfew, but such was the concern over the implications that there were three concurrent opinions. Chief Justice [Harlan] Stone, who wrote the majority opinion, noted that "in time of war residents having ethnic affiliations with an invading enemy may be a greater source of danger than those of a different ancestry." The principal issue was the war power of those charged with the nation's defense, and stating specifically that the Court was not attempting "to define the ultimate boundaries of the war power," Stone pronounced the Court's opinion

"only that the curfew order as applied and at the time it was applied, was within the boundaries of the war power." There was much less agreement on the Court in the *Korematsu* case [1944], when it assented to the relocation order which removed Japanese and Americans of Japanese parentage from the West Coast to relocation centers. Justice Frank Murphy denounced the removal as "one of the most sweeping and complete deprivations of constitutional rights in the history of this nation in the absence of martial law." The crux of the problem confronting the Court was to determine the dividing line between the constitutional rights of the citizen and the nation's power to defend itself. Early in the war the Court showed more concern for the nation's defense; later, as in the case of *Ex parte Endo* [1944], it drew the line somewhat more in favor of individual rights. In this case, although it did not consider the constitutionality of the legislation and executive orders underlying the relocation program, it made a strict interpretation of them and decided that since they did not specifically mention detention, Miss Mitsuye Endo, a loyal citizen, should be released from the relocation center in which she had been detained.

The relocation program on the West Coast was the most widespread disregard of personal rights in the nation's history since the abolition of slavery. It was based on the military's authority to wage war and its insistence that the evacuation was necessary for the defense of the West Coast, although after the initial round-up of suspected subversives the removal of Japanese and Americans of Japanese ancestry was hardly a military necessity. The Washington government approved the action, and the actual removal was administered by a civilian agency. The Court gave sanction to the military error in the belief that in wartime the military should have requisite authority to wage war. At the same time it set a dangerous precedent for further abridgement of personal rights. As the war progressed and as danger to the nation receded, the Court attempted, as in the case of *Ex parte Endo,* to resuscitate some of the rights of the individual. The Court moved slowly; Miss Endo remained in a relocation center for over two years before the Court found that she should not be detained. Similarly, the Court delayed in reaching a decision on martial law in Hawaii, which had been instituted shortly after the attack on Pearl Harbor. Two persons convicted by military tribunals sought redress in the civilian courts. It was not until February, 1946, after the end of the war, that the Supreme Court decided that martial law, although intended to help the military defend the islands, "was not intended to authorize the supplanting of courts by military tribunals."

The question of civil rights arose in other connections, and since the nation's defense was not so closely related, the courts leaned more heavily toward personal liberties. George Sylvester Viereck, a Nazi propagandist, was brought to trial for concealing information while registered as a foreign agent. He had registered and listed the activities for which he had received pay as a German agent, but it was charged that he had failed to disclose certain private ventures, and his conviction would stand only if it were proved that his propagandist activities had been made criminal by the registration statute. The Court not only freed Viereck but criticized the highly emotional tone of the prosecution. [Reaction to] the opinion was sharp, but many considered it a courageous support of civil rights in difficult times. In the case of *Schneiderman v. United States* [1943], the Court held that mere membership in the Communist party did not warrant depriving Schneiderman of his citizenship, athough three justices, including Stone, bitterly dissented. The Court also set aside denaturali-

zation of a German-American citizen charged with continued allegiance to the German government.

The Court strongly supported free speech in wartime. It refused in a five-to-four decision [*Hartzel v. United States,* 1943] to halt propaganda to obstruct the draft and stimulate disloyalty among the armed forces and held that unless such action could be found to violate specifically the Espionage Act of 1917 it should not be outlawed. In another five-to-four decision [*Keegan v. United States,* 1944], the Court threw out the government's prosecution of twenty-five German-American Bund leaders on the ground that by counseling refusal to do military service the Bund was simply awaiting the verdict of a test case on the matter. The Court also found that treason was not proved against Anthony Cramer, who had associated with one of the German saboteurs, since two witnesses to the overt act of treason had not been found. Another case, *Yakus v. United States* [1943], involved a certain curtailment of the right of judicial review. Presumably in an effort not to impede the administration in wartime, the Supreme Court upheld the law in question.

According to the Selective Service Act of 1940 a person who, "by reason of religious training and belief, is conscientiously opposed to participation in war in any form" in place of induction could be "assigned to work of national importance under civilian direction." A person who objected only to combatant service was classified I-A-O; if he objected to both combatant and noncombatant service, his classification was IV-E. Local draft boards made these as they did other classifications, and anyone, including conscientious objectors, who disregarded the instructions of the draft board was subject to arrest and imprisonment. The largest number of conscientious objectors who went to prison were Jehovah's Witnesses, who normally requested exemption from military service not as conscientious objectors, I-A-O or IV-E, but as ministers (IV-D), claiming that they were all ministers. When their claims were denied, since most had other employment in addition to their religious work, they refused to comply with regulations imposed on them and went to prison. As a result three times as many conscientious objectors were imprisoned in World War II as in World War I. . . .

The question of conscientious objectors raised numerous legal problems. The courts upheld the constitutionality of compulsory registration and reaffirmed the Supreme Court's position of World War I that in wartime the government has powers of conscription. The Court did not define clearly "religious training and belief," which was the basis of conscientious objection. It denied the protection of either the First or the Fifth Amendment to conscientious objectors or that there was undue delegation of legislative power to the administrative agencies controlling the Civilian Public Service Camps. Court decisions placed the conscientious objector serving in these camps in a position midway between civilian and soldier; he could be under military control twenty-four hours a day, but if he disobeyed this control he would be tried in a civil rather than military court.

31

Eric Goldman
CONSERVATIVE RESURGENCE

Excerpts from pp. 401–410 of Rendezvous with Destiny, *by Eric F. Goldman. Copyright © 1956 by Alfred A. Knopf, Inc. Reprinted by permission of the publisher.*

Eric Goldman (1915–   ) is a distinguished scholar with unusual experience outside the academy. A professor of history at Princeton University since 1943, he has also been a State Department lecturer in Europe and Asia, a moderator for a network television panel, and, between 1963 and 1966, an informal adviser to President Lyndon Johnson. Among his publications are *Rendezvous with Destiny* (winner of the Bancroft Prize in 1952), *The Crucial Decade—And After: America, 1945–1960* (1961), and *The Tragedy of Lyndon Johnson* (1969).

Liberals were scarcely done cheering Teheran [the inter-allied conference of November 1943] when [President] Roosevelt summoned old Doc New Deal. With a sharp reminder to the country that the Wilsonian postwar should not be repeated, he called on Congress to begin enactment of an "Economic Bill of Rights." The rights were to apply to "all—regardless of station, race, or creed," and they were sweeping.

"The right to a useful and remunerative job in the industries or shops or farms or mines of the Nation;

"The right to earn enough to provide adequate food and clothing and recreation;

"The right of every farmer to raise and sell his products at a return which will give him and his family a decent living;

"The right of every businessman, large and small, to trade in an atmosphere of freedom from unfair competition and domination by monopolies at home or abroad;

"The right of every family to a decent home;

"The right to adequate medical care and the opportunity to achieve and enjoy good health;

"The right to adequate protection from the economic fears of old age, sickness, accident, and unemployment;

"The right to a good education."

"All these rights," the President said, "spell security. And after this war is won we must be prepared to move forward, in the implementation of these rights, to new goals of human happiness and well-being."

In the fourth-term Presidential campaign of

1944, Roosevelt reiterated the Economic Bill of Rights, militantly pledged that "we are not going to turn the clock back! We are going forward," and, when the campaign seemed to lack the old New Deal fervor, brought his liberal following to its feet by the most extraordinary tour de force in the history of American politics. In a tone of grave injury, Roosevelt told how Republican leaders were saying that "my little dog Fala" had been left behind on an inspection trip to the Aleutians and was brought back to Washington at huge cost to the taxpayers, "two or three, or eight or twenty million dollars." Fala's "Scotch soul was furious. . . . Well, of course, I don't resent attacks, and my family doesn't resent attacks, but Fala *does* resent them. He has not been the same dog since." This was the F.D.R., frolicsome, cocky, festooning reform in the gayest of trappings, who had led liberals so long and so effectively. Their confidence was flooding back and they enthusiastically helped to re-elect the President and to increase Democratic strength in both houses of Congress. . . .

To a whole nation that had lived through its grimmest depression and its most frightful war with Franklin Roosevelt in the White House, the news of his death [five months later] came with the force of personal shock. Liberals were not only stunned. Suddenly they realized to what extent their confidence in the postwar had rested on one man. Suddenly all their long-running fears of another debacle swirled back. In the hours following Roosevelt's death, rumors rampaged through liberal circles. New Dealers were being scuttled from high government posts; the San Francisco Conference [at which it was planned to organize the United Nations] would be called off; all economic controls were to be scrapped immediately.

After the first shock, reassurances came.

Publicly before Congress and privately to New Dealers, the new President declared his determination to carry on both the domestic and foreign policies of "that noble soul . . . with all my strength and with all my heart." The whole impression of Harry Truman's first address as President was comforting to liberals. Stoutly controlling his nervousness, radiating modesty, sincerity, and a quiet strength, he made plain that the grand strategy of the war would go on unaltered, that the San Francisco Conference would meet as scheduled, and that domestic reform would be pushed. Within twenty-four hours Truman could even announce a coup important for keeping the United Nations united. The Russians, who had been threatening to snub the San Francisco Conference by sending a second-ranking diplomat, agreed to dispatch Foreign Affairs Commissar Molotov.

In the glow of these events, liberals began looking up the Truman record and found further encouragement. His votes in the Senate had been largely pro-New Deal in domestic affairs and almost unanimously pro-Roosevelt in foreign affairs. His watchdog committee on the defense effort had been the most respected in many years, prodding and scourging with a conspicuous lack of timidity before big business or big brass. And, after all, Franklin Roosevelt himself, who surely must have known that four terms might be too much, had named Truman his heir apparent.

Soon the rush of world news was obscuring the transition from the dazzling Hyde Park patrician to the grayish little country judge from Independence. Twenty-six days after Roosevelt died, the Chief of Staff of the German Army signed his name to a document in a Reims schoolhouse, stood stiffly, then in a strangled voice, like a sob, said: "With this signature the German people and the German armed forces are, for better or for worse, delivered into the victor's hands." Two months later the new President was off for a Big Three conference in Potsdam, and the headlines told both of the upset Labour victory over Winston Churchill and of the loosing of the atomic bomb on Hiroshima. While people were still writing letters to the White House addressed to President Franklin D. Roosevelt, the lights were on again in London and the Japanese were signing surrender papers under the guns of the U.S.S. *Missouri* and the glare of Douglas MacArthur. The infinitely analyzed postwar, so longingly awaited and feared for so long, was at hand.

The postwar looked very much like a postwar. In 1946, the first full year of peace, the President and Congress wrangled endlessly over price-controls, and prices kept going up; by the end of the twelve months, you could pay $2.75 for a hamburger plate and $17.50 for a shirt. More than four million workers, feeling the inflationary squeeze, walked off their jobs, the President of the United States proposed the peacetime drafting of workers to break a strike, and the White House was doing nothing to check assaults on freedom of thinking which approached the hysteria of the days of Attorney General Palmer.

Around the President were gathering a personal circle that Warren Harding would have found thoroughly congenial—the Babbittish John Snyder, hail-fellow George Allen, a master at rowdy stories and at collecting business directorships for himself, the hulking Edwin W. Pauley, who thought politics another, and a lesser, branch of the oil business, and brassy Harry Hawkins Vaughan, always ready to suggest: "You guys will want favors at the White House some day. . . ." New Dealers were fleeing or being pushed out of Washington almost at the rate the gloomiest rumors had predicted. After ten months of the new Administration,

old Harold Ickes, for years a symbol of uncorruptible liberalism, rumbled out with a blast at Pauley that stopped just short of calling him a crook and went the full way of calling him a liar. Seven months later, Henry Wallace, still very much the New Dealer's New Dealer, was gone from the Cabinet, gone from Washington, spending his days convincing *New Republic* readers of their lifelong convictions. On the lower levels the exodus was still more marked. "There isn't any fun working for the government any more," the lesser New Dealers said in their farewells. "No inspiration. . . . No bold adventures."

Congress was hurried into step. In the election of 1946, for the first time in sixteen years, Republicans took over both houses, and a considerable percentage of the new majority were the kind of Republicans who saw dark premonitions of socialism in a bill for free school lunches. Now the Senatorial powerhouse was unquestionably Robert A. Taft, the best mind in the Senate, as liberals wryly commented, until he made it up. The new House was led by Joseph W. Martin, he of the puffed eyes and the policeman's shoes and the glummings about dictatorship, a droning voice straight out of the era of William McKinley. "We have just begun to fight," said the CIO politico, Jack Kroll, bravely whistling as he passed the cemetery.

The 80th Congress, once functioning, was so many months of anguish for liberals. It undercut the Wagner Act with the Taft-Hartley bill, killed effective rent-control, slashed funds for soil conservation and for crop storage, and trimmed all federal pay rolls to the point of forcing the discharge of tax-collectors who took in twenty dollars for each dollar they cost. It tried to enact tax legislation and a tariff that smacked of post-Civil War bonanza days. It ignored the 800,000 displaced persons begging for admittance into America, the estimated

6,000,000 Americans desperate for housing, the demands for extended social security, and an ominous increase of monopoly in the major industries. "This Congress," one liberal newspaperman exploded, "brought back an atmosphere you had forgotten or never thought possible. At first, even the vested interests themselves couldn't believe it. And then you saw them, the Neanderthal Men, lurching forward on hairy feet—the sugar lobby, the wool lobby, the rail lobby, the real estate lobby, the Power trust—tiptoeing back again, fingering things tentatively and then more boldly. Victories fought and won years ago, like the TVA, were suddenly in doubt. Everything was debatable again."

If domestic affairs were dismal for liberals, foreign relations were downright frightening. The San Francisco Conference had no sooner begun than it made public an ominous split between the Soviet Union and the Western powers, and each month seemed to make the division deeper and more dangerous. The Soviet Union went ahead violating its wartime agreements, flatly rejected the American plan for international control of atomic weapons, and talked the blunderbuss language that has so often marked the preparation of totalitarian states for war. The Truman Administration, on its part, turned to the openly anti-Soviet Truman Doctrine in 1947, added the more effectively anti-Soviet Marshall Plan, and began matching the Politburo epithet for epithet. More and more, the violent East-West quarrels threatened to kick the legs from under the young United Nations. And over the flimsy peace played the ghastly knowledge that another world war would be an atomic war.

Hiroshima, more than any other fact in modern history, tore at the minds and hearts of American liberals. It presented in the most urgent possible form the problem that had beset reform-minded men and women since the beginnings of the Industrial Revolution—the

enormous difference in the speed of technological development and the rate at which men learn ways to use industry and science for the benefit of the general population. Liberals poured out a tremendous literature underlining the significance of Hiroshima, articles, speeches, and books which reached temporary climaxes in Norman Cousins's rousingly emotional *Modern Man Is Obsolete* and John Hersey's factually jolting *Hiroshima*. Like soldiers backed into a ravine, the reform-minded threw themselves into the fight to keep control of the development of atomic energy in the United States out of military hands, and when the fight was won, they greeted the victory with the air of men who had been snatched, at the last moment and probably only temporarily, from disaster.

Around everything clung the miasma of another Twenties. . . .

At least, said the *Progressive*, "please, no bathtub gin. Pretty please."

32

Arthur Ekirch
THE DECLINE OF LIBERALISM

From Arthur A. Ekirch, Jr., The Decline of American Liberalism, *pp. 315–318. Originally published by Longmans Green & Co., Ltd., London, 1955. Presently available in paperback from Atheneum, 1967.*

Arthur Ekirch (1915–   ) is a professor of American history who taught at Hofstra College from 1946 to 1965 and who has been at the State University of New York, Albany, since 1965. He is the author of *The Idea of Progress in America* (1944), *The Decline of American Liberalism* (1955), *The Civilian and the Military* (1956), and *The American Democratic Tradition* (1963).

. . . During the early days of the New Deal, and again in the midst of World War II, too many liberals had allowed themselves to be seduced by the illusion of power. Accepting the necessity of planning at home and war abroad, many lost all sense of proportion. They forgot that crusades are seldom liberal. And at the same time the much-diminished American suspicion of a powerful centralized government all but vanished in response to repeated demands that liberals be practical men of action. Denying most vigorously that they had betrayed classical and traditional liberal values, the new totalitarian liberals argued that such liberalism had become outmoded. "The base we want to build our liberalism on is a democratic collectivism," wrote Max Lerner. More honest than most of his contemporaries, Lerner hastened to add: "It will become apparent to the reader before he has read many pages that I am far more a democrat than I am a liberal." The clash between Lerner's views and those of older schools of thought was illustrated in the comment of an historian of Jefferson's liberalism, who pointed out that "A liberal is a catholic-minded democrat, who often opposed a realistic democracy that would ignore minority rights."

In the stress of the war, a number of those who considered themselves liberals had preached a philosophy of vengeance and hate. The Morgenthau Plan to reduce Germany to a pastoral state, the demand for unconditional surrender, and the war crimes trials at Nuremberg and Tokyo were fruits of this policy which later were to prove embarrassing to the United States. This was especially the case when in the postwar era erstwhile disarmed enemies were suddenly desired as newly rearmed allies. At home the doctrine of guilt by association had been invoked by the administration in a mass sedition trial of Americans who had sympathized with the Nazis or who had been members of German-front organizations. In the instance of the two largest wartime minority groups, the Japanese Americans and the conscientious objectors, self-styled liberals in official position had made little protest over unfair or discriminatory treatment. Silent as long as the ugly type of World War I incident was avoided, the war liberals, as Norman Thomas later noted, had been content to let a conservative like Senator Robert Taft assume the onerous task of speaking out most openly in regard to certain aspects of conscription or of the forced evacuation of Americans of Japanese descent.

Thus the thirties and early forties, when liberals under Franklin Roosevelt seemed most strongly entrenched, was actually a period of grave potential peril for traditional liberal values. This, however, was only fully realized after the close of the war, when the liberal retreat was beginning to turn into a rout. Preoccupied by the struggle to gain first economic and then military security, American liberals set the pattern in the 1930's and 1940's for the sacrifice of the very individual freedoms on which all personal, and ultimately national, security is necessarily based. In one of his early messages to Congress before the war, President Roosevelt had indicated the liberals' possible future dilemma in regard to the new instruments of public power that he was helping to fashion. "In the hands of a people's Government," he asserted, "this power is wholesome and proper. But in the hands of political puppets of an economic autocracy such power would provide shackles for the liberties of the people."

As New Deal regulatory powers fell more and more into antiliberal hands, postwar liberals of various shades of opinion were placed on the defensive. Although they could not afford to ignore the popular and official shibboleth of security, it seemed clear that in their concentration on so-called realistic political and economic ends liberals had yielded the less tangible but more important values associated with individual freedom and dissent. The preservation of the Federal bureaucracy had become an end in itself. Accustomed to power and office, New Deal liberals had lost the capacity of self-criticism and vigorous opposition, qualities that might have served them in good stead in the postwar years of hysteria and reaction.

In spite of the undoubted pressures upon American liberals during World War II, it soon became evident that the hardships of the postwar period would prove infinitely more trying. Before the American people could translate the joy of victory into the hope of an enduring peace they were faced with a rapid deterioration in relations between Russia and the West and with the sordid realities of the cold war. Overshadowing the concept of the United Nations and the ideals of the Atlantic Charter was the specter of a third world war and the new means of destruction indicated by the atomic and hydrogen bombs. Meanwhile, permanent world peace, even if remote, seemed all the more necessary as a matter of sheer biological survival. Yet, despite the popular wartime slogan of "One World" and the ready assumption that internationalism had replaced isolationism, it was apparent that the postwar world would still be dominated by considerations of military power, and by a narrow nationalism.

Posing beside one of his campaign posters after having been nominated for the United States Senate in 1946, Joseph McCarthy was only one of the many politicians who capitalized on the fact that he had participated in military service during the war. (Wide World Photos)

These were the signs Negroes carried in a "silent parade" through New York's Union Square, July 25, 1942, in protest against continuing discrimination and a growing number of racial incidents. The demonstration was sponsored by the March on Washington Movement (MOWM), an organization established in 1941 to put pressure on the government on behalf of civil rights.   (Culver Pictures, Inc.)

Chapter Seven

SOCIAL EFFECTS
OF THE WAR

This section is, at least in part, somewhat more specific and detailed than the comparable section for the previous war. Ernest W. Burgess, for example, provides unusually precise statistics in analyzing the impact of World Wars I and II (to 1942) upon the American family, at the same time predicting that the biggest change produced by the second conflict would be "a further rise in the status of women." Similarly, Francis Merrill compiles an extraordinary listing of wartime alterations in society, dividing them into those which represent the intensification of peacetime trends and those which can be described as new or major modifications of older trends. In a less schematic but equally careful fashion, Richard Dalfiume argues that World War II was the great "watershed" of recent Negro history and the seedbed of the "civil rights revolution of the 1950s." Meanwhile, the Report of Committee A (of the American Association of University Professors) for 1943 points up the manner in which the government's reliance on colleges and universities during the war saved many of them financially while at the same time subtly altering their character. Speaking more generally, Isaac L. Kandel suggests that the war served both to demonstrate the need for more federal aid to education and to inspire a variety of educational reforms, curricular and otherwise.

QUESTIONS:
1. In what ways might a war like World War II reinforce the trend toward a "companionship" type of family?
2. How would you explain the odd combination of wartime developments, as reported by Francis Merrill, regarding delinquency, crime, mental disease, and suicide?
3. Why was World War II more of a "watershed" for the American Negro than World War I had been? Or was it?
4. Why do you think there was less public hysteria regarding the enemy in World War II than in World War I?
5. Would you conclude that the Second World War strengthened or weakened American education for its peacetime tasks?

33

Ernest W. Burgess
THE CHANGING FAMILY

From pp. 343–52 of Ernest W. Burgess, "The Effects of the War on the American Family," in American Journal of Sociology, *Vol. 48 (November 1942), published by the University of Chicago Press. Copyright 1942 by the University of Chicago. All rights reserved.*

Ernest W. Burgess (1886–1966) was a Canadian-born sociologist whose career at the University of Chicago spanned the years between 1916 and 1951, when he became emeritus professor. From 1936 to 1940 he was editor of the *American Journal of Sociology*, and during the 1940s he edited *Marriage and Family Living*. He was also the co-author of *The City* (1925), *The Family* (1945), and *Courtship, Engagement, and Marriage* (1954).

War, like any other crisis, has its obvious, although more superficial, and its subtler but more profound, effects upon the family.

The impact of war upon the family is readily observable in its surface manifestations, and these can for the most part be stated quantitatively. They are not to be considered as unimportant in themselves, but they receive added meaning to the extent that they can be related significantly to the ongoing processes of family life. These external effects will be briefly summarized, preliminary to attempting to probe beneath the surface to discover as far as feasible the basic changes taking place under the impact of war upon the modern American family.

Certain readily observable effects of war upon the family flow, first of all, from the withdrawal of millions of young men from civilian life. Recent estimates give approximately four million as the number of men now [1942] in the armed forces. These men are largely but not entirely single and mainly in their twenties or early thirties. The great majority of them have been taken out of families in which they were reared and are required to make adjustment in the army-camp situation. Since a certain percentage of men are not able to make this adjustment, psychiatrists and physicians attempt to weed them out at the time of examination for induction. Of the first two million selectees who were examined for induction into the army under the Selective Training and Service Act of 1940, 57,000, or 2.85 per cent, were rejected for mental and nervous disorders serious enough to disqualify a man for military service.

This withdrawal of men from the primary group controls of the home and of the neighborhood removes restraining influences against socially disapproved forms of behavior. Drinking, gambling, prostitution, and illicit sex behavior are higher among men in military than in civilian life. The increase in sexual irregularity is evidenced not only by reports of the prevalence of prostitution in and near war-camp communities (the trailer and trailer camps representing an innovation of this war) but in the officially released figures showing an incidence of venereal infection in the army at the rate of 42 per 1,000 men for the first six months of 1941 as compared with 27 per 1,000 for 1939. As a result of strenuous efforts to combat this serious impairment of the physical efficiency of our armed forces—including suppression of prostitution by federal agencies and penalties for the nonuse of prophylactics by the soldier—the rate for the first six months of 1942 had fallen to 34 per 1,000 men. These types of behavior may perhaps also, but with less assurance, be taken as an index of the degree to which the military life unfits men to resume their places in the family after the war. Here, however, we are dealing with a rather complicated balance of forces making for and against domesticity. To the great majority of men the war is a disagreeable job, to be finished as soon as possible in order to return to civil life, to settle down, and to enjoy home life, made all the more attractive by contrast with the army camp. Then, too, the discipline of the army and the opportunity to learn a trade are valuable experiences for civilian readjustment to many previously unemployed youth of the depression decade.

The second evident effect of the war upon the family is the entrance of women into war industry and into civilian industry to replace men drawn into the armed forces. Paul V. McNutt, chairman of the War Manpower Commission, estimates that the 1,400,000 women employed in war production in December, 1941, will rise to 4,500,000 by December, 1942, and will reach 6,000,000 by the end of next year. The civilian labor market will require the services of a few additional million women.

The vast exodus of young men from the home into the army and the upsurge of women in industry cannot but have repercussions in the home. First to be evident are reports from all over the country of neglect of small chil-

dren, locked in the house, the apartment, or the trailer during the hours the mother is employed in war industry. This need is now so evident that private and public efforts are being made to meet it by more adequate provision of day nurseries. Although the United States has been in the war less than a year, signs are multiplying that an increase in juvenile delinquency is already in the making. The experience of other countries, including the United States, in World War I indicates that the marked increase in juvenile delinquency does not come until the second year of war. Delinquency rates in England and in Canada are now reported as approximately 40–50 per cent higher than in the pre-war years. Scattered reports from this country indicate that rates are stationary in most communities, but a few cities, like Chicago and Los Angeles, have experienced small increases in youthful crime. There seems little doubt that the removal of the father and more often the older brother from the home and the absence of the mother or older sister from the family during work will result in a piling-up of juvenile offenses during 1943.

The effects of the war upon marriage are already evident. "The 1941 marriage rate— 12.6 per 100,000 population—was the highest rate ever recorded in the United States." The increase in marriages as affected by the war began in 1940 preceding and following the passage of the Selective Service Act in September of that year. There is every reason to believe that the change in the marriage rate during this war will follow the pattern of World War I. . . . The marriage rate rises before and during the early period of the entrance of men in the armed forces, declines during the year or years of war, increases during the first two post-war years, and then returns to normal in the third post-war year.

The first phase of the marriage cycle as affected by the war reached its climax in the increases of the marriage rate in 1941 and the early months of 1942 and may be expected to fall off somewhat during the remainder of 1942. The increase was largely due to hasty and hurried-up marriages. Hasty marriages are of three types: First, there are those entered into on short acquaintance to avoid Selective Service; second, there are the war-camp marriages, typically of the homesick soldier or sailor and of the girl attracted by the glamour of the uniform; and, third, there are the romantic marriages of the men in the expeditionary forces, meeting and falling in love with and marrying Australian, Irish, and English girls. These last, however, do not appear in United States marriage reports, since the weddings take place in foreign countries.

That marriage rates will begin their decline this year and sharply decrease in 1943 is due to postponed unions. These held-over marriages are of two kinds, voluntary and involuntary. Many young people moved more by prudential than romantic reasons have decided to wait until the war is over to marry. Some of these weddings will never take place, either because one or the other will change his mind or because the young man will die or be incapacitated for marriage. As numerous, perhaps, are the involuntary postponed marriages. The great majority of men not engaged before entering the service are disposed to remain single until their return after the war.

World War I was of short duration. The number of casualties in the army during the eighteen months of war was only 50,510 killed and 182,674 wounded. Although the number of casualties so far in the present war are relatively small (45,165, of whom 4,801 are known to be killed, 3,218 wounded, and 1,042 prisoners; of the 36,104 reported missing, the great majority are assumed to be prisoners), the probabilities are that they will greatly exceed those of 1917–18, as the American expeditionary forces move into action on all continents.

The sum total of men killed, of those surviving but incapacitated for marriage, and of those marrying foreign brides will considerably increase the number of American young women of this generation destined to remain single. How great this problem will ultimately become is, of course, contingent upon the duration of the war and the extent and degree of American participation in it.

The divorce rate typically declines during war. Many men temporarily solve their marital difficulties by enlisting. Marriages on the brink of disaster will be saved "for the duration" by the husband's entering the armed forces through Selective Service. Wives who otherwise might sue for separate maintenance or divorce postpone such action until after the war, a prudential course in view of compulsory allowances to dependents of men in the service. Then, too, divorces may be more difficult to obtain when the husband is a soldier, sailor, or aviator.

The deficit in divorces during the war is certain from past experience to be more than made up after the war. The higher proportion of unhappy unions arising from hasty marriages to avoid Selective Service, in war camps, and abroad and, to a lesser degree, those resulting from hurried-up unions, will contribute to the upswing in the divorce rate. Also to be included are the divorces due to all the factors which cause husband and wife to grow apart during their enforced separation.

The effects of the war upon marriage have their inevitable effect upon the birth rate. In World War I the birth rate was nearly as high for the years 1917 and 1918 as for the pre-war year 1916. The pre-war year of 1940, with a higher birth rate (17.9) than any year since 1931, was outdistanced by 1941 (18.9), which in turn is expected to yield to 1942 as the banner year for births. The high rate for 1941 was largely due to the sharp rise in the marriage rate in 1940, which, continuing in 1941, was largely responsible for the anticipated exceptionally high 1942 birth rate. Contributing to the high rate of 1941 and 1942 was the decision of an indeterminable number of previously childless couples to have a child as a ground for deferment of the husband from Selective Service.

Owing to the withdrawal of millions of men from the United States during 1942, the birth rate should show a moderate decline for 1943 and a rather marked decrease for 1944. A recovery in the birth rate cannot be expected upon the basis of experience in World War I until the second and third post-war year periods.

The illegitimate birth rate and the abortion rate may both be expected to rise as a result of the increase of irregular sexual intercourse of men in the armed forces and of single and married women.

These obvious surface changes—while interesting and important—should not blind us to the more fundamental transformation in family structure, functions, and relationships which have been in process for decades. The impact of the war tends to speed up these changes rather than to reverse them or to introduce new trends. Social scientists should, therefore, always be on their guard against the common-sense fallacy of assuming that a given reversal of a trend, due to temporary wartime conditions, is indicative of a permanent change. It is only wishful thinking to project beyond the wartime emergency the revival of neighborliness among urbanites now evidenced in sharing automobiles or in Civil Defense block activities. Victory gardens during the war do not insure home plots after the peace. Nor does the present tendency of many war brides to reside with their parents or parents-in-law forecast a trend after the war to the increased control of the kinship group over the young couple after marriage. Aside from these and other temporary reversals, the safest forecast of the future, unless some counteracting factor is clearly evident, is to project past trends into the future.

The changes now taking place in family organization may best be seen in their long historical perspective and in relation to two contrasting ideal types of family structure. Let us assume that the complete subordination of the individual to the family, on the one hand, and the fullest self-expression of its individual members compatible with the continued existence of the family, on the other, represent the two extreme ideal constructions.

Of the historical and existing types of families, the large patriarchal family most closely approximates the ideal type of the institutional family, where the individual members of the small family unit are completely subordinated to the interests of the large family. The modern American family residing in apartment-house areas of the city approximates most nearly to the ideal type of family in which its members have full freedom of self-expression. The two contrasting ideal types will be named the "institutional" and the "companionship," since the first emphasizes subordination to social control and the second stresses the interpersonal basis of modern matrimony. . . .

For decades the American family has been evolving from a semipatriarchal type revolving around the father and husband as head and authority to the democratic type based upon consensus in making decisions, upon the conception of the equality of husband and wife, and upon the growth of autonomy with age of the children. Accompanying this evolution has been the decreasing size of the family, the diminishing control of the kinship group and of the community over the family unit, and a growing sense of its independence. The external factors making for family stability, such as control by custom and community opinion, have been greatly weakened. The permanence of marriage is more and more dependent upon the tenuous bonds of affection, temperamental compatibility, and common interests. . . .

What, in the light of this analysis, will be the effect of war upon the American family? Without doubt, the trend to the companionship type of family, characterized by equality of the sexes and democratic procedures in the home, will continue with a new momentum under the impetus of the wartime situation.

The biggest change to be anticipated is a further rise in the status of women. World War I gave women the outward symbols of equality with men; namely, the suffrage and a social freedom permitting short skirts, bobbed hair, drinking, and smoking. Abolished also along with the open notorious "red-light" districts was the caste of the prostitute and the rigid line of differentiation between respectable and disreputable women.

The present war and the following reconstruction period bid fair to give women more of the substance of equality than did the last conflict, in part because of its expected longer duration. The formation of the Army and the Navy auxiliary corps of women—the W.A.A.C.'s and the W.A.V.E.'s—is symbolic of the new role conceded to women. Women are being given jobs both in military and in civilian industry previously filled only by men. The big increase in the number of working women spells increased economic independence which lays a solid basis for enhanced social status.

This increase in economic independence will be reflected in the more secure position of equality of women in the home. In fact, the absence of husband and father in the army or in a distant munitions industry will also give many wives a larger role of management in the home, at the same time decreasing the sense of family responsibility on the part of the man.

The changes taking place in familial functions for the period 1900–1929 have been described in convincing detail by W. F. Ogburn and Clark Tibbitts in *Recent Social Change* and need here be only summarized. The family has lost or is losing its historic functions of economic production for the market and for home consumption, care of health, education of its members, protective activities, recreation, and religious rites in the home. The intrinsic functions remaining with the family are the giving and receiving of affection by its members and the bearing, rearing, and informal education of the children. The big surge of women into industry in wartime certainly means further curtailment of economic activities in the home, more reliance upon other institutions for health needs, a great expansion in day nurseries for the care of young children, more dependence upon recreational facilities outside the home, and less time for the mother to give to the educational and religious development of her children. . . .

The loss by the family of its historic functions greatly increased its economic insecurity. With the exhaustion of free land, private charity was largely relied upon to relieve the distress caused by the exigencies of death, accidents, sickness, and unemployment. Although the movement for governmental intervention to deal with these problems was well under way before the thirties, the crisis of the last great financial depression finally brought about a merger of projects and proposals into a federal system of social security. The families of workingmen are now safeguarded by compensation insurance and pension against the contingencies of accident, unemployment, and old age. Most significant, perhaps, for the small family unit, is the provision of pensions for the aged which permits them to live in independence and relieves their children of responsibility for their support.

The war is likely further to augment governmental provision for the security of the family. In the White House Conference on Children in a Democracy, four of the eleven sections of its report were devoted to the family. The Family Security Committee, established in the office of the Director of Defense, Health, and Welfare Services and composed of representatives of voluntary as well as governmental effort, is concerned with safeguarding the values of family life during the period in which the United States is engaged in war. It has first centered its attention upon the strengthening of governmental social services in the field of family security. . . .

Present-day attitudes toward sex and marriage are powerfully affected by the urban way of life, with the high value assigned to rational, standardized, and sophisticated behavior. Corresponding to this shift from rural to urban attitudes are three changes in sex mores which should be specifically mentioned. They all received an impetus from the conditions associated with World War I and are all quite certain to be further affected by the progress of the present conflict.

The lifting of the taboo upon sex and the growth of the movement of sex instruction of children and youth following in the wake of World War I will receive a further push forward from this war.

The social hygiene lectures and the compulsory use of prophylaxis familiarized the soldiers and sailors of World War I with the methods of birth control—lessons that will be repeated for the larger army of this war.

The increase of premarital intercourse following in the wake of World War I, which was accelerated by the depression, appears likely to be further augmented by various conditions accompanying this war, such as glamour of the uniform, patriotic justification in acceding to the desire of a man about to give his life for his country, and the declining value of virginity and chastity.

In the code of sophisticated modern young people the lessening value placed upon chastity does not carry with it the approval of promiscuity. Sexual intercourse is regarded as a privilege of engagement, as permissible when a couple are in love, and to be condoned under certain other circumstances. But promiscuity of the young woman and, to a lesser degree, of the young man draws group disapproval. This code of modern youth seems more likely to be extended rather than restricted under conditions of wartime. The double standard of morals is well on its way out. Moralists still striving to maintain the value of chastity are losing the full force of two of their stock arguments, namely, the fear of pregnancy diminished by the use of contraceptives and the danger of venereal infection lessened by preventives and prophylactics and with the possibilities of cure greatly increased (syphilis by chemical and fever treatments, and gonorrhea by the use of sulpha drugs).

Upon this background of changing sex mores may be sketched the modifications of family relations resulting from the impact of the war.

Because of the decline in the restraining influence of parents upon young people, a higher proportion of war marriages will take place during this than in the preceding war. These comprise not only hurried-up but hasty unions as marriages to avoid Selective Service, war-camp marriages, and marriage of enlisted men in expeditionary forces abroad. The romantic impulses of youth, freed from the prudential restraint of their elders, will lead to many marriages upon short acquaintance, slight knowledge of each other, and insufficient provision for the economic and emotional security of the wife. A high proportion of these unions are certain to turn out unhappily, as indicated by studies of the adverse relation between short acquaintance and adjustment in marriage. Separation while the husband is in the armed forces will also be a disruptive factor, especially upon unions where intercommunication has been insufficient to provide the sharing of experiences and common understanding of feelings, attitudes, and ideas essential to a durable relationship.

During the war all American families are likely to be under considerable stress and strain. There is the shock occasioned by bereavement due to the loss in line of duty of a son, husband, or father. There is the painful readjustment of wife and other relatives to the serviceman returning with physical or mental handicap.

Then, too, wartime is already bringing sudden changes that are disquieting and disrupting. There is mass migration of families and individuals to war-boom communities. Millions of families on stationary incomes already feel the pinch of advancing prices and taxes and are fearful of the menace of inflation. Other millions of families and individuals employed in war industries are experiencing big jumps in income. Both sudden depression and quick prosperity confront the family and its members with changes in habits, attitudes, and roles which contribute to its instability.

A countering factor favorable to family stability is the unifying influence of the sense of participation in the national effort, all the more because of the sacrifices entailed. The balancing of these factors in individual cases requires discrimination between those families which adjust well and those that adjust badly to the wartime situation. . . .

The war, then, will bring great stresses upon marriage and the family, increasing its insta-bility. As an index of this, divorce will markedly increase after the war—an increase that will continue at least for some years with a higher rate than the present, which is one divorce for every six marriages.

Ten years ago a statistician projecting into the future the divorce rate, which since the Civil War has been increasing at the rate of 3 per cent a year, figured that by the year 1965 there would be one divorce for every two marriages. Other writers not statisticians, observing concrete evidences of family instability and unhappiness, have predicted the actual disappearance of the family. Will the war, by increasing family instability, hasten the time of its passing? In reply to these gloomy prophecies certain considerations may be advanced.

1. The companionship type of family still retains the intrinsic and essential functions of the family, namely, the giving and receiving of affection, the bearing and rearing of children, and the guidance of their personality development. It is likely to endure because it is better able to discharge these functions than was the institutional family.

2. Since World War I many services for the family have originated or have been further developed, as family social work, maternal and child health, child guidance, social security, child study, home economics, legal aid for families, associations for family living, education for family life, and marriage and family counseling. These agencies are keenly alive to the effect of wartime conditions upon the family and are actively engaged in taking measures to deal with them. They are orienting their activities to assist in the transition from the institutional to the companionship type of family.

3. Family instability is essentially a phenomenon of the transition from the institutional to the companionship type of family.

The effect of a crisis like war is both to accelerate the transition and to introduce temporary disrupting conditions.

34

Francis Merrill
THE WAR AND SOCIAL PROBLEMS

From pp. 230–234 in Social Problems on the Home Front *by Francis E. Merrill. Copyright 1948 by Harper & Row, Publishers, Inc. Reprinted by permission of Harper & Row, Publishers.*

Francis Merrill (1904–   ), a sociologist and professor, began his career at Central YMCA College in 1932 and moved to Dartmouth College in 1935, where he has continued to teach. During World War II he served on the War Production Board and the Board of Economic Warfare. A specialist on the family and social disorganization, he has published *Social Problems on the Home Front* (1948) and (with Hanford Eldredge) *Culture and Society* (1953).

. . . World War II intensified certain social problems which were already present before the war. These problems may be summarized as follows:

1. The rate of social change was increased.
2. Certain technological changes were accelerated.
3. Corresponding changes in the adaptive culture lagged farther behind than ever before.
4. The rate of social mobility was intensified, with 15 million civilians and 12 million soldiers and sailors on the move.
5. Social congestion was intensified in certain industrial and military centers.
6. The gradual decline in the traditional functions of the family was accelerated.
7. The trend toward the employment of women was intensified by the wartime shortage of labor.
8. Many of the tensions which led to the peacetime disorganization of the family were increased.
9. Desertion probably increased.
10. The long-term trend toward a higher divorce rate and a greater yearly number of divorces was accelerated.
11. The emotional deprivation of children caused by the employment of mothers was increased.
12. Adolescence adjustment was complicated by the accelerated differences between the generations.
13. The trend toward increased sexual freedom was intensified by the wartime decline in the mores.
14. The number of illegitimate births increased, but not as fast as legitimate births.
15. Juvenile delinquency increased sharply, especially among girls.
16. Certain crimes against the person showed a considerable increase.
17. Various minor crimes and offenses against the public morality increased.
18. First admissions to mental hospitals for all psychoses increased.
19. First admissions to mental hospitals for certain organic psychoses of old age increased.
20. First admissions to mental hospitals for the functional psychoses showed a mixed trend, with manic-depressive psychosis decreasing slightly and dementia praecox [schizophrenia] increasing substantially.

Some of these changed social conditions were general, while others were more specific. Each condition, however, represents a situation or combination thereof considered a threat to social values. Each of these problems represents a familiar situation in the dynamic society of peacetime; the war intensified these problems without materially changing them.

. . . [At the same time, the war brought about other situations] which were either substantially new or represented considerable modifications of old ones. . . . [These] included:

1. The increased national consensus on the necessity of winning the war.
2. The high morale resulting from the clear and present danger to national symbols.
3. The increase in prejudice, despite the fact that the war was presumably fought for its abolition.
4. The high level of employment, made possible by the demands for manpower and war production.
5. The high income level, particularly in the manufacturing industries, but partially shared by other employed persons.
6. The large-scale and prolonged separation of millions of families, which was unique both in extent and duration and which brought about significant changes in family roles.
7. The sense of participation in the adolescent generation, whose older brothers had but little possibility for participation during the depression.
8. The increased employment of children and adolescents, which reversed a secular trend toward the progressive abolition of child labor.
9. The decrease in promiscuity for hire (prostitution) because of the more efficient social control thereof.
10. The conflicting trends in venereal disease, with syphilis decreasing and gonorrhea increasing among the civilian population.
11. The decrease in total crimes known to the police, particularly offenses against property.
12. The decline in the suicide rate to its lowest figure in recent years, as many persons merged their personal troubles into the national effort.

. . . [Thus] World War II . . . exerted a differential effect upon the social structure of the United States, intensifying some problems and temporarily reversing others. Certain trends long evident in peacetime were modified by introducing variables which changed the situation in wartime. Even these variables, however, were not something new under the sun, but evolved out of the general cultural and social situation. These wartime variables assumed three general forms, each with its effect upon social problems.

1. *Economic.* In the period from July 1, 1940, to July 1, 1945, the Federal Government spent 323 billions of dollars, largely upon the war and related activities. These expenditures produced virtually full employment, with a minimum low of 630,000 estimated unemployed in October, 1944. These expenditures influenced, directly or indirectly, the following social conditions: individual and national morale; the level of employment and income; the gainful employment of women, children, and adolescents; the rise in the marriage rate; the rise in the birth rate; the decrease in crimes against property; the increase in juvenile delinquency; the increase in offenses against the public morality; and the decline in the number of suicides.

These Federal expenditures and the accompanying boom of the national economy seemingly represented a new situation resulting from World War II. On closer analysis, however, the source of the expenditures emerges as part of a previously established pattern, even if the extent of the expenditures was unprecedented. The spending undertaken by the Federal Government during the depression stimulated business activity by placing a floor under which consumer purchasing power theoretically could not go. These expenditures did not approach in size those made for the prosecution of the war, although many persons expressed alarm lest the national debt become unmanageable when it was less than one-tenth the size of the wartime figure. The purpose of the wartime expenditures was the winning of the war and not the maintenance of employment or increased purchasing power. Some of the effects of this wartime program, however, were similar to those of the depression program. Only in wartime, however, is full employment at high wages considered sufficiently important to warrant adequate Federal expenditures to bring it about.

2. *Psychological.* Co-operative activity toward a common goal is the distinctive feature of high morale. World War II engendered sufficient national sentiment to win the war expeditiously. The principal social grounds co-operated in this effort, whether on the battlefield, in the factory, or in the home. The differential effects of wartime consensus were apparent upon such social situations as the widespread participation in the labor force, the adolescent euphoria toward the war, the decrease in prostitution, the decline in certain crimes against property, the merely nominal increase in neurotic behavior, the comparative stability in the rate of certain functional psychoses, and above all in the decreased number of suicides. Many of these problems were also influenced by economic factors, a situation not inconsistent with the multiple causes of social problems.

In a society which places such a premium upon individualism, the high collective morale

of World War II at first seemed something new. Not since World War I had the nation been mobilized both physically and psychologically in such a supreme effort. The symbols of nationalism have more emotional content during wars than between them. Nevertheless, the psychological mobilization of World War II did not arise full-blown from the great crusade against Fascism. The efforts of the Federal Government during the depression aroused the spirit of national co-operation and individual responsibility. This feeling of participation had a considerable effect upon many social problems through the growing realization that the bell tolled for everyone. National co-operation was not an entirely new phenomenon when the nation entered the perilous decade of the 1940's.

3. *Familial.* The most exceptional effect of World War II upon social problems was the prolonged and extensive separation of families. The total number of broken families during these years is not known exactly, but by April, 1944, the Bureau of Labor Statistics estimated more than 3 million. This figure was later augmented by the induction of married men following the invasion of Europe and the heavy fighting on the continent. Whatever the final figure—whether three and one-half or four million—this situation was unique. Never before were so many American families broken for so long. Many families had been broken during World War I, but for shorter periods and in smaller numbers. Others had been temporarily broken during the depression, as fathers sought work in distant centers. In scope and intensity, however, World War II was the most serious situation the American family ever faced.

The effects of this massive separation were difficult to measure, since they took the form of modifications in family roles. Many effects will not be apparent until the children and adolescents who underwent several years of paternal deprivation have become adults. Many families had developed patterns of reciprocal roles before the war, wherein the relationships between husband and wife and father and children were clearly established. Other families were so recently founded that no such pattern was possible prior to the departure of the husband. Adjustments were necessary, both for the childless wives and those with small children. A considerable segment of the new generation grew up with little initial contact with their fathers.

35

Richard Dalfiume
BEGINNING THE NEGRO REVOLUTION

From Richard Dalfiume, "The Forgotten Years of the Negro Revolution," Journal of American History, *Vol. 55 (June 1968), pp. 90–106.*

Richard Dalfiume (1936–   ) is a young American historian who, after teaching briefly at the University of Wisconsin, Madison, moved to the State University of New York at Binghamton in 1968. His areas of specialization are American politics after World War II and recent Negro history. He has written *Fighting on Two Fronts: Desegregation of the U.S. Armed Forces, 1939–1953* (1969).

The search for a "watershed" in recent Negro history ends at the years that comprised World War II, 1939–1945. James Baldwin has written of this period: "The treatment accorded the Negro during the Second World War marks, for me, a turning point in the Negro's relation to America. To put it briefly, and somewhat too simply, a certain hope died, a certain respect for white Americans faded." Writing during World War II, Gunnar Myrdal pre-

dicted that the war would act as a "stimulant" to Negro protest, and he felt that "There is bound to be a redefinition of the Negro's status in America as a result of this War." The Negro sociologist E. Franklin Frazier states that World War II marked the point where "The Negro was no longer willing to accept discrimination in employment and in housing without protest." Charles E. Silberman writes that the war was a "turning point" in American race relations, in which "the seeds of the protest movements of the 1950s and 1960s were sown." While a few writers have indicated the importance of these years in the recent Negro protest movement, the majority have failed to do so. Overlooking what went before, most recent books on the subject claim that a Negro "revolution" or "revolt" occurred in 1954, 1955, 1960, or 1963. Because of the neglect of the war period, these years of transition in American race relations comprise the "forgotten years" of the Negro revolution.

To understand how the American Negro reacted to World War II, it is necessary to have some idea of the discrimination he faced. The defense build-up begun by the United States in 1940 was welcomed by Negroes who were disproportionately represented among the unemployed. Employment discrimination in the revived industries, however, was rampant. When Negroes sought jobs at aircraft factories where employers begged for workers, they were informed that "the Negro will be considered only as janitors and in other similar capacities. . . ." Government financed training programs to overcome the shortages of skilled workers discriminated against Negro trainees. When government agencies issued orders against such discrimination, they were ignored.

Increasing defense preparations also meant an expansion of the armed forces. Here, as in industry, however, Negroes faced restrictions. Black Americans were assigned a minimal role and rigidly segregated. In the navy, Negroes could enlist only in the all-Negro messman's branch. The marine and the air corps excluded Negroes entirely. In the army, black Americans were prevented from enlisting, except for a few vacancies in the four regular army Negro units that had been created shortly after the Civil War; and the strength of these had been reduced drastically in the 1920s and 1930s.

Although the most important bread-and-butter issue for Negroes in this period was employment discrimination, their position in the armed forces was an important symbol. If one could not participate fully in the defense of his country, he could not lay claim to the rights of a full-fledged citizen. The NAACP organ, the *Crisis*, expressed this idea in its demand for unrestricted participation in the armed forces: "this is no fight merely to wear a uniform. This is a struggle for status, a struggle to take democracy off of parchment and give it life." Herbert Garfinkel, a student of Negro protest during this period, points out that "in many respects, the discriminatory practices against Negroes which characterized the military programs . . . cut deeper into Negro feelings than did employment discrimination."

Added to the rebuffs from industry and the armed services were a hundred others. Negroes, anxious to contribute to the Red Cross blood program, were turned away. Despite the fact that white and Negro blood is the same biologically, it was deemed inadvisable "to collect and mix caucasian and Negro blood indiscriminately." When Negro citizens called upon the governor of Tennessee to appoint some black members to the state's draft boards, he told them: "This is a white man's country. . . . The Negro had nothing to do with the settling of America." At a time when the United States claimed to be the last bulwark of democracy in a war-torn world, the legislature of Mississippi passed a law requiring different textbooks for Negro schools: all references to voting, elections, and democracy were to be excluded from the black student's books.

The Negro's morale at the beginning of World War II is also partly explained by his experience in World War I. Black America had gone into that war with high morale, generated by the belief that the democratic slogans literally meant what they said. Most Negroes succumbed to the "close ranks" strategy announced by the crusading NAACP editor, W. E. B. DuBois, who advocated subduing racial grievances in order to give full support to winning the war. But the image of a new democratic order was smashed by the race riots, lynchings, and continued rigid discrimination. The result was a mass trauma and a series of movements among Negroes in the 1920s which were characterized by a desire to withdraw from a white society which wanted little to do with them. When the war crisis of the 1940s came along, the bitter memories of World War I were recalled with the result that there was a built-in cynicism among Negroes toward the democratic slogans of the new war.

Nevertheless, Negroes were part of the general population being stimulated to come to the defense of democracy in the world. When they responded and attempted to do their share, they were turned away. The result was a widespread feeling of frustration and a general decline of the Negro's morale toward the war effort, as compared with the rest of American society. But paradoxically, the Negro's general morale was both low and high.

While the morale of the Negro, as an American, was low in regard to the war effort, the Negro, as a member of a minority group, had high morale in his heightened race consciousness and determination to fight for a better position in American society. The same slogans which caused the Negro to react cynically also served to emphasize the disparity between the creed and the practice of democracy as far as the Negro in America was concerned. Because of his position in society, the Negro reacted to the war both as an American and as a Negro. Discrimination against him had given rise to "a sickly, negative attitude toward national goals, but at the same time a vibrantly positive attitude toward racial aims and aspirations." . . .

American Negroes took advantage of the war to tie their racial demands to the ideology for which the war was being fought. Before Pearl Harbor, the Negro press frequently pointed out the similarity of American treatment of Negroes and Nazi Germany's treatment of minorities. In 1940, the Chicago *Defender* featured a mock invasion of the United States by Germany in which the Nazis were victorious because a fifth column of southern senators and other racists aided them. Later the *Crisis* printed an editorial which compared the white supremacy doctrine in America to the Nazi plan for Negroes, a comparison which indicated a marked similarity. Even the periodical of the conservative Urban League made such comparisons.

Many Negroes adopted a paradoxical stand on the meaning of the war. At the same time that it was labeled a "white man's war," Negroes often stated that they were bound to benefit from it. For example, [George] Schuyler could argue that the war was not for democracy, but "Peace means . . . a continuation of the status quo . . . which must be ended if the Negro is to get free." And accordingly, the longer the war the better: "Perhaps in the shuffle we who have been on the bottom of the deck for so long will find ourselves at the top."

Cynicism and hope existed side by side in the Negro mind. Cynicism was often the attitude expressed after some outrageous example of discrimination. After Pearl Harbor, however, a mixture of hope and certainty—great

changes favorable to the Negro would result from the war and things would never be the same again—became the dominant attitude. Hope was evident in the growing realization that the war provided the Negro with an excellent opportunity to prick the conscience of white America. "What an opportunity the crisis has been . . . for one to persuade, embarrass, compel and shame our government and our nation . . . into a more enlightened attitude toward a tenth of its people!" the Pittsburgh *Courier* proclaimed. Certainty that a better life would result from the war was based on the belief that revolutionary forces had been released throughout the world. It was no longer a "white man's world," and the "myth of white invincibility" had been shattered for good.

There was a growing protest against the racial status quo by black Americans; this was evidenced by the reevaluation of segregation in all sections of the country. In the North there was self-criticism of past acceptance of certain forms of segregation. Southern Negroes became bolder in openly questioning the sacredness of segregation. In October 1942, a group of southern Negro leaders met in Durham, North Carolina, and issued a statement on race relations. In addition to endorsing the idea that the Negro should fight for democracy at home as well as abroad, these leaders called for complete equality for the Negro in American life. While recognizing the "strength and age" of the South's racial customs, the Durham meeting was "fundamentally opposed to the principle and practice of compulsory segregation in our American society." In addition, there were reports of deep discontent among southern Negro college students and evidence that political activity among the blacks of the South, particularly on the local level, was increasing.

The American Negro, stimulated by the

democratic ideology of the war, was reexamining his position in American society. "It cannot be doubted that the spirit of American Negroes in all classes is different today from what it was a generation ago," Myrdal observed. Part of this new spirit was an increased militancy, a readiness to protest loud and strong against grievances. The crisis gave Negroes more reason and opportunity to protest. Representative of all of the trends of black thought and action—the cynicism, the hope, the heightened race consciousness, the militancy—was the March on Washington Movement (MOWM).

The general idea of exerting mass pressure upon the government to end defense discrimination did not originate with A. Philip Randolph's call for a march on Washington, D.C., in early 1941. Agitation for mass pressure had grown since the failure of a group of Negro leaders to gain any major concessions from President Franklin D. Roosevelt in September 1940. Various organizations, such as the NAACP, the Committee for Participation of Negroes in the National Defense, and the Allied Committees on National Defense, held mass protest meetings around the country in late 1940 and early 1941. The weeks passed and these efforts did not seem to have any appreciable impact on the government; Walter White, Randolph, and other Negro leaders could not even secure an appointment to see the President. "Bitterness grew at an alarming pace throughout the country," White recalled.

It remained, however, for Randolph to consolidate this protest. In January 1941, he wrote an article for the Negro press which pointed out the failure of committees and individuals to achieve action against defense discrimination. "Only power can effect the enforcement and adoption of a given policy," Randolph noted; and "Power is the active principle of only the organized masses, the masses united

for a definite purpose." To focus the weight of the black masses, he suggested that 10,000 Negroes march on Washington, D.C., with the slogan: "We loyal Negro-American citizens demand the right to work and fight for our country."

This march appeal led to the formation of one of the most significant—though today almost forgotten—Negro protest movements. The MOWM pioneered what has become the common denominator of today's Negro revolt —"the spontaneous involvement of large masses of Negroes in a political protest." Furthermore, as August Meier and Elliott Rudwick have recently pointed out, the MOWM clearly foreshadowed "the goals, tactics, and strategy of the mid-twentieth-century civil rights movement." Whites were excluded purposely to make it an all-Negro movement; its main weapon was direct action on the part of the black masses. Furthermore, the MOWM took as its major concern the economic problems of urban slum-dwellers.

Randolph's tactic of mass pressure through a demonstration of black power struck a response among the Negro masses. The number to march on Washington on July 1, 1941, was increased to 50,000, and only Roosevelt's agreement to issue an executive order establishing a President's Committee on Fair Employment Practices led to a cancellation of the march. Negroes then, and scholars later, generally interpreted this as a great victory. But the magnitude of the victory is diminished when one examines the original MOWM demands: an executive order forbidding government contracts to be awarded to a firm which practiced discrimination in hiring, an executive order abolishing discrimination in government defense training courses, an executive order requiring the United States Employment Service to supply workers without regard to race, an executive order abolishing segregation in the armed forces, an executive order abolishing discrimination and segregation on account of race in all departments of the federal government, and a request from the President to Congress to pass a law forbidding benefits of the National Labor Relations Act to unions denying Negroes membership. Regardless of the extent of the success of the MOWM, however, it represented something different in black protest. Unlike the older Negro movements, the MOWM had captured the imagination of the masses.

Although overlooked by most recent writers on civil rights, a mass militancy became characteristic of the American Negro in World War II. This was symbolized by the MOWM and was the reason for its wide appeal. Furthermore, older Negro organizations found themselves pushed into militant stands. For example, the NAACP underwent a tremendous growth in its membership and became representative of the Negro masses for the first time in its history. From 355 branches and a membership of 50,556 in 1940, the NAACP grew to 1,073 branches with a membership of slightly less than 450,000 in 1946. The editors of the Pittsburgh *Courier* recognized that a new spirit was present in black America. In the past, Negroes

> made the mistake of relying entirely upon the gratitude and sense of fair play of the American people. Now we are disillusioned. We have neither faith in promises, nor a high opinion of the integrity of the American people, where race is involved. Experience has taught us that we must rely primarily upon our own efforts. . . . That is why we protest, agitate, and demand that all forms of color prejudice be blotted out. . . .

By the time of the Japanese attack on Pearl Harbor, many in America, both inside and outside of the government, were worried over the state of Negro morale. There was fear that the Negro would be disloyal. The depth of white ignorance about the causes for the Negro's cynicism and low morale is obvious from the fact that the black press was blamed for the widespread discontent. The double victory attitude constantly displayed in Negro newspapers throughout the war, and supported by most black Americans, was considered as verging on disloyalty by most whites. White America, ignorant of the American Negroes' reaction to World War I, thought that black citizens should subdue their grievances for the duration. . . .

By 1942, the federal government began investigating Negro morale in order to find out what could be done to improve it. This project was undertaken by the Office of Facts and Figures and its successor, the Office of War Information. Surveys by these agencies indicated that the great amount of national publicity given the defense program only served to increase the Negro's awareness that he was not participating fully in that program. Black Americans found it increasingly difficult to reconcile their treatment with the announced war aims. Urban Negroes were the most resentful over defense discrimination, particularly against the treatment accorded black members of the armed forces. Never before had Negroes been so united behind a cause: the war had served to focus their attention on their unequal status in American society. Black Americans were almost unanimous in wanting a show of good intention from the federal government that changes would be made in the racial status quo.

The government's inclination to take steps to improve Negro morale, and the Negro's desire for change, were frustrated by the general attitude of white Americans. In 1942, after two years of militant agitation by Negroes, six out of ten white Americans felt that black Americans were satisfied with things the way they were and that Negroes were receiving all of the opportunities they deserved. More than half of all whites interviewed in the Northeast and West believed that there should be separate schools, separate restaurants, and separate neighborhoods for the races. A majority of whites in all parts of the country believed that the Negro would not be treated any better after the war than in 1942 and that the Negro's lesser role in society was due to his own shortcomings rather than anything the whites had done. The white opposition to racial change may have provided the rationale for governmental inactivity. Furthermore, the white obstinance must have added to the bitterness of black Americans.

Although few people recognize it, the war was working a revolution in American race relations. Sociologist Robert E. Park felt that the racial structure of society was "cracking," and the equilibrium reached after the Civil War seemed "to be under attack at a time and under conditions when it is particularly difficult to defend it." Sociologist Howard W. Odum wrote from the South that there was "an unmeasurable and unbridgeable distance between the white South and the reasonable expectation of the Negro." White southerners opposed to change in the racial mores sensed changes occurring among "their" Negroes. "Outsiders" from the North, Mrs. Franklin Roosevelt, and the Roosevelt Administration were all accused of attempting to undermine segregation under the pretense of wartime necessity. . . .

The White House, and it was not alone, failed to respond to the revolutionary changes occurring among the nation's largest minority. When the Fraternal Council of Negro Churches called upon President Roosevelt to end discrimination in the defense industries and armed forces, the position taken was that "it would be very bad to give encouragement beyond the point where actual results can be accomplished." Roosevelt did bestir himself

over particularly outrageous incidents. When Roland Hayes, a noted Negro singer, was beaten and jailed in a Georgia town, the President dashed off a note to his attorney general: "Will you have someone go down and check up . . . and see if any law was violated. I suggest you send a northerner."

Roosevelt was not enthusiastic about major steps in the race relations field proposed by interested individuals within and without the government. In February 1942 Edwin R. Embree of the Julius Rosenwald Fund, acutely aware of the growing crisis in American race relations, urged Roosevelt to create a commission of experts on race relations to advise him on what steps the government should take to improve matters. FDR's answer to this proposal indicates that he felt race relations was one of the reform areas that had to be sacrificed for the present in order to prosecute the war. He thought such a commission was "premature" and that "we must start winning the war . . . before we do much general planning for the future." The President believed that "there is a danger of such long-range planning becoming projects of wide influence in escape from the realities of war. I am not convinced that we can be realists about the war and planners for the future at this critical time."

After the race riots of 1943, numerous proposals for a national committee on race relations were put forward; but FDR refused to change his position. Instead, the President simply appointed Jonathan Daniels to gather information from all government departments on current race tensions and what they were doing to combat them. This suggestion for what would eventually become a President's Committee on Civil Rights would have to wait until a President recognized that a revolution in race relations was occurring and that action by the government could no longer be put off. In the interim, many would share the shallow reasoning of Secretary of War [Henry L.] Stimson that the cause of racial tension was "the deliberate effort . . . on the part of certain radical leaders of the colored race to use the war for obtaining . . . race equality and interracial marriages. . . ."

The hypocrisy and paradox involved in fighting a world war for the four freedoms and against aggression by an enemy preaching a master race ideology, while at the same time upholding racial segregation and white supremacy, were too obvious. The war crisis provided American Negroes with a unique opportunity to point out, for all to see, the difference between the American creed and practice. The democratic ideology and rhetoric with which the war was fought stimulated a sense of hope and certainty in black Americans that the old race structure was destroyed forever. In part, this confidence was also the result of the mass militancy and race consciousness that developed in these years. When the expected white acquiescence in a new racial order did not occur, the ground was prepared for the civil rights revolution of the 1950s and 1960s; the seeds were indeed sown in the World War II years.

36

Committee A, American Association of University Professors
ADAPTING THE COLLEGES AND UNIVERSITIES

From *Report of Committee A for 1943*, "*Academic Freedom and Tenure*," Bulletin of the American Association of University Professors, Vol. 30 (1944), *pp.* 19–20.

As the group responsible for setting standards and investigating violations in the area of academic freedom and tenure, Committee A is the most powerful and prestigious standing committee of the American Association of University Professors

(founded in 1913). It is also, perhaps more than any other, the committee which is most sensitive to and aware of the pressures under which faculties work. For both these reasons, its annual report has been published regularly in the *AAUP Bulletin* for almost half a century.

. . . the generalizations made in the report of last year [1943] still hold. Within the last twelve months hardly a case has raised in any fashion the issue either of pacifism or of subversive expression or action. Our deeper involvement in the war, if the academic world is any barometer, has not yet aroused the unjustified passions and baseless suspicion characteristic of so much campus hysteria twenty-five years ago. On the other hand, a second year of the war has made necessary continued and accelerated adaptation to a diminished civilian student body and to a changed emphasis upon the subjects of the curriculum. Since the Committee's last report, the inauguration of various military programs has greatly stilled the panic over college finances that filled presidents and trustees with a dark despair and professors with apprehension. The government's need for the services of institutions of higher education in connection with the war has had the indirect effect of bolstering the financial position of these institutions very much as banks and other corporate enterprises were bolstered by government action a decade ago. Although, on the present as on the earlier occasion, the benefits have been unequally and sometimes capriciously distributed among institutions in different categories, government largesse has kept many an institution of higher learning as "a college in being" and adjourned "financial exigency" as a justification for wholesale faculty dismissals and educational curtailment.

Such an outcome does not mean that education under contract has no implications for academic tenure. Although such contracts on the whole accept existing salary scales, the negotiators already have established norms for wartime teaching schedules and central officers have prescribed outlines and textbooks. These departures from peacetime procedures are trivial and innocent, perhaps necessary, but the tendency, unless restrained, has disturbing possibilities. Furthermore, the recruitment and training of the staffs required for specialized and prescribed instruction already present questions of peculiar complexity and delicacy. What will be the future tenure status of classics professors who have "retooled themselves"—to resort to the playful vulgarity of the moment—to teach geography, or professors of music who have become, after a month's "refresher course," competent instructors in trigonometry? What will be the tenure status, if the war lasts as long as the habitual probation period, of individuals employed to teach navigation or airplane mechanics to specialized units? A half-lit academic world is in course of creation; to say it will have no repercussions upon the regularized universe of the traditional faculty is nonsense. In the old crafts the importation of outsiders without status was the first step in the destruction of workmanlike standards.

Meanwhile, although income from the government has balanced their budgets, some college administrations still detect a financial exigency sufficiently grave to justify the dismissal of professors whose personalities or performances have long shown they were "not sympathetic with what we are trying to do here." Such individuals—so ran the thought of administrative officers—if they were in disciplines unsubsidized by the military, naturally could not be expected to adjust themselves to the changed circumstances of some other field of instruction; they had already demonstrated they were "unadaptable." If such individuals volunteered to solve the institution's financial dilemma by enlisting in the armed forces or by

seeking employment in some civilian agency and requested leave of absence without pay but with assurance of reengagement, the college wished them God-speed in their patriotic services but could make no commitment in view of the later uncertainties. To conquer a budgetary deficiency of $20,000 by the discharge of a $3,000 professor is hardly evidence of an urgent financial exigency or of the wisdom of measures taken to meet it. The detection of such subterfuges has taken far too much of the Committee's time. In war as in peace, approved academic practice insists that dismissals be made for genuine reasons and follow recognized procedures designed to secure the observance of due process.

37

Isaac L. Kandel
THE CHALLENGE TO EDUCATION

The Impact of War upon American Education (*Chapel Hill: University of North Carolina Press, 1948*).

Isaac L. Kandel (1881–1965) was a Rumanian-born educator who taught at Teachers' College, Columbia University, from 1913 to 1947, and who, from the latter year until his death, served as editor of *School and Society*. His publications include *Comparative Education* (1933), *The Impact of the War upon American Education* (1948), *The New Era in Education* (1955), and *American Education in the Twentieth Century* (1957).

The educational system of the United States was submitted during the war to a nation-wide survey which was far more searching than any deliberately organized survey could have been. World War I had affected higher education only; World War II revealed that no part of the educational system could remain unaffected. The situation was well described in the keynote statement by Paul V. McNutt when he wrote in the first issue of *Education for Victory*, March 3, 1942, that in the days of total war education had a new significance and that "You're in the Army now" was an expression of national necessity.

To this challenge the educational system, with little or no preparation, quickly responded. The speed with which the challenge was met illustrated the flexibility of the educational system and its adaptability to new demands. There was thus illustrated an important aspect of American education. Without waiting for a lead from a government agency, leadership was assumed by state and local administrations and by voluntary agencies—the National Education Association and its Educational Policies Commission for elementary and secondary education, and the American Council on Education for higher education, both of which had already begun to prepare the educational profession against the threat of war through their publications on national defense. In the field of higher education the American Council on Education had in fact prepared plans for the fullest use of colleges and universities in the event of war for some time before the official agencies—the War Department and the Navy Department—reached a decision on the question. Except in higher education the system of education was not seriously dislocated.

The war revealed the strong and the weak points of the educational system. Its general organization was not open to criticism. It responded readily to the new demands placed upon it. The average level of education had been raised by at least two years since World War I. The graduates of colleges and universities proved to be excellent material for appointment or training for the commissioned ranks in the armed forces as well as in manifold civilian activities connected with the successful conduct of the war. Through federal grants provision for the training of personnel for the trade and technological needs of the war effort was quickly organized and successfully developed. And, finally, the teaching profession enlisted voluntarily in a great variety of activities demanded in the war effort.

The ideals and aims of the educational system were proved to be sound. The war revealed a number of weaknesses, however, which indicated that in practice these aims and ideals were not being achieved. The two most serious defects, the existence of which had been known before the war, were, first, the high percentage of men who had to be rejected by the Selective Service System on account of mental and physical deficiencies, and, second, the unsatisfactory status of the teaching profession. Despite the increasing expenditure on education illiteracy had not been eliminated, while the numbers rejected because of physical deficiencies pointed to the inadequate attention paid to health and physical development in the schools and by society in general. The large numbers of teachers who left the profession for better paid employment in war and other industries indicated that the American public was not willing to pay salaries commensurate with its professed faith in education and that conditions of service were not as satisfactory as they might be.

These defects were not always due to the inadequacy of local resources for the maintenance of satisfactory systems of education. In the main, however, they did confirm the fact, already known, that the amount and quality of education could not be improved except by the establishment of adequate minimum national standards, by pooling the resources of the nation, and by the provision of federal aid for education. If any further arguments to support those accumulated since the movement for federal aid began during World War I, they were provided by the objective data revealed during World War II. The fear that an increase of federal funds for education would lead to federal control was allayed during the war years. Federal appropriations were increased for various educational activities during this period but there is no evidence that undue control followed. It became clearer than ever before, as a result of the conditions of education revealed during the war, that the ideal of equality of educational opportunity could only be achieved by the provision of federal funds to remove the inequalities due to accident of residence.

Other shortages were also revealed which reflected on the quality of education. It was found that the supply of personnel with suitable preparation in mathematics, science, and foreign languages was inadequate despite the large enrollment of students in schools, colleges, and universities. The lack of qualified personnel in foreign languages, both the usual and the unusual, was met by the adoption of new methods of instruction, whose value for normal times is still a matter of experimentation. The fact, however, is inescapable that more attention has been devoted to increasing the numbers of students in secondary and higher education than to maintaining adequate standards of quality of achievement.

The future of secondary and higher education received consideration during the war years, but the deliberations had already begun before the war. In secondary education the basic problem was how to meet the varied needs of American youth, the majority of whom were enrolled in high schools. Whether a satisfactory solution can be found in a common program, such as that proposed in the report of the Educational Policies Commission on *Education for All American Youth* without giving adequate attention to those who can profit by an academic attention, will probably continue

to be debatable. At the level of college education, proposals for reform, which had been begun before the war and on which an extensive literature was accumulated during the war, have already been adopted by many colleges. The chief point of attack was the system of electives which led to a demand for general education based on three major areas of study —humanities, social sciences, and natural sciences.

The position of leadership of the United States in international affairs has resulted in the introduction of new areas of instruction in colleges and universities. Courses in international affairs have been introduced; courses in hitherto neglected areas, such as Soviet Russia and the Orient, have been multiplied; not only have new foreign languages been added but a new emphasis has been introduced with more attention given to the social, economic, and political backgrounds than has been the case in the past. Following the new interest in regional or area studies, courses have been organized in American culture or American civilization. The spectacular contributions and advances in science during the war stirred the imagination of the American public and students to such a degree as to lead to some alarm lest this area of study be emphasized at the expense of other areas. The proposed creation of a National Science Foundation with federal support included in its plans the provision of subsidies for students who show talent in the sciences.

Another effect of the international position of the United States has been the official recognition of the importance of international cultural relations as a concern of the government. It is recognized, however, that in this movement voluntary organizations, which have in the past played an important role in promoting international cultural relations, must not be superseded by a government agency, but must be encouraged to continue their activities. The interest of foreign educators and students in American education increased rapidly in the years between the two wars. That this interest will continue is manifested by the large number of foreign students who have come to study in this country on grants from their own government or from American foundations and institutions of higher education, or at their own expense. The use of lend-lease funds for educational purposes under the Fulbright Act will increase the flow of students to and from the United States. Finally, in the field of international cultural relations American educators and laymen played a leading role in promoting the establishment of the United Nations Educational, Scientific and Cultural Organization (UNESCO) with which close relations will be maintained through the National Commission for UNESCO.

World War I was followed by the beginning of a rapid increase in the enrollment of students in high schools. A similar increase has followed World War II at the college and university level as a result of the Servicemen's Readjustment Act (Public Law 346) or the G.I. Bill of Rights. It is expected that the enrollments in institutions of higher education will in all probability become stabilized at three million students, about double the prewar enrollment. The G.I. Bill of Rights indicated that large numbers of young men and women have been enabled to attend colleges and universities, who, because of lack of means, would have been unable to do so. Here again the war has shown that equality of educational opportunity can only be realized, if the inequalities resulting from accident of residence and family circumstances are overcome by the extensive provision of grants from public funds.

Many Japanese-Americans actually intensified their patriotism despite internment in relocation camps like this center in Wyoming. Here on a sub-zero morning in 1943, led by a Boy Scout drum and bugle corp, a group of Nisei raise their arms in the traditional American salute to the flag.　　(Hansel Meith; *Life Magazine* © Time Inc.)

This 1942 poster of the Office of War Information indicates the extent to which World War II had made Americans conscious of the fact that ideas can be manipulated. (National Archives)

Chapter Eight

THE EFFECTS OF THE WAR ON THOUGHT AND CULTURE

The authors in this section tend to agree that the Second World War served to reinforce rather than to alter the pragmatic and optimistic side of the American character. Merle Curti, for instance, emphasizes that our participation in the conflict helped to generate a spirit of nationalism which not only pulled the country together but also dulled the "critical attitude toward American life and values which had marked the 1920's and the 1930's." His views would seem to be corroborated by both John Aldridge and Chester Eisinger, who attest in separate pieces that, even for writers, the war brought little to discover and little to rebel against. In the churches, too, Ray H. Abrams contends, there was a vast difference from 1917–1918, with much less high-flown idealism and with both clergy and congregations tending to remain relatively calm, practical, and hopeful about the future. Only on the level of theology, according to George H. Thomas, did the more disturbing aspects of the situation attract much attention, provoking leading thinkers to attempt to merge continental neo-orthodoxy and American religious liberalism into a more "realistic" view of man.

157

QUESTIONS:

1. Why did the Second World War generate apparently so little self-doubt and self-questioning among Americans?

2. Were Americans more, or less nationalistic in World War II than in World War I? Why?

3. John Aldridge explains the literary situation after the war by saying that "the illusions and causes of war, having once been lost, cannot be re-lost." But were Americans really without illusions about war?

4. According to Ray H. Abrams, there was a greater tolerance of diverse opinions in the Second World War than in the First. Do you believe this to be true, or was it simply that there was a greater consensus in 1941–1945?

5. Would you say that by the end of World War II the trends in American theology were running counter to or in the same direction as the tendencies of the nation at large?

38

Merle Curti
MILITANT NATIONALISM

From pp. 730–734 in The Growth of American Thought, *third ed., by Merle Curti. Copyright 1943, 1951 by Harper and Row, Publishers, Inc. Copyright © 1964 by Merle Curti. Reprinted by permission of Harper & Row, Publishers.*

Merle Curti (1897–   ), one of the deans of American intellectual history, has taught at the University of Wisconsin, Madison, since 1942. Especially known for his Pulitzer Prize-winning work, *The Growth of American Thought* (1943), he has written many other books, including *The American Peace Crusade* (1929), *Peace or War: The American Struggle 1636–1936* (1936), and *The Roots of American Loyalty* (1946).

In the intellectual sphere, as in every other, the years between Pearl Harbor and the sharpening of conflict with the Soviet Union in 1947–1948 were dominated by World War II. Interna-

tionalism seemed to be the theme and to infuse the purposes of that war. "One world" was a slogan heard almost everywhere. And after the fighting stopped, the United States was committed to the manifold international activities of the United Nations and of the administrators of the Marshall Plan, as well as to its own cultural relations programs.

But these activities, whatever their implications for international cooperation, carried strong overtones of nationalism. This was clear, not only in the conquered countries where military government was established, but elsewhere as well. In fact, American policies overseas were reflections of a determined effort to encourage political and economic systems—and loyalties—congenial to the American faith. Nationalism as an active force became dominant in the United States, and indeed throughout the world.

This militant nationalism was supported by the articulate at all levels—by the men on the street and in the country store, by city and rural editors, by magazine writers, preachers, and poets, by college professors and scientists, by officials and diplomats. There was not much analysis of the concept of nationalism itself, except by a few intellectuals. But the renewed vigor and influence of the idea were clear, even though largely implicit and to be inferred from attitudes taken and policies advocated.

Besides this overarching concept of the war decade, other more or less related concepts and doctrines were involved in, and were in various ways affected by, the war. The meanings of individualism, communism, humanism, progress, and democracy were pondered. Esthetic and religious doctrines received new emphases, as did the nature of man and of the universe itself. In the first half of the 1940s the war seemed to give at least a surface unity to almost every aspect of intellectual life.

The resurgence of militant nationalism explains, at least in part, the official nature of much of the intellectual life of the time. The role and weight of government was seen in directed propaganda and information, in the intercultural relations programs, the national monopoly of atomic power, and the federal subsidies to scientific investigation. It was seen in the influence of the military on research and on educational programs and personnel. Official views were reflected in the group reports on schools, universities, the press, and civil liberties. The individual wellsprings of intellectual endeavor and expression did not dry up, as the names of [Reinhold] Niebuhr, [T. S.] Eliot, [Charles A.] Beard, [Robert M.] Hutchins, [David] Lilienthal, [James B.] Conant, and [Albert] Einstein testify. But individual leadership in intellectual life tended to retreat before an expanding officialdom and the mass media of communication. Individual expression became increasingly sensitive to government policy, at least in the discussion of foreign relations. Here, where criticism appeared at all, it was likely to be interpreted as communistic, however far from communist belief the critics might be. In this situation may be found a leading feature of the intellectual history of the later years of the decade and of much of the 1950s—the retreat of the critical attitude toward American life and values which had marked the 1920s and the 1930s. Thus the official aspects of intellectual life take an important place in any survey of the war years and of those that immediately followed.

It seems fair to say that no war had been fought with as much unanimity as World War II. Most of those who, as isolationists or pacifists, had opposed entering the war quietly accepted the situation, whatever their reservations may have been. There were, to be sure, conscientious objectors, officially more than 9000 of them, with an undetermined number who were not put in a position to declare themselves publicly. Of the 9000, some 4000 chose to contribute to the larger ends of society by toiling at peacetime tasks in the civilian camps set up for that purpose. Approximately 5000 refused to register or accept any sort of alternative to military service. Two-thirds of these were Jehovah's Witnesses. Many of them went to prison.

But American patriotism on the whole stood up well under pressure. Only a very small number of Americans could be labeled traitors. In the summer of 1943 a federal court indicted eight persons on the charge of broadcasting for the enemy. The group included Ezra Pound, distinguished innovator of strange stanza forms, who, a rootless expatriate in foreign lands, had long denounced what he called the "degeneracy" of democracy. Subsequently other men and women were indicted, but the number was small. In short, the American public accepted the imperatives of the war effort. To say this is not to say, of course, that business, labor, and ordinary individuals did not often put their own interest above that of country. American patriotism, unlike that of the totalitarian enemies, was undisciplined, something more or less apart from day-by-day life, somewhat sentimental. But it met the test of adversity.

The lack of a clear general understanding of the larger meaning of the struggle did not make this the less true. The Atlantic Charter, for all its idealism, was after all vague, more vague than Wilson's Fourteen Points; the doctrine of unconditional surrender was negative, not positive. There was among the rank and file a wholesome absence of romanticism—to them the war was a job to be done, not a shining crusade. Few faced the underlying issues squarely. Nor was a penetrating light shed on the ideology of the war by business advertisements in the press and on the radio, which implied that the country was fighting in order to get back to bigger and better bathtubs, radios, and automobiles. It was enough for most to understand that America had been attacked, that it was necessary to fight back.

There was still less flag-waving or sentimentalism about patriotic duty within the ranks of the fighting men. Much evidence—personal testimony, letters, and the results of questionnaires—suggests that the great majority neither gave much thought to the larger social and political problems nor basically changed their pre-Army pattern of thought. To be sure, the new environment wrought certain changes. But there was little broadly based patriotic understanding of the larger meaning of the struggle. While the War Department's Information and Education Department dramatized the war for the Four Freedoms, the average fighting man reconciled himself to performing the undesirable but obviously necessary job of overpowering the enemy. Some critics insisted that the timidity of the War and Navy Departments in neutralizing the teaching materials used during training and the failure generally to adopt the British practice of free give-and-take discussion of the issues of the war and the peace, accounted for this state of affairs. But it is possible that the soldier's lack of perspective and his failure to take seriously the official thesis of the nature and objectives of the war reflected rather the fact that "the country had never made up its mind about its relationships to other peoples, but had merely essayed the impossible feat of being in the world but not of it."[1] The indictment by Karl Shapiro, the best-known war poet, was hardly true of the average GI:

He hated other races, south or east,
And shoved them to the margin of his mind.
To him the red flag marked the sewer main.

[1] David L. Cohn, "Should Fighting Men Think?" *Saturday Review of Literature*, XXX (January 18, 1947), 7.

Rather, the GI, like other citizens, tended to ignore, or to hold in mild contempt, peoples other than his own.

Neither the popular war cartoons by Bill Mauldin nor the novels written by veterans cast the conflict in heroic mold. The Mauldin cartoons with good-natured edge featured the prevailing distaste for the big brass, the military routine and protocol, and what appeared to be the senselessness of much that took place. In fiction the war of waiting was best captured in Thomas Heggen's *Mister Roberts*. To some critics it seemed that in many of the novels, dealing as they did with whole divisions and armies, the individual, seldom a hero, was lost in vast, impersonal organization. Norman Mailer's *The Naked and the Dead* labored the thesis that the war merely revealed the worst that was in men in their earlier civilian life. In *From Here to Eternity* James Jones dramatized the problems of a man whose violence was needed by society but who was penalized by the Army when his violence, enmeshed in powerful and chaotic feelings, got him into trouble. The slogan, "One war is enough," made sense to fighting men who spoke or wrote of the war and its dull aftermath in the armies of occupation, an aftermath marked by loneliness, thirst for sex and adventure, and indulgence in black-marketeering. Sometimes the message that one war was enough was phrased in the brutal idiom of Mailer. On other occasions it was reflected in the sensitive stories of Irwin Shaw, or in Major Joppolo's moving struggle to maintain the dignity of man in John Hersey's *A Bell for Adano*. All this helps explain why, once the fighting stopped, the most articulate ex-fighters worked, not as professional veterans, but as civilians. At least some were consciously intent upon building an America in which all might enjoy jobs, freedom, and peace, and where there would be no lost generation.

39

John Aldridge
WRITERS WITHOUT MOTIVATION

From John Aldridge, After the Lost Generation *(New York: McGraw-Hill, 1951), pp. xi–xii, 87–89.*

John W. Aldridge (1922–   ), a literary scholar and novelist, has held teaching positions at the University of Vermont, Sarah Lawrence College, Queens College, New York University, and the University of Michigan. His specialty is American and British literature since 1900, and his works include *After the Lost Generation* (1951), *In Search of Heresy* (1956), *The Party at Cranton* (a novel, 1960), and *Time to Murder and Create* (1966).

. . . The excitement of war was everywhere; and it gave a special brightness and clarity to all that we saw, did, and thought. We were all about nineteen and beginning our second year of college; and looking back, it seems to me that we were very much like the young men Vance Bourjaily writes about in *The End of My Life* with perhaps a touch of the Stephen Dedalus of [James] Joyce's *Stephen Hero* and of Buck Mulligan in *Ulysses*. I remember that there was nothing quite like the taste of the black coffee we drank in the late nights and early mornings of that time, or the green of the trees in the summers, particularly when we had gone for days without sleep, or the sadness of the leaves blowing over the streets in the falls, particularly when we had been reading Thomas Wolfe, which was most of the time, or the parties we went to where we learned to drink and make love, or the poems and stories we wrote that were full of such sincerity and hope. It seemed to us—at least the assumption was implicit in everything we said and did— that we were coming of age in an era of singular crisis and upheaval. The natural excitement of

awakening to life, the normal college experience, was reinforced and heightened by our impending participation in a great world war. The books that were going to be written after that war, the books that we would help to write, would be more magnificent and wise than any ever written in the past. We had read a great deal about the Lost Generation: we could quote pages of [Malcolm] Cowley's *Exile's Return*; we knew [Ernest] Hemingway, [John] Dos Passos, [F. Scott] Fitzgerald, [T. S.] Eliot, [Gertrude] Stein, and Joyce even better than we knew one another; and we were sure that our age would be like theirs—a time of discovery, transition, and revolt. It was not merely that we had the sense of youth, although we had that in abundance. We had as well a genuine sense of inevitability and of new energy getting set to explode.

When my friends and I left college and went to war, we carried with us this feeling about tomorrow; and when we came back from the war we found we had preserved it almost intact. But it was not long before we began to realize that somewhere along the way tomorrow had been lost. Not only had the new age not arrived but there seemed little likelihood that it was going to; and we concluded, not without some bitterness, that we had been keeping alive and making love to an illusion.

During the years that followed, we tried over and over again to discover exactly what had happened. In the letters we wrote to one another and in the conversations we had together, we thought of countless possibilities but never arrived at a final answer. We always had too many emotional associations whenever we tried to reconstruct the past and our memories began playing tricks, so that after a while we couldn't be sure if something had really happened, if that was the way we had really felt, or if we had only read about it somewhere. Finally I think most of us decided we had been partly deluded and partly right, that what we had sensed was true at the time but was no longer true, and that the healthiest thing to do was forget about it.

. . . In the years since Hemingway, Dos Passos, and Fitzgerald began to write, the forces that gave impetus to their development—particularly the forces of disillusionment and denial released by the broken promises of the first war—have declined. The young novelists of the present generation are consequently deprived of that impetus at the same time that their own age and experience offer them nothing comparable. They have come through a war even more profoundly disturbing than the first; but the illusions and causes of war, having once been lost, cannot be relost. Their world, ironically enough, is almost the same world their predecessors discovered; but the fundamental discoveries of modern life can be made but once. America is more than ever a machine-dominated, gadget-minded country. There are more Babbitts now than when Sinclair Lewis invented the term and the expatriates shouted it in their battle cry for freedom, art, and exile. But who cares today to take up that cry, to denounce again with the same fury, or to escape forever into artistic exile?

One aspect of the problem is reflected in the technical differences between the writings of the two wars. Where Hemingway, Dos Passos, and E. E. Cummings (in *The Enormous Room*) were from the beginning innovators of new methods—even of a whole new literary language—with which to present the new experience of war, the new war novelists seem, for the most part, incapable of technical discoveries and resigned to working within the tradition handed down to them from the Twenties. One explanation is that the experience of war is no longer new and, consequently, does not require a new method of presentation. An-

other is that the Lost Generation writers were engaged in a revolution designed to purge language of the old restraints of the previous century and to fit it to the demands of a younger, more realistic time. Idiosyncrasy and defiance were part of their work because the things that had happened to them had happened to no generation before them, and because they were aware of their uniqueness and determined to communicate it to the world.

Today that revolution is over. The innovations of Hemingway, as he himself remarked, were "a certain clarification of the language" and are now "in the public domain." The unique has become the ordinary; young writers using the effects of their predecessors are often not even aware that those effects did not belong to our literature until years after many of them were born. The assimilation into the public domain has, in fact, been so complete that what we have now seems a technical conservatism. Certainly the styles of Vance Bourjaily, Norman Mailer, John Horne Burns, Irwin Shaw, Robert Lawry, Alfred Hayes, Merle Miller, Gore Vidal, Truman Capote, Paul Bowles, and Frederick Beuchner—while they contain overtones of practically everyone from Dos Passos and Hemingway to James T. Farrell and Henry James—show little evidence of new developments and, with the exception of Capote's, Burns's, and Beuchner's, do little to flavor the material they present.

But there has been this change: the single perspective and narrow scope of the World War I novels have given way to huge comprehensiveness in which whole armies and social masses are encompassed. From the individual, neoromantic hero we have progressed to the multiple-hero or, more correctly, to the subordination of all heroes to the group. Mailer carries an entire army division—from general down to private—through a complex military engagement and then goes back to the beginnings of his characters and sketches them against the background of peace. Burns and Shaw take even more characters through action on three or four continents and months of closely packed experience; and all three manage to pay careful attention to detail and to give the actual texture of the background or event described.

This would be achievement indeed if it did not come so often at the expense of insight, form, and power. Taken as a group or singly, the novels of this war simply do not have the impact that those of the first war had—nor, for that matter, do the novels that have been written so far about the aftermath. They are incomparably better written, to be sure. Almost any one of them will show fewer lapses and roughnesses than can be found in the best of the earlier group—*A Farewell to Arms, Three Soldiers, The Enormous Room.* But it is as if they had been written too easily and their authors had had too painless an apprenticeship. Their finish is more often that of a machine-made, prefabricated product than of a finely wrought piece of craftsmanship, the sort that can be obtained if more problems are avoided than are met and overcome.

40

Chester Eisinger
A FAILURE OF IMAGINATION

From pp. 22–26 of Chester Eisinger, Fiction in the Forties, *published by the University of Chicago Press. Copyright © 1963 by the University of Chicago. All rights reserved.*

Chester Eisinger (1915–   ) has taught American literature at Purdue University since 1953. His areas of expertise include seventeenth- and eighteenth-century writing, Nathaniel Hawthorne, and the contemporary novel. In addition to *Fic-* *tion in the Forties,* he has published a section for the anthology *Proletarian Writers of the Thirties* (1968) entitled "Character and Self in Fiction on the Left."

The postwar generation of [Ernest] Hemingway, [John] Dos Passos, and [E. E.] Cummings [had] brought the literature of disenchantment to a very high level. Out of the interaction between the chemistry of their genius and the war [had come] the impressive books that launched their careers. And it was their success that became the curse of the postwar generation of writers in the forties. Critics waited breathlessly but not quietly for the young artists to cast off their uniforms and take up their magic pens, assuming by some quaint analogy to physical laws that the same cause, war, will produce the same results, first-rate novels about the war, written in the same way. These critics suffered from a kind of cultivated blindness: in their orientation toward the twenties, they had prepared themselves for a literature about the war like the literature of the first war. Many young artists, not knowing any better, disregarded their own chemistry and refused to examine the truth of their experience through their own eyes. They tried, instead, to answer to the expectations of the critics. Or if not that, they tried quite self-consciously to see their war as an earlier one had been seen twenty-five years before. This expectation on the part of the literary world and this imitation on the part of the young writers did much to rob the war novel in the forties of originality and freshness of vision and technique.

Hemingway redivivus in the war novels proved to be Hemingway half-baked and half-dead. The trauma of violence and horror in war which he knew, others had come to know. This was a constant in the war experience. But significant differences between Hemingway's time and the forties are easy to find. The twenties emerged from the innocent idealism of Progressivism and the Wilsonian new freedom, from the public avowal of public acts based on principle, to a reality quite suddenly and shockingly different in its unprincipled chaos. Ideals and principles so recently found to be inadequate and inapplicable nevertheless lingered in the consciousness of the writer of the lost generation and gave to his sense of disenchantment the force and pain of a real and anguished loss. The forties was heir to the disillusionments not only of the first war but of the depression and the second war. Innocence thrice violated makes only a spurious protest when it finds the world wicked. The recorded disillusionment of the war novelists in the forties, accordingly, was robbed of much of its strength.

Before the peace of Versailles, [Malcolm] Cowley's young men had gone to war with a sense of high excitement and Hemingway's young men with the military virtues that are much the same as the elements of the code. But writers of the later generation did not share in this kind of excitement and did not admire war virtues. Times had changed. No one expected, or wanted to be embarrassed by, moral heroics. In fact, it was said that America did not provide the moral resources to withstand, as one of the risks of war, the terrors of captivity. Survival, not the thought of danger and death, was what preoccupied young Americans. In war we saw the triumph of those civilian virtues Cowley had spoken of.

Americans have always resented the discipline of the armed forces, the special privileges of officers, the interference with one's freedom of movement. It was true of both wartime periods that Americans, as Denis Brogan wrote, were not merely not military; they were antimilitary. In the first war there was still some response to the romantic conception of war

and the warrior, if not to a military conception. The retreat from romance may be measured in the difference between the recruiting picture of the jaunty doughboy in the first instance and Bill Mauldin's wearily cynical and lugubrious cartoon characters in the second. A drab pall covers the general attitude of Americans toward the second war. An analysis of servicemen's attitudes, *Studies in Social Psychology in World War II*, shows that most men looked upon the war as a defensive or national necessity. It was a detour without context in the national life. It was a forced disturbance of the normal patterns of personal life. Most men failed to achieve a satisfactory relationship with the military organization or a reasonable understanding of their own role in the nation's war aims. They made no personal commitment to the war. It is not surprising to find that most men were not eager for combat. They wanted jobs in the military organization that would not expose them to injury or death. During basic training the men recognized the necessity for learning two kinds of behavior: expedient, or that which pleased their superiors, regardless of the rules; and proper, or that which was acceptable to their fellows. In discussing their officers, enlisted men were less critical of incompetence than they were of special privileges enjoyed by that group. At the end of the war, three-fourths of the enlisted men questioned agreed that most officers had been more concerned with promotion than with doing a good job. Promotion, the prevailing opinion had it, was primarily but not exclusively dependent on what the men delicately called brown-nosing. Most men, it may be concluded, made a cynical and uneasy adaptation to their military environment and regarded their military careers as a suspension of real life activities. If the war novelist did not actually share in these attitudes of the majority, he did live among them or observe them in some way. They were a part of the climate of his sensibility.

Another difference between the two generations is found in the changing nature of war itself. The trench warfare of 1917 was very different from the blitzkrieg tactics of the second war. By using war as an instrument of policy, as Quincy Wright observes in his *A Study of War,* the totalitarian states in the forties had forced the other nations into a more complete organization than ever before of their resources, economy, channels of opinion, and government structure for the purpose of fighting a war. Totalitarian states had succeeded in imposing their own policies and practices upon the others. The doctrine of total war was the result, accepted by fascism and the democracies to an unparalleled extent. Wright quotes Hans Speier and Alfred Kahler: "War always concentrates and reveals the potential forces of collective life as they are embodied in the given social organization." The preparation for war, they say, necessitates disastrous sacrifices of human values. Add to all this the vast geographical scope of the second war and the overwhelming technological complexity of arms and armaments, of organization, none of which had been matched in the earlier conflict. It is clear that war becomes less comprehensible than ever before: it defies the single intelligence that would embrace and order it. Before it, the writer's imagination understandably quails. The writer sees that the individual has to struggle constantly against the impersonality of his military organization and the meaninglessness of his activity. The war and the military take their proper place as prime forces working toward the depersonalization of modern man.

In the light of these encouragements to silence and the sweet sleep of the tongueless singer, what did the writer do? He wrote, and produced, paradoxically, a large body of work

about the war, as I have said, of reasonably high competence. No other war in American history has been so fully recorded in fiction, from a purely quantitative point of view. And writers covered all aspects of the war on all fronts: combat in the army, the navy, the air force; the activities of service and headquarters troops; the problems of command; the period of training in boot camp or air base; the merchant marine during the war; the liberation and the aftermath of the war in Europe; the problems of the home front in America. The generic use of the term war novel applies to books dealing with any of these subjects.

And when the writer wrote, how did he write? Some writers imitated Hemingway. It has been claimed that Hemingway perfected the language of war, that his style and his manner were peculiarly appropriate to combat, and writers naturally fell back on the remembered rhythms of his language, which had given them, possibly, their first idea of war. Those who imitated Hemingway—Vance Bourjaily, Gore Vidal, Robert Lowry are among them— did not often penetrate beyond the manner. They did not try to record combat as the real thing experienced by one who was there; or when, infrequently, they did try, they did not succeed. They did not seek in writing about the war to purge themselves of the war's effects, as perhaps Hemingway did, if we accept Philip Young's conjecture. They did not, like Hemingway and [Stephen] Crane, too, in *The Red Badge of Courage,* find themselves obsessed with the conquest of fear, and so feel compelled to render the experience of war with vivid accuracy as a meaningful gesture in their own lives. Other writers, like Norman Mailer and James Jones, drew upon the naturalistic tradition in American letters. I am speaking now not of the philosophy of naturalism but of the style. Some of these books showed a cultivated and deliberate contempt for the resources of language, and others appear to have been badly written out of sheer inability to do any better. In general the prose contribution of the war novel, like its originality in all formal matters, was minimal.

41

Ray H. Abrams
THE ADJUSTMENT OF THE CHURCH

From Ray H. Abrams "The Churches and the Clergy in World War II," Annals of the American Academy of Political and Social Science, Vol. 256 (March 1948), pp. 114–118.

Ray H. Abrams (1896–   ), now emeritus professor of sociology at the University of Pennsylvania, taught at that institution in an active capacity from 1930 until 1967. In his sociological work he has concentrated his attention on religious customs and on marriage and the family. Among his publications are *Preachers Present Arms* (1933) and *Organized Religion in the United States* (1948).

Up to December 7, 1941, then, the forces of organized religion were divided into several camps ranging all the way from the absolute pacifists to the interventionists who wanted us to declare war at once. . . .

The complete surprise of the Japanese attack on Pearl Harbor settled, for the time being at least, many of the finespun theological and philosophical arguments that had been going on for over two years. War was no longer a possibility. It was a reality.

Correspondence with nearly all the editors of the leading Protestant and Catholic religious periodicals reveals that they accepted the war as a fact and did not attempt to hinder the all-out war effort. Most of these journals seem to have supported our Government, and some

quite actively. A few stood idly by and watched the process of events. . . .

The editors of the *Christian Century*, while not absolute pacifists, nevertheless had so consistently decried all preparation for war that for them Pearl Harbor must have been a terrible psychological blow. In the first editorial written after the fatal December 7, entitled "An Unnecessary Necessity," we read:

> Our Government has taken a stand. It is our Government. It spoke for us as the voice of national solidarity. It is *our* voice. The President is *our* President, all his official acts, even those which we disapprove are our acts. . . .
>
> We stand with our country, we cannot do otherwise. We see no alternative which does not involve national self-stultification. Our country is at war. Its life is at stake. . . .

In a later, more detailed analysis the editor stated that the war was "the judgment of God" and "the terrible fruit of disobedience." Said he:

> It is our necessity, an unnecessary necessity, therefore a guilty necessity. . . . Our fighting, though necessary, is not righteous. God does not command us to fight. His condemnation, written with our own hands, is that we must slay our human brothers and be slain by them. This condemnation, we now affirm, is hell.

The shifting policies of the paper and the above type of reasoning did not appeal to a great many of the brethren. Pacifists did not like it, interventionists ridiculed it. The collected editorials of Dr. [Charles] Morrison were reviewed by Reinhold Niebuhr with what the editors of *Fortune* called "scornful rigor." The editor of the *Christian Leader* commented on the *Christian Century*:

> The erratic editorial policy of that paper, first isolationist and then would-be isolationist, first pacifist and then "wants to be pacifist,"

first against the Government and then for the Government but pulling back on the halter, has destroyed much of its influence.

Considerable attention has been devoted to the *Christian Century* and the opposition to it because nothing portrays so clearly the controversy that raged through Protestantism during those war years. Some day, perhaps, a psychoanalyst will write up the underlying processes at work and there will be laid bare the struggles of religious souls as they grappled with the problem of war. From the institutional point of view, the rationalizations that were resorted to in order to make war more acceptable are worthy of far more space than is herein provided.

One example of this is with respect to the use of the phrase "holy war." In 1917–18 the struggle had frequently been referred to as "the most holy war of all the ages." However, with the events that had intervened between the two wars, the phrase had fallen into thorough disrepute. Karl Barth, the distinguished Swiss theologian, had shocked a great many of the faithful when, addressing the Christians of Great Britain, he declared [that] the war "is a righteous war which God commands us to wage ardently."

The Archbishop of York, Dr. William Temple, solved the theological dilemma by stating: "We are fighting for Christian civilization. I cannot use the phrase 'holy war,' for war in its own nature is always an expression of the sin of man. But without hesitation I speak of this as, for us, a righteous war." . . .

After the United States entered the war as an active belligerent the following major trends seem to be significant as far as the churches are concerned.

When compared with 1917–18, the population in World War II took the conflict and the horrors of war more in its stride. Twenty-four years before, there had been a great deal of hysteria. This time, while there was plenty of denunciation of the "Japs" and of Hitler *et al.*, far less real excitement prevailed. One heard and saw less of the wild-eyed patriot. The clergy in their utterances reflected the same differences. A few bellicose warmongers, yes, but they were not outstanding, certainly. In general, the clergy were calm about the struggle, and, in fact, in their sermons seem to have paid relatively less attention to the current problems of the war than one might have supposed. The generalization is based on data gathered from all over the United States. The war was a grim necessity—something to be gotten over as soon as possible.

Again, a greater toleration of diverse opinions was demonstrated. The Jehovah's Witnesses fared badly, it is true. Yet, the record of civil liberties appears better this time than for the previous war. The churches regarded the pacifist or near-pacifist clergymen with more urbanity than in 1917–18. No one knows how many preachers were pacifists, but they undoubtedly numbered several thousand. A few of them were exceedingly prominent.

The conscientious objectors were more highly regarded than in World War I, when they were damned or spurned by the clergy in general. The pacifist movement of the twenties and the thirties carried right on through the war with remarkable strength. On this point Dr. F. Ernest Johnson comments: "The number of objectors has been extremely small in view of the strength of the pacifist movement, but they constitute a symbol of religious freedom, and the churches in general seem so to regard them."

Approximately 12,000 conscientious objectors served in the Civilian Public Service and in the alternate service to war. About 6,500 spent an average of thirty months in prison for their violation of the Selective Training and Service Act of 1940. They came from 240 religious denominations and sects. The Mennonite group numbered 4,665; the Church of the Brethren, 1,353; the Society of Friends, 951; the Methodist, 673; the Jehovah's Witnesses, 409; and the remainder was distributed through various denominations and small sects.

The furnishing of chaplains to the armed forces was one of the outstanding contributions of the religious bodies. The Army and the Navy recognized the importance of chaplains in maintaining the morale of the men in the service. . . .

So far little has been said with reference to the Catholic and Jewish groups. More space has been given to the Protestant wing of Christendom because it was in that sector of the religious world that the greatest intellectual and spiritual difficulties arose over the war. The Protestant institutions—the established way of doing things—could not meet the impact of the war as readily or as easily as the Catholics and the Jewish organizations did.

While the Roman Catholic Church in this country had for the most part been isolationist prior to that day when our battleships were destroyed at Pearl Harbor, nevertheless the shift from peace to war in a few brief minutes did not constitute a theological nightmare for the Catholics. The hierarchy took care of the role that the church would play. Among the pronouncements of the Catholic bishops was a letter addressed to President Roosevelt on December 23, 1941 by the Administrative Board of the National Catholic Welfare Conference (NCWC), pledging full support of the Nation in the war effort and placing at the President's disposal, in the country's service, "our institutions and their consecrated personnel." The bishops promised to lead their priests and people in the prayer that God "may strengthen us all to win a victory that will be a blessing not for our nation alone but for the whole world." The Roman Catholic hierarchy directed all Catholic churches to pray on December 8, 1942 for "a victory and a peace acceptable to God."

With reference to the question of the conscientious objectors, no official statement of the Catholic bishops as a group or of the Administrative Board of Bishops of the NCWC was issued. A Catholic editor writes that as far as he is able to learn no individual bishop commented on this topic. He continues:

> It is my personal view that the attitude of the Catholic press generally was not sympathetic. However, the Catholic group in New York that publishes *The Catholic Worker* came out strongly in support of conscientious objectors and formed an organization on their behalf.

The role of Pope Pius XII in the war constitutes a study in itself. His statements about the struggle and the various attempts to bring about a peaceful settlement greatly impressed Roman Catholics in this country. Protestants were suspicious. That the Papacy had a most difficult set of problems can scarcely be denied.

Roman Catholic influence in the White House has always been a matter of grave concern for the Protestants. Therefore, when the Roosevelt administration virtually resumed diplomatic relations with the Vatican after a break of seventy-two years, Protestants became indignant.

Thus the war not only called for new adjustments on the part of specific organized religious groups, but frequently complicated their relations to each other in an intense interaction pattern. In the struggle for power, prestige, and the preservation of what was regarded as essential values and institutions within the framework of American culture, historic cleavages, rivalries, and suspicions were intensified.

The Jewish groups—Orthodox, Conservative, and Reform—were able, on a religious plane at least, to accept the war without much difficulty. Dr. F. Ernest Johnson points out that the Jewish community "is too closely bound by its sense of peoplehood to the democratic cause to experience any such shock in the outbreak of war as has come to the Protestant churches."

For the Jewish people in this country there was a more dynamic reason for hoping that some good would come out of the war. The Jews in Germany had suffered such extreme cruelty and torture under Hitler that, for the most part, members of that group in the United States had long hoped to see the Nazis completely defeated. The Allied cause was in a real sense their cause.

A thorough analysis of sermons preached by leading rabbis in the New York area before we were catapulted into the war shows that a considerable proportion of them were definitely preaching against the Nazis and suggesting that something should be done about this "menace." That is not to suggest they were advocating that the United States should declare war, but they were pleading for some form of interventionist policy. On the other hand, there was the haunting fear among them that the Jews in this country would be accused of trying to start a "Jewish war." Of course, that is exactly the accusation which the extreme rightist groups made. As [Harold] Lavine and [James] Wechsler phrased it in their *War Propaganda [and] the United States* (1940):

> William Pelley, leader of the Fascist Silvershirts, was the most bellicose exponent of this creed; Father Coughlin said essentially the same thing in more devious ways; and both of them derived most of their ideological inspiration from the propaganda ministry in Berlin. These slogans were not suddenly fashioned. They were the keynotes of the anti-Semitic drive which had begun many months before in America. It did not matter that the "Jewish conspiracy" was imaginary. . . . The fact that the bulk of American Jewry supported the Allied cause was invoked to sustain the cry of "Jewish war."

It would seem that after the United States got into the war, the Jewish community was about as loyal and active as any cultural-religious group in the country in working for Allied victory.

While it has been possible only to point out relatively a few of the high lights on the broad canvas of the relationship of the churches and the clergy to World War II, it is clear that the forces of organized religion played an important part in the struggle of the ideologies. In the dark hour of war most Christians could not follow or understand those who, like A. J. Muste of the Fellowship of Reconciliation, reaffirmed their sincere belief in "non-violent non-co-operation with the enemy." The great mass of believers in and followers of Jesus were more interested in national survival than in issuing continual statements to the effect that war is a sin.

One fact, however, was characteristic of nearly all the religious groups, pacifist and non-pacifist. They talked and planned for a just and durable peace and some kind of a federation of nations. The Delaware Conference which met in Ohio in March 1942, composed of 377 delegates from twenty-seven American Protestant communions, drafted a statement on "The Bases of a Just and Durable Peace." This proved to be but one of many attempts in various quarters to bring about an end to all wars by planning for permanent peace.

42

George F. Thomas
THE GROWTH OF RELIGIOUS REALISM

From George F. Thomas, "New Forms and Old Faith," in Dixon Wecter, et al., eds., Changing Patterns in American Civilization (Philadelphia: University of Pennsylvania Press, 1962), pp. 165–175. By permission of the University of Pennsylvania Press.

George G. Thomas (1899–   ), a student of both religion and philosophy, has been a professor of religious thought at Princeton University since 1940. His publications include *Spirit and Its Freedom* (1938), *Poetry, Religion and the Spiritual Life* (1951), and *Christian Ethics and Moral Philosophy* (1955).

The disillusionment of the thirties was deepened during the years of the Second World War when man's inhumanity to man and his betrayal of the highest ideals of Western civilization awakened a sense of horror everywhere. The growing influence of neo-scholasticism and neo-orthodoxy [i.e. European Catholic and Protestant perspectives which were themselves in part a response to the experience of the First World War] . . . has been partly due to fear that our civilization may be disintegrating before our eyes. But it has also been due to a growing awareness that our personal lives have been emptied of meaning and dignity by the loss of religious and moral conviction during the period between the two world wars. We have been lacking in a sense of direction, without a purpose to possess us and a passion for something of absolute worth. We have dis-

covered that humanistic devotion to ideals and values of our own making does not satisfy our aspiration for a universal and perfect good which transcends our limited and imperfect goods and at the same time gives them meaning. Even the [religious] liberalism of the twenties has come to seem inadequate because of its mild manner and its defensive attitude in setting forth the claims of Christian faith and love. Are the sweetness and light of the old liberal Christianity, we ask, an adequate substitute for the intense and single-minded faith which moved ancient martyrs to pour out their blood, produced medieval saints and mystics, gave courage to the Reformers, and brought about the Great Awakening and the world-wide missionary movement of the last century?

This has led to a complete abandonment of liberalism by a number of theologians, especially younger men. But the typical reaction against liberalism in theological circles has been less extreme. Almost all liberals have been affected by neo-orthodoxy, but few have been completely converted by it. In 1939, after neo-orthodoxy had become well known in this country, the editor of *The Christian Century* asked a number of Christian thinkers to write their spiritual autobiographies for the last ten years and to record the major changes in their religious thinking. All or almost all showed that they had had to take serious account of neo-orthodoxy. . . .

. . . A new theological attitude [was thereby expressed] which has been steadily growing since that time and which seems to many to point the way American religious thought should follow in the next generation. This attitude has been influenced by the brilliant insights of Professor Paul Tillich of Union Theological Seminary. In certain respects the thinking of Reinhold Niebuhr is closer to it than to neo-orthodoxy, and his brother, Professor Richard Niebuhr of Yale Divinity School, may be regarded as a distinguished representative of it in many ways. It has been called "religious realism," mainly because of its realistic theory of knowledge and its repudiation of the optimistic view of man of the older liberalism. That term is not adequate because it expresses only one aspect of the new attitude. What is equally characteristic of it is its attempt to do justice to the traditional insights revived by neo-orthodoxy and at the same time to retain the essential elements of value in the liberalism of the last two generations. In this sense it may be regarded as a "mediating" type of theology, and some of its representatives have been influenced by British theologians of the *via media* like Archbishop William Temple. Most of all, however, it aspires to develop theology which will do justice to the major insights of the Bible and the great theologians of the past, but in terms relevant to the modern situation. In other words, its representatives believe that theology is important enough to be taken very seriously and that those who wish to make a real contribution to it must free themselves from uncritical allegiance to any particular school of thought and try to think for themselves about the perennial problems. Though this new movement has as yet found no single American spokesman to give it adequate expression, it is represented by a number of men in two theological discussion groups, one composed of older and the other of younger members. From the first of these groups there has already come a volume edited by President Henry Van Dusen of Union Theological Seminary with the title *The Christian Answer*; from the second there will soon appear a volume on the thought of St. Augustine. What do the representatives of this new movement stand for?

First, they share the conviction that there has been a special revelation from God in the series of historical events, culminating in Christ, and that this revelation is ultimate. They gladly accept the fact that there has also been a general revelation of God in nature, history, conscience, and other religions. They also take for granted the critical method of studying the special revelation recorded in the Bible, as well as the testing of its insights by further religious experience and by reason. . . .

Second, the new movement stands for what [John] Bennett calls "moral realism" but not "cynicism or even pessimism" in its doctrine of man. It accepts the fact, stressed by neo-orthodoxy, that man is a sinner and will never eliminate sin from his personal and social life. But it also takes seriously the biblical doctrine of the "image of God" in man and insists that sin has obscured but not destroyed it. . . .

Third, representatives of the new movement agree with the older liberalism on the importance of the social gospel, but they interpret it in the light of the realism about man we have just described. They have abandoned social utopianism and are insisting upon a more adequate theological basis for the social gospel. Some of them believe that Protestantism has been weakened in its social ethic by its neglect of the problem of justice and law. . . .

Fourth, in spite of this critical attitude toward the churches, the new theologians have rediscovered the importance of the church. The castigation of the churches as they *are* for their involvement in our unjust society is itself due to a growing realization of what they *should be*. . . . Liberals in the twenties were inclined to think of religion as a personal affair and to regard the church as a means to their personal development. The continuity of the church with the past, its rich tradition, and the necessity of its solidarity in the face of hostile powers were little recognized. The stern realities of the world situation in the thirties and during the Second World War forced men to a radical revision of this individualistic attitude toward the church. They came to see that they were dependent upon it for the religious experience they enjoyed, that they needed the church to nourish their faith in God in a time of disillusionment with man, that Christians must stand together in the face of persecution abroad and indifference at home. Moreover, Christians saw in the heroic resistance of the church to the Nazis in Germany, Norway, Holland, and elsewhere a proof of vitality that had not been expected. Men in the armed services discovered what Christian missions had meant to the Orient, even in small islands of the Pacific. Meanwhile, Protestant churches for the last two decades have been trying to find a way to overcome their divisions and the narrow sectarianism that has prevented them from cooperating in many fields of common endeavor. The movement for church unity which is known as the "ecumenical movement" has given rise to a number of remarkable world Christian conferences, and has stimulated several successful efforts at organic union between Protestant churches, notably in Canada and South India.

For these and other reasons, the new theology we are describing manifests a deepened appreciation of the church. There has been no tendency to gloss over the defects of the actual churches, their ministers, or their lay members—indeed, we have seen that criticism of them has been very sharp—but the ideal church, the church as it might be, has played a prominent part in recent thinking. Also, Christian thinkers have become more aware both of the importance of the church as a world institution and of the shamefulness of the denominational differences which prevent them from making their common witness more effective at home and abroad. The major developments within theology more and more cut across denominational lines. It has seemed clear for some years that a new consensus of theological thinking is emerging among the Protestant churches and that theologians of each denomination are more conscious of their loyalty to the church as a whole than to their own branch of it. The new theology is, therefore, definitely an ecumenical theology speaking for the whole church.

Part Three

THE IMPACT OF
THE COLD WAR

At first glance, the Cold War might seem to be a very different phenomenon from the world wars that preceded it. After all, as a conflict it has obviously been much less intense, much less concentrated in time, and much less consistently destructive than either World War I or World War II. Furthermore, it cannot be dated with anywhere near the same precision, nor can the participating nations be identified as readily as is the case with the earlier struggles. Some observers have defined the Cold War primarily in terms of Russian-American relations, while others have seen it largely as a confrontation between the Communist bloc of nations and the "free world." Most historians have thought of it as beginning in the period 1945–1947, but a few have pushed it back as far as 1917–1919, and some have even seen it as having ended in the middle 1960s.

In this regard, however, the reader should bear at least two things in mind. The first is that even the most conventional wars, under close scrutiny, are seldom as symmetrical or as easy to delimit as might have been supposed. The Second World War, for instance, contained long stretches like the so-called "phony war" of the winter 1939 when not much was occurring, and even wars of apparently constant fighting, like that of 1914–1918, experience the variation of lull and of campaign. Moreover, as far as chronology and participation are concerned, the historian cannot ignore such peculiarities as the fact that for China, in effect, World War II began in 1937, while for Russia the war against Japan did not begin until August 1945.

A second point worth remembering is that, on a number of occasions at least, "hot" wars have been preceded by something we could call a "cold war." The most obvious example, perhaps, is the extended period of tension in Europe before 1914, but there was a similar, briefer interval there preceding 1939. (The closest the United States has come to such a situation may well have been in 1939–1941.) There have even been "limited wars" within "cold wars" (e.g., in Spain, 1936–1939) which bear a striking resemblance to the Korean and Vietnamese conflicts. If, unfortunately, this anthology does not make "cold war" comparisons possible (primarily because previous "cold war" experiences have been largely European, and because our focus here is upon the United States, and not on particular types of wars), still it is helpful to realize that our own Cold War is not unique, and that in comparing it with World Wars I and II we are doing nothing more than if we were comparing, say, European developments of 1890–1914 with the events of the four years which followed.

When we do make our comparisons we discover that, at least in money and material, the Cold War has surpassed the cost of the "hot" wars which went before. The United States alone, since 1946, has appropriated over $1,000 billion for national defense, and the Soviet Union and other nations have spent almost an equal amount. At the present time the "world war industry" is consuming resources well in excess of $125 billion a year, or, in other words, requiring from 5 to 10 percent of the production of an already impoverished

world. The Korean conflict (1950–1953) cost the American people approximately $53 billion and 157,000 casualties; the Vietnam struggle to date (1959–March 1971) has required more than $130 billion and 340,000 casualties. (Over 5.7 million Americans are listed as having served in the armed forces during the Korean War—out of a population of 150 million; the comparable figure for the Vietnam war is yet to be established, although we know that our standing army numbered 2.5 million in 1965 and reached a peak of 3.2 million in 1969.) China, North Korea, and South Korea together suffered over 3 million killed and wounded in Korea, while North and South Vietnam have lost over 820,000 in military dead alone in the current fighting.

For the United States, the Korean and Vietnamese experiences have meant a variety of change. To an extent, of course, their consequences have been similar. Both conflicts drove the country to the right politically, led it to invest a permanently higher percentage of its income in preparedness, and resulted in a considerable short-changing of domestic programs. Yet despite such parallels, these two "hot" phases of the same "cold" war have also had quite different impacts. Whereas the Korean episode was responsible for new prosperity and boom, surprising consensus in domestic opinion, and a foreign policy of extended commitments, Vietnam has brought us the economic doldrums, polarization of old and young, and a foreign policy of retrenchment.

Indeed, taken as a whole, the Cold War seems to have been somewhat inconsistent in its effects. If it hurt education after Korea, it also helped it after Sputnik. If it assisted the Negro Revolution during the Eisenhower years, it appeared to retard it in the 1960s. If, finally, it distracted both America and the world at large from many more important matters, it also contributed something to an increasing realism among certain groups.

In May 1961, under the prodding of President John Kennedy, the United States embarked upon a ten-year, $20 billion program to land a man on the moon before the Russians. This photograph dates from 1966 and shows an early Saturn V rocket being transported to its launching pad.   (Wide World Photos)

"POOR DEVIL – IF HE COULD ONLY LEARN TO STAY OUT OF WARS..."

By the end of the 1960s it had become apparent that the cold war and the Vietnam conflict were depriving the American economy of its relative advantage over other Western economies. Among the more obvious indications were the mounting domestic inflation, falling rates of productivity, and a seriously adverse balance of payments. (April 23, 1970) (Copyright © 1970, *The Chicago Sun-Times*: reproduced by courtesy of Wil-Jo Associates, Inc. and Bill Mauldin)

Chapter Nine

ECONOMIC EFFECTS OF THE WAR

The authors of this section throw considerable light upon the extent to which a condition of half war/half peace both compounds and obscures the processes of economic change which we have noted previously. Harold G. Vatter examines the American economy at the time of the Korean conflict and concludes that military expenditures played an important role both in sustaining prosperity and in increasing the government's awareness of its own powers. Dumas Malone and Basil Rauch suggest that by the late 1950s the United States and the Soviet Union had begun to develop an economic competition which had unexpected and constructive side-effects for both countries. Bernard D. Nossiter, however, feels that Cold War military expenditures have eroded the distinctions between government and industry, concentrated economic power in the hands of a few large firms, and threatened the principle of free economic competition. Beyond this, Seymour Melman argues that the price of the Cold War "has been the depletion of American society . . . in industry, civilian technology, management, education, medical care, and the quality of life." In more specific terms, Murray L. Weidenbaum analyzes what the war in Vietnam has done, for example, to destroy a stable price situation and to alter the pattern of civilian employment. Finally, on the basis of historical comparison, James L. Clayton demonstrates that the ultimate dollar cost of the Vietnamese war will be at least three times what it has been during the fighting.

QUESTIONS:

1. Compare and contrast the economic effects of the Korean and Vietnamese conflicts, and the effects of both with those of the Cold War in the intervening period (1953–1965). How do you explain the similarities and differences in impact?
2. In what ways has the Cold War weakened the American economy from the standpoint of our peacetime needs, and in what ways has the experience strengthened it?
3. Is it true that the Cold War has blurred the distinction between government and industry in the United States? Has it done this to a greater extent than previous conflicts?
4. What has the Cold War done, if anything, to the distribution of income among the various groups and classes which constitute our population?
5. Aside from the increasing cost of weapons, what other factors have made wars relatively more expensive as the twentieth century has gone on?
6. Which war changed our economy more, the Cold War or World War II? Why?

43

Harold G. Vatter
STABILIZATION AND EXPANSION

Reprinted from The U. S. Economy in the 1950's: An Economic History, *by Harold G. Vatter, pp. 17–18, 72–74, 80–82, 98–99. By permission of W. W. Norton & Company, Inc. Copyright © 1963 by Harold G. Vatter.*

Harold G. Vatter (1910–   ), a professor of economics, taught at Oregon State University and Carleton College before moving to Portland State University in 1965. His special area of concern is business theory, and he is the author of *Small Enterprise and Oligopoly* (1955) as well as co-editor (with Robert E. Will) of *Poverty in Affluence* (1965).

Three major *external* forces in the 1950's significantly raised the sensitivity of the United States to events in the world economy: Soviet-bloc rivalry, increased intervention by less developed countries into international relations, and the rise of powerful competition from Western Europe and Japan.

The "Soviet effect" (by which is meant a direct and often shortsighted countermove in the United States to some initiating Soviet move) penetrated almost every aspect of American economic life—the United States military budget, subsidies to higher education, professional salaries, R & D [research and development] outlays, tariff policy, foreign aid, and numerous others. In the sphere of United States foreign policy in particular, Soviet-bloc rivalry dominated the magnitude and direction of the government's foreign aid program, totaling almost $73 billion between mid-1945 and the end of 1959. After the Korean War, the Soviet effect was clearly represented in grants and loans to foreign countries: military grants accounted for the bulk of the total, and immediate military-strategic considerations dominated the allocation of all types of grants by area. In the case of the less developed countries, long-run, indigenous developmental considerations were generally subordinated in United States aid policy to more immediate measures designed to insure the recipient against actual or anticipated Soviet influences. Direct Soviet-bloc competition in world markets, however, had only begun to emerge as a significant factor by the early 1960's.

It seemed possible that the 1960's would bring a shift in the nature of the United States response to Soviet-bloc rivalry as it impinged upon the less developed world. The 1950's taught many responsible policy-makers the lesson that the people in less developed countries are most responsive to non-military developmental aid to which no political strings are attached. Whether this lesson will be converted into general practice during the 1960's remains to be seen.

The less developed countries exerted a second external influence, which increased as the decade unfolded, on the American economy and American foreign economic policy during the 1950's. The relations between the less developed economies and the industrially developed nations were in many ways analogous to the "agrarian revolt" that originated as far back as the late nineteenth century against the malfunctioning of the private market mechanism in the United States domestic economy. It was clear, for example, by the end of the 1950's that something closely approximating agricultural price parity in principle would have to be established in the foreseeable future in order to protect the terms of trade of the less developed countries, whose exports consist principally of raw materials. And generally, the emerging nations came to articulate ever more cogently their demands for some form of planned international subsidies from the rich nations. United States sensitivity to those demands was strikingly acknowledged in annual appropriations for foreign aid that in 1960 exceeded $4 billion per year. Toward the end of the decade the United States showed some restiveness at bearing the international burden of aid virtually alone; the Eisenhower administration insisted that the German and other Western governments share in the support given to less developed countries. Upon United States initiative the leading industrial nations of the Western bloc formed early in 1960 a Development Assistance Group to share and accelerate the provision of aid to "countries in the process of development."

The decade was also outstanding for the improvement in the international competitive position of Western Europe and Japan in the commodity markets as these areas recovered, partly with United States aid, from the economic impairment of World War II. The relative position of the United States share in commodity markets did not decline in the aggregate, and it remained high compared to the late 1920's; but the American position showed no enlargement. On the basis of a more general measure of long-run competitive position—the ratio to the trade surplus of net foreign commitments on other than trade account—the United States position definitely deteriorated in the 1950's. Western Europe and Japan got the lion's share of the substantial increase in the volume of world exports during the 1950's, a fact which expressed in one way the improved competitive position of those areas. In the case of Western Europe this improvement was emphasized by the formation (1958) and subsequent economic expansion of the European Economic Community (the Common Market), embracing Belgium, France, West Germany, Italy, Luxembourg, and the Netherlands. This was the third major external factor which trespassed upon the traditional comparative immunity of the United States economy from international changes. . . .

Even before Korea the structure of anticipations in the American economy had been changed by the onset of the cold war following the United States Senate endorsement of the Truman doctrine calling for the containment of world Communism in March, 1947. From that time on, a secular rise in the Federal military budget appeared as a built-in feature of the nation's spending stream. About two months prior to the outbreak of the American phase of the Korean War, *Business Week* declared:

> Pressure for more government spending is mounting. And the prospect is that Congress will give in—a little more now, then more by next year.
>
> The reason is a combination of concern over tense Russian relations, and a growing fear of a rising level of unemployment here at home.

Aside from the lasting change in the structure of anticipations . . . represented in persistently large military budgets, it is extremely important to appreciate the concomitant introduction of a powerful new discretionary stabilizer (or destabilizer): the rate of disbursement of already appropriated funds. As the cold war evolved, the Federal spending agencies always operated with a huge fund of authorized defense monies—obligational authority—the disbursement rate and allocation of which were subject to a considerable degree of discretion. It was noticed, particularly after the onset of the 1957–58 recession, that the discretion could be exercised to influence the level of economic activity. By changing the rate of actual disbursement out of the large backlog of unspent appropriations, the executive could very greatly influence the course of the economy in the short and intermediate period. Such discretionary power increased, of course, as the magnitude of authorized defense monies mounted toward the end of the decade. In fiscal 1959, for instance, approximately $74 billion was available for defense expenditure. From this, some $42 billion was expended during the year, leaving an unexpended balance of about $32 billion.

In addition to the open-ended shape of the prospects for military spending at any time, toward the end of the decade it became gradually clearer that "fear of a rising level of unemployment" would also prevent any drastic reductions in the Federal budget. As one editorial writer stated in 1960, the nation had gotten to the point at which nothing would be permitted to go down except unemployment.

The connection between the public budget and unemployment was not made clearer at any time during the decade than it was after the commitment of American forces in Korea. . . . The unemployment rate had remained tenaciously high, though falling under the recovery impetus, through June, 1950, at which time it was still 5.2 per cent of the civilian labor force (3.4 million). Thereafter it continued to drop almost precipitously until it reached around 3 per cent early in 1951. Continued exhilaration under the spending waves in all major sectors pulled the rate down farther until it touched *bottom for the decade*, on a monthly basis, in October, 1953. At that time there were only 1,162,000 unemployed, or 1.8 per cent of the civilian labor force.

Federal cash payments to the public for military services increased $3.3 billion in the second half of 1950 as compared with the first half. However, the increase failed to offset decreases in other components. It was not until 1951 that the large increases came in the military cash payments—from $15 billion in the last half of 1950 to $24 billion in the first half of 1951. Still, the government ran a budgetary surplus of $3.5 billion in the fiscal year ending June 30, 1951, largely because of higher tax rates that became effective in the latter part of calendar 1950 and because of rising prices and incomes after the onset of the war.

The outbreak of war did not, therefore, bring about a boom because of a large immediate stimulus emanating directly from a big deficit-financed increase in the Federal budget. It was the immediate impact of *expectations* of such a war-induced budgetary change that no doubt provided the driving force of the expansion. According to the *Economic Report of the President* for January, 1951, ". . . the effect upon business operations of the anticipated increase in the military program more than offset any counter-inflationary impact of the cash surplus." Expectations prompted a vast wave of buying in nearly all sectors. Consumers, business, and even government rushed to stock up in anticipation of shortages and rising prices, producing of course precisely the result anticipated. In milder form the community later in the decade often exhibited a similar "announcement effect" in response to publicity given Federal spending or taxing plans. This came to be a part of the economic atmosphere.

The expenditure spree and its associated "demand-pull" inflation ran up the GNP by almost $29 billion between the second and fourth quarters of 1950. About $10 billion of this was consumption spending, almost $8 billion government purchases, and most of the rest inventory accumulations. But plant and equipment investment was still not exhibiting any dramatic rise. Prices accounted for much of the increase in all components of the GNP, the wholesale index of all prices other than farm products and foods climbing from 148.7 in June to 166.7 in December. Real GNP (first half of 1951 prices) rose $14 billion. . . .

The increase in military expenditures during the initial phase of the buildup was concentrated in items subject to rapid expansion, such as military payrolls, food, and clothing. The armed forces rose by about 1¾ million during the first year of the war effort—about four-fifths of the ultimate total increase. National security outlays rose from 6 per cent to 11 per cent of GNP.

The expansion of private plant and equipment got underway in earnest after mid-1951. Because of the great overlap between defense and civilian production facilities, the wartime stimulus to fixed capital growth left a lasting stamp on aggregate productive capacity in the economy. In summarizing some of the major industrial effects of the military program, the Joint Committee on Defense Production pointed out that by the end of 1954,

> large expansions in basic industries have materially increased the country's capacity to produce both for war and for peace. Steel has increased from 100 million tons to 124 million tons since 1950. Aluminum production has doubled in 3 years. . . . Electric power capacity has been expanded . . . from 69 million kilowatts in 1950, to an estimated 103 million kilowatts. . . . Petroleum refining capacity has kept pace, too, moving from 5.4 million barrels of crude oil in 1950 to more than 8 million barrels. . . . The chemical industry, committed to the largest expansion in its history, has invested approximately $5 billion since Korea. Goals have been established for about 60 chemical materials calling for 50 to 100 per cent over January 1951. . . . Shipments of machine tools quadrupled in the 3 years after Korea. . . .

It was in this period that the material stockpiling program for strategic and critical materials was firmly established, based on legislation enacted as far back as 1946. As of June 30, 1954, the stockpile was valued in market prices at $4.3 billion. (By 1960 this total had risen to $7.9 billion.) The Office of Defense Mobilization was empowered either to hold in the stockpile or to release to private industry the acquired materials, depending on whichever would be most advantageous for national defense. The assumption of the stockpiling program was that in the event of war such supplies would not be available from foreign sources outside the continental United States and areas immediately accessible. In the early 1960's it was publicly acknowledged by the government that this program had turned out to be another big price-support program, since the stockpile would be practically useless in the event of a global nuclear war and unnecessary in the event of a limited war such as the Korean operation. . . .

A study of industrial growth by the Midwest Research Institute published in 1957 declared that "military demand has been the major and almost exclusive dynamic growth factor in recent years." [Our own] brief survey of the economy from 1949 through the end of the Korean War period has suggested that the conclusion of the Institute does seem consistent with those portions of economic reality selected for the purposes of that survey. . . . Government military spending was undoubtedly the most important general growth factor until the end of the Korean War expansion. Furthermore, it was the major growth factor in most, though not all, of certain large rapidly growing industries throughout the whole decade. . . . Finally, the slowdown in military spending during the later years of the decade was unaccompanied by an offsetting increase in Federal welfare expenditures, shunting the responsibility for growth to other spending streams that failed to rise sufficiently to fill the vacuum thus left. The general retardation in the later years may be attributed in part to this slowdown in overall Federal spending, even as particular growth industries continued to expand under the stimulus of portions of that Federal expenditure stream.

44

Dumas Malone and Basil Rauch
THE RACE FOR ECONOMIC GROWTH

From America and World Leadership *by Dumas Malone and Basil Rauch, pp. 219–222. Copyright © 1965 by Meredith Corporation. Reprinted by permission of Appleton-Century-Crofts.*

Dumas Malone (1892–   ) is an historian and biographer who, after serving as editor-in-chief of the *Dictionary of American Biography* and later as chairman of the board of syndics of the Harvard University Press, held a professorship of history at Columbia University from 1945 to 1959. Appointed Jefferson Foundation professor of history at the University of Virginia in 1959, he received the title of resident biographer there three years later. He is the author of the three-volume *Jefferson and His Time* (1948–1962) and of *Thomas Jefferson as Political Leader* (1963).

Basil Rauch (1908–   ), professor of history at Barnard College, Columbia University, was originally appointed to the faculty of Barnard in 1941, but interrupted his stay at that institution to teach at the United States Naval Academy during World War II. His works include *The History of the New Deal, 1933–1938* (1944), *American Interest in Cuba: 1848–1855* (1947), and *Roosevelt from Munich to Pearl Harbor* (1950).

Late in the fifties a new test of the performance of the nation's economy took center stage in the view of both experts and political leaders. This was the rate of economic growth. Broader than former tests such as capital formation, production of goods, income totals, rate of employment, rate of profit on capital, standard of living, and incidence of poverty, this new way of thinking took it for granted that modern governments could and would prevent major depressions, and made the business cycle itself a short-term factor in judging the performance of a country's economic system. It introduced a new long-term dynamic view of past achievement and future needs. Competition with the Soviet Union in the atmosphere of the Cold War was probably the most important impeller of this change in economic thought. Communist leaders had long proclaimed their intention to "catch up with and surpass" the United States, the leading capitalist nation, and [Nikita S.] Khrushchev bluntly prophesied: "We'll bury you!" But the idea of perpetual economic growth struck a responsive chord in

Americans also because they traditionally believed that immigrants came to the United States to better themselves, that sons must do better than their fathers, that opportunity in education, in access to land, and in freedom to work, to save, and to engage in business enterprise should be open to every individual, with faith that the result would be general economic progress.

This traditional belief had received a severe blow in the Great Depression of the thirties. No sooner had the immediate postwar years been traversed without serious depression and to the accompaniment of immense increases in production and consumption than it received a new blow from the realization that prosperity was very unevenly distributed. Still worse, experts now came forward with studies which proved that the rate of economic growth of the United States had fallen behind that of all the leading industrial nations with the possible exception of Great Britain. Most Americans were not greatly concerned that Japan, West Germany, France, and Italy now for the first time achieved superior rates of growth. But they were deeply disturbed because experts agreed that in the fifties the Soviet Union had one of the highest rates of growth—about 7 per cent per year—while the United States rate fell from its "normal" 3 per cent to about 2 per cent. The Central Intelligence Agency announced that in 1961–1963 the Soviet rate fell to less than 2.5 per cent, largely because of failures in agriculture, but others believed that this estimate was too low, and the CIA warned that the Soviet Union would quickly improve its rate anyway. Americans could scarcely remain indifferent to projections which showed the Soviet Union surpassing the United States in wealth by 1980 if the American growth rate was 3 per cent and Russia's 7 per cent, and which merely postponed the Soviet victory by another twenty years if the United

States succeeded in increasing its rate to 5 per cent.

These calculations were limited to GNP and they were doubtful enough because the Soviet Union did not publish thorough statistical materials and because the differences in economic structures and money systems placed a premium on guesswork. Experts estimated that in the early sixties Soviet GNP reached almost half of United States GNP. The pivotal point of debate was undisputed: that the Soviet rate of growth was greater than the American. It was also indisputable that the Soviet government made arbitrary decisions governing total disposition of GNP which the United States government had to leave very largely in private hands. In Cold War competition this gave the Soviet government several advantages. It could reduce the share of GNP devoted to private consumption, and according to one estimate in 1960 held this below 50 per cent of GNP, while in the United States private consumption absorbed more than 60 per cent of its GNP. The Soviet government could arbitrarily increase capital investment, which made for future economic growth, and this was estimated as 31 per cent of GNP compared with American capital investment chiefly by private decision amounting to only 18 per cent of GNP. And the Soviet government could translate economic into military and political power by concentrating the economic activities of the Russian people on chosen projects such as the development of nuclear energy and spacecraft far more quickly and secretly than could the United States.

The concept of economic growth rate included, however, far more than GNP. It was demonstrable that an increase in education led to an increase in economic output, that the same thing was true of an improvement in people's health, an increase in scientific research and technological development, and many other activities not formerly related to economic measurements. Investments in education, health, and science eventually speeded up a country's rate of economic growth, made it more wealthy and therefore potentially more powerful. The Kennedy-Johnson administration showed itself sensitive to this kind of argument in favor of programs formerly advocated solely as matters of social idealism. Many who were not interested in social reforms for the sake of improving the lot of the least advantaged groups in the nation were willing to accept them as corollaries of Cold War foreign policy. They wanted to bring "wasted" segments of the population into the scales of national power. They wanted to organize human as well as other resources to prevent the Soviet Union from becoming more powerful than the United States. The "War on Poverty" and the Civil Rights Act of 1964 had anti-Communist as well as reformist meanings. If the Cold War motive was uninspiring to some idealists, the United States now engaged in a contest against Communism which at least improved the lot of human beings and was infinitely preferable to a nuclear holocaust.

45

Bernard D. Nossiter
ENTANGLING BUSINESS AND GOVERNMENT

The Mythmakers, pp. 129–133. Copyright © 1964 by Bernard D. Nossiter. Reprinted by permission of the Houghton Mifflin Company.

Bernard D. Nossiter (1926–   ), a journalist and author, received his B.A. degree from Dartmouth College in 1947 and his M.A. from Harvard University in 1948. Since 1948 he has been a reporter and writer for the *Wall Street Journal*, *Fortune Magazine*, the New York *World Telegram and Sun*, and the Washington *Post*. He was a Nieman Fellow at Harvard in 1962–1963.

The Cold War has added a new dimension to [the] problem [of the government's balancing (or countervailing) business power]. One of its principal consequences has been to blur the line between public and private functions. Under the impact of enormous military expenditures, government and private industry have become entangled at an astonishing number of points. The combination is most visible in the flow of top officials who shuttle between high military and government posts to corporate presidencies and directorships. Less apparent but just as important are the new ways in which the government conducts defense business.

The importance of the national security sector in the nation's economy cannot be exaggerated. For the accounting year ending on June 30, 1964, $56 billion was allotted to defense and space tasks, nearly three of every five dollars in the government's conventional budget and about 10 per cent of the economy's total output.

Major industries have grown up almost entirely dependent on government military orders; others draw a substantial portion of their income from military buying. The companies in the aerospace industry receive from two-thirds to 99 per cent of their total business from military purchases. The leading electrical machinery producers, General Electric and Westinghouse, make nearly a third of their sales to defense buyers.

This breeds a dependency that works two ways. Government agencies become as bound to their military suppliers as the military suppliers to their federal customer. So, the Defense Department will deliberately award orders to a less efficient producer to maintain that producer's productive capacity. Officials in charge of the government's stockpile of strategic materials testified they had bought more than they needed to support the prices and profits of their industrial suppliers. A military service or its bureaus will develop as much of a vested interest in one company's weapon design as the company itself. The prestige and power of the service will depend on the appropriations it gets and this in turn may hinge on the approval of its chosen company's design. Just as some trade unions have fought against ending production of an obsolete weapon in order to preserve members' jobs, so too service officers struggle to hold what they have and to expand their domain.

The line between private and public becomes fuzziest, however, in the new administrative arrangements for parceling out defense business. The government does not as a rule award contracts for a rocket engine, a firing mechanism or the construction of a launching site. Instead, it hires a firm to produce a "weapons system" complete from soup to nuts, from blueprints to installation and possibly even operation. Indeed, the firm holding the prime or original contract for such a system will probably draw up the menu itself. The military agency may merely describe what characteristics a new weapon should have and let the prime contractor invent one to fit. The design and production of component parts and the erection of facilities like launching sites will be distributed by this prime contractor downward through successive tiers of subcontractors.

Since no one can reasonably estimate the cost of something that is yet to be invented, the military does not usually award these contracts by competitive bids to the lowest cost firm. Instead, the Defense Department typically negotiates with one firm, or a few selected firms, promising to cover all costs and add on a fixed fee for profit.

In this new twilight world, the government has turned over an endless variety of functions to private groups. Dean Don K. Price of the School of Public Administration at Harvard has noted "that private corporations have contracts to maintain the Air Force's bombers and its missile ranges, private institutions made strategic studies for the Joint Chiefs of Staff and foreign policy studies for the Senate Foreign Relations Committee, universities administer technical-assistance programs for the State Department all over the world, and telephone and radio companies are about to help the National Aeronautics and Space Administration carry our messages through outer space."

One study of the new defense contracting concludes: "While private firms have thus been freed from the restraints of the open market, they have acquired new public responsibilities. They are no longer merely suppliers to the government, but participants in the administration of public functions."

In this new world, arms length bargaining between independent parties disappears. Instead, as E. Perkins McGuire, former Assistant Secretary of Defense, said: "Some of these contractors by the very magnitude of the procurement we are involved in *are in reality agents of the government.*"

The two quotations underline the ambiguity of the new relationship. One suggests that the private firms have become public administrators; the other, that they are really government instruments. In either case, it is clear that they are not simply selling goods and services to a public customer.

The eggs have been so thoroughly scrambled that government officials are becoming worried about a silent abdication of responsibility. In a report to President Kennedy, some of his top advisers generally applauded the new partnership in contracting for research and development. However, the report, signed by Defense

Secretary Robert S. McNamara among others, acknowledged "that in recent years there have been instances—particularly in the Department of Defense—where we have come dangerously close to permitting contract employees to exercise functions which belong with top government management officials."

Apart from the fusing of public and private roles, the great military expenditures undermine the theory of the government countervail in another and central way. The tens of billions of defense dollars contribute substantially to the centralization of American enterprise, to the dominance of the large corporations. This is because the lion's share of military contracts is placed with a relative handful of great firms. Concentration has marked defense outlays since the second world war. If anything, it is currently increasing rather than declining. During World War II, two-thirds of the military orders were awarded to the 100 largest defense contractors. During Korea, the share of the 100 largest dropped slightly to 64 per cent. But in the accounting years from 1958 through 1962, it had risen to nearly three-quarters. The biggest 25 firms alone received more than half of the business during this latest period.

From the standpoint of economic dominance, the most important government dollars are those spent for research and development. These funds finance the search for new knowledge, and new applications of existing knowledge. Firms with the inside track to new technology have the best chance to command the markets of the future. The boxscore of research and development outlays in the United States shows three things. The government provides most of the money for scientific and technological advance. Within the government, the biggest source by far is the military-space-atomic-energy complex, the Cold War agencies. And like defense spending generally, government research and development expendi-

tures are heavily concentrated among a few corporations.[1]

The flow of federal military and research funds to the large corporations erodes the government's countervailing power in direct as well as indirect ways. The most obvious form of countervail is antitrust action, aimed at reducing the strength of large corporations. But under the stress of the Cold War, the Department of Justice will temper antitrust prosecutions at the request of the Defense Department.

[1] In the year 1960–61, for example, the federal government supplied $9.2 billion of the $14 billion spent on research and development. Two years earlier, the federal share was $7.2 billion out of $11.1 billion. In a recent period for which figures were compiled, 1959, the government provided private industry with $5.6 billion for research and development or 59 per cent of all industrial outlays. Of this sum, $4.2 billion went to the three defense-dominated sectors, aircraft and parts, electrical equipment and communications. Large firms, those with 5000 or more employees, received $5.1 billion or nine dollars out of every ten that the government gave industry for research and development.

46

Seymour Melman
THE DEPLETION OF RESOURCES

From Our Depleted Society *by Seymour Melman, pp. 3–12. Copyright © by Seymour Melman. Reprinted by permission of Holt, Rinehart and Winston, Inc. Published in Great Britain by Brandt & Brandt.*

Seymour Melman (1917–   ) is an industrial economist who has held the position of professor of industrial engineering at Columbia University since 1948. Deeply concerned by the impact of the Cold War on our society and its resources, he is an active proponent of disarmament and of conservation. His publications include *Decision Making and Productivity* (1958), *The Peace Race* (1961), and *Pentagon Capitalism* (1970).

Once upon a time the United States was the standout performer, world-wide, as a vigorous, productive society, exceptionally strong in basic industries and in mass-producing consumer goods. American design and production methods set world standards in many fields.

These qualities have been the basis for a confident ideology which proclaims that the combination of technical excellence and money-making incentives is the key to growing affluence for all.

But the United States now is the scene of a drama different from that implicit in her confident ideology. A process of technical, industrial, and human deterioration has been set in motion within American society. The competence of the industrial system is being eroded at its base. Entire industries are falling into technical disrepair, and there is massive loss of productive employment because of inability to hold even domestic markets against foreign competition. Such depletion in economic life produces wide-ranging human deterioration at home. The wealthiest nation on earth has been unable to rally the resources necessary to raise one fifth of its own people from poverty. The same basic depletion operates as an unseen hand restricting America's relations with the rest of the world, limiting foreign-policy moves primarily to military-based initiatives.

This deterioration is the result of an unprecedented concentration of America's technical talent and fresh capital on military production. While United States research programs for civilian purposes are grossly understaffed, and many industries do virtually no research at all, more than two thirds of America's technical researchers now work for the military. We have constructed the most awesome military organizations in human history, with the actual power to destroy what we call civilization on this earth, a power which rational

men dare not use. Military extravagance has been undermining the world value of the dollar and with it the world-banking position of the United States.

The price of building colossal military power, and endlessly adding to it, has been the depletion of American society, a process now well advanced in industry, civilian technology, management, education, medical care, and the quality of life. The prospect of "no future" has become a permanent part of government security policies that depend mainly on the threat of using nuclear weapons. Never before were men made to feel so powerless, so incapable of having a voice over their own fate. . . .

Economic growth has been widely trusted as the yardstick of well-being with too little attention given to the quality of the growth, to economic health. Growth can include parasitic and malignant processes, as well as those that are healthy and productive. Depletion in America, like the increasing inability of many industries to hold their own in competitive markets, is mainly the result of parasitic growth. Replacing this with productive growth is the essential process of reconstruction for America.

By the test of income and the value of goods and services produced, the United States, in 1963–64, was clearly the front-running nation in the world. During 1964 the total value of all goods and services produced in the United States (Gross National Product) was over $600 billion. In 1963, the average value of goods and services per person in the United States was $3,000.

What has become critical for America is the quality of this economic growth. How much is healthy and how much is parasitic? Which parts add to the level of living and to further production, and which parts deplete the quality of life?

The Federal Government's Selective Service Administration, since the Second World War, has maintained a set of minimum standards, physical and educational, for acceptability of men into the armed forces. By these standards, 30% of the young men examined by Selective Service during the Second World War were rejected. Twenty years later, in 1963, the same standards produced a rejection rate averaging 50%. The meaning of this danger signal for deterioration in physical and educational competence among our youth was appreciated by senior officials of the Federal Government, and President Kennedy named a commission to study this development.

In 1950, for every 100,000 Americans, there were 109 physicians in practice. By 1955, this number declined to 102; in 1960 it was 98; and by 1963, there was a further drop to 97. During the same period, the United States imported physicians trained elsewhere in the world. And so 1,600 foreign physicians came to the United States in one year, 1963, representing the equivalent output of 16 medical schools. Their presence has saved the United States from a sharp crisis in medical services. From 1950–63, there were modest increases in the number of doctors graduated in the United States. But they fell far short of the growth in population, with the result that the availability of medical service in this nation has declined.

In the wealthiest country in the world, 1,500,000 school children attend grossly overcrowded classes and schools. Twenty-two million Americans are classified as "functionally illiterate," not having completed eighth-grade education. The following is an inventory of teacher needs in the elementary and high schools of the nation as of September, 1964:

Needs most likely to be met:	
1. To replace those leaving	134,000
2. To serve increased enrollment	54,000
Needs which have not been met and are most likely to continue:	
3. To relieve overcrowding and eliminate half-day sessions	30,000
4. To give instruction and services not now provided	20,000
5. To replace the unprepared	10,000
Total need, September, 1964	248,000
Number of available graduates of 1964	130,000
Estimated shortage	118,000

This National Education Association estimate of the number of teachers required does not even begin to cope with the problem of satisfactory education for our functional illiterates, essential job retraining, and the vast problem of helping millions of Americans overcome disadvantages of segregated education.

Where are the potential physicians and the potential teachers?

An announcement by the Atomic Energy Commission gives us a clue. On December 26, 1964, the AEC publicized a program to recruit for management, technical, engineering, and accounting intern training programs outstanding college students receiving degrees in June of 1965. In the technical-intern program, for which a master's degree or equivalent in science or engineering is required, the starting salary is

$7,950 per year and increases to $8,935 per year —all of this within the framework of an AEC job-training program.

Compare this with the position of teachers and physicians after five years of college training. During 1964, the average teacher's salary in American elementary and secondary schools was $5,963. The starting salary was obviously less than that. I do not know of any school system with a program of teacher internship that approaches the salary level offered by the Atomic Energy Commission. What is the status of a physician in training after five years of college? At that point, he is looking forward to another five years of medical school and hospital training—at no salary at all while a student, and at bare subsistence salary while an intern.

The program announced by the Atomic Energy Commission illustrates the system of rationing by salary which has been operated in the United States, and which has siphoned off a large proportion of talented young people to the service of the defense-space complex. Similar salary differentials between military and civilian work show up in various engineering fields. Military contractors, or the National Aeronautics and Space Administration, offer substantially higher rewards, thereby attracting many of the most talented people.

Whatever worth may be attached to the defense and space program, this much is clear: The work of these men, when completed, does not, by its very nature, contribute to economic health, or to further production. From an economic standpoint defense work only expends manpower and materials. That is why the growth of defense work is parasitic growth, regardless of the fact that the workers buy groceries and services with their salaries. Since we use about two thirds of our prime technical research talent for military-oriented work, the result is a short supply of comparable talent to serve civilian industry and civilian activities of every sort.

Money and manpower continue to be poured into military and related work, creating a superabundance of killing power without precedent. The armed forces of the United States now have six times as many intercontinental missiles and intercontinental airplanes as the Soviets. The U.S. strategic aircraft and missiles alone are able to deliver explosive power equivalent to 6 tons (12,000 pounds) of TNT per person on this planet. But the overkill continues to be piled up. Defense and space budgets continue to take more than half of our tax-dollars each year. Now that we have 6 tons of TNT per person in our strategic missiles and aircraft alone, have we become more secure than when we had only 1 ton of TNT per human being on earth? Will we become more secure when we can deliver 8 or 10 tons of TNT per human being?

There is little doubt about other effects from the incessant and costly pile-up of overkill in America's armed forces. By draining the finite stock of technical talent, the overkill program has depleted our education and health services. The rationing of talent plus capital has resulted in the depletion of entire basic industries in the United States—reducing employment of every sort for Americans, making the United States incompetent in important industrial areas, compelling reliance on foreign sources of supply, and contributing to decay in the quality of our lives by closing off many possible opportunities for productive employment for our young people.

Americans must begin to face the bitter fact that, in many areas of industrial technology, the United States has already become second-rate and that this condition promises to be epidemic if the present concentration of talent and capital on piling up overkill is continued.

In order to learn how to design and operate

really high-speed railroad systems it is now necessary to send a technical mission to Japan to see how it is done. Ditto to Poland and Russia to learn about advanced fishery technology. Similarly, European countries, after the Second World War sent productivity teams to the United States to observe technological methods which they might usefully apply to improve the productiveness of their own industry.

America's twenty major shipyards in 1964 had under construction only 40 merchant ships, totaling 615,000 tons. In the Soviet Union, 673 merchant ships totaling 6,450,000 tons were under construction, or under order. The merchant fleet of every major maritime country in the world—except our own—has been expanding during the last twenty years. In the United States, and in the United States alone, there has been a persistent decline in the size of the merchant fleet and a failure to replace aging vessels.

Merchant vessels are important, complex industrial products. They are required in large numbers by a major industrial society that exports $25 billion worth of goods, as does the United States. In other major maritime countries, between 30% and 50% of the foreign trade is carried by ships under the nation's flag. But of the goods flowing from the United States, only 9% is now carried in American flag ships. This means a decline in jobs for American seamen and declining employment in shipbuilding; it also feeds back into many other industries. Ships require engines, turbines, generators, instruments of many sorts, steel plates, cargo-handling equipment, navigation devices and communications equipment—all, in turn, the product of diverse industries. The decline of shipbuilding therefore means a decline in production and employment in all of these different industries.

Why has the United States shipbuilding industry not been a competent producer of merchant ships? American and foreign shipowners still buy ships, but they do not buy them in the United States. The essential reason is this: The American shipbuilding industry has been unable to compete with the costs and prices of shipbuilders abroad.

Many are quick to say that this uncompetitiveness is due to the high wages paid to American workers. The dramatic fact, however, is that the automobile industry in the United States pays the highest automobile wages in the world, and has also been producing in its low-price lines the cheapest cars in the world measured in price per pound of fabricated vehicle. This was made possible in the auto industry by sustained application of modern production engineering, but it has not been done in the shipbuilding field. This means that the shipbuilding industry has not been introducing in the design of the product and the method of manufacture the technology that would enable it to offset the wages to American workers by high productivity of labor and capital.

During the Second World War, Henry Kaiser operated shipyards at Richmond, California, where 7 million tons of merchant ships valued at $1.8 billion were manufactured in an astonishingly short time and at remarkably low cost. Seven hundred Liberty ships, each of about 10,000 tons capacity, were produced at an average cost of 13¢ per pound of vessel. Ships were launched at the rate of one per day. High-productivity manufacturing techniques were widely applied by the Kaiser shipyard operation. Deckhouses were prefabricated; large sections of ships were built upside down and on continuous line operation to enable simplified working by 300,000 new welders—including a large contingent of former housewives, drugstore clerks, and the like. What happened to all of these high-productivity techniques? Apparently these ideas were promptly scrapped by the shipbuilding industry at the end of the war and we were left with an industry that has become technically retarded.

In the United States a shipbuilding worker was paid about $3.05 an hour in 1964. In Sweden the wage to shipbuilding workers was $1.62 an hour. This means that in order to be competitive with Swedish shipyards American firms must install and utilize production methods which would make the man-hours of American workers about twice as productive as those of Swedish workers.

This is feasible from an engineering standpoint, but the managers of America's shipbuilding industry have not done it. They have been oriented primarily to serving the United States Navy as a principal customer. Ships for the Navy, like destroyers, are produced at a cost of about $5 per pound, and Polaris submarines at $12 per pound. By contrast, a commercial tanker must be manufactured at a cost of 20¢ per pound, or less if possible. By concentrating on military work where cost is of lesser importance, and by concentrating technical talent in the cost-doesn't-matter department as well, the shipbuilding industry has become commercially noncompetitive on the world market. This condition will not be altered until there is a transfer of talent and capital from the military to the civilian sphere.

Until now, there has been no major intervention by any private or public body to save the American shipbuilding industry. From the side of the Government, the major requirement —building up defense—is being satisfied. That is where the talent and the capital have been going. The fiction that the private shipbuilding firms should fend for themselves in a competitive market is maintained despite the fact that the Government, through the Defense Department, has long been the main customer and thereby the main decision-maker for the size and the character of American shipbuilding firms.

Americans have grown up believing in the technological superiority of American industry. We are due for a rude awakening, for the depletion that is visible in the shipbuilding field is also visible in an array of other American industries, notably those that produce basic industrial goods of many sorts.

Americans have believed that our nation is so wealthy and so productive that there is no possible contradiction between massive military buildups and growing affluence for all. The United States can afford guns *and* butter; besides, doesn't defense spending put money into circulation? This was learned from three years of U.S. involvement in World War II—an experience different from twenty years of Cold War. The contradiction between guns and butter is now real and measurable. Our able young men cannot, at once, be trainees for the Atomic Energy Commission and physicians in training; they cannot be teaching the young and also designing missile components. The salary money spent by the missile builder goes into circulation, but that does not in the least add to the stock of talent available for civilian work that needs to be done. "Guns" take away from "butter" even in the United States.

National concentration on the production of overkill, which gives priority to talent and capital for the military sphere, has produced in many industries a deterioration so severe that they are virtually at a terminal condition in terms of economic and technical competence. The point of no return for an industry is reached when it becomes difficult to estimate how long it would take to restore it to economic health. We are approaching that point in the shipbuilding industry and the issue now is: How much second-rate industry is the United States prepared to suffer as the price of accumulating overkill without limit?

How much loss of productive employment should be tolerated? How dependent on foreign countries for the supply of industrial goods should the United States become?

Our economists are quick to remind us that it is efficient to buy things from the cheapest producer. Altogether reasonable. But this rule of reason does not give us instruction about what to do when the noncompetitiveness of American industry has become epidemic, and results in major withdrawals of American firms from productive work in this country.

If the epidemic of noncompetitiveness spreads, we will be left with unassailable leadership in the design and manufacture of Polaris submarines, gadgets, and slick packaging. This direction is the way to an incompetent society, and that is where we are heading fast.

Priority to military and space buildups has continued—despite the fact that the ceaseless pile-up of weapons has, for a long time, not even made military sense.

47
Murray L. Weidenbaum
THE TRANSFORMED ECONOMY

From Murray L. Weidenbaum, "Our Vietnamized Economy," Saturday Review, Vol. 52 (May 24, 1969), pp. 15–17. Copyright 1969, Saturday Review, Inc.

Murray L. Weidenbaum (1927–   ) is an economist whose special interests are the changing nature of the public sector, the structural impact of defense spending, and the process of industrial planning. Currently serving as Assistant Secretary of the Treasury for Economic Policy, he has also worked with the Bureau of the Budget and other federal agencies as well as with the General Dynamics and Boeing corporations. During the 1960s he taught economics at Washington University (St. Louis). He has written *Federal Budgeting* (1964), *Prospects for Reallocating Public Resources* (1967), and *The Modern Public Sector* (1969).

Although American troops have been stationed in South Vietnam since 1954, the major buildup occurred between the middle of 1965 and the middle of 1967. This substantial and rapid expansion in U.S. military spending—from $50 billion before the buildup to $80 billion now—has had many important effects. Fundamentally, it has altered the allocation of the nation's resources between the private and the public sectors. At the end of 1964, 20 per cent of the Gross National Product was purchased by government agencies and the remaining 80 per cent was available to the private economy. By early 1968, the government portion had risen to 27 per cent and the private share had fallen to 73 per cent.

The Johnson Administration consistently underestimated military expenditures, particularly during the crucial buildup period in late 1965 and much of 1966. Most economists and government administrators, moreover, failed to appreciate how quickly the military buildup was influencing the national economy—that the economic impact was occurring as soon as the defense orders were placed and, thus, substantially before the work was completed, paid for, and showing up in the federal budget. Furthermore, policy measures to offset inflationary pressures were not taken soon enough or in a substantial enough way. The January 1966 budget message of the President maintained that the United States could afford simultaneously to wage a two-front war without raising taxes: the domestic war against poverty and the war in Vietnam.

But the program choices made were not as simple as the classroom dichotomy of "guns vs. butter." In a sense, we chose both more guns (military spending) and more butter (more consumer purchases). However, we also chose—in part as tight money began to affect specific parts of the private economy—less housing and fewer automobiles. Simultaneously, the nation was voting for more social welfare programs—thus increasing both the military and the civilian portions of the public sector. As a result, 1966 witnessed what was then the most rapid period of price inflation since the Korean War.

Several major economic problems face the United States as a legacy of 1965–66. With the collapse of the stable price and cost situation prevailing prior to Vietnam, inflation is a major concern. Unusually high interest rates have been set in a thus far unsuccessful attempt to contain the inflation. Income taxes have been raised to reduce unprecedentedly large budget deficits ($25 billion in fiscal 1968). Despite forecasts to the contrary, a serious balance-of-payments situation continues. More basic than all this, the public's confidence in the ability to "fine tune" domestic economic stabilization policies has been undermined. The basic information and analysis released by the federal government to justify its policies has created more suspicion than trust.

There also have been, of course, positive impacts of governmental economic policy during the war. A fundamental imperative was successfully achieved; a large and rapid shift of resources from civilian uses or idleness to military programs was accomplished. At the same time—unlike either the World War II or Korean experiences—the nation managed to avoid direct controls over prices, wages, and materials generally (although relatively small amounts of copper and a few other metals were set aside for use by defense contractors).

Despite the increases in defense spending and the accompanying inflation, economic growth and real improvements in the living standard of the average American continued.

Even after allowing for inflation, the average American has experienced a real growth in income, from $2,123 in 1964 to $2,473 in 1968. Also, expenditures for civilian government programs actually have increased by a larger amount than did the military budget—simultaneously with the $30-billion rise in defense spending due to the Vietnam war, civilian agencies of the Government have increased their expenditures by $35 billion since the war began.

The shift from cold to hot war not only has raised the size of the military budget, but also has changed its composition drastically. The fundamental change was the shift of emphasis from maintaining the potential capability to deal with world-wide or general war situations, in favor of moving toward a military establishment actually waging a difficult but limited war whose dimensions kept evolving.

Three specific shifts in military requirements took place. The amount of funds going for tanks, artillery, rifles, ammunition, and similar conventional battlefield hardware more than doubled from the prewar level. The relative—as well as absolute—importance of missiles was reduced drastically. Meanwhile, the military aircraft budget was reoriented from new long-range bombers to acquiring smaller "tactical" aircraft, particularly helicopters and supersonic fighters, such as the F-4 Phantom.

Once again, the traditional manufacturing industries—automobiles, mechanical equipment, textiles, clothing, tires—have become important suppliers of war material. The most dramatic increases have occurred in ammunition (orders have quadrupled since 1965), artillery and small arms (more than doubled), clothing and textiles (doubled), tanks and vehicles (up 68 per cent), and food (up 66 per cent).

The highly specialized science-oriented aerospace and electronics firms, although still very significant defense contractors, have found their shares of defense business declining. The ten firms with the largest amount of defense contracts in fiscal 1968—General Dynamics, Lockheed, General Electric, United Aircraft, McDonnell Douglas, AT&T, Boeing, Ling-Temco-Voeght, North American Rockwell, and General Motors—received 29.9 per cent of the total awards. This was down from their pre-Vietnam share of 32.2 per cent. It is interesting to note that nine of these ten giants of the military market are aerospace and electronics firms.

Unlike the period of production of large weapon systems—such as ICBMs, which could be supplied only by a few of the industrial behemoths with especially sophisticated capabilities—the economic demands of Vietnam involve numerous smaller contracts with a variety of medium-sized firms. "Small" firms increased their share of defense contracts from 15.8 per cent in fiscal 1963 to 18.4 per cent in 1968. (Companies that made the Pentagon's list of the top 100 contractors in 1968, but were not in that roster earlier, include Atlas Chemical, Colt Industries, Lykes, McLean Industries, Automatic Sprinkler, Harris-Intertype, and National Presto Industries.) But many branches of the industrial economy—including leather, paint, plastic, paper, and furniture companies—have experienced virtually no increase in defense work in recent years.

Large proportions of the companies working on Vietnam orders are in the upper Midwest and in other relatively older industrial states in the East, all of which have long-standing positions in the industrial and consumer markets. The Far West, which since the Korean War had been receiving a dominant share of defense orders, has experienced absolute as well as relative declines as a military supplier. For example, Washington state firms (mainly Boeing) received $530-million worth of defense contracts in 1968, compared to twice that amount in 1964 ($1.1 billion). Colorado's $263 million of Pentagon orders in 1968 were down substantially from the $390-million level of 1964, reflecting a decline in missile work by the Denver Division of Martin-Marietta. Similarly, in 1964 Utah received $340 million in military contracts, down to $263 million in 1968, reflecting lower levels of work on the Minuteman ICBM.

Eight states received defense contracts in 1968 at rates at least twice as high as the pre-Vietnam levels. They are Tennessee, Texas, Connecticut, Illinois, Alabama, Mississippi, Minnesota, and Wisconsin. Six other states were awarded defense contrasts at least 50 per cent greater than in fiscal 1965, before the military buildup in Southeast Asia—Florida, Indiana, Louisiana, New York, Ohio, and Pennsylvania. Most of these states, such as those in the upper Midwest, are major producers of Army ordnance and other battlefield hardware. The most dramatic expansions have been among helicopter manufacturers, notably Bell Aircraft in the Dallas-Fort Worth area, Sikorsky Division of United Aircraft in the Hartford region, and Boeing-Vertol near Philadelphia. A special case of expanding effort is the TFX (F–111) supersonic aircraft being built by General Dynamics in Fort Worth.

Vietnam also has had important effects on the pattern of civilian employment. Overall, out of more than one million new jobs directly generated by the Vietnam war, the great majority has been in highly skilled and highly paid occupations—238,000 more professional and managerial employees vs. 30,000 more service workers (the latter being among the lowest-paid groups in the nation's labor force). While the war effort has resulted in 245,000 more skilled factory workers being hired, there have been only 65,000 more jobs for laborers, 178,000 more office jobs, and 29,000 more sales positions. Thus, indirectly, the war effort has intensified some of our domestic problems—by increasing jobs for the highly skilled and relatively highly paid, rather than for the lower-income, lower-skilled portions of the population. Only one out of every ten defense jobs bears a laborer's classification, while 22 per cent of civilian jobs do.

Early optimistic appraisals of the economic environment following peace in Vietnam have glowed with visions of tax reduction, negative income taxes, federal tax sharing with the states, and massive increases in nondefense governmental activities. However, decisions already being made are strongly shaping the nature of economic adjustments to peace. A return to the prewar dollar "base" of military spending no longer seems feasible.

One reason for this is inflation. Prices on military procurements, and wages and salaries for the armed forces and civilian employees, have increased. Under existing law, the pay of both military and civilian employees of the Pentagon is scheduled to rise by about $2 billion in mid-1969. Several large weapon systems are in early production stages and the large expenditures will come in the next year or so. They include several nuclear carriers and destroyers (about $4 to 5 billion), the Poseidon and Minuteman III missiles (about $7 billion), and the Safeguard ABM system (estimated from $5 billion to several times that amount).

Moreover, because the non-Vietnam portions of the military budget have been squeezed in recent years, considerable "catching up" is needed especially in deferred maintenance, inventory replenishment, and advanced research and development. In 1968, for example, the Department of Defense spent less money than in 1965 on research and development in army ordnance and combat vehicles (tanks, artillery, etc.) and in military science.

This is all aside from future consequences of any new decisions to bolster the nation's long-term arsenal of weapon systems. Two portents of future Congressional action are recent reports by the influential House and Senate Committees on Armed Services. After a year of detailed study and hearings on strategic forces—those designed for all-out nuclear warfare—the Senate Committee urged, "Prompt decisions should be forthcoming for the deployment of additional and more modern weapon systems and improvements to existing weapon systems." The Committee specifically recommended rapid development of a new long-range strategic bomber, and accelerated research and development on an advanced ICBM—each of which could cost $5 billion or more to develop and produce in quantity.

The House Armed Services Committee issued a similar report on seapower, again recommending new hardware. The committee chairman described as "irrefutable" the conclusion that the Navy's most urgent requirement is new ships (nuclear escort ships currently cost about $125 million each, and nuclear carriers more than $500 million).

In addition, a large civilian space program is being recommended for the 1970s. Simultaneous development of a permanent space station plus continued exploration of the moon —after this year's scheduled manned landing— carries a price tag of $45 billion for the next decade. And development of a commercial supersonic transport, if carried out, will cost more than $1 billion. Over the whole economic structure, meanwhile, hangs the threat of inflationary pressures—which, as of this spring, were substantial.

Hence, because of these built-in momentums, the economic environment is not conducive to easy selection of new or expanded domestic social programs, regardless of urgency. Rather, economic factors tend to indicate the need for hard choices among the many pressures for government spending. A tough-minded sense of priorities and a careful weighing of benefits against costs are very much needed.

48

James L. Clayton
THE 200 YEAR MORTGAGE

From James L. Clayton, "Vietnam: The 200 Year Mortgage," The Nation, Vol. 208 (May 26, 1969), pp. 661–663.

James L. Clayton (1931–   ), an economic historian and professor at the University of Utah, is currently devoting himself to the study of America's most recent experience with war. He is the editor of *The Economic Impact of the Cold War: Sources and Readings* (1970) and the author of such articles as "Defense Spending: Key to California's Growth" (*Western Political Quarterly*, 1962) and "The Impact of the Cold War on the Economies of California and Utah, 1945–1965" (*Pacific Historical Review*, 1967).

The war in Vietnam is now the longest war in American history. Taking the date the first U.S. troops were killed in combat as the beginning (July 8, 1959), it is now nearing its tenth year. Even if the most optimistic forecasts come true, and a cease-fire is achieved this year, the Vietnamese conflict will have lasted two years longer than the American Revolution and more than twice as long as the Civil War.

Except for World War II, Vietnam has been by far the most expensive war in American history. In initial dollar costs, according to official figures, it will have cost $110 billion by the end of the next fiscal year. This figure is already double the initial cost of the Korean War and more than three times higher than

the original cost of World War I. If the war continues for another ten months, it will also surpass World War I in the total number of casualties (already more men have been wounded than in World War I) and become our third most costly war in the number of men killed and wounded in action.

But the most striking thing about the price of the war in Vietnam is that the *greatest costs are yet to come.* If history is an accurate guide in these matters—and we have no other—the expenditures for veterans benefits over the next century will be at least 50 per cent more than the initial cost of the war itself. Twenty per cent of the adult population are veterans, and one in every seven is receiving some kind of compensation. Their support now costs the nation almost twice as much as federal public welfare assistance. When one adds to these veteran costs the annual interest payments on debt incurred because of the Vietnamese War, the ultimate cost becomes at least *three times* its initial cost. This kind of accounting is seldom if ever mentioned in debates about the war.

It is extremely difficult to measure the monetary costs of any war. The Executive office of the President has, however, made a valiant attempt to ascertain the costs of the war in Vietnam since 1965. Its findings are printed in the 1970 *Budget of the United States Government* (p. 74). According to these, in fiscal 1970 the war will eat up 13 per cent of all federal expenditures, and will have cost a total of $108.5 billion since 1965. But these figures do not tell the whole story. Actually, only about $100 billion of the federal budget is relatively controllable; the remainder is already committed or in trust funds. Of this $100 billion, no less than 80 per cent is accounted for by national defense. Vietnam accounts for 32 per cent of the 1970 defense budget, and in terms of what the government can actually decide to spend in that year, the war is really costing us 25 per cent of all expenditures, not the 13 per cent that official figures indicate. This percentage, it should be noted, is based on a projected reduction of $5 billion from 1969 costs of the war. It is further assumed that the big increases are over. But that is what we were told in 1968 and costs *increased* by $2 billion. If the war in fact continues at its present rate, almost a third of the disposable federal budget will be committed to Southeast Asia. If the war escalates, the ratio could easily go to one-half.

Official figures also underestimate the costs of the war in other ways. Only American personnel actually stationed in South Vietnam, now approximately 532,500, are generally counted. Since 1967, however, at least 77,000 Americans have been stationed in Thailand or serving offshore as support forces. They would bring the total in the *immediate* zone to 634,000. In addition, more than 250,000 "back-up" men in the United States and elsewhere are probably not counted in cost estimates, and they would raise the total number of men committed to the war closer to 884,000. These additional personnel obviously add to the costs.

Moreover, for reasons that have not been made clear, the official figures measure costs only since 1965. But Americans have been stationed in Vietnam since 1954, and combat troops have been killed there since July 1959. Between 1954 and 1964, 58,885 men served a year apiece and the cost of their support is also omitted from the official estimates. At $25,000 per man year—a figure suggested in 1967 by Robert Anthony, formerly Assistant Secretary of Defense—this would increase the overall war costs by $1.5 billion.

In figuring the costs of war, however, short-run outlays are not nearly so informative as long term. The pattern of long-term costs indi-

cates that the bulk of the money is spent long after the fighting stops. The basic reason is that veterans benefits for our major wars during the past century have averaged 1.8 times the original cost of those wars. The estimated original cost of the Civil War is $3.07 billion (Union forces only). Veterans benefits by 1967 had amounted to $8.57 billion, or an increase over the original cost of 280 per cent. Projected veterans benefits for World War I, World War II and the Korean War will increase the original cost 155 per cent, 125 per cent, and 170 per cent respectively. History, therefore, is a better guide to the real cost of war than contemporary official figures.

If one measures the original cost of our three earliest wars—the American Revolution, the War of 1812 and the Mexican War—as the amount spent by the Departments of the Army and Navy during the war years, one finds that each of these wars cost roughly $100 million. Veterans benefits then began to be paid out and climbed steadily, peaking in the case of the War of 1812 some sixty-eight years later. These benefits continued to be paid for the War of 1812 until 1946, 131 years after that war ended. Veterans benefits for the Mexican War did not drop below $1 million per year until this decade, more than a century later. These benefits have increased the original cost of the first three wars by 68 per cent, 44 per cent, and 65 per cent, respectively.

The reason why veterans costs do not peak until at least two generations *after* the fighting has terminated, and do not stop until well over a century later, is best explained by an example. Suppose a drummer boy, age 14, became a soldier in 1861 and was disabled in that war. Suppose also that he married, had children, his wife died, and he remarried late in life, at say age 60 in 1907. Suppose further that his second wife was 25 years old at marriage and that at age 30 she bore him a child who was mentally or physically incapable of supporting himself. That child would be 57 years old today and still drawing benefits—more than a century after the war ended. The example is not farfetched: in 1967, 1,353 such dependents of Civil War veterans were still drawing benefits that amounted to more than $1 million annually.

Veterans benefits projected for more recent wars are also instructive. Up to 1967, veterans benefits for the Spanish-American War had amounted to $5.3 billion, or *twelve times* the original cost of that war! Moreover, the peak of these payments did not come until fifty-one years after the war ended. World War I veterans benefits probably peaked three years ago or forty-nine years after that war was over. World War II veterans benefits will probably peak at the turn of this century, and dependents of Vietnamese veterans will be drawing benefits until the 22nd century!

After veterans benefits, the interest on money borrowed to fight our major wars is the heaviest long-range cost. Again, any attempt to reach precise figures is extremely difficult, but the pattern is not hard to determine. Before World War I, interest costs probably ranged from one-fifth to three-fourths the original cost of a given war. These are conservatively estimated as follows: Most of the national debt during the early years of the Republic were Revolutionary War debts. If only two-thirds of the interest on that debt between 1790 and 1800 is taken as a fair estimate, the cost of the Revolutionary War is raised by about one-fifth. The increase in interest payments on the national debt from 1816 to 1836, when the debt was paid out, adds about one-third to the 1812 war costs. Prior to the Civil War, interest on the public debt was less than $4 million. During that war it jumped from that figure in 1861 to $144 million in 1867. Interest payments fell gradually over the next twenty-five years

and then leveled off at about $30 million annually. Since very few federal programs that would add to the deficit were undertaken during those laissez-faire years, one may attribute the greater part of the interest payments to the Civil War.

Interest costs for World War I have been much more carefully figured. Some years ago, John M. Clark, in *The Costs of the World War to the American People*, calculated the original cost to be $33 billion. The U.S. Treasury figured the interest to 1929 at $9.5 billion. Total interest amounted to about $15 billion, or approximately 46 per cent of the original cost.

Henry C. Murphy, in *National Debt in War and Transition*, shows that the government borrowed about $215 billion at 2.5 per cent interest to finance World War II. That debt has not been paid off. Indeed, at no time since 1946 has the gross public debt fallen below $252 billion, and it has been increasing rapidly in recent years because of Great Society programs and Vietnam. Assuming that it takes *only* as long to pay off this war debt as it did the Civil War debt—say thirty years— interest payments will amount to approximately $200 billion. That is 53 per cent of the original cost and quite in line with the 46 per cent figure for World War I.

In 1951, the gross public debt was $255 billion; in 1955 it was almost $275 billion. If one-half of that increase is attributable to the Korean War, then in 25 years at 4 per cent the interest costs on the Korean War will have amounted to $10 billion.

The purpose of this exercise in figures is to give some idea of what we may reasonably expect the war in Vietnam to cost. Using the pattern of veterans benefits paid out for World War I, World War II and the Korean War as a guide, we may anticipate that the Vietnamese conflict will eventually cost about 150 per cent of its original cost. This figure is conservative, however, because a much higher percentage of GIs now use their educational benefits, and life expectancy is increasing. Benefits also tend to be more inclusive with time and rise with the cost of living.

Using the Civil War, World War I, World War II and the Korean War as guidelines, we may fairly expect interest costs of the Vietnamese War to be roughly half again as much as the original cost. In short, even assuming a major de-escalation at the end of this year and a total withdrawal next year, the final bill for Vietnam will be about $330 billion.

It should be emphasized that this is a conservative figure, taking account of only the direct major monetary outlays. It does not include war-caused inflation, the loss of services and earnings by the 33,000 men killed in the war to date, the cost of resentment abroad, the depletion of natural resources, the postponement of critical domestic programs, the arrested training and education of our youth, the suspended cultural progress of our nation—and, of course, no price on the death and destruction suffered by the South Vietnamese civilians in the war zone itself.

The estimated ultimate cost of the Vietnamese War is so high that it boggles the mind unless placed in perspective. How much money is $330 billion? Compared with other federal expenditures during the same period (fiscal years 1960–70), the war in Vietnam has cost ten times more than Medicare and medical assistance, sixteen times more than support for education, and thirty-three times more than was spent for housing and community development. We have spent ten times more money on Vietnam in ten years than we have spent in our entire history for public higher education or for police protection. Put another way, the war has cost us one-fifth of the value of current personal financial assets of all living Americans, a third again as much as all outstanding home mortgages, and six times the total U.S. money now in circulation.

When one looks back over the cost of wars in American history, an evil nemesis seems to dog our destiny. Each of the major wars in the past century (the Civil War, World War I and World War II) has cost initially about ten times more than the previous war. The Civil War initially cost $3 billion, World War I $33 billion and World War II $381 billion. Since World War II, our major conflicts have tended to *double* in price. Korea cost $54 billion and Vietnam to date has cost $110 billion. Total federal expenditures, moreover, have tended to increase four to five times after each major war. In the case of Vietnam, government expenditures to date (1960–69) have doubled. If this trend continues, wars may soon be simply too expensive to contemplate, and governments too cumbersome to endure.

American intervention in Vietnam contributed to a political polarization as severe as any this country had experienced in several generations. These scenes are from two opposing demonstrations, one on behalf of "peace" (New York, April 1967), the other espousing "victory" (Washington, November 1969). (Top: Berne Greene; Bottom: United Press International Photo)

Chapter Ten

POLITICAL EFFECTS OF THE WAR

As in previous political sections, the authors here are concerned with the impact of the war upon both governmental institutions and the political mood of the nation at large. The first two selections are intended to give some insight into the structural changes which the Cold War has wrought within the executive branch. But whereas David Wise and Thomas B. Ross assert that a new and "invisible" government has arisen which, through its clandestine operations, threatens traditional democratic procedures, Louis Heren maintains that the principle of responsible civilian control, at least in the Defense Department, was fully achieved by the early 1960s. (In this regard one might also note the articles on the "warfare state" in the following chapter.) A similar difference of opinion (or historical paradox) is evident in the case of other institutions, for though Holbert N. Carroll contends that the "crisis politics" of the Cold War have led Congress to accept a continued growth of presidential power (including its secret aspects), Alpheus T. Mason holds that the international situation of the 1950s acted as a direct prod to the Supreme Court to assert its leadership in certain areas of public affairs. On the political side, while Richard Dudman demonstrates that the Cold

War was a decisive factor in strengthening movements of the far right in the 1950s and early 1960s, Nathan Glazer points out the important, if complicated connection between the Vietnam struggle and the development of the New Left. Lastly, Arthur M. Schlesinger, Jr., suggests that recent Cold War experiences have not only helped to polarize us into right and left, but have also contributed something to what he views as the awakening of the vital middle group in American politics.

QUESTIONS:

1. Does the existence of the so-called "invisible" government seriously weaken the power of the President? Or is it just another way in which his authority is enhanced?
2. Has the Cold War generally affected the prerogatives of the President in ways similar to those in which they were affected by "hot" wars in the past?
3. How do you explain the apparent fact that the war has weakened Congress while rendering the Court stronger? Is this what happened in the last years of World War II?
4. If the Vietnam war has created a polarization in the 1960s, can we look back and see a similar, though milder phenomenon in the 1950s? Or in previous wars? How have such polarizations, when they occurred, been surmounted in the past?
5. To what extent can it be justifiably argued that just as Korea gave us Dwight D. Eisenhower as President, so Vietnam has given us Richard Nixon?

49

David Wise and Thomas B. Ross
INVISIBLE GOVERNMENT

Excerpts from The Invisible Government *by David Wise and Thomas B. Ross, pp. 3–6, 350–352. Copyright © 1964 by David Wise and Thomas B. Ross. Reprinted by permission of Random House, Inc.*

David Wise (1930–   ), writer and newspaperman, was a reporter for the New York *Herald*

Tribune from 1951 to 1966, and chief of the paper's Washington bureau during the last three years of that period. He has collaborated with Thomas Ross to publish *The U–2 Affair* (1962) and *The Invisible Government* (1964).

Thomas B. Ross (1930–   ) served as a junior officer in the Navy during the Korean War, and subsequently worked for the International News Service and the United Press International. In 1958 he became a member of the Washington bureau of the Chicago *Sun-Times*. He was a Nieman Fellow at Harvard University during the 1963–1964 academic year.

There are two governments in the United States today. One is visible. The other is invisible.

The first is the government that citizens read about in their newspapers and children study about in their civics books. The second is the interlocking, hidden machinery that carries out the policies of the United States in the Cold War.

This second, invisible government gathers intelligence, conducts espionage, and plans and executes secret operations all over the globe.

The Invisible Government is not a formal body. It is a loose, amorphous grouping of individuals and agencies drawn from many parts of the visible government. It is not limited to the Central Intelligence Agency, although the CIA is at its heart. Nor is it confined to the nine other agencies which comprise what is known as the intelligence community: the National Security Council, the Defense Intelligence Agency, the National Security Agency, Army Intelligence, Navy Intelligence, Air Force Intelligence, the State Department's Bureau of Intelligence and Research, the Atomic Energy Commission and the Federal Bureau of Investigation.

The Invisible Government includes, also, many other units and agencies, as well as individuals, that appear outwardly to be a normal part of the conventional government. It even encompasses business firms and institutions that are seemingly private.

To an extent that is only beginning to be perceived, this shadow government is shaping the lives of 190,000,000 Americans. Major decisions involving peace or war are taking place out of public view. An informed citizen might come to suspect that the foreign policy of the United States often works publicly in one direction and secretly through the Invisible Government in just the opposite direction.

This Invisible Government is a relatively new institution. It came into being as a result of two related factors: the rise of the United States after World War II to a position of pre-eminent world power, and the challenge to that power by Soviet Communism.

It was a much graver challenge than any which had previously confronted the Republic. The Soviet world strategy threatened the very survival of the nation. It employed an espionage network that was dedicated to the subversion of the power and ideals of the United States. To meet that challenge the United States began constructing a vast intelligence and espionage system of its own. This has mushroomed to extraordinary proportions out of public view and quite apart from the traditional political process.

By 1964 the intelligence network had grown into a massive, hidden apparatus, secretly employing about 200,000 persons and spending several billion dollars a year.

"The National Security Act of 1947," in the words of Allen W. Dulles, ". . . has given Intelligence a more influential position in our government than Intelligence enjoys in any other government of the world."

Because of its massive size and pervasive secrecy, the Invisible Government became the inevitable target of suspicion and criticism. It has been accused by some knowledgeable congressmen and other influential citizens, including a former President, Harry S Truman, of conducting a foreign policy of its own, and of meddling deeply in the affairs of other countries without presidential authority.

The American people have not been in a position to assess these charges. They know virtually nothing about the Invisible Government. Its employment rolls are classified. Its activities are top-secret. Its budget is concealed in other appropriations. Congress provides money for the Invisible Government without knowing how much it has appropriated or how it will be spent. A handful of congressmen are supposed to be kept informed by the Invisible Government, but they know relatively little about how it works.

Overseas, in foreign capitals, American ambassadors are supposed to act as the supreme civilian representatives of the President of the United States. They are told they have control over the agents of the Invisible Government. But do they? The agents maintain communications and codes of their own. And the ambassador's authority has been judged by a committee of the United States Senate to be a "polite fiction."

At home, the intelligence men are directed by law to leave matters to the FBI. But the CIA maintains more than a score of offices in major cities throughout the United States; it is deeply involved in many domestic activities, from broadcasting stations and a steamship company to the university campus.

The Invisible Government is also generally thought to be under the direct control of the National Security Council. But, in fact, many of its major decisions are never discussed in the Council. These decisions are handled by a small directorate, the name of which is only whispered. How many Americans have ever heard of the "Special Group"? (Also known as the "54/12 Group.") The name of this group, even its existence, is unknown outside the innermost circle of the Invisible Government.

The Vice-President is by law a member of

the National Security Council, but he does not participate in the discussions of the Special Group. As Vice-President, Lyndon B. Johnson was privy to more government secrets than any of his predecessors. But he was not truly involved with the Invisible Government until he was sworn in as the thirty-sixth President of the United States.

On November 23, 1963, during the first hour of his first full day in office, Johnson was taken by McGeorge Bundy—who had been President Kennedy's personal link with the Special Group —to the Situation Room, a restricted command post deep in the White House basement.

There, surrounded by top-secret maps, electronic equipment and communications outlets, the new President was briefed by the head of the Invisible Government, John Alex McCone, Director of Central Intelligence and a member of the Special Group. Although Johnson knew the men who ran the Invisible Government and was aware of much of its workings, it was not until that morning that he began to see the full scope of its organization and secrets. . . .

There is a sophisticated notion that the problems raised by a hidden bureaucracy operating within a free society can be resolved by limiting the CIA to intelligence-gathering and setting up a separate organization to conduct special operations. The argument is that when the two functions are joined, as they are now, the intelligence-gatherers inevitably become special pleaders for the operations in which they are engaged.

There is little question that this has happened in the past and that it poses a continuing, basic problem. But the difficulty is that an agent who is running a secret operation often is in the best position to gather secret information. A CIA man involved in intrigues with the political opposition in a given country will very likely know much more about that

opposition than an analyst at Langley, [Virginia, where C.I.A. headquarters are located] or even the ambassador on the scene.

If the CIA were to be prohibited from carrying out secret operational activity and that task were to be turned over to another agency, it might be necessary to create another set of secret operatives in addition to the large number of CIA men already at work overseas. Such a situation would probably reduce efficiency, raise costs and increase the dangers of exposure. The Taylor committee grappled with the problem after the Bay of Pigs [April 1961] and came to the conclusion that the present arrangement is the lesser of two evils.

This problem, as important and complex as it may be, is secondary to the larger question of whether the CIA sets its own policy, outside of presidential control. While this accusation contains some truth, it, too, is oversimplified.

There are procedures which call for the approval of any major special operation at a high level in the executive branch of the government. The public comments of Eisenhower on Guatemala and Kennedy on the Bay of Pigs demonstrated that they not only approved these operations, but took part in the planning for them.

However, many important decisions appear to have been delegated to the Special Group, a small and shadowy directorate nowhere specifically provided for by law. But because the Special Group is composed of men with heavy responsibilities in other areas, it obviously can give no more than general approval and guidance to a course of action. The CIA and the other agencies of the Invisible Government are free to shape events in the field. They can influence policy and chart their own course within the flexible framework laid down by Washington.

In Costa Rica, for example, CIA officers did not see fit to inform the State Department when they planted a fake Communist document in a local newspaper. In Cairo, "Mr. X" slipped in to see Nasser ahead of the State Department's special emissary. In the Bay of Pigs planning, the CIA men selected the political leadership of the Cuban exiles.

Yet because of the existence of the Special Group and a generalized mechanism for approving operations, intelligence men have been able to claim that they have never acted outside of policy set at the highest level of the government. In short, even when a clear policy has been established, a President may find it difficult to enforce. Presidential power, despite the popular conception of it, is diffuse and limited. The various departments and agencies under his authority have entrenched sources of strength. They cannot always be molded to his will.

In his relations with the Invisible Government, the President's problems are compounded. He cannot deal with it openly and publicly. He cannot bring to bear against it the normal political tools at his disposal. He cannot go over the heads of the leaders of the intelligence community and appeal to the people.

A President operates under a constant awareness of the capacity of disgruntled members of the Invisible Government to undercut his purposes by leaking information to Congress and the press. During the deliberations leading to the Bay of Pigs, Kennedy obviously realized the political dangers of canceling a plan to overthrow Castro which had been brought to an advanced stage by a Republican administration. Similarly, during the Cuban missile crisis in 1962, White House officials suspected that someone high in the CIA was attempting to undermine the President by providing the Republicans with information.

This suspicion reflected the fact that the Invisible Government has achieved a quasi-independent status and a power of its own. Under these conditions, and given the necessity for secret activities to remain secret, can the Invisible Government ever be made fully compatible with the democratic system?

The answer is no. It cannot be made fully compatible. But, on the other hand, it seems inescapable that some form of Invisible Government is essential to national security in a time of Cold War. Therefore, the urgent necessity in such a national dilemma is to make the Invisible Government as reconcilable as possible with the democratic system, aware that no more than a tenuous compromise can be achieved.

50

Louis Heren
CIVILIAN CONTROL

From pp. 154–158, 160 in The New American Commonwealth *by Louis Heren. Copyright © 1965, 1968 by Louis Heren. Reprinted by permission of Harper & Row, Publishers, and the author.*

Louis Heren (1919–   ) has been a foreign correspondent for the London *Times* for more than two decades. In the early years of his career he "covered" the Arab-Israeli conflict, the Korean War, and the Indo-Chinese War. Since 1951 he has been the chief of the *Times'* Washington office.

It can be argued that the principle of civilian control in the United States has never been seriously questioned, although there has long been a national weakness for generals as Presidential candidates. Aversion to military influence preceded the Revolution, and can be traced back to the English Civil War. The early English immigrants remembered the history of the Cromwellian period and the New

Model Army. The quartering of troops in colonial homes after the French and Indian Wars became a cause for the Revolution. The Declaration of Independence complained that King George the Third had affected to render the military independent of and superior to the Civil Power. At the Continental Congress of 1787, it was said, despite its earlier lobby for a military dictator, "Standing Armies in time of Peace are inconsistent with the principles of republican Governments, dangerous to the liberties of a free people and generally converted into a destructive engine for establishing despotism."

If the principle was still revered, the high state of preparedness required in the Cold War created obvious difficulties if not dangers. . . . [For example,] civilian control could not be said to exist if the President was unable to ensure that the smallest tactical nuclear weapons—and there were thousands—would not be fired without his express order. Elaborate procedures were worked out for bomber and missile squadrons, but the dangers of nuclear affluence were compounded by technological advances which, for instance, made it impossible to separate the warhead from the missile.

[On the other hand,] many such problems were overcome by electronic devices, and the most complete command and control system man and money could devise was ready by the sixties. If the United States remains prepared to go to any lengths, even to a nuclear exchange, to defend the national interest, it has been made certain that only the President can order it. Nothing has been overlooked, not even Presidential disability or the possibility of insanity.

The process began in 1947 with the enactment of the National Security Act. This most important piece of legislation established the Department of Defense as an executive department of the government, and brought into

being the National Security Council and the Central Intelligence Agency. Its primary objective was not to ensure Presidential command, but rather unification in its widest sense. The experience of the Second World War had driven home a number of lessons. The unification of the armed forces, at least to some degree, was found necessary. Equally important was the realization that the military establishment was but one element in the security of the nation, which was seen to depend as much upon economic growth and the skill and wisdom with which the government conducted its foreign relations. The need was seen for improved organizational means to relate military, foreign, and domestic policies in setting national goals. In possible future conflicts the United States could hardly depend upon time to prepare while allies held back the enemy, and planning for rapid mobilization was seen to be essential.

Much of this, however, combined with nuclear weapons to emphasize the constitutional prerogative of the President as Commander in Chief. The National Security Act therefore provided for the appointment of a civilian Defense Secretary to direct and control the administration of the armed forces under their own departmental secretaries, and to act as the President's principal adviser in all defense matters. The Joint Chiefs of Staff were also established to serve as the principal military advisers to the President, the National Security Council, and the Defense Secretary. The Joint Chiefs, as they are generally known, were to consist of the Chairman, who was to have no vote, the Chiefs of Staff of the Army and Air Force and the Chief of Naval Operations. The Commandant of the Marine Corps was granted the right to be present whenever the Corps was involved. The Joint Chiefs were given their own staff, the Joint Staff. The Chairman, subject to the authority and direction of the President and the Defense Secretary, was to be responsible for the agenda as the presiding officer, and to inform the Secretary when the Chiefs failed to reach agreement.

Subsequent amendments and the Reorganization Plan No. 6 of 1953 strengthened the office of the Defense Secretary. All functions of the Munitions Board, the Research and Development Boards, and some other agencies were transferred to his office. Six additional civilian Assistant Secretaries of Defense were appointed. The appointment of the Director of the Joint Staff had to be approved by the Secretary. A few months later the Key West Agreement further refined the functions of the armed forces and the Chiefs, and the authority of the Defense Secretary was again increased. It established that no function in any part of the Department of Defense would be performed independent of his direction, authority, and control. There was to be the maximum practicable integration of all departmental policies, short of a merging of the armed forces, to bring about an effective and economical organization ensuring military security. The main objectives were the effective strategic direction of the armed forces, the operation of armed forces under unified command wherever possible, the integration of the armed forces into an efficient team of land, naval, and air forces, and the coordination of operations to promote efficiency and economy and to prevent gaps in responsibility. The agreement also laid down that doctrines, procedures, and plans for joint operations would be jointly planned.

The Secretary, acting for the President, was made solely responsible for defending the Constitution of the United States against all enemies, foreign and domestic. He was to maintain, by timely and effective military action, the security of the United States, its possessions, and areas vital to its interest; uphold and advance national policies and interests; and

safeguard internal security. The role of the Joint Chiefs was reduced to one of advice, and their functions were carefully defined. They included the preparation of strategic plans and the provision of strategic direction of the armed forces, including guidance for the operational control of forces and the conduct of combat operations. They were to participate in the preparation of joint plans for logistics and military mobilization, and of combined plans in conjunction with foreign armed forces, as directed by proper authority. They were to establish unified commands whenever necessary, advise the Secretary of Defense and the military departments on the means required for unified commands, and to submit to him for budgetary reasons their requirements based upon agreed strategic considerations, joint war plans, and national security commitments.

It was once bitterly said that the Joint Chiefs were left only sufficient authority to organize military displays and sporting events, but this was something of an overstatement. They cannot move troops except with civilian authority, and the Chairman is a legal anomaly who has no command. They may appeal to the President and Congress, but they are legally dependent upon the judgment of the civilian Secretary of Defense. It could not be otherwise if civilian control is to be something more than a principle, but apart from the Chairman they wear two hats. They are not only advisers. Each is also responsible for the administration and operations of his service, which can hardly be described as a sinecure. Their collective functions are vital to the national security. Upon them depends to a large extent the degree of unification sought, the first objective of the National Security Act. Nevertheless, their subordination to civilian authority is indisputable.

To ensure civilian control, the National Security Act provides that a person who has been on active duty as a commissioned officer shall not be eligible for appointment as Secretary of Defense for a period of ten years. The principle of civilian control, it must be admitted, was not always clear even after the signing of the Key West Agreement until Robert McNamara was appointed as Secretary by President Kennedy. He did not increase the legal authority of the office of the Secretary, but vigorously implemented the broad powers already available. He rejected the essentially passive role of decision-making accepted by some of his predecessors, a mechanistic process of accepting one of the recommendations made by the Joint Chiefs, and instead asserted an aggressive leadership based on questioning, suggesting alternatives, proposing objectives, and stimulating progress. In other words, Mr. McNamara demonstrated that legal authority for civilian control was not enough. The civilian Secretary must exert that authority for the President.

The Defense Secretary is now the vital link in the civilian chain of command from the White House to the missile sites and the most distant infantry post. He is the second most important Cabinet officer, and the distance between him and the Secretary of State is occasionally too narrow to be measured by the human eye. He is a member of the North Atlantic Council as well as the National Security Council and the National Aeronautics and Space Council. Inside the Pentagon, the real power lies in the Office of the Secretary of Defense, a vast civilian hierarchy dominating the entire defense establishment. Its Director of Defense Research and Engineering, for instance, is responsible for unification where it means most, in basic and applied research, and the development, testing, and evaluation of weapons, weapons systems, and all defense equipment. His authority is wider than even these responsibilities suggest. The interaction of research and national security policy and

military strategy is obvious. A recommendation to proceed with a certain weapons system can influence policy and strategy. It can also cost billions of dollars. Such systems can take years to produce, and a wrong evaluation of its role in the circumstances of the next decade or more could prove to be a national catastrophe. . . .

Thus at the apex of military authority stands the Secretary with civilian assistants with a variety of disciplines except military discipline. They depend upon management tools, such as cost and systems analysis and program budgeting, rather than combat experience. It is no exaggeration to suggest that a young mathematician only a few years out of graduate school can influence the shaping of defense policy more than a full general with a chest covered with medals and memories of a lifetime of military service all over the world. Civilian control within the Defense Department is now complete.

51

Holbert N. Carroll
THE CONGRESSIONAL DILEMMA

Holbert N. Carroll, "The Congress and National Security Policy" in David B. Truman, ed., The Congress and America's Future, *pp. 155–160. © 1965 by The American Assembly, Columbia University. Reprinted by permission of Prentice-Hall, Inc., Englewood Cliffs, New Jersey.*

Holbert N. Carroll (1921–   ) is a political scientist who began his career at the University of Pittsburgh in 1946, and has continued to teach there since that time. He is the author of *The House of Representatives and Foreign Affairs* (1958).

The rhetoric of crisis is invoked in every session of the Congress to spur support for programs.

In some circumstances a crisis atmosphere has become almost routine as the leaders work to move bills through a fractured structure that provides . . . many opportunities to delay, erode, or dilute the recommendations of the executive branch. [Sometimes] the Congress generates the crisis atmosphere. On other occasions international events of varying magnitude provoke crises to which the Congress reacts.

The frequency of crises and emergencies since World War II has invariably enhanced presidential power. As the nation has become vulnerable to military attack, the Congress has more willingly conceded extraordinary exercises of executive power. It has no choice. In many situations it now expects to be informed rather than to be consulted. In every emergency, however, lurks the potential of hazardous division and dissension in a political system of separated and diffused power.

On only a few occasions has the President asked the Congress for broad authority in anticipation of a crisis. The risks in asking must be carefully calculated. If the vote is overwhelmingly favorable, potential adversaries are warned that the President has the backing of the nation for whatever he chooses to do. But the debate may be prolonged, division exaggerated, votes close, public confidence shaken, and the backing possibly denied or seriously diluted.

President Eisenhower's request in 1955 for authority to use force, if necessary, to defend Formosa was quickly approved. The resolution was part of a strategy of communicating to Communist China the firm determination of the United States to defend the island stronghold of Nationalist China and vaguely described adjacent areas.

Conveying the unity of the nation and the determination to take risks was evident in resolutions on Berlin and Cuba in 1962. The Berlin resolution expressed the sense of the Congress that the United States was prepared to use any required means to prevent the violation of Allied rights. The Cuba resolution, passed less than a month before the missile crisis of October, 1962, warned the Soviet and Cuban governments that the United States was prepared to use any necessary means, including force, to deal with a Soviet build-up of arms in Cuba and Cuban aggression in the hemisphere. The President did not ask for the Cuban and Berlin resolutions. Once initiated in the Congress, he moved to prevent a narrowing of his discretion and succeeded. The Congress provided constitutional legitimacy for virtually any exercise of executive power. By the Cuba resolution, in particular, the more vigorous congressional proponents, responding to a troubled public, undoubtedly hoped to press the President to take a harder line. When the missile crisis arose, the Congress was not in session, but its resolve to see any crisis through was freshly on record.

The seriousness of the resolutions regarding Formosa and Cuba was underscored in the Senate by joint meetings and reports of the Foreign Relations and Armed Services Committees. The immensely powerful military and foreign policy voices of the Senate were blended. All of the resolutions were approved by huge majorities. They expressed a national consensus.

Congressional resolving in anticipation of crises, whether stimulated by the executive branch or generated within the Congress, entails risks. When President Eisenhower in 1957 asked for approval of his Middle East doctrine, the Congress, under the control of the Democrats, consumed two months to process his proposal. No doubt existed that the Congress would ultimately give him broad authority. The House endorsed the doctrine in only a few hours of debate. Extensive Senate hearings, conducted jointly by Foreign Relations and

Armed Services, were followed by twelve days of Senate debate. The President's proposal was thoroughly analyzed and amended. By its debate the Senate performed an intellectual-political function. It explored alternatives and illuminated areas of doubt. Among other things, the Senate voted for a comprehensive review of Middle East policy and, rather than authorizing the President to use force, simply expressed the view of the Congress that the United States was prepared to use armed force if the President decided that it was necessary. The Senate, in a sense, was preventing the President from diluting his military powers and responsibilities. The House quickly accepted the Senate version.

Resolutions anticipating crises are rare. More commonly the Congress must react to rapidly moving events. The hazards and strengths of separated and diffused power are quickly exposed.

Acute and sudden crises drastically narrow the range of likely congressional behavior. During the most intense period when the uncertainties are greatest, the Congress provides legitimacy for executive responses and reinforces the unity of the nation. As the emergency unfolds and abates, however, elements in the Congress are tempted to exploit the crisis for partisan advantage. In every crisis the Congress by its behavior affects public confidence in men and institutions. The tests of crises are well illustrated by the U–2 incident and the Bay of Pigs failure.

For the Democrats in control of the Congress, the U–2 crisis offered tempting opportunities for partisan gain. It was a presidential election year. The Democrats recalled the bitterness of the 1952 campaign, when Republicans in and out of the Congress had exploited the Korean War for partisan advantage. The principal Democratic contestants for the nomi-

nation were members of the Senate. Vice-President Nixon, who was to become the Republican nominee, presided. And the events were embarrassing—a spy plane shot down in the Soviet Union on the eve of a crucial summit conference in Paris, fake cover stories to mask the purpose of the flight, the Soviet Premier's announcement that the pilot was alive and his general mission revealed, President Eisenhower accepting responsibility for the flight, repercussions in Japan, Turkey, and elsewhere, and the subsequent collapse of the summit meeting. All of these events were telescoped within three weeks.

The Republicans naturally rallied to their President. In retrospect, the reactions of the congressional Democrats were controlled by the behavior of three leaders, Speaker Sam Rayburn, Senate majority leader Lyndon Johnson, and Senator J. William Fulbright, the chairman of the Foreign Relations Committee.

Democratic and Republican leaders were first briefed on the reconnaissance plane's fate on May 9, 1960. From then to the collapse of the Paris meeting and the return of the President to Washington some ten days later, the Democratic leaders called for national unity. When the Soviet Premier suggested in Paris that the conference might be postponed for six to eight months, the three Democrats, joined by the titular head of the party, Adlai Stevenson, cabled President Eisenhower to express to Premier Khrushchev the view of the Democratic party that the conference not be postponed and that "all of the American people earnestly desire peace, an end to the arms race, and ever better relations between our countries." When the Soviet leader's reply assailed the "present Administration," Senator Johnson promptly scorned the attempt to divide the nation. The Democrats, of course, were not solely demonstrating bipartisanship and the essential unity of the nation. They were also avoiding the prospect of being branded as the party the Soviet leader preferred.

Upon the President's return to Washington, the political truce almost collapsed. Democrats in the Congress raised questions about "the blunders" of the preceding weeks. As in all such debates, motives for partisan gain were blended with a desire to learn the facts of a situation that had shaken public confidence.

The Democratic leaders again moved to mute the partisanship of their colleagues by rejecting demands for a full-scale formal investigation in favor of an inquiry by the Senate Committee on Foreign Relations. It was a "self-appraisal," as Senator Fulbright put it, a review and assessment to "learn from the events of the past weeks what we can do to improve our foreign policies and our governmental procedures for their formulation and execution." The inquiry was addressed to the judgments made by the President and his associates and the procedures for making them. Their instrument for the operation, the Central Intelligence Agency, was not investigated. Edited testimony was released daily for public consumption. The Committee's report was sufficiently judicious in drawing conclusions from the facts that four of the six Republican members joined the Democrats to sign it. All of the Republicans expressed mild reservations.

The U–2 affair played only a quite minor part in the presidential election campaign. In retrospect, this largely Senate-managed response to the incident, while illuminating errors of judgment, helped restore public confidence in the competence of government.

Congressional reaction to the abortive Bay of Pigs paramilitary operation in April, 1961, was, in contrast, extraordinarily passive. Leaders of both political parties firmly backed President Kennedy in his exchanges with the Soviet Premier. The Congress provided legitimacy for the operation and conveyed the unity of the nation largely by silence. In the two weeks before the landing the Congress was silent when newspapers reported the training of anti-Castro units in Florida and elsewhere and their movement to forward bases. The President briefed a small bipartisan group of congressional leaders during the three-day period when the invaders were crushed. The leaders were silent. The House and Senate foreign policy committees conducted short, secret hearings two weeks after the event. They did not report. Only in the aftermath, when more information became available about the nature of the invasion and the deep American involvement, were questions raised in the Congress. Even then the criticism was guarded—part of the general stream of debate on what to do about Cuba. Those who got the publicity suggested that the President had not been sufficiently ruthless.

The exceptional congressional restraint may be explained partly by President Kennedy's swift moves to accept responsibility and to form a national front. The President, or a prominent associate, met with former Presidents Eisenhower, Truman, and Hoover, former Vice-President Nixon, General [Douglas] MacArthur, Governor Nelson Rockefeller, and Senator [Barry] Goldwater. "I would say that the last thing you want is to have a full investigation and lay this on the record," said former President Eisenhower. Republican apprehensions about the extent of the Eisenhower Administration's part in planning the affair, fear of war, and, especially, the implication of sensitive agencies, the Joint Chiefs and the Central Intelligence Agency in particular, also contributed to the passivity of the Congress. During the month of April the Congress was also distracted—perhaps with some relief—by a crisis in Laos and the Soviet achievement of whirling a man in space.

The U–2 and Bay of Pigs affairs exposed starkly the unresolved dilemmas of the Congress in performing representative and oversight functions with regard to secret and covert activities. Each affair provoked a dialogue about forming a joint committee on the model of the Joint Committee on Atomic Energy to oversee the Central Intelligence Agency and related intelligence activities of the government. As on past occasions, the proposals met resistance and the debate died.

The Congress has uneasily accommodated itself to the existence of clandestine activities. Most members have no idea where the money for secret and covert intelligence operations lies hidden in the budget or for what purposes the money is spent. Few want to know. Few know much about the Central Intelligence Agency, an agency larger than many government departments over which the Congress seeks to maintain meticulous control.

The Congress had adjusted to mystery by an assumption and by faith in the limited surveillance conducted in secret by a few of its members. The assumption, expressed most clearly in the U–2 hearings, is that the CIA is a servant of the National Security Council, that it does not "make" policy, and that the President and his associates are accountable for the Agency's operations. The surveillance is conducted by subcommittees of the House and Senate Armed Services and Appropriations Committees. Scant evidence exists concerning the extent of their concern and to what degree they monitor the CIA. The chairman of the House money subunit reported that his group had long known about the overflights of Soviet territory. In the Senate U–2 hearings the administration refused to divulge the mission of the particular flight that failed. Senator Fulbright had some advance knowledge about the Bay of Pigs and warned the President against the operation. Most congressmen knew nothing about either vast intelligence operation.

The Congress, in sum, has not devised satisfactory solutions to the many dilemmas posed by the extensive clandestine activities conducted by the executive branch. Its dilemmas are not simply dilemmas of secrecy. Many Congressmen are privy to secrets, and adequate ways have been devised to safeguard secret materials. The dilemmas posed for the Congress go beyond secrecy to the nature of the activities and the questions they raise for democratic government. The democratic ethic proclaims the self-determination of nations, a public voice through representative institutions in the choice of major means to accomplish national ends, and ways for compelling accountability in the continuing operations of government. The consequences of not employing the black arts on a vast scale in a tumultuous world, on the other hand, are incalculable.

How does the Congress resolve these dilemmas? A few members have spoken out vigorously for broader based continuing surveillance through a watchdog committee. Most members evade the dilemmas and are content to let the President and his associates make the ethical judgments and bear the responsibilities. The troubled for the most part are quiet.

52

Alpheus T. Mason
THE JUDICIAL OFFENSIVE

Alpheus Thomas Mason, "Constitutional Limitations in a World of Continuing Crisis" in Marian D. Irish, ed., Continuing Crisis in American Politics, *pp. 121–123. © 1963. Reprinted by permission of Prentice-Hall, Inc., Englewood Cliffs, New Jersey.*

Alpheus T. Mason (1899–   ), a professor of political science and jurisprudence at Princeton University from 1925 to 1968, is now Dougherty Professor of Government and Law at the University of Virginia. He is an expert on constitutional law and American political theory, and has written many books, including *American Constitutional Law* (1954), *The Supreme Court in a Free Society* (1959), and *The States Rights Debate: Anti-federalism and the Constitution* (1964).

Eclipse of constitutional limitations in the period of cold war is reflected in attribution to Congress of indefinite legislative power; concession to the President of power to initiate national legislation for enlarged social objectives; the right of Congress to delegate power *ad libitum* to the President; and recognition of presidential prerogative—power to act in the public interest without a law and even in contradiction of it. Under the quiescent leadership of Chief Justice Fred M. Vinson [1946–1953], the Court seldom challenged these propositions. By 1957, however, it was clear that the judicial backtrack of 1937 had been less complete than generally supposed.

In 1953 Earl Warren, Thomas E. Dewey's running mate in 1948, became the Court's titular head. Warren's appointment coincided with the early years of Eisenhower's moderate Republicanism. Into the serenity of Washington's political life, the new Chief Justice promptly introduced judicial dynamism. He brought to the Court a conviction that "the heart of any constitution consists of its Bill of Rights" and a belief that the Court is under special responsibility to enforce its mandates. "Our Judges," he announced in 1955, "are not monks or scientists, but participants in the living stream of our national life."

On May 17, 1954, within a few months of Warren's appointment, his Court unanimously outlawed racial segregation in the public schools. Cold war tensions were mounting. Racial discrimination was not only creating domestic unrest but also projecting a highly unfavorable image of America to the entire world. As in 1940, when the Court ruled against

Jehovah's Witnesses and upheld Pennsylvania's flag salute in the public schools, the Court may have felt, as Justice [Felix] Frankfurter then said, that it was necessary "to make the adjustment that we have to make within the framework of present circumstances and those that are clearly ahead of us." Both decisions reflect considerations not unrelated to the crises in which they were reached. In the *Flag Salute* case, constitutional limitations were waived in deference to the proposition that "national unity is the basis of national security." In the desegregation case, constitutional limitations were enforced and a half-century-old precedent sacrificed on the altar of national security.

Nor was the judicial order to integrate "with all deliberate speed" the only example of Chief Justice Warren's assertion of constitutional limitations. In June 1957 the Court, despite the pressures growing out of the cold war, proceeded to take on the task of safeguarding civil rights generally. At a single sitting—June 17, 1957—the Court had a field day. It upheld the right of anyone to preach the overthrow of government, as long as the preaching is limited to "abstract principle" and does not openly advocate specific action. It limited the power of congressional committees to make investigations and to require witnesses to testify. It circumscribed the power of states to require witnesses to testify in investigations of subversive activities. It restricted the power of officials to discharge government employees. Revival of constitutional limitations had occurred earlier in the term, when the Justices held that reports of the Federal Bureau of Investigation and other government agencies must be made available to defendants in criminal trials if the persons who made the charge were called as witnesses. In another case, the Court had ruled that past Communist connection, or suspected connection, is not sufficient cause for a state to refuse an admission to the bar. These decisions, all reached by a narrow majority, have not remained unqualified. Subsequent rulings make it clear that a new majority, also narrow, is reluctant to challenge Congress' attempt to cope with subversion. Taking into account this uncertain balance, Chief Justice Warren, speaking in 1962, assayed the security-through-freedom theme:

> Some believe that these cases may be disposed of by the Court balancing the security of the Nation against the freedom of the individual litigant. If these are the appropriate weights to put in the scales, it is not surprising that the balance is usually struck against the individual. If balance we must, I wonder whether on the individual's side we might not also place the importance of our survival as a free nation. The issue, as I see it, is not the individual against society; it is rather the wise accommodation of the necessities of physical survival with the requirements of spiritual survival.

Following closely on the heels of the 1957 decisions, the familiar clamor of judicial usurpation was heard. The Court had once again ignored, as in 1935–36, the salutary self-restraint doctrine. Drastic measures to restrict the Court's power and jurisdiction were introduced in Congress. Individual Justices were singled out for impeachment. Nor was the attack confined to the lunatic fringe. In August 1958, the chief justices of 36 states issued a report expressing grave doubt as to whether we have a government of laws and not of men. The next year a committee of the American Bar Association charged that the Warren Court's decisions encouraged the march of Communism. The shock stimulated by these power-crippling decisions was the more intense in coming so quickly after Chief Justice Vinson's judicial passivism. The Court had been a tame tabby for so many years that some observers were surprised to discover that it still had power, teeth, and muscle.

53

Richard Dudman
THE NEW RIGHT

From Richard Dudman, Men of the Far Right *(New York: Pyramid, 1962), pp. 7–13.*

Richard Dudman (1918–   ) is the chief of the Washington bureau of the St. Louis *Post Dispatch,* and has worked for that newspaper since 1949. His foreign assignments during the period have included a dozen wars and revolutions, numerous international conferences, and extensive survey trips. In 1953 he was the recipient of a Nieman Fellowship for a year of study at Harvard University.

A new mood has come over many Americans, dampening their customary self-confidence and optimism.

Partly it is a mood of resentment—over incomes shrunken by years of inflation; over jobs lost through automation or an efficiency expert's recommendations; over neighborhoods that have become run-down as the patterns of the big cities change; over the "intrusion" of Jews or Negroes or Catholics into communities where they had not been known before; over the innumerable restrictions and endless red tape of a society and an economy growing ever more crowded and complex.

Partly the new mood is one of unease over the struggle with the Soviet bloc, a struggle with recurrent crises, constantly broadening national responsibilities, and no victory in sight.

Some particular jolting experiences like the Korean War, the Soviet space successes, and the development of a communist regime in Cuba have given the new mood special international significance.

To describe it, Thomas L. Hughes, deputy director of intelligence and research in the State Department, has used the term "cold war battle fatigue." The chief symptom is a longing for short-cut answers. It can result in proposals to withdraw from the United Nations, abandon our allies, raise our tariffs, eliminate the income tax, slash the budget, and go to war at the drop of a hat with anyone who disagrees. Its victims, more often than not, have gone in for amateur anti-communism.

The manifestations of the new American mood are highly diverse.

In Washington, D.C., on a spring day this year, a pimply-faced young man carrying a picket's sign paced back and forth in front of the White House. On his sleeve was a red arm band with a black swastika, symbol of something called the "American Nazi Party."

At the other end of Pennsylvania Avenue, a group of gray-haired women listened intently to a Senate hearing on charges that the United States was operating under a secret "no-win" policy. The women wore large buttons saying "In the NIC of time." The initials stood for the National Indignation Convention, organized to oppose the training of Yugoslav air force pilots in the United States.

In Los Angeles, a retired Marine colonel, winner of the Medal of Honor, stood up at a "Project Alert" anti-communism school and said Chief Justice Earl Warren ought to be hanged. He later apologized and retreated to the more moderate position of the rest of the audience, that impeachment was stern enough treatment for Warren's alleged misdeeds.

Out of Dallas, Texas, came a well-printed weekly newsletter called *The Dan Smoot Report* that said solemnly that President John F. Kennedy is a product of Keynesian doctrines, which dominate Harvard University and are basically communism.

All across the country, Dr. Fred C. Schwarz, head of the booming Christian Anti-Communist Crusade, barnstormed from city to city carrying to huge rallies and "anti-communism schools" the message that the United States will be in the hands of the communists in 1973 unless national policies are radically altered.

Into Washington comes a flood of favorable letters encouraging Senator Barry Goldwater of Arizona, with his call for "total victory" over communism; Senator John Tower of Texas, with his denunciation of the Yugoslav pilot-training program; and Senator Strom Thurmond of South Carolina, with his charges that the Kennedy Administration is following a "no-win" policy toward communism.

A powerful tide of right-wing thought and action has been running through the country as a whole for about two years. It has yet to reach a high water mark.

Many different terms have been used to describe the movement. It has been called "ultra-conservatism" and the "ultra-right-wing movement." Some call it the "radical right," to emphasize the fundamental changes sought by many of its members and to carry the implication that they are not really conservatives at all. Alan Barth, writing in the *New York Times Magazine*, has used the term "rampageous right" to convey the idea of belligerence and lack of self control.

The term that will be used mostly here is the "far right." It is general enough to include a broad sweep of individuals and organizations —the educated and the ignorant, the sophisticated and the naive, the fair-minded and the bigoted, the law-abiding and the violent.

How can a collection that includes so many different types be given a name or considered a group at all? Dr. Schwarz suggests that it cannot, at least insofar as he is concerned; he thinks it unfair to call him a member of the "right," let alone the "ultra-right" or the "rampageous right." Barry Goldwater would like to be known as a plain, unhyphenated "conservative."

Despite their differences, those considered

here to be on the far right are alike in their preoccupation with the threat of the Communist movement, especially as an internal threat to the United States government and institutions. They see welfare-state measures and the growth of federal power as steps toward socialism, which they tend to equate with communism.

Abroad, they tend to see all anti-Americanism, neutrality and even mere independent nationalism as signs of communist success in gobbling up the world.

In their opposition to this menace, they tend to regard every setback as the result of a conspiracy that is virtually omnipresent, omniscient and omnipotent. Opponents thus are seen as traitors or, at best, dupes of the conspiracy.

Another broad characteristic of the far right is a general hostility to the two-party system, an unwillingness to make the practical accommodations that enable the Democrats and the Republicans to get together every four years on their respective nominees for President and Vice President.

Finally, the men of the far right see themselves as something of a group, sometimes trying to draw parts of the movement more closely together, sometimes ganging up on one of their number (as in the case of Robert Welch, head of the John Birch Society) who they think has gone too far and is damaging the movement.

Successful politicians are sometimes more difficult to classify according to these standards. The demands of practical politics smooth the rough edges of such men and train them to compromise, get along with their opponents, and smile when they disagree. One of these is Senator Goldwater. So far, for the most part, he has been a good soldier in the Republican Party. But there can be no doubt that his main strength through the country comes from the broad sweep of the far right. Given favorable circumstances one can visualize Goldwater leading a right-wing political crusade to take power from the moderates of the two established parties and impose its own brand of absolutism on domestic and foreign policies. He belongs on any list of men of the far right.

Three figures of speech can help describe the current right-wing movement.

First, as has been suggested, it is a spectrum, running through many shades of belief, strategy and tactics. It runs from the outer range of true conservatism to the wild-eyed vigilantes and fanatics at the outer edge. At the extreme, there are clear indications of a form of insanity, delusions of persecution. This is not to say that members of the far right are alike in the way they think or the way they act. What makes them a group is that they have major goals in common and, given the right circumstances, they could wield great power.

A second figure of speech that helps describe the right-wing resurgence is the reservoir from which the movement draws much of its strength. This reservoir is a number of small organizations and obscure individuals who have been working through the years to document, as they see it, the conspiracy that is trying to take over the United States and the entire world.

Like the burgeoning movement of today, this small but continuing movement also runs across a spectrum. But its spectrum is bunched at the extreme end. Its groups and individuals have been publishing hate-filled pamphlets, often containing a virulent anti-Semitic or anti-Catholic line. In recent years, they have drawn heavily on reports of the House Un-American Activities Committee for help in drawing up their blacklists. Some of them have shown a fascination with the Jewish origins of some of the persons they despise and have gone to great lengths to disclose any cases where a person has changed his name. One source of this anti-Semitic strain, thoroughly discredited but still being circulated, is the *Protocols of the Learned Elders of Zion,* a purported Jewish plan to control the world. Above all, these perennial extremists of the right have promoted a hatred and distrust of everything foreign—foreign governments, foreign trade, foreign thought and literature and especially immigration from foreign countries.

The third figure is, of course, the pendulum. Mass interest in extreme solutions has swung through the years sometimes to the left and sometimes to the right. After World War I, when "bolshevism" was a new and terrifying force in the world, a bitter anti-liberal campaign was waged, climaxed by the mass arrests by Attorney General A. Mitchell Palmer. The 1930s, during the great Depression, saw a swing to the left, in which the Communist Party grew in size, communist-front groups mushroomed, and it was the thing to do to talk extremism of the left.

Almost immediately after World War II, the pendulum swung back toward the right. Leftist groups abruptly lost their magic. Across the country, civic leaders suddenly found it acutely embarrassing to see their names still appearing on letterheads of organizations like the American-Soviet Friendship Council.

In part, this swing was recognition of reality. Competing national interests of the Soviet Union and the United States, glossed over in the wartime alliance, suddenly became painfully apparent again. An iron curtain quickly took shape along the line where the victorious armies of East and West had met. The Soviet Union showed no hesitancy to subvert and overthrow any governments that showed inclinations toward independence on its side of the new line dividing the world.

Later, in the early 1950s, there came a witch-hunting phase that can be explained by the coincidence of the disclosure of Soviet espionage in this country, the jarring experience in

Korea of a war without victory, and the appearance on the anti-communist scene of Senator Joseph R. McCarthy of Wisconsin. McCarthy's censure by the United States Senate and his subsequent decline and death seemed for a time to have marked an end to the era of "McCarthyism," which had become a bad word to most Americans and to much of the rest of the world.

But there were other national setbacks to come, and the pendulum in response, has swung even further right. This time, instead of a single principal leader, there are many leaders. The most extreme are safe in private life. No elected official—no Huey Long or Joseph McCarthy—has risked his future in conventional politics by committing himself fully to the unconventional political force of the resurgent far right.

Several events in the last few years have been profoundly disturbing to the habitual American confidence and optimism. Russia's first sputnik, followed by the Russian success in putting man into orbit for the first time, proved her capability to equal, and in some cases excel, the United States in technological fields where Americans had long taken their supremacy for granted. The Soviet intercontinental rockets, capable of carrying the nuclear bombs developed with surprising speed some years earlier, shifted the military balance, abruptly offsetting the strategic advantage of the ring of air bases of the United States and its allies around the Soviet perimeter.

The United Nations, always viewed with suspicion by the extreme right, changed from a body by and large under control of the Western allies to a huge parliament in which the United States could be outvoted.

Finally, the Monroe Doctrine, that comforting assurance that the Western Hemisphere could be maintained forever as a United States sphere of influence, was shattered by the emergence of a new and unapproved Cuban dictator who thumbed his nose at the United States and openly aligned himself with the Communist-bloc nations. To cap the climax, an ill-concealed United States attempt to use Cuban refugees to invade Cuba and overthrow Fidel Castro's regime ended in humiliating defeat. As everyone keeps saying, there is still a communist state 90 miles off the coast of Florida.

The new young President, in his third month in office, was humiliated by the communists. The circumstances paralleled those of a communist humiliation of President Eisenhower a year earlier, after the U–2 photo-reconnaissance plane was shot down over Soviet territory. Mr. Eisenhower admitted spying and lying, and Soviet Premier Nikita S. Khrushchev used the incident to break up the Paris summit meeting.

As a result of these setbacks and humiliations, Americans were afflicted with an acute sense of unease. Things were going wrong, but no remedy was in sight. Always before, it seemed, war had been available as a last resort. Now, the atomic bomb and the hydrogen bomb had made World War III almost unthinkable. And small, conventional wars promised only a repetition of the Korean episode, with its problem of a privileged sanctuary that could be attacked only at the risk of triggering a major nuclear war.

54

Nathan Glazer
THE NEW LEFT

From Nathan Glazer, "Student Politics and the University," Atlantic Monthly, *Vol. 224 (July 1969), pp. 45–47. Copyright © 1969 by The Atlantic Monthly Company, Boston, Mass. Reprinted with permission.*

Nathan Glazer (1923–   ) was on the editorial staff of *Commentary Magazine* from 1945 to 1953, and later taught at Bennington College and Smith College before moving to the University of California, Berkeley, in 1963. He is joint author of *The Lonely Crowd* (1950) and *Faces in the Crowd* (1952) with David Riesman, and *Beyond the Melting Pot* (1963) with Daniel Moynihan. Other publications include *American Judaism* (1957) and *The Social Basis of American Communism* (1961).

. . . To my mind, if we are to understand the student rebellion, we must go back to 1965 and reconstruct the enormous impact of Vietnam, and we will see that the same lines that began to divide friends on student rebellion reappeared to divide them on Vietnam.

Among all those who were horrified by the beginning of the bombing of the North, and by the increasingly destructive tactics in the South—the heavy bombing, the burning of villages, the defoliation of the countryside—a fissure rapidly developed. It could be seen when, for example, Berkeley radicals sat down in front of trains bringing recruits to the Oakland induction station. Those of us who opposed such tactics argued they would alienate the moderate potential opponents of the war, whose support was needed to bring a change in policy. We argued that to equate Johnson with Hitler and America with Nazi Germany would make it impossible to develop a wide alliance against the war. But actually, the principled basis of our opposition was more important. We did believe there were profound differences between this country and Nazi Germany, Johnson and Hitler, that we lived in a democracy, and that the authority of a democratic government, despite what it was engaged in in Vietnam, should not be undermined, because only worse would follow: from the right, most likely, but also possibly from a general anarchy. Perhaps we were wrong. The reaction from the right was remarkably moderate. The radical tactics did reach large numbers and played finally a major role in changing American policy in

Vietnam. But all the returns are not yet in: conceivably the erosion of the legitimacy of a democratic government is a greater loss than what was gained. Conceivably, too, a movement oriented to gaining wide support—along the lines of early SANE—might have been even more effective.

At Berkeley, the liberal split on Vietnam replicated the liberal split on student rebellion in the university and was paralleled by splits on the question of the summer riots and the whole problem of black violence. Again and again the issues were posed in terms of tactics— yes, we are for university reform of political rules, but we are against sit-ins and the degradation of university authorities; yes, we are against the war in Vietnam, but we will not attack or undermine the legitimacy of a democratic government; yes, we are for expanded opportunities and increased power and wealth for Negroes, but we are against violence and destruction to get them. But of course the split was not really over tactics.

Behind that there was a more basic disagreement. What kind of society, government, and university did we have?, what was owed to them?, to what extent were they capable of reform and change without resort to civil disobedience, disruption, and violence? The history and analysis of this basic division have scarcely been begun. But there is hardly any question as to which side has won among intellectual youth. We have witnessed in the past four or five years one of the greatest and most rapid intellectual victories in history. In the press addressed to the young (whether that press is elite or mass or agitational) a single view of the society and what is needed to change it is presented. Violence is extolled in the *New York Review of Books*, which began with only literary ambitions; Tom Hayden, who urges his audiences to kill policemen, is treated as a hero by *Esquire*; Eldridge Cleaver

merits an adulatory *Playboy* interview; and so it goes, all the way, I imagine, down to *Eye*. . . .

What the liberal critics of student disruption in 1964 did not see was that a storm of violent antipathy to the United States—and indeed to any stable industrial society, which raises other questions—could be aroused in the youth and the intellectuals, and that it could be maintained and strengthened year after year until it became the underpinning of the dominant style, political and cultural, among the youth. The question I find harder to answer is whether we failed to see fundamental defects and faults both in the society and state and the associated universities which had inevitably to lead anyone committed to life and freedom to such a ferocious anger.

Vietnam, of course, could justify anything. And yet the same ferocity can be seen in countries such as Germany, Italy, and Japan, which are really scarcely involved, allies though they are in other respects, in our war in Vietnam, and in a country like France, which actively disapproves of our role. Undoubtedly Vietnam has enormously strengthened the movement of antipathy and anger, and not only because our powerful nation was engaged in the destruction —whatever the reasons for it—of a small and poor one. There were other reasons. Vietnam placed youth in a morally insupportable position. The poor and the black were disproportionately subjected to the draft. The well-favored, as long as they stayed in school, and even out of it, were freed from it. The fortunate middle-class youth, with strong emotional and ideological reasons to oppose violently our war in Vietnam, could escape as long as they stayed in college, just as prisoners could escape as long as they were in jail. They undoubtedly felt guilty because those with whom they wanted to be allied, whom they hoped to help, had to go and fight in Vietnam. In this ridiculous moral position, the university became to many a repulsive prison, and prison riots were almost inevitable—whatever else contributed to them.

And yet, where there was no Vietnam, students could create their own, as in France, or the real Vietnam could serve to make them just as angry at their own, in this case hardly guilty, government.

But the question remains: how do we evaluate the role of Vietnam in directly creating frustrations that led to anger at the university? Did Vietnam serve to teach or remind students, with the assistance of critics of capitalism, that they lived in a corrupt society? Or was it itself the major irritant? How was Vietnam related to the larger society? Was it an appropriate symbol or summary of its major trends or characteristics? Or was it itself an aberration, correctable without "major social change"? The dominant tone of student radicalism was increasingly to take the first position—it reflected the society, and could be used as an issue to mobilize people against it.

55

Arthur M. Schlesinger, Jr.
THE NEW POLITICS

The Crisis of Confidence, *pp. 250–252, 262–269, 272.* Copyright © 1967, 1968, 1969 by Arthur M. Schlesinger, Jr. Reprinted by permission of the publisher, Houghton Mifflin Company. Published in Great Britain by André Deutsch Limited, Publisher.

Arthur M. Schlesinger, Jr. (1917–   ), was professor of history at Harvard from 1946 to 1961, and is presently Albert Schweitzer Professor of Humanities at the City University of New York. During World War II he worked in the Office of War Industries and the Office of Strategic Services, and in later years he served as a member of Adlai Stevenson's campaign staff (in 1952 and

1956) and as special assistant to Presidents John Kennedy and Lyndon Johnson. He is the recipient of two Pulitzer prizes, one for *The Age of Jackson* in 1945, and the other for A *Thousand Days: John F. Kennedy in the White House* in 1965. He has also written three volumes of the *Age of Roosevelt* (1957–60) and *The Bitter Heritage: Vietnam and American Democracy* (1966).

It is important, I think, to distinguish the New Politics from the New Left (and from the New Right). The same conditions—the electronic revolution, the affluent society, the rise of the great organizations, the emergence of the technostructure, the decline of economic issues, the rise of moral and cultural issues—have produced the New Left and the New Right as well as the New Politics. Neither the New Left nor the New Right is a united or homogeneous movement. Each embraces a wide variety of people and doctrine. Within each there are strong disagreements over tactics and goals. Yet the New Left and, less clearly, the New Right share a common view: that is, that the American democratic process is corrupt and phony, that it cannot identify or solve the urgent problems and that American society as at present organized is inherently incapable of providing justice to the alienated groups—for the New Left, the poor, the blacks, the young, the intellectuals; for the New Right, the lower-middle-class whites.

In particular, the New Left and the New Right are agreed in their condemnation of the central institutions of American power, whether real (the national government), semi-mythical (the Establishment) or mythical (the power elite). However much they detest each other, the two extremisms have common methods and common targets. "The real enemy of the radical left in America," writes the New Left *Washington Free Press*, "is and always has been liberalism." Karl Hess, who as Senator Goldwater's speechwriter in 1964 reputedly wrote that "extremism in the defense of liberty is no vice," recently said, "I take my stand with the anti-authoritarians, and so does the New Left. . . . This is one of the reasons I find many of the statements and actions of SDS very satisfying."

It is a happy symbiosis. George Wallace needs Tom Hayden and Eldridge Cleaver; Tom Hayden and Eldridge Cleaver need George Wallace. As Hayden put it in Chicago in August 1968, "America is reaching a point of bankruptcy and decay so complete that only military tools can protect the political institutions. . . . As reform has failed, the reliance on police power has become more visible. . . . Our victory lies in progressively demystifying a false democracy, showing the organized violence underneath reformism and manipulation." This is exactly what Wallace requires for *his* followers; and Wallace's promise to save law and order by stationing paratroopers twelve feet apart on every block is exactly what Hayden and Cleaver require for *their* followers. Thus New Left and New Right verify each other's claims and witness each other's pretensions. For all their vast differences in values and objectives they end as tacit partners in a common assault on civility and democracy.

The idea of the New Politics is very different. The New Politics acknowledges the existence and urgency of the questions that fill the extremists with apocalyptic despair. But it believes that these questions can be met and resolved by democratic means. The point of the New Politics is to force these questions on the national agenda—to make the party system recognize them, take account of them and move to meet them. Some individuals may waver, say, between the New Politics and the New Left, which is why the two are occasionally confused. But no one should ignore the fundamental and radical difference between, on the one hand, the determination to master and use the existing political system and, on the other, the determination to reject and overthrow that system. A test question would be whether the Vietnam war is seen as the result of particular decisions taken by particular men in a situation where other men might have taken other decisions; or whether it is seen as the predetermined expression of an evil system that would have imposed an imperialistic policy on whatever body of men sat in the councils of state. . . .

The New Politics, I have suggested, is the expression of an emerging national mood. . . . Its distinctive impulse is the passion for greater participation in the decisions which determine one's life. For most of those swayed by the New Politics, the critical issue was the Vietnam war—a war that by 1968 had reached proportions which no one outside the National Security Council could remember ever having voted for or been consulted about. The war seemed to compress in itself the secretiveness and dissimulation that made a New Politics imperative. (For those on the right who shared the contempt for the Old Politics and the new passion for self-determination, the critical issue was the Negro revolution which they, for their part, could not remember having voted for or been consulted about.)

Because it represented a national mood, the New Politics began to speak through both major parties (as well as, in distorted and deranged ways, through the New Right and the New Left). It had its greater impact, though, in the Democratic party. This was natural enough. It is an axiom of American history that the great political debates tend to take place first within the majority party. Only if the majority party shows itself incapable of dealing with urgent national issues does the minority party have a serious chance to create a new majority. So the debate over slavery tore the Whig party to pieces in the eighteen-fifties and enabled the Republicans to establish a new political consensus; so too the expulsion from the Republican party in 1912 of its progressive wing prevented the Republicans from meeting the problems of social justice in an industrial society and gave Franklin Roosevelt his opportunity to devise new programs and make the Democrats a new majority party. . . .

. . . The coalition put together by Roosevelt in the thirties was in trouble by the sixties. The city machines had mostly fallen into disrepair. (Chicago was almost the last remaining example of the old-fashioned boss; perhaps the Daley organization should be preserved in the Museum of Natural History—or, since it is a machine, in the Museum of Science and Technology.) Trade union membership had declined both relatively and absolutely; by 1968, only about one fifth of the labor force was organized and, in any case, labor leaders could no longer reliably deliver a labor vote. The south was straggling—in many instances, rushing—out of the party. The ethnic minorities had been turned against each other by the Negro revolution. The intellectuals were disaffected. The combination of the new, non-economic issues with the new means of mass communication was subjecting the New Deal coalition to severe strain. It would have required creative political genius equal to that of Franklin Roosevelt's to reconstruct and revitalize that coalition.

I have no doubt that President Kennedy had precisely that genius and was well on his way to finding new terms for old alliances when tragedy terminated his gallant life. It is an irony of history that his successor, Lyndon Johnson, a devoted son of the New Deal, should have administered the *coup de grâce* to the New Deal coalition. In domestic affairs President Johnson's vision of the Great Society

offered genuine promise of reconstituting the old alliances. But he nullified this wise and admirable effort by his policies in foreign affairs and by his attitudes toward the national Democratic party.

The traditional foreign policy of the Democratic party—the policy of Wilson, Roosevelt, Stevenson and Kennedy—has been a policy that united realism and idealism. These leaders acquired their great influence around the planet because they understand that a fundamental component of national power is the capacity to move the conscience and reason of the world. The traditional foreign policy of the Republican party, on the other hand, has been to deprecate the relevance of world opinion and to base American policy rather exclusively on the theory that military power is the only thing the other side understands. In Vietnam, the Dominican Republic and elsewhere, President Johnson, by casting the United States in the role of an international bully, rejected the traditional foreign policy of the Democratic party in favor of the traditional foreign policy of the Republicans.

In so doing, he badly confused his own party, leaving it torn between loyalty to the Democratic President and loyalty to historic Democratic principles. After holding out his splendid conception of the Great Society with its promise of justice to the poor and the blacks, he now proceeded to sacrifice the Great Society to a squalid and irrelevant war. Vietnam was the essential cause of the Democratic defeat in 1968; and the men who persuaded President Johnson that he should embark on the course of military escalation were the men directly responsible for that defeat. In particular, the Vietnam blunder drove the intellectual community into opposition to the Democratic administration. For better or worse, intellectuals in our society wield a political influence out of all proportion to the votes they cast. No Democratic President of this century has been elected without their active and enthusiastic support. The intellectuals in the thirties had been the linchpin of Franklin Roosevelt's coalition. In estranging them, Lyndon Johnson hastened the demoralization and intensified the crisis of the Democratic party.

Nor could the President save the party by other means. A supreme congressional politician, President Johnson was an incompetent and ineffective national politician. This should not have been too surprising. After all, he had had experience in only two national campaigns: one, when he was the vice presidential candidate; the other, when he was running for President against a man Noam Chomsky could have beaten. In his political instincts, Johnson was more a South American *caudillo* than a North American leader. He had little knowledge of the Democratic party outside the south, little understanding of the forces that animated and inspired it, indeed little interest in its national organization. In the Johnson years, for example, the White House systematically snubbed, spurned and starved the Democratic National Committee. Nor could personal magnetism compensate for party disorganization. The President as a man impressed increasing numbers of Americans as high-handed, devious and disingenuous, the embodiment of a political system that willfully deceived the people and denied them a voice in vital decisions. The President's personal compulsions completed the crisis of the party.

The New Politics was now on the march. The vital question in 1967 was whether the goal of political participation could be pursued within the established political process. The Democratic party of Lyndon Johnson seemed impenetrable; the Republican party of Barry Goldwater and Everett Dirksen unimaginable. The young saw the institutions of American society as organized to shut them out; and the

more radical among them began to conclude that exclusion was inevitable in a system controlled, as they believed, by a military-industrial complex. Thus Mark Rudd of the Columbia SDS viewed the war in Vietnam "as an inherent party of the political-economic system that dominates our country." As the estrangement grew more acute and embittered, the more romantic or irrational students began, with sublime unrealism, to speculate about destroying the system through violent revolution.

This was the situation at the start of 1968. Then in March the New Hampshire primary took place. The nation owes a good deal, I think, to Senator Eugene McCarthy for his demonstration that protest had means of expression within the democratic process. McCarthy's first cause was rationality in Vietnam; but he soon moved beyond this to touch the larger issue of the reassertion of popular control. He coolly attacked the institutions which seemed to deny men mastery over their own lives—the Pentagon, the military-industrial complex, the selective service system, the Federal Bureau of Investigation, even the political machines of his own party. He communicated to people, especially on the campuses and in the suburbs, the idea that it was (I quote Richard Goodwin) "within their power to bring about change." And he displayed himself as entirely his own man in the teeth of the consumer society, unwilling to say a word or make a gesture false to himself for the sake of the mass media.

After New Hampshire, the revolt of the New Politics was strengthened by the decision of Robert Kennedy to enter the contest. Kennedy had been against the war a good deal earlier and more sharply than McCarthy; and he added another essential part of the New Politics to which McCarthy, before 1968, had been indifferent—that is, the need for self-determination by the poor and the blacks. The New Politics scored its first triumph when, two weeks after Kennedy's declaration, President Johnson withdrew from the presidential contest and ended the escalation in Vietnam.

The murder of Robert Kennedy removed the ablest and most powerful leader of the New Politics. But the protest continued to seek outlets within the process—behind McCarthy and later George McGovern in the Democratic party; and, in the absence of its natural leader, John Lindsay, behind Nelson Rockefeller in the Republican party. In the end, though, neither party rose to the challenge. Both conventions selected men of the past—men whose minds had been formed a generation ago and who tended to see the nineteen-seventies in the image of the nineteen-forties. Both candi-

dates represented the Old Politics, and their designations accentuated the sense of mass frustration, a condition dramatized in the disorders of the last days of the Democratic convention. . . .

In the perspective of history, the 1968 election may well go down as the last hurrah of the Old Politics of this period—as, say, the 1928 election in retrospect was the last hurrah of the Old Politics of the twenties. And, as the 1928 election foreshadowed the political developments of the next decade—for example, in the rising Democratic strength in the cities—so the 1968 election may, if we read it aright, tell us something about the shape of American politics to come.

CRISIS IN EDUCATION

BEGINNING A VITAL NEW SERIES

EXCLUSIVE PICTURES OF A RUSSIAN
SCHOOLBOY vs. HIS U.S. COUNTERPART

ALEXEI KUTZKOV
OF MOSCOW

STEVEN LAPEKAS
OF CHICAGO

Russia's launching of the first space satellite (Sputnik I), October 4, 1957, frightened many Americans into believing that the nation had allowed itself to be overtaken by the Communists in basic technological skills. One result was considerable agitation on behalf of better schools, culminating in a wave of curriculum reform and the passage of the National Defense Education Act of 1958.   (Howard Sochurek; Stan Wayman; *Life Magazine* © Time Inc.)

The mood of Sputnik had past when this New York demonstrator of 1967 attempted to point out what the Cold War and Vietnam were costing American education. (Eli Finer)

Chapter Eleven

SOCIAL EFFECTS
OF THE WAR

The variety of interpretation which follows would seem to indicate that the Cold War has had differing effects at different times upon the young, the blacks, and the educational system within our country. A *Time* article written in 1951 attributes much of the responsibility for the reticence of the "silent generation" to the experience of that group in both the "cold" war and the "hot" wars of its lifetime. Moreover, from the standpoint of the early 1960s, Dumas Malone and Basil Rauch suggest that the continuing "possibility of [nuclear] extinction" resulted in an alienation and conformism among adults as well as among the "square" and the "beat" of the younger generation. Yet *Newsweek*, in its profile of the Class of 1969, contends that the Vietnamese conflict has not only helped to radicalize American youth but has gone a long way toward revolutionizing our colleges and universities. Similarly, with regard to racial matters, whereas in 1963 Harold Isaacs could argue that the efforts of the Negro to achieve equality have been very much assisted by the Cold War, more recently Bayard Rustin has asserted that Vietnam, coupled with the declining economic status of the Negro, is fanning both Negro dissatisfaction and the growing movement for "black power." With the schools, on the other hand, things would seem to have gotten better instead of worse, at least for a number of years. While Benjamin Fine demonstrates rather convincingly that the reallocation of funds and materials required by Korea severely damaged the quality of American education, Harold Howe maintains that in the late 1950s and early 1960s the Cold War came to be defined in such a way that it enabled the schools to obtain unprecedented support.

QUESTIONS:

1. Beneath all the apparent changes in effect was there anything constant about the impact of the Cold War in any of the areas which we have surveyed?
2. Why did the Korean War and the Vietnamese War (seem to) have such different impacts? Do the repercussions of either remind you of the impact of the First World War?
3. Why has the Vietnamese War proved to be so devastating to the morale of the American Negro? Or do you agree that it has?
4. What kind of a decade would the 1960s have been without the conflict in Vietnam? Do you agree with Nathan Glazer (Cold War, Politics) that if there were no Vietnam, students would "create their own"?
5. Do you think that the "damage" done to American schools by the Korean War was remedied and rectified in the later 1950s and early 1960s?

56

Time
THE SILENT GENERATION

From "The Younger Generation," Time, Vol. 58 (November 5, 1951), pp. 45–52. Reprinted by permission from TIME, The Weekly Newsmagazine. Copyright Time Inc., 1951.

Is it possible to paint a portrait of an entire generation? Each generation has a million faces and a million voices. What the voices say is not necessarily what the generation believes, and what it believes is not necessarily what it will act on. Its motives and desires are often hidden. It is a medley of good and evil, promise and threat, hope and despair. Like a straggling army, it has no clear beginning or end. And yet each generation has some features that are more significant than others; each has a quality as distinctive as a man's accent, each makes a statement to the future, each leaves behind a picture of itself.

What of today's youth? Some are smoking marijuana; some are dying in Korea. Some are going to college with their wives; some are making $400 a week in television. Some are sure they will be blown to bits by the atom bomb. Some pray. Some are raising the highest towers and running the fastest machines in the world. Some wear blue jeans; some wear Dior gowns. Some want to vote the straight Republican ticket. Some want to fly to the moon.

TIME's correspondents across the U.S. have tried to find out about this younger generation by talking to young people, and to their teachers and guardians. What do the young think, believe, and read? Who are their heroes? What are their ambitions? How do they see themselves and their time? These are some of the questions TIME's correspondents asked; the masses of answers—plus the correspondents' interpretation—contain many clashing shades of opinion, but nevertheless reveal a remarkably clear area of agreement on the state of the nation's youth.

Youth today is waiting for the hand of fate to fall on its shoulders, meanwhile working fairly hard and saying almost nothing. The most startling fact about the younger generation is its silence. With some rare exceptions, youth is nowhere near the rostrum. By comparison with the Flaming Youth of their fathers and mothers, today's younger generation is a still, small flame. It does not issue manifestoes, make speeches or carry posters. It has been called the "Silent Generation." But what does the silence mean? What, if anything, does it hide? Or are youth's elders merely hard of hearing? . . .

The "Korean business"—and a lot of other business that may follow—is the dominant fact in the life of today's youth. "I observe that you share the prevailing mood of the hour," Yale's President A. Whitney Griswold told his graduating class last June, "which in your case consists of bargains privately struck with fate—on fate's terms." The hand of fate has been on the U.S. with special gravity since World War I; it has disturbed the lives of America's youth since the '30s, through depression and war. The fear of depression has receded; the fear of war remains. Those who have been to war and face recall, and those who face the draft at the end of their schooling, know that they may have to fight before they are much older.

But youth is taking its upsetting uncertainties with extraordinary calm. When the U.S. began to realize how deeply it had committed itself in Korea, youngsters of draft age had a bad case of jitters; but all reports agree that they have since settled down to studying or working for as long as they can. The majority seem to think that war with Russia is inevitable sooner or later, but they feel that they will survive it. Reports TIME's Los Angeles Bureau: "Today's youth does have some fear of the atomic age. But he does not feel as though he is living on the brink of disaster, nor does he flick on the radio (as was done in the '40s) and expect his life to be changed drastically by the news of the moment. There is a feeling that the world is in a ten-round bout, and that there will be no quick or easy knockout."

Hardly anyone wants to go into the Army; there is little enthusiasm for the military life, no enthusiasm for war. Youngsters do not talk like heroes; they admit freely that they will

try to stay out of the draft as long as they can. But there is none of the systematized and sentimentalized antiwar feeling of the '20s. Pacifism has been almost nonexistent since World War II; so are Oxford Oaths. Some observers regard this as a sign of youth's passivity. But, as a student at Harvard puts it: "When a fellow gets his draft notice in February and keeps on working and planning till June, instead of boozing up every night and having a succession of farewell parties, he has made a very difficult, positive decision. Most make that decision today." . . .

Perhaps more than any of its predecessors, this generation wants a good, secure job. This does not mean that it specifically fears a depression, as some aging New Dealers claim. The feeling is widespread that anyone who wants to work can find a decent job; the facts confirm that feeling (and the starting pay is better than ever). But youth's ambitions have shrunk. Few youngsters today want to mine diamonds in South Africa, ranch in Paraguay, climb Mount Everest, find a cure for cancer, sail around the world, or build an industrial empire. Some would like to own a small, independent business, but most want a good job with a big firm, and with it, a kind of suburban idyll.

An official of the placement bureau at Stanford University finds college graduates mostly interested in big companies—and choosy about which ones they will work for. "Half the time a guy will turn down a good job because he has to work in the city [meaning San Francisco]. They all figure there's no future in being holed up in a little apartment in town for ten years or getting up at 6 in the morning to commute to work and then not getting home until after dark. So they all want to work down on the peninsula where they can have a little house in the country and play golf or tennis and live the good life."

Says one youthful observer who still likes

his dreams bigger: "This generation suffers from lack of worlds to conquer. Its fathers, in a sense, did too well. Sure, there are slums left —but another Federal housing project can clean up the worst. Most of the fights in labor have simmered down to arguments around the bargaining table. Would-be heroes find themselves padded from harm—and hope—like lunatics in a cell. In business, the tax structure, social security and pension plans promise to soften the blow of depression or personal misfortune—and forbid the building of new empires. In science there is the great corporation (or the Government) glad to furnish the expensive machinery now necessary for the smallest advance—and to give its name, or that of its group research boss, to the new process, while plowing back the profits. A man goes bounding, with no visible bruises, among the pads of an over-organized society."

The facts are that the U.S. is a highly organized society, must be, and will get more rather than less organized; that the big corporation is here to stay (and is a progressive instrument of U.S. capitalism). What is discouraging to some observers is not so much that youth has accepted life within the well-padded structure of organized society and big corporations, but that it seems to have relatively little ambition to do any of society's organizing. What is even more disturbing is youth's certainty that Government will take care of it—a feeling which continues despite a good deal of political distrust of Government. Reports Time's Seattle Bureau: "The Pacific Northwest is only yesterday removed from the frontier, but the 'root, hog, or die' spirit has almost disappeared. Into its place has moved a curious dependence on the biggest new employer—Government. A 28-year-old aerodynamics specialist at·Boeing says: 'I hope to work toward an income of $500 or $600 a month, after taxes. You know, only on a sliding scale for inflation. I'd just like to net $600,

and then my family would always be O.K. You start earning more than that, and it's taxed away from you, so what the hell.' "

Says a 26-year-old promotion manager in Dallas: "Sure, I'd like to do something on my own, but I want to get well fixed first—make plenty of money and then maybe start some innovations."

This cautious desire to be "well fixed" and a little more has many causes: the war; the lingering shock of the Big Depression (which this younger generation felt or heard about in its childhood); and the hard-to-kill belief (still expounded in some college economics courses) that the frontiers of the U.S. economy have been reached. . . .

American young women are, in many ways, the generation's most serious problem: they are emotional D.P.s. The granddaughters of the suffragettes, the daughters of the cigarette-and-short-skirt crusaders, they were raised to believe in woman's emancipation and equality with man. Large numbers of them feel that a home and children alone would be a fate worse than death, and they invade the big cities in search of a career. They ride crowded subways on which men, enjoying equality, do not offer them seats. They compete with men in industry and the arts; and keep up with them, Martini for Martini, at the cocktail parties.

There is every evidence that women have not been made happy by their ascent to power. They are dressed to kill in femininity. The bosom is back; hair is longer again; office telephones echo with more cooing voices than St. Mark's Square at pigeon-feeding time. The career girl is not ready to admit that all she wants is to get married; but she has generally retreated from the brassy advance post of complete flat-chested emancipation, to the position that she would like, if possible, to have marriage and a career, both. In the cities, she usually lives with a roommate (for respectability and lower rent) in a small apartment, fitted with chintz slip-covers, middlebrow poetry and a well-equipped kitchenette. Rare and fortunate is the bachelor who has not been invited to a "real, home-cooked dinner," to be eaten off a shaky bridge table, by a young woman who during the day-time is a space buyer or a dentist's assist-ant. . . .

The younger generation can still raise hell. The significant thing is not that it does, but how it goes about doing it. Most of today's youngsters never seem to lose their heads; even when they let themselves go, an alarm clock seems to be ticking away at the back of their minds; it goes off sooner or later, and sends them back to school, to work, or to war. They are almost discreet about their indiscretions, largely because (unlike their parents) they no longer want or need to shock their elders. The generation has "won its latchkey." It sees no point or fun in yelling for freedom to do as it pleases, because generally no one keeps it from doing as it pleases. It is not rebellious—either against convention or instruction, the state or fate, Pop or Mom. Toward its parents, it ex-hibits an indulgent tolerance. As one young New Yorker put it with a shrug: "Why insult the folks?"

The younger generation seems to drink less. "There is nothing glorious or inglorious any more about getting stewed," says one college professor. Whether youth is more or less pro-miscuous than it used to be is a matter of dis-agreement. Fact is that it is less showy about sex. Whatever its immoralities, it commits them on the whole because it enjoys them, and not because it wants to demonstrate against Vic-torian conventions or shock Babbitt. In that sense, it is far less childish than its parents were. As a whole, it is more sober and con-servative, but in individual cases, *e.g.*, the recent dope scandals, it makes Flaming Youth look like amateurs. . . .

Considering that its parents gave the younger generation few standards, few ideals, and an education increasingly specialized, *i.e.*, without cultural breadth, youth's morals have turned out far better than anyone had a right to hope. Almost of itself, it has picked up the right instincts from an American tradition older than its parents: it wants to marry, have chil-dren, found homes, and if necessary, defend them. . . .

Intellectually, today's young people already seem a bit stodgy. Their adventures of the mind are apt to be mild and safe, and their literature too often runs to querulous and self-protective introspection, or voices a pale, orthodox liberal-ism that seems more second-hand than second nature. On the whole, the young writer today is a better craftsman than the beginner of the '20s. Novelists like Truman Capote, William Styron and Frederick Buechner are precocious technicians, but their books have the air of suspecting that life is long on treachery, short on rewards. What some critics took for healthy revolt in James Jones's *From Here to Eternity* was really a massively reiterated gripe against life. But Jones is not the only young writer to wallow in a world of seemingly private resent-ments. Most of his fellow writers suffer from what has become their occupational disease: belief that disappointment is life's only cer-tainty. The young writers of the '20s were at least original enough to create personal styles. Today the young writer's flair sometimes turns out to be nothing more than a byproduct of his neuroses.

Educators across the U.S. complain that young people seem to have no militant beliefs. They do not speak out for anything. Professors who used to enjoy baiting students by out-rageously praising child labor or damning Shelley now find that they cannot get a rise out of the docile note-takers in their classes. The only two issues about which the younger generation seem to get worked up are race relations and world government; but neither of these issues rouses anything approaching an absorbing faith.

Many students and teachers blame this lack of conviction on fear—the fear of being tagged "subversive." Today's generation, either through fear, passivity or conviction, is ready to conform.

Marxism seems dead among the U.S. young; belief in democracy is strong but inarticulate. The one new movement that has begun in the younger generation is what Poet-Professor Peter Viereck calls the revolt against revolt—an attempt to give youth a conservative credo to stand up against the bankrupt but lingering political radicalism of the '20s and '30s.

One of the most significant facts about the younger generation is that increasingly larger numbers of it are seeking their faith not in secular panaceas but in God. . . .

The soldier in the combat zone is too preoccupied to do much thinking about the underlying reasons for his presence in Korea. He is concerned almost exclusively with personal problems, and the personal problem that overshadows all others is the problem of getting home. To justify his personal yearning to go home, he often subscribes to the thesis that Korea was a mistake (once back in the States, he will probably change his mind). In Korea, he does his job—because of his sense of duty to his country and his buddies, and because of his pride in his country and himself.

G.I. Joe's younger brother is better informed and educated, much better trained and less sorry for himself. Mauldin cartoons today would not find the popularity they did in World War II. The AWOL rate is down, even the use of profanity has fallen off (at least in Stateside camps). "Little Joe" gripes about his officers, distrusts politics and government (it is universally believed that "Harry Vaughan can transfer any man"). He does not go in for heroics, or believe in them. He is short on ideals, lacks self-reliance, is for personal security at any price. He singularly lacks flame. In spite of this, he makes a good, efficient soldier—relying on superior firepower.

The best thing that can be said for American youth, in or out of uniform, is that it has learned that it must try to make the best of a bad and difficult job, whether that job is life, war, or both. The generation which has been called the oldest young generation in the world has achieved a certain maturity.

Young people do not feel cheated. And they do not blame anyone. Before this generation, "they" were always to blame. It was a standard prewar feeling that "they" had let them down. But this generation puts the blame on life as a whole, not on parents, politicians, cartels, etc. The fact of this world is war, uncertainty, the need for work, courage, sacrifice. Nobody likes that fact. But youth does not blame that fact on its parents dropping the ball. In real life, youth seems to know, people always drop the ball. Youth today has little cynicism, because it never hoped for much.

57

Dumas Malone and Basil Rauch
CONFORMISM AND ALIENATION

From America and World Leadership *by Dumas Malone and Basil Rauch, pp. 237–240. Copyright © 1965 by Meredith Corporation. Reprinted by permission of Appleton-Century-Crofts.*

Dumas Malone (1892–   ) is an historian and biographer who, after serving as editor-in-chief of the *Dictionary of American Biography* and later as chairman of the board of syndics of the Harvard University Press, held a professorship of history at Columbia University from 1945 to 1959. Appointed Jefferson Foundation professor of history at the University of Virginia in 1959, he received the title of resident biographer three years later. He is the author of the three-volume *Jefferson and His Time* (1948–1962) and of *Thomas Jefferson as Political Leader* (1963).

Basil Rauch (1908–   ), professor of history at Barnard College, Columbia University, was originally appointed to the faculty of Barnard in 1941, but interrupted his stay at that institution to teach at the United States Naval Academy during World War II. His works include *The History of the New Deal, 1933–1938* (1944), *American Interest in Cuba: 1848–1855* (1947), and *Roosevelt from Munich to Pearl Harbor* (1950).

With the exceptions of educational reform and the civil rights movement, social idealism declined after the Second World War. At first the idealism of the war years found expression in support of the United Nations, the Marshall Plan, and in the Point Four, Atoms for Peace, and Cultural Exchange programs. But increasingly these had to be justified in terms of Cold War strategy. The Kennedy administration tried to put new life into idealism in foreign policy, and won a minor success with the Peace Corps of young people who went out as missionaries to help overcome myriad handicaps of people in underdeveloped countries. Its success led to demand for a "domestic peace corps" on the argument that social sores at home called for the same kind of missionary work. The Anti-Poverty Act of 1964 contained provision for such a corps. The nongovernmental civil-rights workers who went into Mississippi in the same year, risking their lives, represented a high pitch of social idealism. On the other hand, anti-civil rights groups like the Ku Klux Klan, the John Birch Society, and the Minutemen of California, who engaged in paramilitary training against the day when "Communists

and liberals" would be fought, also believed that they were idealists defending the American Way.

The intransigence of Communist Russia and China, the threat of nuclear war, and the growing weight of large-scale public and private organizations, created among most Americans moods of indifference to all public affairs and preoccupation with private goals. Outward conformism and actual alienation were common.

A few young people tried to avoid conformism and to make a cause out of alienation. Dramatizing themselves as the spokesmen of the "Beat Generation," they declined to take part in the "rat race" of ordinary American life, refused to take regular jobs, and scorned to live in the "square" style of Americans at large. But their uniforms of jeans, sandals, and long hair were as standardized as the "gray flannel suit" of the suburban "square," and so was their code of economic and moral lassitude. Even their methods of relief were routinized in alcoholic, narcotic, or hallucinogenic "highs." Some cultivated obliteration of all conceptual thought in the doctrines of Zen Buddhism and Taoism, but they preferred the "instant Zen" of drugs to the arduous route to Nirvana by means of meditation. In new bohemias around Greenwich Village in New York and North Beach in San Francisco, the Beats tried to live up to the great legend of the Lost Generation, but there were two important differences: the Beats produced no first-rate writers or artists, and their style of life was only another kind of conformism. As a rebellion against responsibility, the Beat movement succeeded. As a worthwhile alternative to the stupidities of American life it failed. It fizzled out at about the time of President Kennedy's inauguration.

Conformism and alienation, whether square or beat, were powerfully impelled by McCarthyism. Superpatriots exploited fear of communism to spread fear of all dissent, criticism, and even ordinary liberalism. "The American Way of Life" was an ill-defined object of verbal adoration, infecting administrators of educational institutions, clergymen, popular writers, business executives, editors, and promoters of radical-rightist organizations. Many people purged their minds of any idea which might come under suspicion as "disloyal." The younger generation in particular suffered. To make sure that no career doors would be closed to them, that nothing "controversial" would appear on their records, they suppressed the normal exuberance of youthful thought, carefully avoided organizations which might turn up on the Attorney General's "subversive" list, and concentrated on safe goals of career and family life. "Americanism" came to mean fervent faith in capitalism under the post-Marxist name "free enterprise." To criticize monopolistic violations of economic freedom seemed subversive. To advocate genuine economic freedom, along with the other freedoms guaranteed by the Constitution, above all, to use or advocate the use of the Fifth Amendment guarantee of the right to refuse to be a witness against oneself, seemed dangerously "un-American."

Loyalty to private organizations, especially business corporations, seemed to many ambitious young people identical with loyalty to the United States. All organizations grew larger and as they grew they absorbed larger emotional investments by their employees. Government service and the armed forces provided models for the subordination of self to the organization's welfare. Churches expanded their membership while reducing the theological content of their mission: fellowship, a sense of belonging, the security and status to be gained by respectable affiliation took the place of religious experience. Administrators of educational institutions were less often scholars than in earlier eras, more often executives hardly distinguishable from businessmen. Foundation executives administered enormous amounts of money often according to bureaucratic criteria. The newest and largest of them, the Ford Foundation, as if to admit that its administrators were certain to be too cautious, organized a subsidiary, The Fund for the Republic, to take a few chances. But the chief home of the "organization man" was the large business corporation. Personnel managers scrutinized not only applicants for junior executive posts, but their wives and children, their manners, the interior decoration of their home and the kind of entertainment offered to guests, their make of car, and the suitability to their station of the clothes they wore, as matters relevant to membership on "the team" and promotion.

In the new organizational way of life, the realities of a person's character and thought mattered less than his "image." Indeed, experts worked to create "favorable images" for commercial products, business corporations, and all manner of institutions including political parties. Advertising was the source of not only this expertise but also faith in appearance as the only significant evidence of reality. The influence of advertising and public relations experts over the minds and emotions of the people tended to displace that of educators, clergymen, statesmen, artists and philosophers. "Commercials" on radio and TV and advertisements in newspapers and magazines often showed more talent and commanded more admiration than entertainment programs and editorial matter. Political parties now employed advertising and public-relations firms to conduct their campaigns. Bribery of voters died away only to be replaced by psychological manipulations. "Status-seeking"—working for reputation by maneuvering the symbols of achievement—was the application of image-making to one's own externalities, and this, according to some observers, had become the essence of ambition for many Americans.

Against all this falsification of values, one defense was exposure, and a series of popular books exposed and sometimes exaggerated the power of "other-direction" (Riesman, Denney, and Glazer, *The Lonely Crowd*, 1950), the absorptive power of the business corporation (William H. Whyte, *The Organization Man*, 1957), and the cunning of the image-makers (Vance Packard, *The Hidden Persuaders*, 1957). Such books made people aware of the techniques of those who were trying to manipulate them, with consequent reduction in the power of the manipulators. But for others, such awareness fed keen admiration of the most successful experts in coercion. Another defense was retreat into passivity, privacy, and, in the case of many artists and writers, alienation. Most serious was alienation among the young as evidenced in rising rates of juvenile delinquency. Delinquency was not so confined as formerly to disadvantaged children. It began to appear in "good" suburbs. Some blamed a breakdown of parental standards and discipline, some blamed the schools, some blamed the easy ethics of the community at large. Probably most to blame was the shock young people suffered when they learned that they lived in a society menaced by the possibility of extinction as a consequence of their elders' technical prowess and inability to cope with the problem of war.

It was wrong to judge the America of mid-century as a normal society. The United States had suffered severe social dislocation in the process of fighting two world wars and a major economic depression, besides transforming itself into the most advanced and powerful industrial society on earth. The Cold War perpetuated crisis even during unexampled prosperity. The nation lived as a fortress under siege by Communist nations which had the power and quite possibly the will to use that power to destroy freedom. . . .

58

Newsweek
THE OUTSPOKEN GENERATION

Condensed from "Class of '69: The Violent Years," Newsweek, Vol. 73 (June 23, 1969), pp. 68–72. Copyright Newsweek, Inc., 1969.

. . . Commencement for the 750,000 members of the Class of 1969 found both students and adults divided and angered. The Class of '69 had entered college just after the first wave of student dissent broke loose at Berkeley and swept across the U.S. In the four years since, there have been more disorders on campus than in the comparable years of labor unrest in the 1930s. . . .

The students have forced universities to re-examine their purposes, faculties to re-examine their careers and adults to re-examine their consciences. It is clear that the movement that has done this represents something more than youthful exuberance, more than a transitory stage of growing up ("they'll settle down when they get married"), more than symbolic Freudian parricide, more than Dionysian energies released by sex and drugs—indeed, something more than can be encompassed by any of the other unitary approaches that "explain" the young. It is now recognized that a culturally distinct and apparently permanent youth class is emerging. This grouping is worldwide, but its distinguishing modes of behavior are most evident on U.S. campuses, where the conditions that have created it exist in their most powerful forms.

The emergence of a new class is most easily observed among the non-white U.S. students. Before 1965, they were Negroes; today they are blacks—a profound psychological transformation. Though the break is just as sharp between white youth over and under 25, no one as yet has hit upon a precisely descriptive set of labels. Margaret Mead, for one, calls the young "natives" of a totally new technological world and over-25 adults "foreigners" in this land. Perhaps the most accurate description is contained in Yale psychologist Kenneth Keniston's phrase "post-modern youth"—the first generation to be brought up by modern parents influenced by the emancipating social doctrines of the 1930s.

Post-modern youth, as Yale's Robert Brustein notes, has already been sufficiently praised, even overpraised, for its qualities of commitment, spontaneity, humanitarian values and personal authenticity. America has always valued youth. But now there is a kind of cult of divine youth that suggests that the young are intrinsically superior to the old. The most objective neutral statement that can be made about the new youth class is that modern parents have got the children they professed they wanted. . . .

These new students live in a period of extended youth. Adolescence now begins earlier and lasts longer. The affluence brought on by economic growth and increasing productivity has made it both economically possible and desirable for thousands of individuals to postpone work and a career to the mid- or late 20s. Whereas only one-third of U.S. high-school graduates went on to college in 1940, almost half were entering college by the mid-1960s. In theory, the technological society needed these highly trained people to take their places in the work force along with the machine; California made college, heretofore a privilege of the well-to-do, a right for every resident. But fewer people—and bigger computers—were already producing more goods. College is often a holding pattern for students. But few fidget about a career; the Depression memories of their parents rarely touch them. . . .

This emergence of a new youth class coincides with the emergence of a new kind of university. When the academic envisions the university he sees a disinterested community of scholars devoted to reasoned discourse, the pursuit of truth and the education of the young. The classic statement of this idea of the university was delivered in 1852 by John Henry Cardinal Newman. The university was to be an "alma mater, knowing her children one by one, not a foundry or a mint or a treadmill." The aim was a "liberal education"—and not mere vocational or technical instruction—for the elite leaders of tomorrow. This is the vision that still inspires commencement speakers and mists over the present turmoil on campus. But it is more chimerical than real.

Actually, the American university has followed a different model. The accepted date for the beginning of the modern American university is the appointment of President Charles Eliot of Harvard in 1869. Eliot's Harvard imitated the Germany university with its emphasis on graduate research and study. Yale, Columbia and the newly created universities like Johns Hopkins, Chicago and Stanford also followed the German model. This marked the triumph of "professionalism" in U.S. education, the development hailed by David Riesman and Christopher Jencks as "the academic revolution."

There were efforts to restore the primacy of undergraduate education at the professional, research-oriented universities, most notably at Chicago under Robert Hutchins in the 1930s. These efforts were vaporized, ironically enough, by the atomic bomb which was developed at Hutchins's own school and which ushered in the most recent phase of university development. In July 1930, Enrico Fermi and the other physicists working on the idea of a nuclear chain reaction needed $6,000 worth of graphite. No university physics department in the nation could even consider granting such an astronomical sum—and it took no less than the famous Einstein letter to FDR himself to get the project going.

That was the end of the university's political innocence: the academics went to war; radar developments, proximity fuses, navigation devices—as well as The Bomb—came out of the academy during World War II. Scientific and technical knowledge became, in Clark Kerr's words, "the focal point for national growth." And at the center of the knowledge process, Kerr proudly pointed out, was the new university, or multiversity—a term meant to convey that the academy was now serving a variety of worldly needs. By the mid-1960s, in fact, Kerr's own University of California was itself operating two national nuclear laboratories for the government on a budget of more than $200 million a year. . . .

By this time, too, alma mater had become precisely that foundry and treadmill Newman had abhorred. With 40,000 students on campus, the multiversity had to put the names of its students on IBM cards, send grades out by code number and install TV monitors in the back of vast lecture halls so students could see the tiny creature at the distant podium. Often, this might be the student's only glimpse of the professor. The knowledge business has catapulted the star faculty member and the rising researcher from a local to a national constituency; his time and his loyalty no longer belonged to his university, but to his discipline— and to those in government and industry who wanted to pay for his specialized consultation. With the new academic entrepreneur spending so much time on the shuttle run to Washington, the actual teaching became the responsibility of section heads, often graduate students. "When a man's reputation is national," observes Berkeley Prof. Neil Smelser, "he does

the things that enhance his reputation—and teaching isn't one of them." . . .

The first student complaints about the multiversity were particular rather than general, self-centered rather than cosmic. After the souped-up curriculum of a good high school, the college classroom, grail of all those hardworking years, seemed anticlimactic. Many students had experience with sex and drugs before they reached college, and they objected to rules that required them to live in campus dorms or restricted their hours or visitors. Parietal rules are still among the major causes of white student protest in the South and Midwest. As one student said: "Students don't have the power to get a girl in their room when they want to, and we're talking about ending the Vietnam war!"

The first major mobilization of student dissent came at Berkeley with the Free Speech Movement in 1964. This episode has set the style for subsequent student demonstrations and university responses around the country. FSM centered on a specific grievance—the right for students to have a microphone and political recruiting tables in Sproul Plaza. It involved the tactics of sit-ins and confrontations with authority—techniques that Martin Luther King Jr. used so effectively. At Berkeley, as in Montgomery, authority responded with police, mass arrests, court injunctions, suspensions—and, eventually, negotiations that culminated in the granting of the protesters' demands. Today Sproul at noon is as good a show as "Hair"— and administrators pridefully show it off.

This belated acknowledgement of the reasonableness of the original student demand is part of a pattern too: students protest an injustice; after turmoil and dissension, the university admits that the wrong existed. Moreover, there is evidence that the wrong would have continued to exist uncorrected if the activists, like the boy in "The Emperor's New Clothes," had not insisted: "But the emperor *is* naked." . . .

If many student demands are not unreasonable (in hindsight), then why the failure of so many university officials to grasp this fact? The radical's answer would be that the officials are too corrupt; the cynical might say that they aren't too bright. A more accurate answer might be that administrations, by and large, simply forgot about the students and the professed ideals of the university during the heady, aggrandizing days of the multiversity's growth. At the same time, they failed to appreciate fully the quantum change in student attitudes. The present turmoil is in part the due bill for the years of outward growth and internal indifference.

As a result the administrations on the more volatile campuses have become "crisis managers"—no more than glorified firemen running here and there to put out the conflagrations. Like firemen, these administrators concentrate on each specific emergency as it comes up; they have little time to work out a theory of arson or the design of fireproof communities. Each man is judged by his tactics: Columbia's Grayson Kirk and Harvard's Nathan Pusey "failed" because they called in the police; Cornell's James Perkins erred because he didn't grasp the impact of the news pictures showing black students brandishing guns on campus. Chicago's Edward Levi and Brandeis's Morris Abram, on the other hand, were good tacticians. When student radicals took over Levi's office, Levi simply let them have the building. He mobilized moderate opinion and let the faculty (a body too diffuse to become a target) deal with the nettlesome task of discipline. Abram kept the "lines of communication" open when blacks occupied a Brandeis building—using his powers of persuasion, as lawyers do, rather than bringing on police action. Yale's Kingman

Brewster is credited with "staying one step ahead of trouble" by seeking out students and anticipating their needs. Minnesota's Malcolm Moos, too, is a sympathetic and imaginative administrator. When some funds were needed this year for black-studies activities at state-supported Minnesota, Moos agreed to find private money to pay some of the cost.

This tactical approach, by definition, cannot resolve the campus crisis for several reasons.

First of all, it cannot head off the effectiveness of the Students for a Democratic Society. SDS aims are thought to be generally Marxist, and most discussions center on the tactics of opposition and disruption. Actually Marx wouldn't have approved of SDS any more than contemporary Marxists do: to them, SDS is a band of Bakunin revolutionaries—all action and no organization.

The crisis managers have not yet realized that the revolutionaries' demands can be endless. Columbia's SDS served a list of six demands on the university last year. An SDS leader was asked what the group would do if all six demands were accepted. He replied: make six more demands. The tactic of constant pressure is an old revolutionary strategy; the object is not reform but to bring down the "corrupt" university as a step toward bringing down the "corrupt" society. . . .

Many administrators appreciate how vulnerable the university is. Before the crisis occurs, they are attentive (like Brewster and Moos) to the moderate students' wishes. After trouble begins, they seek (like Levi and Abram) to avoid "radicalizing" the moderates, refusing to call in the police or the guard. But these good tacticians miss the wider meaning of what has been happening to students over the last few years—and this is the second reason they will fail to cool off the campuses. The reputed moderates are really like the SDS: they, too, cannot be bought off with tactical concessions —though for a different reason. The members of the new student class seek a truly radical—as opposed to political—goal. The most unadorned way to phrase this goal is, "They want control of their lives." It is a demand, in its several variations, that is as familiar to parents as to university administrators. . . .

In sum, the present generation of students wants a hand in controlling most phases of university affairs. This goal means demands for an end to the university's role of *in loco parentis* and to other efforts to limit personal freedom, no matter how reasonable to adults. It means demands for "more relevant" courses and a student voice in choosing and promoting faculty. If anything, the moderates' desire for control is more of a "threat" to the university than all the nonnegotiable demands of the political revolutionaries. Unlike the SDS, the moderates are serious about wanting to run the university. . . .

The campus crisis managers cannot be blamed for the third reason for their failure. As more than one commencement speaker noted last week, this is an era of pervasive and passionate questioning of the legitimacy of all who hold power in society. Harvard's Franklin Ford has referred to this as "the particular malaise of the '60s." But it goes beyond recent events. Everyone knows by now that the Vietnam war and the draft are central concerns of the new student class; what is less appreciated is the fact that even if the war and the draft were to end tomorrow, this would not fatally dampen the present assault on authority. Canada has no draft and no war and yet Canadian students are considered perhaps the most militant in the world. What has happened in the U.S. is that the war, the race issue, the befouled environment and all the other perceived gaps between professed ideals and reality have precipitated a crisis for all authority.

This crisis has been building for decades all over the world. It is easier to describe than

explain. At the time of the Sorbonne riots last year one French politician thought society had reached a point when, like Rome, civilizations collapse because belief is dead. For Archibald MacLeish the exact opposite is true. Passionate belief in the value of man, he said recently at the University of California, "had come alive for the first time in the century and with it rage and violence." . . .

In truth many students today are subversive. But theirs seems to be a moral and not a political subversion. If the problem of student dissent were only political, then it would be relatively easy to deal with: the state could uproot the provocateurs; the university could continue to shorten its lines of vulnerability, correct its past ills and make concessions to various student groups in return for tranquillity. The universities have already done a great deal of political trading. Parietal rules have been reduced in many dorms to the vanishing point. Students have been added to disciplinary committees, administrators have re-examined their investment portfolios and military contracts in the light of student criticism and just last week Princeton University named two students—one a black activist—to its board of trustees.

These concessions, however, cannot satisfy the essentially *moral* principles being put forth under the student slogans of "community," "co-control," "relevance" and "legitimacy." There is only so much that the university administration can yield, for example, to satisfy the cry to get "war research" off campus. The point is eventually reached when to meet these claims means diminishing other principles which may not only be moral too, but also rooted in the tradition and the law. Two such principles are now under the most intense pressure. . . .

The first principle is the academic right to free inquiry. The university won the right for its members to pursue the work they chose after bitter battles in the 1930s and the 1940s with heresy hunters, right-wing legislatures, Red baiters and blue-stockings (the late Dr. Alfred Kinsey was hounded mercilessly for his sex research). Now the threat comes from within the campus. In the past year student groups have disrupted the classes of teachers who support U.S. policy in Vietnam, prevented other students from attending interviews with military and industrial recruiters and occupied laboratories doing Pentagon research in order to stop faculty and staff members from going to work.

These coercive acts are clearly extra-legal, a minority imposition on majority rights. They can be "justified" only by appeals to moral aims or to conscience. Thus, violence has come to be regarded by some students—and faculty— as acceptable in the short run (but not as an end in itself) because it dramatizes just grievances and brings them to public attention. Thus, too, free speech and free assembly have become in this view relative rather than absolute. . . .

The second fundamental principle affected by the student claims is the matter of university ownership. The new students have come to regard the university as belonging to them as much as to any other of its constituencies. It is an identification that faculties themselves have presumed to make from time to time. But the legalities are quite incontrovertible. Private schools like Harvard are owned by chartered corporations; public schools like Berkeley, Illinois or CCNY, are operated by regents or boards either appointed by public officials or elected by the voters. The faculty may express its position, as CCNY's did recently on minority admissions, but the decision in the admissions case rests with the Board of Higher Education appointed by the mayor of New York.

The ownership is not likely to change hands bloodlessly. . . .

59

Harold Isaacs
THE NEW WORLD OF THE NEGRO

Copyright © 1963 by Massachusetts Institute of Technology. Reprinted from The New World of Negro Americans *by Harold R. Isaacs, pp. 4–9, by permission of the John Day Company, Inc., publisher.*

Harold Isaacs (1910–   ) is a political scientist who has been a research associate and professor at the Massachusetts Institute of Technology since 1953. As a young man he served as a reporter for the *New York Times*, the Honolulu *Advertiser*, the Shanghai *Evening Post and China Press*, and Agence Havas. From 1943 to 1950 he was associate editor of *Newsweek Magazine*. He is the author of such studies as *No Peace for Asia* (1947), *Emergent Americans* (1961), and *The New World of Negro America* (1963).

From the time of the signing of the Emancipation Proclamation until only a few years ago, the American society was able to deny civil and human rights to millions of its members because of their "race" and yet keep on seeing itself as a striving democracy of free men. For nearly three-quarters of a century, it proved possible to sweep this gross contradiction under the national rug. But the circumstances favoring this massive deception and self-deception began to evaporate about twenty-five years ago. As Sumner Welles observed in 1944: "The thesis of white supremacy could only exist so long as the white race actually proved to be supreme." That thesis was built into the superstructure of Western white-world power; it was used to rationalize and justify on racial grounds the Western white man's sovereignty over the whole of the globe. That system of power and sovereignty had been weakening for decades, barely managed to survive the First World War, began to fall apart with the onset of the

Second World War, and finally came tumbling down in the years of its aftermath. The empires that white Europe had established in Asia and Africa over some 300 years were almost completely dissolved in the 15 years between 1945 and 1960 and were replaced by some 40 new nation-states. To be sure, life-and-death power over the world remained in the hands of the nuclear superpowers and economic power likewise remained heavily concentrated in Western hands, but this was something quite different from the intimate and direct rulership of Western whites over Asian and African nonwhites which was the substance of imperial political sovereignty. The whole basis of their relationship now had to be revised.

For with the collapse of its underpinning political power, the whole superstructure of Western white supremacy began to waver and fall. It has been in these years like watching a slow-motion film of the collapsing of a dynamited building: slowly it falls out into the air, parts of it retaining form and structure even as they sink and are gradually obscured by the dust and rubble into which they fall. Because it is slow motion, some can imagine that these slabs of the familiar facade are still standing there in the air and are not falling at all. But this is illusion becoming delusion, for here they are coming down all around us—all the assumptions we made about each other, about ourselves and about other human beings, about our own and other groups and kinds, "races," peoples, cultures. Here, coming apart amid their fallen power props, are all the myths of white superiority and nonwhite inferiority, all the deeply imbedded notions and emotions, all the patterns of long-practiced behavior. All are being displaced and have to be replaced. All that was *given*, in a word, is now being taken away. Whether we will it, or know it, or like it, or not, we are all participants in this great continental rearrangement of power and human relationships. All Western white men have to get rid of the habits of mastery, and all nonwhites the habits of subjection. This is now the common and nearly universal experience. There is hardly a corner of national or international life now that is not touched by it and hardly anyone, white or black or whatever, who is not now faced by its demands.

In Asia and Africa where the colonies have become nation-states, this process of revision in relationship and mutual image can at least begin with a transfer of political power and thus throw around the new confusions a screen of formal new status relationship. The styles of this transfer have varied greatly—the hasty but relatively skillful improvising of the British, the myopic but brief resistance of the Dutch, the myopic and prolonged resistance of the French, the pell-mell panicking of the Belgians —but the result in every case creates a new formal situation. A new state is proclaimed, a new flag raised, a new government established, a new "power" is established, and from here on out at least the externals of behavior are governed by the protocol of diplomacy and the needs of policy. . . . The shedding of colonial power does not at a stroke relieve the old colonial master of the whole burden of his beliefs about himself, nor Western white people generally of the legacy of what their whole culture taught them for so long about these matters. Similarly, political independence does not at a stroke free either the new nation or its people from *their* legacy of subjection, imposed inferiority, dependence, and self-rejection. But at least now the power of government is in the hands of one's own kind and the most egregious forms of subordination to foreign rulership are forced to disappear. The new national power, no matter how weak, is at least strong enough to put a prohibitive tariff on the return of this kind of foreign domination and under its protection to produce (to resurrect, recreate, or create as the case may be) a new national, cultural or even "racial" identity on which indigenous self-respect can begin to thrive.

In American society, on the other hand, the end of white supremacy has to be signaled not by *separation* but by *integration*. Here there is no simple initial solution like changing the signs at a boundary line and raising a new flag. Here the issue remains locked in the society's unfulfilled promise of democratic pluralism. This promise is perhaps our greatest and most unique virtue and our failure to fulfill it may be our costliest failure, for we have been overtaken by it at last. The gulf between our profession and our practice has become an abyss to whose edge the world has pushed us.

The downfall of the white-supremacy system in the rest of the world made its survival in the United States suddenly and painfully conspicuous. It became our most exposed feature and in the swift unfolding of the world's affairs, our most vulnerable weakness. It was like being caught naked in a glaring spotlight alone on a great stage in a huge theatre filled with people we had not known were there. Here we were now, our vulnerability so highly visible that when hundreds of millions of people all around the world looked in our direction it seemed to be all that they could see.

This was because the "world" in which we now live is no longer the dominant white Atlantic world in which most of us were born. It is a rudely enlarged place that includes Asia and Africa on a wholly new footing. Most of the millions whose scrutiny we are now feeling are the nonwhite peoples coming so dramatically into view with the scars of Western white dominance still heavily marked upon them. These great masses of Asians and Africans turn out to be, moreover, people whose future has become a critical factor in the American future, not to say American survival. For the world-power struggle between the United States and the Soviet Union now turns not only on the balance of economies or weapons, on systems of production or control of strategic resources and territories, but also on the shape of man's political future, the institutions he will choose or be led to build, the conceptions of freedom or unfreedom he will embrace or be embraced by in the next few decades. Unless it is dissolved by resort to the Bombs, the coming shape of things will be largely decided by the choices made by precisely these "new" Asian and African peoples. If, as we insist, the power struggle is not only a confrontation of Bombs and systems of production, but also a confrontation of fundamentally different ways of relating man to his society, then the nature of the American democracy itself becomes a critical issue in this struggle.

The facts are that the American democracy housed slavery for its first 75 years, then freed the slaves and promised them the same constitutional rights enjoyed by all citizens, and then proceeded for nearly another hundred years to deny Negroes those rights. It comes now into this new revolutionary epoch faced abruptly with the need to establish new and more mutually respectful relations with the nonwhite peoples of the earth without being able to show that it has given to its own nonwhite citizens even a minimum measure of the dignity and freedom on which it bases its philosophy and its whole case against the totalitarians. The democratic system itself produced no sufficient self-correction of this profound anomaly. Only the slow trickle of cases through the courts gave evidence of any inward capacity for change, and it was hardly moving at all until it was washed over by the great flood of world events.

So the end of white supremacy in the United States is finally being forced by the end of white supremacy in the rest of the world. We now have to abandon racist practices because we simply can no longer afford to cling to them, any more than we can cling to the idea that there is any security left in continental isolation. No doubt it would have been far better to have reached this point through the working out of the democratic belief in the equality of rights of all citizens or the Christian belief in human brotherhood. It may be that the democratic process works not only as slowly but also as mysteriously as Providence is reputed to do. Nevertheless, both isolationism and racism have had to be blasted out of their deeply imbedded places in American life and history by nothing less than the great world explosions of our time, the technological and political explosions that have transformed all human affairs in this century. Isolationism could not survive the scientific advances that made the globe itself the smallest viable unit of political and social change. White supremacy in America cannot survive the political overturns that have brought to an end the Western white man's sovereignty over the rest of the world. It may be possible to imagine white racist systems persisting in an isolation protected by Super-Bombs. But such systems, even assuming they could survive in a hopelessly hostile world environment, could not remain even nominally democratic. This is what makes the persistence of isolationists and racists among us so perilous and their grip on crucial sections of our national life a drag that threatens to carry us all down with them as they disappear.

There is a certain awesome, almost Biblical irony in the way things have worked out. It is not really very much of an exaggeration to say that as matters stand now, "democrats" must finally become democratic (and "Christians" Christian) or die.

60

Bayard Rustin
GROWING NEGRO DISILLUSIONMENT

*From Bayard Rustin, "Black Power and Coalition Politics," * Commentary, *Vol. 42 (September 1966), pp. 35–38. Reprinted from * Commentary, *by permission; copyright © 1966 by the American Jewish Committee.*

Bayard Rustin (1910–   ), since 1964 the executive director of the A. Philip Randolph Institute, has long been a leader in the black civil rights movement. In the 1940s, as field secretary and race relations secretary for the Fellowship of Reconciliation, he helped to organize the Congress of Racial Equality (CORE). In the 1950s he was special adviser to Martin Luther King and a chief architect of Dr. King's Southern Christian Leadership Conference (SCLC). In 1963 he organized the March on Washington for Jobs and Freedom and a year later he directed the first New York City school boycott.

There are two Americas—black and white—and nothing has more clearly revealed the divisions between them than the debate currently raging around the slogan of "black power." Despite—or perhaps because of—the fact that this slogan lacks any clear definition, it has succeeded in galvanizing emotions on all sides, with many whites seeing it as the expression of a new racism and many Negroes taking it as a warning to white people that Negroes will no longer tolerate brutality and violence. But even within the Negro community itself, "black power" has touched off a major debate —the most bitter the community has experienced since the days of Booker T. Washington and W. E. B. Du Bois, and one which threatens to ravage the entire civil-rights movement. Indeed, a serious split has already developed between advocates of "black power" like Floyd

McKissick of CORE and Stokely Carmichael of SNCC [Student Non-Violent Coordinating Committee] on the one hand, and Dr. Martin Luther King of SCLC, Roy Wilkins of the NAACP [National Association for the Advancement of Colored People], and Whitney Young of the Urban League on the other. . . .

"Black power" is, of course, a somewhat nationalistic slogan and its sudden rise to popularity among Negroes signifies a concomitant rise in nationalist sentiment (Malcolm X's autobiography is quoted nowadays in Grenada, Mississippi as well as in Harlem). We have seen such nationalistic turns and withdrawals back into the ghetto before, and when we look at the conditions which brought them about, we find that they have much in common with the conditions of Negro life at the present moment: conditions which lead to despair over the goal of integration and to the belief that the ghetto will last forever.

It may, in the light of the many juridical and legislative victories which have been achieved in the past few years, seem strange that despair should be so widespread among Negroes today. But anyone to whom it seems strange should reflect on the fact that despite these victories *Negroes today are in worse economic shape, live in worse slums, and attend more highly segregated schools than in 1954.* Thus—to recite the appalling, and appallingly familiar, statistical litany once again—more Negroes are unemployed today than in 1954; the gap between the wages of the Negro worker and the white worker is wider; while the unemployment rate among white youths is decreasing, the rate among Negro youths has increased to *32 per cent* (and among Negro girls the rise is even more startling). Even the one gain which has been registered, a decrease in the unemployment rate among Negro adults, is deceptive, for it represents men who have been called back to work after a period of being

laid off. In any event, unemployment among Negro men is still twice that of whites, and no new jobs have been created.

So too with housing, which is deteriorating in the North (and yet the housing provisions of the 1966 civil-rights bill are weaker than the anti-discrimination laws in several states which contain the worst ghettos even with these laws on their books). And so too with schools: according to figures issued recently by the Department of Health, Education and Welfare, 65 per cent of first-grade Negro students in this country attend schools that are from 90 to 100 per cent black. (If in 1954, when the Supreme Court handed down the desegregation decision, you had been the Negro parent of a first-grade child, the chances are that this past June you would have attended that child's graduation from a segregated high school.)

To put all this in the simplest and most concrete terms: the day-to-day lot of the ghetto Negro has not been improved by the various judicial and legislative measures of the past decade.

Negroes are thus in a situation similar to that of the turn of the century, when Booker T. Washington advised them to "cast down their buckets" (that is to say, accommodate to segregation and disenfranchisement) and when even his leading opponent, W. E. B. Du Bois, was forced to advocate the development of a group economy in place of the direct-action boycotts, general strikes, and protest techniques which had been used in the 1880's, before the enactment of the Jim-Crow laws. For all their differences, both Washington and Du Bois then found it impossible to believe that Negroes could ever be integrated into American society, and each in his own way therefore counseled withdrawal into the ghetto, self-help, and economic self-determination.

World War I aroused new hope in Negroes

that the rights removed at the turn of the century would be restored. More than 360,000 Negroes entered military service and went overseas; many left the South seeking the good life in the North and hoping to share in the temporary prosperity created by the war. But all these hopes were quickly smashed at the end of the fighting. In the first year following the war, more than seventy Negroes were lynched, and during the last six months of that year, there were some twenty-four riots throughout America. White mobs took over whole cities, flogging, burning, shooting, and torturing at will, and when Negroes tried to defend themselves, the violence only increased. Along with this, Negroes were excluded from unions and pushed out of jobs they had won during the war, including federal jobs.

In the course of this period of dashed hope and spreading segregation—the same period, incidentally, when a reorganized Ku Klux Klan was achieving a membership which was to reach into the millions—the largest mass movement ever to take root among working-class Negroes, Marcus Garvey's "Back to Africa" movement, was born. "Buy Black" became a slogan in the ghettos; faith in integration was virtually snuffed out in the Negro community until the 1930's when the CIO reawakened the old dream of a Negro-labor alliance by announcing a policy of non-discrimination and when the New Deal admitted Negroes into relief programs, WPA jobs, and public housing. No sooner did jobs begin to open up and Negroes begin to be welcomed into mainstream organizations than "Buy Black" campaigns gave way to "Don't Buy Where You Can't Work" movements. A. Philip Randolph was able to organize a massive March on Washington demanding a wartime FEPC [Fair Employment Practices Committee]; CORE was born and with it the non-violent sit-in technique; the NAACP succeeded in putting an

end to the white primaries in 1944. Altogether, World War II was a period of hope for Negroes, and the economic progress they made through wartime industry continued steadily until about 1948 and remained stable for a time. Meanwhile, the non-violent movement of the 1950's and 60's achieved the desegregation of public accommodations and established the right to vote.

Yet at the end of this long fight, the Southern Negro is too poor to use those integrated facilities and too intimidated and disorganized to use the vote to maximum advantage, while the economic position of the Northern Negro deteriorates rapidly.

The promise of meaningful work and decent wages once held out by the anti-poverty programs has not been fulfilled. Because there has been a lack of the necessary funds, the program has in many cases been reduced to wrangling for positions on boards or for lucrative staff jobs. Negro professionals working for the program have earned handsome salaries—ranging from $14- to $25,000—while young boys have been asked to plant trees at $1.25 an hour. Nor have the Job Corps camps made a significant dent in unemployment among Negro youths; indeed, the main beneficiaries of this program seem to be the private companies who are contracted to set up the camps.

Then there is the war in Vietnam, which poses many ironies for the Negro community. On the one hand, Negroes are bitterly aware of the fact that more and more money is being spent on the war, while the anti-poverty program is being cut; on the other hand, Negro youths are enlisting in great numbers, as though to say that it is worth the risk of being killed to learn a trade, to leave a dead-end situation, and to join the only institution in this society which seems really to be integrated.

The youths who rioted in Watts, Cleveland,

Omaha, Chicago, and Portland are the members of a truly hopeless and lost generation. They can see the alien world of affluence unfold before them on the TV screen. But they have already failed in their inferior segregated schools. Their grandfathers were sharecroppers, their grandmothers were domestics, and their mothers are domestics too. Many have never met their fathers. Mistreated by the local storekeeper, suspected by the policeman on the beat, disliked by their teachers, they cannot stand more failures and would rather retreat into the world of heroin than risk looking for a job downtown or having their friends see them push a rack in the garment district. Floyd McKissick and Stokely Carmichael may accuse Roy Wilkins of being out of touch with the Negro ghetto, but nothing more clearly demonstrates their own alienation from ghetto youth than their repeated exhortations to these young men to oppose the Vietnam war when so many of them tragically see it as their only way out. Yet there is no need to labor the significance of the fact that the rice fields of Vietnam and the Green Berets have more to offer a Negro boy than the streets of Mississippi or the towns of Alabama or 125th Street in New York.

The Vietnam war is also partly responsible for the growing disillusion with non-violence among Negroes. The ghetto Negro does not in general ask whether the United States is right or wrong to be in Southeast Asia. He does, however, wonder why he is exhorted to non-violence when the United States has been waging a fantastically brutal war, and it puzzles him to be told that he must turn the other cheek in our own South while we must fight for freedom in South Vietnam.

Thus, as in roughly similar circumstances in the past—circumstances, I repeat, which in the aggregate foster the belief that the ghetto is destined to last forever—Negroes are once again turning to nationalistic slogans, with "black power" affording the same emotional release as "Back to Africa" and "Buy Black" did in earlier periods of frustration and hopelessness. This is not only the case with the ordinary Negro in the ghetto; it is also the case with leaders like McKissick and Carmichael, neither of whom began as a nationalist or was at first cynical about the possibilities of integration. It took countless beatings and 24 jailings —that, and the absence of strong and continual support from the liberal community—to persuade Carmichael that his earlier faith in coalition politics was mistaken, that nothing was to be gained from working with whites, and that an alliance with the black nationalists was desirable. In the areas of the South where SNCC has been working so nobly, implementation of the Civil Rights Act of 1964 and 1965 has been slow and ineffective. Negroes in many rural areas cannot walk into the courthouse and register to vote. Despite the voting-rights bill, they must file complaints and the Justice Department must be called to send federal registrars. Nor do children attend integrated schools as a matter of course. There, too, complaints must be filed and the Department of Health, Education and Welfare must be notified. Neither department has been doing an effective job of enforcing the bills. The feeling of isolation increases among SNCC workers as each legislative victory turns out to be only a token victory—significant on the national level, but not affecting the day-to-day lives of Negroes. Carmichael and his colleagues are wrong in refusing to support the 1966 bill, but one can understand why they feel as they do.

It is, in short, the growing conviction that the Negroes cannot win—a conviction with much grounding in experience—which accounts for the new popularity of "black power." So far as the ghetto Negro is concerned, this conviction expresses itself in hostility first toward the people closest to him who have held out the most promise and failed to deliver (Martin Luther King, Roy Wilkins, etc.), then toward those who have proclaimed themselves his friends (the liberals and the labor movement), and finally toward the only oppressors he can see (the local storekeeper and the policeman on the corner). On the leadership level, the conviction that the Negroes cannot win takes other forms, principally the adoption of what I have called a "no-win" policy. Why bother with programs when their enactment results only in "sham"? Why concern ourselves with the image of the movement when nothing significant has been gained for all the sacrifices made by SNCC and CORE? Why compromise with reluctant white allies when nothing of consequence can be achieved anyway? Why indeed have anything to do with whites at all?

61

Benjamin Fine
KOREA AND THE SCHOOLS

From Benjamin Fine, "Rearming Saps School Gains as Rolls and Costs Still Soar," the New York Times, *January 14, 1952, pp. 1, 28. © 1952 by The New York Times Company. Reprinted by permission.*

Benjamin Fine (1905–   ) is a journalist, educator, and author who, upon receipt of his doctorate from Columbia University in 1941, became "education editor" for the *New York Times* and since 1959 has served in the same capacity for the North American Newspaper Alliance. He has also been a member of the faculty at the New School for Social Research (1944–1955) and dean of the Graduate School of Education at Yeshiva University (1958–1960). In 1943 he received the Pulitzer Prize for a series of articles on the teaching of history in the schools. Among his many books are *Democratic Education* (1945), *1,000,-000 Delinquents* (1955), *How to Get the Best*

Education for Your Child (1958), *Teaching Machines* (1962), and *Ways to Study and Learn* (1966).

Once again the nation's public schools are in serious plight. Eighteen months of defense mobilization have taken their toll. Danger signals are flying everywhere, but often are not heeded. Many advances made in the first five years after World War II are being swept away.

The schools, like other aspects of civilian life, are beginning to feel the effects of the Korean conflict. As a result, they face a gloomy year. Many educators are worried lest the gloom continue for another decade.

Reports from state commissioners of education, correspondents of *The New York Times* in each of the forty-eight states, and interviews with leading educators all point to a downward trend.

The schools are caught in a pincers. Four major factors are involved: Increased enrollments, inflationary costs, lack of building materials and an acute teacher shortage.

Each is leaving its imprint on the schools, and on the children, too. It is not a question of tanks versus textbooks. Educators everywhere wholeheartedly support the Government's defense program. They applaud its efforts to make our democracy strong enough to withstand the challenge of Soviet Communism.

They say their problem is not one of more ABC's or more airplanes. They insist our economy is strong enough to provide both. Moreover, they insist that it is just as true today as it was a century ago, when first proclaimed by Horace Mann, that schoolhouses are the first line of our defense.

In the last year it appears schools have made few advances, and many backward steps. A number of communities report unexpected setbacks. Over the nation, 3,500,000 elementary and high school children—one out of eight pupils in the public schools—are suffering an impaired education because of inadequate facilities. A year ago a *Times* study showed 3,000,000 children were being deprived of an adequate education. Thus, there has been an increase of half a million in twelve months.

Incompetent teachers, poorly equipped classrooms, inadequate buildings and poor supervision combine to cheat these hundreds of thousands of young people. The number of pupils on double sessions is growing steadily. An estimated 400,000 boys and girls are not getting a full school day—some are attending school even on triple-session schedules. They go half a day, or a third of a day. What this does to the morale of the children, the parents, the teachers and the community is easy to imagine.

Educators emphasize that a child deprived of his schooling will be unable to regain the years lost—a child is 6 only once. One cannot postpone the growth of a pupil as one might postpone the building of a road or a garage.

This comment by Dr. Walter Maxwell, secretary of the Arizona Education Association, is typical: "At numerous schools I have seen children lined up in front of a schoolhouse door, marching in to take their places in the school as the first shift marched out—just like the changing of shifts in factories."

Inflationary costs are a headache everywhere. School officials are haunted by rising prices. Everything they buy has gone up 50 or 100 or even 200 per cent. Teachers are insisting they get their share, too. Cost-of-living bonuses have been handed out, but not fast enough, the teachers complain, to keep pace with rising food prices. As a result, morale in many communities is poor. Last spring the 500 teachers of Pawtucket, R.I., went on strike for several months, closing all of the city's schools. They won part of the increase they sought—but at a serious cost to the schooling of their pupils.

In other communities the struggle for higher salary schedules goes on in the board rooms rather than on the picket line. The New York City teachers recently ended a year-and-a-half "boycott" of extracurricular activities. Judging from the reaction of their spokesmen, they are far from happy at the compromise salary increases.

But the salary issue is only part of the educational picture. Competition has arisen from higher-paying Government jobs, war-related positions and the demand for skilled and semi-skilled workers in various industries. More teachers are leaving the profession today than at any time since World War II, when 350,000 departed, never to return.

Frequently the community must employ substandard, unqualified teachers because trained personnel are lacking. Many school systems report they are "scraping the bottom of the barrel."

A smoldering discontent is detected. Never before have the schools been under such attacks. Frequently the controversy is artificially contrived, dishonestly designed to wreck the free public school. But there is enough discontent to make thoughtful educators and civic-minded citizens take stock.

The schools are in need of greater financial help—and they are unable to get it. Many communities already allocate a substantial part of their tax funds for the schools. Oftentimes real estate is taxed almost to the danger point. But education costs more today than ever before—and the money frequently is not there to spend.

Enrollment is at its highest peak. *The Times* survey indicates that the 1951–52 school enrollment is 26,525,115—representing a growth of 826,194 in a year. Most of this growth has occurred in the elementary grades, and more particularly the first grade. The private and parochial schools will add another 3,000,000 children or more, thus bringing the total elementary and secondary enrollment close to 30,000,000.

Moreover, the school rolls are going to increase for at least eight years, more likely ten.

Next year—1952–53—the schools will enroll 1,700,000 more children than were registered this year. This is a tremendous number to absorb, particularly since most of the classrooms already are overcrowded. The peak will not be reached before 1957–58, if by then, at which time it is estimated the enrollment in public elementary and secondary schools will exceed 32,000,000, an increase of 6,000,000 over that of today.

Educators are deeply disturbed by this condition. Typical is the view voiced by Dr. Earl J. McGrath, United States Commissioner of Education:

"The tidal wave of children bearing down on our schools bids fair to overwhelm us. We simply are not building enough new schoolhouses or training enough new teachers to meet the situation. We can't go on from year to year on the present makeshift basis without seriously undermining our whole public school system.

"Unless the American people are prepared to take positive action to remedy these deficiencies, millions of children will continue to get a makeshift education."

Today many thousands of children are attending classes in school basements, apartment-house basements, empty stores, garages, churches, inadequate private homes and even trailers. What is more, one out of five of the regular schools is either unsafe or obsolete.

The defense program has played havoc with building plans. Even though the nation spent a record $1,200,000,000 for school construction in 1950–51, the communities were unable to keep pace with the number of children reaching school age. And in 1952, educators warn, [the shortage of] steel and other critical materials will stymie the construction of many badly needed schoolhouses.

More than 1,000,000 school teachers are now employed, 46,000 more than last year. But with more than 1,000,000 children to be added each year for the next several years, the teaching rolls also will have to rise steadily. However, teacher-training institutions are not preparing enough men and women to do the job. All but four states report a teacher shortage even this year. They now could use 71,886 elementary and 15,121 high school teachers.

Despite the need for teachers, young people seem to shy at entering the profession. The teacher colleges report a decrease this year of 16 per cent in their entering classes. This means, in effect, that four years from now, when the school rolls will have increased by more than 5,000,000, there will be fewer trained teachers.

Although the number of teachers holding substandard or emergency certificates has decreased by 5,053, there are still 66,354 of them in the school system. For example, 8,500 of the 24,600 teachers in Missouri are on emergency certificates, and South Dakota reports 1,796 of its 7,159 teachers do not hold regular licenses.

But the "substandard certificates" tell only part of the story. The National Education Association estimates that of the 600,000 elementary teachers in the public schools, 300,000 do not hold college degrees—the minimum standard. Of this number, the N.E.A. says, at least 100,-000 are so inadequately prepared as to make their continued presence in the classroom dangerous to the mental and emotional growth of America's youth.

The Times survey shows that teachers' salaries have risen slightly from an average of $3,097 to $3,290 annually. This $193 increase, or $3.71 a week, has been eaten up, the teachers declare, by increased living costs and higher taxes.

New York State, with an average annual teachers' salary of $4,500, leads the country, followed by the District of Columbia with a $4,300 average and California with $3,967. Mississippi again is at the bottom of the list, paying its teachers an average of $1,475 a year. Arkansas is next to Mississippi with $1,700, and South Carolina is third from the bottom with $2,130.

Six states pay some teachers less than $20 a week—Mississippi, South Carolina, Kentucky, Iowa, Georgia and Missouri. Ten others pay a minimum of $20 to $25 a week.

For the country as a whole, the public schools cost just a little more than five billion dollars, a slight increase over that in 1950–51. Two states—New York and California—spend more than $500,000,000 each. Because of spiraling costs, the funds needed to operate the public schools have risen higher than ever before. Educators complain, however, that the money they get cannot buy as much as their funds of as recently as two years ago.

Once more the effects of the Korean conflict can be seen in the classrooms of every community in the United States.

With Congress in session the N.E.A. and other school organizations again will seek Federal aid for the public schools. One member of Congress who has advocated a Federal aid bill—Senator Lister Hill of Alabama—asserted that the strength and security of the United States against aggression were bound inexorably to education. In a statement to *The Times* he observed:

"Education has given us the widespread, high level of intelligence and general competency by which we have built history's most perfect example of democratic government and preserved it against the winds of alien ideologies. We face a long period of international tensions and big armaments that may last perhaps for five, ten or even twenty years. In terms of sheer numbers of people our potential enemies hold a heavy advantage and our intelligence sources tell us that Russia and her satellites are feverishly working to train large numbers of skilled workers, instructed by industrial experts taken out of East Germany since the last war.

"We must fix our educational sights accordingly and insure that every American boy and girl has the opportunity for maximum development of his or her capabilities. Only in this way can we meet the need for more scientists, more engineers, more chemists, more physicists, more technicians, more skilled workers of every kind, more nurses and doctors and leaders in other professions and business."

62

Harold Howe II
THE NEW FACES OF EDUCATION

"The New Faces of Education," American Education, Vol. 4 (April 1968), pp. 2–3.

Harold Howe II (1918–   ) served as federal commissioner of education and administrator of the Office of Education under President Lyndon Johnson. Prior to 1965 he had been principal of several high schools and the superintendent of schools in Scarsdale, New York. At the present time he is moderator of the Boston television program "College and You," and chairman of the board of trustees of the College Entrance Examination Board.

It was just three years ago—on April 11, 1965—that President Johnson signed the Elementary and Secondary Education Act. Since then, so much has happened in American education that it is difficult, on this third anniversary, to summarize the impact of this historic law. Perhaps one could begin by saying that Harry Brault (as we shall call him here) lost 30 pounds last year.

Your tax money helped him do it. Why?

Because Harry is only seven years old, and when he showed up for the first day of first grade the year before last, he weighed 130 pounds—about twice as much as any other youngster in his class. He was just plain obese, and with the unconscious cruelty of children, his classmates reminded him of it every day. They called him names, excluded him from their cliques, and left him standing on the sidelines when they chose up sides for games. After a while he got the message, and stopped trying to keep up with the other youngsters in anything, in the classroom or out.

Last summer, a nurse whose salary was paid by your taxes (under title I of the Elementary and Secondary Education Act) got together with Harry's school principal, a teaching assistant, and a county health officer. Together they worked out a program of diet and exercise for Harry. Several times during the summer, the nurse visited Harry to examine him and make sure he was sticking to his prescribed regimen.

When he entered second grade last September, Harry was down to 100 pounds. He was still a bit large in comparison with his classmates, but his size coupled with increased speed made him a definite asset to any team that included him. Within a couple of weeks, he was always the first youngster chosen; and having gained acceptance on the playground, he picked up interest in what went on inside the school, too.

The point is that last year, Harry ranked 28th in his class in reading. This year he ranked fourth, and that is why the State of Maryland used a tiny portion of its Federal funds to help him lose weight.

It doesn't seem right to call Harry Brault a "symbol" of Federal programs in education, because he's rather young to have such a heavy and undramatic office thrust upon him. But his case does illustrate in its way what those programs are about: removing, insofar as possible, every impediment that American citizens —young, old, and in between—may encounter in developing their innate abilities.

President Johnson stated that rationale for Federal aid-to-education programs in his January 12, 1965, message to Congress on "full educational opportunity." Asking the 89th Congress to join him in making sure that every American youngster would receive as much education as he could benefit from, the President went on to explain why this was important:

"We want this not only for his sake—but for the Nation's sake.

"Nothing matters more to the future of our country: not our military preparedness—for armed might is worthless if we lack the brain power to build a world of peace; not our productive economy—for we cannot sustain growth without trained manpower; not our democratic system of government—for freedom is fragile if citizens are ignorant."

In essence, this statement amounts to a new concept of "national defense"—and it was a concern for national defense that motivated the first of our contemporary Federal programs for education.

In 1957, the Russians launched their first sputnik. Inquiring into the reasons for this Soviet coup, we decided that American instruction in the sciences was deficient. When the next session of Congress opened the following January, President Eisenhower proposed an educational program that would buttress scientific instruction by allocating Federal funds for student loans, teacher fellowships, the purchase of scientific equipment, and guidance programs to identify especially promising students.

This recommendation later took form as the National Defense Education Act of 1958. Two particularly significant points about it distinguish NDEA from much of the Federal aid-to-education legislation that followed.

First, it was not designed to improve education across the board. NDEA stipulated that the Federal funds had to be used to improve instruction in science, mathematics, and modern foreign languages.

Second, the title of the Act included the word "defense"; NDEA was not for education per se, but had a political and technological emphasis. President Eisenhower underlined this in his message to Congress: "These recommendations place primary emphasis on our national security requirements." Moreover, he said, NDEA was a "temporary" program, an "emergency undertaking to be terminated after four years." Financial support of education, he told the Congress, was "not a Federal responsibility."

NDEA is now 10 years old. Its annual appropriations have risen from $115 million in 1959 to $459 million now, its original four parts have become 11, and the list of subjects it aids has been expanded to include English, economics, reading, arts, history, geography, and industrial arts.

Thus a restricted program intended to end after four years gives every sign of becoming a permanent component of Federal expenditures. Through other aid-to-education measures, two succeeding Presidents and five Congresses have brought the Federal investment in education up from $2.9 billion in 1959 to $11.6 billion for fiscal 1969. President Johnson alone has signed 47 pieces of education legislation, more than his 35 predecessors combined.

These increases in Federal support make it clear that the temper of the American people, as gauged by their representatives in Congress, has changed markedly since 1958. We have decided that education most definitely is a Federal concern, and that States and localities need special assistance from the Federal Government, especially to help them meet the educational needs of our least fortunate people.

President Johnson's statement on "full educational opportunity" means that national defense requires us to be wary of foes within as well as without; it suggests, however, that these home-grown enemies are not communism or other dramatic forms of subversion, but poverty, unemployment, the resentment that stems from opportunity systematically denied, the frustration of a life that offers no prospect except continuing despair for oneself and one's children.

And it says, finally, that the most effective weapon for defeating these domestic enemies is a first-rate education for every American.

The President's statement heralded the most forceful drive ever mounted on behalf of education. During the ensuing 10 months—the first session of the 89th Congress—President Johnson advocated, argued for, and won Congressional approval of 15 aid-to-education measures. These laws started the "War on Poverty," and established such well-known programs as Operation Head Start, the Teacher Corps, and Volunteers In Service To America (VISTA). Such major pieces of legislation as the Economic Opportunity Act of 1964, the Elementary and Secondary Education Act, and the Higher Education Act of 1965 touch every aspect of education from preschool through post-graduate, affect Americans of every time of life from infancy through old age, and—together with the 12 aid-to-education measures passed during the second session of the 89th—certainly justify President Johnson's description of it as "The Education Congress."

Quantity of legislation, of course, is not the ultimate index to the effectiveness of a President or a Congress. What matters is what—if anything—happens after the laws go on the books.

Here are some of the things that have happened as a result of the aid-to-education laws passed since President Johnson took office:

[1] In its first year of operation, title I of the Elementary and Secondary Education Act benefited 8.3 million children—one of every six students from kindergarten through high school. The $987 million expended under this title added an average of nearly $119 to the amount available for the education of each child in areas of large concentrations of low-income families.

[2] Since the Higher Education Facilities Act of 1963 went into effect, 1,359 colleges, universities, and branch campuses in 54 States and Territories have received Federal grants or loans to build and improve undergraduate academic facilities. HEFA funds have helped construct more than 2,500 library, laboratory, classroom, and administrative buildings.

[3] By September 1967, two and one-half years after the College Work-Study program was established, 210,000 students were earning money toward college expenses through federally financed, part-time jobs related to their studies.

[4] In 1964, when the Economic Opportu-nity Act was passed, one of every five Americans 18 years of age and older had less than an eighth-grade education. Last year, 400,000 of those were enrolled in adult basic education programs designed to give them the basic reading, writing, and figuring skills necessary for permanent employment. In the act's three years of operation, federally sponsored basic education programs enrolled nearly a million of the country's most unemployment-prone adults.

[5] Since the Vocational Education Act of 1963 was passed, enrollment in high-school-level programs designed to qualify youngsters for good jobs immediately upon their graduation has increased from 2.1 million to 3.9 million. One of every four public high school students participates in a federally financed vocational program today.

Such statistics convey a fair amount of information about the scope of Federal education programs, but little sense of the impact they have on individuals. Nor do they suggest what may well be the most important result of the Federal aid-to-education laws: a new spirit in education, a new readiness to experiment with both the techniques of teaching and the materials for doing it, and a new determination to extend educational opportunity to those who have been denied it in the past.

The Vietnam War led unprecedented numbers of American churchmen, both clergy and laity, into active opposition to their nation's foreign policies. This rally was held in the Episcopal National Cathedral in Washington, D.C. during the weekend of the so-called "March against death," November 14–16, 1969.   (John Goodwin)

Chapter Twelve

THE EFFECTS OF THE WAR ON THOUGHT AND CULTURE

The six essays of this section seem to offer a repeated proof, if any were needed, that a given war can play different roles in successive periods. In the context of the 1950s, says Harvey Wish, the Cold War made a significant contribution to the anxiety and insecurity which led in turn to an all-embracing conservatism. But a decade later, in the opinion of T. B. Bottomore, the war had become a reinforcement for the swing of the intellectual pendulum toward social criticism and radicalism. In literature, so Robert E. Spiller contends, the effect of the early Cold War was to drive writers into a kind of privatized and instinctual world of the self. Yet by the late sixties, according to Morris Dickstein, our experience in Vietnam was helping to bring back politics into prose and poetry, and to create a new dialectic between the demands of the individual author and those of society. As for religion, Merle Curti finds that, under the first impact of the nuclear age, many intellectuals turned to a search for values more "absolute" than those of our traditional pragmatism. Looking back from 1968, however, Martin Marty suggests that our wars and our anti-communism may well have had a part in bringing on recent and revolutionary changes in religious belief.

QUESTIONS:

1. If war can have such diverse effects as appear to be indicated here, is it possible to speak with any accuracy of such things as a war assisting modernization?

2. Can it be said that the "same" Cold War has had different effects, or would you attribute the differences to the fact that the Cold War itself has changed (e.g., from "cold" to "hot" phases, or from relative success to relative unsuccess)?

3. What would you make of the argument that what war does, above all else, is to reinforce existing trends?

4. Are the beliefs of the Old Right (apparently so popular in the 1950s) and those of the New Left (widely accepted, at least among youth, in the 1960s) so very different? Could war be responsible for some of their similarities?

5. Would you conclude that the Second World War and the early Cold War had similar impacts upon American religion and religious thought? Or were the 1940s more like the 1960s in that regard?

63

Harvey Wish
THE CONSERVATIVE MOOD

From Harvey Wish, Society and Thought in Modern America (2 vols., New York: David McKay, Inc., 2nd ed., 1961), II, 599–602.

Harvey Wish (1900–1968) was professor of history at Western Reserve University from 1945 to 1963, and Benton distinguished professor at that institution during the last five years of his life. He was primarily an American intellectual historian, with special interests in the South and in the twentieth century. His works include *George Fitzhugh, Propagandist of the Old South* (1943), *Contemporary America* (1945), *Society and Thought in America* (1950–1952), and *The Negro since Emancipation* (1964).

The New Conservatism was an arresting phenomenon of the Cold War era, growing out of an effort to formulate traditional certainties against pragmatic liberalism, radicalism, internationalism, and collectivist notions. While some of these writers like the able political scientist Clinton Rossiter, of Cornell, and Russell Kirk, a free-lance author and college lecturer in literature who admired T. S. Eliot, offered well-reasoned conservative theories, the extreme right led by Senator Joseph McCarthy of Wisconsin created havoc in foreign and domestic policies by sweeping charges of disloyalty in the highest places. The senator from Wisconsin, supported by anti-New Dealers, many Irish and German isolationists, oil wildcatters who had struck it rich, and anti-intellectual groups, struck out wildly not only at alleged Communists but at internationalists, scholars like Professor Owen Lattimore of Johns Hopkins University, whom he called a top Soviet espionage agent, our British allies, and the State Department. . . .

Perhaps no one succeeded so well in making the New Conservatism appear intellectually respectable as Russell Kirk, author of *The Conservative Mind* (1953) and *The Intelligent Woman's Guide to Conservatism* (1957). He argued that conservatism was not a fixed and immutable body of dogma but "the preservation of the ancient moral traditions of humanity." To him conscious modern conservatism began in 1790 with Edmund Burke's *Reflections on the Revolution in France*. Burke's social order stressed the continuity of tradition; it was a spiritual union of the dead, the living, and those yet unborn. However, Kirk did not point out that Burke's practical common sense made him impatient with dogmatic theorists who prevented adjustments to everyday realities. But to the conservative, Burke's hostility to liberalism and revolution were his best qualities.

Kirk's conservative man believed in "a divine intent" ruling a society that must be divided into orders and classes. "The only true equality is moral equality." Property and freedom were inseparably connected, for economic leveling was not economic progress. He admired the "proliferating variety and mystery of traditional life" as distinct from the "narrowing uniformity and equalitarianism and utilitarian aims of most radical systems." He attacked the liberals for their idea of the perfectibility of man, the notion that education and social reform could produce men like gods; and their materialistic determinism and exaggerated faith in reason as a substitute for ancestral wisdom. Kirk feared what De Tocqueville called "democratic despotism" and centralization and he attacked Dewey's secularism and his alleged substitution of mere "learning by doing" and group endeavor for intellectual discipline. Education today was not for democracy but for mass submission and descended to catchalls like "social studies" instead of helping the old disciplines. He praised the conservatism of the neo-humanists of the 1920's, Irving Babbitt and Paul Elmer More, and the medievalism of Ralph Adams Cram and Henry Adams. He liked the theories of the Columbia history professor Frank Tannenbaum who believed that trade-unionism was becoming the great conservative force of our time by rediscovering the medieval sense of guild unity free of class conflicts and the dangers of a centralized welfare state.

Much more circumspect in defending traditionalism was Clinton Rossiter's *Conservatism in America* (1955). His ideal of an enlightened conservatism rejected ultra-rightists like William F. Buckley, Jr., editor of the *National Review,* or mere standpattism which tolerated segregation, predatory capitalism, or anti-Semitism. His conservative would defend liberty against experiments that sacrificed real liberty for specious equality. He would heal the rift between the academic and the business world, and discover a middle road, but he left the reader dangling upon the observation that the conservative was committed to no particular policies, but must aspire to an imaginative,

hopeful, and tolerant outlook. Rossiter therefore could not easily be classified with the more outspokenly antiliberal conservatives like Kirk, Friedrich Hayek, James Burnham, and William Buckley. He was too obviously sympathetic to "liberal" causes and had perhaps been overawed by the new aura of respectability for the term "conservative" in this Cold War era.

There was a penetrating explanation of the revolt against liberal individualism in Erich Fromm's *Escape from Freedom* (1941), which had passed through nineteen printings by the spring of 1959. Fromm was an imaginative German psychologist currently resident in New York who used a psychoanalytical technique to understand the character of modern man and the illness of a civilization that could produce fascism and communism. Man had freed himself from the bonds of preindividualistic society which had simultaneously given him security and limited his choices; but he failed to gain freedom in the positive sense of fulfilling himself intellectually and emotionally. Freedom had left him isolated, anxious, and powerless. "This isolation is unbearable and the alternatives he is confronted with are either to escape from the burden of this freedom into new dependencies and submissions or to advance to the full realization of positive freedom which is based upon the uniqueness and individuality of man." Hence the flight to the Leader, the powerful state, and the sadistic programs against minorities. Although Fromm did not actually analyze conservatism, but rather ultra right-wing reaction, he suggested, as Tannenbaum had done, that modern man suffered from an unbearable isolation and must identify himself with a meaningful role in economic production, distribution, and organization.

This theme of "anxiety" discussed by Fromm also absorbed many of the contemporary psychiatrists, psychologists, and philosophers and suggested that this neurotic symptom came out of feelings of helplessness and repression, infantile fears of disapproval, and the insecurity derived from the overwhelming social changes of our time. Conservatives, even without this thesis, gravitated naturally to explanations in a current theology of guilt and original sin, child-like faith, and a renewed hatred of the Age of Reason. Barthian [Karl Barth's] neo-orthodoxy . . . carried to America the emphasis on man's spiritual helplessness and utter dependence upon an unearned gift of God's grace. The current revival of the great nineteenth-century Danish existentialist, Sören Kierkegaard, despite the innumerable conflicting definitions of "existentialism" (most of them antitraditional and individualist), drew attention to man's anxieties and psychological confusion. The distinguished psychiatrist Harry Stack Sullivan reasoned that anxiety grew out of infantile fears and limited the person's activities, awareness, and learning ability. Even in the landmark desegregation case, *Brown v. Topeka*, the Chief Justice had leaned upon the current idea of the effect of anxiety and the feeling of inferiority upon learning ability. Little wonder that this generation spoke so compulsively of "insecurity," looked hopefully to the psychiatrist as the supreme healer, questioned liberal pragmatic experimentation which upset certainties, or on a less intellectual level sought solvents for anxiety and depression in various newly discovered tranquilizing drugs.

64

T. B. Bottomore
DEVELOPING SOCIAL CRITICISM

Excerpts from Critics of Society *by T. B. Bottomore, pp. 51–75. Copyright © 1966, 1968 by T. B. Bottomore. Reprinted by permission of Pantheon Books, Inc. A Division of Random House, Inc. Published in Great Britain by George Allen & Unwin Ltd.*

T. B. Bottomore (1920–   ) is a British-born social scientist who from 1949 to 1965 was affiliated with the London School of Economics, and who since that time has been at Simon Fraser University, British Columbia. He is the author of *Karl Marx: Early Writings* (1963), *Elites and Society* (1964), and *Classes in Modern Society* (1965). He is also the editor of the *European Journal of Sociology*.

The cycle of social criticism in the United States during this century has followed something like a generational pattern, with the peaks occurring in the 1900s, in the 1930s and again in the 1960s. But this regularity is only one aspect of a complicated movement. Another aspect is the changes in the character of social criticism in each of these periods which resulted from the condition of American society, its prevailing ideas, and its relations with the rest of the world.

The progressive era at the beginning of the century was followed by the Jazz Age; pleasure-seeking, light-hearted, at least on the surface, and relatively uninterested in politics. The reforming movement of the 1930s was followed by the sombre and tormented era of McCarthyism, overflowing with political passion. The differences are explicable in part by the changed state of the world and of the United States' place in it. After the First World War there was no immediate new alignment of opposed great powers, and the United States was still not totally involved in world politics. After the Second World War the United States was deeply involved, and had to confront another great power—Russia—which had considerably extended its sphere of influence and directly challenged the American way of life. This was clearly not a time for carefree frolics, even if men's spirits had not already been depressed by the terrible discovery of the atomic bomb.

But McCarthyism also exemplified something more permanent in American life. It was itself a form of social criticism and dissent, though not of an intellectual kind. Indeed, it was rabidly anti-intellectual. In some ways it may be viewed as the Prohibition movement of the 1950s, expressing the same moralizing, censorious and peevish attitudes, and having the same irrelevance to the major problems of the time. It exhibited, as did Prohibition, that strain of intolerance which many observers have found in American life, running alongside and contradicting the tradition of free inquiry and criticism. Only McCarthyism was more intolerant, more virulent and certainly more dangerous to liberty than was Prohibition.

Other elements besides the uncertainties of the international situation and the propensity to intolerance (which itself needs to be explained) contributed to the temporary success of McCarthyism. One of these was perhaps the prevalence of "status anxiety," which Richard Hofstadter has examined closely in an essay dealing with the "radical right." The "rootlessness and heterogeneity of American life, . . . its peculiar scramble for status and its peculiar search for secure identity," have given rise, he argues, to a form of status politics which tend "to be expressed more in vindictiveness, in sour memories, in the search for scapegoats, than in realistic proposals for positive action." Another element was the quiescence of the radical intellectuals, which seems to have resulted from a loss of confidence and excessive feelings of guilt about their earlier Marxist, or even liberal, views, when the enormities of Stalinist rule in Russia and in eastern Europe began to be revealed.

Nevertheless, a revival of self-confidence and of critical thought began to take place in the 1950s, this time not among the philosophers or historians, but among the social scientists and particularly the sociologists. The leading figure in this movement was C. Wright Mills. As a radical critic of American society Mills most closely resembled [Thorstein] Veblen, although he was both less original and more systematic as a thinker. His major purpose, as he often said, was to revive a classical, largely European tradition of sociological thought, which had been created above all by Marx and Max Weber, and which treated large-scale social and historical problems.

The subjects which Mills tackled belong clearly to this tradition. He was interested especially in the massive changes which had taken place in the social structure, and especially the class structure, of the United States since the beginning of the nineteenth century, and in the political consequences of these changes. One of his earliest books, *The New Men of Power: America's Labor Leaders* (1948) dealt with the evolution of the American working class and with the circumstances which had made the leaders of American trade unions aspirants for a place in the national elite rather than critics of the economic and social system of American capitalism.

Mills' next book, *White Collar* (1951), examined the American middle classes and if it did not inaugurate, it certainly re-invigorated and advanced the debate among social scientists upon the significance of the great expansion of middle-class occupations in the industrial societies. . . .

In the third of the books which he devoted to the American class structure, *The Power Elite* (1956), Mills examined the upper class in the United States. This was the book which created the greatest stir, largely because it appeared to re-state and provide evidence for a view which socialists had been expanding ever since the 1880s; namely, that the United States, in spite of its democratic forms and its "classless" ideology, had in fact a ruling class. . . .

One of the first and most influential works of the new criticism [in the postwar decade] was David Riesman's *The Lonely Crowd* (1950). The title itself suggests the theme of "mass society"; the horde of private, unrelated, uncertain, leaderless individuals. The intention of the book was to show how changes in the American character, associated with changes in the social structure, had produced a mass society, and to criticize the quality of its life. In describing types of character, Riesman made use of three terms: tradition-directed, inner-directed, and other-directed. Broadly, these refer to the different ways in which men face the problems of their community life; they may deal with such problems either on the basis of customary rules, or by applying a standard which they have accepted as binding upon their own conduct (a moral imperative), or finally by seeking to conform with what the neighbors are doing, or at least what they think the neighbors are doing. Riesman's chief concern was with the change which he thought had taken place between the early nineteenth century, when Americans, he suggested, were largely inner-directed (by the Protestant ethic), and the mid-twentieth century, when they had become other-directed; that is, anxious to conform as closely as possible with the apparent values of those groups in which they found themselves. Two subsidiary themes of the book were the transition from a work-oriented to a consumption and leisure-oriented society; and the replacement of a ruling class, which might engender an opposition, by a collection of veto-groups to which everyone in some capacity belonged, and which substituted checks, balances and adjustments for the old clash of social and political interests and ideas. . . .

The critical views of Mills and Riesman are alike in certain respects. Both see a tendency toward conformism and a curious collectivism of opinion in the American society of the early 1950s. Both attribute to the new middle classes an important influence in promoting this tend-

ency. Finally, both see a possible way out through the efforts of the intellectuals. Mills exhorts the intellectuals to resume their critical attitude toward the established authorities and ideas; while Riesman concludes that "a vastly greater stream of creative, utopian thinking is needed" before any real progress can be made toward a more autonomous type of social character. Yet neither of them was entirely hopeful about the possible achievements of intellectual criticism. Mills observed often enough that the nineteenth century ideologies of liberalism and socialism—both products of the Enlightenment—were in ruins, and that nothing had yet appeared to take their place. Riesman viewed the mid-twentieth century as a time of disenchantment, when it was "easier to concentrate on programs for choosing between lesser evils" than to propose any new utopias.

In some other respects the ideas of Mills and Riesman diverge quite widely. Mills, although he did not accept Marxism as an adequate theory of society (and even less as a political creed), was still largely concerned with the problems of society and with the bases of political power in the terms which Marx had established. Riesman ignored most of this in order to concentrate upon a cultural transformation which had made leisure more important than work, consumption more important than production in fashioning the nature of American society and its problems. The creative Utopian thought for which he called was to be applied principally to discovering new kinds of leisure activity in a society which already enjoyed material abundance. The problem was seen as one of cultural innovation, rather than political change. . . .

One of the things that prevented the formation of a more integrated body of social criticism in the 1950s was the defection of the philosophers. No thinker of the stature of

[John] Dewey came forward to present a general justification for the diverse lines of criticism, or to link them together in a comprehensive social philosophy. In any case, postwar philosophy in the Anglo-Saxon countries came to be dominated by the linguistic philosophers, who not only showed little interest in social and political doctrines, but held that the elaboration of such doctrines was no concern of a philosopher, and insinuated that there was something reprehensible in dealing with general ideas at all. Such views had a depressing effect in Britain, and I think also in North America; an effect which was in sharp contrast with the quickening influence of Marxism and existentialism in continental Europe during the same period. The editor of an English symposium on philosophy and politics felt able to announce solemnly, and with a certain satisfaction, that "For the moment, anyway, political philosophy is dead"; while an American, Daniel Bell, gave to his collection of essays on political themes the title *The End of Ideology: On the Exhaustion of Political Ideas in the Fifties.*

In North America, these philosophical attitudes, coinciding with the defensiveness of intellectuals under the pressures of McCarthyism, and the absence of any important left-wing social movements, produced an unadventurous, largely conformist state of mind. Writers like Mills and Riesman were at first voices crying in the wilderness, and . . . they were probably more appreciated in Europe than in America. Even in 1960 Mills could write, in a published letter to British Socialists: "When I settle down to write to you, I feel somehow 'freer' than usual. The reason, I suppose, is that most of the time I am writing for people whose ambiguities and values I imagine to be rather different from mine, but with you I feel enough in common to allow us to 'get on with it' in more positive ways."

The one major philosophical thinker who,

at this time, undertook a re-examination of the whole condition of man in modern industrial society—Hannah Arendt—found herself in much the same situation as the sociological critics. Her books, *The Origins of Totalitarianism* (1951), *The Human Condition* (1958), and *On Revolution* (1963), are inspired by German existentialist philosophy, and they have probably made their chief impression upon European thinkers, rather than setting off a new movement of philosophical and social criticism in the United States. This is not to say that they lack any affinity with other critical writings. The theme which Miss Arendt expounds in *The Human Condition*—the dilemma of a society which has glorified labor, and which is about to be liberated from labor —is evidently connected with some of the ideas expressed by Riesman in *The Lonely Crowd,* and with the discussion of work and leisure, from a more strictly economic aspect, by J. K. Galbraith in *The Affluent Society.* . . .

At all events it is plain to see that disagreements over the distribution of economic resources and political power still divide the left from the right in politics, and that in the 1960s they have had a revival with the emergence of a New Left, and on a smaller scale a New Right in the United States. It is fairly easy to date the beginnings of the New Left as an international phenomenon. The crucial year was 1956. That was the year when British and French imperialism had their final, anachronistic and unsuccessful fling at Suez, when the Hungarian intellectuals and workers revolted against Stalinism, when in Poland some of the institutions of the Stalinist system were more quietly dismantled. The Suez affair produced in Britain the most extensive revolt of the intellectuals since the 1930s, while the events in Hungary and Poland led many to give up their allegiance to the Communist Party. These two movements together gave rise to the New Left, which found a practical expression in such movements as the Campaign for Nuclear Disarmament and an intellectual expression in the *New Left Review*. In France, it was not so much the Suez incident as the Hungarian revolution, the war in Algeria and the decay of Stalinism which created the New Left. In the United States it was likewise the events in eastern Europe, and in addition the Cuban revolution, the course of American foreign policy in Latin America and in southeast Asia, and the Negro revolt, which together inspired a revival of the Left. These diverse influences are apparent in the various movements which have emerged in the U.S.A.—the Student Non-violent Coordinating Committee (S.N.C.C.), the Students for a Democratic Society (S.D.S.), the W. E. B. DuBois Clubs, The Free Speech Movement at Berkeley, the Vietnam Day Committees—and in the new journals of the 1960s: *Studies on the Left, Liberation, Ramparts* and others.

What is new about this New Left? First of all, it is less dogmatic in outlook and less exclusively political in its commitment than was the Left in the 1930s. Radical critics today have not accepted any existing social system as an ideal to which they can give their undeviating allegiance with anything like the fervor which some intellectuals of the 1930s displayed in their attachment to the U.S.S.R. At the most, the radical intellectuals have committed themselves to the support of the developing countries in the "third world" and of the revolutionary movements which have appeared there. The avoidance of dogmatism, and in a more extreme form the outright rejection of any ideology, is in some measure a consequence of the lack of any comprehensive and convincing social theory, and of the widespread uncertainty about social ideals. But it also reflects some more positive attitudes—humanism allied with scepticism, or at least with an experimental and empirical approach to problems, an egalitarianism which repudiates the exposition of some orthodox doctrine by infallible teachers; and a strong belief in the importance of personal moral choices. The divergent interpretations of the promise and dangers of affluence and mass leisure, the demonstration of the problems which industrialization and mechanization bring in their wake in every society, whatever the regime under which it lives, have brought into question the uncomplicated faith of earlier generations of radicals and socialists. Hence the concern of the New Left with a great variety of issues outside the economic and political spheres; with education and cultural life, and with social relations in the everyday affairs of the neighborhood or work place. . . .

65

Robert E. Spiller, et al.
A LITERATURE OF THE SELF

Reprinted with permission of The Macmillan Company from Literary History of the United States *by Robert E. Spiller, et al., pp. 1412–1415. Copyright © by The Macmillan Company, 1946, 1947, 1948, 1953, 1968.*

Robert E. Spiller (1896–   ) taught English at Swarthmore College from 1921 to 1945 and at the University of Pennsylvania from 1946 to 1967, where he is now Felix E. Snelling Emeritus Professor. He was the editor of *American Literature* from 1932 to 1939 and has been chairman of the editorial board of *American Quarterly* since 1951. He has published *The Cycle of American Literature* (1955), *The Early Lectures of Ralph Waldo Emerson* (2 vols., 1959–1964), and *The Third Dimension: Studies in Literary History* (1965).

The deaths of [William] Faulkner, [Ernest] Hemingway, and [Robert] Frost mark the end of a period in American letters framed catastrophically by two world wars. A new literature has since come into being. The makers of that literature began to publish during and after World War II. . . . Though the new movement in American letters cannot be evaluated as a completed thing, the centers of its energy, the lines and shapes of its flow, are already discernible.

The character of reality in the postwar world can be described as one of disruptive chaos and equally disruptive organization. The war itself, "hot" or "cold," continued to provide the basic experience of contemporary life: efficient yet senseless violence, alienation from the self as from society, the dehumanization of man. And the experience, shared the world over, served to deepen the affinities between American and European literature, and to anchor both in the concrete predicament of the individual. The new generation discovered, beyond disillusionment, the drab or demonic surrealism of mass society and the modern superstate.

This is not to say that postwar society in America did not develop its distinctive character. Though the world was reputed to have been gradually "Americanized," America itself was not. The surface images of affluence and conformity, in crowded cities and happy suburbs, remained in the public consciousness. But American society, which in some odd way has always permitted both isolation and dissent, reacted against the ballyhoo and lunacies of these images by nurturing pockets of resistance. In the underside of culture, the searches for love and for freedom continued unabated. The search for love sometimes brought men to the threshold of religious experience—Zen or Buddhist thought, Christian mysticism, the I-Thou personal encounter elucidated by Martin Buber. And the search for freedom sometimes ended in crime or anarchy, the burden of [Jack] Kerouac's hipsters, the plight of the "White Negro" described vividly by [Norman] Mailer. The two quests, starting from different points, often met in the idea of the holy goof, the criminal lover, the rebel-victim. Significantly, a kindred concept, that of "the picaresque saint," was used by R. W. B. Lewis to describe the hero of modern European literature. The image of modern man which dominated literature on both sides of the Atlantic was obviously that of the outsider, familiar to Americans for more than a century as Ishmael.

The response of American literature to postwar reality took bitter account of cultural determinism or repression; it drew its power from the inner turbulence of the individual. This is why it is proper to say that the new literature was primarily a literature of the Self. Its main concerns were the private and instinctual imperatives of man. Its morality was personal, existential, therefore ironic and evasive, created in the void left by traditional values which men could no longer accept. Born under the shadow of nihilism, yet dedicated to being and to life, it revealed a will nearly religious in its fervor. Its covert aim was to act as an ironic redeemer of reality.

The moral concerns of the new literature also shaped its sense of form and style. Just as the artistic conscience of the twenties was sharpened by the experience of disillusionment, so was the artistic accomplishment of the fifties influenced by the encounter with nihilism. The forms of literature tended, first, to be elegant, mythical, or intricate, a ceremonious structure of balanced ironies, as in the early work of Richard Wilbur, Jean Stafford, and Frederick Buechner. But as the reaction against the formalism of the forties gained impetus, literary forms began to open themselves freely to the assaults of reality. They became more jagged and irregular; they admitted chance and resorted to improvisation. Such was the character of the work of Jack Gelber and Allen

Ginsberg and of the later work of Norman Mailer and Saul Bellow. The rift between formalist writers, usually labeled Academic, and antiformalist writers, usually termed Beat, was widened by the controversies surrounding the so-called Beat Movement.

Though it is often associated with San Francisco, the Beat Movement was essentially a national, urban phenomenon, and perhaps the only form of overt, even flamboyant, rebellion in mid-century America. Its ultimate significance may reflect on the cultural rather than the literary life of the country. For the Beat Movement went farther in challenging the assumptions of American society than any of the radical movements which preceded it in the thirties. Drawing on European existentialism as on Oriental thought, and drawing, above all, on a native tradition of rhapsodic dissent which harks back to [Ralph Waldo] Emerson and [Walt] Whitman, it spoke primarily for the beleaguered Self, for the holiness and spontaneity of the natural man. This is why, despite its associations with adolescent violence, orgiastic anarchy, and drug addiction, the Beat Movement was a form of religious aspiration even more than of social revolt. In literature, the sympathies of the Beat Movement ran toward freedom, oral improvisation, and even mindlessness; the movement defined itself in opposition to the formal, intellectual, and hieratic tradition of [T. S.] Eliot, [W. H.] Auden, or Wallace Stevens. Patronized from a distance by Henry Miller, championed sporadically by men as different as Kenneth Rexroth and Norman Mailer, a group of writers which included Jack Kerouac, John Clellon Holmes, Lawrence Ferlinghetti, Gregory Corso, Allen Ginsberg, and William Burroughs, struck out to recapture both the openness and the outrageousness of American experience, and to enhance the participation of literary audiences.

When the Beat Movement somewhat subsided—it produced few works of genuine quality—the division between formalists and antiformalists appeared serious enough, though all the authors in one camp were by no means academic, nor were the writers in the other all beat. The urgency and vitality of the antiformalists, the magnitude of their concerns, and the quality of their commitment renewed the promise of American letters. It may very well be that the retreat from formalism, and in some cases the attack on the idea of form itself, will shape the trend of the future.

No one, of course, can predict the future with impunity. In the midst of current confusion, the very idea of an *avant-garde*, which presupposes a coherent, bourgeois order subject to the norms of history, begins to lose its meaning. By 1960, some intriguing trends were nevertheless visible. There were strains in the plays of Edward Albee, Jack Gelber, and even Tennessee Williams of absurd and dark laughter, welling from deep anger. There were affinities in the fiction of John Hawkes and William Burroughs with nightmare and surrealism, which in turn blended into the grotesque visions of Flannery O'Connor, James Purdy, and Carson McCullers. A new raw, roguish quality, inherited from the picaresque, appeared in the novels of Saul Bellow, Norman Mailer, William Styron, and Ralph Ellison; and a new playfulness, more holy than ironic, pervaded the later work of J. D. Salinger. In poetry, the preconscious apprehensions of Theodore Roethke and the explosive power of Robert Lowell created a striking idiom. Also, the modulated passion of Charles Olson and the bardic rage of Allen Ginsberg could occasionally set language singing in a haunting key.

It is hard, of course, to relate these trends and harder still to forecast their viability. One senses behind many of them, however, an emergent comic vision, grim but also antic, a new tolerance of experience that verges on a tolerance for incongruity, and a kind of realism that masquerades in the garbs of surreal humor. The lines which separate comedy from tragedy or pathos from irony, and which distinguish rigid from improvisational forms, begin to vanish. A new concept of "antiform" seems in the process of evolution. Such a creation might carry the dialectic of affirmation and denial which inspires the literary imagination to a tentative conclusion. In the past, the two masters of that dialectic were Melville and Whitman. The new literature has learned from both, from the dark, depth-dredging sense of the one and the intricate loving chant of the other. The new literature has done more: it has sought to unite both in the hope of redefining the American Self, and of discovering a public form commensurate with the terrifying privacy of human desires.

66

Morris Dickstein
A NEW LITERARY DIALECTIC

From Morris Dickstein, "Allen Ginsberg and the 60's," Commentary, *Vol. 49 (January 1970), pp. 67–69. Reprinted from* Commentary, *by permission; Copyright ©* 1970 by the American Jewish Committee.

Morris Dickstein (1940–   ) received degrees from Columbia and Yale, and has taught English at Columbia since 1966, where he is presently an assistant professor. He is particularly interested in Romantic poetry, but has also been concerned with contemporary literature and society. He is the author of *Keats and His Poetry: A Study in Development* (1971).

How did we contrive a unique mixture of 20's bohemianism and 30's politics? The young are promiscuously drawn to both Marx and the occult, Mao and the *I Ching*, politics and pot,

revolution and rock. In the arts the cultural upheaval at large has opened the gates not only to sexual frankness but also to a general revival of experiment the likes of which we have not seen, at least in literature, since the first generation of modernists. (This is not to say that the experiments are as ambitious or as successful, only that we ought to take them seriously enough to make discriminations.)

If I speak of literature it is not only because I know it best or because other arts like painting, more insulated from society by their own modern aesthetic, nurtured vigorous experimental movements in the 40's and 50's, but because I can't agree with the notion popularized by [Marshall] McLuhan that books have been displaced. Literature, even popular literature, has always been the province of a more conscious minority. If books must now share their audience with films and politics and popular music the dispersion is a healthy one (even as far as "content" goes). It's wrong to accuse the young of not reading and also of reading the wrong books. If they've traded in [T. S.] Eliot for [William] Blake, this may be a mistake but it should cause no panic among those who once traded in [Algernon] Swinburne for Eliot or [Percy] Shelley for [John] Donne. I've twice conducted an undergraduate course on Blake, in which even those who came but to get high stayed to sweat out the intricacies of the system. With *The Four Zoas* in one hand and [Northrop] Frye's *Fearful Symmetry* in the other, they could hardly be accused of intellectual laziness.

Young people in the 60's, with a great deal of sophistication, tolerance, and eagerness, have been looking *for* something in literature (as Pauline Kael said recently of young movie audiences), not just looking *at* it. Nor should we scorn their demand for relevance unless it becomes too narrow. So often misapplied, the notion of relevance has taken on a faintly comical air today, but its pitfalls are more visible in the narrowly personal literature exemplified by *The Assistant* and *Seize the Day* than in that which gave us *Catch-22* and *V.* and *Cat's Cradle*. Novelists in the 60's have recovered the gift of fantasy and imaginative excess, as well as an adventurousness of form and technique that rivals [James] Joyce (though not without some loss, as with Joyce himself, of direct human appeal).

The 60's novel has been a hybrid literature, a dialectical literature, like [Allen] Ginsberg's poetry. [Joseph] Heller's *Catch-22* is an odd cross between *No Time for Sergeants* and [Fyodor] Dostoevsky, between a joke-book and [Franz] Kafka. Like Kafka's own work it is a perfect expression of the Jewish imagination of disaster, which means paranoia confirmed by history. [Thomas] Pynchon's *V.* combines a jazzy schlemiel-story with a staggering range of pseudo-Conradian adventures, which are scattered around the book like the pieces of a jigsaw puzzle whose improbable whole takes the shape of our century; or is it just a game? Neither book proceeds directly, both harbor secrets (the secret of Snowden, the mystery of V.), both expand in widening ripples of enigma and disclosure. Similarly haunted by this sense of intricate connection and hidden meaning are [Kurt] Vonnegut's novel *Cat's Cradle*, as clean and spare as a diagram, and Pynchon's *The Crying of Lot 49*, where the game feels more threatening. With their cartoonish characters and weird parodic sects and conspiracies these novels walk a fine line between what Pynchon calls the "orbiting ecstasy of a true paranoia" and the terrible blankness of the quotidian, between the imagination of disaster and no imagination at all. These black-humor fantasies are deeply political, not only because their Kafkaesque anxieties so fully express the sensibility of those who grew up with war and

cold war, the CIA and the bomb, but because their half-mythic appropriation of large chunks of contemporary reality speaks to our political imagination as no propagandist literature could.

Take Donald Barthelme's story "Robert Kennedy Saved from Drowning" side by side with [Norman] Mailer's recent journalism. Who could have predicted that fiction and political reportage would grow together as they have in the 60's? The progress of the literary mind from the anti-Stalinist radicalism of *Partisan Review* in the 30's and 40's to [Lionel] Trilling's still-engaged critique of liberalism in the name of imagination in 1950 to the "tyranny of taste" and the triumph of the New Criticism was toward an increasing disengagement from politics. Somehow Trilling's (and Matthew Arnold's) insistence that the political and literary minds had much to teach each other turned into the notion that they were fundamentally inimical, perhaps because most of the lessons flowed in one direction. Arnoldian disinterestedness came to justify a disdain for ideology and an aloofness from all political commitment, whereas in Arnold it is a mode of cultural criticism, of deeper engagement, directed above all against social complacency and self-congratulation. "Wragg is in custody," people are being quarantined and dehumanized—this is Arnold's prime example of the function of criticism.

Very much marked by this atmosphere of withdrawal, the novels of the 50's oscillated between minute personal concerns and abstract mythic ones; problems of alienation and identity were referred either to the private moral will, to the mysterious chemistry of human interaction, or to metaphysical necessity. Only the ethnic novel, rooted in a small but definable community, preserved a remnant of the social substance of literature. [Bernard] Malamud, [Saul] Bellow, and [James] Baldwin came through honorably if not grandly in their novels. Baldwin's essays and [Ralph] Ellison's *Invisible Man* went further, and adumbrated the new journalism and fiction that followed.

In poetry the 40's and 50's embraced a neo-conservatism of form and an emotional solipsism that went beyond that of the novel. The chief technical models, in addition to the 17th-century poets that [T. S.] Eliot had done the most to revive, were [W. H.] Auden and the early [Robert] Lowell, and the chief theorists were the New Critics. Poets like novelists were retreating from modernism in despair of surpassing it, resuscitating traditional forms as if they were bold new discoveries. Beat poetry, bad as much of it was, made an important break with this constriction of mind, this involution of the self into a distanced object, a well-wrought urn.

One of the New Critics had erected irony, ambiguity, and paradox into a Holy Trinity of the well-made poem. In this rhetorical hall of mirrors direct self-expression and *its* complexities counted for little. In *Howl* Ginsberg reached for what critics once called the Sublime, but John Hollander could only see "a hopped-up and improvised tone" which compared poorly with Ginsberg's "profound and carefully organized earlier writing."

As Paul Zweig has said, "What Ginsberg forced us to understand in *Howl*, twelve years ago, was that nothing is safe from poetry." It was not only that the world flowed through the poem again in all its variety, but also the spirit that greeted the world turned out to be larger than we remembered, as large as Whitman had boasted, able to contain multitudes. After Ginsberg we knew, but still didn't know that we knew: there was real poetry, and then there was what the Beats were doing, which was fun but wasn't Art. When Robert Lowell's *Life Studies* came out in 1959—the same year as Mailer's *Advertisements for Myself* and

[Norman O.] Brown's *Life Against Death*—it should have been clear that the game was up: not only was the shape of the poem broken open again, but the self was about to get a new kind of currency that would thrust American literature back into the Romantic mainstream. But some of Lowell's admirers abused his method: where he had been gritty, prosy, and imaginatively personal, they were literal and "confessional," making histrionic inventories of their inner lives.

It's important to stress that the main direction of American poetry in the 60's has not been "confessional," as has often been supposed, but toward the same dialectic of fantasy and fact, politics and vision, that has marked the new novel. We have seen the birth of a new surrealism—the intense, vatic, turned-on association-of-images of Ginsberg; the visionary kaleidoscope of Bob Dylan's *Blonde on Blonde* songs, much influenced by Ginsberg's style, as by his anger and tenderness; the whimsical surrealism of Kenneth Koch's poems and plays, with their hilarious disproportions of scale and their irrepressible, child-like verbosity; the new pastoral poetry of [Theodore] Roethke and his brood, feeling its way back to a new innocence and quietness, exploring the tangled, irrational roots of the self in the landscapes of nature and the mind.

I refer especially to Robert Bly and others loosely associated with him and his magazine *The Sixties*, such as James Wright, David Ignatow, and Galway Kinnell, who seem to me among the most interesting poets writing today. They are Wordsworthians all, seeking the eye of the storm, what Wordsworth in *The Excursion* called

Authentic tidings of invisible
   things;
Of ebb and flow, and ever-during
   power;

And central peace, subsisting at
     the heart
Of endless agitation.

It is hardly their fault that the contemporary
world and their own burdens of identity within
it have turned these men largely into poets of
disappointment. It was the pastoral poet in
Bly (and a touch of the old public bard) that
compelled him to confront the Vietnam war
by organizing a massive campaign of readings
and even by writing strikingly original political
poems, free of sentimental platitude and direct
appeal. Used often on the stump and finally
included in *The Light Around the Body*
(1967), these poems are angry, charmless mix-
tures of bizarre fact and surreal metaphor. If
the ingredients sometimes fail to coalesce, especially in print, it is nonetheless remarkable
that a poet from Minnesota, populistically mis-
trustful of New York intellectuals, with an
unambiguous sense of both his literary voca-
tion and social responsibility, should have
brought politics back into poetry, where *Partisan Review* and the New Criticism had so
long insisted it could not tread.

67

Merle Curti
THE SEARCH FOR ABSOLUTE
VALUES

From *pp. 767–771 in* The Growth of American
Thought, *third ed., by Merle Curti. Copyright 1943,
1951 by Harper & Row, Publishers, Inc. Copyright ©
1964 by Merle Curti. Reprinted by permission of
Harper & Row, Publishers.*

Merle Curti (1897–   ), one of the deans of
American intellectual history, has taught at the
University of Wisconsin, Madison, since 1942.
Especially known for his Pulitzer Prize-winning
work, *The Growth of American Thought* (1943),
he has written many other books, including *The
American Peace Crusade* (1929), *Peace or War:
The American Struggle 1636–1936* (1936), and
The Roots of American Loyalty (1946).

In the later 1940s and throughout the 1950s
the age-old quest for absolutes was pursued
with fresh zest. Men perennially have longed
for absolute answers and assurances, but several unsettling developments in the postwar
years prompted intellectuals to intensify the
search and expand its scope. On every side,
man's world seemed more and more contingent,
shifting, and elusive. The physical sciences
almost daily revealed the uncertain character
of what was once taken for granted as physical
reality. In human affairs the perilous and increasingly complex quality of life in the age of
the atomic bomb and the Cold War seemed to
threaten every vestige of what men in other
times had been able to count on as sure and
dependable. Even the continued existence of
human civilization was open to realistic
doubt. It appeared obvious, in short, that something had gone seriously awry in the human
career.

To many intellectuals the villain of the
piece clearly seemed to be the relativism and
liberalism dominant in American thought during preceding decades. Some Americans believed, for example, that the liberal concept of
human nature as something plastic and changing was ultimately related to Nazi and Communist attempts to manipulate behavior. Closer
to home, the concept of a plastic human nature
was associated with attempts to control mankind, whether by well-meaning utopian psychologists such as B. F. Skinner of Harvard,
or by mere "servants of power" on Madison
Avenue. Intellectuals, shocked by such efforts
at manipulation and by the vast amount of
actual irrational behavior in the world, searched
for a concept of human nature that was more

realistic than the concept inherited from the Enlightenment and nourished in the Progressive period. They sought a view of man that would be true for all seasons and all places, and that would set limits, as did the Christian doctrine of original sin, to man's presumptions about his perfectibility and rationality.

To find the permanent beneath the flux, to seek out the true man, to discover some kind of enduring justice that might limit man's inhumanity to man, many intellectuals turned—as so often in the past—to religion. Literally interpreted Christian theology did not return to vogue; it had been too much discountenanced in the late nineteenth and early twentieth centuries. Instead, literary historians, critics, and other scholars often identified religious symbols and myths as the highest truths. The great religious myths, sharing common themes and associations, could assure men of the objective validity of their moral, political, and esthetic values, and could harmonize such diverse needs as those for freedom and order, religious satisfactions and rational thought. As Henry B. Parkes put it, the great religions, as sources of enduring social myths, sustained civilizations by revealing the outlines of an ideal justice inherent in the cosmos. Edmond Taylor in *Richer by Asia* (1947) attempted to delineate lasting values of the Orient which should be assimilated into a new world order. In a similar vein Vincent Sheean's *Lead Kindly Light* (1949) found a universal standard in Hindu philosophy as exemplified by Gandhi's teachings and actions.

Another indication of the search for absolute values was the favorable reception given to Arnold Toynbee's *A Study of History*, the twelfth volume of which appeared in 1961. Toynbee's slanted essays sought to prove that the growth of civilizations was a spiritual process and that historical decline was the result of spiritual failure. Toynbee found in a creative elite the key to the rise and prosperity of civilizations; the disappearance of such an elite could result only in decay and decline. The implication plainly was that the challenge to present-day civilization could be met only by a creative minority thoroughly committed to Christian values, faith, and ideals. These doctrinal overtones of Toynbee's work made it an instrument in the ideological warfare of the late 1940s and the 1950s—the conflict, broadly, between those who subscribed to reason, science, democracy, and the process of trial and error, and, on the other side, those who sought guidance and salvation in a return to philosophical or religious absolutes.

The essentially religious emphasis of the reaction against relativism and pragmatism was illustrated in a collection of essays which appeared in 1947 under the title *Our Emergent Civilization*. The contributors—among others Brand Blanshard, George P. Adams, F. S. C. Northrop, and George E. G. Catlin—rejected determinism, opportunism, and materialism. The ills of contemporary life, the fragmentation of the individual and the confusions and tensions, were, the essays argued, the result of the materialistic and irrational postulates of modern psychology and psychoanalysis, the "anchorless inconsistencies" of instrumentalism, the confusions of relativism, the worship of power implied in the mere acceptance of science. As a cure the group of essayists called for a morality that would do more than merely rationalize individual or group interest. They insisted that men abandon uncritical faith in science and material power, which in no case could save mankind from death and destruction. And they urged a renewed faith in the possibility of discovering and cleaving to absolute values and truths that could satisfy man's deepest emotional and spiritual needs. The best clues in the search for a better life for man lay in what religion at its best had always taught.

Direct and indirect support for this revival of supposedly enduring religious values came from many quarters. T. S. Eliot's erudite arguments for Christian tradition and authority continued to appeal to intellectuals. So did the insistence of the followers of Robert M. Hutchins on the "eternal verities" to be found in religion as well as in Aristotelian and Thomistic philosophy. Under the leadership of President Nathan Pusey, the Harvard Divinity School developed from a traditional home of Unitarianism into a distinguished nondenominational center for theological study. Its faculty included Catholic and Jewish scholars, as well as such leading Protestant theologians as Paul Tillich. Reinhold Niebuhr, sometimes called the "Protestant Pope," gained a large following for his neo-orthodoxy. Niebuhr criticized modern liberal Christianity for its sentimentalism, fundamentalism for its rejection of science, and Catholicism for turning to St. Thomas instead of to St. Augustine. He led a widening group of intellectuals in rejecting liberal, optimistic conceptions of human nature and history as entirely too innocent and unrealistic. Only a more realistic Christianity, he insisted, could have honest relevance to contemporary ethical and political problems. An interest in the Christian existentialism of Sören Kierkegaard, a nineteenth-century Danish theologian, reflected a related emphasis on commitment and a fear of moral drift and moral neutrality.

In Catholic circles spokesmen of influence included Thomas Merton, Cardinal Spellman, Bishop Sheen, the Jesuit Gustave Weigel, and the neo-Thomist scholar Jacques Maritain, who visited and taught in America and whose writings were thoughtfully received. Man had too long assumed, Maritain contended, that salvation could be found without religion. He argued that the old world order had collapsed largely as a result of materialism and the selfish competition inherent in secularism. A new world order must revivify "the power of Christianity in its temporal existence." Much in the same spirit, the Catholic magazine *Commonweal* warned that "economic dogmas of liberalism . . . have so deeply permeated all our lives that we accept them unthinkingly as though they were moral or natural laws. . . . Yet this is a profoundly un-Christian nation."

Jewish scholars and theologians also attracted attention in Gentile circles. Will Herberg's *Protestant, Catholic and Jew* (1955), essentially a sociological study, found common ground in all three religions within the frame of American culture. Speaking primarily to Jews, Mordecai Kaplan called for a strengthening of the elements of Hebraic faith that were meaningfully functional in an American environment. And long before Martin Buber of the Hebrew University in Israel visited the United States, his revival of Hasidic mystical enthusiasm found some response among both Jewish and non-Jewish intellectuals.

On the popular level interest in religion seemed to be expanding. An opinion poll in 1948 indicated that 95 percent of those sampled believed in God. In the same inquiry, 90 percent stated that they prayed, and three-fifths expected to go to heaven. Whereas in Lincoln's day, only one out of five Americans belonged to a church, in the 1948 poll three out of five claimed membership in a church or synagogue. Church membership grew with particular rapidity in the millennial and pentecostal sects. As rural folk migrated, especially from "poor white" Southern areas, to cities and to the Southwest, Evangelist Billy Graham, though he did not achieve the following of some earlier revivalists, drew huge crowds. Books on religion, especially those which struck the inspirational and therapeutic note reached by Norman Vincent Peale, made the best-seller lists. At the first Eisenhower inauguration, "God's Float" headed the parade. Congress did its part by setting up a special room in the Capitol for prayer, by inserting the words "under God" into the pledge of allegiance, and by making the inscription "In God We Trust" mandatory on all coins. In 1962 the Supreme Court seemed out of step when it outlawed a simple, nondenominational prayer used in New York schools. But President Kennedy assured the nation that this decision merely provided new reasons to pray more in the home. Several congressmen responded by proposing to amend the Constitution to permit such religious practices in the schools.

Whether all this indicated more than a desire in a highly mobile society to be identified with a church for social advantage or for some other sociological reason, no one could say for certain. But many religious leaders took no satisfaction in outward evidences of piety and faith, and even deplored the frequent association of religion with personal success, prosperity, and health.

68

Martin Marty, et al.
RELIGIOUS REVIVAL AND REVOLUTION

From What Do We Believe? The Stance of Religion in America *by Martin Marty et al., pp. 12–18, by permission of Meredith Press. Copyright 1968 by Martin Marty.*

Martin Marty (1928–   ) is a minister, theologian, and historian who, after serving as a Lutheran pastor for more than ten years, was appointed professor at the University of Chicago in 1962. Somewhat earlier, in 1958, he had become an associate editor of the *Christian Century.* His writings include *The New Shape of American Religion* (1959), *The Infidel* (1961), *Second Chance for American Protestants* (1963), and *The Modern Schism* (1969).

[The comprehensive Gallup polls of 1952 and 1965 would seem to substantiate the view that between those years] America underwent, first, a revival of religion and, second, a revolution in religion. The revival began to be noticed around 1952 . . . ; it seemed to crest somewhere around 1956 or 1958 and began to dwindle and decline by 1960, when a radical change in America's religious interests was evident. There are signs today that that change, often spoken of as a "revolution," itself has been supplanted in the late 1960's. . . . Now [however,] it is more important to notice the interplay of revival and revolution.

After the preoccupations of "the jazz age" of the twenties, the Depression (and religious depression) of the thirties, the distractions of war in the forties, there were good reasons to believe that the age of America's religious revivals had passed by the fifties. Billy Sunday had been the last rough-and-tumble mass evangelist, and he was long forgotten. Harry Emerson Fosdick had been the last of the great fashionable preachers. People foresaw no resurgence of interest in mass religion. Then, in the 1950's, such a resurgence came.

Some scholars, noting how minimal were the institutional and ethical effects of religion in the 1950's, have questioned whether or not a revival ever really existed. Comment on that question depends largely on one's definition of religion and revival. If by it we mean that there was a certifiable gain in authentic religious response, it would be difficult to answer. If by it we mean an increase in public attention to or interest in religion, the signs are more obvious. Almost all the news media and particularly mass-circulation magazines and newspapers called attention to the revival. Perhaps they were celebrating a pseudoevent or a nonevent, were manufacturing news where there had been no "hard" news. But in a media-oriented America these "pseudoevents" serve as well as hard news to fashion people's attitudes.

At any rate, soon they were talking about the subjects to which they [gave their] attention in these polls. Without embarrassment, but usually with considerable vagueness, they talked about the social values of belief in God (often over against atheistic Communism). Church attendance rose, church building became a contagious fever, cover stories of *Life* magazine worried about Sunday school, a new President who typified the revival and the decade's spiritual values spoke in terms of leading a crusade and practiced what he preached even to the point of joining a church and getting baptized himself.

Religious books became best sellers. Collegians, often reputedly resistant to religious appeals, flocked to a pervasive but short-lived event called Religious Emphasis Week. New personalities came on the scene: Bishop Fulton Sheen, Rabbi Joshua Loth Liebman, and—most important of all—evangelist Billy Graham. Mass evangelism under the tutelage of Graham experienced a new birth. The Gallup poll of 1952 reflected a sampling of opinion in the early years of that revival. Civic or societal religion received a great impetus from that revival, as it was generalized, inoffensive, nationalist, noncontroversial religion that was being preached. Even Billy Graham, a would-be particularist who preached the offense of the cross of Jesus Christ, was inoffensive. "Everybody" liked him—secularists, Jews, Catholics, Protestants. Only a few crabby Protestant theologians raised questions.

Looking back, it is hard to recall any ethical achievement growing out of that revival. World and domestic poverty were not being attacked. The great racial crisis was largely overlooked by the revival-minded. The American Business Creed was not called into question. The President assured the people that America was the greatest instrument that God had ever placed on his footstool. When a sour prophet from New York's Union Theological Seminary reminded the nation that the Psalmist says that "he who sitteth in the heavens shall laugh," few listened. Positive thinking, peace with God, peace of soul, peace of mind, brotherhood, success, Americanism—these are the values we recall from the religion of the 1950's.

Not that the revival was without effect. In fact, had it not produced people for the churches, and churches for the people, it is questionable whether there would have been people for the prophets of the 1960's to lead, cajole, harangue, bug, mourn over, or sway. If one takes seriously the cultural impact of the prophets and theologians of the 1960's one is ready for *more* change than will be found in the 1965 poll. Perhaps the preaching of the revival, which helped people insulate themselves against change, served to keep them from being either lifted too high or dropped too low by the revolutionaries of the 1960's.

If the 1950's saw an enhancement of civic and societal religion, the 1960's experienced an attack on it. At the turn between the revival and the revolution there appeared a great number of books by Protestantism's social analysts. Best known of these were Peter Berger's *The Noise of Solemn Assemblies* and Gibson Winter's *The Suburban Captivity of the Church*. They demonstrated the degree to which Protestants had joined their compatriots in celebrating the American Way of Life and giving it the ultimate regard they professedly gave only to God. These prophets either had recourse to historic revelation and tradition or to humanist values in today's revolutionary world in order to gain an angle of vision for judgment or a place of leverage for change.

The "in" people of the 1950's had been the celebrity clerics, the experts at personal pastoral care, the pacifiers of an anxious nation, the sanctioners of a complacent nation. The "in" people of the 1960's, in the field of religion, were social activists, civil-rights leaders, radical experimenters with the liturgies and forms of the church, revolutionary theologians. The collegian who might have his eye on a seminary in the 1950's might very well claim a Peale or Sheen or Graham as a hero. In the 1960's he would more likely have cited a Martin Luther King, a John F. Kennedy, a Pope John as his religious hero. The mass of people, to whom the calls for commitment are less intense, respond less enthusiastically to both types.

The evidences that the 1960's brought about a revolutionary change in public attitudes to religion are on all hands. NBC could title its report on the clergy, "The Quiet Revolution." *Fortune* could ask, "What on Earth Is Happening to Protestantism?" The *New Yorker* sent Ved Mehta in quest of *The New Theologian*. *Time* asked on its Easter cover, "Is God Dead?" *Newsweek* used a Christmas cover in the same liturgical season (1965–66) to feature the unsettlers in Protestantism. *The New York Times* added a religion editorialist to its staff in order to keep up with the change. One journalist put it this way: "In the 1950's we responded to the revival by enlarging the religion section of Saturday metropolitan newspapers. It was full of sermon titles and advertisements for groundbreakings and smorgasbords. In the 1960's we responded to the revolution by decreasing the religion section and by putting religion on the front page of the newspapers."

In education, particularly in higher education, the change from 1952 to 1965 was obvious. The Supreme Court had ruled out school prayer and devotional exercises but had given a new charter for instruction about religion in two decisions designed to spell out "wholesome neutrality" on the part of the state toward religion. The result: During the 1960's there has been a great increase of religious inquiry in colleges and universities even at a time when many a chaplain noted that his chapel was emptying. Clearly, a new style of religious response seemed to be appearing by . . . 1965.

Now that some "backlash" seems to have occurred in reaction to the revolution, it is possible to begin to play the historians' game and to try to determine when, how, and under what circumstances Americans began to relocate the place of religion in personal and national life somewhere halfway between these two Gallup polls. My list is not inclusive, but its parts do illumine the whole change.

The election of John F. Kennedy was one of the symbolic events that represented a turn in American religion. As far as Protestants were concerned, here was the first non-Protestant President. Since the President plays a sort of priestly role in national religion, this change symbolized the displacement of Protestantism from its imperial position. Opposition to Mr. Kennedy's candidacy and election represented the last occasion which brought together old-line Protestant liberals who depended on a kind of nationally taken-for-granted theism with old-line Fundamentalists who were merely anti-Catholic. But Mr. Kennedy's Catholicism, never obtrusive in policy matters, was less significant than was that elusive quality called "style" which he imparted to a new generation. In place of Mr. Eisenhower's revivalist oratory and late-stage idealism, here was a cultivatedly tough and youthful pragmatism, tempered by its own kind of idealism which seemed to endorse a new elite in religion: civil-rights- and activist-oriented, if less pious.

With the Kennedy style, one must cite a hard-news event which more markedly inaugurated change in American religion. This was the racial revolution, which began to gather momentum after the Supreme Court decision of 1954 and the bus boycott in Alabama of

1956 but which reached public consciousness in the long, hot summers of the 1960's and probably crested, so far as Protestant clergy participation is concerned, with the Alabama marches of the spring of 1965. After two hundred years of church-endorsed slavery and one hundred years of church-tolerated segregation, no event did more to embarrass or quicken the conscience of churches. No other event served so readily to rally young activists in quest of a cause. Perhaps the church needed "the movement" more than the movement needed the church; at any rate, after the summer of 1966, the alliance between Negro civil-rights leaders and white churchmen seemed to be threatened. But the race problem remains as the urgent cause, the test of the ethical seriousness of the churches. For Protestantism, all the churchly talk about God and Trinity and Jesus sounded hollow so long as it was not matched by worldly talk about this social problem. Meanwhile, America's societal religion dictated just how much the clergy could become involved in this "secular social issue," and some lay reaction seems evident in the Gallup poll, where people display continued reluctance at seeing the clergy involved in issues of this type.

The discovery of urbanization and metropolis was another factor which brought about change. When the industrial city was first perceived on the American landscape, Protestants began to try to adapt their institutions to serve it. The result was the Social Gospel, Christian Socialism, and Social Christianity on the left and various kinds of institutional churches and the Salvation Army on the right, as it were. But the Protestant forms, the denominations, and the localistic parish church did not easily adapt, and Protestants continued to minister to the city with forms basically accommodated to town and country life.

In the 1960's it was no longer possible to avoid the meaning of the city. The seminaries prepared a new kind of leadership. The churches continued fleeing to the suburbs but making token payments in support of inner-city outpost experiments. While little institutional change came about in white Protestant circles, there was at least much talk about ministering to people who live in slums or the isolation of urban high-rise apartments. Inevitably, tension grew between those who wanted Protestantism to represent village values and those who celebrated secularity, pluralism, and the politics of the city. Reaction to this kind of involvement of the city also is no doubt a factor in ongoing resistance to clerical involvement in social issues, as revealed in the poll.

Talk of a new personal morality characterized religious life in the 1960's. It is clear . . . that most Americans, including younger ones, feel that religion plays a smaller part in determining moral choice than it did in the past. Most regard the old days as times of greater honesty and integrity. This finding would not be significant if we had only the [Gallup] poll of 1952, or only of 1965; it seems almost to be a part of human nature to feel that in earlier times moral integrity was easier to come by, that in the golden days of the past the fathers had it easier in their attempt to apply religion to life. But we have the two polls for contrast, and here is one of the more spectacular changes in all the findings: Clearly, Americans feel that a fundamental change in assessing moral values is coming into being.

The religious leaders have taken part in this revolution. Protestant Episcopal churchman Joseph Fletcher's *Situation Ethics* was only the best known of countless essays at defining what some called "the new morality." The impulses for Protestant advocacy of ethical change were complex and varied. Ordinarily they began with a critique of current and comfortable ethics, a tired legalism which inconvenienced no one but which—within the ceremonies of the religious revival of the 1950's—could be made to look Protestant and godly. The new ethics was to be an inconveniencing one, the removal of the legalist crutch. This critique then moved to the point of an attempted recovery of what these Protestants claimed was at the heart of biblical and Reformation ethical impulses. So advocacy of "situation ethics" grew as much out of the century's theological revival as it did out of assessment of the current moral situation and its possibilities.

Whether the public faulted the religious leadership for their assault on the comfortable if obsolete ethic or for their failure to come up with a satisfactory new ethic, or whether it was being merely nostalgic, it is clear that by the time of the 1965 poll a wider section of the public than in 1952 felt that religious controls over action were weaker. Unfortunately, these polls do not go into detail on complex specific ethical questions, such as the wars (first, in Korea; then, in Vietnam) which have troubled the Protestant conscience. The division within the clergy and between clergy and laity on the military-nationalist issue is itself another factor in the revolution in religion in the 1960's.*

[In 1971, at the request of the author, Mr. Marty added the following postscript to his commentary on recent religious change:]

Following 1965, religious leadership asserted itself ever more vigorously on certain ethical

---

* Editor's note: Perhaps it is of relevance here that, in a poll of 5000 college students carried out by two psychologists in 1970 to determine the impact of the Vietnam war, "two-thirds of those queried reported increased worry, anger and depression" as a result of the conflict; "nearly a third found their commitment to organized religion loosening; and more than a third felt that the war had affected relations with their parents." (The report on this survey is described in *Time*, July 6, 1970, p. 53.)

issues, and public response suggested a generally widening gap between clergy and laity or, better, between a coalition of one kind of clergyman with one kind of layman over against an alliance between another kind of clergyman and layman. One party in this growing denominational "two-party system" favored increasing involvement of religious organizations in social ethical issues; the other advocated ecclesiastical aloofness and passivity, restricting ethical issues to private affairs and personal actions.

The most controversial issues were those that had to do with race relations and the Indo-China War, and the latter in particular contributed to what Jeffrey Hadden called "The Gathering Storm in the Churches." Not long after President Lyndon B. Johnson committed land troops to action in Vietnam, clerical leadership united with antiwar laymen to form a group called Clergy and Laymen Concerned about Vietnam. CALCAV and a number of less well known subsequent organizations united with elements in the academy and the media to form a kind of troika of opposition to military policies. They sought to awaken Christian and Jewish consciences concerning ethical matters involved in the prosecution of the war.

Their success was obviously far from complete. A number of denominational periodicals in the mainline Protestant groups assessed opinions in these church bodies and found that the majority of the laity turned out to be more "hawkish" than the clergy and that an even larger majority opposed the fact that "doves" were speaking up in the name of religion against the war. The 1968 campaign, with the "abdication" of President Johnson, the candidacies of anti-war Senators Robert Kennedy and Eugene McCarthy, and the highly visible dissent at the Democratic Convention led to a further polarization in the churches. (Indeed, eventually the issue came to have to do more with dissent than with the war.) Only after 1970, as the whole nation moved toward a sense of disillusionment and disaffection with the military venture, did the gap on Indo-China attitudes begin to close.

Yet significantly, through the years of the Vietnamese involvement another change had taken place. Roman Catholic bishops, the Lutheran churches, most of the old-line Protestant denominations, and any number of voluntary agencies went on record in support of selec-

tive conscientious objection, a policy according to which a man might refuse to let himself be drafted to fight in particular wars. Since these policies had to be debated on the floor of the representative conventions in church after church, the nation was provided with a barometer for measuring attitudinal change. And by 1971 it was clear that the churches and the public at large had undergone a considerable shift in their views of war in general as well as in their perspective on Vietnam.

Part Four

THE QUESTION OF
THE WARFARE STATE

For more than a decade now, many Americans have believed that the Cold War has generated a coalition of domestic interest groups which acts as an obstacle to peace. Even before President Eisenhower pronounced his famous warning against the "military-industrial complex" in 1961, C. Wright Mills and others had suggested that a new elite was appearing which would have a stake in war. Since that time several hundred books and articles have been written on the subject, the majority of them very critical of the groups involved in our "defense." The most frequent accusation is that, consciously or unconsciously, the politicians, the generals, and the industrialists have found it to their advantage to cooperate in perpetuating international tension.

As we have noted in the introduction to this volume, such charges as these are not unprecedented. Not only were there similar accusations before both of the two world wars, but there are also longstanding traditions of suspicion regarding the "warmongering" of the statesman, the soldier, and the businessman individually. It seems to have required a "cold war" situation to create the image (and perhaps the reality) of the three types coalescing, but even in normal times the anti-political, anti-military, and anti-capitalist traditions have been very much alive in the minds of citizens who strove for peace.

In the section which follows, the reader is introduced both to the (older) suspicions regarding individuals and to the (recent) allegations of merging interests. The three traditional views are each presented separately, organized in three series of selections which range from ancient times down to our own. Since anti-political and anti-military attitudes have long drawn sustenance from Anglo-American liberalism, it has been possible in these instances to turn almost at once to American ex-examples (for example, to Thomas Paine and James Madison). With the anti-capitalist tradition, however, because of its relationship to Marxist thought, it has been desirable to begin the modern period with a statement by a German socialist (Karl Liebknecht). In all three series, the final selection among the readings is a discussion of that particular tradition by a skeptical, contemporary scholar (Kenneth N. Waltz, Samuel P. Huntington, and Quincy Wright).

The assertions regarding merging interests have also been arranged, with one exception, in chronological order. Two pairs of accusation and denial are included for the two world wars, following which the reader enters upon the 1950s–1960s and the full spectrum of today's debate. Here he encounters the *radical* perspective of C. Wright Mills, witnesses its transformation by *liberals* such as Fred J. Cook and H. L. Nieburg, and subjects this to the cross-examination of other *radicals* like Marc Pilisuk and Thomas Hayden, of other *liberals* like Kenneth Boulding, and of *conservatives* like Michael Getler and Richard M. Nixon. The radicals, he discovers, tend to believe not only that American foreign/military policies are basically misguided, but also that they are almost

inevitably the result of our having either a corrupt and obtuse elite (assuming oligarchic control) or false cultural assumptions (assuming a functioning democracy). The liberals, on the other hand, though almost equally offended by our military posture, generally put the blame for it upon that special alliance which they call the "military-industrial complex" and against which they would organize the citizenry. Meanwhile, the conservatives, who usually find themselves defending what America is doing, are far more troubled by the threat which the radical-liberal charges represent to current policy than they are by the (to them, faint) possibility that generals, businessmen, and the like might combine (or have combined) to gain unwarranted influence within the nation.

QUESTIONS:

1. Why was the nineteenth-century liberal less suspicious of the businessman than of the politician or of the soldier? To what extent and why have liberal attitudes been transformed in the present century?

2. Do you detect any substantial difference between the charges of merging interests that were made before the two world wars and those which have been made more recently?

3. Have the authors who make the accusations of connivance proved their case to any extent? Or have they simply demonstrated that the interests of certain groups happen to coincide?

4. Have the authors of the accusations proved that, even with connivance, the "complex" has succeeded in exerting influence?

5. Could it be correctly said of the "military-industrial complex" (or its individual parts) that what it wants is more "cold" and less "hot" war?

6. How much have the desires of the "military-industrial complex" (or its individual parts) had the effect of altering our economic structure and/or our political arrangements? (On this, refer to the article by Bernard D. Nossiter, under Cold War, Economy.)

7. What kinds of cultural assumptions do we as

a people make which might have eased the way (or rendered it more difficult) for the development of a "warfare state"?

8. Do you think that there is any connection between the (possible) existence of a "warfare state" and the imperatives of American foreign policy?

9. If it is true, as Michael Getler argues, that the rate of profit in defense industries is really rather modest, how do you explain the motivation of the people involved to do what they are doing?

10. If you assume that a complex of interests is at work, do you believe that it will become more vulnerable or less vulnerable to public attack over the next few years? Why?

At Algeciras, in 1906, Roosevelt inserted his Big Stick in a Franco-German squabble over control of Morocco.

Theodore Roosevelt, on February 3, 1906, at the time of his intervention in the first Moroccan crisis of the European powers. (Culver Pictures, Inc.)

Franklin D. Roosevelt on October 7, 1940, at the height of the "Battle of Britain" and during his electoral campaign for a third term.   (*The Chicago Tribune*)

"I ADMIRE ALL THE ROOSEVELTS."

Lyndon B. Johnson as he was viewed on the occasion of his sending troops into the Dominican Republic on May 6, 1965.   (Copyright © 1965, *The Chicago Sun-Times*; reproduced by courtesy of Wil-Jo Associates, Inc. and Bill Mauldin.)

Chapter Thirteen

TRADITIONAL SUSPICIONS: POLITICAL

Again, a tyrant is fond of making wars, as a means of keeping his subjects in employment and in continual need of a commander.

—Aristotle

The Politics

69

Thomas Paine
"PART OF THE SYSTEM OF OLD GOVERNMENTS"

Rights of Man, *Part I, in Moncuse Conway, ed.,* The Writings of Thomas Paine *(2 vols., New York, AMS Press, 1967), II, pp. 386–388.*

Thomas Paine (1737–1809), firebrand and pamphleteer, played a highly significant role in the genesis of two revolutions. In America in the 1770s his *Common Sense* and other writings were of crucial importance in mobilizing colonial opinion for the struggle against Great Britain. In Europe in the 1790s his *Rights of Man* was an inspiring rejoinder to Edmund Burke's antagonistic *Reflections on the Revolution in France.* In the passage presented here, which is taken from *Rights of Man,* Paine explains why he thinks that the world is entering upon a more peaceful age.

What were formerly called Revolutions, were little more than a change of persons, or an alteration of local circumstances. They rose and fell like things of course, and had nothing in their existence or their fate that could influence beyond the spot that produced them. But what we now see in the world, from the Revolutions of America and France, are a renovation of the natural order of things, a system of principles as universal as truth and the existence of man, and combining moral with political happiness and national prosperity.

"I. *Men are born, and always continue, free and equal in respect of their rights. Civil distinctions, therefore, can be founded only on public utility.*

"II. *The end of all political associations is the preservation of the natural and imprescriptible rights of man; and these rights are liberty, property, security, and resistance of oppression.*

"III. *The nation is essentially the source of all sovereignty; nor can any* INDIVIDUAL, *or* ANY BODY OF MEN, *be entitled to any authority which is not expressly derived from it.*"

In these principles, there is nothing to throw a Nation into confusion by inflaming ambition. They are calculated to call forth wisdom and abilities, and to exercise them for the public good, and not for the emolument or aggrandisement of particular descriptions of men or families. Monarchical sovereignty, the enemy of mankind, and the source of misery, is abolished; and the sovereignty itself is restored to its natural and original place, the Nation. Were this the case throughout Europe, the cause of wars would be taken away. . . .

Whatever is the cause of taxes to a Nation, becomes also the means of revenue to Government. Every war terminates with an addition of taxes, and consequently with an addition of revenue; and in any event of war, in the manner they are now commenced and concluded, the power and interest of Governments are increased. War, therefore, from its productiveness, as it easily furnishes the pretence of necessity for taxes and appointments to places and offices, becomes a principal part of the system of old Governments; and to establish any mode to abolish war, however advantageous it might be to Nations, would be to take from such Government the most lucrative of its branches.

The frivolous matters upon which war is made, shew the disposition and avidity of Governments to uphold the system of war, and betray the motives upon which they act.

Why are not Republics plunged into war, but because the nature of their Government does not admit of an interest distinct from that of the Nation? Even Holland, though an ill-constructed Republic, and with a commerce extending over the world, existed nearly a century without war; and the instant the form of Government was changed in France, the republican principles of peace and domestic prosperity and economy arose with the new Government; and the same consequences would follow the cause in other Nations.

As war is the system of Government on the old construction, the animosity which Nations reciprocally entertain, is nothing more than what the policy of their Governments excites to keep up the spirit of the system. Each Government accuses the other of perfidy, intrigue, and ambition, as a means of heating the imagination of their respective Nations, and incensing them to hostilities. Man is not the enemy of man, but through the medium of a false system of Government. Instead, therefore, of exclaiming against the ambitions of Kings, the exclamation should be directed against the principle of such Governments; and instead of seeking to reform the individual, the wisdom of a Nation should apply itself to reform the system.

70

Finley Peter Dunne
"WHIN CONGRESS GOES FORTH"

From Finley Peter Dunne, "War and War Makers," in Mr. Dooley's Philosophy (*New York: Harper & Brothers, 1900*).

Finley Peter Dunne (1867–1936) edited the Chicago *Journal* from 1897 to 1900 and the New York *Morning Telegraph* from 1900 to 1911, but his fame rests on his newspaper column and its enormously popular "Mr. Dooley essays." It was in this genre, speaking through the voice of a Chicago Irish bartender, that for many years he maintained a running attack upon corruption in government, American imperialism, and human foibles generally. In the piece reproduced below, "Mr. Dooley" waxes eloquent regarding the mismanagement of the Boer War and the Philippine Insurrection (both 1899–1902).

"I tell ye, Hinnissy," said Mr. Dooley, "ye can't do th' English-speakin' people. Oursilves an' th' hands acrost th' sea ar-re rapidly teachin' th' benighted Lutheryan an' other haythin that as a race we're onvincible an' oncatchable. Th' Anglo-Saxon race meetin's now goin' on in th' Ph'lippeens an' South Africa ought to convince annywan that, give us a fair start an' we can bate th' wurruld to a tillygraft office."

"Th' war our cousins be Sir Thomas Lipton is prosecutin', as Hogan says, again' th' foul but accrate Boers is doin' more thin that. It's givin' us a common war lithrachoor. I wudden't believe at first whin I r-read th' dispatches in th' pa-apers that me frind Gin'ral [Elwell S.] Otis wasn't in South Africa. It was only whin I see another chapter iv his justly cillybrated seeryal story, intitled 'Th' Capture iv Porac' that I knew he had an imitator in th' mother counthry. An' be hivins, I like th' English la-ad's style almost as well as our own gr-reat artist's. Mebbe 'tis, as th' pa-apers say, that Otis has writ himsilf out. Annyhow th' las' chapter isn't thrillin'. He says: 'To-day th' ar-rmy undher my command fell upon th' inimy with gr-reat slaughter an' seized th' important town of Porac which I. have mintioned befure, but,' he says, 'we ar-re fortunately now safe in Manila.' Ye see he doesn't keep up th' intherest to th' end. Th' English pote does betther."

"'Las' night at eight o'clock,' he says, 'we found our slendher but inthrepid ar-rmy surrounded be wan hundhred thousan' Boers,' he says. 'We attackted thim with gr-reat fury,' he says, 'pursuin' thim up th' almost inaccessible mountain side an' capturin' eight guns which we didn't want so we give thim back to thim with siveral iv our own,' he says. 'Th' Irish rig-mints,' he says, 'th' Kerry Rifles, th' Land Leaguers' Own, an' th' Dublin Pets, commanded be th' pop'lar Irish sojer Gin'ral Sir Ponsonby Tompkins wint into battle singin' their well-known naytional anthem: "Mrs. Innery Awkins is a fust-class name!" Th' Boers retreated,' he says, 'pursued be th' Davitt Terrors who cut their way through th' fugitives with awful slaughter,' he says. 'They have now,' he says, 'pinethrated as far as Pretoria,' he says, 'th' officers arrivin' in first-class carredges an' th' men in thrucks,' he says, 'an' ar-re camped in th' bettin' shed where they ar-re afforded ivry attintion be th' vanquished inimy,' he says. 'As f'r us,' he says, 'we decided afther th' victhry to light out f'r Ladysmith!' he says. 'Th' inimy had similar intintions,' he says, 'but their skill has been vastly overrated,' he says. 'We bate thim,' he says, 'we bate thim be thirty miles,' he says. 'That's where we're sthrong, Hinnissy. We may get licked on th' battle field, we may be climbin' threes in th' Ph'lippeens with arrows stickin' in us like quills, as Hogan says, into th' fretful porcupine or we may be doin' a mile in five minyits flat down th' pike that leads to Cape Town pursued be th' less fleet but more ignorant Boers peltin' us with guns full iv goold an' bibles, but in th' pages iv histhry that our childhren read we niver turned back on e'er an inimy. We make our own gloryous pages on th' battlefield, in th' camp an' in th' cab'net meetin'."

"Well, 'tis all r-right f'r ye to be jokin'," said Mr. Hennessy, "but there's manny a brave fellow down there that it's no joke to."

"Thrue f'r ye," said Mr. Dooley, "an' that's why I wisht it cud be fixed up so's th' men that starts th' wars could do th' fightin'. Th' throuble is that all th' prelimin'ries is arranged be matchmakers an' all they'se left f'r fighters is to do th' murdherin'. A man's got a good job at home an' he wants to make it sthronger. How can he do it? Be throwin' out someone that's got an akelly good job down th' sthreet. Now he don't go over as I wud an' say, 'Here Schwartzmeister (or [Paul] Kruger as th' case may be), I don't like ye'er appearance, ye made a monkey iv me in argymint befure th' neighborhood an' if ye continyue in business ye'll hurt me thrade, so here goes to move ye into th' sthreet!' Not that la-ad. He gets a crowd around him an' says he: 'Kruger (or Schwartzmeister as th' case may be) is no good. To begin with he's a Dutchman. If that ain't enough he's a cantin', hymn singin' murdhrous wretch that wudden't lave wan iv our countrymen ate a square meal if he had his way. I'll give ye all two dollars a week if ye'll go over an' desthroy him.' An' th' other la-ad, what does he do? He calls in th' neighbors an' says he: 'Dooley is sindin' down a gang iv savages to murdher me. Do ye lave ye'er wurruk an' ye'er families an' rally ar-round me an' where ye see me plug hat wave do ye go in th' other direction,' he says, 'an' slay th' brutal inimy,' he says. An' off goes th' sojers an' they meet a lot iv la-ads that looks like thimsilves an' makes sounds that's more or less human an' ates out iv plates an' they swap smokin' tobacco an' sing songs together an' th' next day they're up early jabbing holes in each other with baynits. An' whin its all over they'se me an' [Joseph] Chamberlain at home victoryous an' Kruger an' Schwartzmeister at home akelly victoryous. An' they make me prime minister or aldherman but whin I want a man to put in me coal I don't take wan with a wooden leg."

"I'll niver go down again to see sojers off to th' war. But ye'll see me at th' depot with a brass band whin th' men that causes wars starts f'r th' scene iv carnage. Whin Congress goes forth to th' sun-kissed an' rain jooled isles iv th' Passyfic no more heartier cheer will be heard thin th' wan or two that rises fr'm th' bosom iv Martin Dooley. Says I, give thim th' chanst to make histhry an' lave th' young men come home an' make car wheels. If Chamberlain likes war so much 'tis him that ought to be down there in South Africa peltin' over th' road with ol' Kruger chasin' him with a hoe. Th' man that likes fightin' ought to be willin' to turn in an' spell his fellow-counthrymen himsilf. An' I'd even go this far an' say that if Mack [William McKinley] wants to subjoo th' damn Ph'lippeens—"

"Ye're a thraitor," said Mr. Hennessy.

"I know it," said Mr. Dooley, complacently.

"Ye're an anti-expansionist."

"If ye say that agin," cried Mr. Dooley, angrily, "I'll smash in ye'er head."

71

James Andrew Beall
"EACH WITH HIS HAND UPON HIS GUN"

Congressional Record: House of Representatives, *February 15, 1905, 58th Congress, 3rd Session* (Washington, 1905), *pp. 2667–2668.*

James Andrew (Jack) Beall (1866–1929), a lawyer and politician, graduated from the University of Texas in 1890 and served as a member of the Texas State house of representatives (1892–1895) and State senate (1895–1899) before being elected as a Democrat to the 58th and five succeeding Congresses (1903–1915). His comments here were prompted by what he considered the extravagance of President Theodore Roosevelt's demands on behalf of the Navy.

Mr. Beall of Texas. Mr. Chairman, I am not one of those who have lost faith in this Republic. Whatever else may be said about it, and whatever its frailties may be, I believe that it is by far the best Government upon earth. But in some vital respects it is departing from the traditions of the past, and some of the virtues the fathers gave it are being lost. When it was first established it was a simple Government, because the men who wrought its independence and gave it existence were the humblest, the simplest men who ever took upon themselves the awful responsibility of establishing a government. It was established as an economical Government, because the people for whom it was made, wrecked by war and ravaged by conflict, were the poorest people who ever attempted the experiment of government building. The founders of our Government were lovers of liberty, for they had tasted the bitter draught of kingly oppression and they wrote into every line of their Declaration of Independence, of their Constitution, and of their laws the sublime and divine principles that all men were equal and all men entitled to the blessings of self-government.

It seems to me, Mr. Chairman, that in many respects, at least, the simplicity of the past is gone. Our Government to-day pays as much attention to ceremony, as much regard for pomp and display, as much deference to power, as any government in the world. To flatter the pride and tickle the vanity of our President the ships of our Navy are gathered together upon our eastern coast and pass in stately parade before him, greeting him with a royal salute at an estimated cost to our people of $150,000. You see about this city to-day preparations being made for inducting into the office of President him who is already President, and on inauguration day these streets will echo with the tread of infantry, the clatter of cavalry, the rumble of artillery, flags will flutter, swords will flash, bands will play, and cannon will roar, making an occasion as gorgeous in display as

would mark the crowning of any monarch of the Old World. The simplicity of the olden time is gone. . . .

Let us examine for a moment into the naval expenditures. The development of our present Navy began, as stated before, in 1883. In that year the total expenses of our naval establishment were less than $15,000,000. During the next ten years, from 1883 to 1893, we spent $59,000,000 in the construction and equipment of vessels. During the past two years we have spent $64,000,000 for like purposes—$5,000,000 more in the last two years than we spent in ten years, from 1883 to 1893. The last year of [Grover] Cleveland's Administration we spent $29,000,000; the last year of [William] McKinley's $48,000,000. The first year of [Theodore] Roosevelt's required for naval expenditures $65,000,000; the second year $78,000,000, the third year $81,000,000, the fourth year $97,000,-000, besides a deficiency of at least $7,000,000, and this bill carries more than $100,000,000. Thus we have gone on by leaps and bounds increasing our naval expenditures, striving to distance the other nations of the world. . . .

It is this of which I complain, that under the present regime the energy of our Government is being concentrated in the building up of great war machines both on land and sea and the agencies that promote industry and commerce and peace are being ignored and forgotten. Just now this country is disturbed as it never was before over the question as to how the great artificial highways of commerce, the railways, can be made subservient to law and to respect the rights of producers and shippers, and yet when you deepen the harbors and clean out the rivers you develop natural highways which, under the old law of competition, will help to solve this vexing problem better than legislation will solve it.

This bill carries over $100,000,000. During twenty years we will have spent $800,000,000

upon our Navy. If this sum had been left
among the people and spent for education, it
would have put a new song into the mouth of
this nation and made it sweep to new heights
of mental and moral grandeur never dreamed
of before; if it had been spent in the development of agriculture, trade, and commerce, it
would have made the deserts bloom, the barren
fields fertile, the wheels of industry to turn in
a very ecstasy of delight; if spent for humanity
it would have opened the door of poorhouses
and closed up the doors of vice; it would have
kindled a new light in the eyes of little children
and lifted from the backs of weary women
heavy burdens of woe; it would have helped to
bring heaven so close to earth that her weary
ones could catch some of its radiance, but spent
upon the building of great ships and great guns
it may curse us in the days to come. . . .

Many years ago the frontier sections tested
the theory advanced by this Administration
now, and the establishment of private grave-
yards was a thriving industry. Advancing civilization condemned it, but now we are asked as
a nation to adopt that which, tried by the experience of individuals as well as by other nations, has always been condemned.

Yet they say it means peace. The President
on Monday night at a banquet in New York
said that we ought to speak pleasantly about
other nations and at the same time build new
battleships. It is a modification of the expression, "Tread softly, but carry a big stick."

It would be a pleasing spectacle to behold
the English King, the German Emperor, the
Russian Czar, and Uncle Samuel bowing and
smiling at each other, doing the Alphonse and
Gaston act, each with his hand upon his gun.
That is the Rooseveltian idea of brotherly love.

My judgment, Mr. Chairman, is that such
a theory will not apply amongst nations any
more than it will amongst individuals.

There never was a bully who went swagger-

ing about with a chip on his shoulder seeking
a row but what there was found somebody
ready to knock it off. In all time there has
never been a nation that tired of peace and
sought to play policeman for the balance of the
world that did not find some other nation ready
to engage in a death struggle with it, and history, I fear, will repeat itself with us.

72

William Henry Chamberlin
"A DELIBERATE HOAX ON THE AMERICAN PEOPLE"

*From William Henry Chamberlin, "The Bankruptcy
of a Policy," pp. 485–491, in* Perpetual War for Perpetual Peace, *edited by Dr. Harry Elmer Barnes. The
Caxton Printers, Ltd., Caldwell, Idaho, 1953.*

William Henry Chamberlin (1897–   ) is a
writer and former reporter who was Moscow correspondent of the *Christian Science Monitor* from
1922 to 1934, and chief Far Eastern correspondent
of that newspaper in 1939 and 1940. His list of
publications includes *The Russian Revolution,
1917–1921* (2 vols., 1935), *America: Partner in
World Rule* (1945), and *Beyond Containment*
(1953). The following piece is taken from a contribution which he made to the "revisionist" his-
toriography of the Second World War.

According to his own official statements, repeated on many occasions, and with special
emphasis when the presidential election of 1940
was at stake, Franklin D. Roosevelt's policy
after the outbreak of the war in Europe in 1939
was dominated by one overriding thought:
how to keep the United States at peace. One of
the President's first actions after the beginning
of hostilities was to call Congress into special
session and ask for the repeal of the embargo
on the sales of arms to belligerent powers,
which was part of the existing neutrality legis-

lation. He based his appeal on the argument that this move would help to keep the United States at peace. His words on the subject were:

Let no group assume the exclusive label of the "peace bloc." We all belong to it. . . . I give you my deep and unalterable conviction, based on years of experience as a worker in the field of international peace, that by the repeal of the embargo the United States will more probably remain at peace than if the law remains as it stands today. . . . Our acts must be guided by one single, hardheaded thought— keeping America out of the war.

This statement was made after the President had opened up a secret correspondence with Winston Churchill, First Lord of the Admiralty and later Prime Minister in the British government. What has been revealed of this correspondence, even in Churchill's own memoirs, inspires considerable doubt as to whether its main purpose was keeping America out of the war.

Roosevelt kept up his pose as the devoted champion of peace even after the fall of France, when Great Britain was committed to a war which, given the balance of power in manpower and industrial resources, it could not hope to win without the involvement of other great powers, such as the United States and the Soviet Union. The President's pledges of pursuing a policy designed to keep the United States at peace reached a shrill crescendo during the last days of the 1940 campaign.

Mr. Roosevelt said at Boston on October 30: "I have said this before, but I shall say it again and again and again: Your boys are not going to be sent into any foreign wars."

The same thought was expressed in a speech at Brooklyn on November 1: "I am fighting to keep our people out of foreign wars. And I will keep on fighting."

The President told his audience at Rochester, New York, on November 2: "Your national government . . . is equally a government of peace—a government that intends to retain peace for the American people."

On the same day the voters of Buffalo were assured: "Your President says this country is not going to war."

And he declared at Cleveland on November 3: "The first purpose of our foreign policy is to keep our country out of war."

So much for presidential words. What about presidential actions? American involvement in war with Germany was preceded by a long series of steps, not one of which could reasonably be represented as conducive to the achievement of the President's professed ideal of keeping the United States out of foreign wars. The most important of these steps may be briefly listed as follows:

1. The exchange of American destroyers for British bases in the Caribbean and in Newfoundland in September, 1940. . . .

2. The enactment of the Lend-Lease Act in March, 1941. . . .

3. The secret American-British staff talks in Washington in January-March, 1941. . . .

4. The inauguration of so-called naval patrols, the purpose of which was to report the presence of German submarines to British warships, in the Atlantic in April, 1941.

5. The dispatch of American laborers to Northern Ireland to build a naval base, obviously with the needs of an American expeditionary force in mind.

6. The occupation of Iceland by American troops in July, 1941. . . .

7. The Atlantic Conference of Roosevelt and Churchill, August 9–12, 1941. . . .

8. The orders to American warships to shoot at sight at German submarines, formally announced on September 11. . . .

9. The authorization for the arming of merchant ships and the sending of these ships into war zones in November, 1941.

10. The freezing of Japanese assets in the United States on July 25, 1941. . . .

11. When the Japanese Prime Minister, Prince Fumimaro Konoye, appealed for a personal meeting with Roosevelt to discuss an amicable settlement in the Pacific, this appeal was rejected, despite the strong favorable recommendations of the American ambassador to Japan, Joseph C. Grew.

12. Final step on the road to war in the Pacific was Secretary of State Hull's note to the Japanese government of November 26. Before sending this communication Hull had considered proposing a compromise formula which would have relaxed the blockade of Japan in return for Japanese withdrawal from southern Indochina and a limitation of Japanese forces in northern Indochina.

However, Hull dropped this idea under pressure from British and Chinese sources. He dispatched a veritable ultimatum on November 26, which demanded unconditional Japanese withdrawal from China and from Indochina and insisted that there should be "no support of any government in China other than the National Government [Chiang Kai-shek]." . . .

Former Congresswoman Clare Boothe Luce found the right expression when she charged Roosevelt with having lied us into war. Even a sympathizer with Roosevelt's policies, Professor Thomas A. Bailey, in his book, *The Man in the Street*, admits the charge of deception, but tries to justify it on the following grounds:

> Franklin Roosevelt repeatedly deceived the American people during the period before Pearl Harbor. . . . He was like the physician who must tell the patient lies for the patient's own good. . . . The country was overwhelmingly noninterventionist to the very day of Pearl Harbor, and an overt attempt to lead the people into war would have resulted in certain failure and an almost certain ousting of Roosevelt in 1940, with a complete defeat of his ultimate aims.

Professor Bailey continues his apologetics with the following argument, which leaves very little indeed of the historical American conception of a government responsible to the people and morally obligated to abide by the popular will.

> A president who cannot entrust the people with the truth betrays a certain lack of faith in the basic tenets of democracy. But because the masses are notoriously shortsighted and generally cannot see danger until it is at their throats, our statesmen are forced to deceive them into an awareness of their own long-run interests. This is clearly what Roosevelt had to do, and who shall say that posterity will not thank him for it?

Presidential pledges to "keep our country out of war," with which Roosevelt was so profuse in the summer and autumn of 1940, could reasonably be regarded as canceled by some new development in the international situation involving a real and urgent threat to the security of the United States and the Western Hemisphere.

But there was no such new development to justify Roosevelt's moves along the road to war in 1941. The British Isles were not invaded in 1940, at the height of Hitler's military success on the Continent. They were much more secure against invasion in 1941. Contrast the scare predictions of Secretary [of War Henry L.] Stimson, Secretary [of the Navy Frank] Knox, and General [George C.] Marshall, about the impending invasion of Britain in the first months of 1941, with the testimony of Winston Churchill, as set down in his memoirs: "I did not regard invasion as a serious danger in April, 1941, since proper preparations had been made against it."

Moreover, both the American and British governments knew at this time that Hitler was contemplating an early attack upon the Soviet Union. Such an attack was bound to swallow up much the greater part of Germany's military resources. . . .

One is left, therefore, with the inescapable conclusion that the promises to "keep America out of foreign wars" were a deliberate hoax on the American people, perpetrated for the purpose of insuring Roosevelt's re-election and thereby enabling him to proceed with his plan of gradually edging the United States into war.

73

Robert J. Bresler
"A NEW APPRECIATION FOR CONGRESS"

From Robert J. Bresler, "The War-Making Machinery," The Nation, Vol. 209 (August 17, 1970), pp. 105–109.

Robert J. Bresler (1937–   ), a staff member of the Cambridge-Goddard Graduate School for Social Change in Cambridge, Massachusetts, has previously taught at the University of Wisconsin, Green Bay, and at Pennsylvania State University, Capitol Campus. His primary fields of interest are American politics and foreign policy. He has edited a collection of readings entitled *Power in America* (1968) and is presently completing a study on war making by the executive.

The first glimmers of Congressional restiveness were apparent in the summer of 1969. At that time, the Senate passed the National Commitments Resolution calling for Congressional approval of the commitment of troops and financial assistance to any foreign country. The odd coalition of dovish liberals and legalist conservatives which passed the resolution employed arguments similar in tone to those used by Sen. Robert Taft against President Truman's intervention in Korea and deployment of troops to Western Europe. These sentiments were the beginning of a revision of basic concepts of liberal internationalism. The Senate Foreign Relations Committee in its Report on the National Commitments Resolution, for instance, derided "the new generation of foreign policy experts who [encourage] the belief that foreign policy is an occult science which ordinary citizens, including members of Congress, are simply too stupid to grasp." The report condemned the use of crisis diplomacy to place "tremendous pressures upon members of Congress to set aside apprehensions as to the exercise of power by the executive, lest they cause some fatal delay or omission in the nation's foreign policy." In the Senate debate on the resolution, Senator [Frank] Church denounced bipartisanship as a means "to gather more power into the hands of the President by eliminating between elections any semblance of organized opposition in Congress." Sen. Sam Ervin, a Southern conservative and strict constructionist, declared that the revolt against Executive war making meant simply "that the people will not support forever a policy which is made for them but without them."

The implication of such challenges stands on their heads the old arguments for a powerful Executive. For thirty years, American Presidents have exploited the notions of "expertise," "bipartisanship" and "crisis diplomacy" to secure their own supremacy. Presidential control of experts and information has deprived Congress of resources vital to its formation of independent judgments. Bipartisanship, a liberal canon once used quite skillfully to quarantine Congressional isolations, has fudged the lines of political responsibility, baffled voters and immobilized serious and sustained Congressional opposition. But the most potent of these weapons, crisis diplomacy, has frightened a Congress reluctant to risk decisions involving war or peace.

Examples abound. The preamble to the Tonkin Resolution speaks of a "deliberate and systematic campaign of aggression that the

Communist regime of North Vietnam has been waging against its neighbors." Yet the Congress made no such finding, nor did the State Department until early 1965. What *did* happen in Tonkin in 1964? Or at the 38th Parallel in 1950? Or in Santo Domingo in 1965? Were there threats to our national interest in Formosa in 1955, in the Middle East in 1957, in Cuba in 1961 serious enough to justify the sweeping grants of discretionary power Congress· delegated to the President? Historians and ambitious journalists may be able to piece together these events months or years after they occurred, but while they were happening the only facts available were certified by an Executive stamp.

In addition to fearing a recalcitrant and parochial Congress, liberal internationalists and supporters of the Executive state have long feared the vagaries of an aroused public opinion. What if American opinion should one day weary of its global responsibilities and choose "the easy path"? Henry Kissinger, W. W. Rostow and Walter Lippmann, all prominent liberal internationalists of the 1950s, indicated precisely such anxieties. In *Necessity for Choice*, Kissinger warned of Americans' "penchant for choosing the interpretation of current trends which implies the least effort"; Rostow (*The United States in the World Arena*) considered the American people "self-indulgent" because they were apparently so attracted by President Eisenhower's slogan of "peace and prosperity" in the 1956 election; and Lippmann, writing in *The Public Philosophy* in 1955, called public opinion "destructively wrong at the critical junctures . . . and a dangerous master of decision when the stakes are life and death."

These suspicions of the popular mind led to the establishment of institutional arrangements for shaping national security policy in ways which would insulate the "wisdom" of the few from the opinions of the many. Conflicts would be resolved at the top level of leadership and, in the words of V. O. Key, "clusters of public opinion in conflict [would] gradually dissolve because of lack of encouragement from prestigious givers of cues." (*Public Opinion and American Democracy.*)

Dissatisfied with Eisenhower's sluggish leadership, out-of-power liberals argued in the late 1950s for a national security state strengthened through tighter Presidential control, public sacrifice and a revitalization of the chain of command. When they returned to power in the 1960s, there followed the McNamara reforms in the Pentagon and the Churchillian tone of the Kennedy administration. Democracy would be saved, despite itself, from the easy path.

In Vietnam and Cambodia lies bankrupt this elitist thinking and the notion that foreign policy is, at its best, a product of secrecy and expert opinion. Since the Gulf of Tonkin, Americans have been public witness to the indiscriminate and arbitrary use of force, the manipulation of information and the unlimited waste of resources—all in the name of global responsibility and all justified by the transcendent wisdom of Presidential leadership. As Sen. Frank Church recently lamented: "The myth that the Chief Executive is the fount of all wisdom in foreign affairs today lies shattered on the shoals of Vietnam."

Now, after a generation of Executive war making, it begins to be apparent that the major political arguments for Executive domination of foreign policy can be turned against themselves: The destructive force of technology *requires* severe controls on its use rather than its immediate application in time of crisis; the need for expert guidance *requires* its detachment from Executive controls and its use as a public resource. The policy process must be opened up to public scrutiny so as to protect mankind from the "wisdom" of the few.

How did this fascination with Executive power flourish? Americans, especially liberals, should be embarrassed to recall, as Richard Neustadt, author of *Presidential Power*, has acknowledged, that they helped to create the myth which so loosely equated Presidential greatness with the exercise of war powers. A major point of the cold-war consensus, voiced particularly by liberalism and conventional political science, saw a dominant Executive as essential to a modern state and the conduct of contemporary diplomacy. Great Presidents would have to be strong Presidents, and for liberals it was no more than coincidence that strong Presidents invariably became war Presidents.

The liberal academic tradition contributed studies which treated the war making adventures of our Presidents (be it Theodore Roosevelt's exploits in Panama, Wilson's in Mexico, Franklin Roosevelt's in the North Atlantic, or Truman's in Korea) as creative examples of the use of Executive power.

What this point of view neglected was the fact that these dominant Executives accepted public opinion, particularly in relation to war making, as something to be manipulated or structured, and that they treated Congress as an institution to be circumvented or co-opted. For example: after the negative public reaction to his quarantine-the-aggressor speech, Franklin Roosevelt adjusted only the timing of his policy, not its substance. Harry Truman's landmark decisions to build the H-bomb, rearm Germany, intervene in Korea and cross the 38th Parallel were all made within the insulated and rarified atmosphere of the National Security Council, with Congress offering only some advice and little consent, and the public offering only its prayers. John Kennedy's decisions to sponsor the Bay of Pigs invasion and to increase troop support in Southeast Asia were made unilaterally, if not surreptitiously. Lyndon John-

son's invasions of Vietnam and the Dominican Republic were willed by Executive decree and presented to Congress and the public at large as *faits accomplis*.

Liberal internationalists consistently (as during the troops-to-Europe and the Bricker Amendment debates) brushed aside attempts by Congressional conservatives to place strong constitutional and legal controls upon the President's conduct of foreign policy. Liberal rhetoric, such as that which permeated the campaigns of Adlai Stevenson and John Kennedy, spoke of national sacrifice and of the Presidential obligation to make the hard choices and to avoid the easy path. The easy path became inevitably equated with peace and compromise; the hard choices involved sustaining costly military programs and unpopular military adventures. This rhetoric, however, never clearly stated that those hard choices required that the Executive be protected from effective Congressional and public scrutiny. . . .

Where do we go from here? Perhaps a new appreciation for Congress is upon us. Congress remains an anomaly. It is the one major American institution to resist the bureaucratic-managerial norms which pervade our political system and have proven disastrous when applied to foreign affairs. Our bureaucratic foreign policy spawned clandestine wars, as in Laos; and the managerial mentality found the path to Vietnam through its counterinsurgency calculations. Legislative openness, deliberation and delay—characteristic of democratic assemblies and the bane of managerial efficiency—may be the best hope for those who desire a saner foreign policy.

"What would have been on my mind," Senator Church has conjectured, "if President Johnson had said to a joint session of Congress that the government of North Vietnam had by stealth invaded and attacked the government of South Vietnam on a day that would live in infamy? I would have said, 'Where is the evidence?' "

Yet it must be acknowledged that Congressional acquiescence in the expansion of Executive war making stems in large part from the desire *not* to be held politically responsible for crucial decisions. And in spite of the growing new consensus against national commitments made secretly and independently by the Executive, Congressional leadership remains openly in complicity with the national security bureaucracy. Congressional committees on the armed services and on atomic energy jealously guard the privileges of those agencies they are assigned to oversee. In major cold-water crises Congress may continue to shrink from the risks of decision making and permit the President to define both the problem and its solution—invariably in military terms. . . .

The solution, then, is evident. If the Congress is to reclaim its war-making *authority*, it must seek to control the war-making *machinery* and to slow down the process of decision making. The challenge then is to develop procedures which insinuate Congress deep into the very fabric of policy making and, in a sense, force it to accept its constitutional mandate. To do this requires making expert opinion a public resource and information a public commodity. Defense laboratories such as the Lincoln Lab at M.I.T. could be made responsible to Congress, as is the General Accounting Office; it could then provide the legislators with an independent means to evaluate weapons systems.

In the American experience there is a tradition which eschews large standing armies, foreign entanglements, entrenched centralized power and asserts the Congressional prerogative. Possibly a new vision of an open and democratic foreign policy can be defined out of that tradition, so as to hedge power with strong

institutional constraints, expose it to public scrutiny and make its application deliberative. Still needed are new public avenues of participation and clear institutional obstacles to Executive domination.

In William Borah and Robert Taft may be found the strands of such a tradition, combining the Populist Left and libertarian Right and confronting directly the problem of war making. It was Senator Taft's amendment to the Selective Service Act of 1940 that restricted the deployment of conscripts beyond the Western Hemisphere; Sens. Gerald Nye and Robert La Follette, Jr., proposed in 1941 a national advisory referendum on whether Congress should approve the use of land, naval and air forces outside the Western Hemisphere; and Sen. Arthur Vandenberg suggested in 1932 a constitutional amendment clearly defining the power of Congress to prevent defense profiteering.

These thoughts—from the Right and Left—went beyond legalism. This legacy and our grim cold-war past should leave no doubt that if we are to avoid the drift into a Napoleonic state, the assignment will be not simply to relocate the war-making power but rather to dismantle it.

74

Kenneth N. Waltz
LIBERAL ANTI-GOVERNMENTALISM

From Kenneth N. Waltz, Man, the State and War: A Theoretical Analysis *(New York: Columbia University Press, 1959), pp. 97–103.*

Kenneth N. Waltz (1924–   ) taught political science for several years at Columbia University and Swarthmore College before moving to Brandeis University in 1966, where he is now Adlai E. Stevenson Professor of International Politics. His scholarly interests are well represented by the titles of his books, which include *Man, the State and War* (1959), *The Stability of a Bipolar World* (1964), and *Foreign Policy and Democratic Politics* (1967).

In the seventeenth century, [Jean de] La Bruyère asked: "How does it serve the people and add to their happiness if their ruler extend his empire by annexing the provinces of his enemies; . . . how does it help me or my countrymen that my sovereign be successful and covered with glory, that my country be powerful and dreaded, if, sad and worried, I live in oppression and poverty?" The transitory interests of royal houses may be advanced in war; the real interests of all peoples are furthered by peace. Most men suffer because some men are in positions that permit them to indulge their kingly ambitions. Three centuries later, James Shotwell wrote: "The political doctrine of international peace is a parallel to the economic doctrine of Adam Smith, for it rests similarly upon a recognition of common and reciprocal material interests, which extend beyond national frontiers." If real interests were given full play, national boundaries would cease to be barriers. Cooperation, or constructive competition, is the way to advance simultaneously the interests of all people. In a shop or a town, the division of labor increases everyone's material well-being. The same must be true on a national and on a global scale. There are no qualitative changes to damage the validity of the principle as the scale increases. The liberals' free-trade argument, put in terms currently and locally relevant, was as simple as this: Do Michigan and Florida gain by trading freely the automobiles of the one for the oranges of the other? Or would Michigan be richer growing its own oranges under glass, instead of importing the produce of "foreign" labor? The answer is obvious. And since the

principle is clear, it must be true that where natural conditions of production are less spectacularly different, the gain from trade, though smaller, will nevertheless be real. Each side gains from trade, whether between individuals, corporations, localities, or nations. Otherwise no trade would take place.

There was a time when even relatively untutored publicists understood not only this simplified version of the classical free-trade argument but a good many of its more subtle ramifications as well. From the argument it follows not only that free trade is the correct policy but also that attempts to enlarge the territory of the state, whether by annexing neighbors or acquiring colonies, are foolish. The expenses of conquering and holding cannot be balanced by advantages in trade, for the same advantages can be had, without expense, under a policy of free trade. In its most general form, the liberals' argument becomes a simple bit of common sense. Ultimately, they are saying, the well-being of the world's people can increase only to the extent that production increases. Production flourishes in peace, and distribution will be equitable if all nationals are free to seek their interests anywhere in the world. War is destruction and enrichment from war must therefore be an illusion. The victor does not gain by war; he may pride himself only on losing less than the vanquished. This reasoning is the root of the traditional war-does-not-pay argument, an argument dating back at least to Emeric Crucé early in the seventeenth century, developed in detail by [Jeremy] Bentham and both [James and John Stuart] Mill, used by William Graham Sumner to condemn the American war against Spain, and brought to its apogee by Norman Angell who summed up the work of the liberal economists, largely English and French, who came before him.

The liberals had demonstrated, at least to their own satisfaction, the objective harmony of interests among states. Their rational propositions—that war does not pay, that peace is in everyone's real interest—confront the irrational practices of states. The problem is: How can the rational come to prevail over the irrational? But first one must explain why war, the irrational course for all states, characterizes relations among them. Why do governments make war? Because war gives them an excuse for raising taxes, for expanding the bureaucracy, for increasing their control over their citizens. These are the constantly iterated accusations of liberals. The ostensible causes of war are mostly trivial. But the ostensible causes are mere pretexts, ways of committing the nations to the wars their governors want for selfish reasons of their own. [John] Bright, in addressing his constituents at Birmingham in 1858, employed this thesis. It was once England's policy, he told them, "to keep ourselves free from European complications." But with the Glorious Revolution, a revolution that enthroned the great territorial families at the same time that it bridled the king, a new policy was adopted: "We now began to act upon a system of constant entanglement in the affairs of foreign countries." There were wars " 'to maintain the liberties of Europe.' There were wars 'to support the Protestant interest,' and there were many wars to preserve our old friend 'the balance of power.' " Since that time, England had been at war "with, for, and against every considerable nation in Europe." And to what avail? Would anyone, Bright asks, say that Europe is better off today for all this fighting? The implication is clear. The English nation lost by these wars; Europe lost; only the "great territorial families" may have gained.

Though the interest of the people is in peace, their governors make war. This they are able to do partly because people have not clearly perceived their true interests, but more importantly because true interests, where perceived, have not found expression in governmental policy. . . . Democracy is preeminently the peaceful form of the state. Control of policy by the people would mean peace.

The faith in democracies as inherently peaceful has two principal bases. The first was developed by [Immanuel] Kant who, like Congressman Louis L. Ludlow in the 1930s, would have the future foot soldier decide whether or not to commit the country to war. The premise of both Ludlow and Kant is that giving a direct voice to those who suffer most in war would drastically reduce its incidence. The second was developed by Bentham who, like Woodrow Wilson and Lord Cecil, was convinced that world public opinion is the most effective sanction, and in itself perhaps a sufficient sanction, for peace. Thus he proposed a "common court of judicature, for the decision of differences between the several nations, although such a court were not to be armed with any coercive powers." What would give meaning to the court's decisions? Public opinion! The court's proceedings would be open, and the court would be charged with publishing its opinions and circulating them to all states. Refractory states would be put under "the ban of Europe," which would be a sanction sufficient to dissuade a state from ignoring the court's directive. Interest and opinion combine to ensure a policy of peace, for if governors are made responsive to the people's wishes, public opinion can be expected to operate effectively as a sanction.

Faith in public opinion or, more generally, faith in the uniformly peaceful proclivities of democracies has proved utopian. But the utopianism of the liberals was of a fairly complex order. Their proposition is not that at any moment in time war could have been abolished by acts of informed will, but rather that progress has brought the world close to the point where war can be eliminated in the relations of states. History approaches the stage where reason, internationally as well as domestically, can be expected to prevail in human affairs. Utility is the object of state, as of individual, action. For peace, despotism must give way to democracy—so that the utility of the people, and not the utility of minority groups, will be the object sought. . . .

"IT'S A DEAL. YOU SPEAK FOR BATTLESHIPS AND I'LL BACK THE RS-70."

"You see, we had this President who turned everything over to the military...!"

A cartoon of June 8, 1962 during the period of Secretary Robert McNamara's reforms of the defense establishment, depicting a semi-mythical bargain between the navy and the air force to back each other's weapons proposals.   (Copyright © 1965, *The Chicago Sun-Times*; reproduced by courtesy of Wil-Jo Associates, Inc. and Bill Mauldin.)

As the presidential year of 1968 approach there was serious concern among "doves" t the Pentagon might be pressing for a qu "military solution" in Vietnam. (October 1967)   (Los Angeles Times Syndicate)

'. . . AND WE WANT TO THANK YOU, THE TAXPAYER, FOR MAKING THIS ALL POSSIBLE!'

During the Senate debate on the Anti-ballistic missile (ABM) system, opponents often accused the military of wanting armaments simply for the sake of armaments. (October 18, 1969)   (Los Angeles Times Syndicate)

Chapter Fourteen

TRADITIONAL SUSPICIONS: MILITARY

If there be any that delights in war,
King Dionysus, may he never cease
Picking out spearheads from his funny-bones.
If any, seeking to be made a Captain,
Hates to see Peace return, O may he ever
Fare in his battles like Cleonymus.

                        —*Aristophanes*

                           The Peace

75

James Madison
"A DANGEROUS ESTABLISHMENT"

The Federalist, *Number 41 (excerpt).*

James Madison (1751–1836), after participating in the convention that drafted the Constitution (1787), collaborated with Alexander Hamilton and John Jay in writing and publishing those arguments for ratification which have since become known as *The Federalist.* The following passage is from an essay in which Madison discussed the way in which the military would be regulated under the new regime.

. . . the liberties of Rome proved the final victim to her military triumphs; and . . . the liberties of Europe, as far as they ever existed, have, with few exceptions, been the price of her military establishments. A standing force, therefore, is a dangerous, at the same time that it may be a necessary, provision. On the smallest scale it has its inconveniences. On an extensive scale its consequences may be fatal. On any scale it is an object of laudable circumspection and precaution. A wise nation will combine all these considerations; and, whilst it does not rashly preclude itself from any resource which may become essential to its safety, will exert all its prudence in diminishing both the necessity and the danger of resorting to one which may be inauspicious to its liberties.

The clearest marks of this prudence are stamped on the proposed Constitution. The Union itself, which it cements and secures, destroys every pretext for a military establishment which could be dangerous. America united, with a handful of troops, or without a single soldier, exhibits a more forbidding posture to foreign ambition than America disunited, with a hundred thousand veterans ready for combat. It was remarked, on a former occasion, that the want of this pretext had saved the liberties of one nation in Europe. Being rendered by her insular situation and her maritime resources impregnable to the armies of her neighbors, the rulers of Great Britain have never been able, by real or artificial dangers, to cheat the public into an extensive peace establishment. The distance of the United States from the powerful nations of the world gives them the same happy security. A dangerous establishment can never be necessary or plausible, so long as they continue a united people. . . .

76

Alexis de Tocqueville

"DRAWN TO WAR AND REVOLUTION BY THEIR ARMIES"

From Alexis de Tocqueville, Democracy in America, *translated by Henry Reeve (Cambridge, Mass.: Sever and Francis, 1863).*

Alexis de Tocqueville (1805–1859) was a young French nobleman who had served four years as a junior magistrate when he embarked on the tour of the United States which led to the writing of his classic study, *Democracy in America* (4 vols., 1835–1840). His highly perceptive analysis of American society has been an inspiring model for several generations of sociologists. His thoughts on the military profession, some of which are printed here, are as provocative as when they were written.

Among aristocratic nations, especially amongst those in which birth is the only source of rank, the same inequality exists in the army as in the nation. The officer is noble, the soldier is a serf; the one is naturally called upon to command, the other to obey. In aristocratic armies, the private soldier's ambition is therefore circumscribed within very narrow limits. Nor has the ambition of the officer an unlimited range. An aristocratic body not only forms a part of the scale of ranks in the nation, but it contains a scale of ranks within itself: the members of whom it is composed are placed one above another in a particular and unvarying manner. Thus one man is born to the command of a regiment, another to that of a company; when once they have reached the utmost object of their hopes, they stop of their own accord and remain contented with their lot. There is, besides, a strong cause which, in aristocracies, weakens the officer's desire of promotion. Among aristocratic nations, an officer, independently of his rank in the army, also occupies an elevated rank in society; the former is almost always in his eyes only an appendage to the latter. A nobleman who embraces the profession of arms follows it less from motives of ambition than from a sense of the duties imposed on him by his birth. He enters the army in order to find an honorable employment for the idle years of his youth and to be able to bring back to his home and his peers some honorable recollections of military life, but his principal object is not to obtain by that profession either property, distinction, or power, for he possesses these advantages in his own right and enjoys them without leaving his home.

In democratic armies all the soldiers may become officers, which makes the desire of promotion general and immeasurably extends the bounds of military ambition. The officer, on his part, sees nothing which naturally and necessarily stops him at one grade more than at another, and each grade has immense importance in his eyes, because his rank in society almost always depends on his rank in the army. Among democratic nations it often happens that an officer has no property but his pay and no distinction but that of military honors: consequently, as often as his duties change, his fortune changes, and he becomes, as it were, a new man. What was only an appendage to his position in aristocratic armies has thus become the main point, the basis of his whole condition. Under the old French monarchy, officers were always called by their titles of nobility; they are now always called by the title of their military rank. This little change in the forms of language suffices to show that a great revolution has taken place in the constitution of society and in that of the army. In democratic armies the desire of advancement is almost universal—it is ardent, tenacious, perpetual; it is strengthened by all other desires and only extinguished with life itself. But it is easy to see that, of all armies in the world, those in which advancement must be slowest in time of peace are the armies of democratic countries. As the number of commissions is naturally limited while the number of competitors is almost unlimited and as the strict law of equality is over all alike, none can make rapid progress—many can make no progress at all. Thus the desire of advancement is greater, and the opportunities of advancement fewer, there than elsewhere. All the ambitious spirits of a democratic army are consequently ardently desirous of war, because war makes vacancies

and warrants the violation of that law of seniority which is the sole privilege natural to democracy.

We thus arrive at this singular consequence: that, of all armies, those most ardently desirous of war are democratic armies and, of all nations, those most fond of peace are democratic nations. And what makes these facts still more extraordinary is that these contrary effects are produced at the same time by the principle of equality.

All the members of the community, being alike, constantly harbor the wish and discover the possibility of changing their condition and improving their welfare; this makes them fond of peace, which is favorable to industry and allows every man to pursue his own little undertakings to their completion. On the other hand, this same equality makes soldiers dream of fields of battle, by increasing the value of military honors in the eyes of those who follow the profession of arms and by rendering those honors accessible to all. In either case, the inquietude of the heart is the same, the taste for enjoyment as insatiable, the ambition of success as great—the means of gratifying it are alone different.

These opposite tendencies of the nation and the army expose democratic communities to great dangers. When a military spirit forsakes a people, the profession of arms immediately ceases to be held in honor, and military men fall to the lowest rank of the public servants; they are little esteemed and no longer understood. The reverse of what takes place in aristocratic ages then occurs; the men who enter the army are no longer those of the highest, but of the lowest, rank. Military ambition is only indulged in when no other is possible. Hence arises a circle of cause and consequence from which it is difficult to escape—the best part of the nation shuns the military profession because that profession is not honored, and the profession is not honored because the best part of the nation has ceased to follow it. It is then no matter of surprise that democratic armies are often restless, ill-tempered, and dissatisfied with their lot although their physical condition is commonly far better, and their discipline less strict, than in other countries. The soldier feels that he occupies an inferior position, and his wounded pride either stimulates his taste for hostilities which would render his services necessary or gives him a turn for revolutions during which he may hope to win by force of arms the political influence and personal importance now denied him. The composition of democratic armies makes this last-mentioned danger much to be feared. In democratic communities almost every man has some property to preserve, but democratic armies are generally led by men without property, most of whom have little to lose in civil broils. The bulk of the nation is naturally much more afraid of revolutions than in the ages of aristocracy, but the leaders of the army much less so.

Moreover, as among democratic nations (to repeat what I have just remarked) the wealthiest, the best educated, and the most able men seldom adopt the military profession, the army, taken collectively, eventually forms a small nation by itself where the mind is less enlarged, and habits are more rude, than in the nation at large. Now, this small uncivilized nation has arms in its possession and alone knows how to use them, for, indeed, the pacific temper of the community increases the danger to which a democratic people is exposed from the military and turbulent spirit of the army. Nothing is so dangerous as an army amid an unwarlike nation; the excessive love of the whole community for quiet continually puts its constitution at the mercy of the soldiery.

It may therefore be asserted, generally speaking, that, if democratic nations are naturally prone to peace from their interests and their propensities, they are constantly drawn to war and revolutions by their armies. Military revolutions, which are scarcely ever to be apprehended in aristocracies, are always to be dreaded among democratic nations. These perils must be reckoned among the most formidable which beset their future fate, and the attention of statesmen should be sedulously applied to find a remedy for the evil.

77

Oswald Garrison Villard
"PREPAREDNESS IS MILITARISM"

From Oswald Garrison Villard, "Preparedness is Militarism," The Annals of the American Academy, Vol. 66 (July 1916), pp. 217–219.

Oswald Garrison Villard (1872–1949), born in Germany but raised and educated in the United States, was editor and president of the New York *Evening Post* from 1897 to 1918 and editor and owner of the (New York) *Nation* from 1918 to 1932. A crusading reformer and anti-militarist, during 1914–1917 he was one of the leaders in the fight against the "preparedness" movement in this country. His writings include *The German Phoenix* (1933), *Fighting Years: Memoirs of a Liberal Editor* (1939), *Our Military Chaos* (1939), and *Free Trade—Free World* (1947).

. . . we are counselled to take from our possible enemy the very things that have made him efficient and dangerous and become efficient and dangerous ourselves. Not that we shall ever make war—*pace* 1846 and 1898—on anybody; merely that we shall follow in the footsteps of those who believed that the earth is ruled by fear, and that there is no other way to preserve peace than by being so armed that no one shall venture to attack us. And so we have gone about getting a "preparedness" which we are strenuously but falsely pretending will be ours when the legislation now before Congress passes, and so protect us at the close of the war in Europe, and even safeguard us should the present difficulties with Germany result in hostilities. As a matter of fact, the army re-organization proposed will not be consummated for five years, nor the naval program until 1925 or 1927, by which time the present war will be fading into the background like the earth-quakes at St. Pierre and Messina and San Fran-cisco and other great and horrible convulsions of nature, and new world-problems will be upon us.

Now, the real significance of this is that we have all at once, in the midst of a terrifying cataclysm, abjured our faith in many things American. We no longer believe, as for 140 years, in the moral power of an America un-armed and unafraid; we believe suddenly that the influence of the United States is to be measured only by the number of our soldiery and our dreadnoughts—our whole history to the contrary notwithstanding. The ardent ef-forts of both sides in the present European struggle at the outbreak of the war to win for their cause the enormous prestige of the sym-pathy and moral support of the United States —although "unprepared"—we overlook as if it were not the most outstanding fact of the year from August 1, 1914, to August 1, 1915. We are to deprive the world of the one great beacon-light of a nation unarmed and un-afraid, free from the admitted evils of mili-tarism. We are to complete the vicious military circle of the world, so that, if we do not desist, if the oppressed of the nations do not rise in revolt against the whole accursed military sys-tem, the United States will be doing more than any other nation to intensify the race between peoples as to which will be armed most and

at the greatest cost, and it will be one of the most hated and dreaded. As Lord Rosebery has said, nothing since the beginning of the war has been as discouraging, for in Mr. Wil-son's advocacy of our new policy there has not been up to this hour one single phrase to the effect that the United States will be ready and eager to lead the way to disarmament at the close of the war, and our five year naval pro-gram, as its terms signify, is a program for pre-paredness years hence.

Next, the preparedness policy signifies an en-tire change in our attitude towards the military as to whom we inherited from our forefathers suspicion and distrust. A cardinal principle of our polity has always been the subordination of the military to the civil authority as a neces-sary safeguard for the republic, particularly in our national councils, and as to all matters affecting national policy. Today, in our sudden worship of the expert in uniform, we are told that what we need is a national council of defence comprising, as one rear-admiral sug-gests and some of our new-born leagues of safety advise, fifteen military and naval officers with only seven civilians graciously given places at the council board. These men, it appears, sit-ting in secret session and responsible only to themselves, are to formulate the policies of the nation, congressmen to have no other function than to vote the necessary money, ships and men, it not being theirs to reason why. In other words, the council is to be our Great General Staff, and, like its German prototype, it is to make our Congress vote first like the Reichstag and ask questions afterwards—the questions to be answered only if the council deems it wise. Its members are not to be elected, but are to be designated by act of Congress once for all.

Already it is openly stated in the press that the power of the secretary of the navy is to be curtailed by the present Congress, so that he shall not be able to overrule the naval men, thus putting the military directly above the civil. For this purpose the undeserved unpopularity of the present secretary of the navy is being cleverly exploited, while the public is kept in ignorance of the fact that England, the greatest and most efficient naval power on earth, has never, not even in its direst hour, yielded to the navalists, but has kept the control of the fleets in the hands of its civilian Lords of the Admiralty. Simultaneously we hear demands that only our future admirals and generals, and no civilians, shall be permitted to be our secretaries of the navy and of war.

But our sudden worship of the military does not end here. In New York the legislature has just established military drill in all the boys' schools, while all boys between the ages of fifteen and nineteen not at work are to go to camp as soldiers in the summer. There was no public demand for this bill, but the militia wished it, and through it went. Not even in Germany has such a step been advocated, for there, in the home of militarism, gymnastic exercises have been recognized as better preparation for life and military service than military drill. It goes without saying that the smattering of military knowledge the boys will acquire will be of the slightest value, since it is not planned to let them live in trenches, handle bombs, or distribute liquid fire and poisonous gases, and the instruction is bound to be highly superficial. The bill was not debated, and is in its form a model of how not to legislate. It strikes deliberately at one of the most sacred American liberties—the right of freedom of thought, of action, and of conscience—since it excepts not even Quakers, as even England excepts them today. It goes without saying that we of New York owe this favor entirely to the German General Staff. Yet are we told that militarism has and can have no foothold among us! . . .

78

Harold D. Lasswell
"THE GARRISON STATE"

From pp. 455–466 of Harold D. Lasswell, "The Garrison State," in American Journal of Sociology, Vol. 46 *(January 1941), published by the University of Chicago Press. © 1941 by the University of Chicago. All rights reserved.*

Harold D. Lasswell (1902–   ), one of the leading figures of American political science, taught at the University of Chicago from 1922 to 1938, and began his present stay at Yale in 1946. His writings include *The Psychopathology of Politics* (1930), *World Politics and Personal Insecurity* (1935), *Politics: Who Gets What, When, How* (1936), *National Security and Individual Freedom* (1950), and *The Analysis of Political Behavior* (1966). The excerpt which follows, published originally in 1941, is from the second of many articles and essays in which he has dealt with what he sees as the growing danger of militarized government (see the bibliography for references).

. . . The purpose of this article is to consider the possibility that we are moving toward a world of "garrison states"—a world in which the specialists on violence are the most powerful group in society. From this point of view the trend of our time is away from the dominance of the specialist on bargaining, who is the businessman, and toward the supremacy of the soldier. We may distinguish transitional forms, such as the party propaganda state, where the dominant figure is the propagandist, and the party bureaucratic state, in which the organization men of the party make the vital decisions. There are mixed forms in which predominance is shared by the monopolists of party and market power. . . .

To speak of a garrison state is not to predict something wholly new under the sun. Certainly there is nothing novel to the student of political institutions about the idea that specialists on violence may run the state. On the contrary, some of the most influential discussions of political institutions have named the military state as one of the chief forms of organized society. [Auguste] Comte saw history as a succession (and a progression) that moved, as far as it concerned the state, through military, feudal, and industrial phases. [Herbert] Spencer divided all human societies into the military type, based on force, and the industrial type, based on contract and free consent.

What is important for our purposes is to envisage the possible emergence of the military state under present technical conditions. There are no examples of the military state combined with modern technology. During emergencies the great powers have given enormous scope to military authority, but temporary acquisitions of authority lack the elements of comparative permanence and acceptance that complete the garrison state. Military dictators in states marginal to the creative centers of Western civilization are not integrated with modern technology; they merely use some of its specific elements.

The military men who dominate a modern technical society will be very different from the officers of history and tradition. It is probable that the specialists on violence will include in their training a large degree of expertness in many of the skills that we have traditionally accepted as part of modern civilian management.

The distinctive frame of reference in a fighting society is fighting effectiveness. All social change is translated into battle potential. Now there can be no realistic calculation of fighting effectiveness without knowledge of the technical and psychological characteristics of modern productive processes. The function of management in such a society is already known to us; it includes the exercise of skill in supervising technical operations, in administrative organization, in personnel management, in public relations. These skills are needed to translate the complicated operations of modern life into every relevant frame of reference— the frame of fighting effectiveness as well as of pecuniary profit.

This leads to the seeming paradox that, as modern states are militarized, specialists on violence are more preoccupied with the skills and attitudes judged characteristic of nonviolence. We anticipate the merging of skills, starting from the traditional accouterments of the professional soldier, moving toward the manager and promoter of large-scale civilian enterprise.

In the garrison state, at least in its introductory phases, problems of morale are destined to weigh heavily on the mind of management. It is easy to throw sand in the gears of the modern assembly line; hence, there must be a deep and general sense of participation in the total enterprise of the state if collective effort is to be sustained. When we call attention to the importance of the human factor in modern production, we sometimes fail to notice that it springs from the multiplicity of special environments that have been created by modern technology. Thousands of technical operations have sprung into existence where a few hundred were found before. To complicate the material environment in this way is to multiply the focuses of attention of those who live in our society. Diversified focuses of attention breed differences in outlook, preference, and loyalty. The labyrinth of specialized "material" environments generates profound ideological divergencies that cannot be abolished, though they can be mitigated, by the methods now available to leaders in our society. As long as modern technology prevails, society is honeycombed with cells of separate experience, of individuality, of partial freedom. Concerted action under such conditions depends upon skillfully guiding the minds of men; hence the enormous importance of symbolic manipulation in modern society.

The importance of the morale factor is emphasized by the universal fear which it is possible to maintain in large populations through modern instruments of warfare. The growth of aerial warfare in particular has tended to abolish the distinction between civilian and military functions. It is no longer possible to affirm that those who enter the military service take the physical risk while those who remain at home stay safe and contribute to the equipment and the comfort of the courageous heroes at the front. Indeed, in some periods of modern warfare, casualties among civilians may outnumber the casualties of the armed forces. With the socialization of danger as a permanent characteristic of modern violence, the nation becomes one unified technical enterprise. Those who direct the violence operations are compelled to consider the entire gamut of problems that arise in living together under modern conditions.

There will be an energetic struggle to incorporate young and old into the destiny and mission of the state. It is probable that one form of this symbolic adjustment will be the abolition of the "unemployed." This stigmatizing symbol will be obsolete in the garrison state. It insults the dignity of millions, for it implies uselessness. This is so whether the unemployed are given a dole or put on relief projects. Always there is the damaging stigma of superfluity. No doubt the garrison state will be distinguished by the psychological abolition of unemployment—"psychological" because this is chiefly a matter of redefining symbols.

In the garrison state there must be work—and the duty to work—for all. Since all work becomes public work, all who do not accept employment flout military discipline. For those who do not fit within the structure of the state, there is but one alternative—to obey or die.

Compulsion, therefore, is to be expected as a potent instrument for internal control of the garrison state.

The use of coercion can have an important effect upon many more people than it reaches directly; this is the propaganda component of any "propaganda of the deed." The spectacle of compulsory labor gangs in prisons or concentration camps is a negative means of conserving morale—negative since it arouses fear and guilt. Compulsory labor groups are suitable popular scapegoats in a military state. The duty to obey, to serve the state, to work—these are cardinal virtues in the garrison state. Unceasing emphasis upon duty is certain to arouse opposing tendencies within the personality structure of all who live under a garrison regime. Everyone must struggle to hold in check any tendencies, conscious or unconscious, to defy authority, to violate the code of work, to flout the incessant demand for sacrifice in the collective interest. From the earliest years youth will be trained to subdue—to disavow, to struggle against—any specific opposition to the ruling code of collective exactions. . . .

Although the rulers of the garrison state will be free to regularize the rate of production, they will most assuredly prevent full utilization of modern productive capacity for nonmilitary consumption purposes. The elite of the garrison state will have a professional interest in multiplying gadgets specialized to acts of violence. The rulers of the garrison state will depend upon war scares as a means of maintaining popular willingness to forego immediate consumption. War scares that fail to culminate in violence eventually lose their value; this is the point at which ruling classes will feel that bloodletting is needed in order to preserve those virtues of sturdy acquiescence in the regime which they so much admire and from which they so greatly benefit. We may be sure that if ever there is a rise in the production of nonmilitary consumption goods, despite the amount of energy directed toward the production of military equipment, the ruling class will feel itself endangered by the growing "frivolousness" of the community.

We need to consider the degree to which the volume of values produced in a garrison state will be affected by the tendency toward rigidity. Many factors in the garrison state justify the expectation that tendencies toward repetitiousness and ceremonialization will be prominent. To some extent this is a function of bureaucracy and dictatorship. But to some extent it springs also from the preoccupation of the military state with danger. Even where military operations are greatly respected, the fighter must steel himself against deep-lying tendencies to retreat from death and mutilation. One of the most rudimentary and potent means of relieving fear is some repetitive operation—some reiteration of the old and well established. Hence the reliance on drill as a means of disciplining men to endure personal danger without giving in to fear of death. The tendency to repeat, as a means of diminishing timidity, is powerfully reinforced by successful repetition, since the individual is greatly attached to whatever has proved effective in maintaining self-control in previous trials. Even those who deny the fear of death to themselves may reveal the depth of their unconscious fear by their interest in ritual and ceremony. This is one of the subtlest ways by which the individual can keep distracted from the discovery of his own timidity. It does not occur to the ceremonialist that in the spider web of ceremony he has found a moral equivalent of war—an unacknowledged substitute for personal danger.

The tendency to ceremonialize rather than to fight will be particularly prominent among the most influential elements in a garrison state. Those standing at the top of the military pyramid will doubtless occupy high positions in the income pyramid. During times of actual warfare it may be necessary to make concessions in the direction of moderating gross-income differences in the interest of preserving general morale. The prospect of such concessions may be expected to operate as a deterrent factor against war. A countervailing tendency, of course, is the threat to sluggish and well-established members of the upper crust from ambitious members of the lower officers' corps. This threat arises, too, when there are murmurs of disaffection with the established order of things on the part of broader components of the society.

It seems probable that the garrison state of the future will be far less rigid than the military states of antiquity. As long as modern technical society endures, there will be an enormous body of specialists whose focus of attention is entirely given over to the discovery of novel ways of utilizing nature. Above all, these are physical scientists and engineers. They are able to demonstrate by rather impersonal procedures the efficiency of many of their suggestions for the improvement of fighting effectiveness. We therefore anticipate further exploration of the technical potentialities of modern civilization within the general framework of the garrison state.

79

Hanson W. Baldwin
"THE MILITARIZATION OF OUR GOVERNMENT"

From Hanson W. Baldwin, "The Military Move In," Harper's Magazine, *Vol. 195 (December 1947), pp. 481–483. Reprinted by permission of Collins-Knowlton-Wing, Inc. Copyright 1947 by Harper's Magazine, Inc. Reprinted from the December 1947 issue of* Harper's Magazine *by permission of the author.*

Hanson W. Baldwin (1903–   ), a 1924 graduate of Annapolis, served briefly in the Navy and then began a career in journalism with the *New York Times*. In 1942 he became the military editor of the *Times,* and in 1943 he received a Pulitzer Prize for his earlier work as a correspondent. Among his books are *The Price of Power* (1948), *Great Mistakes of the War* (1950), and *The Great Arms Race* (1958). In this article, written as World War II was ending and the Cold War was beginning, one can notice the influence of such apprehensions as those of Harold Lasswell.

Some wise man once wrote that each victorious war costs us a few more of our liberties. Not only does the government, like an octopus, draw to itself during war extensive new powers, many of which are not repealed when peace comes, but the great emotional upsurge of victory inevitably has the double effect of carrying to new positions of authority the military architects of victory, and encouraging in the rest of us dreams of an expanded "manifest destiny" for our country.

Heretofore in our history this trend has rarely been serious, although it can be argued that the damage done to the country by the Grant regime following the Civil War and the brutal reign of the scalawags and carpetbaggers in the conquered South—both of which were in some degree products of the military mind—affected adversely the history of our country and kept us a divided nation for generations. But today the traditional postwar veneration of the military is coupled with the inevitable centralization of economic and political power in the federal government, and with the necessity of preparing the nation for total war and even atomic war. All three of these factors work toward the same end: the militarization of our government and of the American state of mind. . . .

Most of us are pretty familiar with the extent to which the military now sit in positions of American civil authority. The President still has Admiral William D. Leahy as his personal chief of staff—a post of great power and intimate influence. Confidential reports and estimates of the daily situation in the world, which are placed on Mr. Truman's desk each morning, and presumably have their effect on policy, are the product of the Central Intelligence Agency, largely staffed by military men and so far directed (in its brief existence) by two admirals and one general. George C. Marshall, General of the Army, is Secretary of State. The Assistant Secretary of State for Occupied Areas was Major General John H. Hildring and is now Charles E. Saltzman, a former brigadier general. Japan is governed almost unilaterally by General of the Army Douglas MacArthur, who is nominally an Allied commander but in some ways had been a law unto himself. Korea is under a military man. Germany is the domain of Lieutenant General Lucius D. Clay; Austria, of Lieutenant General Geoffrey Keyes. These men ostensibly carry out a policy framed by the civilian State Department, but actually, as administrators of policy in military government, they are also architects of it.

In the foreign service Lieutenant General Walter Bedell Smith is our ambassador to Moscow; Admiral Alan G. Kirk is our ambassador to Belgium; and Lieutenant General Albert C. Wedemeyer has just headed a special mission to China, where our policy has long been influenced by the military. In South Africa and Panama retired generals head the legation and embassy, and throughout South America some thirteen American military missions wield not only military but political power.

Two military men—General of the Army Dwight D. Eisenhower and General of the Army Douglas MacArthur—are potential candidates for the Presidency; and many other less widely known military figures are making themselves politically available for Congressional or other elective positions.

Of course there is nothing insidious in this, *per se*. It is a natural consequence of a victorious war—a public acknowledgment of the debt due these men by a grateful nation, and a tribute to the type of men developed by the armed services and to the orderly administrative qualities of the military mind. Most of the men mentioned are good public servants; many of them are exceptional. Collectively, however, they represent a pattern; they have in common the habit of command and discipline and the mental outlook of years of military training— a tendency to apply in their thinking the yardstick of physical power. It is a pattern to be watched.

Less widely noted, perhaps, has been the extent to which the military influence has already affected our postwar policies. For example, though we frequently stated during the war that we had no territorial or expansionist ambitions, when peace came we virtually annexed the former Japanese-mandated islands. Our proposal to the United Nations was in the form of a "take-it-or-leave-it" notice; we must have a trusteeship validated by the UN or we would "withdraw" our offer—in other words, we would keep the islands anyway. Aside from the fact that it would be difficult to prove the strategic importance to us of *all* the Marshalls, Carolines, and Marianas, since our only potential enemy would seem to be Russia, far to the north, our contention that we must have a most-favored-nation position and be able to prohibit UN inspection visits to the islands certainly weakened our valid opposition to similar Russian privileges in Eastern Europe. We did not even have the grace to link up our policy in the mandates to a Japanese peace treaty. And now the drums are being beaten for Okinawa; we are being asked, with maudlin emotionalism, whether the bodies of our boys who died to take that island are to lie in foreign soil—as if such reasoning would have appealed

to those who died there! These policies in the Pacific—and the MacArthur unilateral policy in Japan—are definitely the product of military influence. A group in the State Department fought, unsuccessfully, the mandated islands policy; others have sought to curb MacArthur, but with singular lack of effect. . . .

So far this trend, as I have indicated, has been noticeable only in a few areas and on a few issues. But unfortunately it coincides with another trend, inevitable in view of the complex economy of our times—the trend toward centralization of power in the federal government.

Let me hasten to disassociate myself from those makers of fairy tales who liken the Roosevelt, or Truman, or any other American administration to that of Hitler or Stalin. We are not that far gone—not by a long shot. Let me add, too, that I do not deny the need for great federal powers in control of interstate commerce, regulation of commercial airlines, the prevention of injurious cartels or monopolies of either capital or labor, and other matters of common consequence. What troubles me is the growing tendency among us citizens to accept without protest extensions of the police power into areas formerly sacrosanct.

When the United States Supreme Court recently virtually abrogated the Fourth Amendment to the Constitution, by endorsing a search by law officers without a search warrant, there was scarcely a rumble in the press. When wiretapping is legalized, as has happened in many states, or when the police adopt the procedure (in the Los Angeles area and elsewhere) of establishing road blocks and searching any and all cars in order to apprehend criminals, we citizens tend to accept these invasions of our liberties as necessary to the public safety. Recently the Presidential Advisory Commission on Universal Military Training, a group of distinguished citizens headed by Dr. Carl T.

Compton, justified such training as a "performance of an obligation which every citizen owes to his country," and added the astonishing observation, "We see no reason why a man should be compensated for undertaking it." In view of the fact that there would be only a slim semantic wall between the forced induction of men into military duties without pay and the forced labor camps of Russia, one might have expected a clamor of public protest at the suggestion. But it seems hardly to have been noticed.

What makes this complacence of ours especially menacing is that it afflicts us at a time when we face the necessity of preparing for total or atomic war.

Here, indeed, the citizens of the United States are confronted with a paradox of frightful mien. Total war means the direction of every phase of the national life to the end of military victory. And preparation for it in time of peace may mean—if the preparations are pushed to full effectiveness—the direction of every phase of national life toward the maintenance of military strength. That might well mean the establishment of a "garrison state" and the destruction of the very qualities and virtues and principles which we originally set about to save.

80

Samuel P. Huntington
LIBERAL ANTI-MILITARISM

Reprinted by permission of the publishers from Samuel P. Huntington, The Soldier and the State, pp. 143– 145, 153–155, Cambridge, Mass. The Belknap Press of Harvard University Press, Copyright 1957, by the President and Fellows of Harvard College.

Samuel P. Huntington (1927–   ) has been an instructor and professor at Harvard University since 1950 except for three years in the early 1960s when he was teaching at Columbia. One of America's leading experts on civil-military relations, Huntington is also interested in defense policy and administration, comparative politics, and political development. His publications include *The Soldier and the State* (1957), *The Common Defense* (1961), and *Political Order in Changing Societies* (1968).

Liberalism has always been the dominant ideology in the United States. The American Constitution, on the other hand, is fundamentally conservative, the product of men who feared concentrated political power and who provided for the widespread dispersion of that power among numerous governmental units. Yet, the outstanding historical fact of American civil-military relations has been the extent to which liberal ideology and conservative Constitution combined to dictate an inverse relation between political power and military professionalism. From the birth of the Republic through the Second World War liberalism and the Constitution were the relatively unchanging environmental constants of American civil-military relations. Together, they delayed the professionalization of officership in America until it had almost been completed in Europe. Together, they made objective civilian control depend upon the virtually total exclusion of the military from political power.

On the first of June 1784 the American Army numbered seven hundred men under the command of Major General Henry Knox. Six months earlier the Revolution had come to an end; Sir Guy Carleton had evacuated New York; Washington had said farewell to his officers at Fraunces' Tavern. The seven hundred men were the only regular military force in the United States, the last remnant of the Continental Army. On June 2, 1784 the Continental Congress, agreeing with Elbridge Gerry that "standing armies in time of peace are inconsistent with the principles of republican Governments, dangerous to the liberties of a free people, and generally converted into destructive engines for establishing despotism," ordered the disbanding of this remnant:

> Resolved, That the commanding officer be and he is hereby directed to discharge the troops now in the service of the United States, except twenty-five privates, to guard the stores at Fort Pitt, and fifty-five to guard the stores at West Point and other magazines, with a proportionate number of officers; no officer to remain in service above the rank of captain . . .

Having thus reduced the regular army to eighty caretakers, the Congress then requested the states to furnish it with seven hundred militia to garrison the western frontier.

A little over 131 years later, in the autumn of 1915, the Acting Secretary of War, Henry Breckinridge, was summoned to the presence of Woodrow Wilson. He found the President "trembling and white with passion," holding in his hands a copy of the *Baltimore Sun.* The President pointed to a story in the paper reporting that the General Staff was preparing plans for the eventuality of war with Germany. When the President asked him if this were true, Breckinridge replied that he did not know. The President then directed him to investigate, and, if he found that it was true, to relieve every officer on the General Staff and order him out of Washington.

These incidents together illustrate two basic points concerning the American political mind. First, liberalism dominated American thinking from the Revolution through the first half of the twentieth century. Second, liberalism does not understand and is hostile to military institutions and the military function.

The universality of liberalism in the United States and its essentially static quality contrast with the variety and dynamism of ideologies in Europe. The Frenchman has had firsthand experience with aristocratic conservatism, revolutionary democracy, Bonapartism, clericalism, monarchism, liberalism, socialism, communism. The American knows only liberalism. The political outlook of the Englishman today, be he socialist or Tory, is fundamentally different from that of the average Englishman at the end of the eighteenth century. The political ideology of Woodrow Wilson was essentially the same as that of Elbridge Gerry. Liberalism in the United States has been unchanging, monotonous, and all-embracing.

The American colonists inherited their liberal ideas from the English tradition of [John] Locke. The dominance of liberalism in America, however, was the product not of inheritance but of economic expansion and international isolation. Steady economic growth diluted class conflict. There were few struggles over the distribution of the pie because the pie was always growing larger. No nascent group ever developed a radical ideology challenging the established order: it was always too quickly assimilated into that order. Nor did any established group (with two exceptions) ever develop a conservative ideology defending its interests against radical onslaught. The oncoming wave always evaporated short of the gates of the castle. Radicalism and conservatism were equally superfluous. Incipient and established groups both adhered to liberalism. In the absence of European feudalism, European classes, and a European proletariat, political struggle in America was restricted to squabbles for limited objectives among interest groups all of whom shared the same basic values. The great political controversies of American history with a few exceptions have been between two or more varieties of liberalism. The isolation of the United States from world politics in the nineteenth century reinforced the dominance of liberalism. National security was a simple given fact—the starting point of political analysis—not the end result of conscious policy. What need was there for a philosophy to explain America's relation with the rest of the world and to suggest the proper course of conduct in international affairs? Not only did every group in American society normally feel economically secure but also American society as a whole normally felt politically secure. American awareness of the role of power in domestic politics was dulled by the absence of class conflict. American awareness of the role of power in foreign politics was dulled by the absence of external threats.

. . . Liberalism is divided in its views on war but it is united in its hostility to the military profession. The function of this profession is the military security of the state, and the legitimacy of this concern is recognized by neither crusader nor pacifist. Both see the military profession as an obstacle to the achievement of their own aims. The pacifist views the professional military man as a warmonger, plotting to bring about conflicts so as to enhance his own rank and power. The crusader views the professional soldier as a sinister drag upon the conduct of war, uninterested and unaroused by the ideals for which the war is fought. The pacifist sees the military man contaminating his peace; the crusader sees him contaminating his crusade.

The pacifist view that the professional military man desires war is a widespread one in western society. More peculiarly American is the opposition to the professional military man in war. In Great Britain, for instance, the military have traditionally suffered in peace but have been relied upon in war: the shifts of British attitude are well reflected in [Rudyard] Kipling's "Tommy Atkins." In America, however, the regular has been rejected in both peace and war. Crusades must be fought by peoples

not by professionals. Those most interested in the ideological objectives of the war have been most vehement in denouncing the conservative, limited policies of the professional military officers. This attitude was well expressed with reference to the Mexican War by Nathaniel Hawthorne in a campaign biography of Franklin Pierce:

> The valor that wins our battles is not the trained hardihood of veterans, but a native and spontaneous fire; and there is surely a chivalrous beauty in the devotion of the citizen soldier to his country's cause, which the man who makes arms his profession and is but doing his duty cannot pretend to rival.

In the Civil War the Radical Republicans, anxious to pursue a vigorous and aggressive policy toward the South, were bitter in their attacks on the cautious behavior of McClellan and other generals. In a similar vein Woodrow Wilson, during World War I, minimized the role of the professional on the grounds that:

> This is an unprecedented war and, therefore, it is a war in one sense for amateurs . . . The experienced soldier,—experienced in previous wars,—is a back number so far as his experience is concerned . . .
> America has always boasted that she could find men to do anything. She is the prize amateur nation of the world. Germany is the prize professional nation of the world. Now, when it comes to doing new things and doing them well, I will back the amateur against the professional every time.

The essential conservatism of the military outlook has caused American liberalism to identify its external and domestic enemies with military professionalism. The Revolutionary War was described as a war of citizen-soldiers against the standing armies and mercenaries of George III. The Civil War was against the West Point directed armies of the South.

President Wilson's words quoted above reflect the American view that German militarism was the principal enemy in World War I. In World War II the American identification of the German Army with the Nazi regime frustrated the possibilities of capitalizing on the opposition of the former to the latter. The professionals, in other words, are always on the other side.

In domestic politics each liberal group tends to identify the military with its own particular enemies. Without any recognized function in a liberal society and standing outside the American ideological consensus, the military have been a universal target group. The identification of the military with the political enemy was initially valid because eighteenth-century military institutions were fundamentally aristocratic and opposed to liberalism. This pattern of thinking persisted, however, after the military had become divorced from the aristocracy and had begun to be professionalized. Each successive emergent liberal group identified the military with the vested interests of the old order. The Jeffersonian Democrats saw the military as the ally of monarchy and a threat to liberty. The Jacksonians saw them as the foundation of aristocracy and a threat to democracy. Business saw the military as the obsolete remnants of a past agrarian age, the refuge of parasites from the competitive ardors of civilian life, and [a] threat to productivity. Labor and reform groups, on the other hand, have pictured a sinister alliance of business and the military. Obviously, all these theories could not be true, and in actual fact, with the exception of their affiliations with the South, the military have had no significant ties with any group in American society. Yet it is precisely this isolation which makes them eligible to be everybody's enemy. The identification of the military with the domestic enemy has a double effect. It enables each liberal group to exaggerate the gap between it and its political opponent by identifying itself with civilian control and its opponent, who was normally within the liberal consensus, with the military profession, which was outside that consensus. This use of the military is thus one manifestation of the tendency of all groups in American society to magnify their political differences by linking their opponents with foreign or "un-American" groups. At the same time, however, this practice also serves to reinforce the anti-military attitudes already present in the American mind.

There could be little doubt who was assigned the ultimate responsibility for war in this cartoon from the Industrial Pioneer, a publication of the Industrial Workers of the World (IWW). (June 1925) (New York Public Library)

BIG BUSINESS (to Labor, generously): "My good fellow, you'll be well paid for your patriotic action in 'tending this glorious plant; you shall have all the fruit above the ground—I'll take ONLY the roots!"

"Uncouth Little Beggars!"

With the defense industries' arrangements for cost-overruns and their requests for guaranteed loans, it is not surprising that they were often thought to be among the most insatiable of those demanding special favors from the government. (June 25, 1970) (© 1970 by Herblock in The Washington Post)

Copyright, 1929, by the New York Tribune, Inc. Courtesy of the N. Y. Herald Tribune

Darling in the New York Herald Tribune

MAYBE THEY DIDN'T DIE SUCH A NATURAL DEATH

The frustrations and suspicions of the Peace Movement of the 1920s were captured well in this cartoon of 1929. (New York Herald Tribune, Inc.)

Chapter Fifteen

TRADITIONAL SUSPICIONS: ECONOMIC

As to weapons of war *and military equipment of all kinds; if military purposes require the importation of any industry, vegetable, mineral substance, material for rope-making, or animal, the cavalry commanders and generals shall have the control of such importation and exportation, the State being both seller and buyer, and the proper and sufficient regulations for the proceeding being imposed by the Curators of Law: there shall be no retailing of these or any other materials for profit anywhere within our territory or among our citizens.*

—Plato
The Laws

81

Karl Liebknecht
"ACTS OF THE RULING CLASS"

From *Karl Liebknecht,* Militarism and Anti-Militarism *(Glasgow: Socialist Labour Press, 1917), pp. 89–93.*

Karl Liebknecht (1871–1919), son of Karl Marx's friend Wilhelm Liebknecht and himself a leading German socialist, played a crucial role before 1914 in awakening wide sectors of opinion to the dangers of the European arms race. It was his pamphlet on *Militarism and Anti-Militarism* (part of which is published here) which in 1907 compelled the Socialists themselves to confront the problem, and six years later he put the entire world on notice when, as a member of the Reichstag, he accused the Krupp munitions firm of promoting Franco-German hostility for the sake of profits. Sentenced in 1916 to forty-nine months' hard labor for demonstrating against the war, he was released from detention in November 1918, only to be arrested and murdered by government troops after the Spartacist uprising of the following January.

"The Communist Manifesto," the most prophetic work in the literature of the world, does not deal specifically with militarism or adequately with its accessory significance. To be sure, it speaks of the revolts "caused in some places by the proletarian struggle," and thus indicates in substance the *role* played by capitalist militarism in the proletariat's struggle for liberation. It discusses in more detail the question of international armed conflicts, or rather conflicts between states, and the capitalist policy of expansion (inclusive of colonial policy). The latter is regarded as a necessary consequence of capitalist development; it is predicted that the isolated condition of nations and nationalist contrasts would tend to disappear more and more *even under the domination of the bourgeoisie*, and that the domination of the proletariat would reduce them still more. One could almost say that the programme of the first measures to be taken under the dictatorship of the proletariat contains nothing laid down with special reference to militarism: the conquest of political power which here is supposed to have already been brought about embraces the "conquest," that is to say, the overthrow of militarism.

Special utterances about militarism begin to be made at the congresses of the [First] International. These utterances, however, refer exclusively to "militarism against the enemy abroad," to the attitude taken up towards war. On the agenda of the Lausanne Congress in 1867 there was the following item: "The Peace Congress in Geneva in 1868." It was decided to work together with the Peace Congress on the supposition which was either naive or ironical, that this Congress would adopt the programme of the International. War was designated as a consequence of the class struggle.

At the third Congress of the International which was held at Brussels in 1868 a resolution, moved by [Jean] Longuet in the name of a commission, was adopted unanimously. In this resolution the lack of economic balance is indicated as the chief and lasting cause of war, and it is emphasized that a change can be wrought only by reforming society. The power to lessen the number of wars by means of agitating and by enlightening the nations is ascribed to the labour organizations, and it is laid down as a duty to work indefatigably with this end in view. In case of war a general strike is advised and the Congress expresses its conviction that the international solidarity of the workers of all countries is strong enough to guarantee their help against war in this war of nations.

Now we come to the "new [Second] International."

The resolution of the Paris Congress in 1889, which deals with the matter, is of the greatest interest. It deals with the standing armies which it stamps as a "negation of democratic and republican *regime*," as the "military expression of the monarchic or oligarchic-capitalist *regime*," as a "tool for reactionary *coups d'état* and social oppression." The resolution characterizes the offensive policy of the armed nations as the cause and consequence of the system of offensive wars, and of the ever present menace of international conflicts. The resolution repudiates both the offensive policy and the armies, from the military-technical point of view, because of their immediate disorganizing and demoralizing properties inimical to all progress of culture, and, finally, because of the unbearable material burdens which the armies impose on the nations. The resolution demands the abolition of the standing armies and the introduction of a universal citizen army, while it looks upon war itself as an inevitable consequence of capitalism.

This resolution as regards characterizing militarism exhausts the subject more than any other drafted before that date.

The proceedings at the Brussels Congress in

1891 were significant. Here the question of war, of international militarism, was exclusively debated. The [Domela] Nieuwenhuis resolution which designated war as a result of the international will of capitalism and as a means of breaking the back of the revolutionary movement, and which enjoined the Socialists of all countries to reply to every war with a general strike, was voted down. The [Edouard] Vaillant-[Wilhelm] Liebknecht resolution which regards militarism as a necessary consequence of capitalism and the peace of nations as an aim to be attained exclusively through the establishment of an international Socialist system of society was adopted. The resolution calls upon the workers to protest, by tireless agitation against the barbarity of war and against alliances which promote it, and to accelerate the triumph of Socialism by perfecting the international organizations of the proletariat: this method of fighting was proclaimed to be the only one to ward off the catastrophe of a world-war.

The Zurich Congress in 1893 confirmed the Brussels resolution and named the following ways of fighting militarism: refusal to vote military credits, incessant protests against standing armies, tireless agitation in favour of disarmament, support given to all associations which strive after a world peace.

The London Congress in 1896 again discussed both sides of militarism. It indicated as the chief causes of war the economic contradictions into which the ruling classes of various countries have been forced by the capitalist mode of production. It regarded wars as acts of the ruling classes in their own interest at the expense of Labour; the struggle against military oppression was looked upon as a duty of the working class and as forming part of the struggle against exploitation; the conquest of political power, in order to abolish the capitalist mode of production and in order to wrench from the hands of the governments the means of power of the capitalist class, the instruments for upholding the existing order, was fixed as the objective. According to the Congress, standing armies increased the danger of war and assisted the brutal oppression of Labour. The immediate demands again were: abolition of the standing armies and the introduction of a citizen army along with international courts of arbitration and the people deciding on war and peace. The resolution concluded that Labour could, however, attain its aim also in this respect only after it had secured a *decisive influence on legislation* and had joined hands internationally to establish Socialism.

The Paris Congress of 1900 passed a comprehensive resolution about the capitalist colonial policy of expansion and the international possibilities of conflict which capitalism bears in its womb; it also condemned the policy of national oppression, quoting a few especially barbarous examples, and devoted especial attention to the struggle against militarism. The resolution referred to the decisions of 1889, 1891, 1896, pointed out the international and national dangers of the imperialistic world policy, called upon the proletariat to take up an international struggle with redoubled energy against militarism and the world policy, and proposed the following practical means: international protest movements, refusal of all military, naval and colonial expenditure, and *"the education and organization of the young people with the object of fighting militarism."*

A survey of these decisions shows a steady growth of practical political insight with regard to militarism against the enemy abroad, and an ever deeper and more specialized recognition of the causes and dangers of war as well as of the significance of "militarism against the enemy at home." . . .

82

*Robert LaFollette, William Kenyon, and
Charles Thomas*
"THE ORGANIZED POWER OF
PRIVATE INTEREST"

From the Congressional Record: Senate, *February 12,
1915, 63rd Congress, 3rd Session (Washington, D.C.:
1915), p. 3633.*

Senators Robert LaFollette (R-Wisc.), William
Kenyon (R-Ia.), and Charles Thomas (D-Colo.)
were among the better known spokesmen for that
intensely provincial, small business-oriented brand
of western radicalism which played so important
a role in the Progressive movement before the
First World War. LaFollette (1855–1925) had
served his state as congressman and governor before beginning nineteen years in the Senate in
1906. Kenyon (1869–1933) had held a brief appointment as district judge and would later become justice of the United States Circuit Court
of Appeals, after his terms of service in the Congress (1911–1922). Thomas (1849–1934) had
been a member of the Democratic National Committee as well as governor of Colorado before his
election to the Senate, where he remained from
1913 to 1921. The following discussion among
them took place in February 1915, on the occasion
of LaFollette's having introduced a resolution
requesting the President to convene a conference
of neutrals for the purpose of promoting an "early
cessation of hostilities."

Mr. LaFollette. . . . It is revolting that we
should encourage or permit traffic in arms and
ammunition by private capital for profit with
organized Governments, thus prompting selfish
interest to influence legislation increasing appropriations in preparation for war and furnishing incentive to intrigue in domestic and foreign
affairs to make a war market for private advantage.

It is repugnant to every moral sense that

Governments should even indirectly be drawn
into making and prosecuting a war through
the machinations of those who make money
by it. Yet the vast capital privately invested in
plants for naval construction and the manufacture of munitions of war necessary for the
equipment of armies has the strongest possible
inducement to employ every means to shape
conditions and influence policies which lead on
to armed conflict. It means business. It means
dividends. It means great accumulations of
wealth in private hands to be again turned,
through organization, into the building of more
plants, more battleships, the manufacture of
more powder, more shot and shell. In the end
it has but one purpose, and that is to sacrifice
human life for private gain.

Back of every big Army and Navy appropriation bill is the organized power of private interest, pressing for larger appropriations, for more
battleships, more armor plate, more powder,
more rifles, more machine guns, a larger standing Army, a bigger Navy; because there follows
in the wake of such legislation fat Army contracts, with attendant opportunity for graft and
easy money.

Mr. Kenyon. Mr. President—

The Presiding Officer. Does the Senator from
Wisconsin yield to the Senator from Iowa?

Mr. LaFollette. With pleasure.

Mr. Kenyon. I do not want to disturb the
Senator, because I am in thorough sympathy
with everything he has said.

Mr. LaFollette. It will not disturb me at all.

Mr. Kenyon. He will remember, too, in this
report from the Secretary of Commerce as to
munitions of war shipped abroad during the
month of November, that it embraced, as I
figure it out, in addition to the cartridges the
Senator has spoken of, about 40,000 rifles,
which have been used in some way to keep
this war going on. Does not the Senator think
we had better stop praying for peace in this

country as long as we are shipping out these munitions of war for profit?

Mr. LaFollette. Yes, Mr. President; I will say to the Senator I think it hardly consistent that we should pray for peace and at the same time supply the ammunition to continue the war. Let me say further that I am indebted to the Senator from Iowa, who has just asked the question, for calling my attention to the report. . . .

Mr. Thomas. Mr. President—

Mr. LaFollette. I yield to the Senator from Colorado.

Mr. Thomas. If it will not disturb the Senator, the remark of the Senator from Iowa reminds me that the recent disclosures of Dr. [Karl] Liebknecht of the extent to which this world-wide aggregation of capital behind the manufacture and sale of war equipment had gone, and which led to a most revolting scandal in German military and naval circles, also disclosed the amazing fact that many of those who are now praying for peace were and doubtless still are interested in furnishing this equipment, and enjoy the dividends that are earned by the blood and tears of humanity.

Mr. LaFollette. I quite agree, of course, with the observation of the Senator from Colorado. We have not escaped the taint which seems to creep into these Army and Navy contracts everywhere. We have had our own armor-plate scandals. Mr. President, over and over again we have heard the same arguments from the same organs of the great special interests, making their hypocritical appeals on the grounds of patriotism; urging that thorough preparation for war is always a sure guaranty of peace.

What State, what city, finds security for peace and good order in allowing every man to "pack a gun"? Why have civilized communities enacted laws and ordinances prohibiting inhabitants from going about armed? States are but aggregations of individuals. Nations are but great groups of human beings. The deadly weapon within easy reach of the hand breeds a murderer. And nations armed to the teeth quickly resort to killing as a means of settling their differences.

83

League of Nations
"OPEN TO GRAVE OBJECTIONS"

From Covenant of the League of Nations, *Article VIII, and* Report of the Temporary Mixed Commission on Armaments, *League of Nations Document No. A. 81, 1921.*

The founders of the League of Nations were very much concerned about the possibility that the activities of arms manufacturers might carry governments into war. Indeed, General Jan Smuts of South Africa urged in 1919 that "all factories for the manufacture of direct weapons of war shall be nationalized and their production shall be subject to the inspection of the officers of the Council," and President Woodrow Wilson included a provision in the first draft of the League Covenant which wholly prohibited the manufacture of munitions and implements of war "by private enterprise or for private profit." Though the Paris Peace Conference ultimately rejected such suggestions, it did stipulate in Article VIII of the Covenant that the arms industry was generally in need of regulation. Moreover, in 1921 a subcommittee of the League's Temporary Mixed Commission on Arms spelled out the particular aspects of the existing situation which were considered most objectionable.

ARTICLE VIII OF THE COVENANT OF THE LEAGUE OF NATIONS (1919)
1. The Members of the League recognise that the maintenance of peace requires the reduction of national armaments to the lowest point consistent with national safety and the enforce-

ment by common action of international obligations.

2. The Council, taking account of the geographical situation and circumstances of each State, shall formulate plans for such reduction for the consideration and action of the several Governments.

3. Such plans shall be subject to reconsideration and revision at least every ten years.

4. After these plans shall have been adopted by the several Governments, the limits of armaments therein fixed shall not be exceeded without the concurrence of the Council.

5. The Members of the League agree that the manufacture by private enterprise of munitions and implements of war is open to grave objections. The Council shall advise how the evil effects attendant upon such manufacture can be prevented, due regard being had to the necessities of those Members of the League which are not able to manufacture the munitions and implements of war necessary for their safety.

6. The Members of the League undertake to interchange full and frank information as to the scale of their armaments, their military, naval and air programmes, and the condition of such of their industries as are adaptable to warlike purposes.

EXCERPT FROM A REPORT OF THE TEMPORARY MIXED COMMISSION ON ARMS (1921)

The Covenant recognizes that the manufacture by private enterprise of munitions and implements of war is open to grave objections. What are these objections? They are not defined by the Covenant; they cannot be extracted from the deliberations of the Committee which drafted the Covenant. It is, however, common knowledge that the public mind is strongly prejudiced against the uncontrolled private manufacture of munitions and implements of

war, and that it is a common belief that wars are promoted by the competitive zeal of private armaments firms, and would be rendered less frequent were the profit-making impulse brought under control or eliminated altogether. In general, the objections that are raised to untrammelled private manufacture may be grouped under the following headings:

1. That armament firms have been active in fomenting war-scares and in persuading their own countries to adopt warlike policies and to increase their armaments.

2. That armament firms have attempted to bribe government officials, both at home and abroad.

3. That armament firms have disseminated false reports concerning the military and naval programmes of various countries, in order to stimulate armament expenditure.

4. That armament firms have sought to influence public opinion through the control of newspapers in their own and foreign countries.

5. That armament firms have organized international armament rings through which the armament race has been accentuated by playing off one country against another.

6. That armament firms have organized international armament trusts which have increased the price of armaments sold to governments.

84

Special Committee of the Senate on Investigation of the Munitions Industry
"DEPENDENT ON THE CONTINUATION OF THE WAR BUSINESS"

From Supplemental Report on the Adequacy of Existing Legislation of the Special Committee on Investigation of the Munitions Industry, 74th Congress, 2nd Session, Senate Report No. 944, Part 6 (Washington, 1936), pp. 2–3.

The Senate Committee Investigating the Munitions Industry, organized in April 1934 in response to increasing fear of war and clamor regarding the "merchants of death," was entrusted by a Democratic Congress to the chairmanship of a western "progressive," Senator Gerald P. Nye (R-N.D.). In the space of less than two years, the "Nye Committee" compiled almost 14,000 pages of exhibits and testimony regarding the activities of the armaments industry at home and overseas during the previous several decades. The following excerpt from one of its reports (which were published in seven volumes, 1935–1936) presents some of its findings concerning changes in American neutrality policy during 1914–1917.

The Committee finds . . . that in August 1914 the Department of State declared that loans by American banks to belligerent governments would be considered unneutral in spirit. This declaration had no legally binding power but the testimony indicates that if it had not been modified such loans would never have been made. The Committee is interested to observe that this ruling was made at a time when the American banks were reluctant to extend such loans. In October 1914 the Department, in a secret ruling officially revealed only to J. P. Morgan & Co. and the National City Bank of New York, made an artificial distinction between loans and credits, permitting the extension of the latter to belligerents. Although rumors of this change were published in the press at the time, no official statement was made until March 31, 1915. Meanwhile in an official letter of January 20, 1915, to the Chairman of the Senate Foreign Relations Committee, the Department failed to mention this distinction, thereby officially misinforming the Senate. The Committee is further of the opinion that this secret and artificial distinction permitted the beginning of the war trade and boom which later in 1915 produced a serious disbalance of American exports.

Loans to belligerents militate against neutrality, for when only one group of belligerents can purchase and transport commodities the loans act in favor of that belligerent. They are especially unneutral when used to convert this country into an auxiliary arsenal for that belligerent who happens to control the seas, for that arsenal then becomes the subject of the military strategy of the other belligerent.

Such loans cannot but profoundly affect the neutrality of mind and spirit of those holding them. When the responsibility for the sale of such loans is placed by foreign belligerents in the hands of any one large banking group, as was done in the case of J. P. Morgan & Co. during the World War where out of some $2,500,000,000 allied indebtedness, J. P. Morgan & Co. arranged for or managed some $1,900,000,000, the concentrated power and influence of such loans on the neutrality of public opinion can be greatly accentuated. When the banking houses floating these loans are also financially interested in munitions companies depending for continued profits on foreign orders, the foreign belligerents have the power of securing the support of these banking houses for loans through favors to the munitions companies.

The Committee finds . . . that the situation in regard to the rifle industry was symptomatic of what was potentially the case in regard to many other industries. It appears, further, that expansion of the rifle factories to fill Great Britain's war orders had produced a situation where not only manufacturers themselves but their bankers were dependent on the continuance of the war business. It appears further in this instance that the relation between finance and industry, war orders and British credit, had become so intimate that it was necessary for the British Government to buy rifles which it did not need in order that the American industrial and financial community should not be angered and refuse to cooperate in British financing in the United States. This refusal would certainly have damaged the British ability to prosecute the war. The Committee is of the opinion that the need of the rifle manufacturers and their bankers for orders from the British Government determined their activity in floating the proposed loans. The Committee is also of the opinion that the de facto ownership of munitions plants by the British Government constituted a violation of American neutrality that should not have been countenanced by the United States Government.

Loans extended to the Allies in 1915 and 1916 led to a very considerable war boom and inflation. This boom extended beyond munitions to auxiliary supplies and equipment as well as to agricultural products. Such loans may be expected to produce a similar situation again. Practically all these loans were partly maintained in price by the expenditure of amounts equal to about one-eighth of their par through the sale of collateral to support them on the market.

The nature of such a war-boom inflation is that, like all inflations, an administration is almost powerless to check it, once the movement is well started. Our foreign policy then is seriously affected by it, even to the extent of making impossible the alteration of our foreign policy in such a way as to protect our neutral rights.

The foreign policy of the United States from 1914 to 1917 was, in fact, affected by our growing trade with the Allies as well as by natural sympathies. The neutral rights we claimed were simply not enforced against our largest customers.

The Committee finds . . . that the development of the export of war commodities to the Allies resulted in a widespread expansion of almost all the lines of American business, an expansion which J. P. Morgan & Co., in their commercial agency contract, specifically undertook to stimulate. As a result by 1916 there was created a tremendous industrial machine, heavily capitalized, paying high wages, and dependent upon the purchasing power of the Allies. The Committee is of the opinion that this situation, with its risk of business depression and panic in event of damage to the belligerents' ability to purchase, involved the administration so inextricably it prevented the maintenance of a truly neutral course between the Allies and the Central Powers. Such a neutral course threatened to injure this export trade.

85

Gabriel Kolko
"THE INEVITABLE COST OF IMPERIAL POWER"

From Gabriel Kolko, The Roots of American Foreign Policy: An Analysis of Power and Purpose *(Boston: Beacon, 1969), pp. 83–87. Copyright © 1969 by Gabriel Kolko. Reprinted by permission of Beacon Press.*

Gabriel Kolko (1932–   ), who specializes in recent American political, economic, and diplomatic history, was appointed professor at York University, Ontario, Canada, in 1970, after having taught briefly at the State University of New York, Buffalo, and at the University of Pennsylvania. One of the most articulate representatives of the new radicalism in historical scholarship, he is the author of *Wealth and Power in America* (1962), *The Triumph of Conservatism, 1900–1916* (1963), *Railroads and Regulation, 1877–1916* (1965), and *The Politics of War, 1943–1945* (1968). Here he presents what he calls "a theory of the United States global role."

In their brilliant essay on the political economy of nineteenth century British imperialism ["The Imperialism of Free Trade," *Economic History Review*, Second Series, VI (August 1953), pp. 5–6], John Gallagher and Ronald Robinson have described a process that parallels the nature of United States expansion after 1945:

Imperialism, perhaps, may be defined as a sufficient political function of this process of integrating new regions into the expanding economy; its character is largely decided by the various and changing relationships between the political and economic elements of expansion in any particular region and time. Two qualifications must be made. First, imperialism may be only indirectly connected with economic integration in that it sometimes extends beyond areas of economic development, but acts for their strategic protection. Secondly, although imperialism is a function of economic expansion, it is not a necessary function. Whether imperialist phenomena show themselves or not, is determined not only by the factors of economic expansion, but equally by the political and social organization of the regions brought into the orbit of the expansive society, and also by the world situation in general.

It is only when the politics of these new regions fail to provide satisfactory conditions for commercial or strategic integration and when their relative weakness allows, that power is used imperialistically to adjust those conditions. Economic expansion, it is true, will tend to flow into the regions of maximum opportunity, but maximum opportunity depends as much upon political considerations of security as upon questions of profit. Consequently, in any particular region, if economic opportunity seems large but political security small, then full absorption into the extending economy tends to be frustrated until power is exerted upon the state in question. Conversely, in proportion as satisfactory political frameworks are brought into being in this way, the frequency of imperialist intervention lessens and imperialist control is correspondingly relaxed. It may be suggested that this willingness to limit the use of paramount power to establishing security for trade is the distinctive feature of the British imperialism of free trade in the nineteenth century, in contrast to the mercantilist use of power to obtain commercial supremacy and monopoly through political possession.

In today's context, we should regard United States political and strategic intervention as a rational overhead charge for its present and future freedom to act and expand. One must also point out that however high that cost may appear today, in the history of United States diplomacy specific American economic interests in a country or region have often defined the national interest on the assumption that the nation can identify its welfare with the profits of some of its citizens—whether in oil, cotton, or bananas. The costs to the state as a whole are less consequential than the desires and profits of specific class strata and their need to operate everywhere in a manner that, collectively, brings vast prosperity to the United States and its rulers.

Today it is a fact that capitalism in one country is a long-term physical and economic impossibility without a drastic shift in the distribution of the world's income. Isolated, the United States would face those domestic backlogged economic and social problems and weaknesses it has deferred confronting for over two decades, and its disappearing strength in a global context would soon open the door to the internal dynamics which might jeopardize the very existence of liberal corporate capitalism at home. It is logical to regard Vietnam, therefore, as the inevitable cost of maintaining United States imperial power, a step toward saving the future in something akin to its present form by revealing to others in the Third World what they too may encounter should they also seek to control their own development. That Vietnam itself has relatively little of value to the United States is all the more significant as an example of America's determination to hold the line as a matter of principle against revolutionary movements. What is at stake, according to the "domino" theory with which Washington accurately perceives the world, is the control of Vietnam's neighbors, Southeast Asia and, ultimately, Latin America.

The contemporary world crisis, in brief, is a by-product of United States response to Third World change and its own definitions of what it must do to preserve and expand its vital national interests. At the present moment, the larger relationships in the Third World economy benefit the United States, and it is this type of structure America is struggling to preserve. Moreover, the United States requires the option to expand to regions it has not yet penetrated, a fact which not only brings it into conflict with Third World revolutions but also with an increasingly powerful European capitalism. Where neocolonial economic penetration via loans, aid, or attacks on balanced economic development or diversification in the Third World are not sufficient to maintain stability, direct interventions to save local *compradors* and oligarchies often follow. Frequently such encroachments succeed, as in Greece and the Dominican Republic, but at times, such as Vietnam, it is the very process of intervention itself that creates its own defeat by deranging an already moribund society, polarizing options, and compelling men to choose—and to resist. Even the returns to the United States on partial successes have warranted the entire undertaking in the form not just of high profit ratios and exports, but in the existence of a vast world economic sector which supplies the disproportionately important materials without which American prosperity within its present social framework would eventually dry up.

The existing global political and economic structure, with all its stagnation and misery, has not only brought the United States billions but has made possible, above all, a vast power that requires total world economic integration not on the basis of equality but of domination. And to preserve this form of world is vital to the men who run the American economy and politics at the highest levels. If some of them now reluctantly believe that Vietnam was not

the place to make the final defense against tides of unpredictable revolutionary change, they all concede that they must do it somewhere, and the logic of their larger view makes their shift on Vietnam a matter of expediency or tactics rather than of principle. All the various American leaders believe in global stability which they are committed to defend against revolution that may threaten the existing distribution of economic power in the world.

When the day arrives that the United States cannot create or threaten further Vietnams, the issue at stake will be no less than the power of the United States in the world. At that point, both the United States and the rest of the world will undergo a period of profound crises and trauma, at home as well as abroad, as the allocation of the earth's economic power is increasingly removed from American control. *If*, in the process of defending their prerogatives, the leaders of the United States during those trying years do not destroy the globe, piecemeal as in Vietnam or in a war with China or Russia, we shall be on the verge of a fundamentally new era for the United States and mankind. The elimination of that American hegemony is the essential precondition for the emergence of a nation and a world in which mass hunger, suppression, and war are no longer the inevitable and continuous characteristics of modern civilization.

86

Quincy Wright
THEORIES ABOUT CAPITALISM AND WAR

From Quincy Wright, A Study of War *(Chicago: The University of Chicago Press, 1942; abridged 1964), pp. 310–316.*

Quincy Wright (1890–1970), America's foremost student of the phenomenon of war, pursued his subject matter in both scholarship and public service. For many years a professor of political science at the University of Chicago, in the last decade of his life he was a professor of international law at the University of Virginia. He also served on several occasions as a consultant for the government: for example, as technical adviser to the International Military Tribunal, Nuremburg (1945) and as assistant to the United States High Commissioner in Germany (1949–1950). Among his writings are *Mandates under the League of Nations* (1930), *The Causes of War and the Conditions of Peace* (1935), *A Study of War* (1942), *Problems of Stability and Progress in International Relations* (1954), and *The Role of International Law in the Elimination of War* (1961).

In spite of the relative peacefulness of capitalistic societies, popular theories have frequently cited capitalism as the major cause of war in modern times. These theories have sprung primarily from socialist writers who have wished to supersede capitalistic systems by socialistic ones and so are to be received with caution. Yet there are tendencies within capitalism which make for war.

Theories have related capitalism to war in general, to imperial wars between capitalistic and agrarian economies, to civil wars between classes within capitalistic economies, to international wars between dominantly capitalistic states, and to general social disintegration within capitalistic economies, providing conditions favorable for war. These theories emphasize, respectively, the problems of (*a*) war profiteering, (*b*) expansionism, (*c*) depression, (*d*) protectionism, and (*e*) materialism.

a) *War Profiteering.*—The theory which attributes wars to the greed of special capitalistic interests, able to profit by war preparations or war itself, may be distinguished from the remaining theories which emphasize the war-provoking tendencies of capitalism as a system.

This theory does not distinguish between classes of war. The war profiteer can gain from war preparations or activities whether in a colonial area, a "Balkan area," or among great powers; whether civil or international; and whether involving his own or other countries. His liability to disadvantages from the war or war scare may, however, vary in these different situations. This type of influence seems to have been important mainly in backward areas and in the relations of small states, though on a few occasions it may have affected the relations of great powers.

The charge of exercising such influence has been leveled especially against arms- and munitions-makers and traders, against international bankers, and against international investors. It is obvious that arms-makers or traders can increase their markets by war scares and wars, and there is evidence that they have on occasion evaded embargoes and international controls, bribed officials to get orders, sold arms simultaneously to both sides in wars and insurrections, stimulated armament races, and maintained lobbies to increase military appropriations and to prevent national or international restrictions on arms or arms trade.

Bankers can make profits from loans to actual or prospective belligerents which may be distributed to the public before defaults occur. Loans by neutral bankers and sales of war materials by neutral manufacturers and traders may eventually create an interest in the victory of the side with the greatest debt and the greatest trade. This interest may extend to farmers, miners, the general investing public, and manufacturers of numerous non-military articles purchased by the belligerent. The evidence indicates that this type of interest has been of relatively slight importance in drawing neutrals into war.

Investors in foreign bonds or enterprises suffering from defaults, from adverse laws, or from inefficient police in the investment area may seek the aid of their government to collect debts or to protect their interests. The practice of diplomatic protection has been fully recognized in international law, as has the danger that it may lead to hostilities. Numerous interpositions by powerful states in the territory of lesser states have occurred, but they have seldom led to major wars, unless associated with political objectives.

The voluminous evidence adduced by the League of Nations, by national commissions, and by private investigators indicates that all these abuses have occurred. Their relative importance in the causation of modern war has probably been greatly exaggerated. . . .

b) Expansionism. — Socialist writers have charged capitalism with the vice of expansionism or imperialism, which, they say, leads not only to exploitative wars by advanced against backward peoples but also to wars between capitalistic nations struggling to exploit the same backward area. The tendency of capitalism to expand in backward areas is said by some to be due to the progressive attrition of the domestic market as the capitalists deprive labor of labor's fair share of the products of industry and decrease its purchasing power. Foreign markets, it is said, must be found to absorb the product of the ever increasing capitalistic plants.

Economists have denied the theoretical reasons adduced for such a development of underconsumption, and some socialists repudiate this theory. Although purchasing power has been inadequate to provide a market for existing productive capacity in periods of depression, it is not clear that serious and protracted depressions are an inherent characteristic of capitalism or that depressions have been the major factor in promoting imperialistic expansion.

The more orthodox socialist theory attributes the alleged expansive tendency of capitalism not to the necessities but to the greed of the entrepreneurs. Opportunities, they say, exist in undeveloped areas to utilize richer resources of raw materials, to exploit more helpless labor, to develop larger markets, and to make more profits out of investment than is possible at home. Consequently, when communication and transportation make it possible, the profit motive urges capitalists and entrepreneurs to exploit such areas and to seek protection through the diplomatic and military power of governments which, according to socialistic theory, the dominant capitalistic class will control.

This theory generalizes from too few facts. A general historical survey indicates that most capitalists and entrepreneurs have preferred domestic to foreign or colonial investment. Bankers and investors have, it is true, sometimes urged governments to assist them in imperial enterprises, but more frequently imperial-minded politicians have utilized bankers and investors as unwilling tools to justify or assist in expansions desired for strategic or political reasons. . . .

c) Depression.—It has also been charged that capitalism tends inevitably toward periodic depressions of increasing amplitude, which, because of the miseries of the unemployed, tend toward civil war or, as a preventive, toward international war.

Depressions have been variously attributed to the extreme commodity price advances and burdens of debt caused by wars themselves, to the tendency of industrialism to decrease the internal market by exploitation of labor, and to fluctuations in the expectation of returns from capital. Explanations such as these in terms of political, industrial, or financial practices do not reach the heart of capitalist economy. If war is the cause of depressions, the difficulty lies in international relations rather than in capitalism.

The economic explanations, which relate

depressions to progressive limitations of competition and to progressive lengthenings of the productive process, both of which may be inspired by the effort toward economic efficiency, suggest inherent weaknesses in capitalism. They assert that capitalism in larger enterprises eventually defeats itself by pursuing its economic end of eliminating inefficiency and increasing division of labor. There can be no doubt that protracted depressions have been a danger to peace. Unless capitalism can succeed in giving steady employment and rising standards of living, it will be in danger. Forms of government intervention have proved to be effective remedies.

d) Protectionism.—Capitalism has led to technologies giving greater control of natural forces, has conquered distance by new means of transportation and communication, and has stimulated trade between all parts of the world. These developments have built up an interdependence of national economies far beyond anything achieved by other economic systems and have also created military techniques greatly augmenting the social and economic costs of war.

The monopolistic tendency inherent in capitalism has urged domestic producers to demand protection through tariff or other economic barriers. National defense demands have added to these barriers. A high degree of economic interdependence of states, when associated with rising national barriers, has produced the problem of "have" and "have-not" states. The latter, unable to trade manufactures for necessary raw materials and foodstuffs, have felt oppressed in an inadequate living-space and have fought for more land. Agricultural countries faced by declining world prices for their products and rising prices for the manufactured goods they need have sometimes resorted to revolution.

Capitalism has contributed to these situations, as has nationalism. Neither is responsible

in itself. The incompatibility of the two has proved disastrous. . . .

e) Materialism.—Perhaps the most serious charge against capitalism has been that it destroys the sense of social values by its emphasis upon individualism and its depersonalization of economic activity. Peace requires effective political organization, and that requires not only respect for and protection of individual rights but also constant loyalty to the symbols of the group. In so far as capitalism has tended to disintegrate all political loyalties, it has tended toward disorder and war.

Capitalism certainly has not built up community loyalties capable of sustaining a political organization operating effectively over the area which it has integrated economically. Instead, by its tendency to concentrate human interest on the business enterprise, on individual profits, and on impersonal productive processes, it has tended to minimize community values and to disintegrate political organizations dependent upon those values. A good economic man tends to be a bad citizen.

As a consequence, political organization during the period of modern capitalism has been sustained by sentiments unrelated to capitalism—sentiments of tribal and cultural solidarity, geographic unity, and historic tradition. The good citizen has tended to be a nationalist and a bad economist.

The natural ethic of capitalism is liberalism and humanism, as was realized by the classical economists who elaborated this ethic in their creed of utilitarianism. In spite of Richard Cobden and Cordell Hull, active capitalism with a laissez faire tradition was lukewarm in its support of those ideals. By accepting protectionist loaves and fishes from national states, it paved the way for its own destruction.

Marxian socialism took up what capitalism had abandoned. It preached internationalism and tried to put the individual and humanity (interpreted as the laboring class) above the nation. Thus the ethic of liberalism continued in the British labor party and in German social democracy. But the natural ethic of socialism is nationalism, since its program can be achieved only by a strong government supported by a powerful sense of group solidarity. Socialism in practice became "national socialism," destructive of both liberalism and humanism. Support for the universal ethical consciousness, essential for the preservation of peace, must be sought outside of either capitalism or socialism.

It may be concluded that, although capitalism and socialism have each claimed to be the most peaceful form of civilized economy, the difficulties of capitalism with depressions and profiteers and of socialism with oppressions and inefficiencies, the subordination of both to nationalism, and the incapacity of either to sustain a universal ethical consciousness in a world of economic and political interdependence, have made each productive of war. Mixed economies have tended to develop in technologically advanced states, converging the two systems and recognizing international objectives.*

* Mr. Wright, in granting permission to reprint this selection, requested that the following word of explanation be appended: The analysis in this book [A *Study of War*] concludes that: "Wars arise because of the changing relation of numerous variables—technological, psychological, psychic, social and intellectual. There is no single cause of war. Peace is an equilibrium among many forces." (p. 351). If the popular classification of the causes of war by such imprecise terms as political, ideological, juridical, psychological, and economic is applied, economic activity (in the sense of rational efforts to increase wealth and welfare), though considered responsible for some wars by some historians, has generally been considered unimportant in the causation of war by both economists and statisticians. The former emphasize that it is "the vice of war that it seldom compares its costs with its achievements" (p. 390) and that "actual or potential war had become costly beyond any value either to national states or to world civilization." (p. 83). The latter believe themselves to have found a "relatively slight correlation of its (war's) occurrence with any definable population or economic changes." (p. 113).

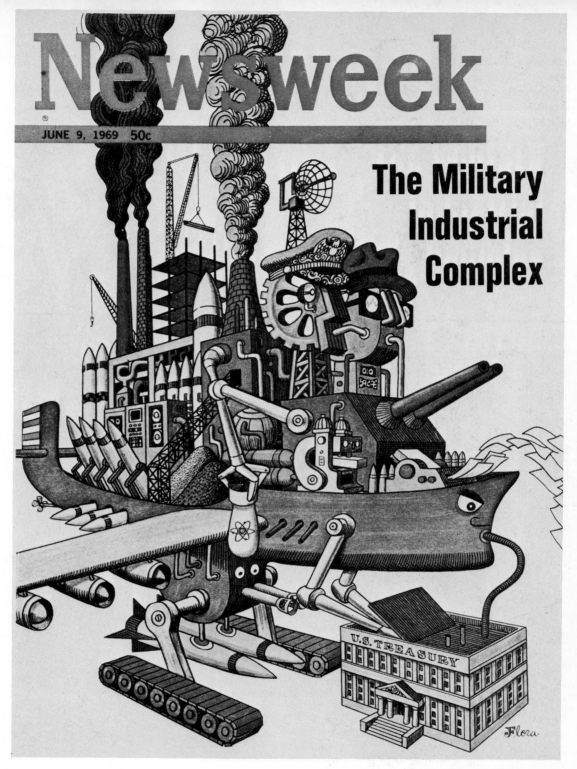

For many Americans, Richard Nixon's quick decision to recommend Anti-ballistic missile (ABM) system only reinforced a conviction that the presidency is but a junior partner in that "complex" which runs the "warfare state." (March 20, 1969) (The Los Angeles Times Syndicate)

"Breaking in a New Mount Is Really Quite Easy, Once You Let Him Know Who's in Charge! I've Never Had Any Trouble"

"They're tryin' to break us up, old buddy!"

When a federal judge ruled that it was unconstitutional for members of Congress to hold reserve commissions in the Armed Forces, many citizens hoped that he had opened the door for a significant attack upon the "military-industrial-congressional establishment." (April 5, 1971) (William Sanders; *The Milwaukee Journal*)

Chapter Sixteen

RECENT ALLEGATIONS REGARDING THE DANGER OF MERGING INTERESTS: PRO AND CON

But we are only at the beginning. Isn't it true that all our actions have now become increasingly amateurish, capricious, and ridiculous by contrast with the high and careful purposefulness of the military way of doing things? The latter is bound to become the model of our existence. For you, my esteemed friend, the most interesting thing will be to observe how the machinery of State and administration is transformed and militarized; for me—how schools and education are given the cure, etc. Of all groups, the workers are going to have the strangest time; I have a premonition that at the moment sounds completely mad, and yet it will not leave me: that the military state will have to become "industrialist." Those great masses of men in the factory areas cannot be left forever in their state of need and lust for riches; a planned and controlled degree of poverty, with a system of promotion and uniforms, begun and ended daily to the roll of drums, that is what logically ought to come. (I know enough history, of course, to know that things do not always work out logically.)
—*Jacob Burckhardt*

From a letter of April 26, 1872

87

Lucia Ames Mead
AMERICA'S DANGER

From Lucia Ames Mead, "America's Danger and Opportunity," Survey, Vol. 35 (October 23, 1915), pp. 90–91.

Lucia Ames Mead (1856–1936), a leader of the American antipreparedness movement during 1914–1917, was a longtime advocate of peace. In the decade before World War I she was a member of the American Peace Society and of the American School Peace League, and served as chairman of the peace committee of the American National Council of Women. After the war broke out she became secretary of the Women's Peace Party and an active agitator in the movement for a League of Nations. Her publications included *Patriotism and the New Internationalism* (1907), *Swords and Plowshares* (1912), and *Law or War* (1928).

Democracy, the world over, stands today in peril. The militarists of Europe are fast ousting civilians and assuming civic functions. A censored press and cowed public, unable in any warring country to freely speak its mind, is accustoming itself to unprecedented governmental control. There is no assurance that the spirit of liberty for which Social-Democrats and labor parties stand will have the power to gain the ascendency.

> Once to every man and nation comes
>   the moment to decide
> In the strife of Truth with Falsehood,
>   for the good or evil side.

Our choice comes now. That money power behind munitions which has for years in many countries largely influenced the press is working desperately to retain after the war the ascendency which this war has given it. It is a terrific power working through vicious moving-picture films, through scare headlines and every shrewd psychologic device to hypnotize the reason and to obsess the imagination. When it once gets its grip upon the schools, as it is trying to do under the plea of patriotism, it may create conditions which will compel the long, bloody fight for democracy to be won over again. This war has revealed within our midst men in high position who are condemning democracy because it will not yield to the militarists' demands, because it will not fall into machine methods. The Prussian conception of the state is getting rooted in the minds of the very men who most bitterly condemn its obvious results. If we give our might toward increased reliance upon force, we may tip the scale downward for all humanity for generations.

If we, on the other hand, make the alternative choice and tip the scale upward, if we put the mighty influence of our rich, safe republic toward creating new and more adequate defences than our physicists have invented, we shall be able to inspire and lead a war-sick world. Let us make no mistake. Our choice is between two courses. We cannot successfully at the same time follow two contrary policies. Years ago, in England, an esteemed friend of mine, a man who loves peace and is a member of the Privy Council, advised me to waste no time in criticizing the mad efforts of the militarists to increase unnecessary armaments. Of course, he declared, these efforts were wasteful and vicious and discouraging, but if only peace workers would confine their efforts to substituting law for war, they would gradually undermine the power of the army and navy leagues. Urge on the work of Hague courts, multiply treaties, improve international law, he counselled, and finally, with world organization complete, militarism would have no leg to stand on and would collapse. I felt at the time that this would be true if reason ruled and no selfish interests upset the logic of events, but I had no faith that men who have made vast profit from armaments and war scares would relinquish their power to hoodwink and to drain the people. As well expect distillers of their own accord to cease making whiskey.

The conflagration of Europe is the outcome of the policy of letting armament makers and the jingo press inflame the fear and jealousy of governments and the people while the sentries of the public who should have been on guard dreamed at their post. They assumed that a thoughtless public would know its own interests and logically work to attain them. The generals and the Krupps, Armstrongs, and DuPonts were perfectly willing to let us read papers on Hague courts and prize courts and sea law and on Caloo and Drago doctrines and laws for neutrals. It amused us and did not hurt them. In fact, in our country the militarists blandly supported it and formed arbitration societies with arbitration and armaments walking abreast arm in arm across their platform. Whether one could serve God and Mammon or not, it was certain that one could serve God and Mars. The one holy thing which they insisted was taboo from all denunciation was any lessening of armaments until human nature had changed and the millennium was in sight. Any one who dared talk of our nation venturing to take an initiative, to be the courageous leader in a new policy in placing more reliance on non-military defences was told that he was no patriot, was "a college sissy" and a contemptible "peace at any price" nonentity. The conceit of the militarist that he alone loves righteousness is characteristic.

The result of Europe's preparedness is apparently teaching no lesson to our own people. "Had England had a million men in arms, this calamity would not have come," they cry. But, as the *Westminster Gazette* well said, "It would simply have come sooner." The worst horror of this accumulation of horrors is that on every hand, even in our country, men seem to be losing their power of reason, their realization of the most impassive facts. A college education gives no proof that the man who has it has any more judgment or perception of relative values, of international ethics and economics than has the man on the street. It gives no proof of power of logic or of imagination, as we are sadly learning.

With the complacent assumption that we could never become militaristic, that we would fight only for righteousness and justice and must be the sole judge in our own case as to what is just, we are with amazing rapidity adopting the very principles of reliance on force which is at the basis of this whole setback to civilization. German military efficiency is what our army and navy leagues have held up as our ideal. The head of the army was reported as saying two or three years ago that he would like to "out-German the Germans" and teach every boy of twelve to shoot. Before this war opened, our military authorities clamored for a great army. Under sharp protest that it is possible for us to be militarized, America under

the sophistry of the panic-stricken press is fast reversing its theories and policies. It is invoking such reliance on force as, if carried out, will end that power of world-leadership which is ours today.

88

Hudson Maxim
PACIFIST ILLUSIONS

From Hudson Maxim, Defenseless America *(New York: Hearst's International Library, 1915), pp. 247–250. Copyright, 1915, by Hearst's International Library Co., Inc.*

Hudson Maxim (1853–1927) was an inventor and mechanical engineer who entered the ordnance and explosives business in 1888 and in 1897 became associated with E. I. DuPont de Nemours and Co. The first to make smokeless powder in the United States, Maxim was also the creator of Maximite, a very powerful explosive. He was a member of the Naval Consulting Board from 1915 until his death, and played a prominent public role during 1914–1917 as an advocate of preparedness.

The pacifists have delved out of the infinite latency a very startling alleged truth, which they are effulging in language of lavish luminosity, to the effect that it is necessary only for a man to have a pecuniary interest or personal advantage involved in order to commit any kind of crime. They have discovered that room for a motive establishes the motive and proves the crime. They have discovered that those things which we call integrity and honor and conscience are no deterrents whatsoever to the commission of the most heinous offense against one's fellow men, so long as there is profit in it. They believe that, if only there is money in the game, an inventor or manufacturer or merchant will scheme for the commission of wholesale poisoning, maiming, and murder. They believe that the inventors and manufacturers of guns necessarily foster war in order to promote the sale of their wares. They surmise that inventors and manufacturers of smokeless powders and high explosives are capable of standing with the "black hand," capable of being gladdened at the dynamite outrage, at the street riot, at the slaughter of song-birds —anything that will consume dynamite or burn gunpowder.

According to the pacifists, the principal lay of makers of war-materials is to connive with the officers of the Army and Navy to stir up international dissension and foment war, in order to create a demand for their products. The pacifists believe that army and navy officers are only too willing to co-operate in the nefarious business, because war brings higher pay and rapid promotion. They believe that it matters not to these "interested parties" how many of their countrymen are sacrificed on the firing line, or how many widows and orphans are made. The groans of the wounded and dying on the battle-field, and the lamentations in the desolated home, are music to the ears of those who supply the war-materials; for, with every shot from a rifle, fifty grains of gunpowder are burned, while bullets enough miss their mark to equal the weight of each man they kill. Consequently, there is substantial profit to the cartridge-maker and the gunpowder-manufacturer for every man killed with a rifle ball. . . .

Look at it any way you will, war, according to the pacifist notion, is a real Klondike for manufacturers of war-materials. The peace sophists have been able to put two and two together, with the conclusions that such an opportunity for profit is too strong for human nature to resist, and that, as they have found room for the motive, they have proved the crime.

Of course, their accusation is a pretty severe arraignment of human nature, after all these years of civilization and Christian enlightenment.

It is strange how human nature can have improved so much lately, as claimed by the pacifists, and how the spirit of brotherhood and good-will can have suddenly become so dominant that the peoples of the earth now despise war, and are so afflicted with the horrors of it that, just as soon as the great European War is over, they are not going to fight any more, while still the makers of war-materials remain in the primitive savagery of the stone age. It seems to me that, if human nature has so improved as to be an efficient bar to a nation against waging war for plunder, regardless of the advantage and the profit, it ought also to be a similar bar to inventors and manufacturers of war-materials, and to army and navy officers, against precipitating war for pecuniary or personal advantage.

But, according to pacifist reasoning, those "interested parties" are more endowed with the spirit of the hyena than with the spirit of brotherhood. Perhaps, however, the manufacturers of war-materials, and army and navy officers, were not home when the great improvement in human nature knocked at their door.

89

John T. Flynn
THE ARMAMENT BANDWAGON

From John T. Flynn "The Armament Bandwagon," New Republic, Vol. 98 (March 8, 1939), pp. 121–123.

John T. Flynn (1882–1964), a political liberal before World War II and later an extreme conservative, was a columnist for the *New Republic* from 1931 to 1940, an associate editor of *Collier's* magazine from 1937 to 1942, and a commentator on the Mutual Broadcasting System from 1954 to 1964. He also served as an adviser to the congressional committees investigating the stock exchange and munitions industries in the early 1930s. He published more than fifteen books, including *Graft in Business* (1931), *Security Speculations—Its Economic Effects* (1934), *The Roosevelt Myth* (1948), and *The Road Ahead* (1949).

When Henry Morgenthau told a Senate committee that the airplane orders from France with their $65,000,000 for American workmen's pockets were "good stuff" he was expressing a belief which is beyond doubt widely held by the American people. It may not look like "good stuff" ten years from now. It is very difficult to believe now that the billions we were supposed to get from Europe in 1915–18 for munitions were really "good stuff," though it looked that way at the time to the people who are in the habit of never looking beyond the ends of their noses.

America at this moment seems to be caught in the drift of powerful forces—too powerful indeed to be resisted. One cannot refuse to look at the phenomenon of men of all parties and all groups and all philosophies from the tip of the right wing to the tip of the left clamoring for war preparations. You see with dismay unquestioned liberal idealists like Lewis Mumford and Nathaniel Peffer demanding armaments and even action, along with old-time Republican reactionaries, professional militarists and political junkers.

There is such a thing as social fatigue. Men grow weary of hard times. Millions out of work become sick of the long struggle against unemployment and the hopeless vista ahead. People on small pay do not settle down complacently to the everlasting treadmill of poverty. Hundreds of thousands of little business men become excessively tired of the endless battle against losses and uncertainty and possible bankruptcy. And so all these very practical groups, not at all vicious but yielding to the commanding voice of self-preservation, come after a while to offer a hospitable ear to any suggestion that promises an improvement in

their condition, even though it be a temporary one. And therefore when a foreign government comes here with an offer to buy planes or ships or guns or dynamite it looks like "good stuff."

Then when leaders propose that the American government itself spend some additional billions on war preparations—that too looks like good stuff to the men who work in steel mills and coal mines and shipyards and chemical plants and copper mills and all sorts of plants where materials will be made "to defend democracy."

In the meantime, the liberal groups, who have always provided the resistance to this sort of thing, dwell upon the fact that democracy too is good stuff. Somehow they have got the notion that the threat to democracy comes from Hitler and Mussolini and that if those two gentlemen were destroyed and their fascist governments with them, democracy would be safe, whereas to me democracy would be a good deal worse off, not because Hitler and Mussolini are good for democracy, but because nothing can be worse for democracy than war—at this time above all others—and vast military preparations. But this clamor of the liberals for war preparations removes the last vestige of resistance to the path of the junker and the fatigued business and labor community which wants business. And so, with all the flags of idealism flying we prepare to destroy ourselves.

In the winter of 1937 I made a continuous tour of the whole country and after that made separate visits to almost every section of the country, some of which I visited several times. If there was one thing that was obvious, it was that Americans everywhere were resolutely opposed to war and to anything that might savor of war. For that reason I, for one, was amazed at the eagerness with which groups everywhere sprang to the bait of preparedness as an avenue toward recovery. And I was even more surprised at the blunt frankness with which they expressed their satisfaction at the recovery elements in the defense of democracy.

The first marked exhibition of this phenomenon came when the President, while the papers were speculating on the extent of his preparedness proposals, brought about a conference between the utilities and the National Defense Power Committee last October. The War Department proposed that the utilities industry make immediate plans for large extensions of generating capacity at strategic spots for war purposes. The government is supposed to have promised financial assistance and the industry responded patriotically to a program of expansion which might run as high as three billion dollars. The chairman of the board of the Electric Bond and Share Corporation hailed it as of great national significance, not only because of its bearing on national defense, but also for its bearing on "the unemployment situation and its doubtless favorable effect in revitalizing business and industry of the country generally. I feel this will be the means of reopening to the utility business the capital markets, particularly for equity financing, which is badly needed."

The *New York Times* reported that "a public-utility executive had estimated that orders for even the first stage of the utility program, now being shaped up, would set leading makers of operating equipment 'operating to capacity within three months.' "

Then came the President's enormous army-and-navy construction program, the full size of which no one yet really knows. Newspapers everywhere pointed out while approving the importance of defending ourselves and squelching the dictators and protecting democracy that this would probably "lead to a sustained recovery for several years enabling business to regain its health."

Then railroad officials began to see the importance of the railroads to national defense. How can we transport armies, how can we mobilize materials at strategic points unless the railroads are put into shape for the strain? Hence Washington and others interested in the roads have been playing with the idea of a billion or so of government credits to enable the roads to get ready for national defense.

Already the shipbuilding industry is booming. With yards rushing work on the naval program and on oil tankers subsidized by government funds for naval auxiliaries in the event of war, and on other merchant vessels also heavily subsidized to provide transports for troops, "construction under way," to quote *The Times*, "in tonnage and in value of contracts, is the greatest in the history of the country save in the brief period while we were in the World War." *The Times* found, after a survey, that "50,000 men will be employed in the private yards by June 1 (1939) and 25,000 in navy-yard construction before the end of the year." This, of course, does not take account of those employed in steel plants and other industries providing materials for construction. And this, the navy proudly informs us, brings business to every state in the Union.

Business executives and observers echo the sentiment expressed by the editor of *Banking*, that "preparations for national defense constitute a business stimulant of the first importance."

And now the purchasing agents of Europe put in an appearance. Not only has a French mission visited us to buy a thousand planes—contenting itself with 600—but an English mission has already bought 100 and is doubtless buying more. Already, we learn from the reports of the secret sessions of the Senate Military Affairs Committee, the French Finance Minister was planning to set up a purchasing corporation here as a preliminary to establishing credits in this country. Mr. Morgenthau refused to countenance that. But as time goes on and we begin to taste more and more of the good stuff, we may yield on that point. It is inevitable that we will. After all, if democracy is worth saving, if democracy is being defended by France and England, if democracy is endangered by the onslaughts of the dictators, is America to refuse to supply to hard-pressed France and England the instruments of defense merely because they cannot lay cash on the line? Is Uncle Sam to put human liberty and the sacred rights of the democratic peoples upon a cash-and-carry basis? Are we, my fellow citizens—and so on. . . .

Thus the great preparedness industry grows. I dare say no one can stop it. The Democrats have come around for it and the Republicans have always been for it. The liberals favor it; the radicals favor it. Business favors it; the idealists favor it. Hence we shall have it. Here I shall merely drop this futile warning—that you cannot prepare for war without doing something to yourselves. You cannot have a war industry without a war scare and having built it and made it the basis of work for several million men you cannot demobilize it and you will have to keep on inventing reasons for it.

90

Nathaniel Peffer
A NECESSARY EVIL

From Nathaniel Peffer, "In an Era of Unreason," Harper's Magazine, Vol. 178 (March 1939), pp. 340–342. Copyright © 1939 by Harper's Magazine, Inc.

Nathaniel Peffer (1890–1964), a newspaper correspondent and research scholar in Japan and China between the wars, accepted an appointment as professor of international relations at Columbia University in 1938, and remained at that institution until his retirement. He was author of *The White Man's Dilemma* (1927), *China: The Collapse of a Civilization* (1930), *Must We Fight in Asia?* (1937), *America's Place in the World* (1945), and *The Far East* (1958).

It is undeniable . . . that a war to stop fascism might bring fascism in its train. America might indeed plunge into a European war to save Europe from fascism and find itself at the end of a victorious war, in which the present fascist nations were crushed, in the grip of an omnipotent state unwilling to remit the absolute powers it had enjoyed during the war. And that there would have to be full centralization of power for the duration of a war exacting the whole of the national energies is self-evident. There is this risk, and it has to be run, whether by Great Britain if it has to fight to ward off fascist control over Europe or by the United States if for one reason or another it elects to cast its lot with Great Britain and France.

Here, however, the argument of those of the school of Norman Thomas can be turned against themselves. They say that the only way to prevent fascism is to eliminate the causes at home. But by the same token if the soil is not right for fascism, then a war need not end in fascism at home. Far too much has been made of this argument in the current controversy on American foreign policy. Fascism may or may not come in America, but if it does, that will be for deeper reasons than participation in war. As a matter of fact, there is far more danger of infection from the prestige and power which further successes would confer on the fascist countries. It is said much too lightly that America can dedicate itself to the preservation of democracy in its own territory and let come what will elsewhere. This is a kind of closet philosophy. It is unreal. No one can seriously believe that a completely fascist Europe would leave America unaffected. A momentum would be put behind the idea that would make it all but irresistible. Not only would the democratic idea be discredited, but those elements in the American population that would find fascism desirable and conducive to their own interests would be tremendously reinforced. Their opponents would be on the defensive. It can already be seen how much impetus has been given fascism everywhere by the recent German successes. America could not remain a democratic island surrounded by fascist states. For if all Europe becomes fascist, so do Latin America and most of Asia. Then assuredly America could not remain socially and politically isolationist.

The essential point is this: can America abstract itself from the rest of the world? If it can its problem is simple. And since simplification of problems and their solution is always tempting, there has been a wide acceptance of the belief that America need only have enough armament to keep invaders at a comfortable distance from its shores and it can let the world go hang. The rest is a matter of persuasion: show the American people they had better not get "involved," partly in their own interest and partly because they can do no good by getting entangled. But the problem is not so simple. As has already been said, under certain circumstances America will not want to abstract itself from the rest of the world—that is, if there is a European war in which Great Britain and France are in danger of defeat by fascist dictatorships. Even if it should want to, there is at least a doubt that it could. It cannot deflect the currents of world ideas and world forces around the American continent. That is the penalty of the time and of America's importance. Its best hope, then, lies in molding the forces and ideas to its liking or, if it cannot, then in cultivating the capacity to deal with them. With respect to international relations its best hope lies in contributing its effort to preventing war.

This was the foundation of the case of the League of Nations advocates, and if the League had made a genuine effort to be a League the case would have been impregnable. But the League is dead.

What is left then? Three lines of progression open up. First, the fascist Powers may win control of Europe by default. That is, the fear which Germany has implanted in the past few months will cause a stampede to its side of all Europe east of the Rhine, and Great Britain and France will continue to capitulate until both have been reduced to second-class Powers, retaining full independence at Germany's pleasure. Second, there may be a war of coalitions—on the one side Germany, Italy, and such allies in Eastern Europe as dare not refuse adhesion; on the other side Great Britain and France, probably Russia, and perhaps some of the smaller nations of western Europe. Third, there may be stalemate—Great Britain and France stiffening up in policy and morale and at the same time increasing their armament so that Germany hesitates to precipitate the test of strength.

Despite recent disquieting evidence, the first of these three alternatives—a stampede to the German side—can still be called questionable. Unless there has been an actual metamorphosis of the British people, one cannot visualize a voluntary British surrender, and nations do not undergo metamorphosis in a few years. It is more plausible to assume that the British have been caught off balance, their poise lost in the inability to decide which they were prepared to risk first—their empire and historical position or the chance of revolution in mid-Europe which might spread to Great Britain and imperil the status of the present ruling groups. Perhaps Great Britain has only not yet become adjusted to the fact that it no longer has international primacy and that it can no longer deal with the rest of the world in nineteenth-century terms. England may be decadent, but one can say with confidence that admission of its decadence will have to be wrested from it. Even a drift into a modified form of fascism would not constitute surrender to Germany. It would only change the banner under which England would fight to maintain imperial status.

If that is true, the second alternative—a war of coalitions—is more likely. At least, from the present drift of events the weight of probability is on the side of war—a war between the fascist coalition and the democratic coalition, with the Soviet Union as an unclassifiable ally of the latter. A Russo-German war or a war between the Soviet Union and the non-communist Powers aligned in a new coalition awaits certain antecedent settlements or understandings in the West.

The hope, a not very sturdy one, lies in the third alternative—stalemate; not because stalemate is a solution but because it at least postpones slaughter and destruction and provides an interval in which some event or development might cut across to avert a war for this generation without capitulation to fascism. This was our best hope after the reoccupation of the Rhineland and the Ethiopian war, but it was lost or thrown away. Skillful diplomatic temporizing and improvisation might have succeeded in warding off a crisis such as shook Europe in 1938. This would have meant not letting the initiative pass to Germany, which would have entailed a resolute front at the beginning. The Spanish affair can be called the dividing line. When the Italo-German intervention was allowed to go unchallenged the way was opened to German aggression. And when the seizure of Austria was followed by Anglo-French complaisance in the face of all signs that Czechoslovakia would go the way

of Austria, a free hand was conferred on Germany and the present crisis was made. For diplomatic temporizing it is not quite too late, though the circumstances are unpromising. Therein, however, lies America's best chance for escape from an ugly choice, a choice which by all the weight of past events and present tendencies will fall on war.

The hope, as I say, is not very sturdy and it can be fortified in only one way—armaments on the grand scale. All the generalizations about the role of armament in history are inapplicable now. Great Britain's military weakness may or may not have been exaggerated to provide an excuse for the debacle of last September [1938, i.e., the Munich Conference]; but with all allowances made, it can hardly be disputed that larger British and French air forces would have precluded the events between February and September. And only a still larger one will prevent an even worse debacle in the not distant future. In the broader sense and over long periods, arms may be an evil; but in specific situations and at particular times they are a necessary evil. The ruling principle of international society now is force. It may be regrettable; it may be mournful testimony that the last war was fought in vain; but it is so. And to ignore this fact, unless one is a philosophical non-resister, is to be doctrinaire and perhaps to invite national suicide. The fact is less compelling for America than for Great Britain and France, but it is one from which America is far from exempt.

There is only one argument to be made against an extensive military establishment for the United States, an argument that rests exclusively on the premise that the United States can hermetically seal itself within its own borders or at most have to defend the two Americas. Seclude itself it cannot, however, and the theory of "hemisphere defense" is a formula of agreeable evasion. The theory of defensive war only is illusory. Nations as powerful as the United States do not get into wars only when they are in danger of being attacked. They become involved in controversies which flame into war. And once engaged in war, a nation must win. It cannot sit secure behind its fortified boundaries with a protective screen of ships and anti-aircraft guns. Or if it can, it will not when it has the might and the pride ,of America. In a time such as ours either a nation as powerful as America resigns itself to non-participation in the world, to self-negation and its consequences, or it must prepare not only to repel attack but to meet an enemy anywhere under any conditions. In doing so it is better to pay more heed to psychology than to geography and classical strategy.

91

C. Wright Mills
THE POWER ELITE

From The Power Elite *by C. Wright Mills, pp. 171, 274–278. Copyright © 1956 by Oxford University Press, Inc. Reprinted by permission.*

C. Wright Mills (1916–1962), a professor of sociology at Columbia University in the years following 1946, was the nation's foremost "neo-Marxist" and a noted critic of American culture at a time when it was none too popular to be so. He was particularly well known for his provocative studies of class relationships in the United States. His works include *White Collar: The American Middle Classes* (1951), *Character and Social Structure* (1953), *The Power Elite* (1956), and *The Causes of World War Three* (1958).

During the eighteenth century, observers of the historic scene began to notice a remarkable trend in the division of power at the top of modern society: Civilians, coming into author-

ity, were able to control men of military violence, whose power, being hedged in and neutralized, declined. At various times and places, of course, military men had been the servants of civilian decision, but this trend—which reached its climax in the nineteenth century and lasted until World War I—seemed then, and still seems, remarkable simply because it had never before happened on such a scale or never before seemed so firmly grounded.

In the twentieth century, among the industrialized nations of the world, the great, brief, precarious fact of civilian dominance began to falter; and now—after the long peace from the Napoleonic era to World War I—the old march of world history once more asserts itself. All over the world, the warlord is returning. All over the world, reality is defined in his terms. And in America, too, into the political vacuum the warlords have marched. Alongside the corporate executives and the politicians, the generals and admirals—those uneasy cousins within the American elite—have gained and have been given increased power to make and to influence decisions of the gravest consequence. . . .

We study history, it has been said, to rid ourselves of it, and the history of the power elite is a clear case for which this maxim is correct. Like the tempo of American life in general, the long-term trends of the power structure have been greatly speeded up since World War II, and certain newer trends within and between the dominant institutions have also set the shape of the power elite and given historically specific meaning to its fifth epoch [the post-New Deal period]:

I. In so far as the structural clue to the power elite today lies in the political order, that clue is the decline of politics as genuine and public debate of alternative decisions—with nationally responsible and policy-coherent parties and with autonomous organizations connecting the lower and middle levels of power with the top levels of decision. America is now in considerable part more a formal political democracy than a democratic social structure, and even the formal political mechanics are weak.

The long-time tendency of business and government to become more intricately and deeply involved with each other has . . . reached a new point of explicitness. The two cannot now be seen clearly as two distinct worlds. It is in terms of the executive agencies of the state that the rapprochement has proceeded most decisively. The growth of the executive branch of the government, with its agencies that patrol the complex economy, does not mean merely the "enlargement of government" as some sort of autonomous bureaucracy: it has meant the ascendancy of the corporation's man as a political eminence.

During the New Deal the corporate chieftains joined the political directorate; as of World War II they have come to dominate it. Long interlocked with government, now they have moved into quite full direction of the economy of the war effort and of the postwar era. This shift of the corporation executives into the political directorate has accelerated the long-term relegation of the professional politicians in the Congress to the middle levels of power.

II. In so far as the structural clue to the power elite today lies in the enlarged and military state, that clue becomes evident in the military ascendancy. The warlords have gained decisive political relevance, and the military structure of America is now in considerable part a political structure. The seemingly permanent military threat places a premium on the military and upon their control of men, materiel, money, and power; virtually all political and economic actions are now judged in terms of military definitions of reality: the

higher warlords have ascended to a firm position within the power elite of the fifth epoch.

In part at least this has resulted from one simple historical fact, pivotal for the years since 1939: the focus of elite attention has been shifted from domestic problems, centered in the 'thirties around slump, to international problems, centered in the 'forties and 'fifties around war. Since the governing apparatus of the United States has by long historic usage been adapted to and shaped by domestic clash and balance, it has not, from any angle, had suitable agencies and traditions for the handling of international problems. Such formal democratic mechanics as had arisen in the century and a half of national development prior to 1941, had not been extended to the American handling of international affairs. It is, in considerable part, in this vacuum that the power elite has grown.

III. In so far as the structural clue to the power elite today lies in the economic order, that clue is the fact that the economy is at once a permanent-war economy and a private-corporation economy. American capitalism is now in considerable part a military capitalism, and the most important relation of the big corporation to the state rests on the coincidence of interests between military and corporate needs, as defined by warlords and corporate rich. Within the elite as a whole, this coincidence of interest between the high military and the corporate chieftains strengthens both of them and further subordinates the role of the merely political men. Not politicians, but corporate executives, sit with the military and plan the organization of war effort.

The shape and meaning of the power elite today can be understood only when these three sets of structural trends are seen at their point of coincidence: the military capitalism of private corporations exists in a weakened and formal democratic system containing a military order already quite political in outlook and demeanor. Accordingly, at the top of this structure, the power elite has been shaped by the coincidence of interest between those who control the major means of production and those who control the newly enlarged means of violence; from the decline of the professional politician and the rise to explicit political command of the corporate chieftains and the professional warlords; from the absence of any genuine civil service of skill and integrity, independent of vested interests.

The power elite is composed of political, economic, and military men, but this instituted elite is frequently in some tension: it comes together only on certain coinciding points and only on certain occasions of "crisis." In the long peace of the nineteenth century, the military were not in the high councils of state, not of the political directorate, and neither were the economic men—they made raids upon the state but they did not join its directorate. During the 'thirties, the political man was ascendant. Now the military and the corporate men are in top positions.

Of the three types of circle that compose the power elite today, it is the military that has benefited the most in its enhanced power, although the corporate circles have also become more explicitly intrenched in the more public decision-making circles. It is the professional politician that has lost the most, so much that in examining the events and decisions, one is tempted to speak of a political vacuum in which the corporate rich and the high warlord, in their coinciding interests, rule.

It should not be said that the three "take turns" in carrying the initiative, for the mechanics of the power elite are not often as deliberate as that would imply. At times, of course, it is—as when political men, thinking they can borrow the prestige of generals, find

that they must pay for it, or, as when during big slumps, economic men feel the need of a politician at once safe and possessing vote appeal. Today all three are involved in virtually all widely ramifying decisions. Which of the three types seems to lead depends upon "the tasks of the period" as they, the elite, define them. Just now, these tasks center upon "defense" and international affairs. Accordingly, as we have seen, the military are ascendant in two senses: as personnel and as justifying ideology. That is why, just now, we can most easily specify the unity and the shape of the power elite in terms of the military ascendancy.

But we must always be historically specific and open to complexities. The simple Marxian view makes the big economic man the *real* holder of power; the simple liberal view makes the big political man the chief of the power system; and there are some who would view the warlords as virtual dictators. Each of these is an oversimplified view. It is to avoid them that we use the term "power elite" rather than, for example, "ruling class."

In so far as the power elite has come to wide public attention, it has done so in terms of the "military clique." The power elite does, in fact, take its current shape from the decisive entrance into it of the military. Their presence and their ideology are its major legitimations, whenever the power elite feels the need to provide any. But what is called the "Washington military clique" is not composed merely of military men, and it does not prevail merely in Washington. Its members exist all over the country, and it is a coalition of generals in the roles of corporation executives, of politicians masquerading as admirals, of corporation executives acting like politicians, of civil servants who become majors, of vice-admirals who are also the assistants to a cabinet officer, who is himself, by the way, really a member of the managerial elite.

Neither the idea of a "ruling class" nor of a simple monolithic rise of "bureaucratic politicians" nor of a "military clique" is adequate. The power elite today involves the often uneasy coincidence of economic, military, and political power.

92

Arnold Rose
CIVILIAN DOMINANCE

From The Power Structure: Political Process in American Society *by Arnold M. Rose, pp. 138–140, 146–147. Copyright © 1967 by Oxford University Press, Inc. Reprinted by permission.*

Arnold M. Rose (1918–1968) taught sociology and social psychology at Bennington College, Washington University (St. Louis), and finally at the University of Minnesota, where he held a professorship from 1949 until his death. He was also a member of the Minnesota House of Representatives from 1963 to 1965. Among his books are *The Negro in America* (1948), *Union Solidarity* (1952), *Theory and Method in the Social Sciences* (1954), and *The Power Structure* (1967).

C. Wright Mills interprets the expanded role of the military in American life by emphasizing the fact that they have joined the power elite. He says, "But they are now more powerful than they have ever been in the history of the American elite; they have now more means of exercising power in many areas of American life which were previously civilian domains; they now have more connections; and they are now operating in a nation whose elite and whose underlying population have accepted what can only be called a military definition of reality. Historically the warloads have been only uneasy, poor relations within the Ameri-

can elite; now they are first cousins, soon they may become elder brothers."[1] Mills goes on to say that while military men have become increasingly involved in politics, they have not shed their military background. He also asserts that it is largely through the default of the civilian politicians that the military have been drawn into the higher political decisions.[2] This is done, Mills states, by politicians who wish to legitimatize their policies by lifting them "above politics." Thus politicians are hiding behind the supposed expertise of military men. Another way in which the military enters politics, according to Mills, is through the lack of a really senior professional civil service. It is the absence of a genuine civil service which makes it easier for the military ascendancy to occur.

Mills slurs over the facts that the military are entering high civilian posts only at the invitation of the Congress or the Executive, and that their role has been primarily advisory rather than decision-making. He also neglects the instances in which the military have been sharply reprimanded by their civilian superiors for occasional participation in right-wing extremist activities. When an Air Force manual charged the National Council of Churches with harboring communists, the Air Force had to make public apologies and remove the manual from circulation. Major General Edwin Walker was dismissed from the service in April 1961 for right-wing extremist activity, including "making derogatory public statements about prominent Americans."

Another questionable assumption made by Mills was that military men, especially major generals and above, are all alike: "More than any other creature of the higher circles, modern warlords, on or above the two star rank, re-

[1] C. Wright Mills, *The Power Elite* (New York, Oxford University Press, 1956), p. 198.
[2] Mills, p. 200.

semble one another, internally and externally."[3] On the contrary, American history suggests there are at least two military traditions.[4] One of these traditions is exemplified by men like Zachary Taylor, U. S. Grant, George C. Marshall, Dwight D. Eisenhower, and Omar Bradley; and is characterized by the friendly easygoing soldier who reflects the ideals of a democratic society and insists that the military must take civilian direction. The other tradition is represented by men like Winfield Scott, George B. McClellan, George Patton, and Douglas MacArthur; this type exemplifies the brilliant, arrogant, and dramatic officer who draws his values and behavior from an older, aristocratic heritage and sometimes finds it difficult to subordinate himself to civilian authority. General MacArthur's insubordination to President Truman is the most spectacular example of this type in modern history. Yet it was the same MacArthur who, in 1962, warned of military usurpation of civilian control over the Armed Services, in a speech to army cadets.

Mills could not have been expected to know, in 1956, when *The Power Elite* was published, that the peak use of military leaders in civilian settings occurred during the Truman and first Eisenhower administrations, but that there would be a sharp deflation in their powers after that. Eisenhower himself, in his "farewell speech" in January 1961, warned against an "industrial-military complex," and beginning in 1961, the strongest civilian Secretary of Defense in modern history—Robert McNamara—reimposed civilian decision-making on all but the technical aspects of the military operations. Military encroachments on civilian authority have actually been very few, and in all cases they have been pushed back without much

[3] Mills, p. 195.
[4] See Harry T. Williams, "The Macs and the Ikes: America's Two Military Traditions," *American Mercury*, 75 (October 1952), 32–39.

difficulty. There is a problem of conflict of interest in military purchasing, . . . but this is found in purchasing by all branches of government, and is more significant for the military only because of its huge size, and hence its significance for the economy as a whole. Congress and the civilian heads of the Executive branch have shown themselves constantly alert to the abuses inherent in military purchasing of supplies, and have succeeded in controlling them. The only uncontrolled problem is that legitimate military purchasing constitutes such a large proportion of American business that its shifts have an impact on the health of the economy. . . .

The major reasons for the increasingly important role of the military in American life have little or nothing to do with alleged efforts of the military to gain power or with an alleged increasing willingness of the economic elite to use them as allies in their own efforts to increase their power. Insofar as the military have had a more salient role in the American scene since World War II, the reasons seem to be the following:

1. The United States has a much more active foreign policy since it emerged from World War II as one of the two leading world powers. The shift from isolationism to internationalism has entailed, among other things, a greater use of military forces. Some of the change has come by necessity: The oceans are no longer wide enough to isolate the United States from her enemies, nor is the British Navy, on which we long tacitly relied, capable of giving us much aid.

2. There has been a tremendous development of military technology, and the need for experts to develop and handle this technology. Politicians are increasingly dependent on scientists and soldiers to advise them on the use of this technology.

3. Some of the newer technology is "secret,"

and there has been a great increase in secret military information generally. This has meant an increased military and civilian organization for the maintenance of secrecy, and a reduction of open debate in Congress, and even in Executive circles, on certain matters.

4. The military has enjoyed increased prestige since just after World War II. As Professor [Samuel P.] Huntington pointed out: "After World War II many military appointments [to civilian posts] were designed primarily to honor or reward military commanders who had distinguished themselves in the war." The organizational skills and knowledge of foreign affairs of certain military leaders, gained or proved in wartime, were welcomed in the civilian sector. But this factor has declined as World War II and the Korean War have receded into history.

5. The expansion of the federal government, and the inability of the President to induce enough qualified civilians to take on some of the new positions because of the low pay and the possibility of public abuse, have occasioned some reliance on the more available military leaders. Some of the new positions—e.g. directing the building of the vast new superhighways —entail technical skills which certain military leaders possess and which will keep them in a condition of top training as much as their military posts do.

93

Dwight D. Eisenhower
THE MILITARY-INDUSTRIAL COMPLEX

From Dwight D. Eisenhower, "Farewell Address," New York Times, *January 17, 1961, p. 22. © 1961 by the New York Times Company. Reprinted by permission.*

Dwight D. Eisenhower (1890–1969) included this famous warning in his Farewell Address of January 1961 after having become increasingly concerned at evidence that vested interests were attempting to expand the nation's military budget. In his eight years as President this former general-of-the-armies had fought continually to reduce defense expenditures, believing as he did that American economic health required that the public sector be held strictly within limits. Indeed, during his last months in office the President had been accused by his opponents of economizing to the point that a "missile gap" had developed to the advantage of the Russians.

Crises there will continue to be. In meeting them, whether foreign or domestic, great or small, there is a recurring temptation to feel that some spectacular and costly action could become the miraculous solution to all current difficulties. A huge increase in newer elements of our defenses; development of unrealistic programs to cure every ill in agriculture; a dramatic expansion in basic and applied research —these and many other possibilities, each possibly promising in itself, may be suggested as the only way to the road we wish to travel.

But each proposal must be weighed in the light of a broader consideration; the need to maintain balance in and among national programs—balance between the private and the public economy, balance between the cost and hoped for advantages—balance between the clearly necessary and the comfortably desirable; balance between our essential requirements as a nation and the duties imposed by the nation upon the individual; balance between actions of the moment and the national welfare of the future. Good judgment seeks balance and progress; lack of it eventually finds imbalance and frustration.

The record of many decades stands as proof that our people and their Government have, in the main, understood these truths and have responded to them well in the face of threat and stress.

But threats, new in kind or degree, constantly arise. Of these, I mention two only.

A vital element in keeping the peace is our military establishment. Our arms must be mighty, ready for instant action, so that no potential aggressor may be tempted to risk his own destruction.

Our military organization today bears little relation to that known of any of my predecessors in peacetime—or, indeed, by the fighting men of World War II or Korea.

Until the latest of our world conflicts, the United States had no armaments industry. American makers of plowshares could, with time and as required, make swords as well.

But we can no longer risk emergency improvisation of national defense. We have been compelled to create a permanent armaments industry of vast proportions. Added to this, three and a half million men and women are directly engaged in the defense establishment. We annually spend on military security alone more than the net income of all United States corporations.

Now this conjunction of an immense military establishment and a large arms industry is new in the American experience. The total influence—economic, political, even spiritual—is felt in every city, every state house, every office of the Federal Government. We recognize the imperative need for this development. Yet we must not fail to comprehend its grave implications. Our toil, resources and livelihood are all involved; so is the very structure of our society.

In the councils of Government, we must guard against the acquisition of unwarranted influence, whether sought or unsought, by the military-industrial complex. The potential for the disastrous rise of misplaced power exists and will persist.

We must never let the weight of this combination endanger our liberties or democratic processes. We should take nothing for granted. Only an alert and knowledgeable citizenry can compel the proper meshing of the huge industrial and military machinery of defense with our peaceful methods and goals, so that security and liberty may prosper together.

Akin to, and largely responsible for the sweeping changes in our industrial-military posture has been the technological revolution during recent decades.

In this revolution research has become central. It also becomes more formalized, complex and costly. A steadily increasing share is conducted for, by, or at the direction of the Federal Government.

Today the solitary inventor, tinkering in his shop, has been overshadowed by task forces of scientists, in laboratories and testing fields. In the same fashion, the free university, historically the fountainhead of free ideas and scientific discovery, has experienced a revolution in the conduct of research. Partly because of the huge costs involved, a Government contract becomes virtually a substitute for intellectual curiosity.

For every old blackboard there are now hundreds of new electronic computers.

The prospect of domination of the nation's scholars by Federal employment, project allocations and the power of money is ever present, and is gravely to be regarded.

Yet, in holding scientific research and discovery in respect, as we should, we must also be alert to the equal and opposite danger that public policy could itself become the captive of a scientific-technological elite.

It is the task of statesmanship to mold, to balance, and to integrate these and other forces, new and old, within the principles of our democratic system—ever aiming toward the supreme goals of our free society.

94

Fred J. Cook
THE WARFARE STATE

Reprinted with permission of The Macmillan Company from The Warfare State *by Fred J. Cook, pp. 20–24.* © *1962 by Fred J. Cook.*

Fred J. Cook (1911–   ), journalist and author, is one of that crusading breed which can perhaps be best described as latter-day "muckrakers." A reporter and feature editor for the New York *World Telegram and Sun* from 1944 to 1959, he has been a freelance writer since that time. He is the author of such books as *The Warfare State* (1962), *The F.B.I. Nobody Knows* (1964), *The Corrupted Land* (1966), and *The Secret Rulers* (1966).

When even a warning as explicit as the one President Eisenhower delivered about the menace of the military-industrial complex leads only to a stronger and greater menace, it would seem only common sense to try to evaluate the resources and the power and the "insidious" influences of the Warfare State. What are some of the yardsticks? How does one assess them?

Anyone trying to answer such questions is promptly overwhelmed by the sheer, fantastic size of the military-industrial colossus. Here are some of the ways by which one may gauge it; but it must be emphasized that, awesome though the figures are, they have been in many instances already relegated to the inadequate past by the continuing upward spiral of military spending touched off by the Berlin crisis.

[1] Property owned by the Defense Department was valued in the Cordiner Report several years ago at $160 billion, "by any yardstick of measurement the world's largest organization." Though Secretary [of Defense Robert] McNamara had initiated a program of closing down some outmoded bases, the Pentagon still owns literally millions of acres of land. Its peak holdings covered more than 32 million acres in the United States and 2.6 million acres in foreign countries. This is an area larger than the combined states of Rhode Island, Delaware, Connecticut, New Jersey, Massachusetts, Maryland, Vermont and New Hampshire. The crowning symbol of military power is the vast Pentagon building, so huge that the Capitol, the seat of the nation's government, could be swallowed up easily in any one of its five principal segments.

[2] In the eight years of the Eisenhower administration, more than $350 billion was spent for defense. In the last Eisenhower years, annual military expenditures were pegged at around $46 billion, a figure that has now been dwarfed. The new Kennedy budget for 1962 calls for a military outlay of $52.7 billion. Another $3.7 billion was allotted to the space program. In the mammoth $92.5 billion total budget, appropriations for defense, space and international aid gobbled up 63 cents of every dollar. An additional six cents was accounted for by veterans services, and eight out of the ten cents spent for interest represents debts of military origin. When these sums are added together, it becomes apparent that some 77 cents of every dollar is being spent for past wars, the cold war and preparations for wars of the future. Inevitably, this cascade of billions funneled into the pockets of the Military has given the Pentagon an economic power that reaches into every nook and cranny of the nation. Military assets are three times as great as the combined assets of United States Steel, American Telephone and Telegraph, Metropolitan Life Insurance Company, General Motors and Standard Oil of New Jersey. The paid personnel of Defense is triple the number of employees of all these great corporations. Ironically, as a people, we have been little con-

cerned about the power and influence of the Pentagon, but we have in the past worried mightily lest General Motors or Standard Oil individually should become powerful enough to dictate national policy.

[3] The two tremendous power complexes of our Warfare State—the Military and Big Business—join in an inevitable meeting of minds over billions of dollars in contracts the one has to award and the other to fulfill. Of the total military budget for the 1960 fiscal year, some $21 billion was spent for the procurement of military goods and hardware. One hundred top corporations carved up three-quarters of this enormous pie. The top ten alone got $7.5 billion. Three corporations got more than $1 billion each—General Dynamics, $1.26 billion, and Lockheed and Boeing, each just over $1 billion. Two others, General Electric and North American Aviation, each got over $900 million.

[4] Such enormous rewards are conferred on a select few top companies at the whim of pro-curement officers: 86.4 per cent of the $21 billion in contracts was awarded without com-petitive bidding. This mere fact has led to inevitable suspicions of influence peddling. So far, proof is lacking, though the grounds for suspicion seem more than ample. Time and again, military officers who have been the cham-pions of a particular weapon or device in their official capacities retire and promptly become well-paid executives of the companies they have championed. The [Representative Felix] Hébert investigating committee of the House of Repre-sentatives found that more than 1,400 retired officers from the rank of major up were em-ployed by the top hundred corporations that feasted on three-quarters of the $21 billions spent for procurement. Included in this list were 261 generals or officers of flag rank. The company employing the greatest number was also—coincidentally, no doubt—the company that received the fattest contracts: General Dynamics. It had on its payroll 187 retired

officers, including 27 generals and admirals, and it was headed at the time by Frank Pace, him-self a former Secretary of the Army.

[5] This concentration of power at the top is reinforced by money benefits that spread throughout the economy. Subcontracts awarded by the top war contractors thread throughout the nation, trickle into virtually every city of any size. The jobs at stake mount high into the millions. The Defense Department alone employs 3.5 million persons, 947,000 of these civilians. Its annual payroll is $12 billion, more than twice that of the automobile industry, customarily considered the bellwether of the domestic economy. In addition, an estimated 4 million persons are employed directly in de-fense industries. This means that a total of some 7.5 million Americans depend for their jobs directly upon the Military—almost pre-cisely one-tenth of the nation's entire labor force. In some areas of especially heavy war plant employment, the percentage is far higher and dependence upon military spending is al-most total. The U.S. Arms Control and Dis-armament Agency, in the only thorough study so far made of the subject, has revealed some startling figures. It found that in 1959 aircraft-missile production accounted for at least 82 per cent of all manufacturing jobs in San Diego, 72 per cent in Wichita, 53 per cent in Seattle. Defense contracts alone accounted for from 20–30 per cent of all manufacturing employ-ment in the states of Kansas, Washington, New Mexico, California and Connecticut. Alaska, Hawaii, Virginia and the District of Columbia got from 10–26 per cent of their income di-rectly from Defense Department payrolls. The secondary effects of such dependence upon the Military as the prime source of jobs and cash is, of course, enormous. Defense industries pour some $5 billion annually into the state of California alone, and in Los Angeles, it has been estimated that fully half of all jobs depend, either directly or indirectly, on the

continuance of arms spending—and the arms race. In the nation as a whole, authorities estimate that between *one-quarter and one-third of all economic activity* hinges upon military spending and that, with further boosts in the military budget, this figure may reach a staggering 50 per cent. Under such circumstances, self-interest in military spending becomes a national disease. Under such circumstances, every food store, every gas station feels that it has a stake in keeping the war plants going. Under such circumstances, any cutback, even any threat of cutback, elicits screams of protest from workers who have jobs at stake, from a wide variety of businesses that have profits at stake, from politicians who have votes at stake.

Such is the face of the Warfare State.

95

Marc Pilisuk and Thomas Hayden
THE COMPLEX AS SOCIETY

From Marc Pilisuk and Thomas Hayden, "Is There a Military Industrial Complex Which Prevents Peace?: Consensus and Countervailing Power in Pluralistic Systems," Journal of Social Issues, Vol. XXI, No. 3 (1965), pp. 67–68, 87–93, 98–99; also published in Robert Perrucci and Marc Pilisuk, The Triple Revolution (Boston: Little Brown, 1968).

Marc Pilisuk (1934–   ), a student of social and clinical psychology, was an associate professor at Purdue from 1965 to 1967, when he was appointed professor of psychology at the University of California, Berkeley. He is co-editor (with Robert Perrucci) of *The Triple Revolution: Social Problems in Depth* (1968).

Thomas Hayden (1940–   ) has been a prominent, if increasingly radical leader of the New Left movement in the United States for almost a decade. In 1962, while a student at the University of Michigan, he helped to write the Port Huron Statement, the founding document of the Students for a Democratic Society (SDS).

At the present time he and four other members of the "Chicago Seven" are appealing conviction for "crossing state lines with intent to incite riot" at the 1968 Democratic National Convention.

The term "military-industrial complex" is very much in the literature. If its most sinister depictions are correct, then the peace researcher who works with the hope that his research may actually improve chances for world peace is wasting his time. A research finding, like a bit of knowledge, is always double-edged in what it portends for application. The project which tells us the surest steps to peace, tells us with equal certainty the steps which must be by-passed if peace is shunned. If there exists an omnipotent elite, committed to militarism, then there is simply no basis for hope that voices for peace have gotten, or can get, an influential channel into inner policy circles. If, on the other hand, the pluralist thesis [that power is scattered among various countervailing groups] can be said to apply in full even to basic policy directions of preparedness for war or for peace, then some influential decision makers must be eagerly awaiting the research findings on paths to peace with intentions to press for their immediate application.

Because we agree with neither of the above positions, because we believe that most research workers in this area tend either to ignore or to over-rate the potential consequences of their work to peace, and because we feel that consideration of the conditions which dictate major directions of policy is essential for an evaluation of any contribution to peace research, we are bringing the concept of the "military-industrial complex" to both the microscope and the scalpel. The implications of this inquiry point to a research approach which does have relevance to the decision process and to the most central agencies of social change, and resistance to change, within American society. . . .

. . . [In contradistinction to the theorists of elitism and pluralism, we believe] that *the constant pattern in American society is the rise and fall of temporarily-irresponsible groups.* By temporary we mean that, outside of the largest industrial conglomerates, the groups which wield significant power to influence policy decisions are not guaranteed stability. By irresponsible we mean that there are many activities within their scope which are essentially unaccountable in the democratic process. These groups are too uneven to be described with the shorthand term "class." Their personnel have many different characteristics (compare IBM executives and the Southern Dixiecrats) and their needs as groups are different enough to cause endless fights as, for example, small vs. big business. No one group or coalition of several groups can tyrannize the rest as is demonstrated, for example, in the changing status of the major financial groups, particularly the fast-rising Bank of America which has been built from the financial needs of the previously-neglected small consumer.

However, it is clear that these groups exist within consensus relationships of a more general and durable kind than their conflict relationships. This is true, first of all, of their social characteristics. The tables which follow combine data from Suzanne Keller's compilation of military, economic, political and diplomatic elite survey materials in *Beyond the Ruling Class* (1963) and from an exhaustive study of American elites contained in [W. F.] Warner, et al., *The American Federal Executive* (1963). Data on elites vary slightly from study to study because of varying operational definitions of the elite population. However, the data selected here are fairly representative and refer exclusively to studies with major data collected within the decade of the fifties. . . .

TABLE 1
Social Characteristics of American Elites

Elite	Nativity % Foreign Born	Rural-Urban % Urban Born[a]	Religion % Protestant	Education % College Grads.
Military	2%	30–40%[c]	90	73–98%[c]
Economic	6	65	85	61
Political	2	48	81	91
Diplomatic	4	66	60	81
U.S. Adult Males	7[b]	42[d]	65	7[b]

[a] Towns of 2,500 or more. [b] 30 years of age and older. [c] Taking the services separately. [d] 1910 U.S. Population

The relevant continuities represented in this data suggest an educated elite with an emphasis upon Protestant and business-oriented origins. Moreover, the data suggest inbreeding with business orientation in backgrounds likely to have been at least maintained, if not augmented, through marriage. The consistencies suggest orientations not unlike those which are to be found in examination of editorial content of major business newspapers and weeklies and in more directly sampled assessments of elite opinions.

TABLE 2
Father's Occupation

	Civilian federal executives	Military executives	Business leaders	Total U.S. male pop. 1930
Unskilled Laborer	4%	2%	5%	33%
Skilled Labor	17	12	10	15
White-Collar (clerk or sales)	9	9	8	12
Foreman	5	5	3	2
Business Owner	15	19	26	7
Business Executive	15	15	23	3
Professional	19	18	14	4
Farm owner or manager	14	9	8	16
Farm tenant or worker	1	1	1	6
Other	1	1	2	2

The second evidence of consensus relationships, besides attitudes and background data indicating a pro-business sympathy, would come from an examination of the *practice* of decision making. By analysis of such actual behavior we can understand which consensus attitudes are reflected in decision-making. Here, in retrospect, it is possible to discover the values and assumptions which are defended recurrently. This is at least a rough means of finding the boundaries of consensus relations. Often these boundaries are invisible because of the very infrequency with which they are tested. What are visible most of the time are the parameters of conflict relationships among different groups. These conflict relationships constitute the ingredients of experience which give individuals or groups their uniqueness and varieties, while the consensus relations constitute the common underpinnings of behavior. The tendency in social science has been to study decision-making in order to study group differences; we need to study decision-making also to understand group commonalities.

Were such studies done, our hypothesis would be that certain "core beliefs" are continuously unquestioned. One of these, undoubtedly, would be that efficacy is preferable to principle in foreign affairs. In practice, this means that violence is preferable to non-violence as a means of defense. A second is that private property is preferable to collective property. A third assumption is that the particular form of constitutional government which is practiced within the United States is preferable to any other system of government. We refer to the preferred mode as limited parliamentary democracy, a system in which institutionalized forms of direct representation are carefully retained but with fundamental limitations placed upon the prerogatives of governing. Specifically included among the areas of limitation are many matters encroaching upon corporation property and state hegemony. While adherence to this form of government is conceivably the strongest of the domestic "core values," at least among business elites, it is probably the least strongly held of the three on the international scene. American relations with, and assistance for, authoritarian and semi-feudal regimes occurs exactly in those areas where the recipient regime is evaluated primarily upon the two former assumptions and given rather extensive leeway on the latter one.

The implications of these "core beliefs" for the social system are immense, for they justify the maintenance of our largest institutional structures: the military, the corporate economy, and a system of partisan politics which protects the concept of limited democracy. These institutions, in turn, may be seen as current agencies of the more basic social structure. We use the term "social structure" as Robert S. Lynd does as the stratification of people identified according to kinship, sex, age, division of labor, race, religion, or other factors which differentiate them in terms of role, status, access to resources, and power. According to Lynd:

> This structure established durable relations that hold groups of people together for certain purposes and separate them for others. Such social structures may persist over many generations. Its continuance depends upon its ability to cope with historical changes that involve absorption of new groupings and relations of men without fundamental change in the structure of the society of a kind that involves major transfer of power (Robert S. Lynd and Helen Merrill, *Middletown*, New York, 1959).

The "renewable basis of power" in America at the present time underlies those institutional orders linked in consensus relationships: military defense of private property and parliamentary democracy. These institutional orders are not permanently secure, by definition. Their maintenance involves a continuous coping with new conditions, such as technological innovation and with the inherent instabilities of a social structure which arbitrarily classifies persons by role, status, access to resources, and power. The myriad groups composing these orders are even less secure because of their weak ability to command "coping resources," e.g., the service branches are less stable than the

institution of the military, particular companies are less stable than the institutions of corporate property, political parties are less stable than the institution of parliamentary government.

In the United States there is no ruling group. Nor is there any easily discernible ruling institutional order, so meshed have the separate sources of elite power become. But there is a social structure which is organized to create and protect power centers with only partial accountability. In this definition of power we are avoiding the [Max] Weber-[C. Wright] Mills meaning of *omnipotence* and the contrary pluralist definition of power as consistently *diffuse*. We are describing the current system as one of overall "minimal accountability" and "minimal consent." We mean that the role of democratic review, based on genuine popular consent, is made marginal and reactive. Elite groups are minimally accountable to publics and have a substantial, though by no means maximum, freedom to shape popular attitudes. The reverse of our system would be one in which democratic participation would be the orienting demand around which the social structure is organized.

Some will counter this case by saying that we are measuring "reality" against an "ideal," a technique which permits the conclusion that the social structure is undemocratic according to its distance from our utopian values. This is a convenient apology for the present system, of course. We think it possible, at least in theory, to develop measures of the undemocratic in democratic conditions, and place given social structures along a continuum. These measures, in rough form, might include such variables as economic security, education, legal guarantees, access to information, and participatory control over systems of economy, government, and jurisprudence.

The reasons for our concern with democratic process in an article questioning the power of a purported military-industrial complex are twofold. First, just as scientific method both legitimizes and promotes change in the world of knowledge, democratic method legitimizes and promotes change in the world of social institutions. Every society, regardless of how democratic, protects its core institutions in a web of widely shared values. But if the core institutions should be dictated by the requisites of military preparedness, then restrictions on the democratic process, i.e., restrictions in either mass opinion exchange (as by voluntary or imposed news management) or in decision-making bodies (as by selection of participants in a manner guaranteeing exclusion of certain positions), . . . would be critical obstacles to peace.

Second, certain elements of democratic process are inimical to features of militarily oriented society, and the absence of these elements offers one type of evidence for a military-industrial complex even in the absence of a ruling elite. Secretary of Defense Robert McNamara made the point amply clear in his testimony in 1961 before the Senate Armed Services Committee:

> Why should we tell Russia that the Zeus development may not be satisfactory? What we ought to be saying is that we have the most perfect anti-ICBM system that the human mind will ever devise. Instead the public domain is already full of statements that the Zeus may not be satisfactory, that it has deficiencies. I think it is absurd to release that level of information. (*Military Procurement Authorization Fiscal Year 1962*)

Under subsequent questioning McNamara attempted to clarify his statement that he only wished to delude Russian, not American, citizens about U.S. might. Just how this might be done was not explained. . . .

Is there, then, a military-industrial complex which prevents peace? The answer is inextricably imbedded into the mainstream of American institutions and mores. Our concept is not that American society contains a ruling military-industrial complex. Our concept is more nearly that American society *is* a military-industrial complex. It can accommodate a wide range of factional interests from those concerned with the production or utilization of a particular weapon to those enraptured with the mystique of optimal global strategies. It can accommodate those with rabid desires to advance toward the brink and into limitless intensification of the arms race. It can even accommodate those who wish either to prevent war or to limit the destructiveness of war through the gradual achievement of arms control and disarmament agreements. What it cannot accommodate is the type of radical departures needed to produce enduring peace.

96

H. L. Nieburg
A CABAL OF VESTED INTERESTS

Reprinted by permission of Quadrangle Books, Inc., from In the Name of Science *by H. L. Nieburg, pp. 184–189, 196–198. Copyright © 1966 by H. L. Nieburg.*

Harold L. Nieburg (1927–   ) has taught political science at the University of Wisconsin, Milwaukee, since 1963, and has devoted himself to such topics as the social implications of technology, the role of pressure and interest groups, and the structure of international affairs. His publications include *Nuclear Secrecy and Foreign Policy* (1964), *In the Name of Science* (1966), and *Political Violence* (1969).

American society has shown considerable resilience in adapting to rapid change. When need arises, an existing institution leaps to meet it, becoming quite a different institution in the process. In recent years the industrial corporation, which "began life as a sort of legal trick to spread the ownership of industrial equipment over a lot of people," has evolved into a routine and immensely powerful method of organizing large undertakings. But the relationship between individuals and corporations has been greatly modified by the overshadowing concentration of corporate power. Government has ceased to be merely a passive arbiter of "the rules of the game" and is forced to become an omnipresent force for balancing the competition for values and controlling the dynamics of social change.

Government has become the economy's largest buyer and consumer. The government contract, improvised, ad hoc, and largely unexamined, has become an increasingly important device for intervention in public affairs, not only to procure goods and services but to achieve a variety of explicit or inadvertent policy ends—allocating national resources, organizing human efforts, stimulating economic activity, and distributing status and power. The government contract has risen to its present prominence as a social management tool since World War II, achieving in two decades a scope and magnitude that now rival simple subsidies, tariffs, taxes, direct regulation, and positive action programs in their impact upon the nature and quality of American life. This evolution has occurred quietly and gradually through a series of improvised reactions to specific problems. Its central role has been achieved without public consideration of far-reaching social and political implications. Even today there is precious little consciousness of the trend; political leaders tend to see each contract as an isolated procurement action, overlooking the general pattern. Just as federal grants-in-aid to state and local governments have (since 1933) become principal means for national integration of divided local jurisdictions, so federal contracting with private cor-

porations is creating a new kind of economic federalism.

The implications of grants-in-aid have acquired some clarity: state taxation still takes care of traditional functions, while new and greatly expanded activities devolve upon local bodies through national decision-making, the states operating more and more as administrative districts for centrally established policies. Here, decision-making is nationalized under the constraints of public attention and democratic politics. On the other hand, economic federalism based upon contracts holds implications that are far from clear. To some degree, the forms and effects of contracting evade the forums of democracy, obscuring the age-old conflict between private and public interests. Mobilized to serve national policy, private contractors interpenetrate government at all levels, exploiting the public consensus of defense, space, and science to augment and perpetuate their own power, inevitably confusing narrow special interests with those of the nation.

Explicit authority for the U.S. government to conduct its business by contract is not found in the Constitution but has historically been accepted as a means of achieving explicitly constitutional objectives. There is ample precedent, such as the use of railroads for troop movements, or General McClellan's arrangements with the Pinkerton Detective Agency for espionage against the Southern Confederacy.

What is new is the persistence and growth of government-industry contract relationships under which, in the words of David E. Bell (then director of the Budget Bureau), "numbers of the nation's most important business corporations do the bulk of their work with the government." The Martin Company, for example, does 99 percent of its business with the government. Bell asked: "Well, is it a private agency or is it a public agency?" Organized as a private corporation and "philosophically . . . part of the private sector," yet "it obviously has a different relationship to governmental decisions and the government's budget . . . than was the case when General Motors or U.S. Steel sold perhaps 2 or 5 percent of their annual output to government bodies." Except in time of war, the government traditionally has not been the dominant customer for any private firm. The contract state of the postwar world must be viewed as a drastic innovation full of unfamiliar portents.

Grandiose claims are heard on all sides for the "unique contribution" that the contract mechanism has made in preserving "the free enterprise system" at a time when it could have been damaged. Atomic energy has been cited as an example of the new collaboration: "Without contracts, it would be government-owned and operated. With contracts, one person in sixteen in the industry works for government; the other fifteen work for contractors." An aerospace journal cites space technology as "the fastest moving, typically free-enterprise and democratic industry yet created," achieving these values "not on salesmanship" (that is, traditional quality/cost competitiveness) but "on what is needed most—intellectual production, the research payoff." Lyndon B. Johnson, while Vice President, argued: "If we want to maintain credibility of our claim to the superiority of a free political system—and a free private enterprise system—we cannot seriously entertain the thought of precipitating now so massive a disillusionment as would follow a political default on our commitments in space exploration."

The government contract has made it possible to perform new tasks deemed essential without direct additions to the size of federal government, thus preserving the alleged rights of private property and profit. But these huzzahs ignore the real ambiguity of the system that is emerging—neither "free" nor "competitive," in which the market mechanism of supply/demand (the price seeking the level which best serves overall productivity and social needs) has been abolished for key sectors of the economy, its place taken by the process of government policy and political influence. Instead of a free enterprise system, we are moving toward a government-subsidized private-profit system.

Unlike older government-fostered industries, the new contractor empire operates without the yardsticks of adequate government in-house capability or a civilian market in areas where research and development has become *the* critical procurement and the crux of the system. As described in the 1962 Bell Report: The companies involved "have the strongest incentives to seek contracts for research and development work which will give them both the know-how and the preferred position to seek later follow-on production contracts." Favored corporations that win R & D work thereafter exploit a number of special advantages: They may achieve sole-source or prime contractor status, which eliminates competition and dilutes all cost and performance evaluation. The open-end, cost-plus nature of the contract instrument, the lack of product specifications, official tolerance of spending overruns, all of which increase the total contract and fee (in a sense rewarding wasteful practices and unnecessary technical complication), permit violation of all rules of responsible control and make possible multiple tiers of hidden profits. The systems-management or prime contractor role enables favored companies to become powerful industrial brokers using unlimited taxpayer funds and contract awards to strengthen their corporate position, cartelize the contract market, and exert political influence.

In less than a decade the area surrounding Washington, D.C., has become one of the nation's major R & D concentrations. Every large corporation has found it necessary to establish field offices in proximity to NASA, the Pentagon, and Capitol Hill. Most of these new installations emphasize public relations and sales rather than research and development. The Washington area now ranks first in the nation for scientific personnel (per 1,000 population), although the major product is company promotion and politics rather than science.

The gross figures provide an index of the economic impact: the 1966 federal budget called for $23.7 billion in new obligational authority for defense and space—$11.4 billion for Defense Department procurement of hardware and control systems, $6.7 billion for R & D; $5.26 billion for NASA (virtually all R & D), and an additional $272 million for space-related R & D conducted by the Weather Bureau, the National Science Foundation, and the Atomic Energy Commission. Over 90 percent of this flows to the highly concentrated aerospace industry. Another $3.3 billion was budgeted for other kinds of R & D, making a total of $27 billion. The 1967 budget allocated more than $30 billion to aerospace. Space, defense, and R & D together now comprise the single most substantial allocation of federal funds, towering over all other programs. In the mid-1960's, government R & D (excluding related procurement) stabilized between 2 and 3 percent of the GNP. Cumulative missile/space spending in the decade which began in 1955 amounted to over $100 billion (Defense Department, $84 billion; NASA, $18 billion), and the remainder of the sixties will add at least an additional $125 billion. Virtually every department and agency of the federal government is involved to some extent in R & D contracting, although the Defense Department and NASA account for more than 96 percent.

The first result of this staggering outpour has been the artificial inflation of R & D costs which has enabled contractors to raid the government's own in-house resources. Officials in the lower reaches of the government bureaucracy (both civilian and military), charged with administration of contracts, find themselves dealing with private corporate officials who often were their own former bosses and continue as companions of present bosses and congressional leaders who watchdog the agencies. A contract negotiator or supervisor must deal with men who can determine his career prospects; through contacts, these industrial contractors may cause him to be passed over or transferred to a minor position in some remote bureaucratic corner, sometimes with a ceremonial drumming before a congressional committee.

The military cutbacks that characterized the Eisenhower years were accompanied by expanding military budgets, a paradox explained by the systematic substitution of private contractors to carry out historically in-house activities. This trend was heralded as a move back to "free enterprise." Government installations and factories built in World War II were sold to industry, usually at a fraction of the taxpayers' investment. Others were leased at low fees to contractors who were then given government business to make the use of these facilities profitable. In some instances government built new facilities which it leased at nominal fees. Such facilities were permitted to be used, without cost, for commercial production as well.

The splurge of mobilizing private contractors for government work occurred as a part of the unprecedented growth of the Air Force. As an offspring of the Army, the new branch lacked the substantial in-house management, engineering, and R & D capability that the Army had built into its arsenal system. The Air Force sought to leapfrog this handicap in competing for jurisdiction over new weapons systems, turning to private contractors to correct the defect. In its rapid climb during the fifties, the Air Force fostered a growing band of private companies which took over a substantial part of regular military operations, including maintaining aircraft, firing rockets, building and maintaining launching sites, organizing and directing other contractors, and making major public decisions. In the area of missilery, junior officers and enlisted men were subordinated to the role of liaison agents or mere custodians.

This had several bonus effects, enabling the Air Force to keep its military personnel levels down in conformity with Defense Department and administration policies, while building an enormous industrial and congressional constituency with a stake in maintaining large-scale funding of new weapons systems. The Air Force's success over her sister services during the Eisenhower years established the magic formula that all federal agencies soon imitated. It set in motion a rush to contract out practically everything that was not nailed to the floor and, in the process, it decimated the government's in-house management, engineering, and R & D capability; inflated the costs of R & D through futile contests for supremacy among contractors financed by contract funds; and as a consequence reduced as well the scientific and engineering resources available to the civilian economy and to the universities. . . .

The quasi-governmental mercantilist corporations, maintained in a position of monopoly power through royal franchises, were anathema to the classical liberals. Thomas Hobbes compared them to "worms in the entrails of man," and [James] Madison in *The Federalist* dealt at length with the problems of limiting their growth. At the end of the nineteenth century Henry Adams emphasized the origin of the corporation as an agency of the state, "created for the purpose of enabling the public to realize some social or national end without involving the necessity for direct governmental administration."

During the second half of the nineteenth century the corporation proved a powerful vehicle for mobilizing and organizing productive resources to achieve rapid economic growth made possible by burgeoning technology. Its very success, the efficiencies of bigness, and the inevitable politics of corporate empire-building thrust into American skies the spires of monopoly power. Since that time sectional and economic interests have shifted and changed, the social and technological landscape has vastly altered, and government has emerged as guarantor of social interests against the claims of private power. Government contracting on its present scale has added another dimension. Business and industry have always been close to the centers of political power, but never before in peacetime have they enjoyed such a broad acceptance of their role as a virtual fourth branch of government—a consensus generated by the permanent crisis of international diplomacy. Sheltered by this consensus, government has accepted responsibility to maintain the financial status of its private contractors as essential to U.S. defense and economic health. Cost competitiveness, the traditional safeguard against corporate power and misallocation of national resources, has been suspended by R & D contract practices.

NASA and the Pentagon use their contracting authority to broaden the productive base in one area, maintain it in another, create more capability here or there for different kinds of R & D, create competition or limit it. Under existing laws they may make special provisions for small business and depressed areas and maintain contracts for services not immediately required in order to preserve industrial skills or reserve capacity for emergency needs. All of this represents national planning.

But without recognition of planning as a legitimate government responsibility, planning authority is fragmented, scattered among federal agencies and Congress, and the makeshift planning that results serves the paramount interests of the most powerful political alignments. In place of forward planning responsible to the broad national community, the nation drifts sideways, denying the legitimacy of planning, yet backhandedly planning in behalf of narrow special interests whose corridors of power are closed to public control.

The result is severe distortion in the allocation of resources to national needs. For almost three decades the nation's resources have been commanded by military needs, consolidating political and economic power behind defense priorities. What was initially sustained by emergency comes to be sustained, normalized, and institutionalized (as emergency wanes) through a cabal of vested interests. The failure of nerve on the part of these interests to redirect this magnificent machine toward a broader range of values denies the nation what may be the ultimate basis of diplomatic strength and the only means to maintain the impetus of a mature economy, namely the fullest enjoyment by all of our people of the immense bounty of equity and well-being almost within our grasp.

The shibboleths of free enterprise perpetuate a system by which, one by one, the fruits of the civilian economy fall into the outstretched hands of the aerospace group. The so-called "Great Consensus" assembled by President Johnson is based on the paradox of support from great corporate giants as well as from labor and the Liberals. The civilian economy and home-town industry have been systematically neglected in the vicious circle of government contracts and economic concentration, leading the small businessman, vast numbers of middle-management, white-collar workers, and

professional groups to embrace the simple formulas of [Barry] Goldwater conservatism, directing the anxieties generated by incipient stagnation against the targets of autocratic organized labor and government spending for welfare and foreign aid. The exploitation of the myths of free enterprise has deflected attention from the feudal baronies of economic power and the tendency of the administration to attack the symptoms of growing inequality of wealth without disturbing the steepening slope itself.

The dynamics of the Contract State require close scrutiny lest, in the name of national security and the science-technology race, the use of the nation's resources does violence not only to civilian enterprise but also to the body politic. In place of sensational claims about the ability of the American system to meet the challenges of new tasks and rapid technological change, it is necessary to judge the appropriateness and adequacy of national policies that increasingly raise a question concerning the relation between government and private contractor: who is serving whom?

97

Kenneth Boulding
ENVIRONMENTAL PRESSURES

From Kenneth Boulding, "The Role of the War Industry in International Conflict," Journal of Social Issues, Vol. XXIII, No. 1 (1967), pp. 52–56.

Kenneth Boulding (1910–   ) is a distinguished economist with many interests outside his own discipline, most notably in the fields of peace research and international systems. A professor of economics at the University of Colorado since 1967, he had previously held teaching positions at Fisk, Iowa State, McGill, and, for eighteen years, the University of Michigan. He has written more than a dozen books, including *The Economics of Peace* (1946), *A Reconstruction of Economics* (1950), *The Image* (1956), *The Meaning of the Twentieth Century* (1964), *The Impact of the Social Sciences* (1966), and *The Organizational Revolution* (1968).

. . . Decisions as to the amount of the defense budgets in any nation emerge as a result of a long and complex process of political compromise, proposals and counter-proposals, rising up through the hierarchy of decision making until some final decision is made at the top. The checks and balances involved in this process are of enormous significance. By and large it is fair to assume that as in any budget-making process, those who are the principal and immediate beneficiaries of budget increases will press for them, and those who are concerned with large issues and larger agendas will tend to cut them down. This seems to be a practically universal principle of budget formation; and as the size of the war industry, unlike that of industries serving consumers, is determined almost entirely by a budget process and not by a market process, budget formation is obviously the key to the overall dynamics of the situation.

There is great need for empirical study of the process of budget formation in military budgets, for as far as I know there has been practically no work, at least of an objective character, in this field. The most one can do is to suggest some hypotheses which might be tested by such studies. One such hypothesis is that there are two large constellations of forces affecting a total budget. One consists of the forces of the internal environment, which almost continuously make for budget increase. Every department within any organization always feels that it could do a much better job if it had a somewhat larger budget. Hence the first step in budget making, which is the col-

lection of proposals from departments and units of an organization, always results in a total budget proposal which will almost certainly be larger than that finally arrived at; and it will almost always result in an increase in budgets over last year, or whatever is the budget period. As these budget proposals move up through the hierarchy of the organization, they are met by another set of forces representing the external environment. At the lower levels of the organization and in its smaller units, these external forces are likely to be weak, though there may be some exceptions to this, in the case of units which are specialized in contact with the external environment, such as, for instance, staff units. Even where the external environment is perceived, however, at these lower levels, there is likely to be distortion of perception which gives a bias towards budget increases rather than budget decreases. As the budget moves up through the hierarchy of the organization from departments to divisions to larger and larger units and aggregates, the external environment becomes more important, and in the final decision the external environment may dominate.

Thus in the case of a state university, the external environment of the legislature is remote at the level of the department, highly salient to the level of the President. Similarly in the case of the defense budget, the external environment may not be very important at the lower levels but becomes extremely important at the top. Generally speaking, therefore, we can suppose that there is an upward bias in budget formation in all organizations, including defense organizations, and that it takes rather an unusual perception of the external environment to bring about budget cuts. In the case of defense establishments, this happens, for instance, at the end of a war, particularly a victorious war, when the international system is suddenly perceived as being much less threatening; decisions to reduce the establishment drastically are made at the top, perhaps in response also to a perception of the internal domestic environment of the country (the "bring the boys home" mood); and the lower echelons of the organization are quite defenseless against the overall budget reduction. Circumstances of this kind, however, are unusual, and in normal circumstances the structure of budget formation, in defense as in other organizations, tends to give an upward bias towards a constant increase.

. . . this means that the coefficients of militarism . . . under ordinary circumstances tend to rise year after year, which leads further to diminishing the chances of stability in the system. The one factor which tends to counteract this is stinginess on the part of civilian government, in response either to the personal prejudices of the decision makers or in response to political pressures from the civilian population. An increase in military budgets must result either in increased taxation, in inflation or in reduction of civilian budgets. There will be political pressures against all these three reactions, and if the ultimate decision-maker is highly sensitive to these pressures, the forces making for increase in military budgets will be correspondingly damped. A study of the Eisenhower period, 1952–1960, for instance, indicates that one of the major factors in damping the arms race in this period was the "stinginess" [of] President Eisenhower, who had strong personal prejudices against increasing public expenditures in general, and who therefore held down military budgets out of sheer parsimony. This substantially increased the stability of the international system, and almost certainly gave us a kind of equilibrium which a more spendthrift, energetic President could easily have destroyed. It is an indescribably tragic commentary on the nature of a system of unilateral national defense that almost the

only way in which it can be workable is through the major decision makers being rather stingy, insensitive and unreactive.

One of the crucial factors in the decision-making and the budget-making process here is the extent to which the defense establishment is under civilian political control or the extent to which the defense establishment itself makes the final decisions about the government budget. By and large, the hypothesis may be put forward that civilian control strengthens the damping forces on budget formation and is likely to result in smaller coefficients and to increase the possibility of an equilibrium of the unilateral defense system; whereas under military control of final budgets, we are likely to see a much greater sensitivity to increase in the budgets of other countries, that is, high reaction coefficients, and we are also likely to see an insensitivity to civilian demands on the budget, which is likely to result in high coefficients of militarism.

The role in a society of what might be called the private sector of the war industry, that is, the industrial part of the industrial-military complex, may also be relevant. . . . In the 1930's, the view that war was mainly a product of the armament manufacturers was very popular. One recalls, for instance, the Nye investigations and the Johnson Acts. This, however, seems now to be a gross oversimplification. It is certainly true that armaments manufacturers represent, as it were, an upward pressure in the formation of military budgets. Under most circumstances, however, this pressure is fairly small compared with the enormous pressures imposed by the external military and political environment and the rest of the internal political environment, as represented by the competing claims on the overall budget. There is, indeed, a dangerous change in this respect in the United States, as we have become a relatively militarized nation. Before the Second World War there was really nothing that could be called a specialized armaments industry. Most of the suppliers of the Department of Defense, such as Dupont, General Motors, and so on, were primarily engaged in the production and sale of consumer goods, and were what might be called consumer-oriented organizations. Since the end of the Second World War, we have seen the rise of firms like General Dynamics and most of the airframe companies, which are not consumer-oriented at all, and which make almost their entire sales to the Department of Defense. There is a recognition among these firms that the defense industry is an unstable customer and that in the interests of their own survival, it would be advisable for them to diversify their activities into civilian markets. Many of them, however, have had some unfortunate experiences with this activity, simply because the kind of organization which is well adapted at selling things to government, which is, shall we say, an understanding and sympathetic customer, is not well adapted to selling things in the hard cold world of the civilian market. Even so, there is not much evidence that as a political pressure group, especially in Congress, the private sector of the war industry in any way dominates defense decisions.

There is a more subtle problem in this connection, which may be of more importance. In the economic folklore of the United States especially, there is a widespread belief that it is only the defense industry which save us from depression. We were half grateful to Hitler and the Japanese for getting us out of the Great Depression of the '30's, and this memory is still strong in the minds of the generation of powerful decision-makers today. The association of peace with unemployment is particularly strong in the labor movement, which accounts at least

in part for its almost total loss of idealism, and the fact that it is the principal drum-beater for the Cold War. The problem of economic adjustments to disarmament, or even to changes within the war industry, is a real one. Nevertheless, with the resources which we now have, it is soluble, given reasonably sensible economic policy. Indeed the American economy is quite astonishingly flexible and adjustable, provided it does not run into deflation; and as deflation can very easily be avoided by monetary and fiscal policy, the association of war with prosperity has now been broken. A good example of this adjustability can be seen in the experience of Michigan. In 1958 the war industry largely moved out of Michigan to California. Temporarily, the results were almost catastrophic. Unemployment in Michigan, for instance, rose from about 5% of the labor force in the summer of 1957 to 16% of the labor force in the summer of '58. By the late summer of '59, however, it had recovered almost to its 1957 level, and after a secondary recession in 1961, under the stimulus of the tax cut it fell to around 3% by the summer of 1965, in spite of the fact that the overall size of the defense industry was fairly stable.

I am not suggesting, of course, that this problem is unimportant. If, for instance, there was a drastic reduction of defense expenditure in the United States, there would be serious local depressions, especially on the West Coast. Unless the reduction in defense expenditure was accompanied by a substantial budget deficit and an easy monetary policy, these local depressions might easily cumulate into an overall deflation. If the overall level of demand, however, is taken care of, the evidence suggests that local adjustments, even without much in the way of government assistance, can be made in about the period of a year. The extraordinary ease with which economic adjustment was made to the great disarmament of 1945–46, which was by far the greatest disarmament in history, is further evidence of the extraordinary flexibility of the American economy. Nevertheless, it is not the reality but the image which dominates behavior, and as long as there is a prevailing folk image of the war industry as a source of prosperity, this is an important factor operating to resist a reduction in military budgets. Furthermore, in order to justify military budgets, we almost have to be reactive, and we have to interpret the messages which come from abroad as hostile. All this increases both the coefficients of militarism and the coefficients of reactivity, and even if it leads to an equilibrium position, the equilibrium has large military budgets.

98

Michael Getler
THE COMPLEX-COMPLEX

From Michael Getler, "The Complex-Complex," Aerospace Technology, Vol. 21 (January 1, 1968), p. 58.

Michael Getler (1935–   ), now of the National Affairs staff of the Washington *Post*, has previously served as editorial director of *Armed Forces Management* magazine, and prior to that, as editor and columnist for *Space/Aeronautics* magazine. He was a 1956 graduate of the City College of New York, and is a former naval aviator. Among his other writings is "The Proxmire-Nossiter Complex" in *Space/Aeronautics* (June 1967).

After eight years of generally unmemorable speechmaking, President Eisenhower, in his farewell address to the nation in January 1961, uncorked one of the most enduring passages of contemporary American politics.

"In the councils of Government," he said, "we must guard against the acquisition of un-

warranted influence, whether sought or unsought, by the military-industrial complex."

In offering this warning, the President also uncorked the longest playing public relations problem the U.S. defense industry has ever had to face.

"The military-industrial complex" has become a sinister phrase, and the attitude of distrust that it implies has created another kind of complex, this one in the minds of some Americans.

Mr. Eisenhower, no doubt, meant well. Unwarranted power anywhere is indeed dangerous, and the enormous growth of a permanent U.S. defense industry in the late 1950s in combination with a large peacetime military establishment was, as he stated, "new in the American experience."

What is most unfortunate about the President's remarks is that instead of being taken as a proper call for vigilance against the *potential* of misplaced power, they have for seven years been taken as established fact by an assortment of columnists and screen writers, politicians and professors to verify their own beliefs that the defense industry is inherently warmongering and profiteering and that the military is inherently brainless and immoral.

Actually, as things have turned out, President Eisenhower might well have been more astute had he warned this country about the medical-drug industry complex, or the legislative-oil industry complex.

If there is any profiteering going on in the U.S. these days, the boys who fret so about the complexes have got the wrong one.

The aerospace industry, which freely translates from what Mr. Eisenhower in 1961 called the defense industry, will show an estimated net profit in 1967, after taxes and expressed as a percentage of sales, of 2.6%, according to figures reported to the Securities and Exchange Commission. This represents a further decline from the 3.25% rate of 1965 and the 3% 1966 figure.

The 1967 figure might well have been even lower, except for the fact that many of the nation's alleged warmongers are trying hard to diversify into commercial markets, where they can make higher profits.

The industry's profit ratio in 1967 is roughly half that of the manufacturing segment of the economy taken as a whole (5.1%).

Profits per dollar of sales by the drug industry this year are running at about 10%. The petroleum industry tops all others, coming in at about 11%.

If there is a danger lurking within the business portion of the military-industrial complex, it may well be that defense will become so unprofitable that it is not worth pursuing at all.

And what of the claims that the moguls of the armaments industry are responsible for keeping the pressure on in Vietnam? Again, the facts do not sustain the charge.

There is a tendency to think that the $30 billion a year for Vietnam gets dumped directly into the coffers of defense firms. On the contrary, the vast bulk of the funds needed to support the war go for such things as paychecks for a larger Army and Marine Corps, for underwear and jungle boots, for shipping and construction and scores of items other than just helicopters and aircraft.

While the war is of course responsible for increased sales in some companies, the industry as a whole has little to fear from a halt in the fighting.

The Aerospace Industries Association estimates that only 12% of aerospace employment is tied to Vietnam, and that production funds flowing in total about $3 billion a year. Surely there is that much new business, both research and development and production, in the defense and space area that has been deferred because of the war spending.

One would be hard pressed, in fact, to define what is meant by a munitions lobby in today's industrial environment.

The U.S. defense industry is too broad to be classified as such. The search for diversification in new commercial markets is too widespread, too obvious. The number of basically commercial firms doing enormous amounts of business for the Dept. of Defense is large and growing.

A look at the list of 100 top Defense contractors for fiscal 1967 bears this out. Is General Electric, No. 4 on the list with military sales of about $1.3 billion, basically a defense contractor or a commercial firm? Is AT&T, No. 8 with $673 million in DOD sales, part of the complex? Is Westinghouse, No. 15 and $453 million, or Honeywell, or IBM, or ITT or Goodyear a party to that black art of military lobbying? Or are they really a part of an advanced technology industry in this country that responds to the requirements of the Dept. of Defense just as it tries to respond to the market for light bulbs and thermostats and computers? Would any of these companies be better off as corporations if the military constituted a large part of their sales? The answer is no.

The defense industry is the most controlled business in the U.S. It is dependent in many cases on one customer. Its profits are controlled and its market is subject to fluctuations over which normal business practices have no effect.

It is used unabashedly as an economic flywheel through which the Government can put money in and take money from the economy to offset other areas where there is less control. This is not altogether a bad thing for the Government, but it is often very difficult for the industry. It has not made this industry a favorite on Wall Street.

Yet it is this same industry upon which we are depending for our survival as a nation. It is this same industry, like it or not, that has fathered the enormous technological revolution of the past two decades and that has created not only an affluent society but a strong one.

The industry, in short, deserves to be treated with a little more respect.

99

Time
A VAST, AMORPHOUS CONGLOMERATION

"What Is the Military-Industrial Complex?" Time, Vol. 93 (April 11, 1969), p. 23. Reprinted by permission from TIME, The Weekly Newsmagazine. Copyright Time, Inc., 1969.

The military-industrial complex is at once more and less than the name implies. As a catch phrase, it may be on its way to surpassing in notoriety "merchants of death," the term that grew out of Senator Gerald Nye's investigation of the arms industry in 1934. But the complex is not a well-organized, centrally directed entity. It is a vast, amorphous conglomeration that goes far beyond the Pentagon and the large manufacturers of weapons. It includes legislators who benefit politically from job-generating military activity in their constituencies, workers in defense plants, the unions to which they belong, university scientists and research organizations that receive Pentagon grants. It even extends to the stores where payrolls are spent, and the landlords, grocers and car salesmen who cater to customers from military bases.

Any important shift of defense spending thus affects many interests and individuals. In fiscal 1968, the Defense Department contracted for $38.8 billion in goods and services, plus $6.5 billion for research and development, amounting to 5.3% of the 1968 G.N.P. These funds went to many thousands of prime contractors and subcontractors.

According to a recent estimate, 21% of skilled blue-collar workers and 16% of professional employees are on payrolls that rely on military spending. Entire communities depend almost totally on a military installation, defense plants, or both. Junction City, Kans. (pop. 20,500), lives off Fort Riley. The post pumps $143 million into the state's economy, most of it in the Junction City area. When an Army division left in 1965, business plummeted 30%.

Communities in this situation grow panicky. Yet some towns have survived the loss nicely. Presque Isle, Me., and Greenville, S.C., for instance, both managed to use land and facilities previously occupied by military installations for industrial development.

Generally, the effect of the M-I complex is to foster heavy defense spending and impede cutbacks, even in an inflationary period. Not at all by coincidence, the legislators who have the most to say about military spending—the chairmen of the Senate and House Armed Services and Appropriations Committees—have been blessed over the years with substantial military business in their states and districts. Congressman George Mahon (House Appropriations) can point to the fact that Texas gets more business from the military than any other state except California (which gets $6.6 billion a year). South Carolina's Mendel Rivers (House Armed Services) can, and frequently does note that his home town of Charleston thrives as a result of its huge shipbuilding facilities and naval installations.

The Defense Department spends almost $4,000,000 a year on congressional liaison, employing about 340 people for the task. One of their functions is to keep in close touch with members of Congress, providing such information as announcements of new contracts or construction in a particular member's bailiwick.

Representatives of the big firms, sometimes called MICs (for military-industrial complex), are often corporate vice presidents with six-figure salaries and generous expense accounts. They are usually not registered lobbyists, and they tend to be discreet in their operations, keeping their names out of the newspapers and avoiding lavish soirees. At private clubs in town, on country-club golf courses, sometimes on a farm in Maryland or Virginia, occasionally on a yacht, they entertain—and gather intelligence. To compete successfully, their companies have to know what the military is likely to want, what project is popular on Capitol Hill, who is really the best man to deal with.

The big contractors find the military an excellent source for such experts. Senator William Proxmire, one of the Pentagon's most persistent and effective critics, notes that 2,072 retired, highranking military officers are now on the payrolls of the 100 top defense contractors, a threefold increase in the past ten years. While Proxmire does not charge any overt impropriety, he and others wonder whether an officer dealing with a particular company is going to drive a very hard bargain if he may go to work for it soon.

What is the overall effect of the M-I complex? That depends on the viewpoint. Dwight Eisenhower warned of its "grave implications," while acknowledging the nation's "imperative need" for a vigorous defense industry. V. J. Adduci, vice president of the Aerospace Industries Association, says that it is not diabolical or secretive but exemplifies the "open, dynamic, fail-safe relationship between two viable segments of our society." Economist Arthur F. Burns, now a senior White House aide, has argued that the complex "has been affecting

profoundly the character of our society as well as the thrust and contours of economic activity." The effects, according to Burns, have been mostly negative: promoting excess government spending, stoking inflation, diverting resources from civilian needs, warping college curriculums, luring professors from teaching into research and breeding a class of civilian managers and scientists whose sole orientation is toward the government. The M-I complex is not really a complex; it is certainly no demon, no Mafia. But in view of the manifold problems it manages to create, without necessarily meaning to, it clearly bears close and constant surveillance.

100

Richard M. Nixon
THE ISSUE AS A STRAWMAN

From Richard M. Nixon, "Speech at the Air Force Academy," New York Times, *June 5, 1969, p. 30.* © *1969 by the New York Times Company. Reprinted by permission.*

Richard M. Nixon (1913–   ) delivered the following remarks in the course of an address at the Air Force Academy in June 1969. They were considered particularly significant at the time because they were pronounced by a new president in a period of heavy accusation regarding the "military-industrial complex" and of rising debate concerning the wisdom of Nixon's plan for an anti-ballistics missile (ABM) system.

. . . I must warn you that in the years to come you may hear your commitment to America's responsibility in the world derided as a form of militarism.

It is important that you recognize that strawman issue for what it is, the outward sign of a desire by some to turn America inward—and to have America turn away from greatness.

I am not speaking about those responsible critics who reveal waste and inefficiency in our defense establishment, who demand clear answers on procurement problems, who want to make sure a new weapons system will truly add to our defense.

On the contrary, you should be in the vanguard of that movement. Nor do I speak of those with sharp eyes and sharp pencils who are examining our post-Vietnam planning with other pressing national priorities in mind. I count myself as one of those.

But as your Commander in Chief, I want to relay to you as future officers of our armed forces some of my thoughts on these great issues of national moment.

I worked closely with President Eisenhower for eight years. I know what he meant when he said "we must guard against the acquisition of unwarranted influence, whether sought or unsought, by the military-industrial complex."

Many people conveniently forget that he followed that warning with another. "We must also be alert to the equal and opposite danger that public policy could itself become the captive of a scientific-technological elite."

And we sometimes forget that, in that same farewell address, President Eisenhower spoke of the need for national security. He said a vital element in keeping the peace is our military establishment. Our arms must be mighty, ready for instant action, so that no potential aggressor may be tempted to risk his own destruction.

And I say to you, my fellow Americans, let us never forget those wise words of one of America's greatest leaders.

The American defense establishment should never be a sacred cow. But on the other hand, the American military should never be anybody's scapegoat.

America's wealth is enormous, but it is not limitless. Every dollar available in the Federal Government has been taken from the American people in taxes. And a responsible government has a duty to be prudent when it spends the people's money.

There is no more justification for wasting money on unnecessary military hardware than there is for wasting it on unwarranted social programs.

And there can be no question that we should not spend unnecessarily for defense. But we must also not confuse our priorities.

The question, I submit, in defense spending is a very simple one. How much is necessary? . . .

101

Sidney Lens
A MEANS TO GLOBAL EXPANSION

From Sidney Lens, The Military-Industrial Complex *(Philadelphia, Pa. and Kansas City, Mo.: Pilgrim Press and the National Catholic Reporter, 1970), pp. 139–147.*

Sidney Lens (1912–   ), a director of the United Service Employees, AFL-CIO, from 1941 to 1966, has established a considerable reputation as a social commentator, journalist, and author. In recent years he has lectured on labor and foreign relations at a number of universities, served as a member of the board of the Chicago Council on Foreign Relations, and edited *Liberation* magazine. He has also written *Left, Right and Center* (1949), *A World in Revolution* (1956), *The Crisis of American Labor* (1959), and *Radicalism in America* (1966).

The debate on the military-industrial complex has begun, and on its outcome may depend not only the survival of the United States but the whole of humanity. It is certainly of greater urgency than the debate over the French Revolution in the 1790's, over slavery from 1830 to

1865, or over the depression of 1929. When the dust clears, the debate will hinge on a single question: Are the assumptions on which the military-industrial complex were created valid, partly valid, or totally false? Proponents of the first position—that the assumptions are valid—will urge economy in spending; proponents of the second position, that the military be "controlled" so that the nation can restructure its "priorities"; and proponents of the third position, that the complex is fighting the wrong war, at the wrong time, with the wrong weapons and must be entirely eliminated.

The argument that the Pentagon is wasteful and inefficient is an attractive one to large numbers of people who are worried about taxes and inflation. "It is responsibly asserted," editorializes the *Wall Street Journal*, "that $10 billion or more a year could be cut from the military budget without impairing national security." If the $10 billion could be chipped away, the economy would be healthier, the burdens on the American people lighter. This thesis may or may not be true (a cut in federal spending can *also* lead to unemployment), but it does not come to grips with more fundamental issues: Are the purposes for which the complex was created justified? Can we avoid a "garrison state" so long as it continues to exist? . . .

Liberals, in and out of Congress, couple their charge of waste with one about distorting national priorities. The problem, as Senator [William] Proxmire sees it, is "how can we balance our military needs and expenditures with our domestic problems and needs?" He accepts the thesis that we need *both* guns and butter, but holds that we are spending too much on one and too little on the other. What the nation requires, as the liberals see it, is not only to curtail waste and arrest inflation, but to meet pressing welfare demands for the underprivileged. A report of congressional dissidents who

met privately in June 1969 argued, therefore, that "if we are to increase substantially our expenditures on domestic needs, we must correspondingly reduce our expenditures on the military." Priorities can be reversed, they said, if Congress were to secure the necessary information to rebut the military and make a concerted campaign to win public support. They propose the formation of a Defense Review Office which would dig out defense information and analyze its significance for the legislators, and a Temporary National Security Committee, made up of congressmen, senators, and private citizens, to "conduct a critical examination . . . of the military-industrial establishment."

John Kenneth Galbraith, statesman, professor, and former national chairman of Americans for Democratic Action, speaks in the same vein. The cover of his recent book, *How to Control the Military*, carries the modest blurb that "when the Vietnam War ends, $6 to $7 billion could be freed to save our cities, feed the hungry, give all Americans a chance at a decent life." One may question whether $7 billion can do—or begin to do—all these wonderful things, but the liberals have concluded that by "controlling" the Pentagon they can redirect money from military coffers to useful social projects. The statement by Daniel P. Moynihan, President Nixon's special adviser for urban affairs, that programs already on the books "are going to eat up any revenue produced by the war's end," has not dissuaded them.

One way to effect the necessary controls, Galbraith suggests, would be through "a special body of highly qualified scientists and citizens to be called, perhaps, the Military Audit Commission." Its task would be "to advise the Congress and inform the public on military programs and negotiations." Congressman Robert L. Leggett of California proposes that the military can be curbed by allocating to it a specific share of the federal budget—"say 50 percent or 60 percent." Prof. Richard A. Falk, former consultant to the Senate Foreign Relations Committee, feels the figure can be trimmed to "between 10 and 25 percent of the present level," in other words to something between $8 and $20 billion a year, if the Pentagon is forced to assess realistically "the kinds of threats that confront the United States." Instead of "working for weapons breakthroughs," says Falk, "and designing against unlikely contingencies, we need to work for a stabilized arms environment sustained at a minimum cost and risk."

Implicit in the liberal critique is the notion that America *does* need a military establishment for defense, but it does not need one so large that it creates in its wake a self-propelling military-industrial bureaucracy which whittles away the power of Congress and the people. John Foster Dulles, oddly enough, made much the same point a long time ago, in a January 2, 1949 interview with *U.S. News & World Report*:

> I am inclined to think that we are exaggerating the percentage of our national income that needs to be diverted into military establishment. I think that there is, as I say, a risk of war, but I think the risk is not so great that we should seriously jeopardize our own economic health as a free society by saddling ourselves with such vast armament.

History shows, unfortunately, that the military spigot can be turned on much easier than it can be turned off. If a nation is ready to accept the simple theorems on which militarism is predicated—whether real or made to look real—each crisis will evoke the demand for "more." The "communist menace" conjured up after World War II made it possible to increase the peacetime military budget from prewar levels of a billion or less to $12 billion and $14 billion in the first postwar years. The Korean crisis of 1950 prompted Congress to give DOD authority to raise spending from $14.5 billion to $53.5 billion in a single year. Actual expenditures doubled from 1951 to 1952, from $20.7 billion to $41.3 billion. The Vietnam crisis in 1965 catapulted the Pentagon's spending from $50 billion a year to $80 billion four years later. If that budget is now slashed by $3 billion or the $7 to $10 billion that *realpolitik* liberals are urging, the *power* of the military-industrial complex will be affected only slightly. And its spokesmen and theoreticians will soon be scurrying for new "crises" on which to peg their argument for more preparedness.

In a world consumed by revolution and power struggles, crises crop up as frequently as the full moon. We must expect, says Prof. C. E. Black in his *Dynamics of Modernization*, "10 to 15 revolutions a year for the foreseeable future in the less developed societies." Each of these revolutions alters the international balance of power to some degree; each can break out into the kind of civil war which resulted in intervention in Vietnam. Henry A. Kissinger, White House national security advisor, has asked the Rand Corporation, according to Flora Lewis, to conduct studies on such subjects as "the danger and extent of insurgency in Thailand," "circumstances in which the government of Brazil might be overthrown if it decides to expropriate U.S. assets," and "circumstances in which U.S. nuclear weapons might be used in the Middle East." Obviously each of these is a crisis area which occupies the thoughts of President Nixon's key foreign policy aide, and under certain circumstances can be manufactured into a synthetic war scare. . . .

Those possibilities are inherent in the purpose of the military-industrial complex. The complex is not a popular force with disinterested goals. It is, instead, a conglomerate of elites—a military elite, an industrial elite, a banking elite, a labor elite, an academic elite—which seeks its own aggrandizement through global expansion. It has sponsored for that purpose what Hanson Baldwin calls "a surge of nationalism," the concept that "America ought to rule the world." Harry Truman defined it more specifically as assuring the dominance of free enterprise economies over regimented ones. In economic terms that means enlarging American trade and investment, as well as finding new sources of raw materials. In political terms it means aiding those regimes favorable to America's economic goals. In military terms it means nuclear deterrence (or damage limitation) to checkmate the only power capable of stymieing those ambitions, the Soviet Union. It translates itself inevitably into military bases around the world, military pacts, contingency agreements, and actual intervention where necessary and feasible, to help friendly regimes that are tottering or friendly forces that aspire to power against neutralists and Communists. The power elite that is now called the military-industrial complex has, in other words, fashioned a blueprint for "pax Americana" that would do for the twentieth century what "Pax Britannica" did for the nineteenth. It would create the international setting in which American private interests could advance unchecked. British historian, Arnold J. Toynbee, by no means anti-American or pro-Communist, describes America's present role as "leader of the worldwide anti-revolutionary movement in defense of vested interests."

It is no accident that Washington has been almost universally on the side of conservative forces in the developing areas—Syngman Rhee in Korea, Chiang Kai-shek in China, the Shah in Iran, the militarists throughout Latin America, the king in Jordan, the king in Saudi Arabia, the military regimes in Thailand, Laos, and Vietnam. These conservative elements, to secure their own "vested interests," have been willing to accept American military and economic support in return for concessions to American "vested interests." Nor is it an accident that by and large the same legislators—[John] Stennis, [Richard] Russell, [L. Mendel] Rivers, [Karl] Mundt, [Barry] Goldwater, [John] Tower, [John] McClellan, to name a few—who are the fiercest advocates of military spending and military ventures, are also the fiercest opponents of social programs such as medicare, higher minimum wages, antipoverty, social security, and favorable trade union legislation.

Put crassly, the military-industrial complex has defined America's goal as being the bastion of the status quo—abroad and at home. Given that national purpose it is folly to expect any *enduring controls* over the military establishment or the complex it fosters. If we believe in taxes we must have tax collectors, and if we believe in global expansion we must have a military-industrial complex. The restructuring of national priorities can only proceed with a repudiation of the complex's definition of national purpose and a re-education of the citizenry as to its folly.

The American people of course are not the authors of the expansionist policy and whatever they have gained from it is ephemeral and illusory. But they have been mobilized behind it by a combination of fear and pride—fear that the Communists, as General Curtis E. LeMay puts it, seek "control of the entire world" including the United States, and pride that military power has made us strong. For a quarter of a century Americans have believed these conventional wisdoms: communism was the implacable enemy, the Pentagon our primary defense against it. America had won World War II through military-industrial power; this was a good enough formula against a new enemy.

But the predigested cliches which have won the people to the Pentagon are in fact dangerous half-truths which, if not repudiated, augur catastrophe. History proves that a nation that prepares for the wrong war has little chance of avoiding defeat. France, for instance, believed that its Maginot Line would protect it from Germany just as its trenches had done in the World War I "war of position." It found to its dismay that the German *blitzkrieg*—war of movement—had upset all the old strategies. Is it possible that the United States too has been preparing for the wrong war against the wrong enemy?

'Just a few more fixes and then I'm going to kick the habit!'

In the spring of 1971, as reports flooded back of increased drug addiction among American troops in Vietnam, some observers wondered if the nation itself were not becoming increasingly habituated to the activity of the war. (May 30, 1971, William Sanders: *The Milwaukee Journal*)

Delinquent Parents Breed Delinquent Children

Copyright, 1947, New York Herald Tribune Inc.

In 1947, with one conflict barely over and another underway, a cartoonist offered these observations about the effects of war as a none too subtle warning for the future. (New York Herald Tribune, Inc.)

Bibliography

IMPORTANT
WORKS ON THE
IMPACT OF WAR

1. WORKS ON CONFLICT, DISASTER, SOCIAL CHANGE

Not surprisingly, both World War II and the Cold War have stimulated social scientists to take up work in a number of areas with relevance to war, although most of what has been done is concerned primarily with the origins of the phenomenon and not its effects. Still, in the realm of conflict studies, for example, one can turn with profit to Jessie Bernard, et al., *The Nature of Conflict* (Paris, 1957), Lewis F. Richardson, *Arms and Insecurity* (Pittsburgh, 1960), Kenneth E. Boulding, *Conflict and Defense* (New York, 1962), Roger Fisher, ed., *International Conflict and Behavioral Science* (New York, 1964), Muzafer Sherif, *In Common Predicament* (Boston, 1966), Lewis Coser, *Continuities in the Study of Social Conflict* (New York, 1967), and for a good overview of the field, Elton B. McNeil, ed., *The Nature of Human Conflict* (Englewood Cliffs, N.J., 1963). Certain classics remain useful, and the student should not overlook Walter Bagehot, *Physics and Politics* (London, 1872), or George Simmel, *Conflict and The Web of Group Affiliations* (Glencoe, Ill., 1955; first published in 1908 and 1922). Lewis Coser presents a helpful analysis of Simmel's essays in *The Functions of Social Conflict* (Glencoe, Ill., 1956).

Much insight into the possible side-effects of war is also to be gained from disaster research. See, for instance, Samuel H. Prince, *Catastrophe and Social Change* (New York, 1920), Pitirim Sorokin, *Man and Society in Calamity* (New York, 1942), Martha Wolfenstein, *Disaster: A Psychological Essay* (Glencoe, Ill., 1957), Fred C. Ikle, *The Social Impact of Bomb Destruction* (Norman, Okla., 1958), G. W. Baker and D. W. Chapman, eds., *Man and Society in Disaster* (New York, 1962), Tom Stonier, *Nuclear Disaster* (Cleveland, 1964), and Allen H. Barton, *Communities in Disaster* (Garden City, N.Y., 1969). Note also Human Sciences Research, Inc., *An Approach to the Study of Social and Psychological Effects of Nuclear Attack* (McLean, Va., 1963).

A rapidly expanding area of study with particular significance for our theme concerns how and why societies change. Here one might begin with Wilbert Moore's *Social Change* (Englewood Cliffs, N.J., 1963) or *Order and Change* (New York, 1967), but for an introduction to the full spectrum of research, consult Amitai and Eva Etzioni, eds., *Social Change: Sources, Patterns, and Consequences* (New York, 1964), and Jason L. Finkle and Richard W. Gable, eds., *Political Development and Social Change* (New York, 1966). Other helpful books are R. M. MacIver and C. H. Page, *Society* (New York, 1949), Pitirim Sorokin, *Social and Cultural Dynamics,*

Vol. 3 (New York, 1957), Egbert deVries, *Man in Rapid Social Change* (Garden City, N.Y., 1961), Don Martindale, *Social Life and Cultural Change* (Princeton, 1962), Richard T. LaPiere, *Social Change* (New York, 1965), S. N. Eisenstadt, ed., *Comparative Perspective on Social Change* (Boston, 1968), and Talcott Parsons, *Societies: Evolutionary and Comparative Perspectives* (Englewood Cliffs, N.J., 1966). For particular reference to the American situation, see Raymond W. Mack, *Transforming America: Patterns of Social Change* (New York, 1967). For assistance in the theoretical problems of comparison, consult Richard L. Merrit and Stein Rokkan, eds., *Comparing Nations: The Uses of Quantitative Data in Cross-National Research* (New Haven, 1966).

As we have noted previously, "modernization" would seem to be a type of social change with extraordinary relevance to the impact of war. The logical starting points in this case are Cyril E. Black, *The Dynamics of Modernization* (New York, 1966), with a fine critical bibliography, Myron Weiner, ed., *Modernization: The Dynamics of Growth* (New York, 1966), and Raymond Aron, *The Industrial Society: Three Essays on Ideology and Development* (New York, 1967). The most comprehensive theoretical studies are Marion J. Levy, Jr., *Modernization and the Structure of Society: A Setting for International Affairs* (2 vols., Princeton, 1966) and S. N. Eisenstadt, *Modernization: Protest and Challenge* (Englewood Cliffs, N.J., 1966). For the political side, see Gabriel A. Almond and James S. Coleman, eds., *The Politics of the Developing Areas* (Princeton, 1960), Lucian W. Pye, *Aspects of Political Development* (Boston, 1966), and John Montgomery and William J. Siffin, eds., *Approaches to Development* (New York, 1966). For the economic and social, note W. W. Rostow, *The Stages of Economic Growth* (Cambridge, Mass., 1960), Everett E. Hagen, *On the Theory of Social Change: How Economic Growth Begins* (Homewood, Ill., 1962), J. A. Salter, *Modern Mechanization and Its Effects on the Structure of Society* (London, 1933), Clark Kerr, et al., *Industrialism and Industrial Man* (Harvard, 1960), Bert Hose-litz and Wilbert Moore, eds., *Industrialization and Society* (New York, 1963), and Karl de Schweiritz, *Industrialization and Democracy* (New York, 1964). For an especially critical group in this process, examine John J. Johnson, ed., *The Role of the Military in Underdeveloped Countries* (Princeton, 1962).

The study of organizations and organizational change is an older field, but another potential key to the understanding of what war does to society. Max Weber's thought is seminal here and can be examined in relation to work that has followed in Robert K. Merton, et al., eds., *Reader in Bureaucracy* (Glencoe, Ill., 1952). A more recent volume which supplements Merton is James G. March, ed., *Handbook of Organizations* (Chicago, 1965). Among individual works, the following are illuminating: Karl Manheim, *Man and Society in an Age of Reconstruction* (London, 1940), Hans Gerth and C. Wright Mills, *Character and Social Structure* (New York, 1953), William H. Whyte, *The Organization Man* (Garden City, N.Y., 1953), Alvin Gouldner, *Patterns of Industrial Bureaucracy* (Glencoe, Ill., 1954), Talcott Parsons and Neil J. Smelser, *Economy and Society* (Glencoe, Ill., 1956), Robert K. Merton, *Social Theory and Social Structure* (Glencoe, Ill., 1957), Arnold M. Rose, ed., *The Institutions of Advanced Societies* (Minneapolis, 1958), Talcott Parsons, *Structure and Process in Modern Societies* (Glencoe, Ill., 1960), Amitai Etzioni, *A Comparative Analysis of Complex Organizations* (New York, 1961), Robert Presthus, *The Organization Society* (New York, 1962), Victor A. Thompson, *Modern Organization* (New York, 1963), Hendrik M. Ruitenbeek, ed., *The Dilemma of Organizational Society* (New York, 1963), Michael Crozier, *The Bureaucratic Phenomenon* (Chicago, 1964), R. M. MacIver, *Power Transformed* (New York, 1964), Jacques Ellul, *The Technological Society* (New York, 1964), and John Kenneth Galbraith, *The New Industrial State* (Boston, 1967). In a class by itself is the brilliant and provocative study by Stanislaw Andrzejewski (later changed to Andreski), *Military Organization and Society* (London, 1954).

2. WORKS ON WAR

Both social scientists and historians have studied war in ways relevant to our theme. For the former, look first to Leon Bramson and George Goethals, eds., *War: Studies from Psychology, Sociology, and Anthropology* (New York, 1964), which introduces the great interpreters from Alexis de Tocqueville, Herbert Spencer, and William Graham Sumner down through the 1950s. Turn next to Quincy Wright, *A Study of War* (2 vols., Chicago, 1942), the standard work of the past generation, and then to Pitirim Sorokin, *Contemporary Sociological Theories* (New York, 1928), which includes a superb summary of nineteenth-century research in the field, Maurice R. Davie, *The Evolution of War* (New Haven, 1929), Sebald Steinmetz, *Soziologie des Krieges* (Leipzig, 1929), Arnold F. Vieth von Golssenau, *Warfare: The Relation of War to Society* (New York, 1939), Jesse Clarkson and T. C. Cochran, *Was as a Social Institution* (New York, 1941), Gaston Bouthoul, *Les Guerres: Elements de Polemologie* (Paris, 1951), Klaus Knorr, *The War Potential of Nations* (Princeton, 1956), Kenneth Waltz, *Man, the State and War* (New York, 1959), and Lewis Richardson, *Statistics of Deadly Quarrels* (Pittsburgh, 1960). Less general studies of merit include R. D. Gillespie, *Psychological Effects of War on Citizen and Soldier* (New York, 1942), Sidonie M. Gruenberg, ed., *The Family in a World at War* (New York, 1942), Anna Freud and D. T. Burlingham, *War and Children* (New York, 1943), John R. Rees, *The Shaping of Psychiatry by War* (New York, 1945), Ross Stagner and Charles E. Osgood, "Impact of War on a Nationalistic Frame of Reference," *Journal of Social Psychology*, XXIV (1946), and Curtis Nettels, "Economic Consequences of War: Costs of Production," *Journal of Economic History*, Supplement (December 1943). Recent social science has preferred to examine war largely in the context of "conflict," but anthropology and psychology provide notable exceptions to this rule, such as Andrew P. Vayda and Anthony Leeds, "Anthropology and the Study of War," *Anthropologica*, III (1961), Michael Haas, "Societal Approaches to the Study of War," *Journal of Peace Research*, II (1965), Paul Bohannon, *Law and Warfare* (Garden City, N.Y., 1967), Morton Fried, Marvin Harris, and Robert Murphy, eds., *War: The Anthropology of Armed Conflict and Aggression* (New York, 1968), Viola W. Bernard, et al., "Dehumanization: A Composite Psychological Defense in Relation to Modern War," in Milton Schwebel, ed., *Behavioral Science and Human Survival* (Palo Alto, Calif., 1965), Jerome Frank, *Society and Survival: Psychological Aspects of War and Peace* (New York, 1967), and Elwin H. Powell, *The Design of Discord: Studies of Anomie, Suicide, Urban Society, War* (Oxford, 1970). See, in addition, the excellent articles on war in the *International Encyclopedia of the Social Sciences* (New York, 1968), and the pathbreaking essay by Berenice Carroll, "How Wars End: An Analysis of Some Current Hypotheses," *Journal of Peace Research*, VI (1969).

On the historical side, a long standing debate as to whether war has assisted human progress finds its classic scholarly antagonists, on the one hand, in Max Jähns, *Ueber Krieg, Frieden und Kultur* (Berlin, 1893), Werner Sombart, *Krieg und Kapitalismus* (Munich, 1913), and Cyril Falls, *The Place of War in History* (London, 1947), who argue the qualified affirmative, and, on the other, in Jakow Novicow, *La Guerre et ses pretendues bienfaits* (Paris, 1894; republished as *War and Its Alleged Benefits* [New York, 1911]), and John U. Nef, *War and Human Progress* (New York, 1942; republished as *Western Civilization since the Renaissance* [New York, 1963]), who take issue with such optimism. Another proponent of the affirmative thesis is Lewis Mumford, *Technics and Civilization* (New York, 1934), but both Oswald Spengler, *The Decline of the West* (New York, 1947; first published 1919) and Arnold Toynbee, *War and Civilization* (New York, 1950) assess war even more negatively than does Nef. J. F. C. Fuller, *War and Western Civilization* (London, 1932) is disinclined to generalization. More interesting, if somewhat more limited in scope, are Hans Speier and Alfred Kähler, eds., *War in Our Time* (New York, 1939), Willard Waller, ed., *War in the Twentieth Century* (New York, 1940), Raymond Aron,

The Century of Total War (Garden City, N.Y., 1954), Edmund Stillman and William Pfaff, *The Politics of Hysteria* (New York, 1964), and John J. Clark, *The New Economics of National Defense* (New York, 1966). For a helpful finding-aid on these and related subjects see Blanche Wiesen Cook, *Bibliography on Peace Research in History* (Santa Barbara, Calif., 1969).

3. WORKS ON NON-AMERICAN WARS
The impact of specific wars on the participating societies has lately received more and more attention from historians. Of special importance for our subject are Arnold Toynbee's superb analysis of the Second Punic War, entitled *Hannibal's Legacy* (2 vols., London, 1965), and such studies as K. B. McFarland, "War, the Economy, and Social Change: England and the Hundred Years' War," *Past and Present* (July 1962), M. M. Postan, "The Costs of the Hundred Years' War," *Past and Present* (April 1964), Theodore K. Rabb, "The Effects of the Thirty Years' War on the German Economy," *Journal of Modern History*, XXXIV (March 1962), Asa Briggs, *The Age of Improvement, 1783–1867* (New York, 1959; republished as *The Making of Modern England* [New York, 1965]), E. J. Hobsbawn, *The Age of Revolution, 1789–1848* (Cleveland, 1962), Olive Anderson, *A Liberal State at War* (New York, 1967), Arno Mayer, *Dynamics of Counterrevolution in Europe, 1870–1956* (New York, 1971), René Albrecht Carrié, *The Meaning of the First World War* (Englewood Cliffs, N.J., 1965), Jack J. Roth, ed., *World War I: A Turning Point in Modern History* (New York, 1967), Arthur Marwick, *The Deluge: British Society and the First World War* (London, 1965), with helpful bibliography, Marwick, "The Impact of the First World War on British Society," *The Journal of Contemporary History*, III (January 1968), Peter Stansky, ed., *The Left and War: The British Labour Party and World War I* (New York, 1969), Philip Abrams, "The Failure of Social Reform, 1918–1920," *Past and Present*, (April 1963), Robert B. Armeson, *Total War and Compulsory Labor: A Study of the Military-Industrial Complex in Germany during World War I* (The

Hague, 1964), Alan Milward, *The Germany Economy at War* (London, 1965), Gerald Feldman, *Army, Industry and Labor in Germany, 1914–1918* (Princeton, 1966), Arno Mayer, *Political Origins of the New Diplomacy, 1917–1918* (New Haven, 1959), Mayer, "Post-war Nationalisms, 1918–1919," *Past and Present*, (July 1966), Mayer, *Politics and Diplomacy of Peacemaking: Containment and Counterrevolution at Versailles, 1918–1919* (New York, 1967), Angus Calder, *The People's War: Britain 1937–1945* (New York, 1969), Gordon Wright, *The Ordeal of Total War, 1939–45* (New York, 1968), with excellent bibliographical essay, Arthur Marwick, *Britain in the Century of Total War: War, Peace, and Social Change* (London, 1968), Alan Milward, *The Economic Effects of Two World Wars on Britain* (London, 1970), and R. von Albertini, "The Impact of Two World Wars on the Decline of Colonialism," *The Journal of Contemporary History*, IV (January 1969).

Older works which deal perceptively with the effects of war are Thucydides, *The Peloponnesian War* (Crawley translation, New York, 1951), Jakob Burckhardt, *Reflections on History* (London, 1943; first published 1906), M. M. Postan, "Some Social Consequences of the Hundred Years' War," *The Economic History Review*, XII (1942), Earl Hamilton, *War and Prices in Spain, 1651–1800* (Cambridge, 1947), A. L. Bowley, *Some Economic Consequences of the Great War* (London, 1930), Samuel J. Hurwitz, *State Intervention in Great Britain, 1914–1919* (New York, 1949), James Westfall Thompson, "The Aftermath of the Black Death and the Aftermath of the Great War," *American Journal of Sociology*, XXVI (1920–1921), Floyd A. Cave, et al., *The Origins and Consequences of World War II* (New York, 1948), Oxford Institute of Statistics, *Studies in War Economy* (London, 1949), and Grayson Kirk, "Nationalism, Internationalism and the War," in Ralph Linton, ed., *The Science of Man in the World Crisis* (New York, 1945). Of particular note is the series of over 130 volumes on the economic and social history of the First World War, edited by James T. Shotwell in the period between the wars. Two of the more interesting studies in this somewhat uneven set are Francis W. Hirst, *The Consequences of the War to Great Britain* (New Haven, 1934), and A. Mendelssohn-Bartholdy, *The War and German Society* (New Haven, 1937).

4. WORKS ON AMERICAN WARS GENERALLY

There is little scholarly writing which deals generally with the impact of war on the United States, although a number of thematic studies and texts touch upon the effects of more than one war. Social scientists and economic historians have ventured farthest toward generalization, as witness W. Lloyd Warner, *American Life: Dream and Reality* (Chicago, 1953), William F. Ogburn and Jean L. Adams, "Are Our Wars Good Times?" *Scientific Monthly*, LXVII (July 1948), Maurice Clark, et al., *Readings in the Economics of War* (Chicago, 1918), Chester W. Wright, "The More Enduring Economic Consequences of America's Wars," *Journal of Economic History*, Supplement (December 1943), Milton Friedman, "Price, Income, and Monetary Changes in Three Wartime Periods," *American Economic Review*, XLV (1955), Marshall A. Robinson, "Federal Debt Management: Civil War, World War I, and World War II," *American Economic Review*, XLV (1955), Bruce Russett, "The Price of War," *Trans-action*, VI (October 1969), and Eliot Janeway, *The Economics of Crisis: War, Politics, and the Dollar* (New York, 1968). Yet others of the economic guild have treated wars on an individual basis and as part of a larger story; see Joseph Dorfman, *The Economic Mind in American Civilization* (5 vols., New York, 1946–59), Victor S. Clark, *History of Manufactures in the United States* (3 vols., New York, 1949), Herman Kroos, *American Economic Development* (Englewood Cliffs, N.J., 1955), William Greenleaf, ed., *American Economic Development since 1860* (New York, 1967), and George Soule, *Planning: U.S.A.* (New York, 1967). The same approach is found in such perceptive, non-economic surveys as Harold Laski, *The American Democracy* (London, 1949), Arthur Link and William B. Catton, *American Epoch* (New York, 1963), Carl Brent Swisher,

American Constitutional Development (2nd ed., Cambridge, 1954), William F. Swindler, *Court and Constitution in the 20th Century* (2 vols., Indianapolis, 1969–1970), and John W. Oliver, *History of American Technology* (New York, 1956). For the effects on political and social reform consult, among others, Eric Goldman, *Rendezvous with Destiny* (New York, 1952), and Arthur Ekirch, *The Decline of American Liberalism* (New York, 1955). For the impact on individual rights see Nathaniel Weyl, *The Battle against Disloyalty* (New York, 1951), John Higham, *Strangers in the Land* (New Brunswick, 1955), John P. Roche, *The Quest for the Dream* (New York, 1963), and Allen Grimshaw, ed., *Racial Violence in the United States* (Chicago, 1969). Opposition/resistance to war is traced in Joseph R. Conlin, ed., *American Anti-War Movements* (New York, 1968), Samuel Eliot Morison, Frederick Merk, and Frank Freidel, *Dissent in Three American Wars* (Cambridge, Mass., 1970), Merle Curti, *Peace or War: The American Struggle* (Boston, 1936), Peter Brock, *Pacifism in the United States: From the Colonial Era to the First World War* (Princeton, 1968), and Lawrence S. Wittner, *Rebels against War: The American Peace Movement, 1941–60* (New York, 1969). The relationship between wars and the American intellectual tradition is examined in Merle Curti, *The Growth of American Thought* (New York, 1943), Harvey Wish, *Society and Thought in America* (2 vols., New York, 1950–62), Robert Spiller, et al., *Literary History of the United States* (New York, 1953), John Aldridge, *After the Lost Generation: A Critical Study of the Writers of Two Wars* (New York, 1951), Malcolm Cowley, "War Novels: After Two Wars" in Lawrence W. Levine and Robert Middlekauf, eds., *The National Temper: Readings in American History* (New York, 1968), and Charles Glicksburg, *American Literary Criticism, 1900–1950* (New York, 1951). For reference to war and religion, note H. W. Schneider, *Religion in Twentieth Century America* (Cambridge, 1945), and Will Herberg, *Protestant, Catholic, Jew* (Garden City, N.Y., 1956). Bibliographic assistance regarding recent studies of American wars is available on a continuing basis in "Consequences of National Defense Policies and War," *Arms Control and Disarmament: A Quarterly Bibliography* (Washington, Library of Congress, 1964–   ).

5. WORKS ON AMERICAN WARS BEFORE 1914

A. COLONIAL WARS

The political, economic, and social significance of America's earliest wars has not been frequently discussed, but Daniel J. Boorstin, *The Americans: The Colonial Experience* (New York, 1958), provides an interesting interpretation, and Herbert Osgood, *The American Colonies in the Eighteenth Century* (4 vols., New York, 1924), offers considerable raw data. See also Wesley F. Craven, *The Colonies in Transition, 1660–1713* (New York, 1967). For the Indian wars, one may turn to Douglas Leach, *Flintlock and Tomahawk* (New York, 1958) and for the intercolonial struggles, to Richard Pares, *War and Trade in the West Indies, 1739–63* (Oxford, 1936) and Edward P. Hamilton, *The French and Indian Wars* (Garden City, N.Y., 1962). There are also several rewarding works on the Seven Years' War, including Lawrence H. Gipson, *The British Empire before the American Revolution* (9 vols., Caldwell, Idaho, 1936–56), Gipson, *The Coming of the Revolution, 1763–1775* (New York, 1954), Gipson, "The American Revolution as an Aftermath of the Great War for the Empire, 1754–1763," *Political Science Quarterly*, LX (1950), and Bernhard Knollenberg, *Origin of the American Revolution, 1759–1766* (New York, 1961).

B. THE REVOLUTIONARY WAR

A colonial revolution, of course, can be defined primarily in terms of rising international tension and finally international war. To what extent this is a valid characterization of the American case has long been in debate, but few historians have focused upon the dynamics or effects of the revolution conceived of as a war situation. Thus, from our standpoint, such basic contributions as J. F. Jameson, *The American Revolution Considered as a Social Movement* (Boston, 1926), and Frederick B. Tolles, "The American Revolution Considered as a Social Movement: A Re-evaluation," *American Historical Review*, LX (October 1954), are at the same time both helpful and considerably misleading. So too is the otherwise admirable compilation of Esmond Wright entitled *Causes and Consequences of the American Revolution* (Chicago, 1966).

To do justice to the impact of war, one must turn to a wide variety of specialized investigations. For the repercussions of prewar hostility, see Arthur M. Schlesinger, *Colonial Merchants and the American Revolution, 1763–1776* (New York, 1918), Schlesinger, *Prelude to Independence: The Newspaper War on Britain, 1764–1776* (New York, 1958), Philip Davidson, *Propaganda and the American Revolution, 1763–1783* (Chapel Hill, N.C., 1941), Bernard Bailyn, ed., *Pamphlets of the American Revolution, 1750–1776* (2 vols., Cambridge, 1965), Edmund C. Burnett, *Continental Congress* (New York, 1941), John Shy, *Toward Lexington: The Role of the British Army in the Coming of the Revolution* (Princeton, 1965), Weldon A. Brown, *Empire or Independence* (University, Louisiana, 1941), and John C. Miller, *Origins of the American Revolution* (Boston, 1943), as well as Gipson and Knollenberg, cited above. Studies of the war itself are invariably military in emphasis, although John C. Miller's *Triumph of Freedom, 1775–1783* (Boston, 1948) and John R. Alden's *The American Revolution, 1775–1783* (New York, 1954) also look behind the battles. For the economic effects of war, consult Curtis P. Nettels, *The Emergence of a National Economy, 1775–1815* (New York, 1962), with a splendid bibliography, Robert A. East, *Business Enterprise in the American Revolutionary Era* (New York, 1938), Victor S. Clark, *History of Manufactures in the United States*, E. James Ferguson, *The Power of the Purse* (Chapel Hill, N.C., 1961), Bray Hammond, *Banks and Politics in America, from the Revolution to the Civil War* (Princeton, 1957), Anne Bezanson, et al., *Prices and Inflation during the American Revolution: Pennsylvania, 1770–1790* (Philadelphia, 1951), and Richard B. Morris, *Government and Labor in Early America* (New York, 1946).

For the impress of war on politics, see Merrill Jensen, *The Articles of Confederation* (Madison, 1940), Jensen, *The New Nation* (New York, 1950), Elisha P. Douglass, *Rebels and Democrats* (Chapel Hill, N.C., 1955), Allan Nevins, *The American States during and after the Revolution* (New York, 1924), and M. B. Macmillan, *The War Governors in the American Revolution* (New York, 1943). On the social and cultural side, note Evarts B. Greene, *The Revolutionary Generation, 1763–1790* (New York, 1943), Russell B. Nye, *The Cultural Life of the New Nation, 1776–1830* (New York, 1960), Jackson T. Main, *The Social Structure of Revolutionary America* (Princeton, 1965), Benjamin Quarles, *The Negro in the American Revolution* (Chapel Hill, N.C., 1961), William H. Nelson, *The American Tory* (Oxford, 1961), and E. F. Humphrey, *Nationalism and Religion in America, 1774–1789* (Boston, 1924).

C. THE UNDECLARED WAR WITH FRANCE, 1798–1800

One must consider here the results of the almost continuous international difficulties from 1793 to 1800. Perhaps the best overview is John C. Miller's *The Federalist Era, 1789–1801* (New York, 1960), while Alexander De Conde's *Entangling Alliance* (Durham, N.C., 1958) and *The Quasi-War* (New York, 1966) concentrate on American-French relations. The economic implications are touched upon in W. B. Smith and A. H. Cole, *Fluctuations in American Business, 1790–1860* (Cambridge, 1935), Douglas C. North, *The Economic Growth of the United States, 1790–1860* (Englewood Cliffs, N.J., 1961), Anna C. Clauder, *American Commerce as Affected by the Wars of the French Revolution and Napoleon, 1793–1812* (Philadelphia, 1932), John D. Forbes, "European Wars and Boston Trade, 1783–1815," *New England Quarterly*, XI (December 1938), and Nettels, Clark, and Hammond, cited above. The results for politics are described in Joseph Charles, *The Origins of the American Party System* (Williamsburg, 1956), Noble Cunningham, *The Jeffersonian Republicans* (Chapel Hill, N.C., 1957), Manning Dauer, *The Adams Federalists* (Baltimore, 1953), and Stephen

G. Kurtz, *The Presidency of John Adams* (Philadelphia, 1957). The meaning for civil liberties is apparent from James M. Smith's *Freedom's Fetters* (Ithaca, 1956), and Dumas Malone, *Jefferson and the Ordeal of Liberty* (Boston, 1962). The impact on foreign policy is discussed in Felix Gilbert, *To the Farewell Address* (Princeton, 1961), Samuel F. Bemis, *Jay's Treaty* (New York, 1923), and Bradford Perkins, *The First Rapprochement* (Philadelphia, 1955).

D. THE WAR OF 1812

This war too was preceded by several years of rising tension (1805–1812) which may have left a greater mark upon the nation than the months of actual belligerency. Henry Adams, *History of the United States during the Administrations of Thomas Jefferson and James Madison* (9 vols., New York, 1889–91) is a good place to start, if simply for the information he has amassed. His work can be supplemented by Irving Brant, *James Madison* (6 vols., Indianapolis and New York, 1941–61), and Raymond Walters, *Albert Gallatin* (New York, 1957), as well as by the economic studies of Smith and Cole, North, Nettels, Clark, Hammond, Clauder, and Forbes (paragraphs B and C). To see specifically what several years of economic warfare had achieved, examine Louis M. Sears, *Jefferson and the Embargo* (Durham, N.C., 1927), Caroline F. Ware, "The Effect of the American Embargo, 1807–1809, on the New England Cotton Industry," *Quarterly Journal of Economics*, XL (August 1926), John H. Reinoehl, "Post-Embargo Trade and Merchant Prosperity: Experiences of the Crowninshield Family, 1809–1912," *Mississippi Valley Historical Review*, XLII (September 1955), Bradford Perkins, *Prologue to War* (Berkeley, 1961), Julius Pratt, *Expansionists of 1812* (New York, 1925), G. R. Taylor, *Agrarian Discontent in the Mississippi Valley Preceding the War of 1812* (Chicago, 1931), and A. L. Burt, *The United States, Great Britain, and British North America* (New Haven, 1940). The internal dissension wrought by the war is described by Samuel E. Morison, *The Life and Letters of Harrison Gray Otis* (2 vols., Boston and New York, 1913), and Roger H. Brown,

The Republic in Peril: 1812 (New York, 1964). The important role of the war and especially the victory at New Orleans in stimulating and abetting American nationalism is dealt with in Kendric C. Babcock, *The Rise of American Nationality* (New York, 1906), George Dangerfield, *The Awakening of American Nationalism* (New York, 1965), Benjamin T. Spencer, *The Quest for Nationality* (Syracuse, 1957), John W. Ward, *Andrew Jackson: Symbol for an Age* (New York, 1955), and Shaw Livermore, *The Twilight of Federalism* (Princeton, 1962). For the war's immediate effect on economic affairs, note Murray N. Rothbard, *The Panic of 1819* (New York, 1962), National Bureau of Economic Research, *Trends in the American Economy in the Nineteenth Century* (Princeton, 1960), and *Output, Employment, and Productivity in the United States after 1800* (New York, 1966), as well as Smith and Cole, North, Clark, and Hammond. For the way in which America's view of the outside world was subtly altered, see Dexter Perkins, *The Monroe Doctrine, 1826–1867* (Baltimore, 1933), Bradford Perkins, *Castlereagh and Adams* (Berkeley, 1964), and Samuel F. Bemis, *John Quincy Adams and the Foundations of American Foreign Policy* (New York, 1956).

E. THE MEXICAN WAR

The impact of the Mexican War on the developing sectional crisis was so profound that it has long obscured almost all the war's other effects. For the standard treatment of the era, see Allan Nevins, *Ordeal of the Union* (2 vols., New York, 1947), Avery Craven, *The Coming of the Civil War* (New York, 1942), and *The Growth of Southern Nationalism, 1848–1861* (Baton Rouge, 1953), Roy F. Nichols, *The Stakes of Power, 1845–1877* (New York, 1961), and Holman Hamilton, *Prologue to Conflict* (Lexington, Ky., 1964). For somewhat more information on economic, social, and political matters, consult Smith and Cole, North, Clark, Hammond, and the two volumes of the National Bureau of Economic Research, as well as Alice Felt Tyler, *Freedom's Ferment* (Minneapolis, 1944), William Goetzman, *Army Exploration in the American West,*

1803–1863 (New Haven, 1959), Eugene McCormac, *James Knox Polk* (Berkeley, 1922), and Kinley J. Brauer, *Cotton vs. Conscience: Massachusetts Whig Politics and Southwestern Expansion, 1843–48* (Lexington, Ky., 1967). The implications of the war for American foreign policy have received considerable attention of late in Frederick Merk, *Manifest Destiny and Mission in American History* (New York, 1963), Merk, *The Monroe Doctrine and American Expansionism* (New York, 1966), and William Goetzman, *When the Eagle Screamed* (New York, 1966). But see also Dexter Perkins, cited above, J. D. P. Fuller, *The Movement for the Acquisition of All Mexico, 1846–1848* (Baltimore, 1936), and Norman Graebner, *Empire on the Pacific* (New York, 1955).

F. THE CIVIL WAR

This is the only American war whose impact has specifically interested scholars, and the reasons become clear when one considers both the scale of mobilization involved and the area of the fighting. Quite naturally, the war-born reconstitution of the South has received the most attention, but developments in the North have also been investigated in detail. What is more, during the centennial of the conflict a series of studies was commissioned to deal in general with "The Impact of the Civil War," and three of these have already appeared: Paul W. Gates, *Agriculture and the Civil War* (New York, 1966), Mary E. Massey, *Bonnet Brigades* (New York, 1966), and Harold Hyman, *Heard Round the World* (New York, 1969). An independent and parallel work of very great merit is Ralph Andreano, ed., *The Economic Impact of the American Civil War* (Cambridge, 1962), which can be supplemented with Pershing Vartanian, "The Cochran Thesis: A Critique in Statistical Analysis," *Mississippi Valley Historical Review*, LI (June 1964), and David T. Gilchrist and W. David Lewis, eds., *Economic Change in the Civil War Era* (Charlottesville, 1965). See also William R. Brock's book of readings entitled *The Civil War* (New York, 1969).

For results of the growing tension during 1850–1860, a period which Avery Craven has called "the first Cold War," the most helpful works are those of Craven, *Civil War in the Making, 1815–1860* (Baton Rouge, 1959), J. G. Randall and David Donald, *The Civil War and Reconstruction* (Boston, 1961), Arthur Cole, *The Irrepressible Conflict, 1850–1865* (New York, 1934), Allan Nevins, *The Emergence of Lincoln* (2 vols., New York, 1950), Louis Filler, *The Crusade against Slavery, 1830–1860* (New York, 1960), Roy F. Nichols, *The Disruption of American Democracy* (New York, 1948), Kenneth Stampp, *And the War Came* (Baton Rouge, 1950), and the previously cited volumes by Smith and Cole, Clark, Hammond, and the National Bureau of Economic Research (2 vols.).

In turning to the effects of the war itself, one finds that most studies are confined to a single section. Regarding the South to 1865, consult E. Merton Coulter, *The Confederate States of America, 1861–1865* (Baton Rouge, 1950), John C. Schwab, *The Confederate States of America, 1861–1865* (New York, 1901), Rembert W. Patrick, *Jefferson Davis and His Cabinet* (Baton Rouge, 1944), Wilfred B. Yearns, *The Confederate Congress* (Athens, Ga., 1960), Louise B. Hill, *State Socialism in the Confederate States of America* (Charlottesville, Va., 1936), Richard C. Todd, *Confederate Finance* (Athens, Ga., 1954), Robert C. Black III, *The Railroads of the Confederacy* (Chapel Hill, N.C., 1952), Bell I. Wiley, *The Plain People of the Confederacy* (Baton Rouge, 1943), Charles W. Ramsdell, *Behind the Lines in the Southern Confederacy* (Baton Rouge, 1944), James W. Silver, *Confederate Morale and Church Propaganda* (Tuscaloosa, Ala., 1957), and Bell I. Wiley, *Southern Negroes, 1861–1865* (New York and London, 1938). For the North in the war, see Allan Nevins, *The War for the Union* (2 vols., New York, 1959), James G. Randall, *Constitutional Problems under Lincoln* (Urbana, Ill., 1951), Burton J. Hendrick, *Lincoln's War Cabinet* (Boston, 1946), T. Harry Williams, *Lincoln and the Radicals* (Madison, 1941), Robert S. Harper, *Lincoln and the Press* (New York, 1951), Wood Gray, *The Hidden Civil War: The Story of the Copperheads* (New York, 1942), William B. Hesseltine, *Lincoln and the War Governors* (New York, 1948), Hesseltine, *Lincoln's Plan of Reconstruction* (Tuscaloosa, Ala., 1960), Emerson D. Fite, *Social and Industrial Conditions in the North during the Civil War* (New York, 1910), Wesley C. Mitchell, *A History of the Greenbacks* (Chicago, 1903), Paul Studenski and Herman E. Krooss, *Financial History of the United States* (New York, 1952), Thomas Weber, *The Northern Railroads in the Civil War, 1861–1865* (New York, 1952), James M. McPherson, *The Negro's Civil War* (New York, 1965), and B. W. Korn, *American Jewry and the Civil War* (Philadelphia, 1951). For both sections, note Randall and Donald, Cole, and National Bureau of Economic Research (2 vols.), cited above, as well as many of the works on economics listed in section 4, above.

For the after-effects of the conflict in the South there are a number of useful books, including Sidney Andrews, *The South since the War* (Boston, 1866), M. L. Avary, *Dixie after the War* (New York, 1906), John T. Trowbridge, *The Desolate South, 1865–1866* (New York, 1956), William A. Dunning, *Reconstruction, Political and Economic, 1865–1877* (New York and London, 1907), E. Merton Coulter, *The South during Reconstruction, 1865–1877* (Baton Rouge, 1947), W. E. B. Du Bois, *Black Reconstruction* (New York, 1935), Francis B. Simkins and Robert H. Woody, *South Carolina during Reconstruction* (Chapel Hill, 1932), Thomas B. Alexander, *Political Reconstruction in Tennessee* (Nashville, 1950), and Vernon Wharton, *The Negro in Mississippi, 1865–1890* (Chapel Hill, 1947).

On the national side, note especially George Fort Milton, *The Age of Hate: Andrew Johnson and the Radicals* (New York, 1930), Eric L. McKitrick, *Andrew Johnson and Reconstruction* (Chicago, 1960), LaWanda and John H. Cox, *Politics, Principle, and Prejudice, 1865–1866* (New York, 1963), W. R. Brock, *An American Crisis: Congress and Reconstruction, 1865–1867* (New York, 1963), Robert B. Sharkey, *Money, Class and Party* (Baltimore, 1959), Irwin Unger, *The Greenback Era* (Princeton, 1964), Kenneth Stampp, *The Era of Reconstruction* (New York, 1966), Joseph B. James, *The Framing of the*

Fourteenth Amendment (Urbana, Ill., 1959), Ralph Morrow, *Northern Methodism and Reconstruction* (East Lansing, 1956), and Mary R. Dearing, *Veterans in Politics* (Baton Rouge, 1952). See also Randall and Donald, and National Bureau of Economic Research (2 vols.).

G. THE SPANISH AMERICAN WAR

The quick success of the Spanish American War meant that its impact was largely limited to the self-esteem it stimulated, the attitudes it confirmed, and the acquisitions it brought. Robert E. Osgood, *Ideals and Self-Interest in America's Foreign Relations* (Chicago, 1953), provides a helpful interpretation of this situation, but should be supplemented with Ernest R. May, *Imperial Democracy* (New York, 1961), Harold Faulkner, *Politics, Reform, and Expansion, 1890–1900* (New York, 1959), and Richard Hofstadter, "Cuba, the Philippines, and Manifest Destiny," in *The Paranoid Style in American Politics and Other Essays* (New York, 1965). Prewar bellicosity and its consequences are discussed in Julius Pratt, *Expansionists of 1898* (Baltimore, 1936), Walter LaFeber, *The New Empire* (Ithaca, 1963), William A. Williams, *The Roots of the Modern American Empire* (New York, 1969), and Dexter Perkins, *The Monroe Doctrine, 1867–1907* (Baltimore, 1937). The impact of victory and empire upon the domestic scene is dealt with in Fred Harrington, "The Anti-Imperialistic Movement in the United States, 1898–1900," *Mississippi Valley Historical Review*, XXII (September 1935), Thomas A. Bailey, "Was the Presidential Election of 1900 a Mandate on Imperialism?" *Mississippi Valley Historical Review*, XXIV (June 1937), William E. Leuchtenburg, "Progressivism and Imperialism," *Mississippi Valley Historical Review*, XXXIX (December 1952), Margaret Leech, *In the Days of McKinley* (New York, 1959), and Merle Curti, *Peace or War*, listed above (section 4). The impact of victory and empire upon American foreign relations and military policies is examined in Charles S. Campbell, Jr., *Anglo-American Understanding, 1898–1903* (Baltimore, 1957), Bradford Perkins, *The Great Rapprochement: England and the United States, 1895–1914* (New York, 1968), Julius Pratt, *America's Colonial Experiment* (New York, 1950), Wilfrid H. Callcott, *The Caribbean Policy of the United States, 1890–1920* (Baltimore, 1962), A. Whitney Griswold, *The Far Eastern Policy of the United States* (New York, 1938), Charles S. Campbell, Jr., *Special Business Interests and the Open Door Policy* (New York, 1951), Raymond Esthus, "The Changing Concept of the Open Door, 1899–1910," *Mississippi Valley Historical Review*, XLVI (December 1959), Akira Iriye, *Across the Pacific* (New York, 1967), Marilyn Blatt Young, *The Rhetoric of Empire* (Cambridge, Mass., 1968), William R. Braisted, *The American Navy in the Pacific, 1897–1907* (Austin, 1958), George T. Davis, *A Navy Second to None* (New York, 1940), Paul Y. Hammond, *Organizing for Defense* (Princeton, 1961), Russell F. Weigley, *Towards an American Army* (New York, 1962), and Richard W. Leopold, *Elihu Root and the Conservative Tradition* (Boston, 1954).

6. WORKS ON WORLD WAR I

A. GENERAL AND PRE-1917

By far the best introduction to the meaning of the war for the United States is Charles Hirschfeld's essay, "The Transformation of American Life," in Jack J. Roth, ed., *World War I: A Turning Point in Modern History*, previously listed, but also valuable are Arthur M. Schlesinger, Jr., *Age of Roosevelt: Crisis of the Old Order* (Boston, 1957), William E. Leuchtenburg, *The Perils of Prosperity* (Chicago, 1958), Leuchtenburg, "The New Deal and the Analogue of War," in John Braeman, et al., eds., *Change and Continuity in Twentieth Century America* (Columbus, 1964), Robert H. Wiebe, *The Search for Order, 1877–1920* (New York, 1967), David F. Trask, ed., *World War I at Home: Readings on American Life, 1914–20* (New York, 1969), and Arthur S. Link, ed., *The Impact of World War I* (New York, 1969), as well as Mayer, Osgood, Laski, and Link and Catton, cited above (see sections 3 and 4).

To be precise about the subject, it is necessary to recognize three distinct phases in the development of the war: pre-1914, 1914–1917, and post-1917. American reaction to growing prewar tension has not yet been adequately studied, but relevant information is presented in George Mowry, *The Era of Theodore Roosevelt, 1900–1912* (New York, 1958), Harold K. Beale, *Theodore Roosevelt and the Rise of America to World Power* (Baltimore, 1956), Raymond Esthus, *Theodore Roosevelt and the International Rivalries* (Waltham, Mass., 1970), William C. Askew and J. Fred Rippy, "The United States and Europe's Strife, 1908–1913," *Journal of Politics*, IV (February 1942), Edward H. Zabriskie, *American-Russian Rivalry in the Far East, 1895–1914* (Philadelphia, 1946), Lionel Gelber, *The Rise of Anglo-American Friendship* (New York, 1938), Alfred Vagts, *Deutschland und die Vereinigten Staaten in der Weltpolitik, 1890–1906* (2 vols., New York, 1935), Outten J. Clinard, *Japan's Influence on American Naval Power, 1776–1918* (Princeton, 1939), Calvin D. Davis, *The United States and the First Hague Peace Conference* (Ithaca, 1962), Merle Curti, *Peace or War*, listed above, Curti, *Bryan and World Peace* (Northampton, Mass., 1931), and the previously cited books by Perkins (*The Great Rapprochement*), Griswold, and Braisted.

The effect of the first three war years on the United States is usually either forgotten in our concern with why we later fought or obscured by our attention to the ensuing mobilization. For the most useful studies of this period, see Arthur S. Link, *Woodrow Wilson and the Progressive Era, 1910–1917* (New York, 1954), Link, *Wilson*, (5 vols., Princeton, 1947–1965), Mark Sullivan, *Our Times* (Vol. 5 of 6 volumes, New York, 1926–1935), Frederic L. Paxson, *The Pre-War Years, 1913–1917* (Boston, 1936), Harold Faulkner, *The Decline of Laissez Faire, 1897–1917* (New York, 1951), Henry F. May, *The End of American Innocence* (New York, 1959), Charles Forcey, *The Crossroads of Liberalism* (New York, 1961), Christopher Lasch, *The New Radicalism in America, 1889–1963* (New York, 1965), Clifton J. Child, *The German-Americans in Politics, 1914–1917* (Madison, 1939), John C. Crighton, *Missouri and the World War, 1914–1917* (Co-

lumbia, 1947), Robert D. Ward, "The Origin and Activities of the National Security League, 1914–1919," *Mississippi Valley Historical Review*, XLVII (June 1960), C. L. King, ed., "America's Interests as Affected by the European War," *The Annals*, LX (July 1915), King, "America's Interests after the European War," *The Annals*, LXI (September 1915), Charles C. Tansill, *America Goes to War* (Boston, 1938), Ernest R. May, *The World War and American Isolation, 1914–1917* (Cambridge, 1959), Edwin J. Clapp, *Economic Aspects of the War* (New Haven, 1915), Richard W. VanAlstyne, "Private American Loans to the Allies, 1914–1916," *Pacific Historical Review*, II (April 1933), Paul Birdsall, "Neutrality and Economic Pressures, 1914–1917," *Science and Society*, III (Summer 1939), Arthur S. Link, "The Cotton Crisis in the South and Anglo-American Diplomacy, 1914–1915," in J. C. Sitterson, ed., *Studies in Southern History in Memory of Albert Day Newsome, 1894–1951* (Chapel Hill, 1957), Ruhl J. Bartlett, *The League to Enforce Peace* (Chapel Hill, 1944), and Charles C. Tansill, *The Purchase of the Danish West Indies* (Baltimore, 1952).

General histories of 1917–1918 and its aftermath include Frederick Palmer, *Newton D. Baker: America at War* (2 vols., New York, 1931), Daniel R. Beaver, *Newton D. Baker and the American War Effort, 1917–1919* (Lincoln, 1966), Peyton C. March, *The Nation at War* (New York, 1932), John B. McMaster, *The United States in the World War* (2 vols., New York, 1918–1920), Preston Slosson, *The Great Crusade and After* (New York, 1930), and Frederic L. Paxson, *America at War, 1917–1918* (Berkeley, 1948) and *Post War Years: Normalcy, 1918–1923* (Berkeley, 1948). For the sake of clarity, more specific works are listed below by the area of their concern.

B. ON THE ECONOMY

The opening chapters of George Soule's *Prosperity Decade* (New York, 1947) offer the broadest view of the impact of war on the American economy, but the student should also examine the excellent monograph by James R. Mock and

Evangeline Thurber, entitled *Report on Demobilization* (Norman, Okla., 1944). The significance of governmental intervention is explained and appraised in Walter Weyl, *The End of the War* (New York, 1918), Grosvenor Clarkson, *Industrial America in the World War* (Boston, 1923), Bernard Baruch, *American Industry in the War* (New York, 1941), James Weinstein, *The Corporate Ideal in the Liberal State, 1900–1918* (Boston, 1968), Rexford G. Tugwell, "America's Wartime Socialism," *Nation*, CXXIV (April 6, 1927), Maxcy R. Dickson, "The Food Administration—Educator," *Agricultural History*, XVI (April 1942), Gerald D. Nash, "Franklin D. Roosevelt and Labor: The World War I Origins of Early New Deal Policy," *Labor History* I (Winter 1960), Gerald D. Nash, "Experiments in Industrial Mobilizations: W.I.B. and N.R.A.," *Mid-America*, XLV (January 1963), Paul A. C. Koistinen, "The Industrial-Military Complex in Historical Perspective: World War I," *Business History Review*, XLI (Winter 1967), Walker D. Hines, *War History of American Railroads* (New Haven and London, 1928), part of the Shotwell series, C. H. Crennan, ed., "War Adjustments in Railroad Regulation," *The Annals*, LXXVI (March 1918), Simon Litman, *Prices and Price Control in Great Britain and the United States during the World War* (New York, 1920), Alexander D. Noyes, *The War Period of American Finance, 1908–1925* (New York, 1926), Sidney Ratner, *American Taxation* (New York, 1942), and Charles Gilbert, *American Financing of World War I* (Westport, Conn., 1970). For the consequences of war to business, see Irving Fisher, "Some Contributions of the War to Our Knowledge of Money and Prices," *American Economic Review*, VIII (March 1918), C. L. King, ed., "Industries in Readjustment," *The Annals*, LXXXII (March 1919), Leonard Ayres, *Turning Points in Business Cycles* (New York, 1939), and John D. Hicks, *Rehearsal for Disaster* (Gainesville, Fla., 1961). For changes in agriculture, see Benjamin Hibbard, *Effects of the Great War upon Agriculture in the United States and Great Britain* (New York, 1919), Theodore Saloutos and John D. Hicks, *Agricultural Discontent in the*

Middle West, 1900–1939 (Madison, 1951), and James H. Shideler, *Farm Crisis, 1918–1923* (Berkeley, 1957). For the effects upon labor, see C. H. Crennan, ed., "A Reconstruction Labor Policy," *The Annals*, LXXXI (January 1919), Samuel Gompers, *American Labor and the War* (New York, 1919), Gordon Watkins, *Labor Problems and Labor Administration in the United States during the World War* (Urbana, 1920), David Brody, *Labor in Crisis* (Philadelphia, 1965), and Rayback, listed previously. Note also, in general, section 4, above.

C. ON POLITICS AND GOVERNMENT

The subject of wartime politics is well introduced by Seward W. Livermore, *Politics is Adjourned: Woodrow Wilson and the War Congress* (Middletown, Conn., 1966), which can be supplemented with such memoirs as Josephus Daniels, *The Wilson Era: Years of War and After* (Chapel Hill, 1946). The interaction of Progressivism and the war is dealt with by Richard Hofstadter, *The Age of Reform* (New York, 1955), as well as Goldman, Ekirch, and Forcey, cited above (sections 4 and 6, A), but see also George E. Mowry, "The First World War and American Democracy" in Clarkson and Cochran, previously listed (section 2), Arthur S. Link, "What Happened to the Progressive Movement in the 1920's?" *American Historical Review*, LXIV (July 1959), Walter I. Trattner, "Progressivism and World War I: A Reappraisal," *Mid-America*, XLIV (July 1962), Charles Hirschfeld, "Nationalist Progressivism and World War I," *Mid-America*, XLV (July 1963), and Allen F. Davis, "Welfare, Reform, and World War I," *American Scholar*, XIX (Fall 1967). The rapid growth of big government during the war is noted by John Dewey, "What Are We Fighting For?" *Independent* (June 22, 1918), W. F. Willoughby, *Government Organization in Wartime and After* (New York, 1919), Wesley Mitchell, *The Backward Art of Spending Money, and Other Essays* (New York, 1950), Sidney Kaplan, "Social Engineers as Saviors," *Journel of the History of Ideas*, XVII (June 1956), and Nathan D. Grundstein, *Presidential Delegation of Authority in Wartime*

(Pittsburgh, 1961). The changes in military organization and thinking are reflected in Hammond and in Weigley, listed above (section 5). The effect on individual liberties is probed by Weyl, and Higham, previously cited (section 4), Zechariah Chafee, *Free Speech in the United States* (Cambridge, 1954), Horace Peterson and G. C. Fite, *Opponents of War, 1917–1918* (Madison, 1957), Harry N. Scheiber, *The Wilson Administration and Civil Liberties, 1917–21* (Ithaca, 1960), Donald Johnson, *The Challenge to American Freedoms* (Lexington, 1963), Robert K. Murray, *Red Scare: A Study in National Hysteria, 1919–1920* (Minneapolis, 1955), Stanley Coben, "Nativism and the Red Scare of 1919–1920," *Political Science Quarterly*, LXXIX (March 1964), Charles Merz, *The Dry Decade* (New York, 1931), and Joseph R. Gusfield, *Symbolic Crusade* (Urbana, 1963). The impact of the war upon America's international ties is touched upon by C. L. King, ed., "America's Relation to the World Conflict," *The Annals*, LXXII (July 1917), Ray Allen Billington, "The Origins of Middlewestern Isolationism," *Political Science Quarterly*, LX (March 1945), Selig Adler, *The Isolationist Impulse* (New York, 1957), Adler, *The Uncertain Giant* (New York, 1965), N. Gordon Levin, Jr., *Woodrow Wilson and World Politics: America's Response to War and Revolution* (New York, 1968), Betty Glad, *Charles Evans Hughes and the Illusions of Innocence* (Urbana, 1966), Herbert Feis, *The Diplomacy of the Dollar: First Era, 1919–1932* (Baltimore, 1950), William A. Williams, "The Legend of Isolationism in the 1920's," *Science and Society*, XVIII (Winter 1954), Harold and Margaret Sprout, *Toward a New Order of Seapower* (Princeton, 1940), and Robert Ferrell, *Peace in Their Time* (New Haven, 1952).

D. ON SOCIETY

Mark Sullivan's *Our Times*, volume 5, cited above, is the most successful attempt at portraying the social changes wrought by war, although Maurice J. Clark, *The Cost of the World War to the American People* (New Haven, 1931), Fred J. Ringel, *America as Americans See It* (New

York, 1932), and W. Lloyd Warner, *American Life*, listed above, are also revealing. What the war did to youth is indicated in John F. Carter, "These Wild Young People: By One of Them," *Atlantic Monthly*, CXXVI (September 1920), and what it did to women is described in Slosson, cited previously (section 6A), and in Eleanor Flexner, *Century of Struggle* (Cambridge, 1959). The repercussions for the Negro are enumerated in E. J. Scott, *The American Negro in the World War* (Chicago, 1919), Scott, *Negro Migration during the War* (New York, 1920), and Louise V. Kennedy, *Negro Peasant Turns Cityward* (New York, 1930). The effect on education is visible in John Dewey, *Vocational Education in the Light of the World War* (Chicago, 1918), Andrew F. West, "The Humanities after the War," *Educational Review*, LVII (February 1919), Bessie Louise Pierce, *Public Opinion and the Teaching of History in the United States* (New York, 1926), L. P. Todd, *Wartime Relations of the Federal Government and the Public Schools, 1917–1918* (New York, 1945), Walter P. Metzger, *Academic Freedom in the Age of the University* (New York, 1955), and Lawrence A. Cremin, *The Transformation of the School* (New York, 1961).

E. ON THOUGHT AND CULTURE

Probably because of the prominence of the "lost generation," literature is one of the few areas in which the consequences of the war have been comprehensively studied, notably by Stanley Cooperman, *World War I and the American Novel* (Baltimore, 1967), Malcolm Cowley, *Exiles Return: A Literary Odyssey of the 1920's* (New York, 1951), Alfred Kazin, *On Native Grounds* (New York, 1942), George Wickes, *Americans in Paris* (New York, 1969), and Aldridge, cited above. Frederick J. Hoffman, *The 20's* (New York, 1955) is also useful, as are Spiller and Glicksburg (see section 4). For the immediate effect of the conflict upon the intellectuals, see Randolph S. Bourne, *War and the Intellectuals: Essays, 1915–1919* (New York, 1964). For the impact upon social thought, note Morton G. White, *Social Thought in America* (Boston,

1957), as well as Curti, Commager, Wish, and Dorfman (Vol. 3), cited previously (section 4). Changes in science are discussed in F. H. Dupree, *Science in the Federal Government* (Cambridge, 1957). The war's effect on religion can be pieced together from Ray Abrams, *Preachers Present Arms* (Philadelphia, 1933), Paul D. Moody, et al., *Religion of Soldier and Sailor* (Cambridge, 1945), Paul A. Carter, *The Decline and Revival of the Social Gospel* (Ithaca, 1954), Donald B. Meyer, *The Protestant Search for Political Realism, 1919–1941* (Berkeley, 1960), Norman F. Furniss, *The Fundamentalist Controversy, 1918–1931* (Hamden, Conn., 1963), Sydney Ahlstrom, "Continental Influence on American Christian Thought since World War I," *Church History*, XXVII (Sept. 1958), and Schneider, and Herberg, listed above (section 4).

7. WORKS ON WORLD WAR II

A. GENERAL AND PRE-1941

There are few general works which deal at all adequately with the impact of World War II upon the United States. Arthur S. Link and William B. Catton, *American Epoch*, cited above, is perhaps the most comprehensive account, although Jack Goodman, ed., *While You Were Gone* (New York, 1946) also gives considerable coverage. Russell A. Buchanan, *The United States and World War II* (2 vols., New York, 1964) is disappointingly military, and neither D. W. Brogan, *The Era of Franklin D. Roosevelt* (New Haven, 1950), nor Richard R. Lingeman, *Don't You Know There's a War On?* (New York, 1970), is thorough or systematic. An interesting if hurried analysis is presented by James McGregor Burns in *Roosevelt: The Soldier of Freedom* (New York, 1970). Revealing compilations of contemporary statements are found in Richard Polenberg, ed., *America at War: The Home Front, 1941–1945* (Englewood Cliffs, N.J., 1968), and Chester Eisinger, ed., *The 1940's: Profile of a Nation in Crisis* (Garden City, N.Y., 1969).

American reaction to the threat of war has been examined in the realm of foreign affairs by Selig Adler, *The Isolationist Impulse*, cited above, Man-

fred Jonas, *Isolationism in America, 1935–1941* (Ithaca, 1966), James J. Martin, *American Liberalism and World Politics* (2 vols., New York, 1964), John K. Nelson, *The Peace Prophets: American Pacifist Thought, 1919–1941* (Chapel Hill, 1967), Charles Beard, *American Foreign Policy in the Making, 1932–1940* (New Haven, 1946), Robert A. Divine, *The Illusion of Neutrality* (Chicago, 1962), F. Jay Taylor, *The United States and the Spanish Civil War* (New York, 1956), Bryce Wood, *The Making of the Good Neighbor Policy* (New York, 1961), William Langer and S. E. Gleason, *The Challenge to Isolation, 1937–1940* (New York, 1952), Donald Drummond, *The Passing of American Neutrality, 1937–1941* (Ann Arbor, 1955), Herbert Feis, *The Road to Pearl Harbor* (Princeton, 1950), and Mark S. Watson, *Chief of Staff* (Washington, D.C., 1950). For the domestic repercussions turn to Goldman, and Ekirch, previously cited, Broadus Mitchell, *Depression Decade* (New York, 1947), James McGregor Burns, *Roosevelt: The Lion and the Fox* (New York, 1956), John A. Krout, "The Effect of the War on America's Idle Man and Idle Money," *Proceedings of the Academy of Political Science*, XVIII (January 1940), Harold J. Tobin and Percy Bidwell, *Mobilizing Civilian America* (New York, 1940), Walter Wilcox, *The Farmer in the Second World War* (Ames, Iowa, 1947), Murray Benedict, *Farm Policies of the United States, 1790–1950* (New York, 1966), Selig Perlman, *Labor in the New Deal Decade* (New York, 1945), Philip Taft, *The A. F. of L. from the Death of Gompers to the Merger* (New York, 1959), Walter Galenson, *The C.I.O. Challenge to the A.F.L.* (Cambridge, 1960), Art Preis, *Labor's Giant Step* (New York, 1964), and Daniel Aaron, *Writers on the Left* (New York, 1961).

The changes wrought by the transitional period 1939–1941 emerge from William Langer and S. E. Gleason, *The Undeclared War, 1940–1941* (New York, 1953), Basil Rauch, *Roosevelt: From Munich to Pearl Harbor* (New York, 1950), Hans L. Trefousse, *Germany and American Neutrality, 1939–1941* (New York, 1951), J. F. Rippy, *The Caribbean Danger Zone* (New York, 1940),

Walter Johnson, *The Battle against Isolation* (Chicago, 1944), Wayne S. Cole, *America First: The Battle against Intervention, 1940–1941* (Madison, 1953), Eleanor Bontecou, *The Federal Loyalty-Security Program* (Ithaca, 1953), Earl Latham, *The Communist Controversy in Washington, From the New Deal to McCarthy* (Cambridge, 1966), Walter Goodman, *The Committee* (New York, 1968), Richard Steele, "Preparing the Public for War: Efforts to Establish a National Propaganda Agency, 1940–1941," *American Historical Review*, LXXV (October 1970), Dwight L. Dumond, ed., "Public Policy in a World at War," *The Annals*, CCXVIII (November 1941), Fletcher Pratt, *America and Total War* (New York, 1941), Roland N. Stromberg, "American Business and the Approach to War, 1935–1941," *Journal of Economic History*, XIII (Winter 1953), J. R. Craf, *A Survey of the American Economy, 1940–1946* (New York, 1947), Simon Kuznets, *National Product, War and Pre-War* (New York, 1944), Lester V. Chandler, *Inflation in the United States, 1940–1948* (New York, 1951), Robert E. Cushman, et al., *The Impact of War on America* (Ithaca, 1942), Seymour E. Harris, *The Economics of American Defense* (New York, 1941), Donald M. Nelson, *Arsenal of Democracy* (New York, 1946), Civilian Production Administration, *Industrial Mobilization for War* (Washington, 1947), Eliot Janeway, *Struggle for Survival* (New Haven, 1951), Joel Seidman, *American Labor from Defense to Reconversion* (New York, 1953), as well as Adler, Jonas, Drummond, Feis, Mitchell, Burns (both books), Goldman, Ekirch, Benedict, Wilcox, Galenson, Taft, and Preis, listed above.

Books and articles on the war and postwar periods are listed below in accord with their respective subjects.

B. ON THE ECONOMY

The best surveys are Craf, listed above, and Seymour E. Harris, *The Economics of America at War* (New York, 1943), but note the works cited previously under section 4. Stuart W. Chase, *The Road We Are Traveling* (New York, 1942), John K. Galbraith, *American Capitalism* (Boston, 1952), and A. A. Berle, Jr., *The Twentieth Century Capitalist Revolution* (New York, 1954), give the reader a broad perspective. On the immediate effects of mobilization, note Nelson, *Arsenal of Democracy*, Janeway, *Struggle for Survival*, and the Civilian Production Administration, previously listed (section 7A), Francis J. Brown, ed., "Organizing for Total War," *The Annals*, CCXX (March 1942), Bruce Catton, *War Lords of Washington* (New York, 1948), Simon Kuznets, *National Product in Wartime* (New York, 1945), Harvey C. Mansfield, et al., *A Short History of O.P.A.* (Washington, 1948), Randolph E. Paul, *Taxation in the United States* (Boston, 1954), David Novik, et al., *Wartime Production Controls* (New York, 1949), and Novik, *Wartime Industrial Statistics* (Urbana, 1949). For consequences to labor, consult Seidman, Taft, and Preis, as well as Herman Feldman, ed., "Labor Relations and the War," *The Annals*, CCXXIV (November 1942), L. P. Adams, *Wartime Manpower Mobilization* (Ithaca, 1951), and David Brody, *Steelworkers in America* (Cambridge, 1960). For agriculture, see Benedict and Wilcox as well as Theodore W. Schultz, *Agriculture in an Unstable Economy* (New York, 1945), Bela Gold, *Wartime Economic Planning in Agriculture* (New York, 1949), A. S. Tostlebe, et al., *The Impact of the War on the Financial Structure of Agriculture* (Washington, 1944), Rainer Schickele, *Agricultural Policy* (Lincoln, Neb., 1964), and Richard S. Kirkendall, *Social Scientists and Farm Politics in the Age of Roosevelt* (Columbia, Mo., 1966).

C. ON POLITICS AND GOVERNMENT

John Dos Passos' *State of the Nation* (Boston, 1944) and Jonathan Daniels' *Frontier on the Potomac* (New York, 1946) show, in general, the impact of war upon American politics. The effect upon the legislature is spelled out by Rowland Young, *Congressional Politics in the Second World War* (New York, 1956), as well as by Brad Westerfield, *Foreign Policy and Party Politics: Pearl Harbor to Korea* (New Haven, 1955), and Fred W. Riggs, *Pressures on Congress* (New York, 1950). The growth of the executive is described in Grundstein, noted above, L. H. Gulick, *Administrative Reflections from World War II* (Birmingham, Ala., 1948), Lawrence Sullivan, *Bureaucracy Runs Amuck* (Indianapolis, 1944), G. M. Kammerer, *Impact of War on Federal Personnel Administration, 1939–1945* (Lexington, 1951), E. S. Corwin, *Total War and the Constitution* (New York, 1947), and Frederick von Hayek, *The Road to Serfdom* (Chicago, 1944). Hammond, and Weigley, previously cited (section 5), show what happened to the War Department. Goldman, Ekirch, and Catton, (listed in sections 4 and 7B), and Barton J. Bernsfein, "America in War and Peace: The Test of Liberalism" in Barton J. Bernstein, ed., *Towards a New Past: Dissenting Essays in American History* (New York, 1967), point up the effect of the war upon the reform movement of the 1930s. The reductions in civil liberties are dealt with in Weyl, Latham, and Goodman, previously cited (sections 4 and 7A), C. H. Pritchett, *The Roosevelt Court* (New York, 1948), Francis Biddle, *Democratic Thinking and the War* (New York, 1944), T. F. Koop, *Weapons of Silence* (Chicago, 1946), Carey McWilliams, *Prejudice* (Boston, 1944), Morton Grodzins, *Americans Betrayed* (Chicago, 1949), D. S. Thomas, et al., *Japanese-American Evacuation and Resettlement* (3 vols., Berkeley, 1946–1954), and M. Q. Sibley and P. B. Jacob, *Conscription of Conscience* (Ithaca, 1952). The consequences of the war for America's view of the outside world are analyzed in Hadley Cantril, "Opinion Trends in World War II: Some Guides to Interpretation," *Public Opinion Quarterly*, XII (Spring 1948), and William G. Carleton, *The Revolution in American Foreign Policy* (New York, 1957). See also Herbert Feis, *The China Tangle* (Princeton, 1953), Feis, *Churchill, Roosevelt, Stalin* (Princeton, 1957), Feis, *Between War and Peace: The Potsdam Conference* (Princeton, 1960), Feis, *Japan Subdued: The Atomic Bomb and the End of the War in the Pacific* (Princeton, 1961), Feis, *From Trust to Terror* (New York, 1970), William H. McNeill, *America, Britain, and Russia: Their Cooperation and Conflict, 1941–1946* (London, 1953), John L. Snell, *Wartime Origins of the East-West Dilemma over Germany* (New Orleans, 1959), Tang Tsou, *America's Failure in China, 1941–1950* (Chicago, 1963), Gabriel Kolko, *The Politics of War* (New York, 1968), Martin Herz, *Beginnings of the Cold War* (Bloomington, 1966), Gar Alperovitz, *Atomic Diplomacy* (New York, 1965), Robert Divine, *Second Chance* (New York, 1967), Ruth B. Russell, *A History of the United Nations Charter: The Role of the United States, 1940–1945* (Washington, 1958), and the recent anthology edited by Robert Divine, *Causes and Consequences of World War II* (Chicago, 1969). Regarding American responsibilities in former enemy countries, refer to Edwin M. Martin, *The Allied Occupation of Japan* (Stanford, 1948), Harold Zink, *The United States in Germany, 1945–1955* (Princeton, 1957), and Edgar McInnis, et al., *The Shaping of Post War Germany* (London, 1960).

D. ON SOCIETY

There are a number of helpful studies on the effects of World War II upon American society, including W. Lloyd Warner's *American Life*, listed above, Selden Menefee's *Assignment U.S.A.* (New York, 1943), William F. Ogburn's *American Society in Wartime* (Chicago, 1943), Jack Goodman's *While You Were Gone*, cited previously, Francis E. Merrill's *Social Problems on the Home Front* (New York, 1948), Dixon Wecter's *Changing Patterns in American Civilization* (New York, 1949), and John W. Chase's *Years of the Modern: An American Appraisal* (New York, 1949). In addition, see Ernest W. Burgess, "The Effects of the War on the American Family," *American Journal of Sociology*, XLVII (November 1942), Ray H. Abrams, ed., "The American Family in World War II," *The Annals*, CCXXIX (September 1943), and James H. S. Bossard and Eleanor S. Boll, eds., "Adolescents in Wartime," *The Annals*, CCXXXVI (November 1944). Case studies of communities are also revealing, as for example, R. J. Havighurst and H. G. Morgan, *The Social History of a War Boom Community* (New York, 1951), L. J. Carr and J. E. Stermer, *Willow Run* (New York, 1952), and R. A. Polson, "The Impact of War on Rural

Community Life," *Rural Sociology*, VIII (June 1943). For the effect of the war upon minorities, see Jeremial Shalloo and Donald Young, eds., "Minority Peoples in a Nation at War," *The Annals*, CCXXIII (September 1942), Lester M. Jones, "The Editorial Policy of Negro Newspapers of 1917–1918 as Compared with That of 1941–1942," *Journal of Negro History*, XXIX (January 1944), John D. Silvera, *The Negro in World War II* (Baton Rouge, 1946), E. Franklin Frazier, *The Negro in the United States* (New York, 1949), Louis Ruchames, *Race, Jobs, and Politics* (New York, 1953), Herbert Garfinkel, *When Negroes March* (Glencoe, Ill., 1959), John Hope Franklin, *From Slavery to Freedom* (New York, 1961), with an excellent bibliography, Richard Dalfiume, "The Forgotten Years of the Negro Revolution," *Journal of American History*, LV (June 1968), and Allen Grimshaw, *Racial Violence*, cited above. Developments in education are described in I. L. Kandel, *The Impact of War on American Education* (Chapel Hill, 1949), but see also American Council on Education, *Higher Education and the War* (Washington, 1942), T. R. McConel, et al., eds., "Higher Education and the War," *The Annals*, CCXXXI (January 1944), and Cremin, cited previously (section 6D).

E. ON THOUGHT AND CULTURE

Alfred Cohn, *Minerva's Progress* (New York, 1946) is a general look at the results of war in this area, but see Curti and Wish also (section 4). Chester E. Eisinger, *Fiction in the Forties* (Chicago, 1963), as well as Aldridge, Spiller, Cowley, "War Novels," and Glicksburg, cited above (section 4), indicate what the experience meant for literature generally. For the effect upon painting, examine E. P. Richardson, *Painting in America* (New York, 1956), and Oliver Larkin, *Art and Life in America* (New York, 1960). For the revolution in science, see Don K. Price, *Government and Science* (New York, 1954), *The Scientific Estate* (Cambridge, 1965), and Daniel S. Greenberg, *The Politics of Pure Science* (New York, 1967). In the realm of religion, note Schneider, Herberg, and Wecter, listed above (sections 4 and 7D), as well as Ray Abrams, "The Churches

and the Clergy in World War II," *The Annals*, CCLVI (March 1948), and R. L. Moellering, *Modern War and the American Churches: A Factual Study of the Christian Conscience on Trial from 1939 to the Cold War Crisis of Today* (New York, 1957).

8. WORKS ON THE COLD WAR

A. GENERAL

Although the Korean and Vietnamese conflicts have fashioned the Cold War into at least four distinct phases (1947–1950, 1950–1953, 1953–1965, 1965–   ), most of the literature relevant to our subject is either general or thematic in scope. There are a number of helpful broader works, including Herbert Agar, *The Price of Power: America since 1945* (Chicago, 1957), Max Lerner, *America as a Civilization* (New York, 1957), Denis W. Brogan, *America in the Modern World* (New Brunswick, N.J., 1960), Eric Goldman, *The Crucial Decade and After* (New York, 1960), David Riesman, *Abundance for What? and Other Essays* (Garden City, N.Y., 1964), George Mowry, *The Urban Nation, 1920–60* (New York, 1965), Dumas Malone and Basil Rauch, *America and World Leadership, 1940–1965* (New York, 1965), Carl Degler, *Affluence and Anxiety* (Chicago, 1968), and Link and Catton, cited above (section 4). There are also several anthologies which include significant articles: Harold F. Harding's *The Age of Danger: Major Speeches on American Problems* (New York, 1952), Joseph Satin's *The 1950's: America's "Placid" Decade* (Boston, 1960), and Ernest R. May's *Anxiety and Affluence, 1945–1964* (New York, 1966). Specifically on the impact of the Vietnamese war, see Arthur M. Schlesinger, Jr., *The Bitter Heritage: Vietnam and American Democracy, 1941–1966* (Boston, 1966), and the special issue of *Newsweek*, July 10, 1967, entitled "The Vietnamese War and American Life."

B. ON THE ECONOMY

For the effect of the Cold War upon our economic institutions and resources generally, consult Robert Heilbroner, *The Future as History*

(New York, 1960), Gunnar Myrdal, *Beyond the Welfare State* (New Haven, 1960), A. A. Berle, *The American Economic Republic* (New York, 1963), John K. Galbraith, *The New Industrial State*, cited above, Seymour Melman, *Our Depleted Society* (New York, 1965), and James L. Clayton, ed., *The Economic Impact of the Cold War* (New York, 1970). For an indication of the repercussions on a less profound level, see Ralph E. Freeman, ed., *Postwar Economic Trends in the United States* (New York, 1960), Bert Hickman, *The Korean War and United States Economic Activity, 1950–1952* (New York, 1955), Hickman, *Growth and Stability of the Postwar Economy* (Washington, 1960), Harold G. Vatter, *The United States Economy in the 1950's* (New York, 1963), Simon Kuznets, *Postwar Economic Growth* (Cambridge, 1964), The Center for Strategic Studies, *Economic Impact of the Vietnam War* (Washington, 1967), Murray L. Weidenbaum, "Our Vietnamized Economy," *Saturday Review* (May 24, 1969), and Russett, listed in section 4 above. John P. Hardt, *The Cold War Economic Gap* (New York, 1961) focuses upon the race which developed between the United States and Russia to increase productivity, while Klaus Knorr and William Baumol, eds., *What Price Economic Growth?* (Englewood Cliffs, N.J., 1961), assess that race from various points of view. America's growing dependence upon defense spending is examined in Seymour Harris, *The Economics of Mobilization and Inflation* (New York, 1951), Aaron Director, *Defense, Controls, and Inflation* (Chicago, 1952), Seyom Brown, "Southern California's Precarious One-Crop Economy," *The Reporter* (January 7, 1960), James L. Clayton, "Defense Spending: Key to California's Growth," *Western Political Quarterly* XV (1962), Murray Weidenbaum, "Where Do All the Billions Go?" *Trans-action*, III (January–February 1966), Weidenbaum, "Measurements of the Economic Impact of Defense and Space Programs," *American Journal of Economics and Sociology*, XXV (1966), Roger E. Bolton, *Defense Purchases and Regional Growth* (Washington, 1966), and William L. Baldwin, *The Structure of the Defense Market, 1955–1964* (Durham, 1967). The meaning of the Cold War for labor and the farmer is studied in Taft, Preis, and Rayback, listed above, and in Lauren Soth, *An Embarrassment of Plenty* (New York, 1965). Edmund Wilson speaks out for the individual citizen in *The Cold War and the Income Tax: A Protest* (London, 1964).

C. ON POLITICS AND GOVERNMENT

Walter Johnson's *1600 Pennsylvania Avenue* (Boston, 1960) is still the best study we have of the impact of the Cold War upon American politics. Joseph Kraft's *Profiles in Power* (New York, 1966) shows how leading individuals have been affected, as does a wide range of semi-biographical literature, including Cabell Phillips, *The Truman Presidency* (New York, 1966), Emmet John Hughes, *The Ordeal of Power* (New York, 1963), Arthur M. Schlesinger, Jr., *A Thousand Days* (Boston, 1965), Theodore Sorensen, *Kennedy* (New York, 1965), and Eric Goldman, *The Tragedy of Lyndon Johnson* (New York, 1969). The institutional changes which have been wrought are discussed in David B. Truman, "The American System in Crisis," *Political Science Quarterly*, LXXIV (December 1959), Richard E. Neustadt, *Presidential Power* (New York, 1960), Henry M. Jackson, ed., *The National Security Council* (New York, 1965), Harry H. Ransom, *Central Intelligence and National Security* (Cambridge, 1958), Allen Dulles, *The Craft of Intelligence* (New York, 1963), David Wise and Thomas B. Ross, *The Invisible Government* (New York, 1964), William R. Kinter, et al., *Forging a New Sword* (New York, 1958), Hammond, and Weigley, previously cited (section 5), James R. Schlesinger, *The Political Economy of National Security* (New York, 1960), Charles J. Hitch and Roland N. McKean, *The Economics of Defense in the Nuclear Age* (Cambridge, 1961), Warner R. Schilling, et al., *Strategy, Politics, and Defense Budgets* (New York, 1962), Edward A. Kolodziej, *The Uncommon Defense and Congress, 1945–1963* (Columbus, 1966), Alain C. Enthoven and K. Wayne Smith, *How Much is Enough? Shaping the Defense Program* (New York, 1971), and Karl Schriftgiesser, *The Lobbyists* (Boston, 1951), as well as the books listed below in the last several paragraphs of the section on "the warfare state." The role of the Cold War in bringing about a political swing to the "right" has been examined in a number of works, among them, Daniel Bell, ed., *The New American Right* (New York, 1955; enlarged and revised, 1962), Clinton Rossiter, *Conservatism in America* (New York, 1962), Ronald J. Caridi, *The Korean War and American Politics: The Republican Party as a Case Study* (Philadelphia, 1969), Theodore H. White, *The Making of a President, 1960* (New York, 1961), and Richard Rovere, *The Goldwater Caper* (New York, 1965). But for specific insight into the relationship of international tension and McCarthyism, see Francis Biddle, *The Fear of Freedom* (Garden City, N.Y., 1951), James Wechsler, *The Age of Suspicion* (New York, 1953), Alan Barth, *Government by Investigation* (New York, 1955), Samuel Stouffer, *Communism, Conformity, and Civil Liberties* (Garden City, N.Y., 1955), Reinhold Niebuhr, "The Cause and Cure of the American Psychosis," *American Scholar*, XXV (Winter 1956), John W. Caughey, *In Clear and Present Danger* (Chicago, 1958), Richard H. Rovere, *Senator Joe McCarthy* (New York, 1959), David Riesman, "Containing Ourselves: Some Reflections on the Enemy Within," *New Republic*, CXLVIII (April 6, 1963), Donald J. Kemper, *Decade of Fear* (Columbia, Mo., 1965), Robert Griffith, *The Politics of Fear* (Lexington, 1970), and Latham, and Goodman, previously cited (section 7A). The impact of these years upon American foreign policy and strategy can be examined in D. F. Fleming, "The Costs and Consequences of the Cold War," *The Annals*, CCCLXVI (July 1966), Desmond Donnelly, *Struggle for the World: The Cold War, 1917–1965* (New York, 1965), James P. Warburg, *The United States in the Post-War World* (New York, 1966), Walter LaFeber, *America, Russia, and the Cold War* (New York, 1967), Ernest R. May, "The Cold War," in C. Vann Woodward, ed., *The Comparative Approach to American History* (New York, 1968), Seyom Brown, *The Faces of Power* (New York, 1968), David Rees, *Korea: The Limited War* (New York, 1964), John W. Spanier, *The Truman-MacArthur Controversy and the Korean War* (Cambridge, 1959), Richard Goold-Adams, *The Time of Power* (London, 1962), Cora Bell, *Negotiation from Strength* (London, 1962), Philip Geyelin, *Lyndon B. Johnson and the World* (New York, 1966), Robert W. Tucker, *Nation or Empire? The Debate over American Foreign Policy* (Baltimore, 1968), George Liska, *War and Order: Reflections on Viet Nam and History* (Baltimore, 1968), Oskar Morgenstern, *The Question of National Defense* (New York, 1961), Samuel P. Huntington, *The Common Defense* (New York, 1961), and Seymour Deitchman, *Limited War and American Defense Policy* (Cambridge, 1964). As signs of the times, see also Gabriel Almond, *The American People and Foreign Policy* (New York, 1950), Arthur M. Schlesinger, Jr., *The Vital Center* (Boston, 1949), Hans Morgenthau, *In Defense of the National Interest* (New York, 1951), George Kennan, *American Diplomacy, 1900–1950* (Chicago, 1951), Reinhold Niebuhr, *The Irony of American History* (New York, 1952), and J. William Fulbright, *Old Myths and New Realities* (New York, 1964).

D. ON SOCIETY

The effects of the continuing crisis upon American society are discussed by Editors of *Fortune*, *U.S.A.: The Permanent Revolution* (New York, 1951), Clarence Morris, *Trends in Modern American Society* (Philadelphia, 1962), R. K. Merton and R. A. Nisbet, eds., *Contemporary Social Problems* (New York, 1966), and Paul Goodman, *Like a Conquered Province* (New York, 1967). For an impressive analysis of several different specific cases, see Gerald Breese, et al., *The Impact of Large Installations on Nearby Areas* (Beverly Hills, Calif., 1965). What the Cold War has meant for the nation's class structure is scrutinized in C. Wright Mills, *White Collar* (New York, 1951), Mills, *The Power Elite* (New York, 1956), Bernard Barber, *Social Stratification* (New York, 1957), Leonard Reissman, *Class in American Society* (Glencoe, Ill., 1959), Richard H. Rovere, *The American Establishment and Other Reports* (New York, 1962), Arnold Rose, *The Power Structure* (Oxford, 1967), and

G. William Domhoff, *Who Rules America?* (Englewood Cliffs, N.J., 1968). The impact of the conflict upon youth is dealt with by Paul Goodman, *Growing Up Absurd* (New York, 1960), Jack Newfield, *A Prophetic Minority* (New York, 1966), and Paul Jacobs and Saul Landau, *The New Radicals* (New York, 1966). There is a wealth of material on the Cold War and the Negro, including Louis Lomax, *The Negro Revolt* (New York, 1962), E. U. Essien-Udom, *Black Nationalism* (Chicago, 1962), Harold Isaacs, *The New World of Negro Americans* (New York, 1963), Martin Luther King, Jr., *Why We Can't Wait* (New York, 1964), Earl Conrad, *The Invention of the Negro* (New York, 1966), Arthur I. Waskow, *From Race Riot to Sit-In, 1919 and the 1960s* (Garden City, N.Y., 1966), and Grimshaw, *Racial Violence*, cited above. For the repercussion of the international competition on education, note James B. Conant, *Education in a Divided World* (Cambridge, Mass., 1948), H. G. Rickover, *Education and Freedom* (New York, 1959), Arthur Trace, Jr., *What Ivan Knows That Johnny Doesn't* (New York, 1961), Richard Hofstadter, *Anti-Intellectualism in American Life* (New York, 1962), and Frank G. Jennings, "It Didn't Start with Sputnik," *Saturday Review*, L (September 16, 1967).

E. ON THOUGHT AND CULTURE

The impress of the Cold War upon thought and culture in America has yet to receive comprehensive treatment, but there are a number of useful studies. Jeff Nuttall, *Bomb Culture* (New York, 1969), gives an impressionistic overview. Norman Podhoretz, *Doings and Undoings: The Fifties and After in American Writing* (New York, 1964), touches upon changes in literature, as does Morris Dickstein, "Allen Ginsberg and the 60's," *Commentary*, IL (January 1970), and Alfred Kazin, "The War Novel: From Mailer to Vonnegut," *Saturday Review*, LIV (February 6, 1971). Rufus Gardner, *The Splintered Stage* (New York, 1965), and Robert Brustein, *The Third Theater* (New York, 1969), survey some of the effects upon the theater. The impact upon painting is described in Larkin, cited above, and

in Franz Schulze, "American Ascendency and European Decline: Painting after World War II," *Modern Age* (Spring 1967). For the relationship of Cold War to social thought, note David Riesman, *Individualism Reconsidered* (Glencoe, 1954), Daniel Bell, *The End of Ideology* (New York, 1961), and John Higham, "Beyond Consensus: The Historian as Moral Critic," *American Historical Review*, LXVII (April 1962). For changes in science, examine H. L. Nieburg, *In the Name of Science* (Chicago, 1966), Richard Barber, *The Politics of Research* (Washington, 1966), Price's two books, and Greenberg, previously listed (section 7E). For what has happened to popular attitudes, see Brand Blanshard, George E. Thomas, Dixon Wecter, et al., *Changing Patterns in American Civilization* (Philadelphia, 1949), Stuart Chase, "American Values: A Generation of Change," *Public Opinion Quarterly*, XXIX (Autumn 1965), Edward L. Long, *The Christian Response to the Atomic Crisis* (Philadelphia, 1950), Arthur R. Eckardt, *The Surge of Piety in America* (New York, 1958), Martin E. Marty, *The New Shape of American Religion* (New York, 1959), Marty, et al., *What Do We Believe? The Stance of Religion in America* (New York, 1968), and an unsigned article entitled "The Unrest in U.S. Churches," *U.S. News & World Report*, LXII (Jan. 23, 1967), as well as Herberg (section 4), and Moellering (section 7E).

9. THE PROBLEM OF THE WARFARE STATE

The ultimate and most difficult question of our study is to what extent war is responsible for creating more war. One could, of course, attempt to answer such a query on the psychological level, turning first to works like William James, "The Moral Equivalent of War," Margaret Mead, "Warfare is only an Invention—Not a Biological Necessity" (both in Bramson and Goethals, cited above, section 2), Bertrand Russell, *Why Men Fight* (New York, 1916), Harold Lasswell, *Psychopathology and Politics* (Chicago, 1931), E. F. M. Durbin and John Bowlby, *Personal Aggressiveness and War* (London, 1939), Frederick S.

Dunn, *War and the Minds of Men* (New York, 1939), Geoffrey Bourne, *War, Politics, and Emotions* (New York, 1941), Edward Tolman, *Drives toward War* (New York, 1942), Mark May, *A Social Psychology of War and Peace* (New Haven, 1943), Gardner Murphy, ed., *Human Nature and Enduring Peace* (Boston, 1945), T. H. Pear, ed., *Psychological Factors of Peace and War* (New York, 1950), Alix Strachey, *The Unconscious Motives of War* (New York, 1957), H. L. Nieburg, "Uses of Violence," *Journal of Conflict Resolution*, VII (March 1963), and Anonymous, *Report from Iron Mountain* (New York, 1968). One could also embark on an analysis of international systems, referring to the studies of John von Neumann and Oskar Morgenstern, *Theory of Games and Economic Behavior* (Princeton, 1944), Hans Kelsen, *General Theory of Law and State* (Cambridge, 1945), Hans Morgenthau, *Politics among Nations* (New York, 1948), John McDonald, *Strategy in Poker, Business, and War* (New York, 1950), Morton A. Kaplan, *System and Process in International Affairs* (New York, 1957), and Klaus Knorr and Sidney Verba, *The International System* (Princeton, 1961). One could even endeavor to combine the previous two perspectives, as Dean G. Pruitt and Richard C. Snyder have done in their anthology entitled *Theory and Research on the Causes of War* (Englewood Cliffs, N.J., 1969). Yet the most common and possibly most fruitful avenue of approach to the problem is what might be termed the "sociological." Here the question focuses upon the extent to which international (inter-tribal, inter-imperial) crises create or strengthen domestic interests of either power, wealth, or relationship, which act in turn to perpetuate the crisis situation. Such a concern quite naturally leads us to an examination of the individuals or groups within society which are exposed to corrupting influence or temptation.

Among these, perhaps the ruler has always been considered the most vulnerable to the lure of war. From the days of the first constitutions and before, men have thought it desirable to limit his warmaking capacities in favor of the aristocrats or the people. Discussions of this problem can be found as far back as Aristotle and Polybius and among such modern students as John Locke, *Of Civil Government: Second Treatise* (Chicago, 1962; first published 1690), Baron de Montesquieu, *The Spirit of the Laws* (New York, 1949; first published 1748), Immanuel Kant, *Eternal Peace and Other International Essays* (Boston, 1914; first published 1795 ff.), Thomas Paine, *The Rights of Man* (New York, 1951; first published 1791), Alexander Hamilton, John Jay, and James Madison, *The Federalist* (New York, 1945; first published 1791), Thomas H. Green, *Lectures on the Principles of Political Obligation* (London, 1901), Arnold Wolfers and Laurence W. Martin, eds., *The Anglo-American Tradition in Foreign Affairs* (New Haven, 1956), Guido de Ruggiero, *The History of European Liberalism* (London, 1927), Harold J. Laski, *The Rise of European Liberalism* (London, 1936), Frederick Watkins, *The Political Traditions of the West* (Cambridge, 1948), and Waltz, cited above. See also, Clarence A. Berdahl, *War Powers of the Executive in the United States* (Urbana, 1921), Howard White, *Executive Influence in Determining Military Policy in the United States* (Urbana, 1925), and Edward S. Corwin, *The President: Office and Powers, 1787–1957* (New York, 1957).

If the ruler has been distrusted for the temptations that he faces, so too has the soldier and military leader. Indeed, a fear of the military establishment dates back to the very beginning of standing armies, and is clearly visible in such Enlightenment thinkers as Jean Jacques Rousseau, *A Lasting Peace through the Federation of Europe*, and *The State of War* (London, 1917; first published 1762), Immanuel Kant, listed above, and Thomas Jefferson, *The Writings of Thomas Jefferson* (see especially vols. 5, 9, 10, and 11, of 12 vols., New York, 1904–1905). American suspicions are particularly longstanding and are well reflected in such works as Alexis de Tocqueville, *Democracy in America* (Cambridge, 1963; first published 1835), Richard H. Thomas, *Militarism; or Military Fever: Its Causes, Danger, and Cure* (Philadelphia, 1899), Oswald G. Villard, *Preparedness* (Washington, 1915), Charles E. Jefferson, "Military Preparedness as Peril to Democracy," *The Annals*, LXVI (July 1916), Charles A. Beard, *The Navy: Defense or Portent?* (New York, 1932), and Burt McKinley, *Democracy and Military Power* (New York, 1934). The anti-militarist tradition has been examined generally in Samuel P. Huntington, *The Soldier and the State* (New York, 1957), and Alfred Vagts, *A History of Militarism* (New York, 1959). Specifically American anti-militarism is discussed in Arthur Ekirch, *The Civilian and the Military* (New York, 1956), Walter Millis, ed., *American Military Thought* (Indianapolis, 1966), Russell F. Weigley, ed., *The American Military* (Reading, Mass., 1969), and Curti, *Peace or War*, Nelson, *The Peace Prophets*, Conlin, Brock, and Wittner, all cited above (sections 4 and 7A). On the meaning of military heroes in American politics, see Frank Weitenkampf, "Generals in Politics," *American Scholar*, XIII (Summer 1944), Dorothy B. and Julius Goebel, *Generals in the White House* (Garden City, N.Y., 1945), Albert Somit, "The Military Hero as Presidential Candidate," *Public Opinion Quarterly*, XII (Summer 1948), Paul Boller, "Professional Soldiers in the White House," *Southwest Review*, XXXVII (Autumn 1952), and Arthur M. Schlesinger, Jr., "Generals in Politics," *The Reporter* (April 1, 1952). On civil-military relations as such, refer to Huntington and Vagts, mentioned above, and to John M. Maki, *Japanese Militarism: Its Cause and Cure* (New York, 1945), John W. Wheeler-Bennett, *The Nemesis of Power: The German Army in Politics, 1918–1945* (London, 1953), Gerhard Ritter, *The Sword and the Scepter; The Problem of Militarism in Germany* (2 of 4 volumes translated, Coral Gables, Fla., 1969—; originally published 1954–1968), Arthur J. Marder, *From the Dreadnought to Scapa Flow* (5 vols., London, 1961–1970), Richard D. Challener, *The French Theory of the Nation in Arms* (New York, 1952), and David B. Ralston, ed., *Soldiers and States: Civil Military Relations in Modern Europe* (Boston, 1966).

The moneylender/businessman has also traditionally been suspected of "warmongering," and socialists have not hesitated to claim that the entire capitalist system is a danger to the peace. Among the earliest non-Marxist critics of capitalist "tendencies" were Walter Rauschenbusch, *Christianity and the Social Crisis* (New York, 1907), Thorstein Veblen, *The Theory of the Leisure Class* (New York, 1912), Veblen, *Absentee Ownership* (New York, 1923), Francis McCullagh, *Syndicates for War* (Boston, 1911), and George H. Perris, *The War Traders: An Exposure* (London, 1913). The classic socialist statement is that of V. I. Lenin (see his *Collected Works*, vols. 19 and 20, New York, 1929), who leans heavily on ideas advanced by J. A. Hobson in the latter's monumental *Imperialism: A Study* (London, 1902). Other Marxist interpreters include Karl Liebknecht, *Militarism and Anti-Militarism* (Glasgow, 1917; first published 1907), Nikolai Bukharin, *Imperialism and World Economy* (New York, 1966; first published 1915), Maurice H. Dobb, *Capitalist Enterprise and Social Progress* (London, 1925), and Paul M. Sweezey, *The Theory of Capitalist Development* (New York, 1942). In the 1930s the debate was joined in the United States and Britain by those isolationist-reformers who, believing that the arms makers had helped to bring on World War I, produced a deluge of such works as Archibald F. Brockway, *The Bloody Traffic* (London, 1933), George A. Drew, *Enemies of Peace* (Toronto, 1933), George Seldes, *Iron, Blood, and Profits* (New York, 1934), H. C. Engelbrecht and F. C. Hanighen, *Merchants of Death* (New York, 1934), **Philip Noel-Baker**, *The Private Manufacture of Armaments* (New York, 1937), and Richard Lewinsohn, *The Profits of War through the Ages* (New York, 1937). For replies to these charges, see Eugene Staley, *War and the Private Investor* (Garden City, N.Y., 1935), Lionel Robbins, *The Economic Causes of War* (London, 1939), and Walter Sulzbach, *"Capitalist Warmongers": A Modern Superstition* (Chicago, 1942). For the conclusions of "official" investigators, examine the *Report* of the Royal Commission on the Private Manufacture and Trading in Arms (London, 1935–36), the reports of the Senate ("Nye") Committee Investigating the Munitions Industry (7 vols., Washington, 1935–

1936), and John E. Wiltz, *In Search of Peace: The Senate Munitions Inquiry, 1934–1936* (Baton Rouge, 1963). One of the few dependable histories of a munitions firm is J. D. Scott, *Vickers* (London, 1962), but see also Clive Trebilcock, "Legends of the British Armament Industry 1890–1914: A Revision," *Journal of Contemporary History*, V (1970).

In the years immediately before the two world wars, as the armament races worsened and as the tension increased, it became plausible to view the political leader, the soldier, and the businessman as allies cooperating in the creation and maintenance of a crisis situation. Among those Americans who "attacked" such an alliance during 1914–1917 were Lucia Ames Mead, "America's Danger and Opportunity," *Survey*, XXXV (October 23, 1915), Arthur Capper, "The West and Preparedness," *The Independent*, LXXXV (January 10, 1916), Allan Benson, *Inviting War to America* (New York, 1916), and David Starr Jordan, *War and Waste* (Garden City, N.Y., 1918). Before World War II perhaps the most outspoken individual was John T. Flynn, who warned of sinister possibilities in a number of articles including "The Armament Bandwagon," *New Republic*, C (March 8, 1939), "Whom are We Getting Ready To Fight?" *New Republic*, CII (January 22, 1940), "Business Warms Up to the War," *New Republic*, CII (June 24, 1940), and "Billions for What?" *New Republic*, CIII (July 1, 1940). Among others who sensed the same danger were M. A. Hallgren, "War," in Harold E. Stearns, ed., *America Now* (New York, 1938), Eugene Staley, "Power Economy versus Welfare Economy," *The Annals*, CXCVIII (July 1938), George Soule, "After the New Deal: The New Political Landscape," *New Republic*, C (May 17, 1939), Hans Speier, "Class Structure and Total War," *American Social Review*, IV (June 1939), and C. Hartley Grattan, *The Deadly Parallel* (New York, 1939).

Another indication that new combinations of forces were being recognized was the way in which the scholarly world turned in the later 1930s to studies of dictatorship and totalitarianism. Among the more significant of these were Alfred Cobban, *Dictatorship: Its History and Theory* (New York,

1939), G. P. Gooch, *Dictatorship in Theory and Practice* (London, 1939), Albert T. Lauterbach, "Roots and Implications of the German Idea of Military Society," *Military Affairs*, V (1940), Ernst Fraenkel, *The Dual State* (Oxford, 1941), R. G. Collingwood, *The New Leviathan* (Oxford, 1942), Franz Neumann, *Behemoth* (London, 1942), and Sigmund Neumann, *Permanent Revolution: The Total State in a World at War* (New York, 1942; republished as *Permanent Revolution: Totalitarianism in the Age of International Civil War* [New York, 1965], with splendid bibliography. More recent works of merit in this area include Hannah Arendt, *The Origins of Totalitarianism* (London, 1952), Carl J. Friedrich, *Totalitarianism* (Cambridge, 1954), Franz Neumann, *The Democratic and the Authoritarian State* (Glencoe, 1957), and Carl J. Friedrich and Zbigniew Brzezinski, *Totalitarian Dictatorship and Autocracy* (Cambridge, 1965).

The hasty industrial demobilization after 1945 coincided so closely with the onset of the Cold War that, for a time, even the skeptics forgot their suspicions of the prewar and wartime period. Indeed, in America the seeming inevitability of the confrontation with Communism left the nation more fearful than suspicious. Thus, pacifists and radicals during these years focused their attention primarily on the military, picking up a theme emphasized by Harold Lasswell in "Sino-Japanese Crisis: The Garrison State Versus the Civilian State," *China Quarterly*, II (Fall 1937), "The Garrison State," *American Journal of Sociology*, XLVI (January 1941), "The Threat Inherent in the Garrison-Police State," in his *National Security and Individual Freedom* (New York, 1950), "The Universal Peril: Perpetual Crisis and the Garrison-Prison State," in Lyman Bryson, et al., eds., *Perspectives on a Troubled Decade: Science, Philosophy, and Religion, 1939–1949* (New York, 1950), "Does the Garrison State Threaten Civil Rights?" *The Annals*, CCLXXV (May 1951), and "The Garrison State Hypothesis Today" in Samuel P. Huntington, ed., *Changing Patterns of Military Politics* (New York, 1962). An early and famous European example of similar concern may be found in George

Orwell's *1984* (New York, 1949). In the United States related warnings included "A Militarized America," *Christian Century*, LXIII (March 27, 1946), Cord Meyer, "What Price Preparedness?" *Atlantic*, CLXXIX (June 1947), Hanson W. Baldwin, "The Military Move In," *Harper's*, CXCV (December 1947), Baldwin, *The Price of Power* (New York, 1947), Oswald G. Villard, *How America Is Being Militarized* (New York, 1947), L. B. Wheildon, "Militarization," *Editorial Research Reports* (May 12, 1948), Ray Jackson, "Aspects of American Militarism," *Contemporary Issues* (Summer 1948), Brig. Gen. C. I. Lapham, "Our Armed Forces: Threat or Guarantee?" in John W. Chase, ed., *Years of the Modern* (New York, 1949), and William O. Douglas, "Should We Fear the Military?" *Look*, XVI (March 11, 1952). See also Louis Smith, "The Garrison State, Offspring of the Cold War," *The Nation*, CLXXVII (December 5, 1953), and Arthur Ekirch, "Toward the Garrison State" in *Civilian and the Military*, cited above. For the opposite points of view, see J. W. Stryker, "Are the Military Moving In?" *U. S. Naval Institute Proceedings*, LXXV (March 1949), and L. B. Blair, "Dogs and Sailors Keep Off," *U.S. Naval Institute Proceedings*, LXXVI (October 1950). More comprehensive studies of the changing ties between the civilian and military included Edward Pendleton Herring, *The Impact of War* (New York, 1941), Jerome Kerwin, ed., *Civil Military Relationships in American Life* (Chicago, 1948), Elias Huzar, *The Purse and the Sword* (Ithaca, 1950), William R. Tansill, *The Concept of Civil Supremacy over the Military in the United States* (Public Affairs Bulletin, No. 94, Library of Congress, February 1951), Burton M. Sapin and Richard C. Snyder, *The Role of the Military in American Foreign Policy* (Garden City, N.Y., 1954), Herman M. Somers, "Military Policy and Democracy," *Current History*, XXVI (May 1954), and Townsend Hoopes, "Civilian-Military Balance," *Yale Review*, XLIII (Winter 1954).

Since the atomic stalemate of the mid-1950s and the advent of more flexible Soviet policies there has been a steadily increasing concern about the extent to which political, military, economic, or other "vested interest" groups may be cooperating to influence American foreign and domestic policy. C. Wright Mills' two books, *The Power Elite* (New York, 1956) and *The Causes of World War III* (New York, 1958), were both pathbreaking in their accusations of collusion. Other commentaries which reflected the changing mood were Matthew Josephson, "The Big Guns," *Nation*, CLXXXII (January 14, 21, and 28, 1956), Franklyn A. Johnson, "The Military and the Cold War," *Military Affairs*, XX (Spring 1956), John Davenport, "Arms and the Welfare State," *Yale Review*, XLVII (Spring 1958), John M. Swomley, "The Growing Power of the Military," *The Progressive*, XXIII (January 1959), and Vagts, *Militarism*, previously cited.

By 1961 President Eisenhower himself had warned of the influence of the "military-industrial complex" (*New York Times*, January 18, 1961) and set the stage for a veritable onslaught of publication. Articles representing significant points of view included "The Military Lobby—Its Impact on Congress, Nation," *Congressional Quarterly Weekly Report*, XIX (March 24, 1961), Julius Duscha, "The Pentagon's Wasted Billions," *The Progressive*, XXV (July 1961), Fred J. Cook, "Juggernaut: The Warfare State," *Nation*, CXCIII (October 28, 1961), William E. Proxmire, "Spendthrifts for Defense," *Nation*, CXCV (August 25, 1962), Fletcher Knebel and Charles W. Bailey, "Military Control: Can It Happen Here?" *Look*, XXVI (September 11, 1962), Norman Cousins, "Sparta and America," *Saturday Review*, XLVI (April 6, 1963), Irving I. Horowitz, "Noneconomic Factors in the Institutionalization of the Cold War," *The Annals*, CCLI (January 1964), Elwin H. Powell, "Paradoxes of the Warfare State," *Trans-action*, I (March 1964), Carl Heuse, "The Aerospace/Defense Complex," *Challenge*, XIII (June 1965), Marc Pilisuk and Thomas Hayden, "Is There a Military-Industrial Complex Which Prevents Peace?" *Journal of Social Issues*, XXI (July 1965), Eugene J. McCarthy, "The United States: Supplier of Weapons to the World," *Saturday Review*, XLIX (July 9, 1966), Walter Adams, "The Military-Industrial Complex and the New Industrial State," *The*

American Economic Review, LVIII (May 1968), John M. Swomley, "Economic Bases of the Cold War," *Christian Century*, LXXXV (May 1, 1968), "Pressures from 'Military-Industrial Complex,'" *Congressional Quarterly Weekly Report*, XXVI (May 24, 1968), Ralph E. Lapp, "The Weapons Industry is a Menace," *Saturday Evening Post* (June 15, 1968), Jack Raymond, "Growing Threat of Our Military Industrial Complex," *Harvard Business Review*, XLIII (May-June 1968), William J. Coughlin, "The Military-Industrial Complex Myth," *Space/Aeronautics* (July 1968), Peter Jones, "The Military Industrial Complex," in Howard Quint, et al., eds., *Main Problems in American History* (Homewood, Ill., 2nd ed., 1968), William D. Phelan, Jr., "Nixon's 'Southern' Strategy: The Authoritarian Prescription," *Nation*, CCI (November 3, 1969), Donald McDonald, "Militarism in America," *The Center Magazine*, III (January-February 1970), James Kuhn, "The Military-Industrial Complex and Its Critics," *Christianity and Crisis*, XXX (March 30, 1970), Bertram M. Gross, "Friendly Fascism; A Model for America," *Social Policy* (November–December 1970), and Keith L. Nelson, "The 'Warfare State'; History of a Concept," *Pacific Historical Review*, XL (May 1971).

The more important books on the subject were Fred J. Cook, *The Warfare State* (New York, 1962), Irwin Suall, *The American Ultras: The Extreme Right and the Military Industrial Complex* (New York, 1962), Harry Howe Ransom, *Can American Democracy Survive Cold War?* (Garden City, N.Y., 1963), Victor Perlo, *Militarism and Industry* (New York, 1963), Tristram Coffin, *The Armed Society* (Baltimore, 1964), John M. Swomley, *The Military Establishment* (Boston, 1964), Jack Raymond, *Power at the Pentagon* (New York, 1964), Julius Duscha, *Arms, Money, and Politics* (New York, 1965), Arthur Herzog, *The War-Peace Establishment* (New York, 1965), Bert Cochran, *The War System* (New York, 1965), Seymour Melman, *Our Depleted Society* (New York, 1965), Donald Cox, *The Perils of Peace* (Phila-delphia, 1965), H. L. Nieburg, *In the Name of Science* (Chicago, 1966), Clark R. Mollenhoff, *The Pentagon: Politics, Profits, and Plunder* (New York, 1967), Ralph E. Lapp, *The Weapons Culture* (New York, 1968), Mike Klare, *The University-Military Complex* (New York, 1969), Erwin Knoll and Judith McFadden, eds., *American Militarism 1970* (New York, 1969), Richard J. Barnett, *The Economy of Death* (New York, 1969), George Thayer, *The War Business* (New York, 1969), Herbert Schiller and Joseph Phillips, eds., *Superstate: Readings in the Military-Industrial Complex* (Urbana, Ill., 1970), Sidney Lens, *The Military-Industrial Complex* (Philadelphia, 1970), Seymour Melman, *Pentagon Capitalism* (New York, 1970), Leonard S. Rodberg and Derek Shearer, eds., *The Pentagon Watchers* (Garden City, N.Y., 1970), with a superb research guide and bibliography, Richard F. Kaufman, *The War Profiteers* (Indianapolis, 1971), Adam Yarmolinsky, *The Military Establishment* (New York, 1971), and Seymour Melman, ed., *The War Economy of the United States* (New York, 1971).

Certain studies on disarmament are also relevant to the central issues. See, for instance, United Nations, *Economic and Social Consequences of Disarmament* (New York, 1962), Seymour Melman, ed., *Disarmament: Its Politics and Economics* (Boston, 1962), Economist Intelligence Unit, *The Economic Effects of Disarmament* (London, 1963), Neil W. Chamberlain, *The West in a World without War* (New York, 1963), Emile Benoit and Kenneth Boulding, eds., *Disarmament and the Economy* (New York, 1963), Seymour Melman, "Economic Alternatives to Arms Prosperity," *The Annals*, CCCLI (January 1964), Roger E. Bolton, ed., *Defense and Disarmament* (Englewood Cliffs, N.J., 1966), Walter W. Heller, "Getting Ready for Peace," *Harper's Magazine*, CCXXXV (April 1968), and Seymour Melman, ed., *The Defense Economy; Conversion of Industries and Occupations to Civilian Needs* (New York, 1970), with impressive bibliography.